ACCESS TO OVER A HUNDRED SOURCES OF INFORMATION!

Link to the latest criminal justice statistics, broaden and deepen your understanding of concepts in the book, and apply your critical thinking skills to criminal justice decision making using the free CD-ROM included in this text! Organized by the chapters and heads in the book, the CD-ROM provides seamless access to criminal justice Web sites, the author's Web site, and activities using online resources.

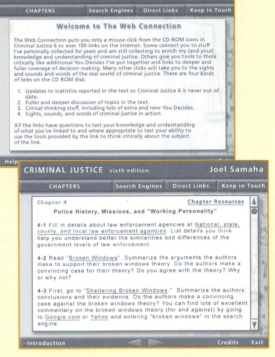

WITH THIS INTEGRATED BOOK AND CD-ROM PACKAGE, YOU NOW HAVE DIRECT ACCESS TO:

- Updated government statistics

- More "You Decide" boxes expanded to the Web that provide an interactive exercise where students can key in their responses and print the entire exercise

- Dr. Samaha's own Web site filled with information that he has personally collected over the years and is still collecting to enrich students' knowledge and understanding of criminal justice

- The latest information and many of the sights, sounds, and words of the real world of criminal justice

- The book companion site at the Wadsworth Criminal Justice Resource Center that includes a Study Guide, tutorial quizzing, chapter outlines, a glossary, Internet activities, glossary flashcards and crossword puzzles, InfoTrac® College Edition exercises (Wadsworth's online journal library included FREE with this text), critical thinking activities, and additional chapter Web links

www.wadsworth.com

wadsworth.com is the World Wide Web site for Wadsworth and is your direct source to dozens of online resources.

At *wadsworth.com* you can find out about supplements, demonstration software, and student resources. You can also send email to many of our authors and preview new publications and exciting new technologies.

wadsworth.com
Changing the way the world learns®

Criminal Justice

SIXTH EDITION

JOEL SAMAHA
UNIVERSITY OF MINNESOTA

THOMSON
WADSWORTH

Australia • Canada • Mexico • Singapore • Spain
United Kingdom • United States

THOMSON
™
WADSWORTH

Executive Editor, Criminal Justice: Sabra Horne
Criminal Justice Editor: Shelley Murphy
Assistant Editor: Dawn Mesa
Editorial Assistant: Lee McCracken
Technology Project Manager: Susan DeVanna
Marketing Manager: Dory Schaeffer
Marketing Assistant: Neena Chandra
Advertising Project Manager: Bryan Vann
Project Manager, Editorial Production: Jennie Redwitz
Print/Media Buyer: Karen Hunt

Permissions Editor: Bob Kauser
Production Service: Ruth Cottrell
Text Designer: Paul Uhl Design Associates
Photo Researcher: Meyers Photo-Art
Copy Editor: Lura Harrison
Illustrator: Judith Ogus
Cover Designer: Yvo Riezebos
Cover Image: Eyewire
Compositor: R&S Book Composition
Text and Cover Printer: Transcontinental/Louiseville

Printed in Canada
1 2 3 4 5 6 7 06 05 04 03 02

For more information about our products, contact us at:
Thomson Learning Academic Resource Center
1-800-423-0563
For permission to use material from this text, contact us by:
Phone: 1-800-730-2214   Fax: 1-800-730-2215
Web: http://www.thomsonrights.com

Library of Congress Control Number: 2002106309

ISBN 0-534-59490-5

Wadsworth/Thomson Learning
10 Davis Drive
Belmont, CA 94002-3098
USA

Asia
Thomson Learning
5 Shenton Way #01-01
UIC Building
Singapore 068808

Australia
Nelson Thomson Learning
102 Dodds Street
South Melbourne, Victoria 3205
Australia

Canada
Nelson Thomson Learning
1120 Birchmount Road
Toronto, Ontario M1K 5G4
Canada

Europe/Middle East/Africa
Thomson Learning
High Holborn House
50/51 Bedford Row
London WC1R 4LR
United Kingdom

Latin America
Thomson Learning
Seneca, 53
Colonia Polanco
11560 Mexico D.F.
Mexico

Spain
Paraninfo Thomson Learning
Calle/Magallanes, 25
28015 Madrid, Spain

For Doug, Dennis, and my students

ABOUT THE AUTHOR

Joel Samaha is professor of history and sociology at the University of Minnesota. He teaches Introduction to Criminal Justice, Criminal Law, Criminal Procedure, and The Supreme Court and the Bill of Rights, 1865 to the present. He is both a lawyer and an historian whose primary research interest is the history of criminal justice. He received his B.A., J.D., and Ph.D. from Northwestern University. Professor Samaha also studied under the late Sir Geoffrey Elton at Cambridge University, England.

Professor Samaha was admitted to the Illinois Bar in 1962. He taught at UCLA before coming to the University of Minnesota in 1971. At the University of Minnesota, he served as Chair of the Department of Criminal Justice Studies from 1974 to 1978. He now teaches and writes full time. He has taught both television and radio courses in criminal justice and has co-taught a National Endowment for the Humanities seminar in legal and constitutional history. He was named Distinguished Teacher at the University of Minnesota in 1974.

Professor Samaha is an active scholar. In addition to his monograph, *Law and Order in Historical Perspective*, an analysis of law enforcement in pre-industrial English society, he has transcribed and written a scholarly introduction to a set of criminal justice records in the reign of Elizabeth I. He has also written several articles on the history of criminal justice and published in a variety of history journals and law reviews. In addition to *Criminal Justice*, he has written two other textbooks, *Criminal Law*, now in its Seventh Edition, and *Criminal Procedure*, now in its Fifth Edition.

Brief Contents

Contents

PART IV   **CORRECTIONS**

CHAPTER 10   **COMMUNITY CORRECTIONS**   173

Preface

The Missions of *Criminal Justice 6*

1. First, describe and explain the basics needed to understand criminal justice.
2. Then, provide the tools to think critically about criminal justice issues.
3. Next, put these into a book you want to read and that fits into one semester.
4. Last, bring the sights, sounds, and research of criminal justice as close as a "click" away.

Introduction

September 4, 2001, was the thirty-first September and the fiftieth time (give or take a few) I went to Anderson Hall 210 at the University of Minnesota to teach "Introduction to Criminal Justice." A lot has changed over those thirty-one years, but one thing has stayed the same: I woke up at 3 o'clock in the morning of that first day of class like all the other first days with butterflies in my stomach. Would it be a good day? I wondered. Maybe, maybe not. But that's the great thing about teaching criminal justice. Every teaching day when I get up, I know it *might* be a good day—even an exciting day—at school. I wrote *Criminal Justice 6* to make the hours you spend studying criminal justice as exciting as my good days teaching it.

Excitement for a Purpose

But there's more for you in *Criminal Justice 6* than a semester (and maybe the start of a lifetime) of excitement. You're studying a social issue that deserves a lot of attention. Who can deny the importance of questions like, What's a crime, and who's a criminal? Which illegal drug users go to prison, and which ones get probation? Why do some murderers get executed and others go to prison for twenty-five years? What happens when prisoners get out of prison? Who decides these questions? Are their decisions constitutional? Are they fair? Are they wise? Do prisons work? And, of course—How much do they cost, and are they worth it?

Three Missions

The *first* mission of *Criminal Justice 6* is huge: **Cover the basics.** And every year it's a bigger challenge to accomplish. Why? Because our knowledge is growing by leaps and bounds. The *second* mission is just as important: Provide you with **tools to think critically** about the big questions raised by criminal justice. (By the way, don't confuse thinking *critically* with thinking *negatively*. By "thinking critically," I mean basing your conclusions on sound information. By "thinking negatively," I mean "dissing" or venting your dislike.) The *third* mission: Write a book that "works" for a one-semester course. The three missions boil down to this: Write a book that covers the basics *and* challenges you to think critically *and* gets you ready for advanced criminal justice courses if you're a criminal justice major *and* makes all of you better informed about an important social issue. How can I accomplish these three missions? That question has nagged me more every year I teach this huge, exciting, growing, and important subject. Writing *Criminal Justice 6* (and it's pretty much all rewritten) gave me the chance to answer this nagging question.

Seven Rules on My Wall

I pasted seven rules on my wall behind my monitor so I could see them while I tried to accomplish my three missions for *Criminal Justice 6:*

1. Keep it conversational and interesting.
2. Keep it lean.
3. Keep it moving.
4. Keep it current.
5. Keep it serious.
6. Describe and explain the basics with clear examples.
7. Present enough (but not *too* much) information on all sides of every question to think about it *critically* (but not *negatively*).

There's something else pasted on my wall, something Thomas Jefferson wrote in 1820:

> I know no safe depository of the ultimate powers of the society but the people themselves; and if we think them not enlightened enough to exercise their control

with a wholesome discretion, the remedy is not to take it from them, but to inform their discretion by education. This is the true corrective of abuses of constitutional power.

Please don't roll your eyes, and forgive me if choosing Jefferson's quote gives away my old-fashioned patriotism about our country and my optimism about your education, but Jefferson's words boil down for me why *I* should be writing and *you* should be reading this book— "to inform" our "discretion by education."

"First Things First": The Basics

Crime Control Agencies

The structure of criminal justice consists of three public agencies of crime control—police, courts, and corrections. These agencies are the structure criminal justice operates in. Whether you're a criminal justice major or not, no budding professional or informed citizen in our constitutional democracy can understand and think critically about criminal justice issues without a solid description and explanation of the *government* crime control agencies. I know you've heard of these public agencies. But today, criminal justice is also operating in a dramatically growing structure of *private* law enforcement, private jails, and private prisons. So, *Criminal Justice 6* includes the basics about public police, courts, and corrections *and* private security and corrections.

Criminal Justice Professionals

What about the people who staff the agencies? Where do they come from? How do they get where they are? One of those people might be you or others in your class who are or someday will become criminal justice professionals. Every year in Anderson Hall 210 where I teach "Introduction to Criminal Justice," I invite police chiefs and officers, prosecutors and defense attorneys, judges, probation and parole officers, corrections officers, wardens, and commissioners of corrections to talk to the class. I've taught so many years I can introduce most of these visitors with words like, "Twenty-five years ago, Commissioner Benson..." or "Twenty-two years ago, Deputy Chief Gardell...," or "Twenty-eight years ago, Judge Bush sat where you're sitting (pointing to a part of the room where they actually sat) and now look where he is."

The entrance requirements, the education and training, the promotion, and, yes, the discipline and removal of criminal justice personnel are also part of the foundation for understanding and thinking *critically* (remember not *negatively*) about criminal justice.

Victims and Offenders

Two other groups of people—the victims of crime and their victimizers—are also part of the structure of criminal justice. Who are the victims? Why are they victimized? What role do they play in criminal justice? How are they affected by and how do they affect criminal justice? And, last but far from least, who are the offenders? Why do they commit crimes in the first place? Who and how many keep committing crimes? Why do most of them stop—most sooner, almost all eventually—committing crimes?

The bottom line: Public and private crime control agencies and the people who populate them—professionals, victims, and offenders—are part of the basics all present and future professionals and all informed present and future taxpayers and voters need to know something about.

Decision-Making Process

Criminal justice is not just a *structure* populated by professionals, victims, suspects, defendants, and offenders. It's a *process,* too—a process consisting of a series of decision points where decision making about committing and controlling crime takes place:

1. **Decisions by offenders** to commit, continue committing, and stop committing crimes
2. **Decisions by victims** to report crimes to the police, help police investigate suspects, and help prosecutors prosecute defendants
3. **Decisions by police** to investigate crimes, apprehend suspects, and hand over to prosecutors the results of their investigations
4. **Decisions by prosecutors** whether to charge suspects with crimes and what crimes to charge them with
5. **Decisions by courts** to try defendants and sentence offenders
6. **Decisions by corrections agencies** to punish offenders, supervise them while they're in custody, prepare them for leaving state custody, and release them from custody

Looking at the criminal justice process as a series of decisions and a process of decision making (called the **decision-making paradigm**) has dominated criminal justice research and teaching for more than half a century. The decision-making paradigm's creators and their followers started almost every criminal justice studies school, department, and course in higher education— probably including the one you're reading this book for and taking right now!

"You Have to Think Critically, Too"

Of course, you have to know the basics about the decision points, the decisions, and the decision makers in criminal justice. But knowing these basics isn't enough to prepare you for advanced criminal justice courses or to set you on the road to becoming informed about the issues of criminal justice. To do that you have to understand decision *making* and be able to think critically about the criteria and the consequences of decision making. *Criminal Justice 6* gives you the tools you need to get behind two aspects of decision making:

1. **The criteria for decision making.** At all decision points—from police decisions to bring cases into the criminal justice system to corrections agency decisions to release offenders from custody—we look at the extent that appropriate criteria (like seriousness of offense and criminal record of the offender) promote sound decision making and inappropriate criteria (like race, ethnicity, and gender) *infect* decision making.

2. **The consequences of decision making.** Here we look at consequences, like how much police decisions to fully enforce the laws against minor crimes (like littering) discourage people from committing serious crimes (like mugging); whether pleading guilty to a crime you know you didn't commit violates the U.S. Constitution; and how cost effective are legislatures' decisions to reduce crime rates by building more prisons.

New and Enhanced Features for *Criminal Justice 6*

Criminal Justice 6 depends on five features to teach you the basics and give you the tools to think critically about criminal justice—a conversational but serious writing style; the most up-to-date information and research; clear and understandable charts, graphs, and tables; "You Decide" boxes; and Internet links.

Writing Style

Serious enough to convey the importance of criminal justice; clear enough to portray the complexity of criminal justice; lean, clean, and interesting enough to get and keep your attention: that's the book I hope the writing style has made *Criminal Justice 6*. I stripped out every section, paragraph, phrase, even every word you don't need to learn the basics and get the tools to think critically.

Up-to-Date

I've cut all out-of-date information and research that's no longer right or useful, replacing them with the latest figures and findings so *Criminal Justice 6* is as current as it can be. But there's more. I've added new topics. For example, the effects of the September 11, 2001, attacks on the World Trade Center and Pentagon are incorporated into appropriate chapters, not just because those events and their effects are "hot button issues," but because

they're relevant to the basic missions of *Criminal Justice 6*. Issues arising out of September 11, 2001, that we look at include:

- Policing high-crime areas when officers are called away to respond to the heavy volume of citizen calls reporting suspected terrorist activities
- Coordinating federal and local law enforcement efforts to investigate terrorist acts and apprehend suspects
- "Profiling" and search and seizure law to find and apprehend terrorists
- Jury selection, deliberation, and verdicts in other criminal cases

I've also expanded many existing topics. Here's a sample:

- Chapter 1: Relationships between race, ethnicity, and gender and crime
- Chapter 2: Elements of criminal liability and defenses to crime
- Chapter 3: Female criminality; spousal homicide rates
- Chapter 4: The police "working personality"
- Chapter 5: Community- and problem-oriented policing
- Chapter 6: Stop and frisk
- Chapter 8: Race, ethnicity, and gender and the decision to charge
- Chapter 9: "Three strikes" laws; and mistakes, public opinion, and the death penalty
- Chapter 10: Race, ethnicity, and gender and community corrections
- Chapter 11: History, causes, and consequences of the prison "population boom"; private prisons; "supermaxes" (supermaximum security prisons); side effects of imprisonment (impact on families and children, loss of income, diversion of resources to and from communities and community services)
- Chapter 12: Prison *as* punishment versus prison *for* punishment; coping with life in prison ("pains of imprisonment"); purposes and evaluation of the effectiveness of prison programs

New and Redesigned Charts, Graphs, and Tables

The graphs, charts, and tables break up the text and give you a break from reading straight text. But that's not the main reason for them. They drive home important points in the text. I'm sure it's an exaggeration to say a picture's worth a thousand words, but there are some facts, trends, and operations that cylinders, pies, lines, and flowcharts can communicate a lot better than words. Every existing chart and graph and every new one has been carefully designed or redesigned to communicate their points as simply and meaningfully as possible. So, they may not be as glitzy as you're used to but they're a lot more effective.

"You Decide" Boxes

The **You Decide boxes** (called Use *Your* Discretion in *Criminal Justice 5*) were unique to criminal justice textbooks when I wrote the first edition of *Criminal Justice*. Reviewers, instructors, and students have consistently singled them out as a favorite, stimulating, and effective tool for actively engaging you in thinking critically about decision making, what drives it, and what its consequences are. In some You Decides, you get to see there really is **more than one reasonable choice** at all the decision points in criminal justice, from legislatures' decisions to "create" crimes to corrections departments' decisions to release offenders from custody. In others, you get to see there are also **reasonable differences** about the missions and strategies of police, courts, and corrections. And, in others you get to evaluate the **effectiveness** of policy decisions regarding the definition, investigation, prosecution, and consequences of criminal behavior.

The You Decides have been carefully reviewed. I've replaced out-of-date ones with new ones and less effective ones with more effective ones; edited existing ones to streamline them; and moved quite a few to the CD-ROM disk. Titles pose a question to focus your attention on the issue to decide, and there are more questions at the end of the box to test your ability to summarize and think critically about the issue "You Decide."

CD-ROM

To keep the book lean, clean, and readable, *Criminal Justice 6* bundles a CD-ROM disk with your book. With the CD-ROM, you're only a mouse click away from **more than one hundred sources.** Some are connections to stuff I've personally collected for years and am still collecting to enrich my (and your) **knowledge and understanding** of criminal justice. Others give you tools to think critically, like additional You Decides I've put together and links to deeper and fuller coverage of **decision making.** Many other clicks will take you to the tremendous wealth of the Internet—the latest information and many of the sights and sounds and words of the **real world** of criminal justice. In short, there are four kinds of links on the CD-ROM disk:

1. Updated government statistics
2. Fuller and deeper discussion of topics in the text
3. Critical thinking stuff, including lots of extra and new You Decides
4. Sights, sounds, and words of criminal justice in action

All the links have questions to test your knowledge and understanding of what you've linked to and, where appropriate, to test your ability to use the tools provided by the link to think critically about the subject of the link.

The Result

What's the result of all this cutting, consolidating, streamlining, updating, and even adding and expanding *Criminal Justice 6*? I'm happy to present you with a book that:

- ■ has 12 instead of 17 chapters
- ■ has 336 instead of 553 pages
- ■ really fits into a one-semester or -quarter course
- ■ motivates you to want to read and maybe even keep it
- ■ is committed to covering the basics of criminal justice—the structure and process of public and private agencies of crime control—with all the information you need to take advanced courses and become a better informed person
- ■ has a clear theme of decision making in criminal justice that concentrates on the question, "What legitimate criteria drive and what unacceptable criteria infect decision making?"
- ■ pays serious attention to the consequences of policy decisions—are they legal? Do they work? Are they fair? How much do they cost? Are they worth it?
- ■ includes a CD-ROM that creates links to (1) the latest criminal justice statistics and other information; (2) deeper and broader knowledge and understanding of criminal justice; and (3) the sights and sounds of the real world of criminal justice.

Supplements

Criminal Justice 6 is accompanied by a wide array of supplements prepared for both the instructor and student to create the best learning environment inside as well as outside the classroom. All the continuing supplements for *Criminal Justice 6* have been thoroughly revised and updated, and several are new to this edition. Especially noteworthy are the new media- and Internet-based supplements. I invite you to examine and take full advantage of the teaching and learning tools available to you.

For the Instructor

Instructor's Resource Manual

This revised and updated *Instructor's Resource Manual* includes the following for every text chapter: learning objectives, key terms, detailed chapter outlines, discussion topics/student activities, Internet connections, media resources, and a test bank. The completely new test bank features the following questions for each text chapter: 50 multiple-choice, 15 true/false, 20 fill-in-the-blank, and 5 essay questions.

Chapter Comparison—*Criminal Justice 5* and *6*

	Criminal Justice 6	Criminal Justice 5
Chapter 1	Formal and Informal Criminal Justice	Criminal Justice in the United States
Chapter 2	Criminal Justice and the Law	Crime, Criminals, and Victims
Chapter 3	Crime, Criminals, and Victims (includes explanations of crime from the 5th edition, Chapter 3)	Explanations of Criminal Behavior
Chapter 4	Police: History, Missions, and "Working Personality" (includes recruitment, training, education, promotion, women and minority policing, and police stress from the 5th edition, Chapter 8)	Criminal Justice and the Law
Chapter 5	Police Strategies	The Missions and Roles of the Police
Chapter 6	Police and the Law (includes use of force and police misconduct from the 5th edition, Chapter 8)	Policing Strategies
Chapter 7	Court Structure and Process	Police and the Law
Chapter 8	Charge, Trial, and Guilty Pleas	Issues in Policing (absorbed into Chapters 4 and 6 of the 6th edition)
Chapter 9	Sentencing	Courts and Courtroom Work Groups
Chapter 10	Community Corrections (absorbs and streamlines Chapter 16, 5th edition)	Proceedings Before Trial (abbreviated and absorbed into Chapter 8, 6th edition)
Chapter 11	Prisons, Jails, and Prisoners	Trial and Guilty Pleas
Chapter 12	Prison Life	Sentencing
Chapter 13		Community Corrections
Chapter 14		Prisons, Jails, and Prisoners
Chapter 15		Prison Life
Chapter 16		Returning to Society (abbreviated and absorbed into Chapter 10, 6th edition)
Chapter 17		Juvenile Justice (abbreviated and absorbed into relevant chapters of the 6th edition)

ExamView® Computerized Testing

ExamView helps you create and customize tests in minutes! You can easily edit and import your own questions and graphics, edit and maneuver existing questions, and change test layouts. Tests appear on screen just as they will when printed. *ExamView* offers flexible delivery and the ability to test and grade online.

InfoTrac® College Edition

With InfoTrac College Edition, the premier online library of current publications, instructors can ignite discussions and augment lectures with the latest developments in corrections and criminal justice. Available free with this newly purchased text, InfoTrac College Edition gives instructors and students four months of free access to an extensive online database of reliable, full-length articles (not just abstracts) from hundreds of top academic journals and popular sources that go back as far as twenty-two years. By entering a single key word, users instantly search the entire InfoTrac College Edition database for related articles that can be read online or printed. This is available only to colleges and universities.

Criminal Justice Faculty Development: Teaching Professors to Teach, Second Edition
by Laura B. Myers, *Sam Houston State University*

This helpful fifty-page guide includes suggested teaching tips and lecture outlines for the introduction to criminal justice course. The author proposes a teaching model, which can be used to develop a teaching course in criminal justice graduate curricula, to assist graduate students who do not have the benefit of such courses, and to help veteran faculty members improve their teaching skills.

Classroom Presentation Tools for the Instructor

Introduction to Criminal Justice 2003: A Microsoft® PowerPoint® Presentation Tool

This set of over five hundred slides will help you enhance your classroom presentations quickly and easily.

Introduction to Criminal Justice 2003 Transparency Acetates

This set of fifty full-color transparencies will help you effortlessly enhance your discussion of key concepts and research findings.

CNN® Today: Criminal Justice Video Series

Now you can integrate the up-to-the-minute programming power of CNN and its affiliate networks right into your course. These videos feature short, high-interest clips perfect for launching your lectures. A current new volume is available to adopters each year. Ask your Thomson/Wadsworth representative about our video policy by adoption size.

Introduction to Criminal Justice: Vol. I: 0-534-55951-4. Vol. II: 0-534-56819-X. Vol. III: 0-534-56829-7. Vol. IV: 0-534-56830-0. Vol. V: 0-534-56833-5

Customized Criminal Justice Videos

Produced by Wadsworth and *Films for the Humanities,* these videos include short 5- to 10-minute segments that encourage classroom discussion. Topics include white-collar crime, domestic violence, forensics, suicide and the police officer, the court process, the history of corrections, prison society, and juvenile justice. Vol. I: 0-534-52528-5. Vol. II: 0-534-57335-5

The Wadsworth Criminal Justice Video Library

So many exciting, new videos . . . so many great ways to enrich your lectures and spark discussion of the material in this text! Your Thomson/Wadsworth representative will be happy to provide details on our video policy by adoption size. The library includes these selections and many others:

- *Court TV Videos*—one-hour videos presenting seminal and high-profile court cases
- *Plus* videos from the *A & E American Justice Series, Films for the Humanities,* and the *National Institute of Justice Crime File Videos*

For the Student

Study Guide

For each chapter of the book, this helpful guide contains learning objectives, detailed chapter outlines, chapter summaries, key terms with definitions, key names and cases (where applicable), critical thinking exercises, and a self-test with an answer key. The practice test questions include 25 multiple choice, 20 true/false, 15 fill-in-the-blank, and 3 essay questions.

Careers in Criminal Justice Interactive CD-ROM, Version 2.0

Updated with many new career profile videos, the *Careers in Criminal Justice CD-ROM* is filled with self-exploration and profiling activities. It is designed to help students focus on the criminal justice career choices right for them. Features include the following:

- **Careers Rolodex** features video testimonials from practicing professionals in the field and information on hundreds of specific jobs, including descriptions, employment requirements, and more.
- **Interest Assessment** gives students a direct link and FREE online access to the Holland Personalized Self-Assessment Test, designed to help them decide which careers suit their personalities and interests.
- **Careers Planner** features helpful tips and work-sheets on resume writing, interviewing techniques, and successful job search strategies.
- **Links for Reference** offers direct links to federal, state, and local agencies where students can get contact information and learn more about current job opportunities.

Crime Scenes: An Interactive Criminal Justice CD-ROM

Recipient of several *New Media Magazine Invision Awards,* this interactive CD-ROM allows your students to take on the roles of investigating officer, lawyer, parole officer, and judge in excitingly realistic scenarios! An *Instructor's Manual* is also available.

Mind of a Killer CD-ROM

Voted one of the top 100 CD-ROMs by an annual *PC* magazine survey, *Mind of a Killer* gives students a chilling glimpse into the realm of serial killers with over 80 minutes of video, 3-D simulations, an extensive mapping system, a library, and much more.

Internet Activities for Criminal Justice, Second Edition

This completely updated booklet shows how to best utilize the Internet for research through fun and informative exercises, searches, and activities.

Internet Guide for Criminal Justice, Second Edition

Intended for the less-experienced Internet user, the first part of this completely revised booklet explains the background and vocabulary necessary for navigating the Internet while the second part focuses on Internet applications in criminal justice, doing criminal justice research online, and criminal justice career information on the Web.

InfoTrac College Edition Guide for Criminal Justice

This booklet provides detailed user guidelines for students, illustrating how to use the InfoTrac College Edition database. Special features include log-in help, a complete search tips worksheet, and a topic list of suggested key word search terms for criminal justice.

The Criminal Justice Internet Investigator,
Third Edition

This colorful trifold brochure lists some of the most popular Internet addresses for criminal justice–related websites.

Internet-Based Supplements

Criminal Justice Resource Center at **http://cj. wadsworth.com** This website provides instructors and students alike with a wealth of FREE information and resources, such as:

- The Criminal Justice Timeline
- What Americans Think
- BookFinder
- Terrorism: An Interdisciplinary Perspective
- National Criminal Justice Reference Service Calendar of Events
- And so much more!

The Criminal Justice Resource Center also includes text-specific websites with chapter-specific resources for instructors and students. For instructors, the websites offer password-protected instructor's manuals, Microsoft PowerPoint presentation slides, and more. For students, there is a multitude of text-specific study aids. These chapter-specific features are available for students using many of Wadsworth's criminal justice and criminology texts:

- Tutorial practice quizzes that can be scored and emailed to the instructor
- Internet links and exercises
- InfoTrac College Edition exercises
- Flashcards
- Crossword puzzles
- And much more!

To access all these exciting text-specific Web resources, go to *The Wadsworth Criminal Justice Resource Center* at http://cj.wadsworth.com and follow these steps:

- Click either **Student Resources** or **Instructor Resources** on the left navigation bar. If you are an instructor, you will be prompted to enter a user name and password.
- Click the text cover that you use.

Acknowledgments

Criminal Justice 6 bears the marks of instructors from all over the country who reviewed previous editions. The list of my creditors is long and just mentioning their names far from repays my debt to them. The following instructors reviewed *Criminal Justice* and provided thoughtful and serious evaluations of it:

Reviewers of the Sixth Edition are:

William J. Cook, Jr.
Westfield State College

Greg Matoesian
University of Illinois—Chicago

Terry Miller
Valencia Community College

Joseph Peterson
University of Illinois—Chicago

Daniel F. Postingle
Lorain County Community College

William Ruefle
University of South Carolina

Gregory D. Russell
Washington State University

The instructors who reviewed previous editions include James A. Adamitis, Bonnie Berry, John S. Boyd, Susan Brinkley, Stephen Brown, Orman Buswell, Dave Camp, Paul V. Clark, Walt Copley, Jerry Davis, Dana C. DeWitt, Marlon T. Doss, Edna Erez, Walter M. Francis, Peter Grimes, John E. Harlan, Patricia Harris, Vincent Hoffman, Nicholas H. Irons, Michael Israel, Mark Jones, Gary Keveles, Peter B. Kraska, Robert Lockwood, Matthew Lyoncs, Robert McCormack, Joseph Macy, Stephen Mastrofski, G. Larry Mays, William Michalek, JoAnn Miller, Robert Murillo, Gordon E. Meisner, Donald R. Morton, Charles E. Myers II, John Northrup, H. Wayne Overson, Gary Perlstein, Mario Peitrucci, Harry L. Powell, Joel Powell, Archie Rainey, Christine Rasche, Philip Roades, Ronald Robinson, Glenda Rogers, John Scarborough, William Selke, Edward Sieh, Stan Stodkovic, Kenrick Thompson, Myron Utech, Neil R. Vance, Timothy Vieders, Allen Wagner, Mervin White, Thomas Whitt, Warren M. Whitton, Keven Wright, and Stanley Yeldell.

I'm really pleased to acknowledge how much two colleagues at the University of Minnesota helped me improve *Criminal Justice 6*. Professor Candace Kruttschnitt provided me with her own invaluable latest research in press and list of up-to-date references on gender and crime that have definitely enriched the sections on gender and crime. Chris Uggen probably doesn't even know how much conversations with him helped me to formulate my overall plan for focusing and streamlining *Criminal Justice 6*. I'm delighted also to acknowledge those whose influence on previous editions still shows. Professor David

Ward, professor in the Department of Sociology, my loyal friend for over thirty years, knew all the answers to my questions about corrections research. The book is richer because of his knowledge, his experience, and his unlimited generosity in taking the time and energy to share his vast knowledge and experience with me. Professor Joachim Savelsberg, who carefully reviewed earlier editions, made copious notes and discussed his experiences in using *Criminal Justice* in his sections of our introductory course in criminal justice at the University of Minnesota. Joachim offered not only editorial advice but has also continued to engage me in constructive thinking about the theory and sometimes not too subtle biases that appear in the text. I haven't taken all his suggestions but I've always listened to them. Norm Carlson, former director of the Federal Bureau of Prisons and until his retirement my colleague at the University of Minnesota, has taken me to correctional facilities, gotten me information and photos I couldn't have gotten on my own, and helpfully criticized the text. But more than that, he set an example that all of us should follow—he remained generous, optimistic, cheerful, and open-minded in the face of what would have soured many others in less challenging positions. His advice, encouragement, and example have all enriched *Criminal Justice*. His advice to me to "show the positive side of criminal justice," I've taken to heart even when it wasn't easy.

It's also my pleasure to acknowledge my former students who are now experienced and respected criminal justice professionals in their own right, who enriched my classes when they took them, and who now influence my teaching and writing: Deputy Chief Richard Gardell, St. Paul Police Department; Sergeant James De Concini, Minneapolis Police Department (retired); Martin Costello, esq., Hughes and Costello; John Sheehy, esq., Meshbesher and Spence; Judge Phil Bush; David Schwab, United States Probation Office; Deputy Commissioner of Minnesota Department of Corrections Dennis Benson; and David Crist, warden of the prison at Stillwater, Minnesota. Following their careers, sharing their experiences, listening to their stories, and arguing with their positions has kept me young in mind and in touch (at least secondhand) with the "real world" of criminal justice.

Criminal Justice 6 has also profited from the now thousands of my former students. Undergraduates, graduate students, law students, and criminal justice professionals whose names aren't mentioned in the last paragraph have changed a lot since 1971, but they haven't changed at all—they inspire me to give them the most I can and the best I have.

Criminal Justice 6 owes much to the expertise, devotion, and effort of the people at Wadsworth. Criminal Justice Editor Sabra Horne—always there to reassure me and keep me going—she's not only a great editor but a good friend. Even when she had her own problems, Ruth Cottrell never lost her cool with me. She's a glaring exception to the rule that no one's indispensable. She's kind, generous, efficient, smart, and on top of all that, she's really nice. Lura Harrison deserves a lot of credit for careful editing and excellent suggestions, even when—to put it mildly—I didn't want to hear them. Jennie Redwitz could always tell me who to go to for what I wanted and needed; that's not easy because I'm not what you call organized on these important matters. Shelley Murphy helped me clarify how we'd accomplish the missions of putting the basics of criminal justice and the tools to think critically about criminal justice decision making into a book that would fit realistically into a one-semester course, that students want to read, and that put them a mouse click away from the latest statistics about the basics and the sounds and sights and public debate about criminal justice issues.

My assistant Doug drives me here and there so I can physically do my work. But he does a lot more—he puts up with my mercurial temperament day by day. Speaking of putting up with me, my best friend Steve does all the things I can't or won't do because I'm researching, writing, and/or getting ready for class. And my counselor Dennis—Dennis knows how much he contributed to *Criminal Justice 6*.

Thanks to everybody mentioned—and many more who aren't—for making *Criminal Justice 6* a better book. But of course blame me for its shortcomings.

Joel Samaha
Minneapolis

CHAPTER 1

Formal and Informal Criminal Justice

© Michele Burgess/Stock Boston

CHAPTER OUTLINE

A Native American found drinking cheap red wine and eating a tuna fish sandwich in a city park was arrested and found guilty of the offense of "drinking in the park." In the same city, a gourmet club, which had prepared a meal of salmon mousse and bought an expensive imported white wine to go with it, dined in another park that provided "the right atmosphere." The police saw the event but didn't arrest anyone. On the following Sunday, the society page even wrote a glowing description of the club's event. A local public defender, with tongue in cheek, quipped, "What's the problem? They were eating and drinking in the park, even from the same food groups."

MINNEAPOLIS IN THE MID-1970S (AUTHOR'S RECOLLECTION)

As a young law graduate I found that the real world of the prosecutor's office differed sharply from what one would expect if formal law was applied in practice. Prosecutors used informal, extralegal methods for dealing with minor frauds and other community problems that affected the poor, who were unable to afford legal assistance. In handling a case involving a poor person who had been defrauded by conduct that may or may not have constituted a violation of the criminal law, the prosecutor commonly notified the suspect that a criminal prosecution was being considered. The hope was that the suspect would respond by returning the money obtained from the poor victim. Ultimately the objective was to solve the problem. It was thought less important to decide whether the problem was a criminal fraud. . . .

FRANK REMINGTON (REMINGTON 1993, 73–74)

[Three criteria for decision making in criminal justice] . . . play a persistent and major role throughout the system: the seriousness of the offense, the prior record of the offender, and the personal relationship between the victim of the crime and the offender. Other . . . [criteria] are also influential . . . but none characterizes the process to a greater degree.

MICHAEL GOTTFREDSON AND DON GOTTFREDSON
(GOTTFREDSON AND GOTTFREDSON 1988, 257–258)

■ INTRODUCTION

The three quotes above deal with something you're going to be reading a lot about in the pages and chapters that follow. It's called **discretion,** meaning decision making according to professional judgment based on training and experience. The first two quotes are examples of good and bad discretionary decision making. The third identifies criteria for *good* decision making.

Throughout the book we concentrate on discretionary decision making in different criminal justice agencies—police, courts, and corrections. As we focus on these differences in decision making in these agencies, it's easy to lose sight of four common characteristics of discretionary decision making throughout criminal justice:

1. *Decision making operates on two levels*—formal decision making "by the book," according to written rules, and informal decision making "in action," based on the training and experience of criminal justice professionals.
2. *Decision making is complicated* because it has to respond to an almost endless variety of people and circumstances, involving delicate matters calling for sensible judgments by criminal justice personnel.
3. *Decision making is interdependent* because decisions made in one agency affect decisions made in the other agencies.
4. *Decision making boils down to four* main *criteria*—the three noted in the Gottfredson quote (the seriousness

of the offense, the criminal history of the offender, the relationship between victims and offenders) and the strength of the legal case against suspects and defendants.

■ FORMAL AND INFORMAL CRIMINAL JUSTICE

Formal criminal justice is criminal justice "by the book"; **informal criminal justice** is criminal justice "in action." The "book" refers to written rules:

1. U.S. and state constitutions
2. Statutes (written laws) created by the U.S. Congress, state legislatures, and city councils
3. Court decisions of state and federal courts
4. Rule books and other written policies of criminal justice agencies

Formal criminal justice is public, and its decisions are usually written and almost always published. One famous example of formal decision making is so embedded in our culture almost everybody can recite it—the *Miranda* warnings—and if we watch crime news stories or dramas on TV, we're likely to see these rules followed or talked about (Chapter 6). Formal criminal justice represents the need for certainty and predictability—we should know what to expect and be able to count on it happening (Walker 1993, 18–20).

Criminal justice in action (informal criminal justice) consists of decision making by professionals who rely on their specialized training and real-world experience. This informal decision making is barely visible, and the rules it applies are unwritten. Informal criminal justice recognizes the need for flexibility because individual cases don't fit neatly into the rules in the book. So, there's a need for "play in the joints" of formal criminal justice, or **discretionary decision making** (a phrase you're going to see a lot in this book). Discretionary decision making lies at the heart of the day-to-day reality of criminal justice.

Despite the emphasis on discretionary decision making in this book and its importance in day-to-day criminal justice, remember two important points. First, *both* informal and formal decision making are essential. Criminal justice "rests on, indeed is created and enabled by . . . law" wrote one of the great authorities on criminal justice decision making and author of his own criminal justice textbook, the late Donald J. Newman (Remington 1993, 279). Second, just because the rules aren't in writing and decision making according to them is invisible doesn't mean discretion is *bad*, as we'll shortly see and be reminded of throughout this book.

Decision making is a complicated business in the real world of criminal justice. The "book" doesn't have a list of simple rules telling police officers, prosecutors, defense lawyers, judges, and corrections officers how to solve most of the problems they run into. Only judgment, hopefully developed through training and experience (with maybe a little luck thrown in), will do.

Also, the goals of criminal justice are multiple, vague, and often in conflict. Prosecutors are formally told to "do justice." Informally, they pursue other goals like winning cases, cracking down on specific crimes, improving efficiency, and saving the people's tax dollars. Judges have to impose sentences that are supposed to punish, incapacitate, and reform individual defendants while protecting the community by sending a message to prevent criminal wannabes from committing crimes. Probation officers are supposed to police and counsel offenders in the community. Corrections officers are supposed to maintain order and prevent escapes from prison, discipline prisoners, and turn them into people who can return to society ready to work and play by the rules. Adding further to their difficulties, professionals don't have the luxury of time to consider their decisions. They have to decide *right now* how to accomplish their goals. By now, I think you're beginning to see how complex decision making in criminal justice really is. There are no simple solutions written in books to solve most of the problems criminal justice professionals have to deal with in their daily work (Walker 1992, 47).

■ CRIMINAL JUSTICE: STRUCTURE AND PROCESS

Criminal justice is both a structure and a process. The structure consists of criminal justice agencies and the professionals in them. The process consists of decision making by the professionals who work in the agencies. The decision makers include law enforcement officers and management, prosecutors, judges, court professionals who aren't lawyers, and corrections professionals. The process also includes the people decisions directly affect—suspects, defendants, convicted offenders, and victims (Figure 1.1) (Bottomly 1973, xiii).

 1-1 The system in depth*

The Structure of Criminal Justice

The criminal justice system consists of three types of government agencies:

1. *Law enforcement:* Municipal police departments and county sheriff's offices
2. *Courts:* District lower criminal and trial courts and state courts of appeals
3. *Corrections:* County and sometimes municipal jails and state prisons (National Institute of Justice 1983, 45)

*Each time you see the icon for a CD-ROM, go to the Criminal Justice CD-ROM that came with this book to read more about the topic.

What is the sequence of events in the criminal justice system?

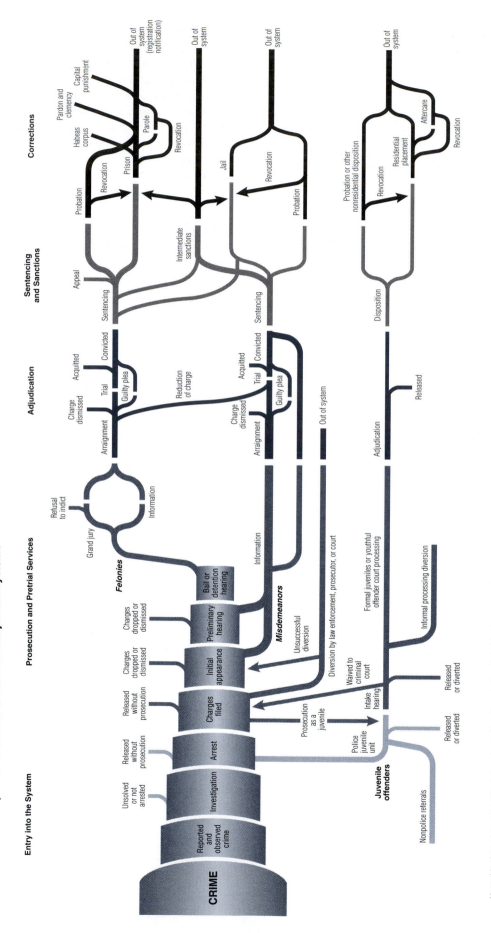

Note: this chart gives a simplified view of case flow through the criminal justice system. Procedures vary among jurisdictions. The weights of the lines are not intended to show actual size caseloads.

FIGURE 1.1

Criminal Justice Structure and Process

SOURCE: Adapted from President's Commission on Law Enforcement and Administration of Justice 1967.

Law enforcement, courts, and corrections agencies exist at all three levels of government: local, state, and federal.

State and local agencies

The principal state and local criminal justice agencies include

1. *Law enforcement:* Municipal police departments and county sheriff's offices
2. *Courts:* Lower criminal courts, criminal trial courts, state courts of appeal, and probation offices
3. *Corrections:* County and sometimes municipal jails, state prisons, and community corrections agencies

Local agencies employ 60 percent of all criminal justice employees; most are law enforcement officers (Figure 1.2).

Federal agencies

Criminal justice is (and it's *supposed* to be) a state and a local affair. But the role of federal criminal justice has grown steadily since the 1960s; it increased more quickly during the 1980s and 1990s when new federal drug, gun, and violent crime laws were passed. The increasing federal role in law enforcement is sure to continue in the wake of the September 11, 2001, attacks on the World Trade Center and the Pentagon and the spread of anthrax cases in several states that followed. These acts produced the "largest criminal investigation in the government's history"—7000 agents and employees were put on the case (Savage and Lichtblau 2001). The American Patriot Act, signed by President George W. Bush in October 2001, expanded the definitions of federal terrorist crimes and the power of the FBI to investigate and apprehend suspects in these cases. At the signing of the act, the president said federal law enforcement's highest priority would be to prevent, investigate, and bring violators of terrorist laws to justice.

These federal law enforcement agencies include familiar names:

- Federal Bureau of Investigation (FBI)
- Drug Enforcement Agency (DEA)
- Bureau of Alcohol, Tobacco, and Firearms (ATF)

Anyone who watches many TV cop shows and movies knows that turf wars exist between the "feds" and local law enforcement. Rivalry between federal and local law enforcement is old and natural in our federal system, which divides power between national and state and local governments. So, it's not surprising the new emphasis on federal enforcement of laws against terrorism immediately caused a turf war in the investigation of the September 11 attack.

The federal court system consists of names that probably aren't as familiar to you as federal law enforcement agencies:

- *U.S. Attorney's offices:* The federal prosecutors
- *U.S. Public Defenders' offices*
- *U.S. Marshals:* The federal law enforcement officers responsible for transporting and supervising federal suspects and defendants

The federal courts include

- *U.S. Magistrates:* Judicial officers who issue warrants and conduct pretrial proceedings
- *U. S. District Courts:* The federal criminal trial courts
- *U.S. Courts of Appeals:* The federal intermediate courts of appeals; they hear appeals both from federal district courts and often from state courts involving constitutional questions
- *U.S. Supreme Court:* The nation's court of last resort

Federal correctional agencies include the

- *U.S. Probation Office:* Supervises persons convicted of federal offenses who aren't sentenced to prison
- *Federal Bureau of Prisons:* Supervises incarcerated federal offenders

The Process of Criminal Justice

The process of criminal justice consists of a series of decision points (Figure 1.1). Law enforcement starts the process by deciding whether to investigate crime and apprehend suspects. Prosecutors continue the process by deciding whether to charge suspects and what crimes to charge them with. Next, prosecutors, defense counsel, and judges

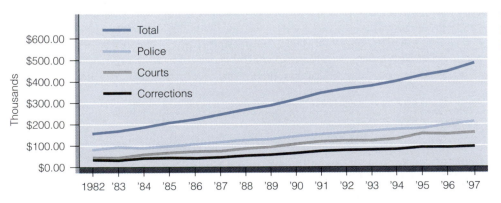

FIGURE 1.2

Per-Capita Criminal Justice Expenditures, 1982–1997

SOURCE: Bureau of Justice Statistics 2000b.

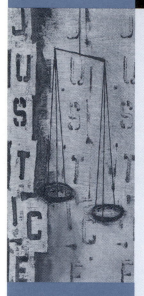

YOU DECIDE

Who should investigate the attack on the World Trade Center?

Adapted from Epstein and Gibson, 2001.

On October 6, 2001, Baltimore Mayor Martin O'Malley and Police Commissioner Edward T. Norris testified before the U.S. House of Representatives Committee on Government Reform. They criticized the FBI for cutting them out of the investigation of the suspects in the September 11 attack on the World Trade Center. "We have to know what the FBI knows about threats, tips, and even just rumors. Why aren't we all working together to find the people the FBI is looking for?" asked Commissioner Norris.

The comments were an unusually public signal of discord in what has become a huge investigation with partners worldwide. They came just a day after FBI Director Robert S. Mueller III and Attorney General John D. Ashcroft publicly thanked local police, saying they had played a "critical role" in the probe nationwide. "As we all realize, no one institution has enough resources or expertise to defeat terrorism," Mueller said. "It must be a joint effort across agencies, across jurisdictions, and even across borders."

FBI officials say they have notified local police and officials across the country when they have received specific threat information deemed credible, and they say they have employed local officers to help check thousands of tips and track information. But the bureau is not showing its hand to local police by any stretch— and that is by design. Much of the information that the bureau is tracking is so sensitive, officials say, that agents tracking the leads must have security clearances to work on the case.

O'Malley and Norris said in interviews that they recognized the political risk in publicly questioning the FBI's procedures—"None of us want to look like we're unpatriotic," the mayor said—but they called the issue urgent. "We all need each other if we as a nation are going to successfully counter threats that can come from virtually anywhere, at any time, in any form, including those that could destroy whole cities," Norris testified. "I think the threat is so great we should use every police officer in America in this fight. . . . I believe the life of the nation may depend on it."

Norris said that the only item the FBI had shared with his department is a "watch list" with hundreds of names but no photographs or aliases to aid local patrol officers and detectives. "We don't expect them to travel under their God-given names," Norris said. O'Malley noted that Oklahoma City bomber Timothy McVeigh was apprehended after a traffic stop: "How many of the 500 people that the FBI is looking for are perfect drivers?" . . .

Police agencies have long grumbled about the FBI at times "big-footing" investigations. But in the sweeping probe of the September 11 attacks, with the stakes incredibly high and the volume of information enormous, the bureau appeared to be taking care to avoid those turf battles. . . . Most significantly, law enforcement sources say, the bureau is working in almost lockstep with its longtime rival, the Central Intelligence Agency, as agents try not only to find out who was behind last month's attacks in New York and Washington but also to stop any new terrorist violence. . . .

As part of its strategy in the case, the bureau has purposely kept some details private. When photographs of the 19 suspected hijackers were made public, Justice Department officials said one reason that the pictures hadn't been released sooner was that agents wanted to be sure that sources they were interviewing would not falsely recognize the faces after seeing them on the media or from another law enforcement agency.

---

all participate in deciding bail, disposition (trial or plea of guilty), and sentencing of offenders. Corrections professionals decide how to supervise offenders in their custody and participate in deciding if, when, and how prisoners return to society. The process boils down to deciding whether to move people further into the system and when and under what conditions to remove them from it (Table 1.1).

■ THE CRIMINAL JUSTICE "SYSTEM"

The structure and processes of criminal justice together are what we call the **criminal justice system.** The dic-tionary defines a system as a "collection of parts that make up a whole." The parts of criminal justice—police, courts, and corrections—fit this definition: Together, they make up the structure, or public agencies, engaged in crime control; and they process people as part of their efforts to control crime. Like most processes, decisions in criminal justice produce "products." What are the "products," and who makes them?

1. *Law enforcement* officers produce *suspects* when they arrest them.
2. *Prosecutors* produce *defendants* when they charge suspects with crimes.
3. *Courts* produce *offenders* when they convict defendants.

Agencies that have independently divulged information about the probe have been rebuked. In Portland, Maine, Police Chief Michael Chitwood released a photograph in the first week of the investigation that showed two of the hijackers passing through an airport security checkpoint. After that, Chitwood said, local FBI agents stopped speaking to him. Chitwood said he is frustrated that his 160-officer department continues to turn over leads and information to the bureau but hears nothing in response. "It's elitist and territorial," Chitwood said in an interview. "When they say they're sharing, it's not happening."

Chitwood said O'Malley and Norris were right to speak up. He is particularly troubled because two of the hijackers spent their last night in Portland, boarding a commuter plane the next morning to Boston, where they boarded one of the planes that crashed into the World Trade Center. "I don't have to know what's going on in Baltimore, but if it impacts Portland, Maine—and obviously it does since two of the hijackers left from here— then I need to know what's going on," Chitwood said.

Several of the hijackers also spent time in Maryland, and investigators have combed Prince George's County, where some of the hijackers on the plane that crashed into the Pentagon had shopped and worked out at a gym. The Maryland investigation has been focused mostly on the areas around Laurel and College Park, sources have said; the hijackers' path in the state does not appear to include Baltimore.

Special Agent Peter A. Gulotta Jr., spokesperson for the FBI's Maryland field office, would not comment on details of the investigation. But he said agents at the local office in Woodlawn have enjoyed an "excellent relationship" with Baltimore police—a point Norris made as well, even as he raised broader concerns. Norris

noted his officers have turned over several suspects for questioning by the FBI, including an 18-year-old man who was arrested by CSX police September 20 for trespassing after he emerged from the Howard Street railroad tunnel with a camera and spray paint. During the arrest, he allegedly made a statement that "America got what it deserved."

Norris said that the FBI might have received information before September 11 that could have aided his department in protecting the city. He and O'Malley also said that the nation's nearly 650,000 local law enforcement officers, who are closer to the ground in their communities than are federal agents, could play a greater role in tracking down lower-priority leads. "Some of the things that look like they're nothing at first turn out to be something, and you really don't know unless you follow up," O'Malley said.

Gulotta said local police will play an increasingly important role in the investigation as agents move away from tracking specific information in the criminal case to gathering broader information and intelligence to prevent further violence. "We will certainly utilize them and appreciate their assistance, whatever assistance they can give us, when we ask for it," Gulotta said. "And we will be asking for it."

Questions

1. What are local law enforcement's complaints, and what are the FBI's defenses against them?
2. Is this a turf war, or is it necessary for the FBI to keep tight wraps on what they know? Defend your answer.
3. How would you resolve the problem? Defend your answer.

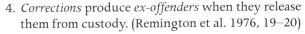

4. *Corrections* produce *ex-offenders* when they release them from custody. (Remington et al. 1976, 19–20)

The parts of the system are interdependent because decisions of one agency affect decisions in other agencies. Take, for example, state laws that say police officers have to arrest suspects in all alleged domestic assault cases. Before these mandatory arrest laws, *police officers* took things like age, mental illness, and amount of aggressiveness into account in deciding whether to arrest. Since the laws have been passed, do things like age, mental illness, and amount of aggressiveness matter? Of course they do. However, now *prosecutors,* rather than police officers, use them in their discretionary decision whether to charge ar-

rested men (the assailants are almost always men) with assault. We call this shifting of discretion from one agency to another the **hydraulic effect.** It means when you compress discretion at one point in the system it'll pop up somewhere else. The criminologist Lloyd E. Ohlin nicely sums up the interdependence that makes criminal justice a system, describing it as

a system of complex individualization of justice, adaptively balanced, not easily controlled, and certainly not inevitably improved by attempts to mandate choices, remove discretion, or impose well-meaning but simplistic panaceas on such a highly complex process. (Ohlin 1993, 10)

TABLE 1.1

Formal and Informal Decision Making

FORMAL RULES	Constitutional provisions	■ U.S. Constitution and Bill of Rights
		■ State constitutions and bill of rights
	Statutes	■ U.S. Code
		■ State codes
	Court decisions	■ Decisions of federal courts interpreting constitutional provisions and statutes
		■ Decisions of state courts interpreting constitutional provisions and statutes
	Rules of procedure	■ Federal Rules of Criminal Procedure
		■ State rules of criminal procedure
	Department and agency rules and regulations	■ Federal law enforcement agency rules
		■ U.S. Attorney General rules
		■ Federal Bureau of Prisons rules and regulations
		■ State and local police departments' rules and regulations
		■ County and district attorneys rules and regulations
		■ State and local prison and jail rules and regulations
INFORMAL DISCRETION	Police	■ Do nothing
		■ Investigate crime
		■ Report and record crime
		■ Arrest criminal suspect
		■ Search criminal suspect
		■ Interrogate criminal suspect
		■ Release criminal suspect
		■ Verbally warn criminal suspect
		■ Use force against individuals
		■ Intervene to maintain the peace by ordering people to "break it up," "move on," or "keep it quiet"
		■ Provide service to people by recommending other social services, helping lost persons find their way, helping parents find their children
	Prosecutor	■ Take no action
		■ Divert case or person to another agency
		■ Charge suspect with a criminal offense
		■ Recommend bail or detention
		■ Negotiate a guilty plea
		■ Go to jail
		■ Recommend harsh or lenient sentence
	Judge	■ Bail
		■ Detain prior to trial
		■ Accept negotiated plea
		■ Reject negotiated plea
		■ Suspend sentence
		■ Sentence to probation
		■ Minimum sentence
		■ Maximum sentence
	Probation department	■ Little or no supervision
		■ Minimum supervision
		■ Medium supervision
		■ Maximum supervision
		■ Report probation violations
		■ Don't revoke probation for violations
		■ Revoke probation for violations
	Prisons	■ Classify prisoners for type of prison and program
		■ Place minimum restrictions on prisoner's liberty and privacy
		■ Place medium restrictions on prisoner's liberty and privacy
		■ Place maximum restrictions on prisoner's liberty and privacy
		■ Issue disciplinary reports
		■ Take disciplinary actions
		■ Release prisoners
	Parole board	■ Grant parole
		■ Deny parole
		■ Revoke parole for violations
		■ Don't revoke parole for violations
	Parole department	■ Little or no supervision
		■ Minimum supervision
		■ Medium supervision
		■ Maximum supervision
		■ Report probation violations
		■ Take little or no action regarding revocation of probation

"System" isn't a completely accurate description of criminal justice for two reasons. First, criminal justice agencies have a lot of independence. They get their authority and their budgets from different sources. Police departments get their power and money from cities and towns. Sheriff's departments, prosecutors, public defenders, jails, and trial courts get their power and money from county budgets. Appeals courts and prisons get theirs from the state.

Second, agencies set their own policies, rarely if ever coordinating them with other agencies. And even less do individuals within these agencies think about the effects of their decisions on other agencies. For example, when police officers arrest suspected drunk drivers, child molesters, burglars, and thieves, they're not thinking about how their arrests are going to affect the "system" (giving prosecutors more work, courts heavier caseloads, and prisons more prisoners). Why? Probably because the consequences of their decisions are too far down the line to worry about them. So, each agency becomes its own little subcriminal justice system. In reality, Professor Ohlin writes:

> [T]he criminal justice process reduces the cases processed from its broadest net of police intervention to final incarceration in jail or prison. Certainly the cases that go all the way demonstrate the system as a system. But absent rigid legislative mandates or other external controls on discretion, most . . . criminal cases are not subject to maximum processing. So although full enforcement does exist as a total system, other more abbreviated systems exist within it to respond to the different problems and the infinite variety of persons dealt with by enforcement officials. (Ohlin 1993, 11)

■ MODELS OF CRIMINAL JUSTICE

Some useful models will help us picture the essence of the criminal justice system. Keep in mind models are simplifications of reality, because to highlight the essentials they dim the details of total reality. Let's look at four widely used models:

- The criminal justice "wedding cake"
- The criminal justice "funnel"
- The crime control model
- The due process model

Decisions Before the Criminal Process Begins

Before we get to the models, we need to consider four decisions that have to be made *before* the criminal justice process can begin:

1. Legislatures have to decide to make certain actions crimes. (Chapter 2)
2. Offenders have to decide to commit crimes. (Chapter 3)
3. Victims have to decide to report crimes. (Chapter 3)
4. Law enforcement officers have to decide to arrest people. (Chapter 5)

Other chapters cover legislative, offenders, and police decisions, so we'll discuss only victims' decisions here.

In colonial times, crime victims played a central part in criminal justice. They conducted their own investigations, got warrants, paid witnesses, and hired lawyers as their private prosecutors. Colonial law was generous to victims who wanted to sue offenders, allowing victims to collect damages, and even going so far as to let them make offenders their personal servants—a form of involuntary servitude. If they could afford it, victims could pay the government to keep their victimizers in jail. So, colonial criminal justice was victim-centered. However, by 1900, criminal justice had become society-centered. Punishment was measured by the harm to society as a whole, not to individual victims. Formally, victims pretty much lost their legal place in criminal justice, and offenders were relieved of their legal responsibility to individual victims (Elias 1986, 11–12).

Informally, the importance of victims is another matter. Today, the government depends on victims to identify, prosecute, and convict criminals. According to the political scientist James Q. Wilson, "The most important person in the criminal justice system may not be the judge, police officer, or prosecutor—it may be the victim." Why? Because if victims don't report crimes to the police (Chapter 3), most crimes won't enter the criminal justice system; and if they won't testify in court, prosecutors probably won't charge suspects; and if they aren't effective witnesses, defendants probably won't be convicted. When victims *do* report crimes, they have to get involved in the criminal process. Getting involved means spending time, possibly losing hours, or even days, of work. And the time and money spent might all come to nothing because the police can't find the suspect, the punishment doesn't satisfy the victim, or the stolen property isn't even found (Wilson, 1983b).

With these preliminary but vital decisions *before* the criminal process begins in mind, let's look at the models depicting decision points *after* the process kicks in.

The Criminal Justice "Wedding Cake"

The **wedding cake model** depicts a process in which criminal justice officials decide how to deal with cases by ranking them according to their seriousness. Professionals distinguish between "real crime" and "garbage" (also called "bullshit") cases. What determines the difference?

1. The seriousness of the charge
2. The past criminal record of the offender

3. The relationship of the victim to the offender
4. Whether the victim was injured
5. Whether the offender used a gun
6. The strength of the case

We can boil down these six criteria into the four noted earlier (see pp. 2–3). All we have to do is absorb victim injury and the use of a gun into seriousness of the charge. Judged by these criteria, it's no surprise that "real crimes" get more attention (as well they should) than "garbage" cases (Gottredson and Gottfredson 1988; Mather 1974, 187–216; Spohn and Cederblom 1991, 306).

A wedding cake with its tiers, narrow at the top and increasingly wider toward the bottom (Figure 1.3), is one way to look at criminal justice decision making.

Each of the four tiers in the wedding cake model represents a different type of crime:

1. On the small top tier are a few "celebrated cases."
2. In the second tier are larger numbers of "real crimes."
3. Most "ordinary felonies" are in the third tier.
4. The broad fourth tier represents the vast number of minor crimes.

All three top tiers are **felonies,** serious crimes that can result in a year or more in prison. The "celebrated cases" are those few felonies that grab public attention because the crime is particularly grisly (Timothy McVeigh who blew up more than a hundred men, women, and children is a good example) or a famous person (such as O. J. Simpson) is charged with committing it. In celebrated cases defendants get all the protections the law allows, including a

trial. Don't be misled into thinking these full legal protections and a trial are typical; they're the rarest event in real-life criminal justice (Chapter 8). A story will make my point. A former student, now a successful criminal lawyer, defended a man charged with the horrific crime of murdering his girlfriend and her little girl by cutting them up with a hatchet. As you might expect the case was all over the TV news and newspapers. Because it was a grisly crime and got so much publicity, the case was definitely going to trial. Discouraged at the prospect of having no defense, he complained, "I can't even count on the cops screwing up by violating his rights. They know this case is going to trial and they want a conviction, so they'll handle this sucker with kid gloves so they can put him away."

The second tier is made up of "real crimes" (serious felonies like rape, aggravated assault, and armed robbery). They're in this layer because they're committed by people who have past criminal records, are strangers to their victims, use guns, and injure their victims. "Real crimes" are less likely than celebrated cases to go to a full formal trial but more likely than less serious felony and misdemeanor cases.

Third tier cases are "ordinary felonies," like burglaries, thefts, and unarmed robberies where no one got hurt and the victim knew the offender. "Technically," serious felonies where the event is also a private dispute are "ordinary." Suppose Doug asks his roommate Eli for $25. At the time Eli gives Doug the money, Doug believes the $25 is a gift. A few months later, Eli asks Doug for his $25. When Doug says, "No way, you gave me that $25," Eli grabs Doug's wallet and takes all the money in it, $40. "I'm taking my $25 plus the rest in interest." Police and prosecutors don't call this a "real" robbery no matter what the law says. So, they either divert it out of the system completely or go for a guilty plea to ordinary theft.

The vast majority of cases are fourth tier, misdemeanors like simple assault, petty theft, shoplifting, and disorderly conduct. Samuel Walker calls this bottom tier the "lower depths." Practically none of these cases go to trial; they're not worth the cost and effort of formal proceedings. So, they're disposed of quickly either in preliminary proceedings or in agreements among prosecutors, defendants, and lawyers. In many, there are no criminal charges at all; they're considered "problems" the parties should settle between themselves (Walker 1994, 29–37).

The Criminal Justice "Funnel"

Wide at the top, narrow at the bottom, a funnel is opposite in shape to a wedding cake; however, both models represent the reality of day-to-day decision making. The wedding cake depicts how a few celebrated cases and serious felonies move through the whole formal criminal justice system and how the many ordinary felonies and the vast majority of misdemeanors are disposed of by informal discretion early in the criminal process. The funnel

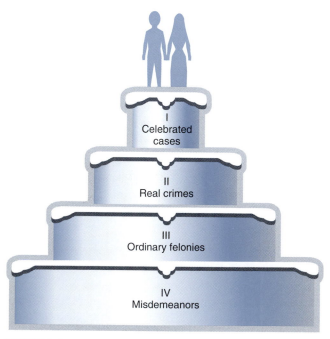

FIGURE 1.3
The Criminal Justice Wedding Cake
SOURCE: Based on Walker 1994.

I
Celebrated cases

II
Real crimes

III
Ordinary felonies

IV
Misdemeanors

shows that decisions made at each stage in the criminal process sort out those people who shouldn't go further from those who should continue. We call this sorting operation **case attrition**, because at each stage, the numbers of people in the system shrink.

Some decisions remove people by releasing them outright with no charges. Some decisions remove people by **diversion**, transferring them to other agencies for alcohol and other treatment or family counseling programs. The rest are sent on to the next stage. Figure 1.4 shows how in this sorting operation, more people are arrested than charged with crimes; more people are charged with crimes than convicted; more people are convicted than sentenced; and more people are sentenced to probation than to prison. Put another way, there are more suspects than defendants, more defendants than convicted offenders, and more convicted offenders than prisoners.

Don't think of case attrition as "letting criminals off" because you assume every arrest would end in conviction and punishment if it weren't for "technicalities," incompetence, softhearted judges, or even corruption. In the old days, this view was reflected in the phrase "case mortality." Empirical research has repeatedly proven the case mortality view was wrong. Why? Because the decisions to arrest, charge, and convict depend on how much evidence backs them up (the strength of the case criterion). Arrest doesn't mean guilt (proof beyond a reasonable doubt); it means *probable cause* (Chapter 6, "Probable Cause" section) to *believe* arrested people are guilty. Prosecutors need more proof to charge defendants, and of course they have to prove guilt beyond a reasonable doubt to convict (Chapter 8, "Decision to Charge" and "Proving Guilt" sections). And judges weigh the three other criteria—seriousness of the offense, criminal history of the offender, and relationship between offender and victim—when they decide whether to sentence offenders to prison (Chapter 9, "Sentencing"). So, there will

always be more arrests than charges, more charges than convictions, more convictions than prison sentences, and more short than long prison sentences. And that's the way it *should* be.

The Crime Control and Due Process Models

In an influential article written in 1964, Stanford University law professor Herbert Packer built two models of criminal justice on two values of our constitutional democracy—crime control and due process (Packer 1964, 113). According to the value of **crime control**, criminal justice exists to reduce crime for the good of the whole society. According to the value of **due process**, criminal justice exists to guarantee fair procedures for every individual. Most people put crime control high on their list of priorities when it comes to criminal justice. But crime control doesn't mean controlling crime at any price. We have to respond to crime within limits placed on government power by the values of our constitutional democracy. So, officials fighting crime have to respect the life, liberty, privacy, property, and dignity of all people no matter how much we hate them or what they do.

The crime control model

The crime control model focuses on the need to protect people and their property, partly for the victims' sake but also for the good of society. If people don't feel safe, they lose their capacity to function and enjoy the rewards that should come from playing by the rules. At the end of the day, crime control guarantees social freedom by protecting people and their property.

To make good on this guarantee, criminal justice decisions have to sort out the guilty from the innocent, let the innocent go as soon as possible, and convict and punish the guilty, also as soon as possible. Notice speedy decisions

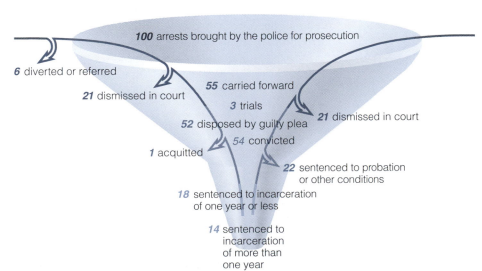

FIGURE 1.4

The Criminal Justice Funnel

The funnel shows that decisions made at each stage in the criminal process sort out those people who shouldn't go further from those who should continue.

SOURCE: Bureau of Justice Statistics 1989a.

100 arrests brought by the police for prosecution

6 diverted or referred

21 dismissed in court

55 carried forward

3 trials

52 disposed by guilty plea

21 dismissed in court

54 convicted

1 acquitted

22 sentenced to probation or other conditions

18 sentenced to incarceration of one year or less

14 sentenced to incarceration of more than one year

aren't enough; they have to be right too. We don't want to convict innocent people and let guilty ones go free, not just because it's unfair but also because it leads to time wasting, expensive second-guessing of decisions already made. In other words, we also want decisions to be right because we want them to be final (Packer 1968, 158).

Informal decision making is the best way to ensure speed and accuracy. In Professor Packer's words, "[T]he process must not be cluttered up with [the] ceremonious rituals" of a formal legal contest. For example, police interrogation gets to the truth faster and better than examination and cross-examination during a trial. Negotiations out of court between prosecutors and defense lawyers are more efficient and fairer than time-consuming, formal court proceedings. According to Packer, the crime control model operates like

> an assembly line conveyer belt down which moves an endless array of cases, never stopping, carrying the cases to workers who stand at fixed stations and who perform on each case as it comes by the same small but essential operation that brings it one step closer to being a finished product, or, to exchange the metaphor, a closed file. (Packer 1968, 159) (Figure 1.5)

The **presumption of guilt** (people caught up in criminal justice are *probably* guilty) fits in with the premium placed on fast and accurate crime control. The presumption comes from the notion the police wouldn't have arrested a suspect and prosecutors wouldn't have charged her unless she'd done something wrong. So, courts shouldn't "handcuff" the police and stymie prosecutors by putting up expensive, time-consuming hurdles to their efforts to find the truth. Give police officers leeway to detain, search, and interrogate suspects so they can sort out the guilty from the innocent. Let prosecutors bargain for guilty pleas to get the guilty to punishment and hopefully redemption as soon as possible. As you can

see, the crime control model emphasizes the early stages in criminal justice—police investigation and guilty pleas.

One final point: The model isn't too worried about mistakes and unfairness. Why? First, because of three assumptions based on confidence in government power: police and prosecutors rarely make mistakes; they don't base their decisions on personal prejudices even if they *are* prejudiced; and most suspects really are guilty of *something*. Second, the need for crime control outweighs the suffering of the few innocent people who get caught up in the system—it's better that a few innocent people get convicted than guilty people go free. Third, sooner or later the innocent are vindicated—usually sooner rather than later. At the end of the day, the model expresses more fear of criminals than government.

The due process model

According to the due process model, it's more important to guarantee the rights of individuals to fair procedures than to catch criminals. In fact, the best definition of due process is fair procedures. "Fair procedures" means decision making according to formal rules growing out of the Bill of Rights and the due process clauses of the U.S. Constitution and state constitutions (Chapter 2). The commitment to decision making by formal rules is based on a distrust of government power and the need to control it. In Professor Paul Bator's harsh words, "The criminal law's notion of just condemnation and punishment is a cruel hypocrisy visited by a smug society on the psychologically and economically crippled" (Bator, 1963). So, we have to throw up barriers to government power at each step in the criminal process to prevent further involvement in this risky business of criminal justice. It shouldn't surprise us that the due process model resembles an obstacle course, not an assembly line (Packer 1968, 170) (Figure 1.6, Table 1.2).

Creating due process obstacles is based on the idea that you can't find the truth informally because human

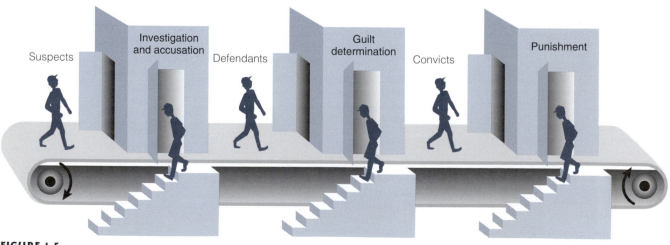

FIGURE 1.5
Crime Control Conveyer Belt

FIGURE 1.6
The Due Process Obstacle Course

failings—like our faulty powers of observation, our motivation of self-interest, our emotions, and our prejudices—stand in the way. The model puts great confidence in the **adversary process**—getting to the truth by fighting in court according to the formal rules of criminal procedure (Chapters 7–8). So, in the due process model, the trial is the high point of criminal justice. Why? Formal public proceedings reduce the chances that mistakes, emotions, and prejudices will infect decision making because skilled lawyers argue their side of the story in front of neutral judges acting as umpires, and impartial juries decide who's telling the truth.

Distrust of government power and the need to control it also means operating according to the presumption of innocence. The government always has the burden to justify its use of power even against people who turn out to be guilty. When all is said and done, the due process model expresses more fear of government than criminals.

The History of Crime Control and Due Process

The tension between the values of due process and crime control is as old as criminal justice. The history of criminal justice in Western cultures can be described as a pendulum swing between a commitment to crime control and a commitment to due process (Figure 1.7).

TABLE 1.2

Comparison of Crime Control and Due Process

Crime Control	Due Process
Control crime	Fair procedures
Society's needs	Individual's rights
Confidence in police and prosecutor	Distrust of all government power
Negotiation	Adversary court proceedings
Reliability of informal fact finding	Reliability of formal fact finding
Discretion in police and prosecutors	Limited discretion of police and prosecutors
Presumption of guilt	Presumption of innocence
Emphasis on early stages of investigation	Emphasis on trial
Conveyer belt	Obstacle course
Fear of criminals	Fear of government

At one extreme is the fear of government abuse of power and demands for rules to control it. At the other is the fear of crime and demands for discretionary power to eliminate it. Fear of government abuse of power has always led to more rules and less discretion. Fear of crime has always produced more discretion and fewer rules. No one has stated more eloquently the problem of crime control in a constitutional democracy than James Madison, during the debate over the Bill of Rights in 1787:

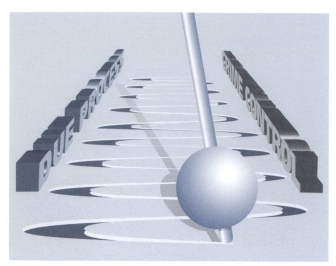

FIGURE 1.7
The Crime Control/Due Process Pendulum

If men were angels, no government would be necessary. If angels were to govern men, neither external nor internal controls on government would be necessary. In framing a government which is to be administered by men over men, the great difficulty lies in this: You must first enable the government to control the governed; and, in the next place oblige it to control itself. A dependence on the people is no doubt the primary control on the government; but experience has taught the necessity of auxiliary precautions. (Cooke 1961, 349)

The early history of criminal justice

In the ancient Roman republic, citizens enjoyed strong safeguards against government power. During the later years of the empire, Rome swung to the opposite extreme. The Emperor Hadrian boasted that merely sending a suspect to trial was conclusive proof of guilt (Pound 1921, 1–16; Strachan-Davidson 1912, 114, 168).

English history also experienced this swing of the pendulum between discretionary power and formal checks upon it. After the Norman Conquest in 1066, the Norman kings wielded enormous power; by 1185 the great Angevin King Henry II had consolidated and centralized royal power. In the thirteenth century, a reaction occurred, provoked by Henry II's power-hungry son, John. In 1215, King John's barons forced him to accept and sign the Magna Carta, or Great Charter. Among other restrictions, King John agreed to a historic limit on royal power:

> No freeman shall be taken or imprisoned . . . or in any wise destroyed, nor will we go upon him, nor will we send upon him, unless by the lawful judgment of his peers, or by the law of the land. (Plucknett 1956, 24)

These curbs on royal authority emboldened the English nobility into great lawlessness that went on for more than 200 years. Finally, royal authority reemerged under the Tudor monarchs in the late 1400s and throughout the 1500s, especially during the reigns of Henry VII (1485–1509) and his son, Henry VIII (1509–1547). Complaints that the ordinary courts protected criminals, rioters, and disturbers of the peace led to the creation of special royal courts like the famous Court of the Star Chamber. Unlike Norman kings, the Tudor monarchs were checked by the rule of law (Elton 1974).

The case in 1575 of George Dibney (Samaha 1974, 1979), an Elizabethan gentleman, illustrates the balance between law and royal discretionary power in late Tudor England. Queen Elizabeth suspected Dibney had published seditious libels against Benjamin Clere, one of her supporters. She called on the local constables to go to Dibney's house and search for the libels. When the constables arrived at his door, Dibney demanded to know what authority they had to search his house. They replied, "the Queen's authority."

"Not good enough," Dibney replied; they had to have a warrant backed up by probable cause to enter his house and search it.

"We have probable cause."

"Of what does it consist?" Dibney demanded.

"We're credibly informed" that he had the libels in his house, they responded.

Who credibly informed them? Dibney wanted to know. On hearing the name of the informer, Dibney scoffed at them; the constables and everyone else knew that their informant was a "liar and a knave."

Now impatient, the constables replied that they were coming in whether or not Dibney liked it. Dibney demanded to know the names of everyone who was about to enter.

"Why?" they demanded.

So that when he sued them he would be sure to collect damages for their illegal entry, just as he had done with the "last lot" who had illegally searched his house. Because the record ends at that point, we don't know whether the constables searched his house, or, if they did, whether Dibney sued them and collected damages. However, we do know "mere suspicions," even those of the powerful Queen Elizabeth I, weren't enough to back up entering a private home without probable cause to search.

The resurgence of royal power under the Tudors emboldened the Stuart monarchs in the 1600s to aggrandize their power. The Stuarts upset the precarious Tudor balance between royal discretionary power and legal limits. By the reign of King Charles I, in the early 1600s, the royal Court of Star Chamber had abandoned procedural safeguards in favor of the royal power to punish troublemakers. Furthermore, royal domination of common-law judges ensured decisions favorable to royal interests and to the members of the aristocracy who supported the Stuart kings. This aggrandizement, and the abuses accompanying it, eventually led to the English Civil War and later to the Glorious Revolution. Both were fought in part to resolve the struggle between those who favored royal discretionary power (some even claiming the monarch had absolute power above the law) and those who maintained that the law—not kings, queens, and their minions—ruled England (Kenyon 1986).

The colonial American balance

The first New England colonists came to America not only to establish their own church but also to escape the harsh Stuart criminal law and its arbitrary administration. They established the Massachusetts Body of Liberties, which reduced the number of capital offenses and guaranteed defendants several procedural safeguards. John Winthrop, the leading founder of the Massachusetts Bay Colony, devoted a major part of his life to working out the proper balance between the power of the government to enforce the criminal law and the rights of those charged with committing crimes (Chapter 9, "History of Sentencing" section) (Walker 1980).

The influence of the American Revolution

The American Revolution, fought in part over the colonists' perception of George III's tyranny, led to the creation of a government of checks and balances, separation of powers, and constitutionally prescribed limits on government's power over individual citizens. All these actions bespoke a hostility to government power, expressed in Victorian historian Lord Acton's famous aphorism, "Power tends to corrupt and absolute power corrupts absolutely."

The authors of the Constitution believed they could create in a written document a perfect balance between security and liberty, goals expressed in the Preamble as "insure the domestic tranquillity" *and* "secure the blessings of liberty." But many refused to trust the document unless it included specific guarantees limiting the power of the government to enforce the criminal law. These guarantees included the rights against unreasonable searches and seizures, self-incrimination (Chapter 6), and cruel and unusual punishment (Chapters 2 and 9) and the guarantees of the rights to jury trial, to confront witnesses, and to counsel (Chapters 7–9). These guarantees appeared as amendments and are among those in the Bill of Rights.

The safeguards written into the Bill of Rights and into similar bills adopted by all the states for their own constitutions established a criminal procedure with strong formal safeguards against government power. This structure existed with minimal complaints as long as a relatively homogeneous, widely scattered, mainly agrarian population dominated American society and its institutions (Pound 1921, 1–16).

In this inspiring story of individual rights and limits on government power in our history, let's remember five groups excluded from the enjoyment of these rights—Blacks (both free and slaves), Native Americans, women, poor people, and immigrants.

Industrialization, urbanization, and immigration

Industrialization, urbanization, and immigration transformed American society and its institutions during the nineteenth century. An agricultural society made up of farmers and small towns was transformed into a manufacturing society made up of wage laborers from widely differing cultural heritages, crowded into cities of teeming millions and causing enormous problems of public order. Although no one at the time was aware of it, the response to the growing disorder was the creation of what would later become the modern criminal justice system. The modern bureaucratic agencies of criminal justice—police, courts, and corrections—were begun in the nineteenth century (we will discuss the particular histories in the appropriate chapters on police, courts, and corrections). The United States was not unique in these responses to industrialization, immigration, and urbanization; most of the industrial nations of Western Europe and Japan formulated a similar response to similar historic developments (Walker 1998, 49–50).

By the early years of the twentieth century, many influential Americans believed they were in the midst of an epidemic crime wave. The widespread fear of crime led to the questioning of restrictions on the power of government to establish order and to demands that police, prosecutors, and judges crack down on crime and criminals. Some, such as Samuel Untermeyer, a prominent New York attorney, advocated the abolition of the Fourth Amendment's protection against unreasonable searches and seizures and the Fifth Amendment's guarantee against self-incrimination (American Academy of Political and Social Science 1910). Others demanded harsher punishments for even minor offenses, such as life imprisonment and even death for hardened drunkards and prostitutes. This tough stance toward criminals prevailed from the 1920s through the 1950s, when the public feared gangsters, mobsters, and juvenile delinquents more than they feared abuse of government power (Brown and Warner 1992, 296–305; Howe 1910; Walker 1998).

The due process revolution

Then came the due process revolution of the 1960s. Prior to this time, the U.S. Supreme Court had interpreted the Bill of Rights to apply only to federal criminal proceedings. During the 1960s the Court adopted an ambitious (some say too ambitious, even unconstitutional) agenda:

1. Expand the rights of criminal defendants.
2. Apply these expanded rights to both federal *and* state criminal proceedings.
3. Include "outsiders"—like poor, minority, and other suspects, defendants, and offenders—within the protection of these expanded rights. (Chapter 2)

The 1960s were turbulent times when "the establishment" was under siege. (I remember, when I was a young lawyer-turned-"do-gooder"-high school teacher in

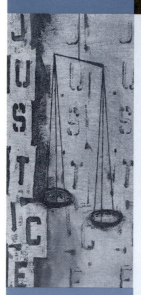

Public opinion surveys consistently show a huge gap between Blacks' and Whites' views about the fairness of the criminal justice system. Most Whites believe the system provides "justice for all"; most Blacks believe "justice means 'just us.'" According to the research, it's not race (or ethnicity, or gender, or sexual orientation) but four other criteria that govern *most* decision making: the seriousness of the offense, the criminal history of the offender, the relationship between the offender and the victim, and the strength of the case against the offender. Consider the following quotes concerning this empirical research:

- "The bottom line of most of the best research is that America's justice system is *not* racist . . ." (Professor John DiIulio, Jr. in Russell 1998, 29–30)
- "There is racial prejudice and discrimination *within* the criminal justice system . . . there are individuals, both black and white, who make decisions . . . on the basis of race. I do not believe that the *system* is characterized by racial prejudice or discrimination against blacks." (Wilbanks 1987, 4–5)
- "The principal conclusion of . . . [our research] was not that racial discrimination does not exist—there are too many anecdotal reports of such discrimination to dismiss that possibility—but, rather, that the *bulk* [my emphasis] of the racial disproportionality in prison is attributable to differential involvement in arrest, and probably in crime, in those most serious offenses that tend to lead to imprisonment." (Blumstein 1993, 743, 750)

Professor Blumstein compared the racial distribution of arrests for the crimes that account for most prison populations with the racial mix of prisoners for the same crimes (Figure 1.8). According to Professor Blumstein, "If there is no discrimination after arrest, then one would expect the fraction of black arrestees for each type of crime to be reflected in a similar mix in prison for that crime type" (Blumstein 1993, 746). Here's what Professor Blumstein found:

1. In the two most serious offenses—murder and robbery—"both had a fraction of blacks in prison that was *almost identical* [emphasis mine] to the fraction of blacks at arrest." (1993, 746)
2. For less serious offenses, the fraction of Blacks in prison is larger than at arrest. Since there's more room for discretion in these less serious crimes, "[D]iscretion *could* [my emphasis] invoke considerations other than the seriousness of the crime, which is most likely to dominate the sentencing

decision for murder and robbery." Some are appropriate (prior conviction record of the offender); others might be (prior record of arrests and employment history). "Of course, the room for discretion also offers the opportunity for the introduction of racial discrimination." (1993, 746)
3. "For homicide (murder and manslaughter), blacks are significantly *under*-represented in prison compared to their presence in arrest. For most of the other crime types, there is *some degree* [my emphasis] of over-representation of blacks in prison. . . ." Overall, 76 percent of all arrests were based on arrests, and arrests are probably a good measure of actual offending. That leaves 24 percent that *might* be based on discrimination. (1993, 750–751)
4. The widest gap between Black arrests and imprisonment is in drug offenses. Two reasons, having nothing to do with direct discrimination, may explain this:
   a. More police are in Black neighborhoods because there's more crime there, and so they're more likely to discover drug crimes there.
   b. Drug markets operated by Blacks are more often outdoors and therefore more vulnerable to police discovery than drug markets operated by whites, which tend to be indoors. (1993, 752–753)

However, according to Professor Katheryn K. Russell:

Professor Blumstein surmises that a 20 to 25 percent gap is no great cause for alarm because eliminating this gap would not change the incarceration picture dramatically. By Blumstein's calculation, the 20 to 25 percent gap of unexplained disparity between arrest and incarceration figures represents about 10,000 black prisoners. Although 10,000 prisoners is a statistical drop in the bucket of the overall prison population (less than 1 percent), socially it is no small number. Ten thousand blacks, who may have been more harshly treated by the criminal justice system *because* of their race, constitutes an enormous social problem. If 10,000 blacks have been subjected to discrimination, this means that some were unjustly convicted and unjustly sentenced to lengthy prison terms.

Further, the impact of the race discrimination would extend beyond those blacks who were direct victims of discrimination. There would be the social and economic impact on their families (e.g., children, spouses, and parents). By what logic could we excuse

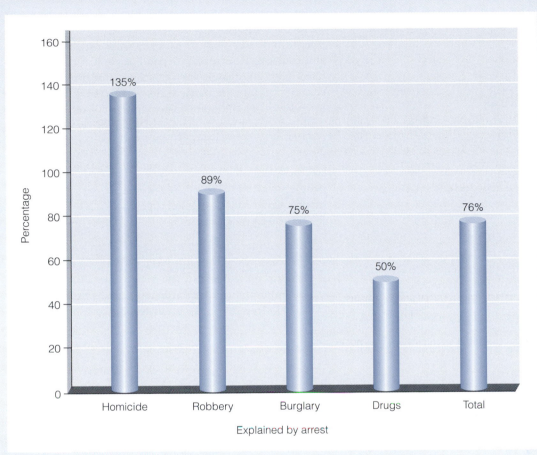

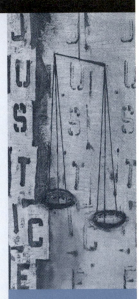

FIGURE 1.8

Percentage of Disproportionality Between Black Arrests and Imprisonment Due to Arrest, 1991

SOURCE: Blumstein 1993.

or, worse, ignore this unexplained 20 to 25 percent gap? Blumstein states that the high rate of black incarceration is "not so much due to racial discrimination." How could he know this to be true? Can the issue of discrimination be dismissed so easily? It is likely Blumstein did not intend to belittle the impact of racial discrimination." (Russell 1998, 31)

Questions

1. In answering the question "How much discrimination is too much?" how important is it that Blacks are underrepresented in imprisonments for homi-

cide and then overrepresented in imprisonments for less serious crimes?

2. How much weight do you give to Professor Russell's response to Professor Blumstein?

3. In your opinion, how much discrimination is unacceptable in real-world criminal justice decision making as opposed to ideal decision making? Defend your answer.

Chicago's inner city, an older teacher who began almost every conversation by wringing her hands and saying, "In these times of upheaval and disorder. . . .") Soaring crime rates; an increasingly militant civil rights movement; growing dissension over an unpopular war in Vietnam; a highly publicized youth counterculture; and rioting in the streets and cities left law-abiding citizens reeling (Cronin, Cronin, and Milakovich 1981; Halberstam 1998; Skolnick 1994, 241).

The return to crime control

One popular interpretation of the problems of the 1960s was that a permissive society with too many safeguards for criminal defendants and not enough punishment for offenders emboldened budding criminals to mock the standards of decency, hard work, and "playing by the rules." These "antisocial renegades" lived for sex, drugs, rock and roll, riots, and, eventually, for crime. The popular and political answer was to declare and fight an all-out "war on crime." The elements of this war consisted of more police, more punishment, and fewer rights for criminal defendants. This resurgence of the value of crime control continued throughout the 1980s and 1990s. And, despite reduced crime rates and some public disenchantment with all "domestic wars"—including those on crime and drugs—the belief that law-abiding people are still at war with crime, particularly violent crime and drugs, is very much alive in 2002 (Currie 1998, 3–11; Flanagan and Longmire 1996).

■ RACE, ETHNICITY, GENDER, AND CRIMINAL JUSTICE

Why are we outraged if race, ethnicity, gender, sexual orientation, and other characteristics we were born with affect police officers' decisions to investigate, prosecutors' to charge, juries' to convict, judges' to sentence, and corrections authorities' to punish? Because decisions based on them violate two of our deepest held values—equality and fairness. It wouldn't be an outrage if there were an *acceptable* reason for treating individuals in these groups differently, like having enough facts to back up police officers' arrests, prosecutors' charges, juries' verdicts, and judges' sentences. So, throughout this book we'll try to answer (as much as existing evidence allows) two questions about criminal justice decisions where race, ethnicity, gender, and sexual orientation are involved:

1. Are there disparities?
2. If so, are disparities caused by discrimination, by something else, or by a combination?

The answer to the first question is almost always, yes; there is **disparity**. All serious scholars and nearly all empirical research demonstrate the percentage of racial and ethnic minorities in the criminal justice system consistently and sometimes greatly exceeds the percentage of these groups in the general population.

The tougher question to answer is *why?* First, individual prejudice of criminal justice professionals has to account for some of the disparity, but it's hard to prove in these days of political correctness when we've learned how to hide our prejudices, even from our best friends, and sometimes ourselves. Second, even if different treatment isn't motivated by conscious discrimination, researchers point to **statistical discrimination** (attributing to individuals the stereotypes of their group) as a real problem. According to Professor Michael Tonry, who has studied race and criminal justice, statistical discrimination in criminal justice means "because young black men are members of a group in which crime is high, many people of all races react to the stereotype and unfairly judge individuals." Professor Tonry (1995, 50–51) recounts the following incident:

> Brian Roberts, a . . . law student in a three-piece suit, visiting a white St. Louis judge as part of a class project, was pulled over by the police soon after his rental car entered the judge's affluent neighborhood. He was then followed, the squad car leaving only after he was admitted to the judge's home.

Many professional Blacks tell similar stories. Brent Staples, a member of the *New York Times* editorial board, has written of numerous instances in which he was stereotyped in college, graduate school, and afterward. The journalist Ellis Cose (1995), in *The Rage of a Privileged Class,* says he was thrown out of a restaurant because the waiter mistook him for another Black man who had caused trouble there in the past. In *Race Matters,* the Harvard philosopher Cornel West (1994) tells of how he was stopped three times in his first ten days at Princeton "for driving too slowly in a residential neighborhood."

Newark Judge Claude Coleman, a police officer turned judge, tells of how he was arrested while he was Christmas shopping in Bloomingdale's because of mistaken identity. Earlier that day, another Black man had tried to use a stolen credit card. Even though Coleman bore no resemblance to the man, the police arrested him. When the officers arrived, Judge Coleman protested his innocence, asked to see his accusers, and showed identification. He was nonetheless handcuffed—tightly behind his back—and then dragged through crowds of shoppers to a police car. At the stationhouse, he was chained to the wall and was prevented from calling a lawyer. Judge Coleman was eventually released. His response to the incident: "No matter how many achievements you have, you can't shuck the burden of being black in a white society" (Margolick 1994).

Despite these and many anecdotes, empirical research spanning more than twenty-five years, conducted by a wide range of scholars from all parts of the ideological spectrum, has repeatedly demonstrated that the *bulk* of decisions throughout criminal justice—arrest, charge, bail, conviction, sentence, punishment, and release from custody—are based on seriousness of the offense, criminal history of the offender, relationship of the victim to the offender, and the strength of the case against the defendant, the criteria we laid out earlier in the chapter (Russell 1998).

The research has also found that discriminatory decision making is concentrated in *minor* offenses (disorderly conduct, public drunkenness, and prostitution). The more serious the offense (murder, rape, and robbery), the less race and other unacceptable criteria infect decision making. Of course, as we've already learned in this chapter, a lot more people commit minor offenses than murder, rape, and robbery.

But there are problems with the empirical research. Social factors—particularly education, job opportunities, families, and class—relate strongly to criminal behavior, and race and ethnicity are strongly tied to the distribution of the benefits or disadvantages of these social factors. So, legitimate criteria (seriousness of the offense, criminal history of the offender, and amount of proof) may well explain decision making *inside* the criminal justice system because class, family, job opportunities, and education *outside* the criminal justice system affect the seriousness of offenses and the criminal history of offenders.

Also, the empirical research focuses on the decisions themselves, not on the circumstances surrounding them. Just because discrimination doesn't infect the *decision* to arrest, to search, to convict, to sentence, and to incarcerate doesn't mean criminal justice professionals aren't prejudiced. William Wilbanks, whose own research and survey of others' research on racism in criminal justice emphatically concluded a "racist criminal justice system" is a "myth," nonetheless concedes:

> To argue that there is no systematic bias against blacks in formal decisions does not speak to the issue of whether the police are more likely to "talk down" to black citizens or to show them less respect. The fact that a police officer may call a 40-year-old black man "boy" [however] does not necessarily mean that the officer will be more likely to arrest that man (or, if he does, that his decision is based primarily on the racist stereotype). Harassment of minorities by system personnel, less desirable work assignments, and indifference to important cultural needs could exist, but not be systematically reflected in formal criminal justice processing decisions. (Wilbanks 1987, 6)

Knowledge and Understanding Check

Introduction
- ✔ What is discretion?
- ✔ Identify and describe four characteristics decision making in all criminal justice agencies has in common.

Formal and informal criminal justice
- ✔ Explain the difference between formal and informal decision making in criminal justice.
- ✔ What role does discretionary decision making play in criminal justice?

Criminal justice: structure and process
- ✔ Identify and briefly describe the parts of the structure of criminal justice.
- ✔ Identify and briefly describe the decision points in the criminal justice process.

The criminal justice "system"
- ✔ Explain how criminal justice is a *system* and why "system" isn't a completely accurate description.
- ✔ Explain the hydraulic effect.

Models of criminal justice
- ✔ Identify four decisions that have to take place *before* the criminal justice process can begin.

- ✔ Trace the history and explain the significance of victims' decisions.
- ✔ List the characteristics of the criminal justice wedding cake and funnel.
- ✔ Compare and contrast the criminal justice wedding cake and funnel.
- ✔ Describe the major goals of the crime control and the due process models.
- ✔ Describe the major characteristics of the crime control and the due process models.
- ✔ How is the crime control model like a conveyor belt assembly line? How is the due process model like an obstacle course?
- ✔ Identify and trace the developments of the major eras in the history of crime control and due process.
- ✔ Explain why the history of crime control and due process is one of "pendulum swings."

Race, ethnicity, gender, and criminal justice
- ✔ Explain the difference between intentional and statistical discrimination.
- ✔ Summarize the findings and the weaknesses of empirical research on the effects of discrimination on criminal justice decision making.

KEY TERMS

adversary process
case attrition
crime control
criminal justice system
discretion

discretionary decision making
diversion
due process
felonies
formal criminal justice

hydraulic effect
informal criminal justice
presumption of guilt
statistical discrimination
wedding cake model

INTERNET PROJECT

 What is the state of our knowledge about discrimination in criminal justice? Using InfoTrac College Edition, enter the keyword "discrimination." You can research the topic generally or concentrate on race, gender, sexual orientation, disability, or even obesity. Unfortunately, you won't find anything about ethnicity.

CHAPTER 2

Criminal Justice and the Law

© Reuters NewMedia/Corbis

CHAPTER OUTLINE

> **Our crime control system rests on, indeed is created and enabled by law. . . . This is not simply a system of informal social behavior . . . without formal controls. . . . The whole significance . . . [is] to counterpoint the law in action with formal legal . . . controls. . . .**
>
> DONALD J. NEWMAN (1993, 281)

■ INTRODUCTION

"No crime without law" and "no punishment without law" are two ancient principles of our criminal law. In a *pure* democracy, the majority can make anything it pleases a crime. But ours is a *constitutional* democracy, where even a 100 percent majority can't make anything it pleases a crime. The U.S. Constitution says crime control has to operate within the framework of law, and these two ancient principles are part of the framework. No behavior, however harmful, can be made criminal without a specific law defining it as a crime and prescribing a punishment for it. No action taken or decision made by any police officer, prosecutor, defense attorney, judge, jury, probation officer, corrections officer, or parole officer (discussed in the remaining chapters of this book) is allowed unless the law says so.

At least, this is the formal side of criminal law and procedure. But, just as there are both a formal and an informal criminal justice, there's also an informal discretionary decision making side to criminal law and procedure. So, although decision making has to take place inside the framework of formal law, there's plenty of room to allow for informal social, ideological, and political influences. In this chapter, we'll look closely at both sides of criminal law and criminal procedure.

■ CRIMINAL LAW

Criminal law tells private individuals what behavior is criminal and defines the punishment for criminal behavior. In every society there are people whose behavior society should condemn. Some of this behavior (for example, murder, rape, and robbery) is clearly offensive and should be a crime. But no society makes crimes out of *all* offensive behavior. Criminal law distinguishes *reprehensible* behavior from *criminal* behavior. To put it bluntly, we distinguish between creeps and criminals. For example, creeps cheat on their girlfriends and boyfriends, and they lie to friends, but they shouldn't go to jail for it. Why? Because criminal law is society's last resort in controlling crime. It's expensive and unwieldy and intrudes deeply

into privacy and liberty, often with limited or no effect. So, we rely on less expensive, less restrictive social control mechanisms like disapproval of family, friends, and others we love and respect; informal discipline within social institutions like schools and workplaces; and private lawsuits. We call this reliance on the least expensive or invasive response to misbehavior the principle of economy. The bottom line: In a constitutional democracy, there are limits to the power of government to define and control crime.

The principle of economy is only one way we limit the power of government to define crime. Let's look at three others:

1. U.S. Constitution
2. **General principles of criminal liability** (the elements of crime prosecutors have to prove beyond a reasonable doubt)
3. General principles of justification and excuse (defenses to criminal liability)

Constitutional Limits

Four provisions in the U.S. Constitution limit the power of government to create criminal laws and set punishments:

1. "No . . . *ex post facto* law shall be passed." (Article I, Section 9)
2. "No person shall be . . . deprived of life, liberty, or property without due process of law. . . ." (Amendment V)
3. "No state shall . . . deny any person life, liberty, or property without due process of law." (Amendment XIV)
4. "No state shall . . . deny any person within its jurisdiction the equal protection of the laws." (Amendment XIV)

The **ex post facto clause** prohibits retroactive criminal laws. (Retroactive criminal laws make a crime out of behavior that wasn't criminal before the law was passed.) For example, if a state passes a statute on January 2, 2002, raising the drinking age from 18 to 21, the state can't prosecute a 19-year-old who bought a beer on New Year's

Eve in 2001. Why? People have to have fair warning their behavior is a crime; ex post facto laws obviously don't do that.

Vague laws deny individuals life, liberty, and property without due process of law, according to the **void-for-vagueness doctrine.** They don't give individuals fair warning. In the words of the U.S. Supreme Court, a law

> which either forbids or requires the doing of an act in terms so vague that men [and women] of common intelligence must necessarily guess at its meaning and differ as to its application violates the first essential of due process of law. (*Lanzetta v. New Jersey* 1939, 453)

The Nebraska supreme court struck down a Lincoln, Nebraska, city ordinance prohibiting "any indecent, immodest, or filthy act in the presence of any person," because it violated the Fourteenth Amendment due process clause. (The Fifth Amendment due process clause applies to the federal government; the Fourteenth Amendment due process clause applies to state governments.) A passerby saw Doug Metzger standing naked in front of his window eating a bowl of cereal for breakfast. According to the Nebraska supreme court:

> We know of no way in which the standards required of a criminal act can be met in those broad, general terms. There may be those few who believe persons of the opposite sex holding hands in public are immodest, and certainly more who might believe kissing in public is immodest. (*State v. Metzger* 1982)

The Fourteenth Amendment also prohibits states from denying individuals equal protection of the laws. Equal protection doesn't mean laws have to treat people *exactly* alike. But it does mean laws can't make *unreasonable* distinctions, especially those based on race but also on gender and ethnicity. For example, a statute making it a crime for women (but not men) to smoke in public violated the equal protection clause. On the other hand, the U.S. Supreme Court ruled California's statutory rape law, which applied only to men, didn't violate the equal protection clause. Why? Because California has a "compelling interest" in reducing "the tragic human costs of illegitimate teenage pregnancies" (*Michael M. v. Superior Court of Sonoma County* 1981).

Due process also protects the controversial right of privacy. But, don't look for the word *privacy* in the U.S. Constitution—it's not there. Nevertheless, the U.S. Supreme Court says there is such a right. The right is based on the idea that a free society maximizes human autonomy—the right of the people to be let alone by government, especially when it concerns their bodies, their homes, and their family relationships. So, the U.S. Supreme Court, in *Griswold v. Connecticut* (1965), struck down a Connecticut statute making it a crime for married couples to use contraceptives. According to Justice William O. Douglas, the Constitution creates a "zone of privacy" around the "intimate relation of husband and wife," and the statute had a "destructive impact upon the relationship." Although the Court created the right of privacy, it has made clear it's far from absolute. For example, in 1986 the Court in *Bowers v. Hardwick* (1986) let stand a Georgia sodomy law against a challenge that the right of privacy protected sexual acts in private between two consenting adult homosexuals.

However, several state constitutions do have specific provisions protecting privacy. The Alaska constitution, for example, provides "the right of the people to privacy is recognized and shall not be infringed." Relying on the right to privacy provision in the Alaska constitution, the Alaska supreme court ruled that in Alaska the right to privacy includes the right of an adult to possess a small amount of marijuana for personal use in her home. According to the court:

> The privacy amendment . . . was intended to give recognition and protection to the home. Such a reading is consonant with the character of life in Alaska. Our . . . state has traditionally been the home of people who prize their individuality and who have chosen to settle or to continue living here in order to achieve a measure of control over their own lifestyles which is now virtually unattainable in many of our sister states. (*Ravin v. State* 1975)

The people of Alaska later overruled the decision by changing the law through a referendum.

 2-1 Right to privacy in your state

The Principles of Criminal Liability

Prosecutors have to prove defendants guilty beyond a reasonable doubt to convict them (Chapter 8, "Charge, Trial, and Guilty Pleas"). Specifically, this means prosecutors have to prove every element of the crime beyond a reasonable doubt. All serious crimes (homicide, rape, robbery, burglary, and theft) require proof of three elements:

1. Criminal act
2. Criminal intent
3. Concurrence of the criminal act and the criminal intent

A few crimes, like criminal homicide, require a fourth element

4. Causing a particular result (for example, causing death in homicide)

Criminal act

Our criminal law can't punish people for what they wish, or hope, or intend, or might do, or who they are; it can only punish them for what they *do*. However, this doesn't mean you have to complete a crime for it to be a criminal act. For example, the Wisconsin supreme court ruled it was attempted murder when a man chased his wife with a gun he forgot to load, caught up with her, pointed the gun at her head, and pulled the trigger several times. "It won't shoot! It won't shoot!" he shouted (*State v. Damms* 1960). It's also a crime to agree to commit a crime even if you never start to commit it. So, a woman who agreed to buy "X" (the drug Ecstasy) was guilty of conspiracy even though the deal fell through. It's even a crime to encourage someone else to commit a crime, even if they turn you down cold. So, when Harold Furr offered Donald Owens $3000 to kill his wife Earlene, he was found guilty of solicitation even though Owens flatly refused the offer (*State v. Furr* 1977). It's also a crime to even have in your possession a long list of things, including certain types of weapons, drugs, and pornography, even if you don't use, sell, or for that matter *do* anything with them. It's enough that you took some action to get them. But notice what all these crimes have in common—they all include some action: *pulling* the trigger, *agreeing* to buy Ecstasy, *asking* a friend to kill, and *taking* possession of, say, a gun.

"Criminal act," as defined by the law, also includes failure to act but only if there's a legal duty to act. These are called **criminal omissions.** There are two kinds. Most common are failures to report when required by law, like not filing your income tax return. Less common is failure to intervene to help someone in danger, like a father who stands by while a mother abuses their baby. Legal duties can arise out of specific statutes (like income tax laws); contracts (an agreement to take care of a sick person); and special relationships (parents and minor children, doctors and patients).

 2-2 Special relationship

One critical limit to this generous definition of "act" is the act has to be voluntary. So, forcing Doug with a loaded gun to take Sally's Ecstasy wasn't stealing. Nor, a court decided, was it murder in one bizarre case when a mother killed her daughter with an ax while she was dreaming she was killing a man who was attacking the daughter.

 2-3 Sleep walking as a criminal act

Criminal intent

In all serious crimes like murder, rape, robbery, burglary, and theft a criminal intent has to trigger the criminal act. The mental element is complicated because there are four levels of criminal intent:

1. Purposeful
2. Knowing
3. Reckless
4. Negligent

Purposeful, sometimes called specific, intent means you committed the criminal act (or caused the harm) on purpose. Knowing means you *know* you're committing an act or causing a harm but you're not acting for that purpose. For example, a doctor who performed a life-saving hysterectomy on a pregnant woman to save her life knew he would kill the fetus but he didn't remove the uterus for the very purpose of killing the fetus. Reckless means consciously creating a risk of harm. Consider the man who didn't tell his partner he had AIDS because he was afraid his partner wouldn't have sex with him if he did. They had sex regularly. The man didn't want his partner to get AIDS, but he knew he was creating the risk of giving him AIDS by having sex with him, and he did it anyway. Negligent is like reckless in that it means actions creating a risk of causing harm. But negligent is *unconsciously* creating a risk, meaning you *should* know you're creating a risk but you don't. Consider the man who bought a car from a newspaper ad and drove it home without checking the brakes, which he didn't know were faulty. He struck and killed a pedestrian when the brakes failed on the way home. He was negligent; he didn't know but he should've known not to drive a car he wasn't familiar with.

Criminal intent, unlike action, isn't required in lesser crimes carrying light punishments like fines. We call these crimes without intent **strict liability offenses.** Our criminal law didn't recognize strict liability until the Industrial Revolution when public transportation, factories, and large-scale consumer purchasing created high risks to health and safety. Shared managerial responsibility characterized these new enterprises and made the requirement of personal and individual culpability meaningless. The requirement of criminal intent prevented the punishment of these serious injuries, incurable diseases, and deaths. Legislatures responded by adopting strict liability offenses.

Concurrence

The element of concurrence means criminal intent has to trigger the criminal act. For example, Doug hates Nathan. He plans to kill him but changes his mind because he doesn't want to go to prison. As luck would have it, two months after he abandons his plan to kill Nathan, Michelle accidentally hits Nathan with her new VW and kills him. Doug's delighted when he hears Nathan's dead, but he's not guilty of murder. Why? Because his intent to kill Nathan didn't trigger Michelle's running over him (LaFave and Scott 1986, 267–277).

Causing a harmful result

The prosecution has to prove two types of cause led to a "harmful result": cause in fact and legal cause. **Cause in fact** means that "but for" the actions of the defendant, the result wouldn't have happened. For example, Kibbe and his companion rob Stafford and leave him on a country road. Blake, a college student on his way to a class, accidentally runs over Stafford and kills him. "But for" Kibbe and his companion leaving Stafford on the road, Blake wouldn't have run over and killed him. So, Kibbe and his companion were the cause in fact of Stafford's death.

Cause in fact is necessary but not sufficient to prove causation; there also has to be legal cause. **Legal cause** asks the question: Is it fair to blame the defendants for the results of actions they set in motion? It's up to the jury to decide the "fair to blame" question. For example, in a jealous rage Cameron stabs Rob. Rob refuses to go to the doctor because he doesn't want to spend the money. Finally, after nearly a day, he's so weak from loss of blood he goes to an emergency room where he receives a transfusion. He develops an infection from a dirty needle used in the transfusion and dies three weeks later. The jury has to decide whether it's fair to blame Cameron for Rob's death because stabbing Rob set in motion a chain of events that ended in Rob's death but would *not* have led to Rob's death if he'd gotten help earlier and the hospital hadn't used a dirty needle.

Defenses to Criminal Liability

Legally, defendants can escape criminal liability in four ways:

1. Failure of the government to prove all the elements of the crime beyond a reasonable doubt
2. Defense of alibi
3. Defense of justification
4. Defense of excuse

As we've already learned, the government has to prove all the elements of the crime. Defendants have to prove their defenses. In defenses of **alibi,** defendants prove they couldn't have committed the crime because they were somewhere else when the crime was committed. Defenses of **justification** focus on the rightness of the defendant's *actions*. Defendants admit they committed the acts they're charged with but argue that under the circumstances what they did was justified. The best example of a justification is self-defense: "I killed Cruz because he was about to kill me." The defenses of **excuse** focus on the competence of the *actors*. Defendants admit what they did was wrong but argue that under the circumstances they weren't responsible: "Killing Mai was wrong but I was insane when I killed her." We'll take a closer look at the latter two types of defenses: justification and excuse.

Defenses of justification

Defenses of justification include self-defense, defense of home and property, and consent.

Self-Defense   "Kill or be killed" is the general idea behind self-defense. It's an example of what societies ruled by law abhor—letting you take the law into your own hands. Only the law can't help you at that moment. So, a more accurate way to express the defense is, "Kill or be killed *right now!*

You're legally justified in using force against an attacker only if you can prove three conditions:

1. You didn't provoke the attack.
2. You reasonably believed you were going to be attacked right then.
3. You used only enough force necessary to repel the attack.

These conditions rule out two reasons for using force that are utterly unacceptable under the rule of law: (1) to prevent future attacks (preemptive strikes) like killing someone who's going to kill you next week and (2) paying back someone who tried to kill you last week (retaliation). Preemptive strikes and retaliation are the government's business, not private individuals.'

One example of the preemptive strike (and maybe retaliation too) is battered women who can't take their battering anymore but who aren't in imminent danger of death when they kill their batterers. In one case, Peggy Stewart and her daughters suffered years of unspeakable physical, sexual, and emotional abuse from Peggy's husband Mike. On the day of his death, Mike raped Peggy and repeatedly threatened to kill her. That evening, Peggy and Mike went to bed at about 8 o'clock. Mike fell asleep while Peggy lay beside him agonizing over her situation. At about 10 o'clock she went into the room where Mike kept his gun, came back, and shot him to death. She obviously wasn't in danger of Mike killing her at the moment she shot him, so she didn't fit into one of the conditions qualifying her for self-defense (danger of imminent death). In *State v. Stewart* (1988), the jury acquitted her anyway (probably an instance of jury nullification, see Chapter 8).

 2-4 Battered woman defense

Defense of Home and Property   Under the **common law,** killing nighttime home intruders was justifiable homicide. (The common law translated the traditions, customs, and values of the English people into legal rules.) Modern law still follows the common-law rule by granting occupants the right to use force to defend their homes. For example, Colorado's "make-my-day law" grants immunity from all legal action—including criminal prosecution—to occupants of homes who use force, including deadly force, against "one who has made an unlawful entry into the dwelling"(*Colorado Statutes* 1986).

In most states, you can also use force to protect personal property. If you're in Texas, you can even shoot to kill to protect your "tangible property" and "movable property" (like cars, cameras, MP3 players, or any other personal belongings) *if* you can't protect it "by any other

YOU DECIDE

Was she justified in killing her batterer?

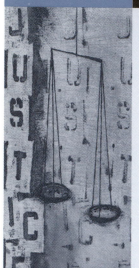

State v. Cramer, 17 Kan.App.2d 623, 841 P.2d 1111 (Kan. App. 1993)

Facts

Janette Cramer and William Cramer were married in July 1987. William began to beat Janette nine days before their wedding, and he continued to beat her regularly up to the time of his death. Some of these beatings were so violent Janette was hospitalized. On one occasion, William picked Janette up and tried to "hang" her on a nail on the wall. The nail punctured her back and left a scar running up to her shoulder. Frequently, both parties were drinking when these violent episodes took place.

Finally, Janette sued William for divorce. She obtained a restraining order, but it didn't restrain William, who continued to beat and threaten her. After one of these beatings put Janette in the hospital, a friend gave her a handgun for protection. On the night of William's death, Janette put the handgun in a strategic position in her house.

On the evening of William's death, he came to Janette's home with her permission. He came to discuss their divorce and brought along a supply of beer and liquor. The two parties sat down at the table and began to drink and discuss the terms of their divorce. As the evening wore on, William became more angry and, finally, began to pound on the table. He started to verbally abuse Janette and stood up and stepped toward her. According to Janette, she got up and retrieved the handgun. She pointed the gun at William and said, "You're not going to beat on me again." William laughed, took one step forward, and Janette shot him in the chest. As a result of the gunshot, William bled to death.

Janette was charged with second-degree murder. Her defense was self-defense, based on the battered woman's syndrome. After a three-day trial, the jury returned a verdict, finding her guilty of involuntary manslaughter. At her sentencing, Janette argued that to deny her probation amounted to "manifest injustice" under K.S.A.1991 Supp. 21-4618(3). After listening to defendant's arguments, the trial court denied her probation because of her use of a firearm and the provisions of K.S.A. 21-4618(1) and (2). She appealed her conviction and sentence. After careful consideration, we affirm on both counts.

Opinion

In order to prove her battered woman's syndrome defense, defendant introduced the expert testimony of Dr. Stephen E. Peterson, a psychiatrist at the Menninger Clinic. He testified that, in his opinion, defendant was suffering from the battered woman's syndrome. Dr. Peterson prepared an extensive report that gave specific details about defendant's past life and experiences. A portion of this report described several instances of violent conduct between defendant and other parties. The State of Kansas countered Dr. Peterson's testimony by introducing testimony of Dr. Alice Brill. Dr. Brill is also a psychiatrist, and she testified that, in her opinion, defendant did not suffer from the battered woman's syndrome. Dr. Brill's opinion was based in large part on the evidence of specific instances of past conduct, to which defendant objects.

Defendant is particularly aggrieved by the testimony of Melvin Fox. Fox testified he had had a relationship of sorts with defendant. He described in graphic detail one occasion when he was in the bathroom, throwing up

means," or if "the failure to use deadly force" would expose you or others to a "substantial risk of death or serious bodily injury" (*Texas Criminal Code* 1988, Section 9.42).

Consent Are you justified in committing a crime against someone who gives you permission to commit the crime against him? A few courts say consent is a justification for criminal behavior. The reason is the value placed on individual autonomy in a free society. If a mentally competent adult wants to be a crime victim, so the argument for the defense of consent goes, no paternalistic government should interfere with her choice. Consent may make sense in the larger context of individual freedom and responsibility, but the criminal law is hostile to consent as a justification for committing crimes. Individuals can take their

own lives and inflict injuries on themselves, but they can't authorize others to kill them or beat them.

The few courts that allow this defense place three limits on its use: no serious injury results from the consensual crime; the injury happens during a sporting event; or the conduct benefits the consenting person, such as when a surgeon operates on a patient. Not only is consent limited to these three circumstances, but the consenting persons have to know they're consenting and consent of their own free will. Forgiveness *after* the crime's committed doesn't count.

 2-5 You Decide: Are you justified in committing a crime against a consenting "victim"?

after a drinking spree. He testified that, while he was in this rather vulnerable state, defendant entered the bathroom wearing only steel-toed biker boots and proceeded to kick him several times. Dr. Brill referred to the incident described by Fox in support of her opinion that defendant was not suffering from the battered woman's syndrome.

[According to the court, the evidence was admissible.] Testimony concerning the specific instances complained of by defendant was elicited by the State in an effort to cast doubt upon Dr. Peterson's diagnosis of the battered woman's syndrome. On cross-examination, Dr. Peterson was cross-examined about an incident at a wedding party where defendant physically fought with another woman. Another incident concerned an altercation between defendant and a male bouncer at a tavern. Dr. Brill, the State's expert witness, referred to these incidents as inconsistent with those characteristics associated with the battered woman's syndrome.

The defense in this lawsuit was self-defense. This was based on the contention that defendant suffered from the battered woman's syndrome and perceived she was protecting herself from imminent danger in shooting William. The record is replete with evidence of repeated beatings inflicted upon defendant by William. Both expert witnesses agreed that defendant was a battered woman. Defendant's circumstances in this case were those of a battered woman being advanced upon by her battering spouse.

The defendant in this case was convicted of the crime of involuntary manslaughter, as defined by K.S.A. 21-3404. This crime was committed with the use of a firearm. Under these circumstances, the mandatory sentencing provisions of K.S.A.1991 Supp. 21-4618 are applicable. This statute requires mandatory imprisonment under the circumstances shown. The trial court sentenced defendant under K.S.A.1991 Supp. 21-4618(1) and (2) and denied her application for probation or assignment to a community corrections program.

We have reviewed the record carefully in the instant matter. We conclude that the trial court considered all of the necessary sentencing factors required by statute in making its decision. It is not our position to second-guess the trial court in matters of sentencing. The trial judge heard all of the testimony, observed the witnesses, and had the opportunity to evaluate their credibility based on personal observance. The trial court is in the best position to evaluate the sentencing factors involved, and we respect the trial court's superior knowledge and its primary responsibility in pronouncing sentence.

Affirmed.

Questions

1. Do you think the evidence of Janette Cramer's past history of violence against other people proves she didn't suffer from battered woman's syndrome? Defend your answer.
2. Do you think that the evidence of her violent history should play a part in sentencing her? Defend your answer.
3. Would you sentence her to probation? Defend your answer.

Defenses of excuse

Now that we've examined some of the justifications, let's look at the excuses (the act was wrong but the defendant wasn't responsible). The defenses of excuse are based on the idea that the law should make allowances for the imperfections and frailties of human nature. In the real world, excuses aren't popular. I hear excuses from students almost every day. I often think (and sometimes say), "Excuses, excuses, excuses, I'm sick of excuses!!" The criminal law doesn't like them either, even though there's a long list of them, including age; duress; entrapment; intoxication; the best-known excuse, insanity or diminished capacity; and a number of so-called syndromes, like PMS (premenstrual syndrome), PTS (posttraumatic stress syndrome), and the culture of violence syndrome. The law's hostility to them is formally hidden. But, you can clearly detect it in the failure of almost every defendant who pleads them to escape conviction.

Age Immaturity has excused criminal liability since the earliest days of the English common law. The common law recognized three categories of maturity:

1. Individuals too young under all circumstances to be criminally responsible
2. Individuals mature to the extent that they might or might not be criminally responsible
3. Individuals mature enough to be criminally responsible in nearly all circumstances

The law still recognizes these categories. In most states, the categories are synchronized with the jurisdiction (authority) of juvenile courts. So, juvenile courts have exclusive jurisdiction up to age 15 or 16. Between 16 and 18, juveniles can either be tried as juveniles or certified (transferred) to the regular criminal courts for trial as adults. Certification is most common when juveniles are accused of murder, rape, aggravated assault, robbery, and drug-related offenses.

Old age has occasionally provided an excuse to criminal liability. In one case, a husband asked his wife of fifty years to get him some bagels. She forgot. According to the prosecutor, "The guy goes berserk and he axes his wife; he kills the poor woman with a Boy Scout–type ax!" The prosecutor did not charge the man, saying: "What do we do now? Set high bail? Prosecute? Get a conviction and send the fellow to prison? You tell me! We did nothing. The media dropped it quickly and, I hope, that's it." Incidentally, this case provides another excellent example of discretion adapting law to social reality. The formal law provided no excuse of advanced age. But the prosecutor exercised his independent judgment as to what justice required in this individual case and how best to allocate scarce resources and balance the law and broad community values (Cohen 1985, 9).

Duress   If another person forces you to commit a crime, you might have the excuse of duress. In some states, duress is a defense to all crimes except murder; in others, it excuses only minor crimes. States also differ as to the definition of duress. Some say only threats to kill the defendant are enough to excuse the crime; others say threats to seriously injure will do. Threats to damage reputation or to destroy property aren't enough in any state. Most states say defendants have to face immediate harm if they refuse to commit the crime.

Entrapment   "Make it *easy* to do right and *difficult* to do wrong," Prime Minister William Gladstone told the English government. "Lead us not into temptation, but deliver us from evil" implores the Lord's Prayer. Entrapment—official efforts to get people to commit crimes—defies both the great prime minister's advice and the Lord's Prayer. But the practice has an ancient pedigree. From the reign of Henry VIII, to Hitler and Stalin, to Slobodan Milosevic and Saddam Hussein, police states have relied on government agents (*agents provocateurs*) to trap opponents of the regime (Carlson 1987, 1011).

Entrapment is a defense to crimes that are investigated even though there are no complaining witnesses (prostitution, gambling, pornography, official wrongdoing, and drug crimes). Law enforcement has to use deception to investigate these crimes. The argument in favor of entrapment (and against entrapment as an excuse for criminal behavior) was nicely summed up by one court more than a hundred years ago:

> We are asked to protect the defendant, not because he is innocent, but because a zealous public officer ex-

ceeded his powers and held out a bait. The courts do not look to see who held out the bait, but to see who took it. (*People v. Mills* 1904, 791)

The excuse of entrapment represents an intolerance of government pressures on law-abiding people to commit crimes they wouldn't have committed without the pressure (Marcus 1986, 5).

Encouragement isn't entrapment. So, for the purpose of getting people to commit crimes, officers can ask people to commit crimes; form personal relationships with them; promise them benefits; and supply or help them get contraband. How do we separate encouragement from entrapment? Most courts use the **predisposition test** to decide when officials have crossed the line between encouragement and entrapment. According to the test, if the defendant was ready and willing to commit the crime (predisposed) and the officer only provided her with the opportunity to commit it, that's encouragement, not entrapment. The crucial question is, Where did criminal intent originate? If it originated with the defendant, then the government didn't entrap but only encouraged the defendant (Tiffany et al. 1967).

Sherman v. United States (1958) is a good example of entrapment. In this case, a government undercover agent, Kalchinian, met Sherman in a drug treatment center, made friends with him, and eventually asked Sherman to get him some heroin. Sherman, an addict in treatment, at first refused. After several weeks of Kalchinian's pleading, Sherman broke down and got the requested heroin. The U.S. Supreme Court ruled that Kalchinian entrapped Sherman, arguing that Sherman's reluctance and his being in treatment refuted the claim he was predisposed to commit the crime.

Intoxication   Johnny James was executed by lethal injection for kidnapping two women, forcing them to perform sex acts on each other, and then shooting them both in the head. One died, the other survived and identified James at trial. The criminal justice system turned a deaf ear to James's claim he was too drunk to know what he was doing when he committed the crime so he didn't deserve to die (Gibeaut 1997, 56).

According to Professor George Fletcher, the defense of intoxication is "buffeted between two conflicting principles":

1. *Accountability.* Those who get drunk should face the consequences of their actions.
2. *Culpability.* You can't punish someone who isn't responsible for his or her actions. (Fletcher 1978, 846)

The common law focused on the first principle:

> As to artificial, voluntarily contracted madness, by drunkenness or intoxication, which, depriving men of their reason, puts them in a temporary frenzy; our law looks upon this as an aggravation of the offense, rather

than as an excuse for any criminal misbehavior.
(Blackstone 1803, IV, 25—26)

The Johnny James case proves the common law principle is alive and well. John Gibeaut (1997) notes this contemporary emphasis on the principle of accountability in his article on the James case entitled, "Sobering Thoughts": "Legislatures and courts increasingly are just saying no to intoxication as a defense of mitigating factor" (56—57).

We've been talking about *voluntary* intoxication, which isn't an excuse. *Involuntary* intoxication *is*. Involuntary intoxication refers to defendants who either don't know they're taking intoxicants or know but are forced to take them. So, Augustus Penman was allowed the defense of intoxication when he killed a friend after taking breath mints he didn't know were laced with cocaine (*People v. Penman* 1915).

As for forced intoxication, only *extreme* force is an excuse. According to one authority, "[A] person would need to be bound hand and foot and the liquor literally poured down his throat, or . . . would have to be threatened with immediate serious injury." In *State v. Burrows* (1931), Richard Burrows was 18 and stranded on an Arizona highway with no money. He hitched a ride to Phoenix with Jack Martin. Shortly after they got on the road, Martin began drinking beer and asked Burrows to have some. Burrows, who'd never had a drink, turned him down. Martin got belligerent and threatened to throw Burrows out in the desert if he didn't drink some beer with him. Burrows took a drink because he was afraid of being stranded in the desert. Later, Martin started drinking whiskey and threatened to throw Burrows out again when Burrows said he didn't want to drink anymore. So, Burrows took some. The situation quickly deteriorated after that, the man got more belligerent and Burrows now drunk, got more scared, and finally shot and killed Martin. At his trial for murder, Burrows contended "[A]ny suggestion or influence which induces another to become intoxicated, when, if he had been left entirely to himself, he would have remained sober, excuses him from the consequences of a crime." The state argued that "the influence must go to the extent of actual coercion and abuse." The jury convicted Burrows of murder. On appeal, the Arizona supreme court wrote:

> We are of the opinion that the true rule is that the influence exercised on the mind of a defendant must be such as to amount to duress or fraud. The law has always jealously guarded the effect of drunkenness as a defense in criminal cases, and, even with all the restrictions surrounding it, the doctrine is a dangerous one, and liable to be abused. In this case there is no suggestion of fraud, and it was for the jury to decide whether or not there was coercion and abuse to the extent of duress.

Insanity   The insanity excuse attracts a lot of public, philosophical, religious, and scholarly attention. But, it plays only a tiny part in the day-to-day operations of criminal justice. Defendants rarely plead insanity and rarely succeed if they do. Also, if they do succeed, they don't automatically "walk." In some jurisdictions, the verdict is "not guilty by reason of insanity"; in others, it's "guilty but insane." Guilty but insane means they will go to prison but with the chance for treatment while incarcerated. Not guilty by reason of insanity means they're not guilty but not free to go. Special proceedings to decide whether defendants are mentally ill and dangerous follow the verdict of not guilty by reason of insanity. If they are (and it's a rare court that finds they aren't), they're confined to maximum security hospitals (really just prisons). They're confined until they're no longer dangerous, which usually means a long time and often for life. John Hinckley, who attempted to assassinate President Reagan in the early 1980s, is typical. He's still detained in a maximum security hospital (although he's allowed occasional weekend furloughs).

 2-6 John Hinckley video clip

Insanity is a legal, not a medical, term; it means a mental disease (for example, paranoia) or defect (retardation) that impairs reason and/or will. There are three main tests of insanity:

1. The right-wrong test
2. The right-wrong test supplemented by the irresistible impulse test
3. The substantial capacity or American Law Institute (ALI) test

The **right-wrong test** focuses on reason. The test, sometimes called the *M'Naughten* rule, comes from a famous English case. In 1843, Daniel M'Naughten had the paranoid delusion that the prime minister, Sir Robert Peel, had masterminded a conspiracy to kill him. M'Naughten shot at Peel in delusional self-defense, but mistakenly killed Peel's personal secretary. The jury acquitted M'Naughten. On appeal, the House of Lords—England's highest court of appeal—formulated the right-wrong test. The test evaluates whether two necessary elements were present at the time the crime was committed: (1) A mental disease or defect caused such damage to defendants' capacity to reason (2) that *either* they didn't know what they were doing, *or* if they knew what they were doing, they didn't know it was wrong (*M'Naughten's Case* 1843).

Several jurisdictions have supplemented the right-wrong test with the **irresistible impulse test.** The irresistible impulse test focuses on defendants' willpower, or their capacity to control their actions at the time of the crime. The test evaluates whether two necessary elements

YOU DECIDE

Was his intoxication an excuse for murder?

State v. Hall, 214 N.W.2d 205 (Iowa 1974)

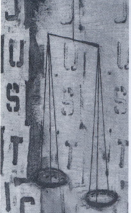

Facts

Allen Hall was hitchhiking in the West, and Gilford Meacham offered him a ride from Oregon to Chicago if Hall would drive. Hall was supposed to split off and hitchhike to his home in North Carolina, while Meacham was to drive on to Connecticut to get married. Hall drove all the way to Iowa without rest and was exhausted. When they got to Des Moines, Hall took a pill (later determined to be LSD) casual acquaintances in California had given him. (They told Hall it was a "little sunshine" and would make him feel "groovy.") It made him "feel funny, and the road turned different colors and pulsated." Meacham was sleeping on the passenger side. Hall testified he heard strange noises from Meacham's throat, like growling. Meacham's face grew and his nose got long, and his head turned into a dog like the one defendant's stepfather had shot. Defendant testified he got scared, picked up Meacham's gun, and shot him three times.

Hall said he didn't remember much that happened for awhile. The next time he clearly remembered anything he was in a cemetery at What Cheer, Iowa. He testified he had periods thinking Meacham was human and periods thinking Meacham was a dog. He drove Meacham's car to Davenport, abandoned it, took a bus to Chicago, hitchhiked through the Southwest, and turned himself in to officials in the State of Nevada. He voluntarily told officers about the incident.

The County Attorney of Jasper County, Iowa, charged defendant with murder. A jury found him guilty of first-degree murder. Hall appealed, claiming involuntary intoxication was an excuse for the murder.

Opinion

Voluntary intoxication from alcohol does not constitute a complete defense. Is the rule the same when the mental condition results from voluntary ingestion of other drugs? We think so. Defendant does not contend that extended use of drugs caused him "settled or established" insanity. He does argue that he did not take the pill voluntarily. But assuming he did take a drug, according to his own testimony no one tricked him into taking it or forced him to do so. Such is the language of defendant's own citations involving involuntary intoxication. Defendant did not take the pill by mistake—thinking, for example, it was candy. If his own testimony is believed, he knew it was a mind-affecting drug.

Defendant's next contention takes us another step into the legal effect of voluntary use of drugs. The trial court submitted to the jury forms of verdict for both first- and second-degree murder, for manslaughter, and for acquittal. In its instruction on defendant's claimed mental condition from taking a pill, the trial court instructed that "no amount of voluntary use of drugs can entirely excuse a Murder and thereby entitle a slayer to an acquittal."

Does voluntary drug intoxication permit a jury to reduce a homicide to manslaughter? Turning again to the analogy of intoxication resulting from alcohol,

> It is now generally held that intoxication may be considered where murder is divided into degrees, and in many states, may have the effect of reducing homicide from murder in the first degree to murder in the second degree. In fact, in most states the only consideration given to the fact of drunkenness or intoxication at the time of the commission of the homicide is to enable the court and jury to determine whether the prisoner may be guilty of murder in the second degree, rather than of murder in the first degree. The rule followed by most courts is that intoxication will not reduce a homicide from murder to manslaughter.

Affirmed.

---

existed: (1) Defendants suffered from a mental disease or defect, and (2) it caused them the loss of power to choose between right and wrong. In other words, defendants know what they're doing, they know it's wrong, but they can't stop themselves from doing it.

The **substantial capacity test** focuses on both reason and will. Formulated by the American Law Institute, it evaluates whether two necessary elements existed: At the time of the crime (1) defendants had a mental disease or defect that caused them to lack substantial capacity (2) to *either* appreciate the wrongfulness (criminality) of their conduct *or* to conform their conduct to the requirements of the law. Notice the test focuses on *substantial* capacity; in other words, the mental disease or defect doesn't have to totally destroy their reason or will.

Syndrome Defenses   Since the 1970s, a range of "syndromes" supposedly affecting mental states have led to some bizarre excuses, including the policeman's, love, fear, chronic brain, and holocaust syndromes. Law professor and defense attorney Alan Dershowitz (1994, 3) wrote a book listing dozens of these syndrome excuses. The title, *The Abuse Excuse and Other Cop-Outs, Sob Stories, and Evasions of Responsibility,* makes clear his opinion of

Dissent

My first disagreement with the majority opinion deals with its premise that drug intoxication and alcohol intoxication are legally the same when considering them as a possible defense to the commission of a crime. The fallacy in the majority's position is that it puts the issue on a Time basis rather than an Effect basis. It says the use of drugs is no defense unless mental illness resulting from long established use is shown because that's what we have said of alcoholic intoxication. But we have said that about alcohol because ordinarily the use of alcohol produces no mental illness except by long continued excessive use. On the other hand that same result can be obtained overnight by the use of modern hallucinatory drugs like LSD. The reason for our alcohol-intoxication rule disappears when we discuss the use of these drugs. LSD can cause a breakdown in the normal functioning of the mind because hallucinations and a complete break with reality is one result of the use of the drug. The LSD reaction may be equated, for legal purposes, with delirium tremens. In many ways they have the same effect on the human mind, and it would appear that both should render the subject legally insane.

Our intoxication rationale as applied to alcohol simply does not fit the use of modern hallucinatory drugs; and it was never meant to. It was adopted before such drugs, as we now know them, were in common use. That is why I would say they are dissimilar and should be so regarded. There is no justifiable reason for equating the effects of so-called "hard" drugs, particularly those classified as hallucinatory, with the use of alcohol.

In the case of alcohol, we have long experience which teaches us the usual and ordinary effects of alcohol upon the human mind and body. We are therefore justified in formulating general rules as to alcoholic intoxication, even though they may not operate with precise fairness in every case. We do not yet have the same scientific reliability on the effect of the use of drugs as far as criminal responsibility is concerned. But this should not tempt us to slough the matter off by lumping all drugs together with alcohol, where obviously many of them do not belong.

Assuming, however, there is no merit to what I have said, there is still another reason why I cannot agree with the majority opinion. Even under that view, it is only Voluntary intoxication which may not be relied upon as a defense to the commission of a criminal act. The majority finds that the use of drugs here was voluntary. I believe that finding entirely overlooks the real import of the evidence. The testimony shows defendant took a pill which he knew to be a drug but which he did not know to be LSD and which he testified he thought to be harmless, although he had been told it would make him feel groovy. There is nothing to indicate he knew it could induce hallucinations or lead to the frightening debilitating effects of mind and body to which the doctors testified. The majority nevertheless holds the defendant's resulting drug intoxication was voluntary. I disagree.

Questions

1. Summarize the arguments of the majority and the dissent.
2. Is the majority or the dissenting opinion a better basis for decision making? Defend your answer.

---

them. Dershowitz worries these excuses are "quickly becoming a license to kill and maim." His is probably a needless worry because defendants rarely plead these excuses, and except for a few infamous cases, defendants don't escape conviction by pleading "abuse excuses."

One famous syndrome excuse case took place in the late 1970s when Dan White, a San Francisco police officer and member of the city council, shot and killed gay activist and fellow official Harvey Milk and Mayor George Moscone. White's lawyer introduced the junk food syndrome, popularly called the "Twinkie defense." He argued junk food had diminished White's mental faculties. According to one psychiatrist's testimony:

> During these spells he'd become quite withdrawn, quite lethargic. He would retreat to his room. Wouldn't come to the door. Wouldn't answer the phone. And during these periods he found that he could not cope with people. Any confrontations would cause him to kind of become argumentative. Whenever he felt things were not going right he would abandon his usual program of exercise and good nutrition and start gorging himself on junk foods. Twinkies, Coca Cola.

> Mr. White had always been something of an athlete, priding himself on being physically fit. But when something would go wrong he'd hit the high sugar stuff. He'd hit the chocolate and the more he consumed the worse he'd feel, and he'd respond to his ever-growing depression by consuming even more junk food. The more junk food he consumed, the worse he'd feel. The worse he'd feel, the more he'd gorge himself. (Weiss 1984, 349–350)

The defense argued these depressions, which eating junk food aggravated, diminished White's capacity enough to reduce his responsibility. The jury returned a verdict of manslaughter, and White was sentenced to a relatively short prison term. After his release from prison, he committed suicide.

Occasionally, women have used premenstrual syndrome (PMS) to excuse their crimes. In a New York case, Shirley Santos called the police, telling them, "My little girl is sick" (*Newsweek* 1982, 111). The medical team in the hospital emergency room where she was taken found welts on the girl's legs and blood in her urine and diagnosed them as resulting from child abuse. The police arrested Santos, who explained, "I don't remember what happened. . . . I would never hurt my baby. . . . I just got my period." At a preliminary hearing, Santos asserted PMS as a complete defense to assault and endangering the welfare of a child, both felonies. She admitted beating her child but argued that because of PMS she had blacked out; hence, she could not have formed the intent to assault or endanger her child's welfare. After lengthy plea bargaining, the prosecutor dropped the felony charges and Santos pleaded guilty to the misdemeanor of harassment. Santos received no sentence, not even probation or a fine, even though her daughter spent two weeks in the hospital from the injuries. The plea bargaining prevented a legal test of the PMS defense in this case. Nevertheless, the judge's leniency suggests that PMS affected the outcome informally.

There are three obstacles to successfully pleading the PMS defense:

1. Defendants have to prove that PMS is a disease; little medical research shows it is.
2. The defendant has to actually suffer from PMS; there are hardly ever any medical records to document it.
3. PMS has to cause the mental impairment; there's still too much skepticism about PMS to accept that it excuses criminal conduct. (Note 1983, 263–269)

■ CRIMINAL PROCEDURE

Criminal law is a list of don'ts directed at private individuals. **Criminal procedure** tells public officials what power they have to enforce this list of criminal don'ts and what consequences they face for abusing that power. The law of criminal procedure is the formal side of decision making in criminal justice agencies. It lays down rules for decisions made by officials at each step in the criminal process (discussed in Chapter 1). We'll examine the law of criminal procedure as it affects decision making in law enforcement, courts, and corrections in later chapters where that law specifically applies. Table 2.1 contains a list of the specific provisions in the Bill of Rights and the stages of the criminal process to which they relate. Here, we focus on the principles that apply to all stages—due process and equal protection.

Due Process of Law

The bedrock of the formal law of criminal procedure is the principle of "due process of law." Due process in the law of criminal procedure means the right to fair procedures (Chapter 1). As we saw at the beginning of the chapter, both the Fifth and Fourteenth Amendments to the U.S. Constitution guarantee that neither the federal nor state governments can deny any person "life, liberty, or property without due process of law." (See also Chapter 1 on the tension between crime control and due process.)

But, as early as 1833, the chief justice of the U.S. Supreme Court, John Marshall, made clear that criminal procedure is a state and local matter. If Congress had meant to take the extraordinary step of applying the Bill of Rights listed in Table 2.1 to the states, "they would have declared this purpose in plain . . . language." So, Marshall concluded, whether the Bill of Rights applied to state and local procedure is a question "of great importance, but not of much difficulty": The federal Bill of Rights did *not* apply to the states. The states had their own bills of rights, which they could enforce as each state saw fit (*Barron v. Baltimore* 1833, 250).

TABLE 2.1

The Bill of Rights and Criminal Procedure

Agency	Amendment	Rights
POLICE	Fourth	Guarantee against unreasonable search and seizure
	Fifth	Right to a grand jury indictment
		Right against double jeopardy
		Right to due process
		Right against self-incrimination
COURTS	Sixth	Right to a speedy and public trial
		Right to an impartial jury
		Right to notice of charges
		Right to confront witnesses
		Right to a lawyer
COURTS AND CORRECTIONS	Eighth	Prohibition against excessive bail
		Prohibition against cruel and unusual punishments

Following the Civil War, a number of amendments were added to the U.S. Constitution to bring former slaves into full citizenship. As far as criminal justice is concerned, the Fourteenth Amendment due process clause is the most important of the "Civil War Amendments," because it specifically says, "[No] *state* shall deny any person of life, liberty, or property without due process of law." Despite this specific prohibition, states continued to make all decisions about criminal justice within their own borders, just as they'd done since the Revolution. This hands-off state criminal justice approach began to break down in the 1930s. It's probably not a coincidence that just as Hitler rose to power in Germany, the U.S. Supreme Court decided its first case applying the Fourteenth Amendment due process clause to the states. The German war machine of the First World War, and the rise of fascism in its aftermath, revived suspicions held by Americans since the days of George III of arbitrary government.

That first case began in northern Alabama one morning in March 1931, when seven scruffy White boys came into a railway station and told the stationmaster a "bunch of Negroes" had picked a fight with them and thrown them off a freight train (*Powell v. Alabama* 1932). The stationmaster phoned ahead to Scottsboro where a deputy sheriff deputized every man who owned a gun. When the train got to Scottsboro, the posse rounded up nine Black boys and two White girls. The girls were dressed in men's caps and overalls. Five of the boys were from Georgia and four from Tennessee. They ranged in age from 12 to 20. One was blind in one eye and had only 10 percent vision in the other; one walked with a cane; all were poor; and none could read or write. As the deputy sheriff was tying the boys together and loading them into his truck, Ruby Bates told him the boys had raped her and her friend, Victoria Price. By nightfall a mob of several hundred people had surrounded the little Scottsboro jail, vowing to avenge the rape by lynching the boys.

When the trial began on Monday morning, April 6, 1931, 102 National Guardsmen struggled to keep several thousand people at least 100 feet away from the courthouse. Inside the courtroom, Judge Alfred E. Hawkins offered the job of defense attorney to anyone who would take it. Only Chattanooga lawyer Stephen Roddy accepted. Roddy, an alcoholic already drunk at 9:00 A.M., admitted he didn't know anything about Alabama law. Judge Hawkins then appointed "all members" of the local bar present in the courtroom as counsel. By Thursday, eight of the boys had been tried, convicted, and sentenced to death. The jury was divided on 12-year-old Roy Wright, with seven demanding death and five holding out for life imprisonment. Judge Hawkins declared a mistrial in Roy Wright's trial and sentenced the others to death by electrocution.

Liberals, radicals, and Communists around the country rallied to the defense of the "Scottsboro boys," as the case was popularly known. In March 1932, the Alabama Supreme Court upheld all of the convictions except for Eugene Williams, who was granted a new trial as a juvenile. In November, the U.S. Supreme Court ruled in *Powell v. Alabama* that Alabama had denied the boys due process of law. According to Justice Sutherland:

> It has never been doubted by this court . . . that notice and hearing are preliminary steps essential to the passing of an enforceable judgment, and that they, together with a legally competent tribunal having jurisdiction of the case, constitute the basic elements of the constitutional requirement of due process of law. The words of [the great lawyer, Daniel] Webster . . . that by "the law of the land" is intended "a law which hears before it condemns" have been repeated . . . in a multitude of decisions. . . . The necessity of due notice and an opportunity of being heard is . . . among the "immutable principles of justice which inhere the very idea of free government which no member of the Union may disregard."

There were passionate debates about just what the decision meant for state criminal justice, but by the end of the 1960s the meaning boiled down to this: The federal Bill of Rights sets a minimum standard all states have to follow. They can raise the minimum by expanding rights, but they can't fall below it. For example, in one leading case, the U.S. Supreme Court ruled that DWI (driving while intoxicated) checkpoints at which all motorists are stopped and checked for signs of intoxication aren't "unreasonable seizures" under the Fourth Amendment to the U.S. Constitution (*Michigan v. Sitz* 1990). But, the Michigan Supreme Court decided the Michigan constitution's seizure provision guaranteed more protection than the U.S. Constitution and that according to the state constitution DWI roadblocks *are* unreasonable seizures (*Sitz v. Department of State Police* 1993). According to the Michigan supreme court:

> [O]ur courts are not obligated to accept what we deem to be a major contraction of citizen protections under our constitution simply because the United States Supreme Court has chosen to do so. . . . This court has never recognized the right of the state, without any level of suspicion whatsoever, to detain members of the population at large for criminal investigatory purposes. . . . In these circumstances, the Michigan Constitution offers more protection than the United States Supreme Court's interpretation of the Fourth Amendment. (*Sitz v. Department of State Police* 1993, 218)

Equal Protection of the Law

It's an uncomfortable fact we have to live with, but our Constitution recognized Black slavery, excluded Native Americans from its protection, and provided no rights for women. But standing beside this caste system written into the Constitution is the value of equality, which is deeply embedded in our ideology. In the years just before the Revolution, one commentator wrote, "The least considerable man among us has an interest equal to the proudest nobleman, in the laws and constitution of his country." In the 1960s, we described equality in criminal justice in harsher terms: "If the rich can beat the rap, then everyone should get to beat the rap" (Inbau 1980, 209).

Since 1868, as we've already seen in our discussion of the constitutional limits on criminal law, equality has been more than a hope of the excluded or a slogan in criminal justice—it's a constitutional command. According to the Fourteenth Amendment to the U.S. Constitution, "[N]o state shall . . . deny to any person within its jurisdiction the equal protection of the laws." In the law of criminal procedure, equal protection doesn't mean officials have to treat suspects, defendants, and offenders exactly alike in their efforts to control crime. It does mean they can't investigate, apprehend, convict, and punish people for unacceptable reasons. So, courts look suspiciously at certain classifications, particularly those based on race and ethnicity, at least when they're the only reason for decision making.

But police officers can take ethnic background into account when they stop and frisk a Hispanic suspect, as long as being a Hispanic isn't the *only* reason for the stop and frisk. Prosecutors can take race into account when they decide to prosecute a Black crack dealer as long as it's not the only reason for the decision. (By the time you read this, you may be able to apply the "not the only reason" test to the investigations, detentions, charges, and prosecutions surrounding the September 11, 2001, attacks on the World Trade Center and the Pentagon.) As we move through the criminal justice decision-making process in the chapters on police, courts, and corrections, we'll run into other examples of treating people differently without violating the equal protection clause.

■ INFORMAL CRIMINAL LAW AND PROCEDURE

Criminal law and procedure don't exist in a vacuum of formal decision making. They're living institutions that respond to social, ideological, and political reality. So, we won't find the answers to the *hows* and *whys* of day-to-day decision making in these formal rules, although they draw for us the outer boundaries of informal decision making. Analyzing the words of statutes, court decisions, and legal principles can't explain why legislatures pass specific criminal statutes, can't reveal the reasons for courts' interpretations of these codes, and can't account for why criminal law excludes many social harms from its scope.

To find the answers to these hows, whens, and whys, we have to look to social science. Social scientists don't accept the proposition that specific statutes simply apply

neutral principles embodied in criminal law and the law of criminal procedure. They look for the informal influences on decisions to define behavior as criminal and whether to, when to, and how to enforce the criminal law. In other words, formal criminal law and procedure don't explain discretionary decision making in criminal law and procedure (Friedman 1985, 36–56).

Consensus and Conflict Perspectives

Our pluralistic society has greatly influenced both the creation of criminal law and the administration of criminal justice. The diverse values of racial, ethnic, and cultural groups make it impossible to explain criminal law and its enforcement without accounting for the influence of pluralism. This requires an exploration of the connection between society and criminal law and procedure.

Throughout history, two contrasting views of the nature of society and social change have prevailed among social theorists. According to the **consensus perspective,** harmony is the normal state of society because we all share common values and by and large the state represents and protects these common values. True, there are groups with competing values and conflict arises sometimes. But when it does, the state mediates among groups with competing values, finally reaching a compromise that best represents an agreement of society as a whole. According to the **conflict perspective,** conflict is normal. Society is composed of groups with conflicting values and interests. Conflict isn't always violent and out of control. Revolution and civil war only rarely resolve conflicts; more frequently, debate and consultation do. But the dominant group usually wins the revolutions, civil wars, debates, and consultations. At the end of the day, the state represents the values and interests of the group or groups with enough power to control social institutions (Bernard 1983; Chambliss 1975, vii; Dahrendorf 1958, 126; Hay 1980, 45–84).

Consensus theory

Consensus theory has an ancient heritage, going back at least to Plato and Aristotle. Its modern version owes much to Emile Durkheim, the great nineteenth-century French sociologist whose ideas have greatly influenced the sociology of law and contributed to criminal justice theory. Durkheim enunciated two fundamental propositions relevant to understanding the sociology of criminal law:

1. Crime is conduct "universally disapproved of by members of each society. Crimes shock sentiments which, for a given social system, are found in all healthy consciences."
2. "An act is criminal when it offends strong and defined states of the collective conscience." (Durkheim 1933, 73–80)

Based on these ideas, Durkheim suggested two broad hypotheses of the consensus theory:

1. Criminal law is a synthesis of a society's essential morality, based on values that are shared by all "healthy consciences."
2. Society defines crime in order to establish moral boundaries that, if violated, threaten society's basic existence. Defining certain behaviors as criminal notifies ordinary people how far they can go without undoing social order. (Chambliss and Seidman 1982, 171–206)

The American sociologist Kai Erikson's classic study *Wayward Puritans* tested Durkheim's boundary hypothesis. Erikson studied witchcraft among seventeenth-century New England Puritans. He analyzed evidence about creating, prosecuting, and punishing witchcraft, concluding that the community created "crime waves" to solidify moral boundaries in order to keep the community from disintegrating. Puritans needed witchcraft to keep society from wandering outside settled behavioral boundaries (Erikson 1966).

Empirical evidence from modern times also supports Durkheim's synthesis hypothesis. Blacks and Whites, men and women, rich and poor, young and old, well-educated and poorly educated people agree about what conduct amounts to serious crime. In 1983, researchers asked a selected sample to rank the seriousness of various crimes. The answers displayed broad consensus on the following: Violent crimes were considered most serious, property crimes less serious, and public-order crimes least serious. This compares favorably with rankings in most criminal codes. Table 2.2 contains the results of this comprehensive survey of American opinion concerning the seriousness of offenses. Do your own rankings agree with these findings (Rossi et al. 1974, 224–237)?

Conflict theory

Consensus theory dominated mainstream criminology in the 1940s and 1950s. Then, in the late 1950s, social conflict theories reemerged. The conflict theorists challenged the notion that consensus is the "normal" state of society. Instead, conflict theory—which enjoys a history in social thought as old as consensus theory—assumes conflict is the normal state of society. It also assumes social control requires active constraint, sometimes in the form of coercion. Common values and interests don't produce social control because they don't exist in real life. In real life, society is divided into competing classes and interest groups, the most powerful of which dominate social institutions, including legislatures, criminal justice agencies, and their decision making. The dominant group writes criminal laws that further their interests and impose their values on the whole society. These laws then become an instrument enabling the dominant classes and interest groups to maintain their dominance and to prevent conflict (Chambliss 1984, 16–31).

Conflict theory has many variants, but all shift the emphasis from law *breaking* to law *making* and law *enforc-*

TABLE 2.2

Consensus on the Seriousness of Crimes

Severity Score Offense—10 Most Serious
72.1 Planting a bomb in a public building (the bomb kills 20 people)
52.8 Forcibly raping a woman, who dies from the injuries
43.2 Robbing a victim at gunpoint, who dies from the robber's shots when the victim struggles
39.2 Husband stabbing a wife to death
35.7 Stabbing a victim to death
35.6 Intentionally injuring a victim, who dies as a result
33.8 Running a drug ring
27.9 Wife stabbing her husband to death
26.3 Skyjacking a plane
25.9 Forcibly raping a woman with no *physical* injury resulting

Severity Score Offense—10 Least Serious
1.1 Disturbing the neighborhood with noisy behavior
1.1 Taking bets on the numbers
1.1 Group hanging around a street corner after police tell them to move on
0.9 Running away from home when under 16
0.8 Being drunk in public
0.7 Breaking the curfew law when under 16
0.6 Trespassing in the backyard of a private home
0.3 Being a vagrant
0.2 Playing hooky from school when under 16

ing (Chapter 3, "Labeling Theory" section). Until modern conflict theory reemerged in the late 1950s, most criminologists began their study with criminal law that was already in place. They considered *criminals,* not criminal *law* and criminal law *enforcers,* to be the social problem. Conflict theory changed all that. The emphasis on law making and law enforcing led to an examination of criminal law and its enforcement in a new and different light. Conflict theory maintains criminal law doesn't reflect absolute, agreed-on principles or universal moral values. Instead, criminal law defines, and criminal justice agencies preserve and protect, the interests and values of the dominant social groups. Criminal law and procedure are means of preserving the dominant group or groups' definition of social order (Greenberg 1981, 1–26, 190–194).

Radical Theory

Dissatisfaction with both consensus and conflict theory, and with mainstream criminology and criminal justice in general, produced a "new," or radical, criminology in the 1960s. It wasn't exactly new, however. It drew on the tradition of social conflict theory and on Marxist theory. Radical criminology maintains that mainstream criminologists and criminal justice professionals are apologists, if not lackeys, for a capitalist ruling class that dominates the state.

Radicals disagree over whether the dominant class consciously exploits the working class, or whether the structure of capitalist society inevitably determines their exploitative actions. *Instrumentalists* contend the ruling class consciously decides to exploit. *Structuralists* maintain capitalists don't exploit by conscious design but because capitalism by its nature requires exploitative class relationships and class conflict. They believe capitalist social and economic structure requires exploitation to operate; criminal law is just a tool of that structure.

Although the rhetoric often ran high in the 1960s and 1970s, radical criminologists developed a criminal justice theory based on the following propositions:

1. The primary purpose of the state is to protect the interests of the dominant class.
2. Dominance requires controlling the working classes.
3. The dominant class exploits the working class by wringing profit from overworked laborers.
4. Criminal law controls workers so capitalists can get richer and secure protection for their accumulated riches.
5. Brute force isn't always or even usually necessary to protect these interests and control the workers.
6. Capitalists sometimes have to commit crimes to maintain the existing power arrangements. So, police officers violate individuals' rights, government abuses its power, corporations fix prices, and so on. They try not to do this too often because it threatens the myth that law is neutral, evenhanded, and fair.
7. Workers commit crimes mainly out of necessity. They prey on other workers, and sometimes capitalists, to survive: They steal what they cannot earn. Or, out of frustration with existing unjust arrangements, they erupt in violence against others. Occasionally, they commit "heroic crimes," like attacking the power structure. Their crimes are not bad or evil; they are utilitarian actions necessary to survive in a capitalist society. (Quinney 1977)

Summary of Social Theories

These brief descriptions oversimplify the consensus, conflict, and radical social theories. Consensus theorists don't maintain that harmony and negotiation *always* prevail in politics and society; nor do they claim their theories explain *everything* in criminal justice. Conflict theorists don't demand an interpretation of social interaction that *totally* excludes agreement and social cohesion. Radical criminologists don't contend class determines *all* laws or capitalists *always* win and workers *always* lose. Consensus, conflict, and radical theorists *do* maintain criminal law reflects their theoretical view of social reality.

The Politics of Criminal Law and Procedure

The consensus, conflict, and radical theories suggest but don't elaborate on the political process involved in making criminal law and criminal procedure. The decisions to define certain behavior as a crime and to establish rules of criminal procedure depend not only on the ideological approaches to law but also on the interaction of individuals, public and private interest groups, and criminal justice professionals. Scholars long ago revised the theory that laws reflect the unaltered will of the majority. True, public outrage *sometimes* gets translated into criminal law. During the 1940s, outrage over a few heinous sex crimes led to the enactment of sexual psychopath laws. In the 1980s, the fear of the spread of crack cocaine use and the violence surrounding its trafficking created some of the most severe drug crime laws in history (Chapter 9, "Sentencing"). In the 1990s, outrage over a spate of carjackings spurred Congress and the president into rare quick action when they passed specific federal legislation dealing with taking cars by violence. But these are rare and not pure examples of popular will deciding the content of criminal law.

An **interest group theory** has replaced the pure democracy explanation of criminal law and procedure enactments. According to this theory, public and private groups, led by moral entrepreneurs, or reformers, put pressure on legislators by a variety of means to purify society. Prohibition and antiprostitution crusades are two examples of how the theory can explain the politics of criminal law.

But there's more to the making of criminal law than either public outrage or moral crusades. In most legislation, criminal justice professionals decide the content of criminal law and criminal procedure. This happened in the revision of most states' and the federal government's criminal procedure codes that took place during the 1960s and 1970s. Barton Ingraham (1980), in an analysis of the enactments of these revisions, concluded:

> **Legislative reform of criminal procedure . . . is usually initiated by some agency or official of the state with law-making or law-enforcing authority. The job of drafting the new code is then placed in the hands of a group consisting mostly of lawyers, judges, and law professors. (28)**

Timothy Lenz (1986, 282) reached a similar conclusion in a detailed analysis of sentencing reform in Indiana, Minnesota, and Mississippi. He found that although conditions might bring legislation into public view and generate heated opposition, the public "is not constantly watching over" the legislative process. As a result, "policy is usually the domain of a narrow set of political and professional interests."

Richard Hollinger and Lonn Lanza-Kaduce (1988, 101) examined the enactment of computer crime legislation that rapidly spread throughout the country during the 1970s. They found, except for one organization linked to the private security industry and the American Bar Association, few interest groups influenced this legislation. They concluded neither interest groups nor moral entrepreneurs were responsible for most computer crime legislation. Instead, computer crime experts and legislators wrote most of the laws.

Knowledge and Understanding Check

Criminal law
- ✔ Define criminal law.
- ✔ What is the principle of economy?
- ✔ Identify and describe three limits on the power of the government to define crime.
- ✔ List and explain the principles of criminal liability.
- ✔ Explain the difference between defenses of justification and excuse.
- ✔ List and identify the elements of the defenses of justification.
- ✔ List and identify the elements of the defenses of excuse.

Criminal procedure
- ✔ Explain the difference between criminal law and criminal procedure.

- ✔ Define "due process of law," and explain how it applies to the law of criminal procedure.
- ✔ Define "equal protection of the law," and explain how it relates to the law of criminal procedure.

Informal criminal law and procedure
- ✔ What types of answers don't we find in formal criminal law and procedure?
- ✔ Compare and contrast consensus, conflict, and radical theories of criminal law and procedure.
- ✔ What does politics have to do with decision making in criminal law and procedure?

KEY TERMS

alibi
cause in fact
common law
conflict perspective
consensus perspective
criminal law
criminal omissions
criminal procedure

entrapment
ex post facto clause
general principles of criminal liability
general principles of justification and excuse
interest group theory
irresistible impulse test

legal cause
predisposition test
right-wrong test
strict liability offenses
substantial capacity test
void-for-vagueness doctrine

INTERNET PROJECT

 Using the Internet or InfoTrac College Edition, search for information about "the intoxication defense." What do you find? Can you find any cases that used this defense? How successful was this defense?

CHAPTER 3

Crime, Criminals, and Victims

Leonard Detrick Photo © *New York Daily News*

■ INTRODUCTION

A newspaper headline warns, "Serial Rapist Strikes Again." A judge has ordered a young woman to walk up and down in front of the local Kmart wearing the sign "I stole $5 from Kmart," the local TV news informs us. A student was arrested for "drunk and disorderly" conduct when he got obnoxious in a bar after drinking one beer too many, he tells me. A "deadbeat dad" is barred from having more children until he pays his child support. A local resident is sentenced to thirty days in jail for returning library books late. My neighbor reports me to the local police because I parked my car on my own lawn (a "crime" in the Minnesota town where I live). And the last time I checked, it's still a crime in Minnesota to "fornicate with a bird." Years ago, a Bloomington, Minnesota, police officer told me, "We should have a billboard at our city limits reading, 'Welcome to Bloomington, you're under arrest.'"

"Why?" I asked.

"Because everything in Bloomington is a crime."

Of course, he was joking but he had a point: The word *crime* covers an enormous range of behavior—technically, whatever the law calls a crime.

Now that we've gotten a good grounding in the criminal justice system as a whole (Chapter 1) and the constitutional and legal framework it operates under (Chapter 2), we need to get some understanding of the subjects and objects of criminal justice decision making—crime, criminals, and victims—and how to measure and explain them. These are the topics of Chapter 3.

■ TYPES OF CRIME

What's the first thing you think of when you hear the word *crime*? I'm sure it won't be parking on your front lawn. It'll probably be murder, rape, or mugging. After all, they're the crimes that really hurt you and the people you care about. And, of course, they're the only crimes you see on TV news. But, the truth is violent crimes are only a tiny slice of the total amount of crime—a few mur-

ders, a few more rapes, still a few more robberies and burglaries, lots of thefts, and a deluge of drunk and disorderly conduct charges and "other" crimes like parking on my front lawn (Figure 3.1). This breakdown is nothing new; it's similar to the types of crimes committed in sixteenth-century Essex, the English county, during the reign of Elizabeth I that I studied when I was a young historian (Samaha 1974).

How can we get a grip on this hodgepodge we call crime? Let's begin by dividing it into sensible categories, or to get a little technical, by classifying it. A respected and experienced sixteenth-century justice of the peace from the county of Kent, which neighbors Essex, gave us a classification that (with a little tinkering) still works. In the many editions of his widely used practical manual for justices of the peace, JP William Lambarde (1583) divided crimes into six categories, from the most to the least serious:

1. *Crimes against the state:* Treason and sedition
2. *Crimes against persons:* Murder, rape, sodomy, and assault
3. *Crimes against property and persons:* Robbery

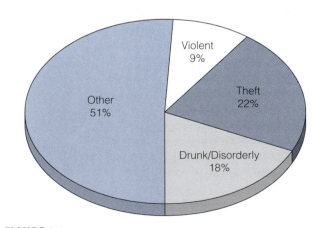

FIGURE 3.1
Arrests in 2000
SOURCE: FBI 2001, Table 29.

4. *Crimes against habitation:* Burglary and arson
5. *Crimes against property:* Stealing
6. *Crimes against public order and morality:* Disorderly conduct

 3-1 FBI crime rates

Lambarde's list tracks well with modern-day divisions in our formal criminal law (Chapter 2); the categories that make up our published national crime statistics (see "Measuring Crime" section); and the subjects of most criminological research on crime. Of course, we need to add to the list to cover the more than four centuries of history that take us from a rural English county in the 1500s to the postindustrial United States in 2002. Let's look at three additional categories: crimes associated with occupations, hate crimes, and crimes without complaining victims.

Occupational Crimes

The manager at a Beall's Outlet store in the Southeast was stealing money in small amounts—$50 here, $90 there. She would take it from the cash register when no one was looking and then fill out a refund form for the same amount, writing in a name and number taken from the phone directory. Or she would give the money to a friend posing as a customer and split it with her later. She would even place fake refunds on her credit card. Before long, she had taken more than $1,000, a big dent to the store's bottom line in an industry where profit margins are razor thin. (Lee 2001)

Employee theft, the example of **occupational crime** (crimes related to employment, business, or profession) related here, doesn't make it into the national crime statistics (the UCR and NCVS, discussed later on); but according to one estimate, it costs retailers more than $20 billion every year—even more than shoplifting (Lee 2001).

Employee theft isn't the only occupational crime. At the 1939 annual meeting of the American Sociological Association, its president, Edwin Sutherland, told the members that just as there is blue-collar crime, there is "crime in the upper- or white-collar class, composed of respectable or at least respected business and professional men." We generally think of corporate occupational crime as price-fixing or other forms of bilking people out of their money. But, corporate crime can also hurt and even kill people, even if the only intent of the corporation is to make money. For example, an Elkhart, Indiana, prosecutor charged Ford Motor Company with reckless homicide when three teenagers were killed when their Ford Pinto exploded after the car was hit in the rear. Company documents proved that Ford knew that the Pinto gas tank was located where it could explode but had decided it would be cheaper to risk paying damages for wrongful deaths

than redesigning the car. Ford was acquitted because the documents were dated before Indiana passed the law that permitted this type of prosecution.

Hate Crimes

Hate crimes (also called bias crimes) are crimes motivated by prejudice against groups based on differences in race, ethnicity, religion, physical or mental capacity, or sexual orientation. In 2000, there were 8152 hate crime incidents reported to the FBI; most were motivated by race (4368), followed by religion (1483), sexual orientation (1330), ethnicity and national origin (927), and disability (36). Two-thirds of the hate crimes reported in 2000 were violent crimes, and most of the rest were property crimes. Sixty-four percent of the known hate crime offenders were White and 18 percent were Black (FBI 2001).

 3-2 Hate crimes

Why make a crime a special crime when it's motivated by group prejudice? After all, isn't murder murder, rape rape, and so on? There are at least two reasons, both of them controversial. First, hate crimes are based on the idea that committing crimes because of group characteristics reverberates beyond individual victims to whole groups, communities, and even the entire nation. Second, groups protected by hate laws are especially vulnerable to crime. So, we have to compensate these vulnerable victims by harsher punishment.

Opponents have their own arguments. First, we don't need special hate crime statutes because all crimes are hate crimes. Second, current statutes are discriminatory because they leave out many vulnerable groups, like the elderly, children, the diseased, ex-offenders, and so on. Third, where will including vulnerable groups stop? Will it include broad categories like neighborhood, social class, and education? Fourth, hate crime statutes are not constitutional because they violate our right to free speech. Words and thoughts are free; you can't punish people for what they believe or how they feel, only for what they do (Chapter 2). Finally, it's impossible to prove hate: we can't see into the human mind, especially in this age of political correctness when we're all clever enough to hide our prejudices.

Victimless Crimes

The term **victimless crimes** doesn't mean exactly what it says; all crimes hurt the community that passed the laws making them crimes. Furthermore, the families and friends of criminals are potentially harmed by victimless crimes. What we really mean by the term is crimes with no *complaining* victim (gambling, prostitution, and illegal drug use).

■ MEASURING CRIME

Societies have kept track of crime for centuries. In 1730, Aarhus Denmark conducted a survey asking people if they'd been crime victims. And, in the 1800s, an English constable went door to door asking Midlands villagers if they'd been victimized. Today, there are two main sources of crime statistics—police reports and victim surveys— and one less widely used—offenders' self-reports of crimes they've committed. Each of these statistics has its strengths and weaknesses (Sparks 1981, 2). Measuring occupational crime presents special challenges for law enforcement.

Police Reports

Basing crime statistics on police reports stems from the belief that the best way to find out about crime is to ask the police. Certainly, this was the belief of the International Association of Chiefs of Police, a police reform organization that planned the first nationwide collection of crime statistics in the United States. In 1930, the FBI collected its first set of data based on official police records, the **Uniform Crime Reports (UCR).** Since then, the FBI has depended on voluntary cooperation from local police departments to collect and report to them two major statistics: numbers and kinds of crimes known to the police, and the numbers of people the police arrested and the crimes they were arrested for committing. The FBI reports these statistics every year in its UCR publication, *Crime in the United States.*

 3-3 Several years of the UCR

The most widely publicized statistic in the UCR (and the basis for crime news reports) is crimes known to the police (Figure 3.2). This statistic, the Crime Index, is a list of raw numbers and rates (the number for every 100,000 people) of eight serious crimes: murder, forcible rape, robbery, aggravated assault, burglary, theft, motor vehicle theft, and arson.

UCR statistics (not surprisingly) aren't perfect. Why? Most important, the Crime Index doesn't include crimes police *don't* know about (the **dark figure in crime**). Also, the UCR overrepresents serious crime because it counts attempts and completed crimes and people report serious crimes more often than minor crimes to the police. Finally, the UCR overrepresents **street crime** (crimes committed by poor and minority criminals). White-collar crimes— price fixing, embezzlement, causing death by unsafe products, and the like—don't make it into the Crime Index (Brownstein 1996, 19–25; Schneider and Wiersema 1991, 333–335).

Victim Surveys

Eager to close the gap (which many guessed to be large) between how many crimes the police know about and how much crime there really is, criminologists called for a more complete measure of crime. Believing the best method to find out how much crime there really is was to ask victims, criminologists developed victim surveys. The most extensive (and most expensive) victim survey in history, the **National Crime Victimization Survey (NCVS),** was launched in 1972. The NCVS collects detailed information about violent and property crimes. Obviously, it doesn't include homicides because the victims are dead (Figure 3.3).

How does the NCVS operate? Every six months, U.S. Census workers take a telephone poll of a national sample of more than 40,000 households. They ask questions about five topics:

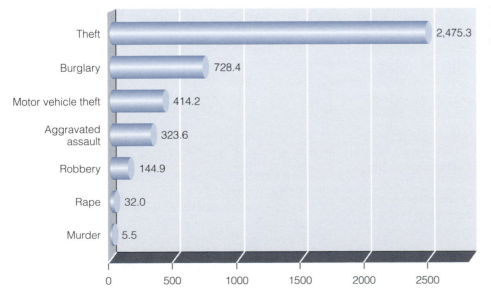

FIGURE 3.2
UCR Index, 2000
SOURCE: FBI 2001, Section II.

FIGURE 3.3

NCVS 2000 Rates (per 1000 persons age 12 or over)

SOURCE: Bureau of Justice Statistics 2001c, Table 1.

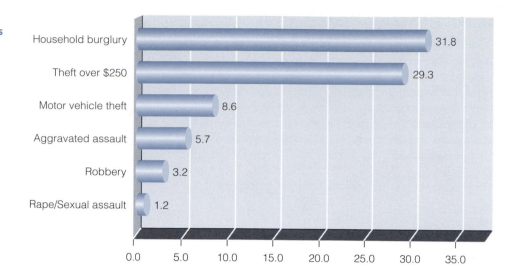

FIGURE 3.4

Percentage of Victimizations Reported to the Police, 2000

SOURCE: Bureau of Justice Statistics 2001c, Table 7.

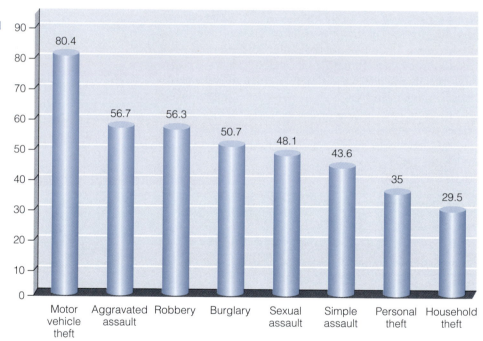

1. *Victimization:* Whether the person was a victim of a crime within the past six months
2. *Victims:* Age, race, sex, educational level, and income of victims
3. *Crime:* Location, amount of personal injury, and economic loss suffered from the crime
4. *Perpetrator:* Gender, age, race, and relationship to the victim
5. *Reporting:* Whether victims reported the crimes to the police and the reasons why they did or didn't report

 3-4 NCVS questionnaire

In its first annual report, *Criminal Victimization in the United States 1972,* the NCVS proved what researchers and policymakers had always said: There are a lot more crimes committed than get reported to the police. But how many more? And, do victims report more of some kinds of crimes than others? The NCVS gives us the answers:

1. Victims report less than 40 percent of all NCVS offenses.
2. Victims report violent crimes more often than property crimes.
3. Victims report completed crimes more than attempts.

Every annual report since 1972 has backed up these findings (Figure 3.4).

TABLE 3.1

Comparison of the UCR and the NCVS

	Uniform Crime Reports (UCR)	National Crime Victimization Survey (NCVS)
CRIMES INCLUDED	1. Index crimes (attempted and completed) • Homicide • Rape • Robbery • Burglary (personal and commercial) • Aggravated assault • Theft (personal and commercial) • Motor vehicle theft • Arson 2. Arrests in all other offenses	1. Rape 2. Robbery 3. Aggravated assault 4. Simple assault 5. Household burglary 6. Personal theft 7. Motor vehicle theft
SCOPE	1. Reported to the police by victims and witnesses 2. Discovered by the police	1. Nonfatal violent and property crimes against persons 12 or older 2. Victims' age, sex, race, ethnicity, marriage status, income, and educational level 3. Offenders' sex, race, age, and relationship to the victim
EXCLUDES	1. White-collar crimes	1. Homicide 2. Commercial crimes 3. White-collar crimes
METHOD	Local police departments record crimes reported to and discovered by them and then report raw numbers to the FBI	U.S. Census Bureau surveys a representative sample of households, asking about crimes committed against members of the household during the last six months
SOURCE	Federal Bureau of Investigation (FBI), a federal law enforcement agency	Bureau of Justice Statistics (BJS), the research arm of the U.S. Department of Justice

Like the UCR, the NCVS isn't perfect; the dark figure may be lighter but it's still there. Why? First, the most serious violent crime, homicide, isn't included in the NCVS. Neither are commercial burglaries and thefts or occupational crimes. Second, victims don't tell interviewers about all their victimizations. Why not? According to criminologist Wesley Skogan, "Most victimizations are not notable events. The majority are property crimes in which the perpetrator is never detected. The financial stakes are small, and the costs of calling the police greatly outweigh the benefits." Interviewers have found other reasons, including embarrassment, apathy, forgetfulness, and knowing the perpetrator. All of these reasons tell us why victims don't report *minor* offenses. But what about serious crimes? Victims *do* report more violent crimes than property crimes. Still, only a little more than half of the victims report robbery and aggravated assault. So, there's still a dark figure in crime in the NCVS, but it isn't as dark as it is in the UCR (Table 3.1) (Skogan 1990b, 256–272).

A number of sampling problems also distort the figures in the NCVS. Young Black males and illegal immigrants are consistently underrepresented among those interviewed. So are people with particular lifestyles, like drifters, street hustlers, and homeless people. Also, the NCVS doesn't survey people in prisons, jails, or juvenile corrections facilities. (We know that prisoners have higher victimization rates than the general population.) Wealthy people escape the NCVS by insulating themselves from all kinds of interviews. Another sampling problem is the small number of rapes, robberies, and aggravated assaults reported; for example, the year 2000 sample turned up only 92 rapes and 160 robberies with victim injury. Basing national estimates on these low numbers is risky (Brownstein 1996, 1–2; Bureau of Justice Statistics 2001c; Garofalo 1990, 81–82).

Self-Reports

Self-reports are based on the idea that if you want to know about crimes, ask the people who commit them. Self-reports grew out of a distrust of official statistics. During the 1960s crime boom (see "Crime Trends" section), some criminologists explained the steep increase in crime figures as not so much a real increase but a reflection of biased, greater enforcement against racial minorities, poor people, and the youth counterculture. In a pioneer selfreport survey in the late 1950s, James F. Short and F. Ivan Nye asked both school kids and kids in juvenile institutions about their delinquent acts. Both groups admitted similar behavior—truancy, stealing less than $2, buying and drinking alcohol, driving without a license, and having sex. Self-reports grew rapidly until by the end of the 1960s they dominated the study of juvenile delinquency (Lafree 1998, 15).

Beginning in the 1980s, a number of self-reports concentrated on adult felons, most of them prisoners. In *The Armed Criminal in America,* James D. Wright surveyed more than 1800 convicted adult male felons incarcerated in ten states. Prisoners were asked if, how, and why they obtained, carried, and used firearms, especially in committing crimes. The largest group (39 percent), "unarmed criminals," had never committed a crime while armed. About 11 percent, "knife criminals" and "improvisers," had carried a variety of ready-to-hand weapons. The other half were "gun criminals." More than half of the gun criminals (28 percent) had used a gun only once or sporadically. The rest (about 22 percent)—"handgun predators" and "shotgun predators"—had committed almost half the self-reported crimes (Wright 1986).

Gun criminals reported they'd lived around guns all their lives and that it was easier to commit crimes when they had a gun. A majority reported their guns were always loaded and they had shot them a lot—half said they'd shot at other people. Half also said someone had fired at them. Many said a man armed with a gun is "prepared for anything that might happen." When asked how they'd respond to a ban on small, cheap handguns, they said they'd just get bigger, more expensive handguns. Asked about their response to a total ban on handguns, a majority of gun criminals—and more than three-quarters of the "predators"—said they'd carry sawed-off shoulder weapons (Wright 1986).

There are obstacles to finding out about crime by asking prisoners. First, convicted prisoners don't represent all criminals. They overrepresent multiple offenders and "unsuccessful" criminals. Second, even a representative sample doesn't guarantee accuracy. Some prisoners exaggerate their "expertise" and minimize the harm they inflicted on their victims. Many don't trust the researchers or just want to "play games" to liven the monotony of life in prison (Chapter 12). Also, no matter what promises of confidentiality interviewers make, many prisoners still believe what they say will affect their chances for release. So, they paint the best possible picture of themselves (Hough 1987, 356; Wright and Decker 1994, 5–6).

The Canadian criminologist Gwynn Nettler had this to say about self-report surveys after he'd reviewed many of them:

> Asking people questions about their behavior is a poor way of observing it. . . . It is particularly ticklish to ask people to recall their "bad" behavior. Confessional data are at least as weak as the official statistics they were supposed to improve upon. (Braithwaite 1979, 21)

Measuring Occupational Crime

Neither the UCR nor the NCVS includes *occupational crime* (crimes committed by persons in the course of their employment), because it's so difficult to uncover. Practically no one reports occupational crime to the police, and police departments don't have occupational crime units. The NCVS doesn't ask questions about occupational crime because of the difficulties of getting information about it. There's usually no identifiable, single victim. In many cases, individual victims don't even know they've been victimized.

Measuring **white-collar crime** (crimes committed by corporate officers and managers under the authority of the corporation) by extracting data from official records of formal proceedings in white-collar crime cases has all the shortcomings of the UCR, plus one more: Isolated court cases don't begin to show the extent of harm done to many victims by corporate crime (Sparks 1978, 163–164).

The ability to measure blue-collar crime depends partly on self-reports of employee theft. Richard Hollinger and John P. Clark, for example, combined anonymous questionnaires and face-to-face interviews with both executives and employees in several industries and communities. Some studies of blue-collar crime are based on information supplied by informants—namely, researchers who work in particular business places and report what they observe. To study employees' "cheating" at work, Gerald Mars interviewed more than one hundred informants selected simply because they were available, rather than according to any rational selection criteria (Hollinger and Clark 1983; Mars 1982).

■ CRIME TRENDS

A crime *boom*—that's the best way to describe the trend in crime from the 1950s to the early 1990s (Figure 3.5).

Here's the way Professor Gary Lafree (1998) describes the boom:

> Murder rates doubled; rape rates quadrupled; robbery and burglary rates quintupled. By the early 1990s, nearly 25,000 Americans were being murdered each year. In just two years, more Americans were murdered than were killed in the Vietnam War; in twelve years more were murdered than died during World War II. . . . Taken together, there was an eightfold increase in rates of murder, robbery, rape, aggravated assault, burglary, and theft reported to the police between the end of World War II and the early 1990s. (15)

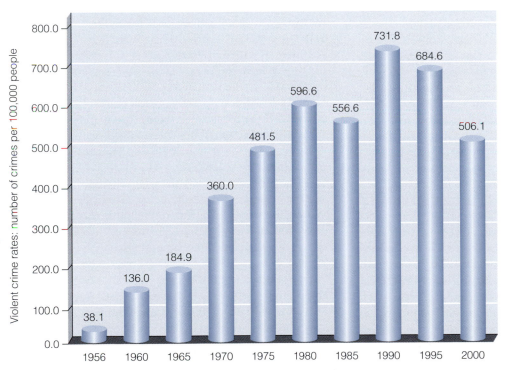

FIGURE 3.5
UCR Crime Index, 1956–2000
SOURCE: FBI 2001, Section II.

FIGURE 3.6
UCR Violent Crime Index,
1956–2000
SOURCE: FBI 2001, Section II.

Then came the 1990s crime *bust*. Violent crime (murder, rape, robbery, and aggravated assault) rates dropped 31 percent, from a high of 758.1 in 1991 to 524.7 in 1999. Still, this is a long way from the low of 38.1 in 1956, clearly demonstrating the 1990s bust can't match the 63 percent increase during the 1960s boom (Figure 3.6) (Lafree 1998, 1).

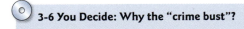

3-5 Crime trends 1980–1999

3-6 You Decide: Why the "crime bust"?

■ CRIMINALS

There are seven things we can say with some confidence about the people who commit crimes:

1. Most aren't violent (fewer than 1 out of 100).
2. Seventy-four percent are men.
3. Almost half are under 25.
4. Almost none are over 50.
5. Over two-thirds are White.
6. Over half know their victims.
7. Many are both criminals and crime victims. (Bureau of Justice Statistics 2001c, Table 4)

Let's look more closely at what we know about female criminals, the relationship between race and crime, and the relationships between criminals and their victims.

 3-7 Details from the numbered list on characteristics of criminals

Female Criminals

We can say at least three things with confidence about women and crime. First, women commit only 10 percent of violent crimes. Second, that small number of female criminals begin committing crimes earlier than men, stop committing crimes sooner, and return to committing crimes much less frequently than men. Third, female crime is increasing. Female arrests for violent crimes grew 36 percent during the 1990s, whereas arrests of men fell 15 percent. These figures sound dramatic, but before we make too much of what looks like a boom in female violent crime, we should beware of percentages based on small numbers. We're talking about 410 murders, attempted murders, and voluntary and attempted voluntary manslaughters out of a female population of 135 million in 1990 and more than 140 million in 2000 (FBI 2001e, Table 53; Kruttschnitt 2001, 1–37).

What accounts for the enormous differences between female and male criminality and the shorter life of crime for women? Traditional criminologists said it's because women are biologically and psychologically different from men. The great sociologist Emile Durkheim said women faced less strain from bad social and economic conditions because "being a more instinctive creature than man, woman has only to follow her instincts." Also, "they are much less involved in collective existence; thus they feel—[the effects of economic and social conditions] good or evil—less strongly." The great psychoanalyst Sigmund Freud said female criminality stemmed from biological problems brought about by the odd functioning of women's genitals, which limited them to family roles. So, these distinguished men and a long string of their followers looked to women's biology and psychology to explain their criminality (Steffensmeier and Haynie 2000, 403, 407).

A second school of thought about women criminals, more congenial to social scientists, says women are affected by social and economic conditions just like men. So, poverty, income inequality, race, and other "structural determinants" link women *and* men to crime. Darrell Steffensmeier and Dana Haynie used arrests in 178 U.S. cities with populations of over 100,000 in 1990 to determine whether things like race, poverty, unemployment, and female-headed households affected arrest rates of men and women. What did they find?

1. Poverty, income inequality, joblessness, and female-headed households affect arrest rates for *both* Black women *and* Black men.
2. But these structural disadvantages affect men more in one crime—homicide of all types *except* killing spouses or partners. (Steffensmeier and Haynie 2000, 428–429)

Let's examine this homicide exception closely. This exception is huge because almost all women who kill kill people they're intimately involved with (unlike men, who kill not only their wives and girlfriends but their "friends" and strangers, too). In fact, it was a dirty little secret until 1992 that wives kill their husbands as often (and in some places more often) than husbands kill their wives, at least in the United States. Margo I. Wilson and Martin Daly examined spousal homicide in the United States and other countries. They found what they call the **sex ratio of killing (SROK)** (SROK = homicides committed by women for every 100 homicides committed by men) was 75 in the United States, 31 in Canada, and only 6 in parts of Africa. In some cities in the United States, women kill their husbands *more* often than husbands kill their wives. The Chicago SROK was 102, Detroit's 119 (another study found it was 200!), and Houston's, 137 (Wilson and Daly 1992, 189, Table 1).

How can we explain this major spousal homicide exception in light of the generally low criminality of women? Wilson and Daly say there might be three reasons. First, increased marital conflict takes the form of increased male coercion, which limits women's options which in turn leads women to take drastic forms of escape and self-defense. Second, women kill their husbands when they feel socially empowered to retaliate. For example, in Chicago where the SROK is 102, many Black underclass women maintain strong ties with their relatives and not their husbands' families. This might explain why Latinas have a low SROK; their ties are mainly to their husbands' families. According to Wilson and Daly, in societies where

> **women are cut off from their kin and may be treated like household servants by their mothers-in-law, an abused wife may feel she has no recourse other than suicide or flight; violence against the husband is futile and almost unthinkable. Conversely, an abused wife who is surrounded by supportive relatives has more assertive options available for changing her situation,**

and she may be especially tempted to react violently. . . . However, the majority presence of the wife's relatives might be expected to deter husbands from seriously assaulting wives, so that the incidence of serious wife battering might be lower in matrilineal kinship systems. (Wilson and Daly 1992, 208)

Third, women's deadly actions overtake men's when women are defending their children from prior relationships against their current partners. So, Wilson and Daly (1992) say:

Higher SROK values . . . may reflect a greater prevalence of stepfathers. . . . If black children in Chicago, for example, experience higher rates of their fathers' absence and of new men in their mothers' life than white children, and if Latino children experience lower rates of substitute fatherhood than either blacks or whites, this could largely account for the ethnic contrasts in SROK values [blacks, 131; whites 43; and Latinos, 29]. (202, 209)

 3-8 Female crime and criminality

White and Black Criminals

According to Figure 3.7, almost twice as many Whites are arrested for violent, property, and drug offenses as Blacks. Arrested Whites make up about 15 percent *less*

than their percentage of the general population. On the other hand, arrested Blacks make up about three times *more* than their percentage of the general population. Why are there so many more Blacks than Whites arrested compared with their percentage of the general population? Does the criminal justice system (in this case the police) discriminate against Blacks? Or, do Blacks commit crimes at higher rates than Whites?

We'll talk about discrimination in several other chapters. Here, we have to answer other important questions. First, why are we only talking about Blacks and not other minorities, too? Unfortunately, the arrest statistics lump Whites and Hispanics together, so we can't get those numbers, and the numbers for Asian and Native Americans are so small that they're not reliable. Second, why are we looking at *arrest* rates? Well, to be honest, it's partly because they're easy to get. But, there's more to it than that. The NCVS data back them up. Remember, the NCVS asks *victims* about the crimes committed against them. One of the questions the NCVS asks is the race of victimizers. (Of course, victims have to *see* their victimizers, which happens only in rape, robbery, and assault.) Victim identifications match up well with police statistics in cases victims report to the police. This is important because two very different sources—police and victim reports—corroborate each other on race statistics.

 3-9 More discrimination statistics

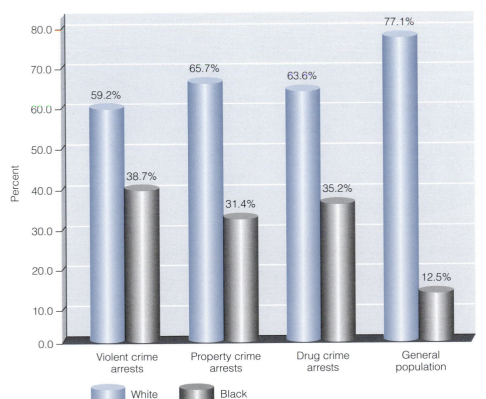

FIGURE 3.7
Percentage of Whites and Blacks Arrested and in General Population, 1999
SOURCE: FBI 2000; U.S. Census 2001.

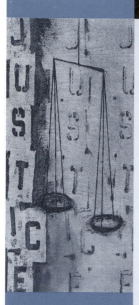

Consider the following excerpts from a *New York Times* article:

> Drug arrests on the 10 o'clock news tend to show inner-city blacks and Latinos being led away in handcuffs. But Federal health statistics show only slight differences in the rates of drug use for whites and people of color [Figure 3.8]—and define the typical drug addict as a white male in his 20's who lives in a suburb where drug busts almost never happen.
>
> The Partnership for a Drug-Free America expects to spend nearly $200 million this year to convince policy makers and affluent Americans that the drug problem crosses racial, economic, and geographic lines. This point would seem self-evident. But the myth that drug use is confined to the black inner city will be difficult to dislodge.
>
> The *Hartford Courant* learned how deep the myth runs when it published a series . . . that examined the lives of drug addicts who supported their habits through prostitution. Conditioned to think of drug abuse as a minority problem, some readers were stunned that 70 percent of the drug-addicted prostitutes shown in the series turned out to be white. Some doubted that the story was true. The refusal to believe that white heroin addicts exist was particularly self-deceptive in a state that is almost 90 percent white. . . .

Speaking at a national conference last week, Dr. Dawn Day, an addiction specialist from the Dogwood Center in Princeton, N.J., drew a connection between racial profiling of intravenous drug users and the rapid spread of AIDS in the black community. The

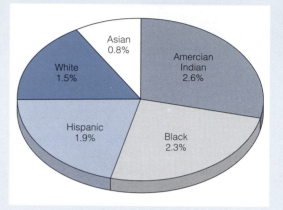

FIGURE 3.9

Percent of the General Population of Each Group Dependent on Drugs in 1999

SOURCE: Substance Abuse and Mental Health Services Administration (SAMHSA) 2000, *1999 Annual Survey*. http://www.samhsa.gov/oas/NHSDA.htm.

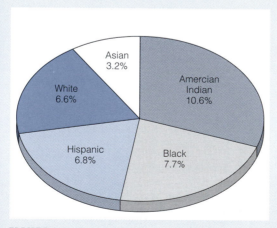

FIGURE 3.8

Percent of the General Population of Each Group Using Drugs in 1999

SOURCE: Substance Abuse and Mental Health Services Administration (SAMHSA) 2000, *1999 Annual Survey*. http://www.samhsa.gov/oas/NHSDA.htm.

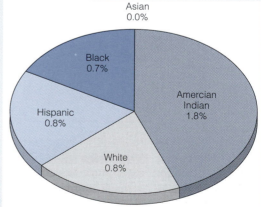

FIGURE 3.10

Percent of the General Population of Each Group Selling Drugs in 1999

SOURCE: Substance Abuse and Mental Health Services Administration (SAMHSA) 2000, *1999 Annual Survey*. http://www.samhsa.gov/oas/NHSDA.htm.

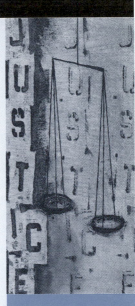

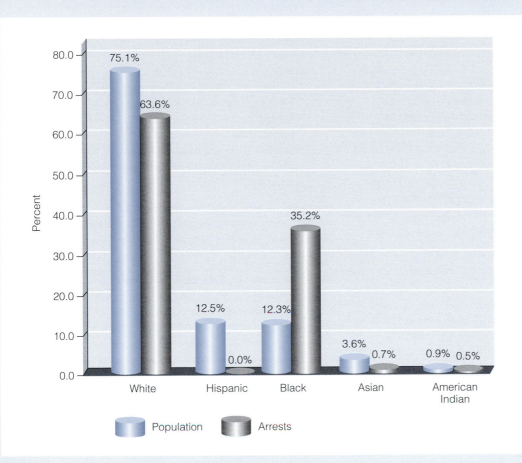

FIGURE 3.11

Percentage of General Population and Arrests for Drug Offenses

*There are no arrest figures for Hispanics.

SOURCES: FBI 2001, Table 43; U.S. Census 2001, Table DP-1.

most conservative estimates suggest that white intravenous drug users outnumber black users by at least 5 to 1. Even so, drug sweeps tend to be concentrated in inner cities, which are widely viewed as the sole source of the problem. Dr. Day's calculations, based on Federal data, show 5 arrests for every 100 white addicts, but 20 arrests for every 100 black addicts. (Staples 1999, 22)

Now, consider Figures 3.8 through 3.11.

Questions

1. Summarize your findings from the article excerpt and graphics.
2. What do you find about the relationship between race and illegal drug use and selling, drug dependency, and arrests for drug offenses?
3. How do you explain the disparities? What more would you want to know before answering?
4. What, if any, criminal justice policy changes would you recommend in view of your findings?

Third, do Blacks commit crimes at higher rates than Whites? Or, to put it technically, is there more Black criminality than White criminality? A mass of research too powerful to dismiss says yes, Blacks commit more crimes than Whites compared with their numbers in the general population. But, let's be clear about two things this *doesn't* tell us. First, it doesn't tell us Blacks are by nature more crime-prone than Whites. According to respected experts on race and crime, Robert J. Sampson and Janet L. Lauritsen (1997):

> The idea that I.Q., temperament, and other individual characteristics explain the race-crime connection is anathema . . . on political and policy grounds. But there are better reasons to reject the constitutional arguments—empirical validity. . . . The reason is simple; there are more variations *within* any race or ethnic group than *between* them. . . . "Race" is socially constructed, and the explanation of apparent differences is linked to the fact that race is serving as a proxy for some other set of variables. (331)

Second, it doesn't mean criminal justice doesn't discriminate against Blacks. In fact, two theories (strain and labeling) we'll discuss later (and several other theories not discussed) look to social structure and the agencies of criminal justice (not race) to explain criminal behavior (Gottredson and Hirschi 1990, 149–153; Hindelang 1978, 92–109; Tonry 1995, 52–56; Walker, Spohn, and DeLone 2000, 37–48).

Traditional explanations of crime focus on the individual level; they try to separate offenders from nonoffenders. Another old idea in criminology focuses on the community level. This is not to explain why individuals get involved in crime but to identify characteristics in neighborhoods, cities, states, and countries that lead to high rates of criminality. The founders of the **social ecology** theory, Clifford Shaw and Henry McKay, identified three community characteristics of Chicago neighborhoods—low social economic status, racial or ethnic heterogeneity, and high residential mobility—that led first to social disorganization and then to high crime and delinquency rates. Perhaps their most important finding was high crime rates continued for many years in such neighborhoods no matter how much population turnover there was. Because of this finding, they rejected individual explanations and focused on how community characteristics linked to transmitting criminality from one generation to the next (Sampson and Lauritsen 1997, 351–352).

Later research has backed up Shaw and McKay's social ecology theory to explain higher rates of Black criminality. In an important study, Robert J. Sampson established a link between joblessness among Black males and murder and robbery rates in 150 U.S. cities. He found high numbers of unemployed Black men compared with Black women is directly linked to single-parent families headed by women, and Black family disruption is significantly connected to murder and robbery rates (Sampson 1987, 348–382).

In a later comment on the study and other related research, Sampson and Lauritsen (1997) conclude:

> Despite a large difference in mean levels of family disruption between black and white communities, the percentage of *white* families headed by a female also had significant effect on white juvenile and adult violence. The relationships for white robbery were in large part identical in sign and magnitude to those for blacks. As a result, the influence of black family disruption on black crime was independent of alternative explanations (e.g., region, income, density, age composition) and could not be attributed to unique factors within the black community because of the similar effect of white family disruption on white crime. (335)

What does this mean? First, there's no homogeneous Black community. Second, there's no unique "Black subculture of violence." Otherwise, the variations *within* race don't make sense.

> For example, if a uniform subculture of violence explains black crime, are we to assume that this subculture is three times as potent in, say, New York as Chicago (where black homicide differs by a factor of three)? In San Francisco as in Baltimore (3:1 ratio)? These distinct variations exist even at the state level. For example, rates of black homicide in California are triple those for whites in Maryland. Must whites then be part of the black subculture of violence in California, given that white homicide rates are also more than triple those for whites in Maryland? We think not. The sources of violent crime appear to be remarkably invariant across race and rooted instead in the structural differences among communities, cities, and states in economic and family organization. (Sampson 1995, 41)

The debate over the link between race and crime is far from over and is hampered by political correctness and ideological stubbornness, but Shaw and McKay's followers have put aside both to advance our knowledge of this important and touchy subject (Sampson and Wilson 1995).

 3-10 Latest SAMHSA report

Relationship Between Criminals and Victims

"You always hurt the one you love" goes the old song. It's more true of criminals and their victims than we like to admit. When it comes to criminals, relationships *do* matter, especially four:

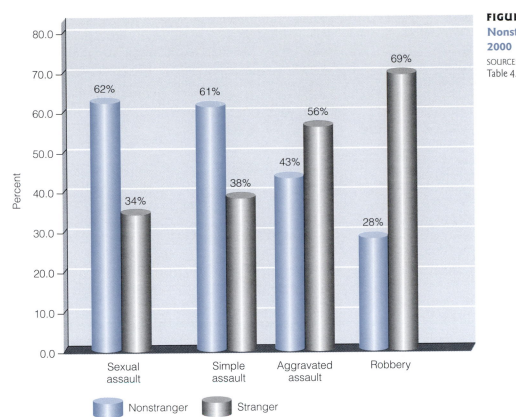

FIGURE 3.12
Nonstranger/Stranger Relationships, 2000
SOURCE: Bureau of Justice Statistics 2001c, Table 4.

1. *Intimates:* Spouses, ex-spouses, same-sex partners, boyfriends, girlfriends

2. *Relatives:* Parents, children, siblings, grandparents, in-laws, cousins

3. *Acquaintances:* People who know each other, like friends; people from work, where they shop, where they go for fun

4. *Strangers:* People who don't know each other (Figure 3.12)

3-11 Details behind Figure 3.12

Murray A. Strauss and others interviewed more than two thousand husbands, wives, children, brothers, and sisters. They found:

- Fifty to 60 percent of all husbands assault their wives at least once during marriage. (Finkelhor et al. 1983)
- Husbands and boyfriends are a lot more likely to kill their wives and girlfriends than wives and girlfriends are to kill their husbands and boyfriends. (Langan and Innes 1986)
- Husbands and boyfriends kill 70 percent of women homicide victims! (Bureau of Justice Statistics 1998b, 1; Gove et al. 1986, 464–465)

Some researchers estimate parents physically assault 100,000 to 200,000 children every year, sexually abuse 60,000 to 100,000, and kill 5,000! (Strauss, Gelles, and Steinmetz 1980, 49). The kind of abuse varies by social class. Stephen Brown (1984, 259–278) used an anonymous questionnaire to survey 110 high school freshmen about parental abuse. He found lower-class parents abused their children more often physically and middle-class parents abused their children more often emotionally ("guilt trips" and shaming).

Family violence receives most of the attention, but property crimes also occur within families. In a pilot study, Alan J. Lincoln and Murray A. Strauss administered a voluntary anonymous questionnaire to 450 randomly distributed New England college students. The questionnaire asked about property crimes—including forgery, fraud, vandalism, and extortion—committed by one family member against another. Property crimes occurred in 73 percent of the families (Lincoln and Strauss 1985, 71–87).

■ CRIME VICTIMS

Here are the bare facts of criminal victimization reported by the NCVS for the year 2000 (Bureau of Justice Statistics 2001c):

- There were 25.9 million victimizations.
- Almost 6.6 million were violent crimes and a little more than 19 million were property crimes.
- Young people were violent crime victims at higher rates (60.1 for 12–15 year olds and 64.3 for 16–19 year olds) than any other age group (13.7 for 50–64 year olds).
- There were 32.9 male victims and 23.2 female victims of violent crime in every 1000 households.
- There were 27.1 White violent crime victims in every 1000 households; 35.3 Blacks; and 28.4 Hispanics.
- The violent crime rate in households with incomes less than $7500 was 60.3 for every 1000 households; it was 22.3 in households with incomes over $75,000. The rate went up 5 percent in poor households from 1999 to 2000; it went down 2.5 percent in wealthy households.
- Households with incomes of less than $7500 were the only income group in the country to suffer *increases* in violent crime.
- Most violent crime victims didn't face an armed attacker.

These are the raw numbers. But, what about the experience of being a crime victim? Numbers can't capture the fear, helplessness, anger, and the desire for revenge—like this husband and wife whose house was burglarized experienced:

WIFE: That made me angry inside, that someone would do that and upset my children. . . . It was somewhat revenge, anger toward that person and feeling like they had no business in my home. . . . The more I thought about it . . . the more revenge I felt.

HUSBAND: It's unfair that you work for something, like this lawn mower was nothing of value really, but you work hard for it and somebody takes it away from you when you're about to enjoy it or continue to enjoy it. (Greenberg, Ruback, and Westcott 1983, 81)

Another victim went even further:

Six young men rob a teenager of his gold jewelry while he waits for a subway train. The next night the victim chances upon the offenders at the same station. He comes up to them and simply utters, "Remember me?" Although they don't recognize him and look puzzled he takes out a pistol and shoots three of them before fleeing. (Karmen 1990, 2)

Criminals aren't the only cause of victim suffering. A bank teller found this out when she handed over money to a robber. The robber had handed her a note that read, "This is a stickup. Put all the money in a bag and no one will get hurt." In her panic she forgot to slip in a specially treated bundle of bills to set off shots of red dye and tear gas at the robber when he tried to leave the bank. The

next morning her boss gave her a choice: She could either take a demotion and pay cut or an unpaid indefinite leave of absence. She quit. "I did what any normal person would do—I gave the man the money. For three years I've been a loyal employee and this is what I get" (Karmen 1990, 2).

Let's look at types of victims and programs for protecting and assisting victims.

Types of Victims

I've been mugged six (or was it seven) times in my life. Does this mean I'm victim-prone? Probably not. I haven't been mugged since I've gotten older and stopped going to places and doing things at times I probably shouldn't have. In other words, I was in the right place at the right time (see the "Situation Theories" section). My own experience illustrates what research clearly demonstrates—victimization isn't a random experience. Take the elderly. The common perception is they're crime-prone. In fact, people 65 or over are five times less often victims of violent crime, four times less often victims of car theft, and half as often victims of home burglaries. Of course, this doesn't mean older people don't suffer from crime. Victimization and the fear of it traumatize older people more than they do younger victims. This fear erodes the quality of their lives, forcing them to stay at home rather than venture outside (Cook 1979, 123; Eve and Eve 1984, 290; Miethe and Meier 1994, 2).

Some empirical research supports victim proneness. Marvin E. Wolfgang, Terence P. Thornberry, and Robert M. Figlio asked birth cohorts (people the same age) about the crimes they committed and the victimizations they suffered between the ages of 12 to 18 and 18 to 26. The responses showed they were both victims and victimizers in violent crimes but not property crimes (Reiss 1980, 47–57; Wolfgang, Thornberry, and Figlio 1987, chap. 13).

Occupation also affects victimization. More than one million people a year are the victims of violent crime on the job. Every year, someone steals personal belongings from more than two million workers while they work, and the cars of another 200,000. These victimizations cost an average of about 3.5 days of work per person every year. Among those victimized while working, men are more likely to be the victims of violent crime, but women are just as likely to be the victims of theft (Bureau of Justice Statistics 1994; *Wall Street Journal* 1994).

Victimization is also related to race. In 2000, the violent crime victimization rate for Whites was 27.1 per 1000 persons over 12 years of age and for Hispanics slightly higher, 28.4. For Blacks it was 35.3. The National Institute for Occupational Health and Safety (OSHA) found the rate of work-related homicides for Blacks was nearly twice that of White workers. Black taxi drivers and gas station attendants have especially high homicide rates. Finally, most crime is intraracial (within races) not interracial (between races). In other words, most crime is White on White, Black on Black, Hispanic on Hispanic, Asian on Asian, or American Indian on American Indian (Bureau of Justice Statistics 2000, 3; Walker, Spohn, and DeLone 2000, 24–25).

Victimization strongly correlates with lifestyle. Criminologists have developed theories built around this correlation (Miethe and Meier 1994, 2). The earliest theorists faced strong opposition on ideological grounds. During the 1970s, feminists and victims' advocates complained such theories blamed the victims. Despite opposition, one of these theories, the **lifestyle-exposure theory,** has received considerable acceptance among criminologists. Michael S. Hindelang, Michael Gottfredson, and James Garofalo (1978) found different victim lifestyles explain different rates of victimization. Gender, race, and income are linked to different lifestyles and to chances of victimization. According to the theory, crimes take place disproportionately against young, single, low-income Black men because this group spends more time away from home at night, taking part in activities during which crimes often occur (Hindelang, Gottfredson, and Garofalo 1978; Meier and Miethe 1993, 459–465).

Lawrence W. Sherman, Patrick R. Gartin, and Michael E. Buerger identified "hot spots" in Minneapolis (places where most crimes take place). On the basis of more than 300,000 emergency calls for one year, they found most calls reporting robberies, rapes, and thefts came from hot spots. Because older people, married couples, and others with steady employment rarely go to hot spots, particularly at night, they're rarely victims (Chapter 5) (Sherman, Gartin, and Buerger 1989, 27–55).

Protecting and Assisting Victims

The U.S. Victims of Crime Act created a $100 million crime victims' fund drawn from criminal fines in federal offenses. The money supports state victim-compensation and other programs to assist victims. States have also passed laws to assist crime victims. Most of these statutes compensate violent crime victims who report crimes and cooperate with investigation and prosecution for medical expenses, funeral expenses, lost wages, and the support of deceased victims' dependents. However, the caps on the allowable amounts are too low to make compensation meaningful.

Some states have established victim-witness assistance programs, usually supervised by prosecutors. These programs provide services like

- *Personal advocacy:* Helping victims receive all the services they're entitled to
- *Referral:* Recommending or obtaining other assistance
- *Restitution assistance:* Urging judges to order, or probation authorities to collect, restitution and helping

violent crime victims fill out applications to receive compensation
- *Court orientation:* Explaining the criminal justice system and their participation in it
- *Transportation:* Taking victims and witnesses to and from court, to social service agencies, and, if necessary, to shelters
- *Escort services:* Escorting witnesses to court and staying with them during proceedings
- *Emotional support:* Giving victims support during their ordeals with crime and with the criminal justice proceedings following it (National Law Journal 1990, 12)

Thirteen states have even written victim's rights provisions into their constitutions. Typical provisions require the criminal justice system to:

- Treat victims with compassion and respect
- Inform victims of critical stages in the trial process
- Invite victims to attend and comment on trial proceedings

"I feel as if our movement is picking up the steam it needs to carry through all fifty states," said Linda Lowrance, chair of the Victims' Constitutional Amendment Network.

No one has evaluated the effectiveness of these provisions, according to John Stein, deputy director of the National Organization for Victim Assistance. However, some evidence shows victim impact statements make people "feel better" about the criminal justice system, even though the statements have little or no effect on sentencing or punishment of convicted offenders. Roberta Roper, whose daughter was raped and murdered, couldn't attend the trial of her daughter's murderers because Maryland has no victims' rights law. Forced to watch the trial by pressing her nose against the small pane of glass in a wooden courtroom door, Roper felt she'd let her daughter down by not being in court. "By being a presence at the trial, we could as a family bear witness to the fact that Stephanie lived, and she mattered. We were denied that" (Bureau of Justice Statistics 1989; *New York Times* 1992, 156).

At the time of the crime, victims have to depend on self-protection. According to the NCVS, three-quarters of victims reported taking self-protective measures against offenders, including resisting, trying to capture the offender, persuading the offender, and running away. More than half of those who took self-protective measures reported that their actions had a positive effect. About 7 percent reported that the measures made the situation worse, while 6 percent reported that both positive and negative effects resulted (Table 3.2).

 3-12 You Decide: Is fear of robbery racist?

TABLE 3.2

Victim Self-Protective Measures, 1999*

	Both Sexes	Male	Female	White	Black
ATTACKED WITH WEAPON	1.0	1.4	0.6	1.0	1.3
ATTACKED WITHOUT WEAPON	10.4	12.5	8.1	9.8	14.4
THREATENED WITH WEAPON	1.2	1.7	0.6	1.3	0.5
THREATENED WITHOUT WEAPON	2.5	3.5	1.4	2.4	2.6
RESISTED OR CAPTURED OFFENDER	20.2	22.4	17.8	20.0	21.8
SCARED OR WARNED OFFENDER	9.8	6.9	12.8	10.1	8.0
PERSUADED OR APPEASED OFFENDER	10.9	11.3	10.5	10.7	11.5
RAN AWAY OR HID	15.0	15.5	14.4	15.2	14.1
GOT HELP OR GAVE ALARM	11.5	8.4	14.8	11.8	9.0
SCREAMED FROM PAIN OR FEAR	2.3	0.8	3.9	2.3	2.2
TOOK OTHER MEASURES	15.3	15.5	15.0	15.4	14.5

*Columns may not sum to 100% due to rounding errors.

SOURCE: Bureau of Justice Statistics 2000b, Statistical Tables, Table 71.

■ EXPLAINING CRIMINAL BEHAVIOR

Why do people commit crimes? This question has fascinated and puzzled moralists, political leaders, legislators, and policymakers for centuries. According to the distinguished criminologists Michael Gottfredson and Travis Hirschi (1990), the explanation requires recognition of a simple fact:

> Force and fraud are ever present possibilities in human affairs. Denial of this fact promotes the development of theories of crime that are misleading guides to policy. Awareness of this fact allows the development of a theory of crime consistent with research and the needs of sound public policy. (4)

Criminologists consider the origins of criminal behavior fundamental to the discipline of criminology, but knowing the causes of crime is also of great practical importance. We can't control crime if we don't know what causes it. Unfortunately, social scientists haven't found the *causes* of crime, but they have identified a number of *relationships* (correlates) between crime and individual characteristics and social conditions. We can divide the explanations into two categories: (1) individual responsibility explanations and (2) social explanations.

Individual Responsibility Explanations

The earliest explanations of criminal behavior focused on individual offenders. In the Middle Ages, criminals were believed possessed by Satan or other demons who caused them to commit their crimes. During the eighteenth century Age of Reason (Enlightenment), explanations turned to free will and the capacity of individuals to choose between committing crimes and obeying the law. English philosopher Jeremy Bentham—influenced by the ideas of Italian criminologist Cesare Beccaria—developed the **utilitarian theory of crime causation.** The theory is based on two assumptions: First, it's human nature to seek pleasure and avoid pain. ("Nature has placed mankind under two sovereign masters, *pain* and *pleasure*," in Bentham's words.) Second, individuals are free to choose to commit (or not commit) crimes. So, if the pleasure from committing crimes outweighs the pain of getting caught and punished, then criminal behavior will result (discussed later in the "Rational Choice Explanations" section) (Gottfredson and Hirschi 1990, 5).

Opposition to the idea of free will grew during the 1800s when **determinist theories** based on the idea that forces beyond individual control determined behavior took root. "Criminals are born not made," concluded the nineteenth-century Italian psychiatrist turned criminologist Cesare Lombroso. "It's in the genes," we might say today. As a young doctor at an asylum in Pavia, Lombroso performed an autopsy on an Italian Jack the Ripper. In the course of his examination, he detected an abnormality in the dead man's skull. Describing his discovery, he wrote:

> At the sight of that skull, I seemed to see all at once, standing out clearly illumined as in a vast plain under a flaming sky, the problem of the nature of the criminal, who reproduces in civilised times characteristics, not only of primitive savages, but of still lower types as far back as the carnivora. (Lombroso-Ferrero 1972, 6–7)

So the **biological explanation** was born in Lombroso's lab, and it survives today but modified by more sophisticated analyses that pay attention to the interaction between environment and heredity.

Perhaps the most sensationalized, modern offender-focused biological explanation of crime links violent behavior to abnormal chromosomes. Until 1960, it was widely accepted that males have two sex-linked chromosomes, one X and one Y. Then, biologists discovered some men have two or sometimes even three Y chromosomes. Then, in 1965, Scottish researchers reported an astonishing correlate: A high proportion of tall, violent, male mental patients had an extra Y chromosome. In a subsequent wave of studies in mental hospitals and prisons, researchers tried to trace violent behavior to these newly identified "supermales" with "chromosomes of criminality." These studies yielded mixed results: Some found a chromosome-violence link; others didn't (Rennie 1978, 224).

Some twin studies also attempted to link biology to crime. Karl Otto Christiansen investigated all Danish twins born between 1881 and 1910. He found if one fraternal twin was a criminal, there was a 12 percent chance the other twin was too. In identical twins, the chance was three times greater. So, the links established a definite, but weak, link between twins and criminal behavior (Mednick and Christiansen 1977).

The National Research Council, the research arm of the prestigious National Academy of Sciences, added credibility to theories of biological origins of crime in its report *Understanding and Preventing Violence* (Reiss and Roth 1993). The report, which compiles the work of nineteen prominent scholars and scientists from a range of disciplines, finds that biological, genetic, and criminogenic factors should be considered in the search for the causes of violence. A detailed survey of sociology, psychology, psychiatry, law, genetics, and biology, the report recognizes the complexity of the causes of crime:

> [R]esearch strongly suggests that violence arises from interactions among individuals' psychosocial development, their neurological and hormonal differences, and social processes. Consequently, we have no basis for considering any of these "levels of explanation" any more fundamental than the others. (Reiss and Roth 1993, 102)

However, Mark Moore, professor of criminal justice policy at Harvard's John F. Kennedy School of Government, offered this bleak assessment of the National Research Council report on the link between violence and biology:

> You come to the important point of view that the causes of violence are complex and therefore elusive. The hope that we might be able to base policy on definite knowledge of the causes of violence is receding. (Butterfield 1992, 12)

The **psychoanalytic explanation** also grew out of the nineteenth-century determinist intellectual tradition. Under the influence of Austrian psychoanalyst Sigmund Freud, psychoanalytic psychology became a significant force in the 1920s. It reached its high point during the 1950s and 1960s. During the 1980s, critics from all over the political and intellectual spectrum joined in an assault on psychoanalytic psychology. The critics charged (fairly or unfairly) the theory itself caused crime by giving criminals an excuse for their behavior. "It's not my fault, blame my cruel father and my domineering mother" captures the gist of the criticism. These withering attacks on the psychoanalytic explanation dealt a fatal blow to the psychoanalytic explanation of criminal behavior.

Sociological Explanations

Criminologists are wary of explanations of criminal behavior based on individual biology and psychology and free will (see the "Rational Choice Explanations" section). They look for the explanations of criminal behavior in the structure of and interactions in social institutions like family, neighborhoods, churches, and schools; demographics like social status, race, gender, age, and education; and community values. Let's look at some of these explanations, including social structure theories, social process theories, rational choice explanations, the seduction of crime, and situation theories.

Social structure theories

Social structure theories link individual criminal behavior to social conditions such as poverty, unemployment, and poor education. According to social structure theorists, crime is located mainly in the lower-income classes because flaws in the social structure increase the odds individuals in that part of society will commit crimes. The nineteenth-century sociologist Emile Durkheim (1951) explained crime as the result of weakening social norms—the **anomie theory.** Durkheim formulated the anomie theory when France was changing from a rural agricultural society to an industrialized nation. A society in transition, said Durkheim, weakens the bonds that ordinarily control behavior; crime follows. Two forms of the theory, the strain and opportunity theories, were developed to describe conditions specific to the United States.

Strain Theory   In 1938, during the Great Depression, sociologist Robert K. Merton (1968, 185–214) formulated a U.S. version of anomie in a paper entitled "Social Structure and Anomie." The sociologist Gilbert Geis has called Merton's paper "the single most influential formulation in the sociology of deviance, and . . . possibly the most quoted paper in modern sociology." According to Merton, society establishes goals we all try to achieve. At the same time, for some people, social structure blocks achievement of these goals. In the United States, the goals are wealth, power, and prestige based on hard work. **Strain theory** explains why some people commit crimes when they work hard but fail to attain the American dream. The prototypical success story in the United States is rags to riches. You may be a Burger King employee today, but if you work hard and stick to it, you'll soon manage a Burger King, and eventually start your own chain of restaurants. The trouble is, many people work hard and play by the rules, but they don't get wealth, power, or prestige. According to Merton, society praises only success and winning, not fair play.

Some theorists have extended strain theory to crime in organizations. Feeling deprived when others around them are doing better causes strain for less successful members of the organization. They may be doing exceptionally well by the standards of people below them, but they don't look down; instead, they yearn for the salary, power, and prestige of those above them. This **anomie of affluence** leads some people to put rules aside to reduce their deprivation (lack of success) (Lafree 1998, 57; Simon and Gagnon 1976, 356–378; Thio 1975, 135–158).

Does strain affect crime rates? Strain theory doesn't fit the crime trends of the last fifty years. The theory treats strain caused by trying to get ahead and roadblocks to it like a permanent characteristic, but crime trends have been anything but constant. Our biggest crime boom (the 1960s) took place when there were both more opportunities to get ahead and fewer roadblocks to getting there (Lafree 1998, 64–65).

Opportunity Theory   In 1960, Richard Cloward and Lloyd Ohlin expanded strain theory and developed what they called opportunity theory. According to **opportunity theory** when you can't get money, power, and prestige legally, you break the law to get them. So, criminal behavior depends on criminal opportunities available to obtain widely shared goals. For example, poor neighborhoods where juveniles get a poor education provide criminal opportunities for them to get what they're not equipped to get legally (Cloward and Ohlin 1960).

In Clifford Shaw's classic book, *The Jack-Roller,* the delinquent youth Stanley describes a community with criminal opportunities:

> Stealing in the neighborhood was a common practice among the children and approved by the parents. Whenever the boys got together they talked about robbing and made more plans for stealing. I hardly knew any boys who did not go robbing. The little fellows went in for petty stealing, breaking into freight cars, and stealing junk. The older guys did big jobs like stick-up, burglary, and stealing autos. The little fellows admired the "big shots" and longed for the day when they could get into the big racket. (Shaw 1966, 54)

Social process theories

Social structure theory doesn't pretend to explain all criminal behavior. After all, crime occurs in all social classes, and most people in the lower classes don't commit crimes. Social process theories look at **social processes** (interactions among members) of families, peer groups, schools, churches, and other social institutions. There's a lot of empirical research linking experiences with these institutions to criminal behavior. For example, most prison inmates come from single-parent homes, have relatives and friends who have served time in prison, are school dropouts or underachievers, and have poor work skills and employment records (Chapter 11).

Social process theorists agree that criminogenic forces in society affect behavior, but they disagree over *how.* **Social learning theories** assume individuals are born like blank slates and can learn any values and behavior. **Social control theory** assumes everybody is born with the desire to break the rules. **Labeling theory** assumes the criminal justice system creates criminals. Whether individuals have actually broken the law doesn't matter. Society's actions shape the self-image and behavior of people who have been labeled criminals.

Learning Theories   When I was a boy, a neighbor told her son to stay away from that Joel Samaha because, I'd "put bad bugs in his head." The commonsense notion that people learn criminal behavior from others underlies social learning theory. This notion in turn depends on the assumption that we're blank slates at birth and our parents, friends, teachers, religious leaders, and government write the attitudes, beliefs, and values on our behavioral slates.

The criminologist Edwin Sutherland formulated the most prominent social learning theory: **differential association.** According to Sutherland, criminal behavior, just like any other behavior, depends on our associations with other people. If we associate more with lawbreakers than law-abiders, chances are we'll commit crimes. Some associations are stronger than others. The more intense the relationships the more we learn from them and the longer we retain what we've learned. So, our families and our friendships teach us the most enduring lessons about how to behave. People in low-income neighborhoods who associate with "street criminals" learn to act like street criminals, not because people who live in poor neighborhoods are "bad," but because that's the way social beings behave. By the same reasoning, corporate criminals learn criminal behavior too (Sutherland and Cressey 1978, 83–87).

3-13 You Decide: Did violent criminals learn their violent behavior from their abusive parents?

Control Theory   Social control theory assumes that people are rule breakers by nature. As Travis Hirschi (1969), the leading proponent of social control theory, put it:

> The question "Why did they do it?" is simply not the question the theory is designed to answer. The question is, "Why don't we do it?" There is much evidence that we would, if we dared. (34)

Why do we obey rules when we're rule breakers by nature? Because our ties to established institutions of social control, such as families, peer groups, churches, and schools, check our natural desire to break rules and satisfy our selfish interests. When ties to these institutions weaken, criminal behavior is likely to follow. Social bonds don't reduce our desire to get what we want; they reduce the chance we'll give in to our desire (Cullen 1983, 134–142).

Hirschi identified four elements in the social bond that curb the natural desire to break rules. First, attachment to others makes us sensitive to their opinions. Attachment to those whose opinions we care about (parents, teachers, coaches, neighbors, and friends) predicts best whether we'll follow rules. Second, commitment to the conventional order keeps us in line. The stronger our desire to get a job, get an education, and protect our reputation, the greater the chances we'll follow the rules. Third, involvement in legal activities leaves us less time to get into trouble; "idle hands are the devil's workshop." Fourth, the stronger we believe in the conventional order, the less likely we are to break its rules. Hirschi reports the results of testing his theory in *Causes of Delinquency* (1969). Police reports, self-reports, and schools for more than three thousand boys in a California youth project backed up Hirschi's theory. Further empirical studies have yielded similar results.

Control theory explains both street crime and organizational crime. When applied to organizations, the theory goes like this: Organizations don't provide controls on deviance. Rules don't apply; especially at the top. The ends justify the means. According to control theory, the rules are seen as obstacles to a greater goal. So, organizational criminals are freed from the bonds that would keep them in line (Stotland 1977, 179–196).

Control theory is an appealing explanation for crime trends since 1950, a period that saw ties to traditional institutions weakened. Empirical evidence strongly supports the argument that juveniles and young adults with strong ties to their families and schools are less likely to commit crimes. Of course, this doesn't explain what caused the weakening of ties in the first place and why ties were stronger in the 1950s than they were in the 1990s (Lafree 1998, 66–67).

Labeling Theory   In his classic *Outsiders,* Howard Becker (1973) developed the influential labeling theory. According to Becker, individuals don't commit crimes because they can't manage the stresses in society, or because they associate with other criminals and learn crime from them, or because their social bonds keep in line their urges to break rules. Instead, deviant episodes are turned into criminal careers by outsiders—"moral entrepreneurs" like police, courts, and corrections officers trying to control crime. In other words, the criminal justice system creates criminals. Whether "criminals" have actually broken the law doesn't matter. What *does* matter is once the "system" says they're criminals, they act like criminals. Society's actions shape their self-image.

Labeling theory shifts the emphasis from lawbreakers to lawmakers and law enforcers. This shift draws attention to the possible harmful effects of contacts with criminal justice agencies. The theory had a direct influence on public policy during the 1960s and 1970s in the creation of programs that diverted people out of the criminal justice system into alternative social programs (Cullen 1983, 125–128).

Rational choice explanations
Rational choice theorists have returned the individual to center stage in explaining crime. Since the late 1960s, several studies by economists have prompted criminologists to study a theory embraced by criminal justice officials and the public since the eighteenth century: People are rational and make decisions according to what they believe is in their self-interest. This behavior doesn't have to be *completely* rational—*somewhat* rational is good enough. The theory also allows for both irrational and pathological components in criminal behavior. Rational choice theory consists of three elements:

1. A reasoning criminal
2. A crime-specific focus
3. Separate analyses of criminal involvement and criminal events (Cornish and Clarke 1986)

The **reasoning criminal element** assumes offenders commit crimes to benefit themselves. Getting benefits requires rational decision making, however rough and affected by irrationality and pathology it may be. In short, criminals have specific goals, alternative means of obtaining them, and at least some information for choosing the best alternative to achieve their goals.

The **crime-specific element** assumes decision making is different for each crime. Burglary, for example, requires decision making different from robbery. And, different kinds of burglaries and robberies require different decision making. So deciding to rob a convenience store, or a bank, or to mug a person on the street all demand separate analyses. The decision to commit a commercial burglary isn't like the decision to commit a residential burglary. Burglars who target public housing, middle-class neighborhoods, and wealthy enclaves differ as to individuals, motivations, and methods.

The third element divides criminal involvement and criminal events. **Criminal involvement** refers to three stages: (1) deciding to get into crime generally, (2) continuing to be involved, and (3) deciding to get out of involvement in crime. The **criminal event** refers to the decision to commit a specific crime.

Empirical research into a variety of crimes, including shoplifting, burglary, robbery, and illegal drug use, has demonstrated some support for all three elements. Richard T. Wright and Scott H. Decker's sample of 105 St. Louis residential burglars found

> the decision to commit a residential burglary arises in the face of what offenders perceive to be a pressing need of cash. Previous research consistently has shown this to be so and the results of the present study bear out this point. More than nine out of ten of the offenders in our sample—95 out of 105—reported that they broke into dwellings primarily when they needed money. (Wright and Decker 1994, 36)

Wright and Decker found that burglars needed the money to "solve an immediate problem." Burglary for them was a "matter of day-to-day survival." Two burglars put it this way:

> Usually what I'll do is a burglary, maybe two or three if I have to, and then this will help me get over the rough spot until I can get my shit straightened out. Once I get it straightened out, I just go with the flow until I hit that rough spot where I need money again. And then I hit it . . . the only time I would go and commit a burglary is if I needed it in that point in time. That would be strictly to pay light bill, gas bill, rent. (Dan Whiting in Wright and Decker 1994, 37)

> You know how to stretch a dollar? I'll stretch it from here to the parking lot. But I can only stretch it so far and then it breaks. Then I say, "Well, I guess I got to go put on my black clothes. Go on out there like a thief in the night." (Ralph Jones in Wright and Decker 1994, 37)

The need for cash isn't always to buy food and pay the rent. Sometimes it's to "keep the party going." When Wright and Decker asked the burglars in their sample what they spent the money on, almost 75 percent said for "high living." As Janet Wilson, one of the burglars put it, "Long as I got some money, I'm cool. If I ain't got no money and I want to get high, then I go for it." A substantial number of burglars said they "needed" money for "keeping up appearances"—buying brand-name clothes and expensive cars (Wright and Decker 1994, 37–38).

Do criminals consider the risks of getting caught? The evidence is mixed. Neal Shover and David Honaker question whether their sample of repeat property offenders in Tennessee state prison were "reasoning criminals." Most of the prisoners (62 percent) said they didn't consider the risk of getting arrested; the rest said they thought about getting arrested briefly but then quickly got on with their planned burglaries. One burglar put it this way: "You think about going to prison about like you think of dying" (Shover and Honaker 1992, 281).

On the other hand, Julie Horney and Ineke Haen Marshall found their sample of more than one thousand men in Nebraska prisons for property offenses *did* think about

getting caught and accurately perceived the risk of getting caught and punished. They've learned through experience that "what actually happens when rules are violated is often nothing." They take this into account in their decision to commit crimes, which is what we'd expect a reasoning criminal to do according to rational choice theory (Horney and Marshall 1992, 572–592).

A sample of Washington, D.C., drug dealers adds further support to rational choice theory. Rand Corporation researchers selected a sample of persons charged with drug offenses in the District of Columbia between 1985 and 1987. They found drug dealing was profitable. Even if dealing doesn't lead to big fortunes, it pays a lot more than the legitimate jobs available to most urban youths with poor education and job skills. The Rand researchers estimated that drug dealers made an average of $30 an hour and if they wanted them, free drugs. Of course, the risks are high. In a year of dealing, dealers face a 1 percent chance of getting killed, a 7 percent chance of serious injury, and a 22 percent chance of going to prison. They took the risks (Reuter, MacCoun, and Murphy 1990, viii–xix).

Choosing to make profits in the face of the real risks of getting killed, injured, or going to prison supports rational choice theory, but it presents major problems for law enforcement agencies. "Drug selling is an important career choice and a major economic activity for many Black males living in poverty," according to the Rand study. Improving employment prospects would probably do little to reduce drug selling, because many dealers have developed expensive drug habits. Raising legitimate wages by 50 percent, to about $10.50 an hour, is unrealistic in view of the low education and job skill level of most dealers. Besides, even $10.50 an hour falls far short of the $30 an hour they can make dealing drugs. According to researchers, society must teach young people to avoid the lure of short-term gains. The realities of frequent imprisonment and expensive drug dependency are not worth it (Reuter, MacCoun, and Murphy 1990, xiv).

Forty-two out of sixty career robbers and burglars in Kenneth Tunnell's sample couldn't see any realistic alternative to committing crimes. Approximately equal numbers of the remaining inmates said they'd already tried to live without crime, tried to borrow money, or tried to find a job, and failed at all of them (Tunnell 1990, 45).

Rational choice doesn't apply to all crimes. Crimes of passion *do* happen; some criminals are psychotic or suffering from biological defects affecting their behavior. Furthermore, rationality plays a larger role in the decision making of experienced criminals than of amateurs. Finally, criminals committing the same type of crime act with varying degrees of rationality. Contrast the following statements by robbers to Floyd Feeney as to why they committed a particular robbery:

ROBBER 1: There wasn't no food in the house, you know. Scrounging. And I'm forced into having to do something like this. I know I was desperate. Besides, I was going out stealing anything I could get a hold of, get a little money to get some food.

ROBBER 2: I have no idea why I did this. Well, guess it was for some money, but I didn't have no problem, really, then. You know, everybody got a little money problem, but not big enough to go and rob somebody. I just can't get off into it. I don't really know why I did it. (Cornish and Clarke 1986, 57)

Rational choice theory can lead to two policy approaches to reducing crime. One is to raise the cost of illegal behavior by more arrests, convictions, and stiffer punishments. We've followed this approach in the past and it's widely used today. Raising the price of crime enjoys wide public support. We'll "get tough on criminals" politicians promise. The second approach, to increase the gains from lawful behavior, we haven't often tried, and it enjoys little support. Why? For one thing, we'd have to make major changes—some say unwarranted invasions—into areas that are not the government's business. For example, government could set wage controls, guarantee job security, and order more chances for advancement for car washers. This might well make washing cars attractive enough that former car thieves would rather wash cars than steal them. But, that amount of government interference is out of the question in our free market economy.

Seductions of crime

In his fascinating book *Seductions of Crime* (1988), Jack Katz explores what he calls the **foreground forces in crime,** "the positive, often wonderful attractions within the lived experience of criminality." He goes beyond rational choice theory by exploring the "thrill" of committing crimes. Katz doesn't reject the "background" forces of traditional sociological theory we've examined, but he contends there is more. Katz argues traditional criminologists have neglected foreground forces:

> The social science literature contains only scattered evidence of what it means, feels, sounds, tastes, or looks like to commit a particular crime. Readers of research on homicide and assault do not hear the slaps and curses, see the pushes and shoves, or feel the humiliation and rage that may build toward the attack, sometimes persisting after the victim's death. How adolescents manage to make shoplifting or vandalism of cheap and commonplace things a thrilling experience has not been intriguing to many students of delinquency. Researchers of adolescent gangs have never grasped why their subjects so often stubbornly refuse to accept the outsider's insistence that they wear the "gang" label.
>
> The description of "cold-blooded senseless murder" has been left to writers outside the social sciences. Neither academic methods nor academic theories seem to be able to grasp why such killers may have been courteous to their victims just moments before the killing, why they often wait until they have dominated victims in sealed-off environments before coldly executing them, or how it makes sense to kill them when only petty cash is at stake. Sociological and psychological studies of robbery rarely focus on the distinctive attractions of robbery, even though research has now clearly documented that alternative forms of criminality are available and familiar to many career robbers. In sum, only rarely have sociologists taken up the challenge of explaining the qualities of deviant experience. (Katz 1988, 3)

Katz says studying foreground forces might explain why most people escape the criminogenic forces identified by theories of social structure, process, and control they're exposed to. And foreground forces might also shed light on why many of those who fit the causal profiles of biological, psychoanalytic, and sociological theories "go for long stretches without committing the crime to which theory directs them." "Why," asks Katz, "are some people who were not determined to commit a crime one moment determined to do so the next?" Katz (1988, 4) says it's the "seduction," the "thrill," of crime.

The foreground approach looks at what stops people from committing or seduces them into committing crimes that their social, biological, and psychological background can't explain. According to Katz, at the moment of crime the criminal feels seduced, drawn to, compelled to commit the crime. Seduction isn't special to criminals—everyone gets seduced into something or by someone. What *is* special is the seduction of committing a crime. Compelled doesn't mean there was no choice. At the moment of the crime, says Katz, there's a transition from the choice to commit crimes rationally to a compulsion to do so, driven by the seductive thrill of crime. The criminal controls the *transition* from choice to compulsion.

Situation theories

Situation theories study the "location of targets and the movement of offenders and victims in time and space." Situation theories are based on the early twentieth-century human ecology perspective. This perspective focused on plotting the distribution of crime by place and time—namely, neighborhoods according to hour, day, and month. (See the "White and Black Criminals" section.)

Central to situation explanations of crime are opportunity and temptation. Situation theories assume offenders' decisions are "not calculated to maximize success, but rather to meet their needs with a minimum of effort." This explanation assumes most criminals (like most people) are "middling in morality, in self-control, in careful effort, in pursuing advantage." Therefore, criminal behavior depends on the situation—specifically, on time, space

YOU DECIDE

Should rational choice theory be the basis for criminal justice policy?

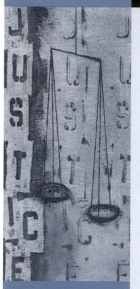

Critics have found much to criticize about the rational choice theory. Some have challenged the free will and rationalist assumptions on which the theory rests. Respected sociologists like Michael Gottfredson and Travis Hirschi say rational choice theory treats criminal behavior like a job. But it's not, they say. The decision to commit crimes, unlike the decision to go to work, doesn't have career characteristics such as specialization; it's not a source of lasting income; its pursuit conflicts with legitimate activities; and criminals don't "respond to fluctuations in risk created by crime-control bureaucrats." Besides, data on property crime simply don't support the "view of crime derived from economic models of work." As an example, Gottfredson and Hirschi (1990) point out that data on burglars refute the rational choice theory:

> The model age for burglars is about seventeen, and the rate of burglary declines rapidly with age. The most likely "pecuniary" outcome for a burglar is no gain, and his next offense is likely to be something else than burglary. Shoplifting of something he does not need and cannot use is high on the list of probabilities, or an offense likely to terminate his legitimate and illegitimate careers—such as rape, assault, or homicide—for (again) no pecuniary gain is also highly probable. In the unlikely event that he is legitimately employed, his most likely victim will be his employer, an act difficult to reconcile with maximization of long-term utility or the equation of legitimate work with risk avoidance. Because research shows that offenders are versatile, our portrait of the burglar applies equally well to the white-collar offender, the organized-crime offender, the dope dealer, and the assaulter; they are, after all, the same people. (74)

According to criminologists Ronald V. Clarke and Marcus Felson (1993), "the economist's image of the self-maximizing decision maker, carefully calculating his or her advantage, did not fit the opportunistic, ill-considered, and even reckless nature of most crime" (5).

Others have criticized the economic model by treating self-interest as the only motive for human behavior. According to Amitai Etzioni, "Individuals are simultaneously under the influence of two major sets of factors—their pleasure, and their moral duty . . ." (Forst 1995, 5–6). Robert H. Frank, in *Beyond Self-Interest*, argues that we often ignore our self-interest when we

> trudge through snowstorms to cast our ballots, even when we are certain they will make no difference. We leave tips for waitresses in restaurants in distant cities we will never visit again. We make anonymous contributions to private charities. We often refrain from cheating even when we are sure we would not be caught. We sometimes walk away from profitable transactions whose terms we believe to be "unfair." We battle endless red tape to get a $10 refund on a defective product. And so on. (Quoted in Forst 1993, 5–6)

Mitchell B. Chamlin and John K. Cochran (1998) point out:

> The question remains . . . whether . . . downturns in the business cycle have much of an effect on the life-style choices of individuals. If . . . progressive transformations of the social, physical, and economic structure of post–World War II society have produced life-style patterns that embody a greater penchant for the consumption of consumer goods and the enjoyment of leisure activities away from the home . . . short-term downturns in the economy may have little effect on the day-to-day activities of individuals. Rather than abandoning behavioral patterns that have become ingrained over time, individuals may choose to maintain their life-styles but do so in a more frugal manner (e.g., eat more at fast-food restaurants and less so at more elegant establishments). . . . (426–427)

Others have attacked the highly sophisticated equations that are an essential element in econometric models, claiming they're too mechanistic, too cold, calculated, and unemotional to reflect what most people are really like. Clarke and Felson maintain that "the formal mathematical modeling of criminal choices by economists often demanded data that was unavailable or could not be pressed into service without making unrealistic assumptions about what they represented."

Still other critics say even if highly refined equations can accurately explain human behavior, they require a lot more sophisticated data than their creators have used up to this point (Clarke and Felson 1993, 5).

Questions

1. Summarize the major criticisms of the economic explanation of crime.
2. In light of these criticisms, would you recommend spending money on policies based on the economic explanation of crime?
3. Would you ask for more research? If so, what would you specifically want to learn from this research?

(perhaps more properly, place), opportunity, and temptation. Situation explanations look at the *modus operandi* (MO) of offenders "not merely as interesting material for undergraduate classes, but rather as central information for professional criminologists."

According to Lawrence E. Cohen and Marcus Felson (1993):

> No matter at what level data were measured or analyzed, that approach kept returning . . . to specific points in time and space . . . and to changes from moment to moment and hour to hour in where people are, what they are doing, and what happens to them as a result. (3, 10–11)

In 1979, Cohen and Felson (1979) introduced **routine activities theory**, which argued that crimes are committed when three elements unite:

1. A motivated offender (never mind what that motivation is)
2. A suitable target (can be a person, a place, or a thing)
3. The absence of a capable guardian (doesn't have to be a police officer and usually isn't)

A likely offender is "anybody who for any reason might commit a crime." A suitable target is "any person or object likely to be taken or attacked by the offender." This includes anyone or any property in the right place at the right time. The capable guardian isn't usually a police officer or a security guard. Cohen and Felson (1993) offer this explanation for omitting the police as capable guardians:

> This was the result of a conscious effort to distance routine activity theory from the rest of criminology, which is far too wedded to the criminal justice system as central to crime explanation. . . . Widespread media linkage of the police and courts to crime [is incorrect]. . . . In fact most crime involves neither agency. Indeed, the most likely persons to prevent a crime are not policemen (who seldom are around to discover crimes in the act) but rather friends, relatives, bystanders, or the owner of the property targeted. (2–3)

Routine activities theory brings time and space into the foreground and pushes into the background both the individual motivation of criminals and the agencies of criminal justice. Whether money, power, status, sex, or thrills motivate offenders to commit crimes is not the significant inquiry; any motivation will do. According to Cohen and Felson, people are

> treated virtually as objects and their motivations scrupulously avoided as a topic of discussion, in stark contrast to the heavy motivational emphasis of virtually all contemporary criminology at that time [1970s]. . . . Thus, at the outset the approach distinguished clearly between criminal inclinations and criminal events and made that distinction a centerpiece rather than a footnote. (Clarke and Felson, 1993, 1–14; Cohen and Felson 1979, 588–608; Felson 1998, 2)

What have we learned from routine activities theory? Crime is more likely to occur when targets are more attractive, aren't as well guarded, and are more exposed to motivated offenders. For example, Americans have increasingly spent more time away from home since World War II. As more people spent more time away from home (women working and single-parent families), homicide, robbery, rape, assault, and burglary rates climbed. The number of property crimes has also increased with the number of light portable electronic gadgets (Lafree 1998, 68).

Routine activities theory has stretched criminology beyond motivation and demonstrated the importance of informal social control. But, according to the criminologist Gary Lafree (1998):

> Situational theories do not offer a ready explanation for the observed timing of observed changes in crime rates. . . . It seems unlikely that the situational variables identified by Cohen and Felson were not also changing when crime rates were . . . high and constant in the 1980s and 1990s. By concentrating on the supply of suitable crime situations, situational theorists end up treating all motivated offenders as equally motivated and all capable guardians as equally capable. (68)

Knowledge and Understanding Check

Types of crimes
- ✔ List the six types of crimes listed in early classification systems.
- ✔ List the three types of crimes added to modern classification systems.
- ✔ Which crimes are committed the most often? the least?
- ✔ Identify the arguments for and against making some crimes hate crimes.

Measuring crime
- ✔ List and describe the three main crime statistics and their sources.
- ✔ List the strengths and weaknesses of each crime statistic.

Crime trends
- ✔ Summarize the trend in crime from the 1950s to 2000.
- ✔ What are the main theories explaining the crime bust? Which one do you think is most likely? Why?

(continued)

Knowledge and Understanding Check (continued)

Criminals

✔ What are seven things we can say about people who commit crimes?

✔ List and describe the major characteristics and explanations of female crime.

✔ Describe the "homicide exception" to female criminality, and explain the possible reasons for it.

✔ What is the "new female crime type"? Does it exist?

✔ List the major characteristics of Black criminality, and explain the social ecology theory of Black criminality.

Crime victims

✔ What does lifestyle have to do with criminal victimization?

✔ List and describe the services provided by victim-witness assistance programs.

✔ List the self-protective measures taken by victims, and summarize the effects the measures have had.

Explaining criminal behavior

✔ Identify and explain the difference between the two main categories of crime theories.

✔ Trace the history of crime causation theories.

✔ Identify and list the characteristics of the social structure theories discussed in the text.

✔ Identify and list the characteristics of the social process theories discussed in the text.

✔ Explain the difference between social structure and social process.

✔ Identify and explain the three elements of rational choice theory.

✔ Summarize the research on the theory.

✔ Describe and explain the significance of Jack Katz's "seduction of crime" perspective.

✔ State the three elements of routine activities theory and the assumptions underlying it

✔ Summarize what we've learned from the routine activities theory.

KEY TERMS

anomie of affluence
anomie theory
biological explanation
crime-specific element
criminal event
criminal involvement
dark figure in crime
determinist theories
differential association
foreground forces in crime
hate crimes

labeling theory
lifestyle-exposure theory
National Crime Victimization
   Survey (NCVS)
occupational crime
opportunity theory
psychoanalytic explanation
reasoning criminal element
routine activities theory
sex ratio of killing (SROK)
situation theories

social control theory
social ecology
social learning theory
social process
strain theory
street crime
Uniform Crime Reports (UCR)
utilitarian theory of crime
   causation
victimless crimes
white-collar crime

INTERNET PROJECT

Examine the explanations for criminal behavior. Run a key word search "causes of crime." List the causes that appear in your search and tabulate the number of articles on each. Which causes are emphasized most, least, and not at all? In your search did you find causes that are discussed in the text? If so, which ones? Should the text have discussed them? Why? Why not?

CHAPTER 4

Police: History, Missions, and "Working Personality"

© David Young-Wolff/Photo Edit

> When one looks at what police officers actually do, one finds that criminal law enforcement is something that most of them do with the frequency located somewhere between virtually never and very rarely.
>
> EGON BITTNER (1970)

■ INTRODUCTION

Every profession has a mission. The mission of armies is to win wars, of doctors to cure the sick, and of teachers to educate the young. Professionals play roles, become part of organizations, adapt to the group's subculture, and follow strategies to accomplish their missions. Yet, in reality, no profession sticks to a single mission or plays a single role. Armies sometimes "keep the peace." Doctors sometimes play the role of "ministers of mercy" by allowing or even helping terminally ill patients to die. Teachers help students through crises by assuming the role of counselor. Perhaps no profession has more missions than policing. And, perhaps none has faced more controversy both from inside and outside as to what its missions should be and what strategies it should follow to accomplish them.

To the public, to politicians, in most of the news media, on television, and in movie dramas, the police mission is simple and clear—prevent crime and catch criminals. But, the reality is a lot more complicated.

■ HISTORY OF POLICING

To give us some perspective on the history of policing, let's note how ancient the idea of policing really is. As far back as 1500 B.C., Egypt and Mesopotamia established police forces. We don't know much about them except they were efficient and effective, tortured suspects to obtain confessions, and mistreated prisoners. We also know that in 27 B.C. the Roman Emperor Augustus appointed an urban officer armed with the power to "maintain public order," and by A.D. 6, the Romans had established a "24/7" police force that patrolled the streets of Rome (Adamson 1991, 1–2).

The Constable/Night Watch System, 1066–1850

Fast forward to England after the Norman Conquest in 1066, when King William created the **constable/night watch system,** a police structure based in the local community. It consisted of two elements—constables and night watch—in every local community. That system lasted until 1829 in England, came to the American colonies, and endured until the 1850s.

Constables worked for the courts. They were paid fees for serving warrants and summonses and arresting suspects. They also made money by helping to prosecute criminals. Prosecution was private and widely used, especially by the poor, Black, and immigrant communities in 1800s' cities. Victims had to bring their own cases to court—they often did—and they paid constables to help them, even when it cost more to hire them than the value of the property stolen (Lane 1992, 7).

Night watchmen (they were all men) were supposed to patrol the neighborhood from dusk to dawn, calling out the hours ("8 o'clock and all is well!"); making sure the street lamps were lit; watching for fire; breaking up fights; and arresting "suspicious persons." Night watch was a public duty, but you could hire substitutes to do it for you. Watchmen were the objects of ridicule at least from the time of Shakespeare. The usual criticisms were they slept when they should've been watching; they shook their "rattles" only to scare off criminals instead of apprehending them; and they ran away from *real* danger. One newspaper said they were "idle, drunken, vigilant snorers," who never stopped a disturbance "in their lives; but would . . . be as ready to join in a burglary as any thief in Christendom" (Monkkonen 1992, 549). There's no way to tell how true these criticisms were, but it's hard to believe these amateurs or their substitutes were an effective law enforcement organization. Still, for all its faults, the constable/night watch system had two things going for it: It was cheap and it was weak. So, it reduced the fear of two things mid-1800s Americans hated as much as crime: government taxes and government power.

But fear of disorder, especially mobs of urban rioters that grew in number and intensity between 1830 and 1860, led to less fear of government and more of disorder. There was plenty to spark outbursts from rioting mobs: "out" groups like the newest immigrants, unpopular politicians, merchants who sold food at high prices in times of scarcity, and as the Civil War approached, slavery. The change to a market economy with its cycles of boom and bust; swarms of warring foreign immigrants and domestic "hayseeds" fresh from rural America pouring into cities; and growing hostility to free Blacks as the country approached civil war all contributed to make the period from 1830 to 1860 the most riotous in our history (Lane 1992, 7–8).

The Municipal Police Department Era, 1850–1920

After three major riots in four years, Boston had had enough. In 1838, the city established a **municipal police department,** a formalized police force responsible to a central office and on duty "24/7." Most cities rapidly followed Boston's example. Riots precipitated the creation of police departments, but city residents and city government quickly found them a convenient tool for missions other than riot control. According to police historian Roger Lane (1992):

> The men on the beat gave directions, unsnarled traffic, returned lost children, aided victims of sudden accident, and escorted drunks either to the station house or home. . . . Homeless drifters . . . were given nightly lodging in the station houses. . . . In hard times policemen sometimes ran soup kitchens for the hungry. (9)

The new police introduced four new features. First, they were organized (at least formally) like a military hierarchy with orders issued from the chief at the top and carried out by officers on the beats below. Informally, except for riot control and unlike soldiers who act under specific orders in groups, patrol officers spent most of their time alone walking beats acting on their own initiative with no orders (see "Law Enforcement" section).

Second, the new departments were part of the executive branch of city government, not the courts as the constable/night watch system had been. This meant the end of fees collected for serving court documents. Instead, police officers were paid salaries—good ones, good enough to lure many skilled laborers onto the force. As part of the executive branch, police were divorced from preparing and prosecuting cases, isolating them from courts and prosecutors and creating antagonism among these three major criminal justice agencies (Lane 1992, 13).

Third, officers wore uniforms. This made them the first, and for a long time the only, public official everybody identified as a public official. However, officers bitterly fought wearing uniforms. Mass protests, resignations, and lawsuits greeted New York's introduction of uniforms in 1853 (Lane 1992, 12). Why such opposition? First, it was un-American. Uniforms were for lackeys of kings and queens, not for Americans who believed part of being an American was being able to wear what you wanted. As one Philadelphia officer who refused to wear a uniform explained, it was "derogatory to my feelings as an American." Second, uniforms identified them not only to residents who needed them but to "street toughs looking for trouble" and probably, more important, to superior officers making sure officers were walking their beats

and not hanging out in saloons and billiard rooms (Monkkonen 1992, 556–557).

Fourth, police were **proactive,** meaning they were supposed to prevent crime before it happened and investigate it and apprehend suspects when it did. This was in stark contrast to the constable/night watch system where constables and watchmen only acted when they were asked and paid to do it. Walking the beat (patrol) was supposed to scare off criminal wannabes, and salaries were supposed to make officers want to investigate crimes and victims to report crimes to the police (Monkkonen 1992, 556–557).

Municipal control had its downside. Police departments were the arms of the dominant political machines. So they participated in partisan politics, and that participation was often corrupt—like manipulating ballot boxes. Partisan politics wasn't the only corrupting influence. Money too often lured departments as well as individual officers into making deals with vice operations, like houses of prostitution, saloons, and gambling establishments. One New York City officer was delighted by his assignment to the vice district because it meant he'd be eating tenderloin instead of chuck steak. (I never knew until I heard this story why a friend who took me to an establishment in Chicago I won't identify told me we were going to the "tenderloin.")

Nevertheless, on balance, police departments could claim several strengths. They enjoyed community support because officers were almost always from the neighborhoods they policed. They took charge of "whatever emergencies and crises crossed their paths." They provided needed services, such as ambulances, soup kitchens, garbage collection, and homeless shelters. Malcolm K. Sparrow, Mark H. Moore, and David M. Kennedy (1995) summed up their contributions this way in their excellent book on the police: "In a time before widespread and well-supported social work and social programs, and before municipalities had assumed many of their routine obligations, the police often filled important vacuums" (34).

Still, police reform was swept up in a new wave in the early twentieth-century called the Progressive Era. A rash of investigations in cities throughout the United States from about 1895 to 1920 uncovered widespread incompetence and corruption in most city police departments. At the same time, policing was undergoing a fundamental change from all-purpose public service to criminal law enforcement. This shift reflected a change in thinking by social welfare reformers and some police chiefs who were beginning to stop looking at unemployed people as members of the "dangerous classes," saving the description for criminals only.

This was not just a change in viewpoint; it was a change in police officers' behavior. Until the late 1800s, the police didn't see any difference between housing the homeless, feeding the hungry, arresting drunks, and arresting murderers, rapists, and robbers because they were all part of their mission to control the dangerous classes. But historians Catrien C. J. H. Bijleveld and Eric H. Monkkonen (Monkkonen 1992) showed in their analysis of arrests in the largest cities in the country that as early as 1894 police departments were concentrating more on criminal law enforcement against murder and other felonies and less on broader social services like housing the homeless and minor public order offenses. According to Bijleveld and Monkkonen, "[B]y the end of World War I, police were in the business of crime control. Other city- or state-run agencies had taken over their former non-crime control activities" (Monkkonen 1992, 556–557).

Police missions may have changed but police officers stayed the same. As the twentieth century opened, the typical urban police officer in the United States was a recent immigrant with little or no education, appointed by a local politician, and expected to enforce the law according to the ward's wishes. According to Richard A. Staufenberger (1980), officers

> knew who put them in office and whose support they needed to stay there. Their job was to manage their beat; often they became completely enmeshed in the crime they were expected to suppress. Corruption, brutality, and racial discrimination, although not universal, were characteristic of most big city departments. (8–9)

The Reform Model Era, 1920–1960

Recognizing this political dominance, corruption, and lack of training, three California police chiefs in the 1920s, August Vollmer, O. W. Wilson, and William Parker, encouraged what they called the **reform model of policing.** According to this model, the police are the "gatekeepers" of the criminal justice system; they decide who enters the system and who doesn't. So the police mission is clear and narrow: Arrest people for committing the FBI's Index Crimes (Chapter 3) (Sparrow, Moore, and Kennedy 1995, 37–38).

By the 1950s, all of the following elements in the reform agenda were at least *formally* in place:

1. *Centralization of police authority:* Police chiefs began to really run their departments.
2. *Shift from foot to motorized patrol:* Officers moved into squad cars.
3. *Use of technological advances:* Fewer officers could cover more territory because of squad cars, two-way radios, and telephone call boxes.
4. *Paramilitary organization:* Chiefs were in charge of a strictly disciplined hierarchy with formal authority descending from the top through the ranks to patrol officers.
5. *Specialized units:* These were mainly vice squads with the power to control police corruption throughout the department.

6. *UCR data:* FBI Uniform Crime Reports data (Chapter 3) became the measure of police performance.
7. *Reactive, incident-driven policing:* Responding to calls became the distinctive method of policing.
8. *Restriction on police discretion:* Department rules, such as those regarding use of force and high-speed chases, lessened police discretion.
9. *Focus on criminal law enforcement:* As opposed to maintaining order and providing service, the focus became enforcing criminal law. (Sparrow, Moore, and Kennedy 1995, 38–40)

According to Malcolm K. Sparrow and his colleagues (1995):

> The reformers produced a conception of policing whose purpose has been largely focused on crime control and whose methods have been limited to law enforcement. Every discussion of the purpose of the police begins with crime control. For many the discussion ends there as well. Crime control is widely taken, both inside and outside the police, as the only important police function, with everything else they might do not only secondary but a dangerous and wasteful distraction. This is not in itself new; much thinking about the police has taken more or less this form for the last century. But the degree to which the reform model . . . has narrowed the debate is unprecedented. . . . (41)

Public confidence in the reform model remains high and support from police professionals and politicians remains strong—but not without challenge. A small band of police chiefs around the country are fighting the reform model. These chiefs and their supporters in academic circles list the following reasons for their lack of confidence in the reform model.

1. Despite some reduction in the mid- to late 1990s, crime rates taken in the long run remain at historic highs. (Chapter 3)
2. Criminal justice is ineffective because even if the police arrest suspects, the likelihood is small they will serve time in prison. (Chapter 8)
3. Police tactics such as patrol, rapid response, follow-up investigation, and arrest don't work well to either control crime or reduce fear of crime.
4. Private security is outpacing public police as a means to control crime, fear, and disorder. (See the "Private Police" section.) (Sparrow, Moore, and Kennedy 1995, 44–50)

The 1960s

During the 1960s, a predominantly urban, industrial, pluralist, and highly vocal group of protesters challenged the values of White Anglo-Saxon Protestant men and their dominance. The challengers demanded their share of the promises of American life—material abundance, freedom, and justice. Their hopes were raised and quickly dashed. The belief that a "quick fix" could assure everybody an opportunity to share the good life evaporated. Understanding the police in the 1960s requires appreciating the false hopes and the resulting frustration, anger, destruction, and, ultimately, adoption of more modest goals that were the legacy of those turbulent times of protests, riots, and soaring crime rates (Chapter 3) (Cronin, Cronin, and Milakovich 1981; Matusow 1984).

The police became easy scapegoats caught in the middle of disorder, riots, and crime-plagued cities. Of course, police couldn't remove or even significantly reduce deep racial, ethnic, class, and gender inequalities. Nor could they be realistically expected to calm the culture wars between social conservatives and social liberals that had ebbed and flowed long before the 1960s and continue today. Police actions, of course, didn't create these divisions even if they sometimes did bring them into sharp and painful focus. It's not surprising "law and order" was a major theme of the 1964 presidential election campaign. The significance of the Republican candidate Barry Goldwater's appeals for law and order were not lost on Lyndon Johnson, despite his enormous landslide victory. In the aftermath of the election, President Johnson created the President's Commission on Law Enforcement and the Administration of Justice. The Crime Commission, as it was called, gave serious attention to six police problems:

1. Multiple missions of the police
2. Fragmented nature of law enforcement
3. Poor training and minimal education of police officers
4. Police corruption, brutality, and prejudice
5. Separation of the police from the communities they serve
6. Lessening of the public support on which effective policing ultimately depends (President's Crime Commission 1967; Staufenberger 1980, 13–18)

By the late 1960s, police officers were frustrated, angry, and fed up with highly publicized and unrelenting criticism by the "reformers." But they had other complaints, including poor pay, dictatorial chiefs, urban riots, unrealistic demands to solve the nation's social problems, and U.S. Supreme Court opinions that "handcuffed the police instead of the criminal" (Chapter 6). These complaints had one lasting effect—police unionization. Regardless of whether their complaints were justified and whether unions were the answer to their complaints, departments in almost all large cities, with the notable exception of the South, became unionized.

Unionization had a major impact on police administration. Chiefs had to share their power by negotiating with unions. Furthermore, according to police historian Samuel Walker (1992b, 27–28), the union movement "won dramatic improvement in salaries and benefits for officers along with grievance procedures that protected the rights of officers in disciplinary hearings." Not everyone favored unionization—and it still has its share of critics. Some reformers believed unions "resisted innovation and were particularly hostile to attempts to improve police community relations." Nevertheless, the union movement represents a major concrete result of the troubled 1960s.

The Legacy of Twentieth-Century Reform

The achievements of all reform movements fall short of their promise, and surely twentieth-century police reform movements are no exception. In the more than three decades since President Johnson's Crime Commission issued its report, we've witnessed considerable progress, despite problems that have plagued American policing since colonial times. In 1969, President Richard Nixon launched a major federal effort to help local police departments that had (or wanted to start) programs to reduce specific crimes like robbery and burglary. Education and training have increased. Police have formulated and adopted more and better-articulated policies, and they've developed rules governing police practices. Most important, we've advanced enormously our knowledge of policing. More than courts and corrections, police departments have participated in evaluations of their work, even when research has criticized their practices. They've also established experiments producing changes in policies and practices. So, clearly, the legacy of the 1960s includes more than riots, crime, and disorder. Of course, there's still a lot to criticize, and we'll examine some of those criticisms in this and the next two chapters (Feeley and Sarat 1980).

■ LAW ENFORCEMENT STRUCTURE AND PROCESS

During the discussion that follows, remember two basic features of the structure of law enforcement (also called police organization) we outlined in Chapter 1. First, it's part of our federal system of government, so there are national and local (state, county, and municipal) law enforcement agencies. The best-known federal law enforcement agencies are the Federal Bureau of Investigation (FBI) and the Drug Enforcement Agency (DEA). At the local level, we're all familiar with the state police, county sheriff's department, and municipal police departments.

Second, law enforcement agencies are part of the executive branch of each level of government (president, governor, and mayor). So the FBI and DEA are answerable to the president of the United States; the state police to the governors of the states; the sheriff to the county supervisors; and police departments to the mayors of the municipalities they serve.

To further examine the structure and process of law enforcement, we'll look at its formal structure and informal process, private police, and various police management styles.

 4-1 Further details about law enforcement agencies

Formal Structure and Informal Process

Formally, law enforcement agencies resemble military organizations; we call this the **military model of policing.** First, there's a hierarchical command structure, meaning authority flows from the chief who gives orders at the top down to officers on the beat who carry out the orders. Officers wear uniforms, and they're divided into ranks with military-sounding names like commander, captain, lieutenant, and sergeant. Also, disobeying orders is called insubordination and leads to punishment just like in the military. Further, the police mission is defined as fighting "wars" against "enemies" who commit crimes, use drugs, and otherwise cause trouble. The following description of the New York City Police Academy nicely captures this military model of police agency structure:

> "Attention," the drill sergeant yelled at 200 men and women. One man slouched. Another saluted with his left hand. "About face." A few turned the wrong way. A few more stumbled. The sergeant was not amused. "This is unbelievable!" the sergeant bellowed at a new crop of police recruits on their first day of gym class at the Police Academy. "Look straight ahead when you're at attention. Do things in unison. You're not civilians anymore," he told them. "You're in a semimilitary outfit." (Nix 1987)

Although the military model describes the formal, outward appearance of police organization, the informal reality of the decision-making process in its day-to-day operations is very different. Whereas soldiers wait for specific orders from officers before they act, and most orders are highly specific ("Go over that hill and attack that house"), police officers are left on their own to carry out vague commands like "keep the peace," "settle problems," and so on. Soldiers work together. They can't, don't, and shouldn't decide whether to move into an area, shoot at the enemy, and so on. In contrast, except for large public gatherings, demonstrations, disturbances, and riots, police officers work alone or with a single partner.

> Every day, out of their supervisors' sight, police officers at the lowest levels of their departments make . . . "low visibility decisions" that have great effects on . . . individuals. . . . At any moment . . . police officers throughout the United States are deciding whether to ticket or merely to warn this motorist; whether or not to destroy the marijuana cigarette that kid was found holding and send him on his way without marking his life history with a record of arrest; whether or not to arrest this abusive husband; whether to back off a bit or stand firm and shoot the oncoming emotionally disturbed person wielding the knife. (Skolnick and Fyfe 1993, 119)

In day-to-day operations, police departments are more like hospitals, universities, and law firms than military organizations. Police chiefs, hospital administrators, college deans, and managing partners in law firms make sure there are enough personnel, money, and support so the officers, doctors, professors, and lawyers can do their jobs. But the "big" decisions are left to the doctors ("medicate or operate"), professors (pass or fail), trial lawyers (plead guilty or go to trial), and officers (arrest or let go) (Skolnick and Fyfe 1993, 118).

The military model *does* describe our image of the police as well as their image of themselves. But that image causes problems. The military image and the belief that "all's fair in war" leads some police officers to use excessive force or illegally invade the privacy and liberty of anyone they consider the "enemy" (Chapter 6). The enemy—people in the community in this case—may adopt the same maxim, putting the police in danger. According to Jerome Skolnick, a highly respected police expert, and James Fyfe (1993), a former police officer and now a criminal justice professor:

> However stirring this call [for a war on crime], it relies upon an inexact analogy and is far more likely to produce unnecessary violence and antagonism than to result in effective policing. The lines between friend and foe were clear in the Arabian desert, but police officers on American streets too often rely on ambiguous cues and stereotypes in trying to identify the enemies in their war. When officers act upon such signals and roust people who turn out to be guilty of no more than being in what officers view as the wrong place at the wrong time—young black men on inner-city streets at night, for example—the police may create enemies where none previously existed. (114)

Private Police

The first private security officer in the United States was Allan Pinkerton, who founded the legendary Pinkerton Agency in the mid-1800s mainly to protect business interests. He started out working for railroads because once trains left the station, they were open targets for train robbers. Soon, Pinkerton was also working for factory owners during the industrial strife of the 1880s. Although he was pro-labor, Pinkerton was against strikes. Modern private security has also grown mainly in response to business needs. However, residents in large-city apartment complexes, condominiums, and suburban gated communities have also stepped up their use of private security guards.

Private security is a for-profit industry. It provides personnel, such as guards, investigators, couriers, and bodyguards. It also supplies equipment, including safes, locks, alarm systems, and closed-circuit television. In addition, it furnishes services, including monitoring, employee background checks, polygraphs, and drug testing. Businesses or others can either hire private security directly or contract for specific services and equipment (Bureau of Justice Statistics 1988, 66).

In many states, private security personnel have the power to arrest, and they're not subject to the same restraints as public police officers. For example, private police don't have to give arrestees the *Miranda* warnings (Chapter 6). Some states have special legislation authorizing private security to act as "special police" within a specific jurisdiction such as a plant, store, or university campus (Bureau of Justice Statistics 1988, 66).

Sworn police officers can (and frequently do) "moonlight" for private security firms during their off-duty hours; most police departments permit moonlighting. Some departments even contract with private concerns to provide personnel and use the revenue for department needs. For example, Miami and St. Petersburg, Florida, allow off-duty police officers to work armed and in uniform; the departments even arrange jobs for their officers (Bureau of Justice Statistics 1988, 66).

New York City allows companies to form "business districts" that pay special taxes for private security. A number of private security forces patrol various parts of the city to augment public police. For example, 29 uniformed but unarmed security guards patrol a fifty-block section of Manhattan. A former police borough commander directs the force, and a self-imposed surtax by property owners pays for it. Security guards start at about $10 an hour, take a special thirty-five-hour training course at John Jay College of Criminal Justice, and spend two more weeks training on the street. Squads patrol from 8 A.M. to midnight. Similar private security forces patrol other areas: A 285-member unit patrols Rockefeller Center; a 49-member unit patrols South Street Seaport; and Roosevelt Island has an unarmed 46-member force commanded by a former police official. New York City police officers are allowed to moonlight but not in the department's uniform (Blumenthal 1989).

In some precincts, there are more off-duty public police officers acting as private security officers than on-duty officers. Because they wear uniforms, off-duty employment increases both the availability and visibility of police officers. On the other hand, off-duty employment raises concerns about conflict of interest in serving private interests, fears of corruption, and possible lawsuits for alleged misconduct. To reduce the risk of these problems, department orders and regulations frequently limit the kinds of employment officers can accept (Reiss 1988).

Public police protection grew rapidly during the 1960s and 1970s but stabilized during the 1980s. *Private* security, on the other hand, continued to grow. By 1990, private security had become the "nation's primary protective force," outspending public law enforcement by 73 percent and employing two and a half times the workforce. Spending for private security in 1990 reached $52 billion, and private security agencies employed 1.5 million people. Public law enforcement spent $30 billion and employed 600,000. Expenditures for private security were supposed to more than double that for public law enforcement by 2000 (but there are no numbers to confirm this estimate made in 1991, the most recent I could find) (Cunningham, Strauchs, and Van Meter 1991).

Police Management Styles

For all of the visible bureaucratic formality of law enforcement agencies, individual departments vary in management style according to:

1. The community they serve
2. The goals their chiefs set
3. The values and ambitions their individual officers hold

In other words, the formal structure of police departments adapts to serve the informal professional, ideological, political, and societal needs of its personnel and the community. A survey of Kentucky police chiefs found more than half felt political pressure from mayors, city managers, city council members, and business leaders. This pressure affected their decision making in many areas, including hiring, promotion, and demotion of officers; arresting offenders; enforcing specific laws; and providing services to specific groups in the community (Tunnell and Gaines 1992, 10).

Political scientist James Q. Wilson's landmark *Varieties of Police Behavior* (1968) identified three basic styles in police departments—the watchman, the legalistic, and the service styles. The style depends on the mission the political culture of the community wants their police to accomplish (see "Police Missions" section). The **watchman style** emphasizes maintaining order and providing public service. In watchman-style departments, officers' decision making doesn't depend on whether offenders' behavior violates the criminal law but on whether it threatens to cause disorder. Watchmen-style officers avoid formal arrests; they settle disputes informally.

Legalistic-style departments emphasize criminal law enforcement. Uniform, impartial arrests for all violations of law characterize the legalistic style. It places a premium on formal criminal justice, reducing informal discretionary decision making to an absolute minimum. **Service-style** departments, like legalistic-style departments, rely on formal rules, but all rules not just those found in the criminal law. They take all requests for service seriously, regardless of whether they stem from criminal law violations, maintaining order, or just providing information. Officers often intervene but rarely arrest, particularly for minor violations. Instead, they counsel, issue written warnings, or make referrals to social service agencies (Langworthy 1992, 103).

■ POLICE MISSIONS

"The police in modern society . . . have an "impossible task," wrote police expert Peter K. Manning (1995, 103) in 1977. This is still true. So is his next comment:

> To much of the public the police are seen as . . . crime-fighters . . . that keep society from falling into chaos. The policeman himself considers the essence of his role to be the dangerous and heroic enterprise of crook-catching and the watchful prevention of crimes. . . . They do engage in chases, in gunfights, in careful sleuthing. But these are rare events. (1995, 103)

As we've already learned from the history of policing and management styles today, there are three police missions:

1. Criminal law enforcement
2. Order maintenance
3. Public service not related to either criminal law or maintaining order

Criminal law enforcement may be the most publicized mission, but it is in order maintenance and providing other public services not related to crime or disorder that discretionary decision making looms largest, officers spend most of their time, and most taxpayers' dollars go.

Criminal Law Enforcement

Criminal law enforcement may be the "rare" police mission, but rare doesn't mean unimportant. Just because there's more (a lot more) to policing than safekeeping the gates of the criminal justice system, deciding who will and who won't pass through those gates and starting the criminal process in motion is still important. The police produce the first product of criminal justice decision making—the criminal suspect. Without that product, the criminal process never starts. The **criminal law enforcement mission** consists of four duties:

1. Preventing crime from ever happening
2. Investigating crimes and identifying suspects after they've been committed
3. Finding and catching suspects after they're identified
4. Helping prosecutors build a case against defendants

Formally, police are supposed to enforce all the criminal laws; this is known as **full enforcement.** Informally, officers never make the impossible—and really stupid—effort to enforce every criminal statute all the time by setting the criminal process in motion. Legislatures pass laws

based on the silly idea "there oughta be a law" to deal with every social and moral problem. In their day-to-day work, officers practice **selective enforcement**: using their discretion to arrest *some* people, *sometimes,* for breaking *some* laws (Goldstein 1977, chaps. 3–4).

Selective enforcement doesn't mean police officers can do as they please in deciding when, how, and against whom they enforce the criminal laws. This is especially true of decision making about serious felonies. As gate-keepers of the criminal justice system, law enforcement officers always "open the gates" to serious felonies. So, they always arrest suspected murderers, rapists, and armed robbers no matter what their race, ethnicity, gender, or social class (Chapter 1). In less serious felonies and minor offenses, their decision making is more discretionary. This is an example of how important the seriousness of the offense is in decision making at every point in criminal justice. And, of course, the more discretion, the more room for unacceptable criteria to infect decision making (Chapters 1 and 3).

Order Maintenance

Maintaining order calls upon the police to "do something right now to settle problems." Notice three major differences between maintaining order and criminal law enforcement:

1. "Do something" calls for a wide range of discretionary decision making about problems that go far beyond just arresting someone.
2. "Settle problems" also allows a wide range of discretionary decision making. Problems include more than crimes, and "settle" means more than putting the criminal justice process in motion.
3. "Right now" means to settle the problem in minutes. Criminal law enforcement takes days—sometimes weeks or even months—stretching from investigation before arrest and the arrest itself by patrol officers to follow-up investigation by detectives. (Chapters 5 and 6)

In order maintenance, law enforcement officers have to use their judgment to "do the right thing," sometimes without clear guidelines and with little agreement about just what the right thing to do is (Wilson 1968, 4–5). One thing officers do know: They have the power to back up their decisions with force. This **monopoly of force** is the defining feature of police work (Bittner 1970, 36–47). According to Skolnick and Fyfe (1993):

> [T]he risk of physical injury is greater in many lines of industrial work than in policing, but cops are the ones to whom society accords the right to use, or to threaten to use, force. This assignment and the capacity to carry it out are said to be the central feature of the role of police in society. (94)

YOU DECIDE

Which laws should the police enforce?

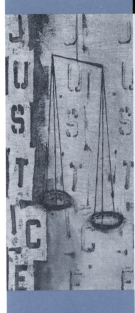

All of the following incidents took place in Chicago:

1. A 19-year-old fired three shots from the street at a woman standing in her doorway. Several neighbors saw the shooting. The woman asked the police not to arrest him.
2. A police officer witnessed an armed robbery. The victim asked him not to arrest the robber.
3. A police officer witnessed a shoplifting. The store owner asked the officer not to arrest the shoplifter.
4. An officer caught a juvenile throwing rocks through large windows. The youth agreed to pay for the damages.
5. A patrol officer saw a juvenile drinking.
6. An officer witnessed a man paying a prostitute for services.
7. A patrol officer saw a 21-year-old woman riding her bicycle on the sidewalk.
8. An officer saw customers smoking in the "no smoking" section of a restaurant.
9. A group of neighbors gathered in an apartment for a Saturday night poker game for money. A police officer, in the building on another call, saw the game in progress through an open door.
10. Two patrol officers saw a man spit on the sidewalk.
11. Two patrol officers came upon a young couple having sexual intercourse in their car while parked in a city park.
12. A patrol officer caught a 21-year-old man smoking marijuana. The only marijuana he had on him was the "joint" he was smoking when he was caught.
13. The police caught a cocaine user with cocaine in her possession. She was well known among big drug dealers and would make an excellent "snitch."
14. The police witnessed a physician and a lawyer engaging in homosexual sodomy in their car in a city park.

All of these incidents broke a state law and/or a city ordinance. And, police board rules and general orders issued by the chief of police clearly stated officers have to enforce *all* the laws and city ordinances. The police didn't arrest *anyone* (Davis 1975, 3–7).

Questions

1. Which of the people in these incidents should the police have arrested? Why?
2. Who should decide whether to arrest?
3. Should the officers be punished for breaking their own rules, the chief's orders, city ordinances, and state laws? What should the punishment be?

There are lots of definitions of *order,* but in this book we mean behaving according to ordinary standards of decency when we're in public. This sounds like an awfully broad definition and open to all kinds of mischief in the hands of officers whose mission is to maintain these "ordinary standards of decency." But we shouldn't be too alarmed. People in all kinds of neighborhoods, of all ages, both sexes, across racial, ethnic, and economic groups believe order is central to the quality of life and disorderly conduct threatens it. Disorderly conduct is sometimes called a **quality-of-life crime** (Skogan 1990a, 10).

The long list of behavior most people agree does *not* comport with ordinary standards of decency (quality-of-life-crimes) includes:

- Public drinking and drunkenness
- Begging and aggressive panhandling
- Threatening behavior and harassment
- Obstruction of streets and public places
- Vandalism and graffiti
- Street prostitution
- Public urination and defecation
- Unlicensed vending of most kinds, including the more aggressive forms such as "squeegeeing"—

washing the windshields of stopped cars and demanding money for the "service"

In their article "Broken Windows," Professors James Q. Wilson and George L. Kelling (1982) set off a debate about quality-of-life crimes when they suggested these "petty offenses" not only upset law-abiding people but are also linked to serious crime. In the **broken windows theory,** according to Professor Wilson:

We used the image of broken windows to explain how neighborhoods might decay into disorder and even crime if no one attends faithfully to their maintenance. If a factory or office window is broken, a passerby observing it will conclude that no one cares or no one is in charge. In time, a few will begin throwing rocks to break more windows. Soon all the windows will be broken, and now passersby will think that, not only is no one in charge of the building, no one is in charge of the street on which it faces. Only the young, the criminal, or the foolhardy have any business on an unprotected avenue, and so more and more citizens will abandon the street to those they assume prowl it. *Small disorders lead to larger and larger ones, and perhaps even to crime.* [emphasis added] (Kelling and Coles 1996, xiv)

 4-2 Complete "Broken Windows" article

Notice Wilson only cautiously suggests a possible link between disorder and serious crime. However, in research empirically testing the broken windows theory, Professor Wesley G. Skogan (1990a) confirms this link:

> Our concern with common crime is limited to whether disorder is a cause of it. . . . [N]eighborhood levels of disorder are closely related to crime rates, to fear of crime, and the belief that serious crime is a neighborhood problem. This relationship could reflect the fact that the link between crime and disorder is a causal one, or that both are dependent on some third set of factors (such as poverty or neighborhood instability). (10)

Notice how Skogan carefully avoids saying disorder *causes* crime. What he *does* say is his data "support the proposition that disorder needs to be taken seriously in research on neighborhood crime, and that both directly and through crime, it plays an important role in neighborhood decline" (Skogan 1990a, 75).

 4-3 Critique of broken windows theory

The weeks following the September 11, 2001, attacks on the World Trade Center and the Pentagon and the discovery of anthrax-contaminated mail had an immediate effect on local policing. Local departments found themselves "responding to hundreds of reports of spilled powder" and providing extra security in public buildings. Local departments worried they might "become slower in responding to crimes and might not be able to close as many cases" as they usually do (Sack 2001). The burden on local law enforcement will get even heavier if the FBI carries out its plan to drop bank robbery and drug trafficking from its scope of responsibilities so it can fight terrorism.

It's too early for statistics to show us how "9/11" has affected local policing, but some city departments say it's already affected them. Philadelphia Police Commissioner John Timoney believes at least some of the thirty-seven homicides in Philadelphia in September 2001 were caused by the decision to put narcotics detectives on city center patrol. According to Commissioner Timoney, over half the killings were drug-related:

> The homicides that are most amenable to police prevention are drug-related because there will be a shooting followed by a retaliatory shooting followed by another retaliatory shooting. So, to the extent you can get

in there and stop it quickly, you may prevent future shootings of a retaliatory nature. (Sack 2001)

The attacks have led some departments to say they've had to begin "rethinking the very nature of policing" (Sack 2001); the rulebook has been thrown out. But in reality, decision making to maintain the quality of life depends more on experience, community standards, and personal values than on the mechanical application of rules found in manuals, ordinances, statutes, constitutions, and court decisions. Officers can't say, "Hold everything until I check the book on this one." Even if they have time, the answer won't be in the book. It can't be; no book can spell out how to respond to the countless kinds of problems officers face every day.

Public Service

Police departments are the only government agency on call every day, all day, all year. It's useful to point out that in the 1800s the word *police* meant local government. (To this day the legal term "police power" refers to state and local government power to make all laws, not just criminal laws [Black 1980, 29–32].) So, it makes sense for people to call the police to solve all kinds of problems: to report fights, drunkenness, rowdy kids, prostitution, and panhandling on the streets; to stop a feud between neighbors outside; to settle a domestic disturbance and a noisy party inside; to find lost children and animals in distress anywhere; or to find the nearest hospital, football field, or dog show.

Calling the police for every imaginable reason is nothing new. In 1910, Brand Whitlock, the reform mayor of Toledo, Ohio, recognized this reality in his city. Whenever anything "bothered" people, their instant reaction was, "It's time to call the police," the exasperated mayor complained (Whitlock 1914, 239). This **community service mission** is a central part of the history of policing (see the "History of Policing" section). So, it's clear, whether the police like or want to get involved in people's problems, the public wants (no demands!) that they *do* get involved. In reality, police touch the lives of more people in more ways than any other public agency. And that's just the way most people want it. It's not surprising police funding eats up the largest share of criminal justice expenditures (Figure 1.2).

Overlap of Missions

Police missions don't fit neatly into their own boxes of law enforcement, order maintenance, and miscellaneous other public services. In reality, the three missions reinforce each other. Police expert James Q. Wilson (1983) puts it this way:

> Though the law enforcement, order maintenance, and service provision aspects can be analytically distin-

guished, concretely they are thoroughly intermixed. Even in a routine law enforcement situation (for example, arresting a fleeing purse snatcher), how the officer deals with the victim and the onlookers at the scene is often as important as how he handles the suspect. The victim and onlookers, after all, are potential witnesses who have to testify in court; assuring their cooperation is as necessary as catching the person against whom they will testify. The argument about whether "cops" should be turned into "social workers" is a false one, for it implies that society can exercise some meaningful choice over the role the officer should play. Except at the margin, it cannot. (111–112)

Others have suggested the crime-fighter image makes maintaining order and community service more effective. Police effectiveness boils down to respect for the *potential* power to use force. For example, Elaine Cumming and her colleagues found wife beaters were less willing to obey unpleasant orders given by service-oriented police officers than by crime-fighter officers who make clear they're prepared to arrest and put them in jail. Cumming and her colleagues also found individuals "needing help" follow crime fighters' orders better than community service agents' commands (Cumming, Cumming, and Edell 1965, 285).

According to police expert Herman Goldstein (1984), who for decades has studied what police really do out there in the field:

> We've learned that what the police do in their "order maintenance" function may have a very important bearing on their capacity to deal with crime; that citizen attitudes and cooperation are heavily influenced by the effectiveness of the police in providing the wide range of services that the public has come to expect from them. (11)

⊙ **4-4 You Decide: What do police do, and how do they do it?**

⊙ **w4-5 Evansville, Indiana, police department job description**

Possible Shifts in Mission Priorities

When I called St. Paul Assistant Police Chief Richard Gardell to ask him to talk to my "Introduction to Criminal Justice" class about the missions of the police, I began, "I'm sorry to interrupt you in your war on crime, which I know you spend all of your time fighting. . . ." He interrupted me with a laugh and said, "Not anymore, at least not in *this* department where we have all kinds of other

things to do." This exchange was just banter with my former student from the 1970s. But there's some evidence to suggest the myth of the crime-fighting mission may have started to lose its grip even in the days when Assistant Chief Gardell was a young student here at the University of Minnesota.

Professor James Q. Wilson (1968, 236) noted in his study of police departments during the 1960s that at least some police administrators were aware of, and willing to talk openly about, maintaining order and providing services as higher priorities than law enforcement. Another study based on observing three California departments found patrol officers willing, even eager, to nurture their community service functions. They openly admitted they get a lot of satisfaction from pursuing the mission of community service. Some departments issue clear policy statements regarding the importance of maintaining order and providing service.

Twenty years ago, police expert George Kelling offered the following excellent summary of the complexity of police functions—and it's still accurate:

> Although the crime-related functions of the police were historically important and continue to be so, it is insufficient to define the police either predominantly or exclusively on the basis of those functions. Their functions are far broader, and consist of peace-keeping and management functions essential to urban life. Taking this point of view the police are not just a part of the criminal justice system, but also are a key element of urban government. They are the primary contact citizens have with government. . . . [P]olice services constitute more than 30% of the cost of city government. The police are available 24 hours a day. They resolve conflicts between families, groups, interests and individuals. All police rhetoric about crime fighting aside, it is clear, from observing the needs of citizens and what the police actually do, that the order and service functions are the functional heart of policing. (Police Foundation 1981, 112)

Not everyone agrees police should perform such a wide variety of services. Many criminal justice professionals, the public, and politicians call for the police to narrow their focus to concentrate on serious crime. In 1967, Professors Norval Morris and Gordon Hawkins (1967) wrote what many believe is still true:

> [T]he immense range of police obligations and duties must be drastically reduced. A variety of means are suggested here [transferring traffic control, most misdemeanors, and minor violations to other agencies] for both diminishing the range of their responsibilities and enabling the more effective use of their resources in the prevention and control of serious crime [murder, rape, robbery, and burglary in particular]. (9)

POLICE "WORKING PERSONALITY"

> The day the new recruit walks through the door of the police academy he leaves society behind to enter a profession that does more than give him a job, it defines who he is. For all the years he remains he will always be a cop. (Skolnick and Fyfe 1993, 91)

This insight from New Haven, Connecticut, police chief James Ahern in 1972 described how policing becomes what Skolnick and Fyfe (1993, 91) call the "defining identity" of police.

The sociology of occupations teaches us that our job affects the way we look at the world. Social scientists who've studied police all over the United States, in Europe, and in Asia have found three elements of police work always the same—danger, authority, and the power to use force. The combination of these three elements creates the **police working personality**—the way police look at the world; their standards of right and wrong; their behavior while they carry out their missions (Chapter 4), strategies (Chapter 5), and the law (Chapter 6); and the way they face critical issues in policing (Chapter 6) (Skolnick and Fyfe 1993, 92).

How Police Look at the World

The way the police working personality develops goes something like this: Danger makes them suspicious. Suspiciousness combines with their authority and the power to back up their authority with force to isolate them. This isolation makes police stick together, especially when they're in trouble. Let's fill in some details.

The world cops work in is "unkempt, unpredictable, and sometimes violent." Police experts David H. Bayley and Egon Bittner (1989) write:

> Police continually deal with situations in which physical constraint may have to be applied against people who are willing to fight, struggle, hit, stab, spit, bite, tear, hurl, hide, and run. People continually use their bodies against the police, forcing the police to deal with them in a physical way. While police seem to be preoccupied with deadly force, the more common reality in their lives is the possibility of a broken nose, lost teeth, black eyes, broken ribs, and twisted arms. Few officers are ever shot or even shot at, but all except the rawest rookie can show scars on their bodies from continual encounters with low-level violence. (93)

One officer put it this way:

> You never know what's going to happen. The whole world can come to an end in your last few minutes of duty, right before you leave your watch. Or—right before you retire from the force. We've had cases of police officers working their last tour before going on pen-

sion. And they've run into a situation where they're killed. (Baker 1985, 211)

This potential for danger makes officers look for signs of danger, especially the chance of violence but also of other law breaking and disorder. Police manuals teach officers where to look for the signs of danger: An adult hanging out where children play; several kids hanging out on street corners; known troublemakers in large groups of people; dirty cars with clean license plates; clean cars with dirty license plates; lights on in an office building at night. In other words, be suspicious of the unusual, the out of place (Baker 1985, 97).

When officers use their authority in unusual circumstances, it's usually applied to someone who at the very least doesn't like it and probably resents it (sometimes a lot!). Of course, officers would like to deal with "stable, well-dressed, normal, and unthreatening" people. Unfortunately, because they're our designated force users, they're probably going to run into unstable, badly dressed, threatening, and all-around not very nice people. So, every exercise of authority is a volatile situation.

We have to add to this mixture of danger, suspiciousness, and authority, the power to back up authority with force. According to sociologist Egon Bittner (1970), who probably knows more about what police actually do than most observers:

> Whatever the substance of the task at hand, whether it involves protection against an undesired imposition, caring for those who cannot care for themselves, attempting to solve a crime, helping to save a life, abating a nuisance, or settling an explosive dispute, police intervention means above all making use of the capacity and authority to overpower resistance. (40)

 4-6 Police stress and the police working personality

Working Personality and Discretion

Steve Herbert (1998) rode along with Los Angeles police sergeants who supervise patrol officers and senior lead officers who monitor problem areas (like corners where drugs are sold and houses where gang members hang out). Herbert was interested not just in defining police subculture but in connecting it to police discretionary decision making. He found the following formal and informal subculture influences on police discretion:

1. Adventure/machismo
2. Safety
3. Competence
4. Morality
5. Solidarity
6. Law and department rules

These influences interact and affect their standards of right and wrong and their behavior while they carry out their missions.

Adventure/machismo

Los Angeles police officers see one another as either "hardchargers" or "station queens." **Hardchargers** are "willing to rush into dangerous situations" and look for "the adrenaline high" from a dangerous call. They "volunteer" to handle incidents that "threaten their well-being." They're "police warriors and exemplify such typically masculine characteristics as courage and strength." The LAPD has had a long reputation for being aggressive, especially in policing minority neighborhoods; hardchargers are sometimes called "ghetto gunfighters." **Station queens** are "wary of danger. They seek instead the refuge of inside to avoid the hazards of the streets. The term 'queen' clearly feminizes such officers—they do not possess sufficient strength to pass muster in accordance with the adventure/machismo normative order" (Herbert 1998, 355–356).

Safety

Hardchargers may relish dangerous calls, but they don't want to die answering them. "It's better to be judged by twelve than carried by six," Herbert (1998, 357–358) heard officers say. Concern for their own safety shapes how they define situations and neighborhoods. Officers distinguish between "pro-police" and "anti-police" neighborhoods. When officers enter what they've decided is an anti-police neighborhood, they take their seat belts off for more mobility; they roll down their windows so they can hear better; they unlatch their shotguns; and they tell the dispatcher where they are in case they need backup. The Christopher Commission (1991) suggested an overconcern for safety made police overly suspicious of even remote threats by anyone. This in turn hurt their relations with neighborhoods, especially minority neighborhoods. So, safety not only defines police subculture, it also explains tensions between police and some communities in Los Angeles.

Competence

Competence means doing a good job. Doing a good job means getting the approval of other cops but, more important, it means pulling your own weight. Pulling your own weight means getting and keeping control of every situation officers run into without asking for help unless you really need it (Herbert 1998, 359–360).

Getting and keeping control isn't just a matter of solving problems, it means making sure the people they deal with respect police authority. Researchers have repeatedly found the high premium officers place on respect for their authority and the consequences for people who defy it. According to Paul Chevigny's (1969, 136) classic study of police in New York, "the one truly iron and inflexible rule" in all the cases of police abuse of power he reviewed

was, "[A]ny person who defies the police risks the imposition of legal sanctions, commencing with a summons, on up to the use of firearms."

John Van Maanen (1978) describes how the importance of authority affects police decision making in his study of a large police force of over 1500 officers. Officers divided the people they dealt with into three groups. Most people are **know-nothings,** ordinary people who aren't police and don't know anything about the world the police inhabit. Officers treat these "good citizens" with courtesy and efficiency. **Suspects** don't fit in their surroundings, like tall, energetic, athletic, dreadlocked, Black disk jockey, promoter of rock music concerts Edward Lawson walking late at night in a White San Diego neighborhood, who the police usually treat in a brisk professional manner. They just want to confirm or remove their suspicion. Unless the suspicious person crosses the line into the third group, what Van Maanen says police call "assholes."

An **asshole** is anyone who questions police authority. Van Maanen gives this example: A cop stops a car for speeding and politely asks the driver for license and registration. "Why the hell are you picking on me and not somewhere else looking for real criminals?" "Cause you're an asshole, but I didn't know that until you opened your mouth."

Morality

Seeking adventure, trying to stay alive, and maintaining their authority isn't all there is to the informal influence of the police working personality on decision making. There's also a powerful moral sense in the police working personality—the age-old struggle between good and evil. Steve Herbert (1998, 360) says "bad guy" comes up all the time in talk among LAPD officers. Of course, if there are bad guys there have to be good guys too. And, police officers see themselves as the good guys who fight the bad guys.

Sociologist Carl Klockars (1991a, 413) writes about a dilemma caused by this powerful moral component in the police working personality: Does the end justify the means? Klockars calls it the **Dirty Harry problem.** The name comes from the 1971 movie *Dirty Harry,* in which Clint Eastwood plays Dirty Harry Callahan, a cop who's on a psychopathic killer's trail. The psychopath is demanding ransom for a 14-year-old girl he kidnapped and buried alive with only enough air to live for a few hours. Dirty Harry brings the ransom to the kidnapper; the kidnapper takes back the offer, wounds Harry's partner, and escapes. Harry tracks him down, illegally searches his apartment, finds enough evidence to convict him, and captures the kidnapper on a football field. Harry shoots him in the leg and twists the injured leg until the kidnapper confesses where the girl is. Unfortunately, she's already dead, and almost as bad, the killer has to go free because Harry got the evidence and the confession illegally.

The movie presents a tough enough moral dilemma—breaking the law to save an innocent girl from an evil monster we know is guilty. Tougher still is when the evil isn't one clearly guilty person but a group (like a gang) and a mistake hurts innocent people. Skolnick and Fyfe (1993, 107–108) relate the tragedy of the LAPD Gang Task Force raid on four apartments they believed were crack houses controlled by gangs. Police also believed the gangs were terrorizing families who lived between the apartments and that the gang members were heavily armed. A few days before the raid, the captain at roll call told officers to "hit hard" and he wanted the apartments to look "leveled" and "uninhabitable" after the raid. The police officers did just that. They raided the apartments with guns, axes, and sledgehammers. Nobody was killed but they destroyed the apartments. They broke the toilets and tore them out of the floor, and water ran everywhere. They smashed the walls with their sledgehammers. They broke everything they could find—VCRs, TVs, and the bedroom and living room furniture. They cut the wires. They emptied wine and baby food on clothes and bedding. And, they spray-painted "LAPD rules" on what was left of the walls. Unfortunately, no gang members lived in the apartments, only a small amount of marijuana and cocaine was found, and there were no guns at all. An honest but tragic mistake. (Or, very bad police work "outsiders" might say, behavior the officers should be held accountable for.)

Newsweek columnist Jonathan Alter (2001) poses the Dirty Harry dilemma as it relates to the investigation of the September 11 attacks and suspects who *might* have information about future attacks:

> **In this autumn of anger, even a liberal can find his thoughts turning to . . . torture. OK, not cattle prods or rubber hoses, at least not here in the United States, but something to jump-start the stalled investigation of the greatest crime in American history. Right now, four key hijacking suspects aren't talking at all. Couldn't we at least subject them to psychological torture, like tapes of dying rabbits or high-decibel rap? (The military has done that in Panama and elsewhere.) How about truth serum, administered with a mandatory IV? Or deportation to Saudi Arabia, land of beheadings? (As the frustrated FBI has been threatening.) Some people still argue that we needn't rethink any of our old assumptions about law enforcement, but they're hopelessly "Sept. 10"—living in a country that no longer exists. (45)**

4-7 The entire *Newsweek* article and a longer debate on the use of torture

Solidarity

Danger, authority, and the power to use force—these three elements of the police subculture set the police apart, creating solidarity among them and isolating them from the people they police. The Christopher Commission (1991), which investigated the riots following the police

use of force against Rodney King in Los Angeles in the early 1990s, picked up on what it called the siege mentality of the Los Angeles police— "*us* against *them*." Isolation and the us-against-them attitude is especially strong when police are being criticized and the police **code of silence** (don't ever tell on another cop) kicks in. However, codes of silence aren't unique to police work (Skolnick and Fyfe 1993, 110). Do you know of at least one student who's cheated on an exam or plagiarized a paper? Did you turn him or her in? I think I know your answer.

4-8 International Association of Police study on the police code of silence

Next, we often hear police officers that break the code risk their lives. This has probably happened sometime in someplace besides cop shows and movies, but Skolnick and Fyfe say they know of only one case where police shot other officers to punish them for "squealing."

In the isolation of the us-against-them world of police, there's enormous pressure to remain loyal so there's no need to shoot people to guarantee their loyalty. The most common ways to enforce the code are the threat of shunning and blowing the whistle on informants' own wrongdoing. Robert Leuci's testimony put his whole squad and about seventy other NYPD narcotics officers in jail. Here's a conversation Leuci had with his wife before he talked:

LEUCI: I'm not going to implicate anyone close to us.
GINA LEUCI: Do you think they will allow you to do whatever you choose to do? Do you think they will say: Okay Bob, whoever you want to tell us about. You decide. I don't think they will allow you to do that [short pause]. I know you feel guilty. Other people are responsible, not you. They are guiltier than you are.
LEUCI [*in a low voice*]: I want to end this life I have been living.
GINA: Then quit the Police Department.
LEUCI: And do what? Sell insurance? Work in a bank?
GINA: I know you. It's going to kill you. They will force you to hurt friends, people who have done no harm to you, only good. When you were sick they all came. They called me every day. I know what kind of man you are. I know what you can live with and what you can't live with. This will kill you. You tell me the feelings you have for informants, and now you are going to be an informant. How are you going to live with that? (Skolnick and Fyfe 1993, 111–112)

Notice Leuci doesn't mention safety. Why? Because he didn't believe—and he turned out to be right—the people he "hurt" would *physically* shut him up. At the end of the day he had to face the reality that he could never be what he once was—the "Prince of the City," a hotshot member of the most envied and prestigious detectives in the biggest police department in the country (Skolnick and Fyfe 1993, 112).

YOU DECIDE

Was the law or subculture behind the decision?

Steve Herbert (1998) relates the following incident from his "ride alongs" with LAPD sergeants and senior lead officers.

A sergeant is summoned to an apartment building by a group of patrol officers. A woman is charging her husband with domestic abuse. Because the officers are choosing to take no action, she is now threatening a lawsuit. This threat captures the sergeant's attention, and he responds.

He arrives to discover one officer guarding an obviously intoxicated man sitting on the front steps of the building; the man is the husband in question. The other officers are inside with the woman. They are refusing to arrest the man because there is no evidence of physical abuse—the woman sports no cuts or bruises despite her claims that he abused her, the apartment is in good order even though she said he went on a rampage. The sergeant interviews the

woman and then calls a group huddle in front of the building.

A discussion ensues about what, if any, law can be invoked. The sergeant agrees that a domestic abuse charge is not warranted. They briefly discuss arresting the man for drunkenness in public, but they acknowledge that he is outside only because they ordered him there. The discussion is over, the sergeant informs the woman that she will have to obtain a restraining order for them to have legal power to arrest her husband. She is dissatisfied, but the officers leave the scene. (352–363)

Questions

1. Did the officers decide what they should do and look for a law to back them up? Or, did they look for a law to tell them how to settle the problem? Defend your answer.
2. Did they make the right decision? Why or why not?

Law

It should be clear by now how much discretion police officers have and how important the informal influence of the police working personality is on individual officers' discretionary decision making. But broad and important as police subculture is, law (and department rules) is also key to decision making (Herbert 1998, 352–363). First, law creates and defines police power; it sets the boundaries of discretionary decision making. Second, law defines order—the "disorderly conduct" ordinances. Third, law is the way officers define a problem. And fourth, it tells them how to resolve a problem. Many have written how officers handle an incident and find some law to back up how they handled it. But, often it works just the other way around: Officers use the law to decide whether and how to respond. Of course, broad terms like "disorderly conduct" leave officers lots of room to roam according to their occupational values and sometimes thumb their noses at the law they're sworn to uphold (Chapter 6), but these excesses don't mean law isn't important.

Knowledge and Understanding Check

History of Policing
✔ Compare and contrast the constable/night watch system and the municipal police departments that replaced the system.
✔ Describe the elements of the reform model of policing, and explain the driving forces behind the model.

Law Enforcement Structure and Process
✔ Describe the formal structure and the informal process of police organization.
✔ Trace the origins and development of private police.
✔ List and explain three styles of police management.

Police Missions
✔ List three police missions and the characteristics of each.
✔ Contrast the public image with the reality of police missions.
✔ Describe how the missions overlap.
✔ Describe possible shifts in police missions.

Police "Working Personality"
✔ Identify and describe the elements of the police working personality.
✔ List the formal and informal subcultural influences on police discretionary decision making, and explain how they influence decision making.
✔ Describe and explain the significance of the police code of silence.

KEY TERMS

asshole
broken windows theory
code of silence
community service mission
constable/night watch system
criminal law enforcement mission
Dirty Harry problem
full enforcement

hardchargers
know-nothings
legalistic style of policing
maintaining order
military model of policing
monopoly of force
municipal police department
police working personality

proactive
quality-of-life crime
reform model of policing
selective enforcement
service style of policing
station queens
suspect
watchman style of policing

INTERNET PROJECT

 Examine the "broken windows" theory and police enforcement of quality-of-life crimes. In separate searches, enter the key words "broken windows" and "disorderly conduct."

CHAPTER 5

Police Strategies

© Bob Daemmrich/Stock Boston

CHAPTER OUTLINE

> Can police reduce crime? The answer is in the eye of the beholder. In the "get tough" climate of the 1980s, victims' advocates . . . demanded more of police actions they were certain would help reduce specific types of crime, such as more arrests for drunk driving and domestic violence. At the same time sociologists and social reformers reacted with increasing stridency about the inability of the police to control crime in the face of "root causes" of crime: family structure, unemployment, and poverty.
>
> LAWRENCE SHERMAN (1992, 159)

INTRODUCTION

Patrol and investigation, the two strategies at the heart of crime control, have dominated American policing since the 1800s. Uniformed police officers patrol the streets to prevent crimes. Detectives investigate crimes to catch suspects for conviction and punishment. Both strategies once took a one-size-fits all approach to crime control—react the same way to all crimes in all places at all times. However, empirical research found definite limits to this approach. This research; public frustration and anger over illegal drugs and violence; fear of crime; and impatient demands to "do something" led to refinements in patrol and investigation. But it also led to the introduction of crime-attack, or proactive, strategies to supplement preventive patrol and criminal investigation strategies. Crime-attack strategies home in on specific problems in specific places at specific times, involving specific types of people; some call them "smarter law enforcement." But, empirical questions about their effectiveness; constitutional questions about whether they violate rights of privacy and liberty; and ethical questions about whether they intrude upon dignity and autonomy in a free society raise questions about how "smart" crime-attack strategies really are.

PATROL: THE BACKBONE OF POLICING

The medieval word *patrol* meant "to walk or paddle in mud or dirty water." Today, patrol officers move through the streets, sometimes on foot, but mostly in vehicles. Patrol cars move either slowly (prowling) to prevent crime or speeding through the streets, with sirens screaming and red lights flashing, to pursue suspects. More than 60 percent of all officers are assigned to patrol (Sherman 1992, 172).

Let's look more closely at the decision points that lead patrol officers to mobilize, the issues that determine their response time to calls, and some of the debates over how effectively different forms of patrol (preventive, foot, and single-officer) help fight crime.

Mobilizing Patrol

Ninety percent of the time, the police go into action, or **mobilize,** only after victims report crimes. In the remaining 10 percent, officers actively look for crimes and go into action when they find them. There are four decision points in police mobilization:

1. Victims and witnesses decide to call the police. (Chapters 1 and 3)
2. Civilian police operators decide whether to forward calls to dispatchers (Figure 5.1). About half the callers don't get beyond the operators. Their decisions aren't reviewed, but we know their main criterion—the more serious the crime the more likely operators will forward the call to dispatchers.
3. Dispatchers decide whether to mobilize the police. They have wide discretion, too, but the seriousness of the crime determines whether they assign cars at all, and if they do, what priority to give the calls.
4. Patrol officers decide how to respond to the calls dispatchers give them. They can drop some calls, hurry to the scene in others, or proceed with no particular urgency, depending on their reading of the situation. (Scott 1980, 59–67)

Response Time

Faster is better. At least, that's what police used to think about their response to calls. They assumed the faster they got to crime scenes the more criminals they could catch, the more injuries they could prevent, and the more satisfied

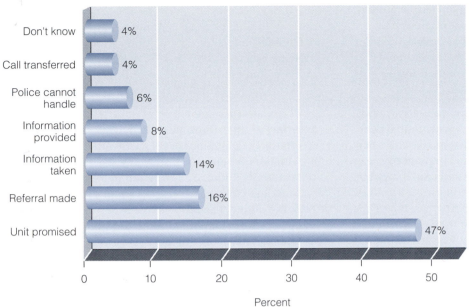

FIGURE 5.1
Responses to Calls for Service
SOURCE: Scott 1980, 62.

the public would be. Departments relied on two tactics to speed up response time: (1) the emergency 911 telephone number and (2) computer-assisted automobile vehicle monitoring (AVM) system (National Advisory Committee on Criminal Justice Standards and Goals 1973, 193).

Then came several empirical studies shattering the belief that faster is better. Researchers discovered police response time has no effect on apprehension, charge, and conviction rates. They also found people's satisfaction doesn't depend on how fast police answer calls (Forst et al. 1982; Forst, Lucianovic, and Cox 1977; Kelling and Fogel 1978, 166–167; U.S. Department of Justice 1978).

These discoveries led police departments to drop the one-size-fits-all approach to calls. Instead, they adopted a **differential response** approach, varying their response according to the type of crime. They used rapid response for serious crimes like rape and robbery and other responses for less serious offenses, like 30-minute delays, telephone reporting, walk-in reporting, and scheduled appointments (Petersilia 1989, 234).

The respected Police Executive Research Forum (PERF) designed a model response system. In this model, civilian complaint-takers answer all calls and classify them as critical or noncritical. They transfer the critical calls to dispatchers for immediate response and ask callers to file reports of their noncritical calls later. Evaluation of the model found:

- Fast police response accounted for less than 5 percent of arrests for serious crimes.
- Most service calls don't require a fast response.
- Different responses don't alienate people if they know in advance how the police will handle their calls.

- The differential response approach saved the Garden Grove, California, Police Department 8000 labor-hours (more than $223,000) during its first year. (Petersilia 1989, 235)

■ TYPES OF PATROL

There are many strategies of how patrol should most effectively be implemented to reduce crime. We'll look at three issues in this discussion: preventive patrol, foot patrol, and single-officer patrol.

Preventive Patrol

The famous reform era chief O. W. Wilson believed police cars cruising randomly through the streets, **preventive patrol,** creates the impression the police are everywhere and can appear any time. According to police experts Jerome Skolnick and James Fyfe (1993), preventive patrol "is based on the premise that the presence of uniformed cops and marked police cars will send would-be criminals elsewhere, will keep jaywalkers on the sidewalk, and will cause motorists to check their speedometers" (251–252).

Officers spend about half their time patrolling. What do they do on patrol? It depends on the city, the beat, the time of day, and the officer. According to Gary Cordner and Robert Trojanowicz (1992):

Patrolling can be stationary or mobile; slow-, medium-, or high-speed; and oriented toward residential, commercial, recreational, or other kinds of areas. Some patrol officers intervene frequently in people's

lives by stopping cars and checking out suspicious circumstances; other officers seem more interested in . . .
parked cars and the security of closed businesses;
still other officers rarely interrupt their continuous
patrolling. Some officers devote all of their uncommit-
ted time to loafing or personal affairs. (5)

Technology—vehicles, telephones, two-way radios,
and computers—has isolated police by changing policing from a personal operation of individuals who knew
the communities they policed into a bureaucratic, mechanical, centralized operation. For example, computers
can pinpoint the exact location of patrol cars at all times,
helping supervisors control officers on patrol. But at the
same time, computer terminals (found in most patrol cars
now) let officers gather information without getting out
of their squad cars to talk to the people they police and
police for.

Isolating police from the communities they police has
contributed to poor police-community relations (Police
Foundation 1981, 11). This is especially true in poor
urban neighborhoods where many residents see police
as a hostile occupying force, isolated in their "rolling
fortresses, unable to communicate with the people they
presumably serve" (Skolnick and Fyfe 1993, 240). According to the eminent sociologist of the police Albert J.
Reiss, Jr. (1992):

> Insulation of the police came at a high price. The pa-
> trol officer in his air-conditioned and heated car no
> longer got out of the police vehicle to do preventive
> patrol or to learn more about the community being
> policed. . . . No longer did the public have confidence
> that the police were handling, or could handle their
> problems, and many, particularly minority groups,
> felt alienated from the police. (3)

Beginning in the 1970s, a series of empirical evaluations uncovered several deficiencies in preventive patrol. Prisoners told interviewers the presence of police
didn't frighten or deter them (Kelling et al. 1974, 9–10).
Attempts to increase perceived police presence by letting officers use squad cars for their personal use had
little, if any, deterrent effect. Patrol can't stop crimes
committed inside buildings. Even when preventive patrol deters, its effect is limited to main streets and buildings, leaving side and back streets, alleys, and even the
backs of buildings on main streets unaffected (Goldstein
1977, 49–54).

These evaluations also found crimes of passion are
largely beyond the reach of preventive patrol. Enraged or
demented individuals don't take patrol officers into account when their impulses explode into violence. Also,
skilled criminals quickly discover where the police concentrate their efforts and avoid those places or at least
wait until a squad car drives by before they make their
moves. According to Andrew Halper and Richard Ku

(1975), a police officer "performs the functions of a scare-
crow. . . . In this respect his presence can be as reassuring
to criminals as to the law-abiding. The potential felon,
knowing where a policeman is, can safely deduce where
he is not, and guide himself accordingly" (1–2).

David Bayley (1998) adds:

> The relatively small effects of police patrolling on
> crime, arrests, or the fear of crime may be due to the
> relatively small numbers of patrol officers compared
> with population. . . . Most people are unaware just
> how thinly police are spread out in most places. . . . In
> American cities, the average is about 400 people per
> police officer. The ratio of visible patrol officers—cops
> on the street—to population at any given moment is,
> however, much less. In fact, it is less than one-tenth of
> total police strength. There are several reasons for this.
> In the first place, only about 60% of police officers are
> assigned to patrol. So visible strength is already four-
> tenths less than the total. But all patrol officers do not
> work all the time; they work in shifts. Usually, there
> are four shifts—three 8-hour shifts on duty, and one
> shift off duty. This means that only 15% of police
> strength is available during most 8-hour periods
> (60% divided by 4). (29)

The Kansas City Preventive Patrol Experiment

The most famous and perhaps the most influential study
of preventive patrol, the **Kansas City Preventive Patrol Experiment,** tested the effectiveness of this strategy. Researchers divided fifteen beats into three groups
matched for similar crime rates and demographic characteristics. For one year, the police applied three patrol
strategies to each group. In the control group, they
applied traditional preventive patrol; one car drove
through the streets whenever it wasn't answering calls.
In group 2, **proactive patrol,** they greatly increased patrol activity; cars drove through the beats two to three
times more often than in the control group. In group 3,
reactive patrol, they eliminated preventive patrol entirely; a patrol car stayed at the station until someone
called for assistance.

Before and after the experiment, interviewers asked
businesspeople and neighborhood residents if they'd
been crime victims; their opinion about the quality of
law enforcement; and about their fear of crime. To the
surprise of many, no matter what the strategy:

- Crime rates stayed the same.
- Rates of reporting crime to the police remained
  constant.
- People's fear of crime stayed the same.
- Opinions about the effectiveness of police services
  didn't change.
- Respect for the police increased in the control beats
  (traditional preventive patrol!). (Kelling et al.1974)

YOU DECIDE

Is preventive patrol a waste of police time and taxpayers' money?

Some critics have rushed to the conclusion the Kansas City Preventive Patrol Experiment was a waste of police time and taxpayers' money. But, Gary Cordner and Robert Trojanowicz (1992) caution that the Kansas City study merely "demonstrated that varying the level of motorized patrol between zero cars per beat and 2–3 cars per beat, for one year in one city, had no effect" (6–7). And, James Q. Wilson (1983, 65–66), author of the influential *Varieties of Police Behavior,* warns the experiment didn't prove police presence of all kinds is useless in controlling crime. It only showed patrol in marked cars did little good. Results might have been different if officers had responded to calls faster in unmarked cars or on foot. Reported crime did decline in Flint, Michigan, when the Flint Police Department adopted foot patrols (Sherman 1992, 153–154).

The Kansas City Preventive Patrol Experiment did have several definitely positive effects:

1. It showed the willingness of police departments to engage in research to evaluate the effectiveness of their programs. According to police expert Herman Goldstein (1977), the experiment also "demonstrated that the police can undertake complex experiments that require altering routine operations with results that are beneficial to the agency . . . and to the entire police field" (52).
2. The experiment also opened up the possibility of freeing expensive patrol resources for other police activities; administrators might be able to divert as much as 60 percent to investigation, surveillance, and community service without diminishing the effectiveness of patrol.
3. By challenging traditional practices, according to J. L. Ray LeGrande of the Miami Beach Police Department, "It was a breakthrough in research—as important as using the police radio for the first time" (Petersilia 1989, 232).

4. The experiment set off a wave of empirical studies pointing out the shortcomings of reactive policing, spurring the increase of variations on existing proactive strategies, and introducing several new ones.

Most of the discussion of evaluations of the reactive strategies of preventive patrol and criminal investigation and the analyses of proactive strategies in the rest of this chapter stem from the findings and questions raised by the Kansas City Preventive Patrol Experiment.

The findings of the Kansas City Preventive Patrol Experiment were and still are widely accepted. Nevertheless, according to policing expert David H. Bayley (1998):

> Motorized patrol is still the mainstay of policing, with police departments continuing to assign the bulk of their personnel to random motor patrolling. . . . In sum, the Kansas City preventive patrol research is famous; its findings are generally accepted as being true; its research strategy is considered to be seriously flawed; it has never been replicated; it has not lessened appreciably the reliance of the police on random patrolling, but it has encouraged a rethinking of police purposes and methods. The curiously mixed, indeed paradoxical impact of the Kansas City research represents a failure, in my view, of police professionals, as well as social scientists. One group or the other should have acted on it, and neither really has. (15)

Questions

1. Summarize the findings of the evaluations of preventive patrol.
2. List the positive and negative findings regarding preventive patrol.
3. Do you favor preventive patrol as a strategy? Defend your answer.

Foot Patrol

Police returned to the old practice of patrolling on foot in the 1970s and 1980s because it brought them closer to the community. Why does getting closer to the community matter? According to Stephen Mastrofski (1990):

> Imbued with a proprietary interest in the neighborhood's well-being and armed with a rich knowledge of its people and places, the officer is expected to enlist citizens' assistance and thus reinforce the informal social control mechanisms of the community. Ultimately these efforts are expected to contribute to more positive police-community relations, less fear of crime and disorder, and an actual reduction in crime and disorder. (37)

Does foot patrol make police street smarter, reduce crime and disorder, and reduce the fear of crime too? Two major evaluations tried to answer these questions. In Flint, Michigan, foot patrol reduced the fear of crime *and* actual crime rates. It was so popular that in spite of

Flint's severe financial problems, the city voted three times for special tax increases to expand the program. On the other hand, the Newark Foot Patrol Experiment produced mixed results. Fear of crime went down and public satisfaction with police went up, but crime rates stayed the same (Cordner and Trojanowicz 1992, 10).

Single-Officer Patrol

Patrol is labor-intensive; it relies heavily on people, not labor- and cost-saving equipment. Salaries make up 80 percent of police budgets, making patrol the most expensive police operation. This is particularly true of two-officer patrols, which prevailed in American policing until the 1980s. Faced with declining budgets, the cost effectiveness of one-officer patrols appealed to budget-conscious administrators. Administrators saw the chance to cut the cost of patrol in half by moving from the two- to one-officer patrols. But, officers vigorously opposed the idea because of their strong belief that partners backing each other up increased their safety. However, when the respected Police Executive Research Foundation evaluated one-officer patrols in San Diego it found this wasn't true. The study reported that compared to two-officer units, one-officer units:

- Saved money
- Were less often involved in resisting arrest situations
- Resulted in fewer assaults against officers
- Resulted in fewer injuries to officers
- Generated fewer citizen complaints
- Completed about the same number of traffic warnings, field interrogations, business checks, arrests, and crime report filings (Mastrofski 1990, 31)

■ CRIMINAL INVESTIGATION

Crime stories, whether on TV or in novels, always start with detectives. From Sherlock Holmes in the 1800s to *NYPD Blue* in 2002, detectives sleuth clues in dirty, dangerous places; subject their clues to laboratory analysis and their own intuition; and, lo and behold, catch the bad guy. To most people, police work *is* criminal investigation. Detectives, who make up about 15 percent of officers, are also the prestige elements in police subculture. They don't have to wear uniforms, keep their own hours, get paid more, and are the envied group.

Research, however, generally complicates the popular image of criminal investigation. Since the 1960s, research has found "detective work is often boring, usually requires only normal decision-making powers, and seldom leads to solutions." But, is detective work really that boring and useless? Research from the 1980s and 1990s

indicates criminal investigation isn't as exciting as the crime stories depict it, but it's more effective than the 1960s and 1970s research suggested (Brandl and Frank 1994, 149–168; Eck 1992, 19). Let's look more closely at what really happens during preliminary and follow-up investigations and the roles of patrol officers and detectives in each.

Preliminary Investigation

Most departments divide criminal investigation into preliminary investigation by patrol officers and follow-up investigation by detectives. In **preliminary investigations,** patrol officers collect information at crime scenes and write **incident reports** describing what they learned. Police departments and prosecutors rely heavily on incident reports in deciding whether to continue the criminal process. Incident reports that contain "good" information, such as (1) the names and addresses of several witnesses, (2) the names and addresses of suspects (or at least good descriptions of them) and (3) detailed descriptions of stolen property, raise the chances of successful prosecution and conviction. Police incident reports containing the names of two witnesses instead of one raise conviction rates by 60 percent! Furthermore, good preliminary investigation also reduces the chance of involving innocent people as suspects (Forst et al.1977, 24–32; 1982, 23).

Patrol officers make most arrests. They either arrest suspects at the scene of the crime or later based on identifications from victims or witnesses. Detectives, on the other hand, make only a small number of arrests, and detective investigations almost never lead to the identification of unknown criminals. As a result of these findings, many police departments train patrol officers to conduct more extensive investigations. Some departments even provide patrol officers with feedback from prosecutors' offices regarding the final outcome of cases that officers have investigated (Brandl and Frank 1994; Eck 1983; Greenwood, Chaiken, and Petersilia 1977; Greenwood and Petersilia 1975).

Follow-up Investigation

TV and movies tell stories where the detectives always solve the crime and catch the bad guys, but researchers who've studied detectives in real life tell a more complicated story. First, most cases aren't solved by detective work, according to researchers who examined arrests in Los Angeles, Miami, and Washington, D.C. How *are* they solved?

1. Patrol officers have already arrested the suspect.
2. Detectives have identified suspects before they get the case.

3. Arrested suspects confess to *other* crimes they've committed. (Greenwood, Chaiken, and Petersilia 1977, 72)

In a study of the importance of detective work in solving crimes, John Eck (1983) collected data from four police departments: DeKalb, Illinois; County, Georgia; St. Petersburg, Florida; and Wichita, Kansas. Cases fell into three categories. In two of the categories—weak cases with little evidence and strong cases with a lot of evidence—police effort didn't matter. They didn't have to do anything in the strong cases and no matter how hard they worked on weak cases they couldn't solve them. In the third group—cases with moderate evidence—the more time detectives spent the greater their chances of making an arrest.

Police experts Jerome H. Skolnick and David H. Bayley (1986) sum up detective work this way:

> Crimes are not solved—in the sense of offenders arrested and prosecuted—through criminal investigations conducted by police departments. Generally, crimes are solved because offenders are immediately apprehended or someone identifies them specifically—a name, an address, a license plate number. If neither of these things happens, the studies show the chances that any crime will be solved fall to less than one in ten. Despite what television has led us to think, detectives do not work from clues to criminals; they work from known suspects to corroborating evidence. Detectives are important for the prosecution of identified perpetrators and not for finding unknown offenders. (5)

🔘 **5-1 Audio discussion of the effectiveness of detective work**

PROACTIVE POLICING

Can police reduce crime? The public thinks so. So do politicians, but criminologists are skeptical. Their research has clearly demonstrated the limits of preventive patrol and criminal investigation. But it goes deeper than that. Some criminologists doubt the police can do *anything* about crime. According to these criminologists, police can answer emergency calls and maintain order, but they can't control crime. Why? Because they believe cops can't do anything about the "root causes" of crime (discussed in Chapter 3). But not all criminologists believe this. They concede preventive patrol and criminal investigation have their limits. But those limits are mainly due to strategies based on a one-size-fits-all approach to crime control—respond to all crimes in all places at all times the same way. We've already seen how research led to refinements in pa-

trol and investigation to make decision making "smarter." It also led to adopting crime-attack strategies tailored to specific crimes and types of criminals, in particular places, at certain times. Let's look at some of these strategies, including hot spots patrol, police crackdowns, field interrogations, and crime-specific lines of attack.

Hot Spots Patrol

"Hot spots" patrol is based on a simple idea: Some addresses at certain times need special attention. Why? Because crime is not evenly distributed in place and time. For example, in Minneapolis, more than half the 911 calls reporting serious crimes came from only 3 percent (hot spots) of its 115,000 addresses. All rapes came from 1.2 percent of the addresses; all robberies from 2.2 percent; all car thefts from 2.7 percent; and all domestic disturbances from 9 percent. So, deciding to give every resident an equal share of patrol wasn't smart. Lawrence Sherman (1995, 331) assisted the Minneapolis Police Department in designing a major experiment to test how "smart" hot spots patrol is.

Sherman and his colleagues at the Crime Control Institute (Sherman 1995) evaluated the experiment. They collected addresses based on calls for assistance and crimes reported to the police during one year for the Minneapolis Hot Spots Patrol Experiment. Then, the police applied "three hours a day of intermittent, unpredictable police presence" to a random selection of the "worst" hot spot intersections in the city (333). Robbery fell 20 percent, and crimes overall fell 13 percent in these intersections. The number of fights and disturbances was cut in half in the experimental areas. The Minneapolis police officers on hot spots patrol just drove around; they didn't get out of their cars to talk to people or to interrogate suspects. According to Sherman (1995), "More aggressive efforts may have reduced crime even further—or made it worse" (333–334).

🔘 **5-2 Policing drug hot spots**

Police Crackdowns

Sherman and his colleagues (1995) also found calls to the police came on "hot" days of the week at "hot" times of the day. According to Sherman, "[M]ost addresses, and even most blocks, in any city go for years without any crime—even in high-crime neighborhoods" (331). **Police crackdowns** consist of sudden increases in police activity at places during these hot days and times. How effective are crackdowns? The evidence is mixed. Some research shows crackdowns on drunk driving, robbery, drug dealing, and prostitution reduce crime. But—and it's a big but—only at the crackdown location and only

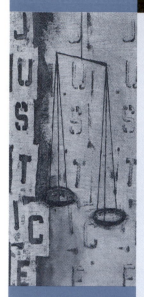

YOU DECIDE

Were the field interrogations appropriate?

Reproduced here are two field interrogations conducted by New York City Police officers as part of the NYPD "zero tolerance" for quality-of-life violations (Chapter 4). Keep in mind these are written from the perspective of two individuals who were interrogated, not the police who conducted them.

Personal Narrative

A. JOHN REYES

John Reyes is a 22-year-old Hispanic male who resides in East Harlem with his ill mother and teenage sister. Mr. Reyes graduated from a New York City public high school in 1996 and matriculated at a community college in Westchester that same year. After only one semester, he could no longer afford the school and was forced to leave. To pay for college, Mr. Reyes entered the federal Americorps scholarship program. In accordance with the program's requirements, he worked at a community-based program site for approximately 1200 hours to earn scholarship money. Mr. Reyes' "stop & frisk" experience occurred late one night in the summer of 1997.

After working a late shift, Mr. Reyes left the community center at approximately 12:30 A.M. He arrived at his building at approximately 1:00 A.M. Mr. Reyes entered his apartment building, walked to the elevator bank, and was waiting for the elevator when four or five men appeared. "I felt like they came from nowhere. Although they were not in uniform, a few of the men had their badges on, so I knew that they were police officers." The police officers questioned him about where he was coming from. They frisked him and searched his bag. In the midst of a search of his bag, the officers asked Mr. Reyes if he lived in the building. He told them that he did.

"Once the police officers seemed satisfied that I was not in possession of any contraband, and that they were going to let me go on my way, I felt comfortable to ask them what was going on. . . . They told me that they had received a report that shots had been fired, and that I fit the description of the perpetrator. They didn't give me any more details."

Mr. Reyes reported that this was his first encounter with the police. As he explained, "I was nervous about being stopped and searched. I thought that only happened to criminals." The officers searched his bag. He was embarrassed and somewhat afraid. "It felt strange when the police told me to place my hands against the wall, patted down my body, and then rifled through my things. I was somewhat embarrassed because I knew I had done nothing wrong. . . . I was also glad that none of my neighbors witnessed this incident, because they might have gotten the wrong idea." Mr. Reyes added, "I did not tell my mother what had just happened because I didn't want to upset her."

B. JEAN DAVIS

Jean Davis is a 54-year-old African American woman who resides in Brooklyn. Davis works as a home health aide for elderly persons. Her encounter with the NYPD occurred in March 1999 at about 10:30 P.M. That evening, Ms. Davis had worked as an aide at a client's home five blocks away from her house. At the end of her shift, she left the client's home and walked on foot toward her house.

Two blocks from her home, she noticed a White man walking in the street. Ms. Davis thought it was strange to see a White person in her predominately Black neighborhood. Since there recently had been reports of crimes in

---

for a short time. Why? Because crime moves to another location (a result called **displacement**) and then comes back to its old location after the crackdown. However, Sherman's review of evaluations of crackdowns in eighteen U.S. locations and five other countries shows fifteen worked with little evidence of displacement. For example, in London, England, there was no evidence a crackdown on prostitution pushed prostitutes to other areas of London (Sherman 1995, 332).

Sherman (1995) contends crackdowns have the opposite effect of displacement:

> Rather than displacing crime to surrounding areas, crime prevention measures reduce crime in nearby

areas where they had not been implemented. . . . [T]he key to making crackdowns work is to keep them short and unpredictable. Long-term police crackdowns all show a "decay" in their deterrent effects over time. Short-term crackdowns, in contrast, show a free bonus of "residual deterrence" after the crackdown stops, while potential offenders slowly figure out that the cops are gone. Random rotation of high police visibility across different short-term targets can accumulate free crime prevention bonuses and get the most out of police visibility. Even if displacement to other spots occurs, the unpredictable increases in police presence

the area, Ms. Davis quickened her pace. She was almost at her home when the man suddenly approached her from behind and grabbed her around her neck. "I screamed. I thought I was being attacked, so I screamed. I was only a few houses away from where I lived, and I thought I could scream loud enough that my son would hear me, and come to my rescue."

"The man told me to be quiet because he was a police officer, but I really didn't know whether to believe him because he did not show me any identification . . . the next thing I knew, the man was forcing me to walk down the street, back towards the direction he came from. He pulled me down the street towards a car. As we got closer to the car, I saw another man get out of it. The man who was holding me forced me to put my hands on the hood of the car, and patted down the sides of my body and legs."

By this time, Ms. Davis knew that the two men were police officers. Her original fear began to subside as her anger grew. Ms. Davis stated that the officer then conducted a full search of her person, removing the contents of her jacket pockets, shaking her pants legs, removing the baseball hat she was wearing, and shaking that out as well.

At this point, Ms. Davis asked the officers for an explanation. One officer explained that the officers had gotten a call informing them that someone had purchased drugs in the area, and that she fit the description of the alleged purchaser. The officer was not specific about the description. The officer then walked up and down the street looking for drugs. Ms. Davis, now suspicious of the officers and irritated by her continuing detention, feared that an officer might plant drugs on her

to cover up his mistake. Ultimately, the officer told Ms. Davis that she was free to go.

"I was shocked and humiliated at being treated like a common criminal," Ms. Davis said. She went home immediately and called her co-worker, who in turn called their employer. The employer accompanied Ms. Davis to the police precinct, where she filed a complaint. She also filed a complaint with the Civilian Complaint Review Board. "I don't trust police officers. Following the incident, I couldn't sleep well for months . . . Eventually, I went to the doctor who prescribed sleeping pills." Ms. Davis added that, rather than walk the five blocks to her job site, now she takes a taxi.

Questions

1. Do you think John Reyes has a legitimate complaint against the field interrogation NYPD officers used in his case? Defend your answer.
2. Do you think Jean Davis has a legitimate complaint against the field interrogation she experienced? Why or why not?
3. Which, if either, of the interrogations is more appropriate? Explain your answer.
4. To get a more complete answer, explore the Final Report of the San Diego Field Interrogation and the description of the NYPD's field interrogation practices in the links on your CD-ROM.

at any hot spot may create generally higher deterrent effects from the same number of police officers. (332)

Crackdowns raise questions about the right balance between crime control and due process in a constitutional democracy (Chapter 1). Crackdowns intrude deeply into people's daily lives. As a result, they interfere with everybody's right to come and go as they please and to be let alone by government. Some residents complain about crackdowns turning their neighborhoods into "police states." Young Black men complain officers "hassle" them simply because they're young, Black, and in the neighborhood. Inevitably, crackdowns affect inno-

cent people who have no intention to commit crimes or cause trouble (Sherman 1990, 2–6).

Field Interrogation

Field interrogation means to stop, question, and sometimes search people who "don't look or act right." Does field interrogation reduce crime? The San Diego Field Interrogation Experiment tried to find out. The experiment compared three patrol areas. One area continued field interrogations as usual. In the second, only officers specially trained to reduce conflicts with people they stopped did the questioning. The third area stopped all field interrogations for nine months and then started it up again. Total reported crime stayed the same in both areas where field interrogation continued. But total crime went up 20 percent during the nine months that interrogation stopped in the third area, and then went down when interrogation started up. Quality-of-life crimes like disorderly conduct, public drunkenness, petty theft, and prostitution went up even more during the suspension of field interrogation (Boydstun 1975).

But did the benefits of field interrogation come at the expense of bad relations with the community? No. Surveys showed reducing interrogation had no effect on people's attitudes toward the police. But, attitudes toward police were most favorable in the area where specially trained officers did the questioning. So, it looks like aggressive field interrogation can reduce crime *and* maintain good relations with communities where it's practiced professionally (Boydstun 1975).

 5-3 San Diego Field Interrogation Final Report and an evaluation and critique of the NYPD's field interrogation practices

 5-4 You Decide: When is undercover police work ethical?

Proactive Strategies to Attack Specific Crimes

We've emphasized that proactive policing tries to provide "smarter law enforcement" by moving from one-size-fits-all strategies to crime-attack strategies that focus on times, places, and people. Now let's look at how police used smarter law enforcement to attack three types of crimes—gun violence, drugs, and domestic assault.

Gun violence

Most gun research focuses on *how many* guns there are (gun density), but it takes gun *carrying* to translate the number of guns into gun violence. So, cities with a high gun density can have lower gun crime rates than cities with a low gun density. James Q. Wilson hypothesized police can reduce gun violence by seizing guns in "gun hot spots" (high-crime neighborhoods at certain times). However, most police departments count on reactively finding guns during routine searches following arrests for other crimes. Departments don't use the number of guns seized as a measure of police performance and "few officers go out of their way to try and find guns on the street" (Sherman and Rogan 1995, 673, 675).

The Kansas City Gun Experiment tested the hypothesis that greater enforcement of gun-carrying laws in gun crime hot spots could reduce gun crimes overall in

two Kansas City, Missouri, Police Department beats (144 and 242) with identical drive-by shooting rates. The control beat, 242, did business as usual, while beat 144 directed extra patrols on gun crime hot spots. Here are three examples of what the extra patrol officers actually did:

- *Safety frisk during traffic stop*: When the officer asked the driver for his license, the driver leaned over to the glove compartment, revealing a bulge under the jacket on the left arm. The officer grabbed the bulge, felt a hard bulk in the shape of a gun, and reached into the jacket to pull the gun out.
- *Plain view*: As the officer approached a car he had stopped for speeding, he shined a flashlight onto the floor in front of the back seat and saw a shotgun. Ordering the driver and the passenger out of the car, he found the shotgun was loaded.
- *Search incident to arrest on other charges*: After stopping a driver for running a red light, the officer asked for his driver's license. A computer check revealed that the driver was wanted for a failure to appear on domestic assault charges. The officer arrested the driver, searched him, and found a gun hidden under his shirt. (Sherman and Rogan 1995, 681)

The results: Hot spots patrol officers increased the total guns found in beat 144 by 65 percent in six months (29 guns). Most of the guns never went back to the streets; they were destroyed by the police. Gun crimes fell by 49 percent in the same six months, including reductions in drive-by shootings and homicide. Residents said they were less afraid and more satisfied with their neighborhoods. There was no sign of displacement either. Rather than moving gun crime to the beats next to 144, gun crimes went down in two of them. The results of the control beat told a different story: Gun seizures fell slightly and gun crimes went up slightly; homicide and drive-by shootings stayed the same. Residents felt more fear and less satisfaction than residents in beat 144 (Sherman and Rogan 1995, 688–689).

Despite these favorable results, Sherman and Rogan (1995), who conducted the research, caution:

> We offer our findings with appropriate cautions. Intensified gun patrols in some neighborhoods conceivably could harm police-community relations, even though no complaints and no legal challenges to the experiment were ever filed in Kansas City. . . . Gun hot spot patrols could pose great risks to officers' safety, although no officers were injured in the limited period of the experiment. Most worrisome is the possibility that field interrogations could provoke more crime by making young men subjected to traffic spots more defiant toward conventional society and thus commit more crimes. (692)

5-5 Full report of the Kansas City Gun Experiment

Drug hot spots

Policing drug crimes has created the most innovative strategies in police work since the 1980s: police crackdowns; raids on crack houses; and new tactics like "jump-out" squads intercepting public drug deals, condemning buildings, and fining landlords for drug dealing. Which police strategies work in drug law enforcement? To find out (and to be honest to answer public pressure), the National Institute of Justice established the Drug Market Analysis Program (DMA).

David Weisburd and Lorraine Green (1995, 715–717) evaluated a DMA experimental strategy to enforce drug laws in Jersey City, New Jersey. Drug hot spots were responsible for a "substantial portion" of calls for service, drug-related crimes, and arrests. For example, the hot spots amounted to only 4.4 percent of streets and intersections but 46 percent of drug sales arrests and emergency calls for narcotics. Before the project, the Jersey City Police Department narcotics squad had relied on unsystematic tactics, including surveillance, arrests, search warrants, and "street pops" (field interrogations of suspected dealers on street corners). Although these activities increased, they didn't have any impact on the drug problem.

According to Jersey City Captain Frank Gajewski, the traditional drug enforcement strategy maintained the street-level drug problem as much as it combated it:

> One can look at these drug markets as vineyards. The arrests made within their borders can be symbolized as the fruit from the vine. Each vineyard is capable of producing a continual supply of "fruit" as long as the vine is left intact. Some vineyards are larger than others. The arrest strategy sees the pickers (the police) traveling from vineyard to vineyard harvesting the fruit. There are many vineyards so the pickers never stay too long at any particular site. As demand increases from irate citizens . . . the police respond by picking more fruit. Police administrators seeking to assuage the public, display the high harvest numbers as evidence of their commitment and the efficiency of their organization. But the vines are never uprooted, indeed police activity may contribute to their health. (Weisburd and Green 1995, 717)

The ineffectiveness of their traditional strategies frustrated the Jersey City Police Department. That's when they turned to DMA and the creation, implementation, and evaluation of the drug hot spots experiment. The experimental strategy aimed at getting business owners and residents involved; cracking down on drug hot spots; and creating a maintenance program to patrol the hot spots after the crackdowns. Comparing the seven months before and after the experiment, Weisburd and Green (1995, 714–717) found:

1. Significant reductions in emergency calls to the police
2. Little displacement of crime to areas near the experimental hot spots
3. Reduced crime in areas around the experimental hot spots (**diffusion of benefits**)

According to Weisburd and Green (1995, 721), the reduction in emergency calls is important because "recent studies suggest emergency calls are a more reliable measure of crime and crime-related activity than are other official indicators."

 5-6 Full report of the Jersey City DMA experiment

 5-7 You Decide: Is DARE a "good" drug prevention program?

Domestic violence

"I hate those domestic disputes. There's not a thing you can do with them" (Black 1980, 146). What can police do about domestic violence disputes? A 1968 study found some New York City Police officers specially trained to handle domestic violence calls believed counseling batterers was more effective than arresting them. A report by the National Institute of Law Enforcement and Criminal Justice endorsed the NYPD approach. However, by the 1970s, many law enforcement officials had started rejecting the counseling approach, claiming it didn't work. At the same time, the growing women's movement rejected it as "soft" on batterers (Brown 1988, 289).

During the 1980s, states began to change ancient laws that only allowed officers to arrest suspects without warrants if they witnessed a misdemeanor firsthand. About the same time, police departments began to adopt policies allowing officers to arrest batterers even if they hadn't witnessed misdemeanor assaults or didn't have evidence a felony was committed. These new laws and policies made it easier for police to arrest batterers.

In 1980, the Minneapolis Domestic Violence Experiment tested the effectiveness of nonarrests in domestic assault cases. Officers agreed to give up their discretion and decide according to a random system whether to arrest, mediate, or temporarily separate couples. Using victim interviews and official police records of assaults, experiment evaluator Lawrence Sherman and his associates reported arrests cut assaults by 50 percent in the six months after the first assault (Sherman, Schmidt, and Rogan 1992).

Scholars claimed this was one of the "most influential results ever generated by social science" (Maxwell, Garner, and Fagan 1991, 3). But, six replications of the Minneapolis

Experiment in other places between 1981 and 1991 failed to duplicate these results. In three studies, assaults by arrested batterers went *up*; in three others, assaults by arrested batterers went *down*—a little bit (Maxwell, Garner, and Fagan 1991, 1). However, when researchers reworked the data from the replication studies, they found the following:

■ Arresting batterers was related to fewer aggressive acts against female intimate partners.

■ Age and criminal history were more strongly related to future assaults than arrests.

■ Arrests reduced future aggression about equally in all locations.

■ Most suspects committed no new crimes against their original victim whether they were arrested or not.

■ There was no association between arresting the offender and an increased risk of subsequent aggression against women generally. (Maxwell, Garner, and Fagan 1991, 2)

5-8 The latest research on the effects of arrest on intimate partner violence

■ PROBLEM-ORIENTED AND COMMUNITY-ORIENTED POLICING

The improvements in patrol and criminal investigation and the effectiveness of crime-attack strategies are *real* but *limited*. Problem-oriented policing (POP) and community-oriented policing (COP) are ambitious efforts to go beyond these limits. **Problem-oriented policing** focuses on *solving problems* of crime, disorder, and fear by forming partnerships with residents, businesses, and other local agencies to get at the underlying causes of these problems. **Community-oriented policing** focuses on the *sources* of crime, disorder, fear of crime and disorder, and relations between police and the neighborhoods they police.

Think of problem-oriented and community-oriented policing not just as new strategies to control crime but as a whole new philosophy to improve the quality of neighborhood life. Police expert Professor Mark Moore (1992) says compared with patrol, criminal investigation, and crime-attack strategies, problem-oriented and community-oriented policing provide police with "broader opportunities to prevent and control crime *and* to promote security and ease some of the danger, pain, and frustration of living in today's cities" (127).

Problem-oriented Policing

Problem-oriented policing consists of several elements:

1. The focus is to solve *problems,* not just settle *incidents.*
2. Problems include not just specific crimes but also disorder, fear, and other threats to the quality of neighborhood life.
3. Police try to form partnerships with residents, businesses, and other agencies to identify and solve problems. (Figure 5.2)

"Problems" alludes to more than the incident of the moment, such as a loud party or the burglary of a particular house. Police are more likely to view a series of burglaries on a particular street or ongoing loud parties in a large apartment complex near a college as "problems." Here's a description of one partnership to identify and solve one problem:

In the spring of 1985, Gainesville, Florida, was hit by a rash of convenience store robberies. The police thought the robberies were the work of one or two repeat offenders. A review of suspect descriptions proved otherwise: many different offenders were suddenly knocking over convenience stores. Officers assigned to analyze this problem observed that the convenience stores that were being robbed differed from the others in that their interiors (and particularly their cash registers) were less visible from the street, tended to hold more cash in their registers, and were staffed by only one person during the late night hours. They then interviewed offenders who had been convicted of convenience store robberies and learned that robbers always avoided convenience stores staffed by more than one clerk.

These findings were presented to an association of local merchants that had been formed to help deal with the problem. The police were surprised by the fact that the merchants rejected the police requests to change their practices to make their stores less vulnerable. Undeterred, the police designed a local ordinance requiring the owners to remove window advertising that blocked the view of the store's interior from the street, to place cash registers in full view of the street, to install security cameras in the store and outside lighting in the parking lot, to limit the amount of cash in the registers, and to staff the stores in late night hours with two employees trained in crime prevention techniques. Despite continuing opposition from the merchants, the City Commission approved the ordinance. Following the implementation of the ordinance, robberies fell 65 percent overall, and 75 percent at night. (Eck and Spelman 1987, 4–5)

FIGURE 5.2
**Groups Police Met with to
Discuss Problems, 1999**
SOURCE: Bureau of Justice Statistics,
2001b, Figure 4.

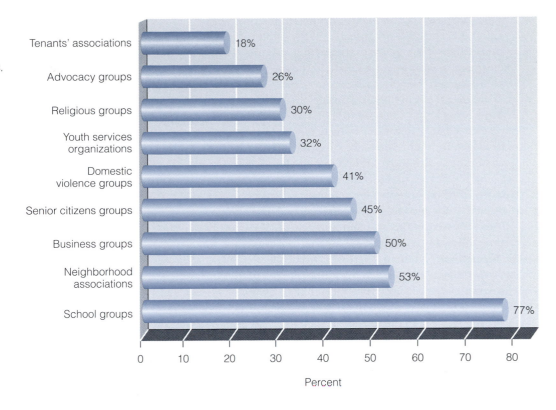

Tenants' associations	18%
Advocacy groups	26%
Religious groups	30%
Youth services organizations	32%
Domestic violence groups	41%
Senior citizens groups	45%
Business groups	50%
Neighborhood associations	53%
School groups	77%

Percent

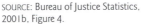 **5-9 You Decide: Is problem-oriented policing good
policy?**

Community-oriented Policing

The idea of community-oriented policing is that partnerships between police and the community can help reduce crime and increase security. It emphasizes that residents are the main line of defense against crime, disorder, fear, and the deterioration of the quality of life in their neighborhoods. So, in community-oriented policing, residents identify and participate in the solutions to the problems in their neighborhood. When police talk to residents, they find residents don't always put serious crime at the top of their list of concerns; they often say fear is as important as victimization, and what to police seems like minor stuff (kids hanging out on corners, drunks in the street, and graffiti) usually triggers their fear more than serious crime (Moore 1992, 123). (In Chapter 4, see the "broken windows" discussion in the Order Maintenance section.)

Crime control isn't the only mission in community-oriented policing; so is community satisfaction and harmony. This doesn't mean police do whatever neighborhood residents want. Suppose angry neighbors want to drive a suspected child molester out of the neighborhood. The police can't allow it because they have to up-

hold the suspect's rights. Police can't just listen to the most outspoken individuals or groups in the neighborhood either. The "squeaky wheel" doesn't "get the grease" in community-oriented policing unless the police believe it should. And, residents have to help in the solutions too. They can't just nominate a problem and expect the police to solve it alone. So, police listen to neighborhood demands, but they don't (and shouldn't) automatically give in to them (Moore 1992, 123).

Here's an excellent example of community-oriented policing:

> In New York in April 1987, a representative of a tenants' association called a Community Patrol Officer with specific information about drug dealers and locations in the housing project in which he lived. The informant complained that the building was inundated with dealers and purchasers who occupied apartments and loitered in the halls making deals. The building's residents were frightened and frustrated, as were other members of the community. . . . The officer's first move was to call a meeting with the tenants' association. There was a good turnout of the residents, and the officer initiated a discussion in which conditions in the building were described clearly. He insisted that no specific details be given or accusations made, however, since some of the building's drug dealers were attending in order to observe and intimidate the others. . . . The meeting showed clearly that most of the building's

residents shared a common attitude toward the problem, but that, because drug dealing is illegal, it is the responsibility of the police department to eliminate it. Their demand was clear; they wanted the police to clean up the building by more frequent patrolling and evictions or arrests of the drug dealers.

The officer believed it essential that he convince the tenants they could not wait passively for the problem to be solved for them, but had to become active participants in the solution. He argued that the police could not possibly devote to one building as much time and attention as these tenants were requesting. He explained that the building's residents needed to act not only as reporters of the problem, but also to take some responsibility for eliminating it. The officer suggested the formation of a tenants' patrol . . . to supplement police activity and promised his support of the patrol. The tenants came around; they formed their own patrol unit.

Within two weeks the tenants' association had been transformed from a rather limited and fragmented organization to a far more cohesive and powerful group. The association established an around-the-clock patrol of the building, which monitored and recorded the presence of every person who entered it. . . . The officer conducted vertical patrols of the building five or six times a day . . . and regularly informed special narcotics units in the Police Department about the situation. In addition, he met with representatives of the Department of Housing Preservation and Development, the local City Councilman, the Bureau of Family Services. . . . These different resources collaborated in providing information to the tenants, worked on renovating apartments, and assisted in responsibly choosing future tenants in order to assure that the problem would not simply begin again with new faces when the present dealers were evicted. (Vera Institute of Justice 1988, 11–12)

Does community-oriented policing work? That is, does it reduce crime, disorder, and fear and improve the quality of life in neighborhoods where it's adopted? It's hard to say. For one thing, no department has fully implemented community-oriented policing. This is probably because it's such a major change that it takes years, maybe even decades, to implement. Still, some evaluations are somewhat encouraging. For example, one experiment in community crime prevention was found to have reduced burglaries; another reduced burglaries and robberies and increased residents' sense of security (Rosenbaum 1986).

Knowledge and Understanding Check

Patrol: The backbone of policing
- ✔ List and briefly describe the four stages of police patrol mobilization.

Types of patrol
- ✔ Define and list the strengths and weaknesses of preventive patrol.
- ✔ Summarize the findings and explain the importance of the Kansas City Preventive Patrol Experiment.
- ✔ Explain the differences between reactive and proactive policing.
- ✔ Describe response time, differential response, foot patrol, and one-officer patrol.
- ✔ Summarize the findings of the evaluations of response time, differential response, foot patrol, and one-officer patrol.

Criminal investigation
- ✔ Distinguish between preliminary and follow-up investigations.
- ✔ Explain the significance of the evaluations of both.

- ✔ List the three kinds of facts collected for incident reports.
- ✔ Who is mainly responsible for preliminary investigations?
- ✔ Describe the major findings of empirical research regarding follow-up investigation.

Proactive policing
- ✔ List and describe the crime-attack strategies discussed in this section.
- ✔ Summarize and explain the significance of these crime-attack strategies.

Problem-oriented and community-oriented policing
- ✔ List and describe the characteristics of problem-oriented policing.
- ✔ List and describe the characteristics of community-oriented policing.
- ✔ Do problem-oriented policing and community-oriented policing work? Explain.

KEY TERMS

community-oriented policing
DARE
differential response
diffusion of benefits
displacement
field interrogation

hot spots patrol
incident reports
Kansas City Preventive Patrol
  Experiment
mobilize
police crackdowns

preliminary investigations
preventive patrol
proactive patrol
problem-oriented policing
reactive patrol

INTERNET PROJECT

 Deepen your understanding of problem- and community-oriented policing. Enter the key words "community oriented policing," "community policing," and "problem oriented policing." List what you think are the main points you learned that added to your understanding of and the effectiveness of these strategies.

CHAPTER 6

Police and the Law

© Ted Spiegel/Corbis

CHAPTER OUTLINE

> Courts offer to police the opportunity, if they wish to take advantage of it, to seek the state's capacity to punish. In effect, the courts say to the police that if they wish to make use of that capacity, they must demonstrate to the courts that they have followed certain procedures in order to do so. . . . Only on those occasions that the police wish to employ the state's capacity to punish do courts and police have any relationship of any kind. Despite the enormous growth in police law in the past quarter century, the courts have no more "control" over the police than local supermarkets have over the diets of those who shop there.
>
> **CARL B. KLOCKARS, POLICE EXPERT (1991B, 532)**

■ INTRODUCTION

Police officers don't usually take advantage of the opportunity to bring cases to prosecutors, as discussed by Professor Klockars in the opening quotation. One year, half the officers assigned to a high-crime neighborhood in New York City didn't make a single felony arrest; 68 percent made only three. Sociologist Donald Black (1980) found officers usually don't arrest suspected violent felons even when they've got plenty of evidence. So, police, the gatekeepers to the criminal justice system, don't usually open the gates to criminal prosecution. Instead, they exercise their discretionary decision making against starting the formal criminal justice process. This shouldn't surprise us or lead us to conclude that the police aren't doing their job. Remember, maintaining order and providing 24/7 services take up most of their time (Chapter 4).

■ LAW ENFORCEMENT AND THE CONSTITUTION

Under our constitutional system, police can't on a hunch interfere with our rights to come and go as we please and be let alone by the government. They have to back up their interferences with facts. We call this requirement the **objective basis**. So, when police officers stop, search, arrest, interrogate, and conduct lineups they have to back them up with an objective basis. Getting evidence and backing up how they got it allows plenty of room for informal decision making by individual officers. But, it's limited by the formal requirements of the U.S. Constitution.

It's no exaggeration to say information controls the *formal* criminal justice process. Naturally, the police would like the power to manage the discovery and the use of this information. Suspects and defendants, of course, would like to manage if, when, what, and how the police get the information. And innocent people, understandably, don't want to be arrested, searched, put in jail, interrogated, or stand in lineups unless the police can objectively justify their right to interfere with their liberty, privacy, and property.

The U.S. Supreme Court settles conflicts between the need to get information to enforce the criminal law and the rights of individuals to come and go as they please and to be let alone by the government—a balance created by the U.S. Constitution. We're concerned with four provisions in the Constitution the Court has to settle disputes over:

- *Fourth Amendment:* The right of the people to be secure in their persons, houses, papers, and effects against unreasonable searches and seizures shall not be violated, and no warrants shall issue but upon probable cause, supported by oath or affirmation, and particularly describing the place to be searched and the persons or things to be seized.
- *Fifth Amendment:* No person . . . shall be compelled in any criminal case to be a witness against himself, nor be deprived of life, liberty, or property, without due process of law. . . .
- *Sixth Amendment:* In all criminal prosecutions, the accused shall enjoy the right . . . to be confronted with the witnesses against him . . . and to have the assistance of counsel for his defense.
- *Fourteenth Amendment:* No state shall make or enforce any law which shall abridge the privileges or immunities of citizens of the United States; nor shall any state deprive any person of life, liberty, or property, without due process of law; nor deny to any person within its jurisdiction the equal protection of the laws.

YOU DECIDE

Should the right against "unreasonable seizures" be reduced during emergencies?

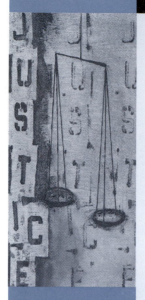

In the first few weeks after the September 11, 2001, attacks on the World Trade Center and the Pentagon, the FBI began an investigation and search for the killers. Within days, the FBI had arrested and detained as many as one thousand people on minor traffic and immigration violations and as "material witnesses" who weren't charged with any crime. The government conducted proceedings connected with the detentions in secret on the ground that it was necessary to protect the country and not tip their hand to other attackers.

Consider the following episodes involving arrests, detentions, and secret proceedings.

1. Hani Khoury, an immigration attorney in Hackensack, N.J., represents two neighbors of men detained in the case. Both were detained without bond because they overstayed their visas. "In the nine years I've been practicing, I've never seen them hold a non-criminal overstay for ten days," Khoury said. "You know, they generally just hold them, if they hold them, a day, two at most."

2. In Jersey City, Sousan Achou's husband, Abdoul Salam Achou, was detained after authorities raided the apartment next door. She said her spouse, whose visa expired September 1, was being held at the local jail. Since the raid on September 15, Sousan Achou said, she has been able to visit with her husband once, but she has no idea when or if he will be released. She said it took more than a week to find out where he was being held.

3. In Oklahoma City, immigration lawyer Mitchell Gray had difficulty meeting with Hussein al-Attas, a 23-year-old Saudi detained for alleged visa problems. Al-Attas, a student at the University of Oklahoma until May, reportedly is a former roommate of Zacarias Moussaoui, a suspected terrorist. Gray was asked to represent al-Attas by a friend, but he said the INS barred him from contact because he could not produce a form signed by al-Attas to authorize

the representation. The problem, said Gray, was that the INS refused to let him see al-Attas in order to show him the form. "I talked to the INS several times, and nobody would tell me where he was," said Gray. "They said, 'Do you have a G-28 signed by this man? We can't let you see him without a G-28.' Well, how can I get a G-28 signed unless I see him?"

4. In Orlando, a man who runs a check cashing and international money transfer business was arrested as a material witness. Asserting a need for secrecy, authorities didn't confirm the man's identity and erased his name from jail records. After a quick secret hearing before a U.S. magistrate, the man was held for three days in the Seminole County Jail. Then, in the middle of tight security—which included a 4 A.M. ride from the jail to the federal courthouse in Orlando—he was taken to another secret hearing, flown to New York to testify before a grand jury, and then released. "We have every reason to believe he is not guilty of a crime," said Joe Palmer, chief investigator for the Federal Public Defender's Office, which represented the Orlando man. "This is an innocent citizen the government believes has some information critical to the investigation."

5. Albader Al-Hazmi's lawyer, Gerald H. Goldstein, said his client was held incommunicado after his arrest as a material witness right after the attack. It took six days for his lawyer to get to see him. "This is a good lesson about how frail our processes are," Goldstein said. "It's how we treat people in difficult times like these that is the true test of the democracy and civil liberties that we brag so much about throughout the world." (Slevin and Sheridan 2001, A10)

Some experts contend the horrible nature of the attacks justifies these actions. Others argue this could

---

 6-1 "Arrest for minor offense to investigate serious crime"

■ ARREST

Arrests are one kind of seizure in the Fourth Amendment ban on "unreasonable seizures" of persons. What's an unreasonable seizure? The U.S. Supreme Court has filled

many pages in its written decisions trying to answer this complicated question. But, for us, the answer boils down to this. Most arrests are reasonable if officers:

1. Back them up with probable cause.
2. Get a warrant before they go into a house to arrest someone.
3. Don't use excessive force to make the arrest. (See the "Excessive Force" section)

deny individuals the right to bail and to a lawyer. The government responds that it has to keep the proceedings secret to protect innocent people and not tip off other attackers.

Now consider these comments from lawyers and journalists:

1. Jeanne Butterfield, director of the American Immigration Lawyers Association, expressed concern that attorneys and legal aid organizations have not heard of many people seeking counsel. "That leads me to believe they have not been allowed to contact lawyers, or they don't know what lawyer to contact," she said.

2. Justice Department spokesperson Susan Dryden said that everyone arrested on a criminal charge or as a material witness is told of their right to a lawyer and to appointed counsel if they are indigent.

3. Immigration and Naturalization Service spokesperson Russ Bergeron said every detainee is given a list of attorneys and support organizations. But he pointed out that people held for administrative violations don't have a right to free counsel.

4. Attorney General John D. Ashcroft reported (on September 25, 2001) that 352 people were being held as part of the investigation. Of that number, 98 were being detained on suspicion of violating immigration laws, while 254 were held on other charges, including traffic offenses, misdemeanors, and identification fraud.

5. A former Deputy Attorney General said, "It's really just a question of degree. You're talking about the largest criminal investigation in the history of the United States." They're using tactics that have been used in other cases, but on a much smaller scale."

6. A group of lawyers and legal scholars said they couldn't remember when so many people had been arrested and held without bond on charges—particularly minor charges—unrelated to what the gov-

ernment was really arresting them for. However, they pointed out, the Supreme Court permits such detentions when authorities believe an individual has information important to another case.

7. Beth Wilkinson, who prosecuted Oklahoma City bomber Timothy McVeigh, said, "It is not inappropriate to detain people for legitimate violations. The Supreme Court in prior cases has allowed law enforcement to arrest people for relatively minor violations when they were investigating larger crimes."

8. *Washington Post* reporters said the Justice Department is using a section of the criminal code to arrest material witnesses—"individuals who may have significant information about the attack. Even if not a suspect in a crime, the person may be held without bond if a court rules that nothing else will guarantee that the witness will be available to supply essential testimony."

9. The same reporters wrote, "The detention of material witnesses was considered startling in 1995, when prosecutors in the Oklahoma City case used the tactic. It has been used since, lawyers say, but until now typically involved the arrest of very small numbers of people." (Slevin and Sheridan 2001, A10)

Questions

1. List and rank the seriousness of the restrictions placed on these arrested individuals' freedom and rights. Explain your ranking.

2. Summarize the points and arguments of the lawyers and journalists. Which do you agree with? Why? Which do you disagree with? Why?

3. How much should government be able to limit people's rights against unreasonable seizures (arrests) and to see a lawyer in times of national security? Defend your answer.

The Definition of Arrest

Police actions affecting our right to come and go as we please include everything from voluntary encounters to locking people up in jail without their consent. **Arrest**—seizing people by taking them into custody without their consent—is only one of these encounters. An officer who comes up to you and asks you questions has *not* arrested you. An officer who comes up to you and says "You're

under arrest," takes you to the station, books you, and locks you up overnight *has* arrested you. But, you're protected by the Fourth Amendment in the second example (the officer has to show probable cause); in the first example you're not. In the second, the officer is exercising discretionary decision making, which is another way of saying officers are free to use to use their judgment without later review of their decisions.

How do we know when cases that don't fit so neatly into our two examples are arrests? The U.S. Supreme Court dealt with one of these harder cases in *Florida v. Royer* (1983). Two narcotics detectives went up to Mark Royer in the Miami, Florida, airport and asked him if he had a "moment" to talk to them. "Yes," Royer answered. The detectives identified themselves as narcotics officers and asked Royer to go with them to a "large storage closet," about 40 feet away. Royer followed them without saying anything. Fifteen minutes later, after they searched Royer's luggage and found marijuana in it, the officers told Royer he was "under arrest."

Was Royer arrested *before* the officers told him he was under arrest? According to the Supreme Court:

> Law enforcement officers do not violate the Fourth Amendment by merely approaching an individual on the street or in another public place, by asking him if he is willing to answer some questions, by putting questions to him if the person is willing to listen. . . . Nor would the fact that the officer identifies himself as a police officer, without more, convert the encounter to a seizure. . . . But . . . what had begun as a consensual inquiry in a public place had escalated into an investigatory procedure in a police interrogation room, where the police, unsatisfied with previous explanations, sought to confirm their suspicions. The officers had Royer's ticket, they had his identification, and they had seized his luggage. Royer was never informed that he was free to board his plane if he so chose, and he reasonably believed that he was being detained. At least as of that moment, any consensual aspects of the encounter had evaporated. . . . As a practical matter Royer was under arrest.

The dissent read the facts differently:

> The [Court] concludes that somewhere between the beginning of the forty-foot journey and the resumption of the conversation in the room the investigation became so intrusive that Royer's consent evaporated, leaving him as a practical matter under arrest. But if Royer was legally approached in the first instance and consented to accompany the detectives to the room, it does not follow that his consent went up in smoke and he was arrested upon entering the room. . . . Royer, who was in his fourth year of study at Ithaca College . . . simply continued to cooperate with the detectives as he had from the beginning of the encounter.

 6-2 Full opinion in *Florida v. Royer*

Probable Cause

The Fourth Amendment says arrests are unreasonable unless officers back them up with probable cause. **Probable**

cause to arrest means there are enough facts and circumstances for a reasonable officer in light of her expertise to believe the person arrested has committed, is committing, or is about to commit a crime. Probable cause is more than a hunch, but it's not proof beyond a reasonable doubt (Chapter 8) or even the probability the person is more guilty than not. Practically speaking, arrest lets officers "freeze" a situation to give prosecutors time to decide if there's enough evidence to charge suspects.

 6-3 You Decide: Did the officers have probable cause to arrest?

■ SEARCHES

The right against unreasonable searches is ancient. In 57 B.C., Cicero spoke of citizens' homes as "sacred." Under Byzantine Emperor Justinian's Code of A.D. 533, a "freeman could not be summoned from his house" because it is "everyone's safest place, his refuge, and his shelter." In 1505, John Fineux, chief justice of the English Court of King's, held "the house of a man is for him his castle and his defense" (Cuddihy 1990, xc–xcvi).

But, the *power* of government to search is as much a part of history as is the lofty rhetoric claiming the *right* against unreasonable searches. Most of the early controversy over searches in England was about religion and politics. When Catholics were in power they ransacked the houses of Protestants to find proof of their blasphemy; when Protestants were in power they did the same to Catholics' houses. When subjects criticized the kings and queens, their ministers ransacked the subjects' houses looking for "seditious libels." (Seditious libels are written criticisms of the government.) No one cared much about the rights of ordinary criminals—the subject of our book; the power to search them and their "houses, papers, and effects" (to use the words of the Fourth Amendment) was pretty much unlimited.

In the 1700s, the numbers of seditious libels increased because of the low respect the English had for their imported German kings, the four Georges. The kings granted general warrants (blank checks good for the life of the king issued to officials) authorizing their officers to break into shops and homes to look for seditious libels. General warrants also became a weapon in the war against smuggling a growing list of taxable goods—most of them very popular, like salt, beer, and cider—into the American colonies. The use of general warrants provoked William Pitt in 1777 to speak the most famous words ever uttered against the power of government to search the houses of its people:

> The poorest man may in his cottage bid defiance to all the forces of the Crown. It may be frail; its roof may shake; the wind may blow through it; the storm may

enter; but the king of England may not enter; all his force dare not cross the threshold of the ruined tenement without a lawfull warrant. (Hall 1993, 4)

In the British American colonies, the great colonial trial lawyer James Otis argued a famous general warrant case in Boston in 1760. He claimed the general warrants were illegal; only searches with specific dates, naming the places or persons to be searched and seized, and based on probable cause were lawful where free people lived. The future president John Adams was at the trial. Many years later Adams recalled how moved he was by Otis's words: "There was the Child Independence born" (Smith 1962, 56). Hostility to general warrants led to the adoption of the Fourth Amendment. But, remember the opposition was about their use in religion, politics, and taxation—not what we call ordinary crime.

The Fourth Amendment "unreasonable searches" clause limits the power of law enforcement to get information to control crime, but it still leaves the government with plenty of power. According to former prosecutor John Wesley Hall, Jr. (1993):

> The raw power held by a police officer conducting a search is enormous. An officer wielding a search warrant has the authority of the law to forcibly enter one's home and search for evidence. The officer can enter at night and wake you from your sleep, roust you from bed, rummage in your drawers and papers and upend your entire home. . . . The power of an officer conducting a stop or warrantless search is also quite intense. Nothing can be more intimidating or frightening to a citizen than being stopped by the police and being asked or told to submit to a search. (ix)

The Definition of Search

Wherever people have a *reasonable* expectation of privacy, government intrusions are **searches.** Remember, the Fourth Amendment only bans *unreasonable* searches. What's a reasonable expectation of privacy is left to the Supreme Court to decide on a case-by-case basis. In *Katz v. U.S.* (1967), FBI agents bugged a public telephone booth to listen to bookie Charles Katz giving odds on college football games in his gambling operation. According to the U.S. Supreme Court, "One who occupies a public telephone booth, shuts the door, and pays the toll that permits him to place a call is entitled to assume that his conversation is not being intercepted."

This sounds like a boost for privacy, but the Court has defined narrowly what a reasonable expectation of privacy is. According to the Court, *none* of the following is a search, so each depends on the discretion of individual law enforcement officers:

- Looking for evidence in plain view
- Obtaining bank records, including savings and checking accounts and loans
- Going through trash looking for criminal evidence
- Wiring a paid informant for sound so law enforcement officers can listen to conversations

According to the **plain view doctrine,** it's not a search if officers' discovery of evidence meets three conditions:

1. Officers discover the evidence by means of their *ordinary* senses—sight, smell, hearing, and touch.
2. Officers discover the evidence *inadvertently.*
3. Officers have a right to be where they are and are doing what they have a right to do.

Applying these conditions, the U.S. Supreme Court decided that it was a plain view search when officers stopped a car for running a red light and saw a plastic bag of marijuana on the front seat. But it wasn't a plain view search when officers used a high-powered telescope to see into the apartment of a suspect hundreds of feet away or turned a TV set upside down to get its serial number and check to see if it was stolen. Why? According to the Court, the first was a plain view search because officers discovered the marijuana by their ordinary sense of sight while they were doing what they had a right to do in a place they had a right to be. In the second case, officers relied on a technological enhancement of their sense of sight to look into the apartment. In the third case, the discovery wasn't accidental: they had to upend the TV to get the serial number.

In *Kyllo v. U.S.* (2001), the Court decided it *was* a search when officers parked outside Danny Kyllo's house and employed a thermal imaging device to detect heat lamps he used to grow marijuana in his house. By a bare majority of 5–4, the Court decided the home is a special place where the reasonable expectation of privacy is so high officers need a warrant to sit outside and point the device at someone's home.

> 6-4 Transcript of the oral arguments before the U.S. Supreme Court and the Court's entire opinion in *Kyllo v. U.S.*

The Meaning of Unreasonable Search

Like the question of what's an unreasonable arrest, the question of what's an unreasonable search is complicated, and the answer fills even more pages of the Supreme Court's written decisions. But for us, the answer boils down to this. In the everyday work of police officers, searches are reasonable if they:

1. Back them up with probable cause
2. Get a warrant before they search houses
3. Get consent to search if they don't have probable cause or want to search a house without a warrant

Probable cause to search is similar to probable cause to arrest except the facts and circumstances have to support a reasonable belief officers will find evidence of crime, weapons, or contraband on the person or places they search.

Searches of houses are reasonable only if officers get warrants and in most cases only if they knock, announce their presence, and give occupants a chance to get to the door before they go in. They don't have to wait long because suspects might run out the back door, grab a weapon, and/or destroy evidence or contraband. So, according to the **knock-and-announce rule,** a search is reasonable if officers get a warrant; knock on the door saying, "Open up, police"; wait 10 seconds; knock down the door; enter; and arrest the suspect (*Wilson v. Arkansas* 1995).

However, officers don't always have to follow the knock-and-announce rule. According to the U.S. Supreme Court: "The Fourth Amendment's flexible requirement of reasonableness should not be read to mandate a rigid rule of announcement that ignores countervailing law enforcement interests. . . ." There are three exceptions to the rule: when there's a threat of violence; when officers are in hot pursuit of a fleeing suspected felon; and when there's a threat that occupants will destroy evidence (*Wilson v. Arkansas* 1995).

 6-5 Full opinion in *Wilson v. Arkansas*

Officers don't need either probable cause or warrants if the person they search consents to the search. According to the **consent search rule,** you can give up your right against unreasonable searches—but only if you do it voluntarily. In the leading U.S. Supreme Court consent search case, *Schneckloth v. Bustamonte* (1973), police officers didn't have either a warrant or probable cause to search a car so they asked if it was "okay to look in the trunk of the car."

"Sure, go ahead," the driver said.

The Court ruled the consent was voluntary, so the Fourth Amendment warrant and probable cause requirements didn't kick in. The dissent argued consent searches are only legal if officers warn people they have a right to say no to the search (like the *Miranda* warnings discussed later on). Why? Because to ordinary people, requests by police officers are really polite commands backed up by the power to use force.

 6-6 Complete opinion in *Schneckloth v. Bustamonte*

Stop and Frisk

Stopping suspicious persons and demanding to know who they are and why they're out and about is an old practice. Ancient statutes and court decisions empow-ered English constables to detain "suspicious nightwalkers" and hold them until morning to investigate their suspicious behavior. We've already learned about this old practice in its modern form—the proactive police strategy of field interrogation (Chapter 5). The legal term for field interrogation is stop and frisk. **Fourth Amendment stops** are briefer detentions than arrests, and they take place in public; **Fourth Amendment frisks** consist of outer clothing pat downs for weapons and are less invasive than full-body searches. Constitutionally, stops are Fourth Amendment seizures and frisks are Fourth Amendment searches. Stops and frisks that begin and end on the street are a lot more frequent than arrests, which take suspects to the station. For example, the New York City Police Department recorded 175,000 stops between January 1998 and March 1999; only 19,000 of these stops led to arrests (Spitzer 1999, 112).

6-7 NYPD's "Stop and Frisk Practices" and a critical review of the practices

The objective basis for backing up stops and frisks is less than probable cause; it's called reasonable suspicion. **Reasonable suspicion to stop** consists of facts and circumstances that would lead a reasonable officer in the light of her training and experience to *suspect* that a crime *might* be afoot. Compare this definition with probable cause, which requires enough facts and circumstances to *believe* that a crime *is* being committed. "Suspect" isn't as strong a conclusion as "belief"; and "might" isn't as certain as "is." **Reasonable suspicion to frisk** consists of facts and circumstances that would lead an officer to suspect that a person lawfully stopped might be armed (*Terry v. Ohio* 1968).

■ INTERROGATION

According to the Fifth Amendment, "[N]o person shall be compelled in any criminal case to be a witness against himself." Supporters of interrogation believe a safe society depends on questioning suspects. Critics argue a free society doesn't convict people with evidence out of their own mouths. Supporters of interrogation reply interrogation doesn't just convict the guilty, it frees the innocent, too. Critics argue police use unethical tactics like lying, deceit, and tricks to get confessions; officers reply interrogating criminal suspects isn't (and shouldn't be treated like) a conversation between friends and pressure isn't the same as force.

Empirical data will probably never fully resolve this debate, partly because we don't know what really goes on in interrogation rooms. According to U.S. Supreme Court Chief Justice Earl Warren, an experienced former prosecutor, "Interrogation takes place in privacy. Privacy results in secrecy and this in turn results in a gap in our knowledge as to what in fact goes on in the interrogation room." Fortunately, sociologist Richard Leo's (1996) research has begun to close the gap. After spending more than five hundred hours inside the interrogation rooms of a major urban police department and analyzing videotaped custodial interrogations from two other departments, Leo made the following important findings:

- Very few interrogations are coercive.
- One in five suspects invokes one or more *Miranda* rights to avoid cooperating with the police.
- Interrogators use tactics advocated in police training manuals (fabricated evidence, "good guy–bad guy") to undermine the confidence of suspects and overbear their rational decision making.
- Interrogators have become increasingly skilled in eliciting incriminating evidence during custodial interrogation.
- The overwhelming majority of custodial interrogations last less than one hour.
- Suspects who provide incriminating information are likely to be treated differently at every stage of the criminal process from suspects who don't. (1996, 266, 302)

Miranda v. Arizona

In one of the most famous cases in U.S. Supreme Court history, *Miranda v. Arizona* (1996), the Court decided police have to give suspects in custody four warnings before they interrogate them: (1) You have a right to remain silent; (2) anything you say will be used against you; (3) you have a right to a lawyer; and, (4) if you can't afford a lawyer one will be provided for you.

"*Miranda* has become embedded in routine police practice to the point where the warnings have become part of our national culture," said Chief Justice of the U.S. Supreme Court William Rehnquist on June 26, 2000. What was the occasion for the Chief Justice's comment? He was reading the Court's decision in *Dickerson v. U.S.* (2000), a case that decided whether Congress had overstepped its power when it overruled *Miranda v. Arizona* in 1968. In that year, in a burst of "get tough on criminals" legislation, Congress overruled the requirement that police officers had to give the now famous warnings. The law was ignored until 1997 when a Virginia federal court relied on the statute to admit Charles Dickerson's confession, obtained by FBI agents after giving him defective warnings. The 1968 law, the 1997 case relying on it, and the Supreme Court's decision declaring the law unconstitutional are part of a long and impassioned debate over the right against self-incrimination (Levy 1968).

6-8 *Miranda* and *Dickerson*

Miranda is part of our culture, but it's also part of our culture wars. Perhaps no procedure has generated more hostility among the public. On *NYPD Blue,* the good cops, Andy Sipowitz and his partner, wage an unrelenting "war on *Miranda.*" In almost every episode, a "scumbag" murderer—or his lawyer—makes a "mockery of the system" by taunting the cops with his rights. Then Sipowitz and his partner threaten, shove, and often beat a confession out of the "worthless animal" called a suspect. We all know he's guilty (it's always a man), and we're invited to hate not just the murderer but also the system that gives rights to such lowlifes.

This pop culture picture of saintly cops handcuffed by *Miranda* in their war against satanic criminals hides the complexity of the real picture of interrogation in at least three ways. First, police don't have to warn suspects unless they do two things: take them into custody (almost always the police station) *and* interrogate them. Second, most suspects talk even when they've been warned. Third, police coercion has to *cause* suspects to incriminate themselves.

The Voluntariness of Confessions

Remember the Fifth Amendment bans *compelling* suspects to confess. A confession is only compelled if the facts of the case prove (1) *coercion* by law enforcement officers and (2) a *causal link*—that is, coercion by law enforcement officers has to cause the incriminating statements.

According to Chief Justice Rehnquist in an important confession case, *Colorado v. Connelly* (1986):

> Cases considered by this Court over . . . 50 years . . . have focused on the crucial element of police overreaching. While each confession case has turned on its own set of factors justifying the conclusion that police conduct was oppressive, all have contained a substantial element of coercive police conduct. Absent police conduct causally related to the confession, there is simply no basis for concluding that any state actor has deprived a criminal defendant of due process of law. . . . As interrogators have turned to more subtle forms of psychological persuasion, courts have found the mental condition of the defendant a more significant factor in the "voluntariness" calculus. But this fact does not justify a conclusion that a defendant's mental condition, by itself apart from its relation to official coercion, should ever dispose of the inquiry into constitutional "voluntariness."

6-9 You Decide: Should officers be allowed to use force in interrogating September 11 suspects?

IDENTIFICATION PROCEDURES

In most cases, proving a crime was committed is easier than identifying the perpetrator. But not always. Some suspects are caught red-handed; victims and witnesses personally know other suspects; and others confess. Technological advances have led to the increasing use of novel scientific evidence to identify criminals. For example, bite-mark evidence helped convict the notorious serial rapist and murderer Ted Bundy. Fiber evidence helped convict Wayne Williams of the murders of 2 of 30 murdered young Blacks in Atlanta. Still, the best known is DNA (deoxyribonucleic acid) testing, which lifts samples of body fluid from the victim, much like lifting fingerprints, and then matches these samples with the body fluids of the suspect. Although best known for proving the innocence of convicted people, it's also a means for proving the guilt of defendants.

The Dangers of Mistaken Identifications

According to one expert, faulty identifications present the "greatest single threat to the achievement of our ideal that no innocent man shall be punished." Best guesses are eyewitness error accounts for half of all wrongful convictions. In one famous example (*National Law Journal* 1979, 1), seven eyewitnesses swore Bernard Pagano, a Roman Catholic priest, robbed them with a small, chrome-plated pistol. In the middle of Pagano's trial, Ronald Clouser admitted that he, not Father Pagano, had committed the robberies. Improper suggestion by law enforcement officers probably accounts for some errors. But, according to widely accepted findings of psychologists (Note 1977, 970), the biggest problem is we're just not very good observers, and our memories too often add to our inaccurate observations. This is particularly true when we're under stress, which most crime victims are.

Psychologists have known for more than a century that the eye isn't like a video camera that records exact images on the brain. Cameras have no expectations; people do. And their expectations influence what they *think* they see. Add to these problems the troubling finding of psychologists that we're even worse at identifying strangers of a different race. Blacks can identify Whites better than Whites can identify members of other races, because Whites are more prone to the "they all look alike" phenomenon. In one famous experiment, researchers showed observers a photo of a White man brandishing a razor blade in an altercation with a Black man on a subway. When asked immediately afterward to describe what they saw, over half the observers reported that the Black man was carrying the weapon (Note 1977, 982).

Memory fades over time, and it fades most in the first few hours after seeing a stranger and then remains stable for several months. What happens after seeing the stranger can dramatically alter what witnesses remember seeing; they can be highly susceptible to the power of suggestion. The mind stores all information about an event—whether it was learned at the time of the event or later—in the same "bin." According to the highly respected eyewitness research expert Elizabeth Loftus, in a study she conducted witnesses embellished their stories depending on how she described an incident. Later, they drew this information out of the bin during the identification process (Yant 1991, 91).

Steven Penrod, identification researcher at the University of Wisconsin, says this embellishment is natural. "A witness tells his story to the police, to the family, then to friends, then to the prosecutor." As the story gets retold, it becomes less reality and more legend. "Witnesses feel very confident about what they now think happened and that confidence is communicated to the jury" (Yant 1991, 100).

Unfortunately, witnesses' confidence about the image grows while their memory is fading. That false confidence is especially dangerous because witness confidence has such a strong effect on judges and juries. For once TV has it right: When the prosecutor asks, "Do you see who did this to you?" and the witness, pointing directly at the defendant, strongly proclaims, "There he is," it's usually all over.

Now add the pressure created by police lineups and photographic displays. Witnesses think the suspect *has* to be in the lineup or in the mug shots or the police wouldn't have bothered to call the witnesses in. So, they treat the procedure like multiple-choice tests without a "none of the above" choice. They're afraid they might look foolish if they "don't know the answer." Despite knowing of these problems, courts hardly ever reject eyewitness identification testimony.

The Supreme Court and Identification Procedures

In *Manson v. Brathwaite* (1977), the Court ruled that identification procedures violate the Constitution only if (1) the procedure was unnecessarily suggestive *and* (2) this caused a "very substantial likelihood of . . . misidentification."

 6-10 *Manson v. Brathwaite*

POLICE MISCONDUCT

Police misconduct can include everything from something as minor as accepting a free cup of coffee in a local restaurant to things as serious as arresting someone just because she's Hispanic and selling drugs. There are many explanations of police misconduct. First, there's the **rotten apple theory,** which says there are a few bad officers that recruitment and training can't identify. Second, there's the theory that some officers start out as idealists but become "bad" because of the socialization processes of training and field experiences (Chapter 4). Let's look at two kinds of police misconduct, use of excessive force and corruption, and the remedies for police misconduct.

Excessive Force

The defining characteristic of police is the **legitimate use of force** (Chapter 4). Police use legitimate force to gain control of resisting or fleeing suspects and to protect themselves or others from injury and death (Williams 1993, 5–6). **Excessive force** means officers use more than the amount of force necessary to get control of suspects and protect themselves and others. It is the *perception* of the use of excessive force that has contributed to some of the worst riots in American history—Harlem in 1935, Watts in 1965, Miami in 1980, and Los Angeles in 1992.

The police use of force against Rodney King and the riots sparked by the acquittal in 1992 of the officers who used that force brought out the public's mixed feelings about police use of force. We actually saw the police use force instead of just descriptions of it, because, by chance, a young guy trying out his new camcorder recorded a group of LAPD officers using clubs, boots, and other means to keep King down. Seeing the tape night after night on TV etched the picture in our minds. And it provoked a huge public debate over police use of force.

The beating, the acquittal, and the death and destruction caused by the riots brought out three points about police use of force:

1. The defining characteristic of police work—the *legitimate* use of coercive force—is critical to effective police work. (Chapter 4)
2. The need for *legitimate* force creates the central problem of police misconduct—the *excessive* use of force.
3. The *perception* of excessive force is held by many members of racial minority groups. (Kerstetter 1985, 149–182)

Bringing these points out into the open produced research showing us what we know—and *don't* know—about the kinds and amounts of force police use; about policies and practices regarding the use of force; and about the effectiveness of these policies and practices. But the debate over police use of force didn't begin with Rodney King. New York journalist Lincoln Steffens opened the twentieth century with a series of articles reporting the brutality of NYPD officer "Clubber Williams." In 1930, President Hoover's Wickersham Commission reported shocking abuses of police use of force. In 1967, President Johnson's Commission on Law Enforcement found some police were still abusing their power to use force. The debate started by Lincoln Steffens in 1900 continues in 2002, and I'm sure will continue for as long as there are police. Let's look at the types of police force and what the Constitution says about those uses.

Types of use of force

The respected Police Foundation conducted the most thorough study yet of the kinds and amounts of police use of force (Pate and Fridell 1993, 21–25, 73–78). Figure 6.1 shows the results of this survey.

The types of force we'll discuss include knockdown force, deadly force, and high-speed chases.

Knockdown Force   **Knockdown force** is enough force to "cause the suspect to fall to the ground." Greg Meyer (1991), a Los Angeles Police Department officer, examined the types of force used by LAPD officers, the success of each in getting control of suspects, and the injuries caused to officers and suspects by each. He found Tasers and chemical sprays, two types of knockdown force, are as (or more) effective than other kinds and also a lot safer. Meyer's data showed Tasers and tear gas didn't injure a single suspect or officer (Meyer 1991, 29). According to the Police Foundation, using more Tasers, stun guns, and tear gas would result in "fewer citizen injuries and deaths, fewer officer injuries and deaths, improved police-community relations, reduced exposure to departmental liability for wrongful police actions, and improved police morale" (Meyer 1991, 29).

Deadly Force   Police kill on average about 600 people every year, shoot and wound another 1200, and fire at, but miss, another 1800. However, the numbers vary from city to city and from neighborhood to neighborhood in the same city. For example, New Orleans police are 10 times more likely to kill people than Newark police. Chicago's near west side, for example, is 27 times more likely than the near north side to experience a police shooting in an average year. Deadly force not only kills suspects, officers die as well; 65 were killed in 1999. Contrary to what you might think, it's not always suspects who kill officers; they often die in friendly fire—officers accidentally shoot other officers (Geller and Scott 1992, 59–60; O'Donnell 1983, 14).

Departments that adopt strict deadly force rules and enforce them show steep drops in citizen *and* officer deaths. After the Kansas City, Missouri, department adopted a rule banning police from shooting juveniles except in self-defense, the number of youths under 18 shot by the police dropped dramatically. Former NYPD officer and now criminal justice professor James Fyfe showed that not only police shootings dropped sharply after the New York City Police Department adopted a rule, but the numbers of police *officers shot at* also

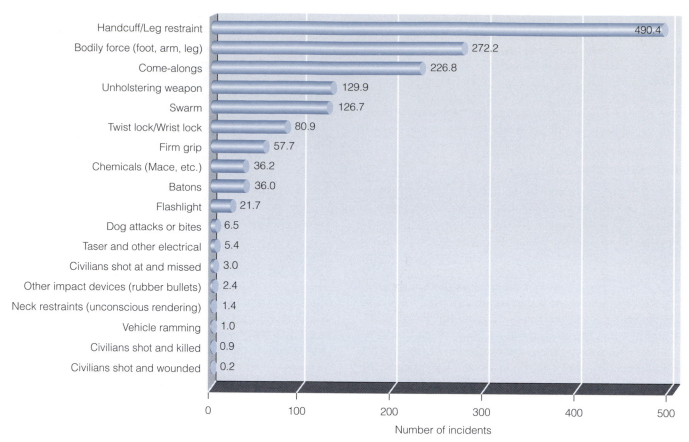

FIGURE 6.1
Types of Force Used by City Police
SOURCE: Pate and Fridell, 1993, based on Table 6.1.

dropped (*Criminal Justice Newsletter* 1996, 5; Geller 1985; Milton 1977, 10).

Formulating, implementing, and enforcing deadly force rules is difficult. Patrol officers suspect changes, and police unions fight them. Administrators don't want to put firearms policies in writing because they're worried about lawsuits. In fact, some courts have given them reason to worry. The California Supreme Court (*Grudt v. Los Angeles* 1970) allowed the LAPD written firearms policy to be used as evidence by a plaintiff who was suing an officer for wrongful death. (The officer had broken the deadly force rule.)

However, compared with the total number of contacts police have with individuals, shootings are rare. A study of New York City patrol officers found officers used force of all kinds in less than one-tenth of 1 percent of all encounters with private individuals. Civilians were shot at 5 of the 1762 times observers saw officers use any physical force (Geller and Scott 1992, 60). We have to be careful not to give the impression that rare means not serious because, of course, every death, every wound, even every miss is serious.

Does race play a differential role in the use of deadly force?

The most common type of incident in which police and civilians shoot one another in urban America involves an on-duty, uniformed, white, male officer and an armed, black, male civilian between the ages of 17 and 30 and occurs at night, in a public location in a high-crime precinct, in connection with a suspected armed robbery or a "man with a gun" call. (Geller and Scott 1992, 143)

Nearly all related studies report that the police shoot at more Blacks than Whites:

- Chicago police officers shot at Blacks 3.8 times more than at Whites during the 1970s.
- New York City police officers shot at Blacks 6 times more than at Whites during the 1970s.
- Dallas police officers shot at Blacks 4.5 times more than at Whites during the 1970s and 1980s.
- St. Louis police officers shot at Blacks 7.7 times more than at Whites from 1987 to 1991.
- Memphis police officers fatally shot at Blacks 5.1 more times than at Whites from 1969 to 1974; 2.6 times more from 1980 to 1984; and 1.6 times more from 1985 to 1989. They were 9.4 times more likely to shoot at Blacks than at Whites in relation to sus-

pected property crimes from 1969 to 1974 and 13 times more from 1980 to 1984; and Blacks were the only property crime suspects shot at from 1985 to 1989. (Geller and Scott 1992, 147–48)

Is the decision to shoot suspects infected with racism? The numbers definitely show there's a disparity between decisions to shoot Blacks and Whites. But we know *disparity* doesn't have to mean *discrimination*. The empirical research is mixed. In their widely cited *Split-Second Decisions,* when William A. Geller and Kevin J. Karales (1981, 119) controlled for violent felonies (murder, rape, armed robbery, and aggravated assault and battery) in decisions to shoot, racial disparities disappeared.

But, James Fyfe (1982, 707–722) found shooting data in Memphis showed race *did* infect decisions to shoot in some kinds of cases. The data strongly supported

> the assertion that police did differentiate racially with their trigger fingers, by shooting blacks in circumstances less threatening than those in which they shot whites. . . . [The] black death rate from police shootings while unarmed and non-assaultive (5.4 per 100,000) . . . 18 times higher than the comparable white rate (0.3). (715)

After Memphis police officer Elton Hymon shot and killed 13-year-old Edward Garner, Memphis adopted a strict shooting policy—police could only shoot to apprehend suspected "violent felons" who "posed a threat of serious physical harm to the officer or to others unless he is immediately apprehended." Jerry R. Sparger and David J. Giacopassi (1992) reviewed records of police shootings before and after the restriction. They found after the strict policy was adopted:

1. Overall police shootings dropped sharply.
2. Racial disparity in shootings almost disappeared.
3. Black deaths from police shootings declined.

However, they also found the *rate* of Black deaths from police shootings was still 56.5 percent higher than the rate for Whites (211–225). Also, few will disagree with the Black officer who voiced this opinion after the Rodney King case:

> There are many fine white officers who are doing their job and do not harbor racist sentiments. However, there is still a significant group of individuals whose old line, deep-seated biases continually manifest themselves on the job. (Christopher Commission 1991, 80)

High-Speed Chases

> During our years in police cars, we have been at the cop's end of more than thirty high-speed chases. Younger cops, hotshot cops, aggressive cops, relish the exhilaration of these pursuits. People who haven't rid-

den in patrol cars for a full shift cannot appreciate how tedious policing can be even in the world's most crime-ridden cities. Patrol policing, like military combat and the lives of cowboys, consists mostly of periods of boredom, broken up by interludes of excitement and even of terror. For police, a chase is among the most exciting of all work experiences: the sudden start of a chase is a jolt not unlike that experienced by the dozing fisherman who finds suddenly that he has a big and dangerous fish on the other end of his line. (Skolnick and Fyfe 1993, 11)

Why is the topic of high-speed chases in this section on police use of force? Because vehicles are deadly weapons that can hurt and kill people. According to police specialist Gordon E. Misner (1990), "If the circumstances don't reasonably permit the use of deadly force, they also do not warrant engaging in a high-speed chase!" (15).

Is the risk of injury and death worth the chase? Geoffrey P. Alpert and Roger G. Dunham (1990, 38; Alpert 1987, 298–306) found 54 percent of high-speed chases in Florida's Metro-Dade County Police Department were for traffic violations; 32 percent were for suspected felonies; 12 percent were because of calls "to be on the lookout for" a named suspect; and 2 percent were for driving while intoxicated (DWI). Accidents occurred in more than half the pursuits. But, Alpert also found many traffic violation chases produced arrests for unrelated serious felonies (Figure 6.2).

Still, Lee P. Brown, when he was chief of the Houston Police Department, in a cover message to a new pursuit policy, wrote:

> Remember the criminals will continue to be out there in the future and they can be found and arrested by other means. So if you decide not to chase based on the risks involved, you will not be subject to criticism. However, if you decide that you should chase, we will support you and offer acceptable standard operating procedures to assist you. The safety and well-being of our officers and the public we serve is the first and foremost priority in our minds, and we will continue to work toward that end with you. (Misner 1990)

Use of force and the constitution

Constitutionally, the use of force is a seizure. Remember, the Fourth Amendment bans "unreasonable" seizures, so, legitimate force is reasonable and excessive force is unreasonable. What this means in practice is police can use the amount of force reasonably necessary to get control of fleeing and resisting suspects and to defend themselves and others against forced used by civilians.

 6-11 You Decide: Did the officers use excessive force?

FIGURE 6.2
Results of High-Speed Chases, Dade County Police Department, 1985–1987
Source: Alpert and Dunham 1990, based on Table 1, p. 37.

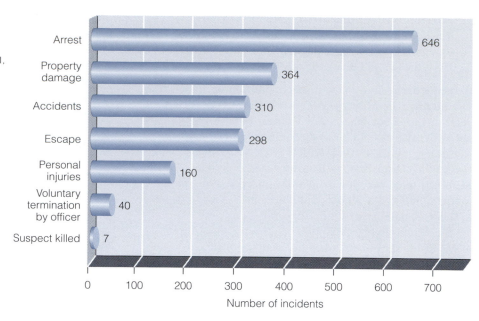

Police Corruption

Police corruption is a form of occupational crime: misusing police authority for private gain (Chapter 3). Corruption can be limited to one or two officers or spread throughout a whole department. And, it can include everything from a top official extorting thousands of dollars a month from vice operations to a patrol officer accepting a free cup of coffee from a neighborhood restaurant (Sherman 1978, 30–31). In former New York Police Commissioner Patrick Murphy's broad definition, "Except for your paycheck, there is no such thing as a clean buck" (Goldstein 1977, 201).

The most common corrupt practices include:

- *Mooching:* Free meals, alcohol, groceries, or other items
- *Chiseling:* Demands for free admission to entertainment
- *Favoritism:* Getting immunity from traffic violations
- *Prejudice:* Giving non-Whites less than impartial treatment
- *Shopping:* Stealing small items from stores left unlocked after business hours
- *Extortion:* Demanding money in exchange for not filing traffic tickets
- *Bribery:* Receiving payments of cash or "gifts" for past or future assistance in avoiding arrest or in falsifying or withholding evidence
- *Shakedown:* Taking expensive items for personal use and attributing their loss to criminal activity during the investigation of a break-in or burglary
- *Perjury:* Lying to provide an alibi for fellow officers apprehended in illegal activity.

- *Premeditated theft:* Executing a planned burglary to gain forced entry to acquire unlawful goods (Stoddard 1983, 340–341)

Police corruption damages public confidence and lessens residents' willingness to help the police. It also hurts policing from inside. Officers "on the take" have less time for police work and even resent how it interferes with their money making. Corrupt supervisors also weaken administrative control over patrol officers. Weak supervisors encourage officers to "respond more slowly to calls for assistance, avoid assigned duties, sleep on the job, and perform poorly in situations requiring discipline" (Goldstein 1977, 190–192).

We can't write off the cause of corruption as simply greed (Goldstein 1977, 197–199). Police officers deal with not very nice people in a day's work. So, it may not be surprising that some officers believe everybody's "on the take." Officers sometimes also look at criminal justice as hopeless. They watch offenders pass through the lower courts. They see prosecutors, defense attorneys, and judges take their share of "dirty money." And they swallow the bitter pill of seeing these prosecutors and judges immune from scandalous exposure (Knapp Commission 1972, 5–6; Rubenstein 1973, 282). But, does seeing corruption by other public officials justify or excuse their own corruption? Of course not. This is especially true when we take into account what this chapter teaches us: Police officers *are* different from the rest of us—only they have the *legal* power and the technology to take away what we dearly prize—our right to come and go as we please *and* even our lives—before there's proof beyond a reasonable doubt that we're guilty of crimes. As every Spiderman® comic book reader knows because it appears in every issue: "With great power goes great responsibility."

Exposing and correcting corruption are difficult. For one thing, discretionary decision making *not* to enforce laws (necessary as this may be) is usually hidden from public view. Further, "a code of silence brands anyone who exposes corruption a traitor. . . . It is easier for . . . a rookie to become corrupt than to remain honest" (Chapter 4) (Knapp Commission 1972).

Remedies for Police Misconduct

One day, when I was a member of a Minneapolis mayor's committee to examine police misconduct, we held a neighborhood meeting. One resident posed this issue: "We all know what happens when *we* break the law—*we* get arrested and prosecuted. What I want to know is what happens when the *police* break the law against us? What recourse do we have?" The answer is there are four possible remedies for police misconduct:

1. *Criminal law:* Prosecute the officer.
2. *Civil law:* Sue the officer, the police department, or the government.
3. *Administrative:* Discipline the officer as a result of internal or external review.
4. *Procedural:* Throw illegally obtained evidence out of court.

Formally, all four can be used in the same case. For example, the state can prosecute a police officer for breaking and entering when he illegally searches a house. The homeowner can sue the officer for damages. The police department can fire or suspend the officer. Finally, if the "victim" of the illegal entry is prosecuted, the court can throw out any evidence the officer found during the illegal search. However, in practice, it's rare to see all of these remedies pursued in the same case.

Criminal punishment

Most police misconduct is also a crime. A police officer who *illegally* shoots and kills a person has committed criminal homicide. Illegal arrests might be false imprisonment. Illegal searches can be breaking and entering or trespassing. Corruption might be theft, extortion, or even robbery. But, how likely is it police officers will be charged with crimes, convicted, and punished when they break the law? Not very. Why? First, witnesses are hard to come by and when they are they usually don't get much jury sympathy. Many people who are the objects of police illegality are probably criminals themselves. Rarely will a prosecutor or a jury (or, for that matter, the public) side with a "real" criminal over police officers who, after all, are "only trying to do their job." Even totally innocent people run up against the thick wall of resistance to criticizing police officers. There's a strong presumption they're acting properly and it's tough to show they're not.

Civil lawsuits

Most police criminal misconduct is also a private injury (**tort**). Plaintiffs can go into a state court to sue individual officers and sometimes their departments and municipalities to recover money (**damages**) to compensate them for their injuries. But, just like it's hard to convict police officers of crimes, it's also hard to win lawsuits in state courts. According to the **doctrine of official immunity**, police officers aren't liable unless their misconduct was intentional and malicious. Why? Because as the Minnesota supreme court (*Susla v. State* 1976, 912; *Pletan v. Gaines et al.* 1992, 40) put it, "[T]o encourage responsible law enforcement . . . police are afforded a wide degree of discretion precisely because a more stringent standard could inhibit action." So, the court decided, a police officer wasn't liable for the death of a small boy killed during a high-speed chase where the officer was trying to catch a fleeing shoplifter. Official immunity protected the officer; otherwise, the court maintained, officers in the future might hold back in their vigorous enforcement of the law.

Plaintiffs can also sue in federal courts if officers violate their constitutional rights. The Civil Rights Act gives individuals the right to sue state and local governments, their agencies, and their agents for violations of rights guaranteed by the U.S. Constitution. The act provides:

> Every person who, under color of any statute, ordinance, regulation, custom, or usage, of any State or Territory, subjects, or causes to be subjected, any citizen of the United States or other person within the jurisdiction thereof to the deprivation of any rights, privileges, or immunities secured by the Constitution and laws, shall be liable to the party injured in an action at law, suit in equity, or other proper proceeding for redress. (U.S. Code 1994)

It's even harder for plaintiffs to recover damages under the Civil Rights Act than it is in state courts. The U.S. Supreme Court has created a **defense of qualified immunity** for officers whose actions are "objectively reasonable." According to the Court, qualified immunity has to strike a balance between protecting individuals' constitutional rights and law enforcement's power to do its job. In the leading qualified immunity case, *Anderson v. Creighton* (1987), FBI agents searched the Creightons' home without a warrant and without probable cause, looking for one of their relatives. The Court agreed FBI Agent Anderson violated the Creightons' rights when he illegally came in and searched their house. But unreasonable searches don't automatically translate into civil liability under section 1983. If Anderson could have believed his unreasonable search was reasonable, he wasn't liable. So, the Creightons lost their case.

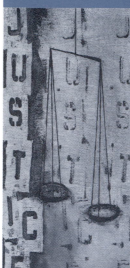

Thurman v. City of Torrington

Facts

OCTOBER 1982

Charles Thurman attacked Tracey Thurman at the home of Judy Bentley and Richard St. Hilaire in the city of Torrington. Mr. St. Hilaire and Ms. Bentley made a formal complaint of the attack to a police officer and asked him to keep Thurman's husband, Charles, off their property.

NOVEMBER 5, 1982

Charles Thurman went to the Bentley–St. Hilaire residence and took by force their son Charles J. Thurman, Jr. Tracey Thurman and Mr. St. Hilaire went to police headquarters to make a formal complaint. At that point, police officers refused to take a complaint—even of trespassing.

NOVEMBER 9, 1982

Charles Thurman screamed threats to Tracey Thurman while she was sitting in her car. Officer Neil Gemelli stood on the street watching Charles Thurman scream threats at Tracey Thurman until Charles Thurman broke the windshield of her car as she sat inside. Officer Gemelli then arrested Charles Thurman.

NOVEMBER 10, 1982

Charles Thurman was convicted of breach of peace. He received a suspended sentence of six months and a two-year "conditional discharge," during which he was ordered to stay completely away from Tracey Thurman and the Bentley–St. Hilaire residence and to commit no further crimes. Thurman was informed of the sentence.

DECEMBER 31, 1982

While Tracey Thurman was at the Bentley–St. Hilaire residence, Charles Thurman came to the house and threatened her again. She called the Torrington Police Department. Although informed of the violation of the conditional discharge, the officer who took the call made no attempt to find out where Thurman was or to arrest him.

JANUARY 1–MAY 4, 1983

Officers took numerous telephone complaints from Tracey that Charles threatened to hurt her and repeated requests that the officers arrest him because of his threats and violations of the terms of his probation.

MAY 4 AND 5, 1983

Tracey Thurman and Ms. Bentley reported to the Torrington Police Department that Charles Thurman threatened to shoot Tracey. Officer Storrs took the written complaint of plaintiff Tracey Thurman and her request that they get an arrest warrant for her husband because of his death threat and violation of his "conditional discharge." Officer Storrs refused to take Ms. Bentley's complaint and he told her to come back three weeks later (June 1, 1983), when Storrs or someone else would try to get the warrant.

MAY 6, 1983

Tracey Thurman filed an application for a restraining order against Charles Thurman in the Litchfield Superior Court.

That day, the court issued a restraining order forbidding Charles Thurman from assaulting, threatening, and harassing Tracey Thurman. The City was informed of this order.

MAY 27, 1983

Tracey Thurman asked for police protection to get to the Torrington Police Department, and when an officer brought her to the department, she asked for a warrant for her husband's arrest. The officer told her she had to wait until after the Memorial Day holiday weekend and was advised to call on Tuesday, May 31, to pursue the warrant request.

MAY 31, 1983

Tracey Thurman appeared once again at the Torrington Police Department to pursue the warrant request. She was then advised by an officer that Officer Schapp was the only policeman who could help her, and he was on vacation. She was told that she had to wait until he got back. That same day, Tracey's brother-in-law, Joseph Kocsis, called the Torrington Police Department to protest the lack of action taken on Tracey's complaint. Although Mr. Kocsis was told Charles Thurman would be arrested on June 8, 1983, no arrest took place.

JUNE 10, 1983

Charles Thurman appeared at the Bentley–St. Hilaire residence in the early afternoon and demanded to speak to Tracey Thurman. Tracey, remaining indoors, called the police department asking that Charles be picked up for violation of his probation. After about 15 minutes, Tracey went outside to try to persuade him not to take or hurt Charles Jr. Charles suddenly stabbed Tracey repeatedly in the chest, neck, and throat.

Twenty-five minutes after Tracey's call to the Torrington Police Department and after her stabbing, a single police officer, Officer Petrovits, arrived on the scene. Charles Thurman was holding a bloody knife. Charles dropped the knife and, in the presence of Petrovits, kicked Tracey in the head and ran into the Bentley–St. Hilaire residence. Charles came back holding Charles Thurman, Jr. and dropped him on his wounded mother. Charles then kicked Tracey in the head a second time.

Soon thereafter, Officers DeAngelo, Nukirk, and Columbia arrived on the scene but still permitted Charles Thurman to wander about the crowd and continue to threaten Tracey. Finally, upon approaching Tracey once again, this time while she was lying on a stretcher, Charles Thurman was arrested and taken into custody.

From the first to the last of these episodes, Charles Thurman lived in Torrington and worked as a counterman and short order cook at Skie's Diner. There he served many members of the Torrington Police Department, including some of the officers in this case. While at work, Charles Thurman boasted to the officers that he intended to "get" his wife and that he intended to kill her.

Opinion

Tracey Thurman sued the city for the violations of her rights under the U.S. Constitution. The City brought a motion to dismiss her claims. The City . . . argues that the equal protection clause [no state shall deny any person the equal protection of the laws] "only prohibits intentional discrimination that is racially motivated." The City's argument is clearly a misstatement of the law. The application of the equal protection clause is not limited to racial classifications or racially motivated discrimination. . . . Classifications on the basis of gender will be held invalid under the equal protection clause unless they are substantially related to strike down classifications which are not rationally related to a legitimate governmental purpose.

Tracey Thurman alleges that the city uses an administrative classification that manifests itself in discriminatory treatment that violates the equal protection clause. Police protection in the City of Torrington, they argue, is fully provided to persons abused by someone with whom the victim has no domestic relationship. But the Torrington police have consistently afforded lesser protection, plaintiffs allege, when the victim is (1) a woman abused or assaulted by a spouse or boyfriend, or (2) a child abused by a father or stepfather. The issue to be decided, then, is whether the plaintiffs have properly alleged a violation of the equal protection clause of the Fourteenth Amendment.

City officials and police officers are under an affirmative duty to preserve law and order, and to protect the personal safety of persons in the community. This duty applies equally to women whose personal safety is threatened by individuals with whom they have or have had a domestic relationship as well as to all other persons whose personal safety is threatened, including women not involved in domestic relationships. If officials have notice of the possibility of attacks on women in domestic relationships or other persons, they are under an affirmative duty to take reasonable measures to protect the personal safety of such persons in the community. Failure to perform this duty would constitute a denial of equal protection of the laws.

Tracey Thurman alleges there is an administrative classification used to implement the law in a discriminatory fashion. It is well settled that the equal protection clause is applicable not only to discriminatory legislative action, but also to discriminatory governmental action in administration and enforcement of the law. Here the plaintiffs were threatened with assault in violation of Connecticut law. Over the course of eight months the police failed to afford her protection against such assaults, and failed to take action to arrest the perpetrator of these assaults. She alleges this failure to act was pursuant to a pattern or practice of affording inadequate protection, or no protection at all, to women who have complained of having been abused by their husbands or others with whom they have had close relations. Such a practice is tantamount to an administrative classification used to implement the law in a discriminatory fashion.

A city may be sued for damages under § 1983 when "the action that is alleged to be unconstitutional implements or executes a policy statement, ordinance, regulation, or decision officially adopted and promulgated by the body's officers" or is "visited pursuant to governmental 'custom' even though such a custom has not received formal approval through the body's official decision-making channels."

Some degree of specificity is required in pleading a custom or policy. A plaintiff must typically point to the facts outside his own case to support his allegation of a policy on the part of a municipality. In the instant case, however, the plaintiff Tracey Thurman has specifically alleged in her statement of facts a series of acts and omissions on the part of the defendant police officers and police department that took place over the course of eight months. From this particularized pleading a pattern emerges that evidences deliberate indifference on the part of the police department to the complaints of the plaintiff Tracey Thurman and to its duty to protect her. Such an ongoing pattern of deliberate indifference raises an inference of "custom" or "policy" on the part of the municipality. Furthermore, this pattern of inaction climaxed on June 10, 1983 in an incident so brutal that under the law of the Second Circuit that "single brutal incident may be sufficient to suggest a link between a violation of constitutional rights and a pattern of police misconduct." Finally, a complaint of this sort will survive dismissal if it alleges a policy or custom of condoning police misconduct that violates constitutional rights and alleges "that the City's pattern of inaction caused the plaintiffs any compensable injury."

For these reasons, the City's motion to dismiss the complaint for failure to allege the deprivation of a constitutional right is denied . . . ; the City's motion to dismiss claims against it for failure to properly allege a "custom" or "policy" on the part of the City is denied.

[Note: Tracey Thurman was left partially paralyzed and received $2.3 million in damages in 1985.]

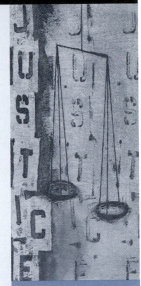

Questions

1. Do the facts in this case prove "custom" or "policy"? Explain.
2. Assume there is proof of a policy. Was the policy the cause of the injury? Defend your answer.
3. If this happened today, would the damage award she received be enough? too much? not enough? Explain your answer.
4. Should lack of training be considered a "policy"? Defend your answer.

6-12 More on Tracey Thurman, the battered wife in the You Decide. (Caution: Some of the sites you'll find contain graphic pictures of battered women.)

Internal review

The most common and systematic accountability procedure for police misconduct is **internal review.** In most large and mid-sized departments special internal affairs units (IAU) review police misconduct. According to Professor Douglas W. Perez (1994, 88–89), a former deputy sheriff, "Most cops do not like internal affairs." They don't trust IAU, and some even think IAU investigators are traitors. Still, most officers believe IAU operations are a necessary evil. For one thing, they're a good defense against external review (see next section). The famed Chicago chief of police O. W. Wilson said, "It is clearly apparent that if the police do not take a vigorous stand on the matter of internal investigation, outside groups—such as review boards consisting of laymen and other persons outside the police service—will step into the void" (Griswold 1994, 215–221).

There are four stages of internal review:

1. Intake
2. Investigation
3. Deliberation
4. Disposition

The Internal Affairs Section of the Oakland, California, Police Department is considered an excellent unit, so we'll use it as an example of how internal review proceeds through these four stages. Although the unit is housed in the department building, the department's intake policy is "anyone anywhere should accept a complaint if a citizen wishes it taken." All complaints alleging excessive force, police corruption, and racial discrimination are followed up (Perez 1994, 92–93).

Someone besides the intake officer investigates complaints. The investigator gathers evidence, usually interviewing the officer involved last. If officers refuse to cooperate, they're subject to discipline, like dismissal for refusing to obey an order of the chief.

Completed investigations go to the IAU supervisor. If the supervisor approves, complaints go to the decision-making or deliberation stage. There are four possible decisions (Figure 6.3):

1. *Unfounded:* The investigation proved that the act did not take place.
2. *Exonerated:* The acts took place, but the investigation proved that they were justified, lawful, and proper.
3. *Not sustained:* The investigation failed to gather enough evidence to clearly prove the allegations in the complaint.
4. *Sustained:* The investigation disclosed enough evidence to clearly prove the allegations in the complaint. (Perez 1994, 96)

If the decision is "unfounded," "exonerated," or "not sustained," the case is closed. If the decision is "sus-

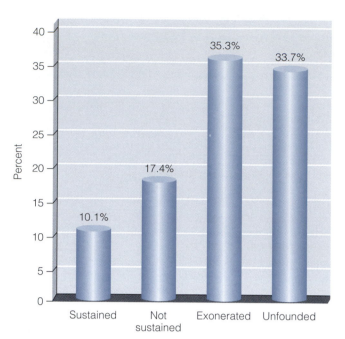

FIGURE 6.3

Disposition of Excessive Force Complaints

SOURCE: Pate and Fridell, 1993, 116.

tained," the supervisor recommends disciplinary action. Recommended disciplinary actions ranked from least to most severe include (1) reprimand, (2) written reprimand, (3) transfer, (4) retraining, (5) counseling, (6) suspension, (7) demotion, (8) fine, and (9) dismissal.

After the initial disposition, the case goes up the chain of command until it finally reaches the chief. In about half the cases, there's a discrepancy between the chief's recommendations and those of the immediate supervisor. These discrepancies are important because the immediate supervisor, usually a sergeant of patrol, works on the street with other patrol officers. The supervisors of sergeants usually go along with the recommendations of sergeants. Chiefs of police, on the other hand, are removed from the day-to-day street operations of patrol officers and their immediate supervisors. They have departmentwide perspectives and are responsible to "local political elites" for their department's performance. So chiefs may find the disciplinary penalty too light and make it heavier. According to Perez, "Oakland chiefs are often seen from below as abusive of police officers, always increasing punishments, never going along with the lighter recommendations." Oakland, however, may not be typical in this respect. Figure 6.4 shows the distribution of disciplinary measures taken in a national sample of city police departments (Perez 1994, 96–97).

External review

The fundamental objection to internal review is that police shouldn't police themselves. To the question, "Who will watch the watchmen?" the answer is, "Not the watchmen!" In response, we've seen the external review

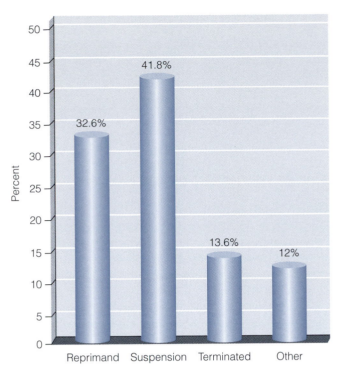

FIGURE 6.4
Distribution of Disciplinary Actions
SOURCE: Pate and Fridell 1993, 116.

grow. In **external review,** individuals who aren't sworn police officers participate in the review of complaints against the police. Usually called civilian review, it's sparked controversy for nearly half a century. Police oppose external review because it invades their independence; they have no confidence outsiders know enough about police work to review it; and they know outside scrutiny would pierce the "blue curtain" that hides their "real" work from public view (Chapter 4).

Strong police unions, chiefs who opposed external review, and the creation of internal review procedures (discussed in the last section) successfully prevented external review during the 1960s, when it became a popular proposal of some reformers and citizen groups. However, by 1994, 72 percent of the fifty largest cities had created civilian review procedures of some sort (Walker and Bumpus 1992, 1, 3–4).

Types of External Review   The differences among civilian review procedures all turn on the point in the decision making process when nonofficers may participate, including

1. The initial investigation to collect the facts
2. The review of the investigation reports
3. The recommendation for disposition to the chief
4. The review of decisions made by the chief

Still, no matter at what point nonofficers participate, civilian review boards can only *recommend* disciplinary action to police chiefs because under civil service laws

only police chiefs can decide on disciplinary action against police officers (Walker and Bumpus 1992, 3–4).

Does Civilian Review Work?   The answer depends on the *definition* and the *measures* of effectiveness. *Effectiveness* can mean at least four things, all of which are important in determining the value of civilian review procedures:

1. Maintaining effective control of police misconduct
2. Providing resolutions to complaints that satisfy individual complainants
3. Preserving public confidence in the police
4. Influencing police management by providing "feedback from consumers" (Walker and Bumpus 1992, 8)

It's difficult to measure the effectiveness of civilian review because official data are ambiguous. Take the number of complaints, for example. A large number of complaints might mean a large volume of police misconduct. But it can also indicate confidence in the review procedures. Following the Rodney King incident in Los Angeles, observers noted that San Francisco, a city known for its strong review procedures, received more complaints than the much larger city of Los Angeles. In contrast, the Independent Commission heard a number of citizen complaints that the LAPD created "significant hurdles" to filing complaints, that they were afraid of the process, and that the complaint process was "unnecessarily difficult or impossible." The ACLU collected evidence suggesting that the LAPD "actively discouraged the filing of complaints." The beating of Rodney King, in fact, would never have come to public attention without the video, according to the Independent Commission because, the efforts of his brother Paul to file a complaint following the beating were "frustrated" by the LAPD (Pate and Fridell 1993, 39).

The numbers and rates of complaints are also difficult to assess because we don't know the numbers of incidents where people don't file complaints. In one national survey, of all the people who said the police mistreated them, only 30 percent said they filed complaints. One thing, however, is clear. Misconduct isn't distributed *evenly* among individuals and neighborhoods. In one survey, only 40 percent of the addresses in one city had any contact with the police in a year. Most contacts between private individuals and the police occur in poor neighborhoods. In New York City, the rate of complaints ranges from one to five for every 10,000 people, depending on the neighborhood.

Official data have consistently indicated racial minority males are disproportionately represented among complainants. So, the perception of a pattern of police harassment is a major factor in conflict between the police and racial minority communities (Walker and Bumpus 1992, 10).

Whatever the ambiguity of numbers and rates in the official statistics, observers have noted civilian review procedures rarely sustain complaints. Furthermore, the rates of complaints sustained in civilian review are about the same as the rates in internal affairs units (Walker and Bumpus 1992, 16–17).

The exclusionary rule

The **exclusionary rule** throws out "good" evidence because of "bad" police behavior. It bans the government from using confessions obtained in violation of the right against self-incrimination; evidence gathered by unreasonable searches and seizures; evidence gotten in violation of the right to counsel; and eyewitness identifications gotten by unreliable procedures.

No other country does it, so why do we? There have been several justifications for the exclusionary rule over the years, but the U.S. Supreme Court says only one is acceptable—to deter unconstitutional police behavior.

The Supreme Court weighs the social cost of letting criminals go free by throwing out good evidence of guilt against the possible deterrent effect throwing out evidence has on law enforcement officers. If the social costs outweigh the deterrent effect (which in virtually every case the Court says it does), then the evidence can come in (Schroeder 1981, 1378–1386).

Empirical research, however, doesn't support the U.S. Supreme Court's view that throwing out evidence has hardly any effect on deterring police misconduct. In an extensive study of the exclusionary rule among Chicago narcotics officers, Myron W. Orfield, Jr. (1987), reported several important findings:

- Chicago narcotics officers are *always* in court when judges suppress the evidence.
- They *always* understand why the court excluded the evidence.
- This experience has led them to seek search warrants more often and to be more careful when they search for and seize evidence without warrants.

Prior to the decision in *Mapp v. Ohio* (which applied the exclusionary rule to state and local law enforcement), police officers rarely obtained warrants. By 1987, the narcotics division of the Chicago Police Department ordered that "virtually all preplanned searches that are not 'buy busts' or airport-related searches occur with warrants." Orfield's study also demonstrated the exclusionary rule "punishes" officers. Getting evidence thrown out can negatively affect both assignments and promotions (Orfield 1987, 1017–1018, 1029).

Orfield found some officers lie in court so their illegally seized evidence won't be thrown out. Admittedly, this limits the effectiveness of the exclusionary rule. But strong responses to police perjury by both the police department and the courts have reduced the instances of perjury. Finally, every officer in Orfield's study believed the courts should keep the rule. They said the rule has just about the right amount of a deterrent element. They believed a tort remedy (suing the police) would "overdeter" the police in their search for evidence (Orfield 1987, 1027–1028).

The social costs of excluding evidence aren't nearly as high as the Supreme Court (and most people) thinks. Researchers have shown the rule affects only a tiny number of cases in just a few crimes. Less than one-tenth of 1 percent of all criminal cases will be dismissed because the police illegally got the evidence. And most of these are drug offenses, not murder, rape, and other violent crimes. Property crimes too are unaffected (National Institute of Justice 1982, 12) (Figure 6.5).

Other responses to misconduct

One positive approach to dealing with police misconduct relies on training and other socialization measures to improve police-community relations. For example, advocates for the positive approach argue the effectiveness of convincing officers to use unflappable responses to unpleasant behavior. Taking an insult without reaction wins more respect and obedience than responding emotionally to insults. James Q. Wilson (1983), a supporter of the positive approach, recommends that recruitment, training, and the police subculture should aim at producing police officers

> who can handle calmly challenges to their self-respect and manhood, are able to tolerate ambiguous situations, have the physical capacity to subdue persons, are able to accept responsibility for the consequences of their own actions, can understand and apply legal concepts in concrete situations, and are honest. (112)

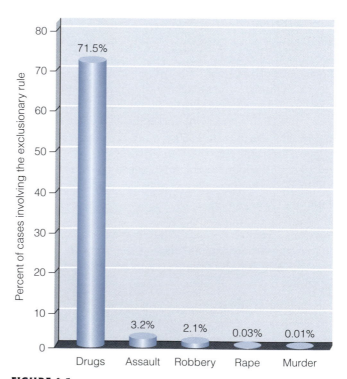

FIGURE 6.5

The Exclusionary Rule in California

SOURCE: National Institute of Justice 1982, 12.

Knowledge and Understanding Check

Law enforcement and the constitution

✔ Why can't police interfere with people's rights based on hunches?

✔ Describe the balance created by the U.S. Constitution.

✔ List the amendments to the U.S. Constitution responsible for settling disputes over the balance.

Arrests

✔ List three elements required in "reasonable" arrests.

✔ Define and explain the significance of probable cause.

Searches

✔ Define search, and explain when searches are unreasonable.

✔ Compare arrests and searches with stops and frisks.

Interrogation

✔ When do police officers have to give *Miranda* warnings to suspects?

✔ Under what two conditions are confessions involuntary?

Identification procedures

✔ List and define the police identification procedures and what constitutional amendments apply to them.

✔ What are the dangers of eyewitness identification? What can be done to reduce these dangers?

✔ When are identifications unconstitutional?

Police misconduct

✔ List the kinds of force police use, and summarize the research on the effectiveness of these kinds of force.

✔ What's the relationship between race and the use of deadly force? What effects do deadly force policies have on this relationship?

✔ When is the use of police force unconstitutional?

✔ Define police corruption.

✔ List the types.

✔ Describe the causes of police corruption.

✔ Why is it difficult to expose and correct police corruption?

✔ Identify the four types of actions open to individuals who have suffered unconstitutional invasions conducted to obtain evidence.

✔ Describe the rationale of the exclusionary rule.

✔ Summarize the research on the social costs of the exclusionary rule.

KEY TERMS

arrest

consent search rule

damages

defense of qualified immunity

doctrine of official immunity

excessive force

exclusionary rule

external review (civilian review)

Fourth Amendment frisk

Fourth Amendment stop

internal review

knock-and-announce rule

knockdown force

legitimate use of force

objective basis

plain-view doctrine

police corruption

probable cause to arrest

reasonable suspicion to frisk

reasonable suspicion to stop

rotten apple theory

searches

tort

INTERNET PROJECT

Examine police corruption here and around the world to enrich your knowledge and understanding of police misconduct. Enter the key words "police corruption." If you're interested in the famous Los Angeles Ramparts scandal, enter the key words "rafael perez corruption."

CHAPTER 7

Court Structure and Process

EQUAL JUSTICE UNDER LAW

© Joel Gordon

CHAPTER OUTLINE

> Most citizens expect . . . the courthouse to live up to the promise of its marble interior—a palace of justice, with no secret closets or hidden corridors. Anyone should be able to walk in and see the rules of law uniformly applied. Prosecutors and defense lawyers are vigorous advocates, but they have to place their commitment to truth and law above everything else. Judges and juries wisely and justly apply the law to the facts of each case. But most people also know the courthouse has to deal with the brutish and bloody aspects of life. Now the courthouse is not a majestic palace. It's a harsh and seamy place. So when people read about courthouse deals they're confused, shocked, and disappointed.

ADAPTED FROM ROSETT AND CRESSEY (1976, 1–2)

■ INTRODUCTION

After arrest, decision making moves from police departments to courts. *Formally,* courts are legal institutions—"palaces of justice." In the courtrooms, aggressive prosecutors fight for the "people" and vigorous defense lawyers fight for their clients, umpired by neutral judges who make sure they fight hard but fair according to the rule of law. Juries convict the guilty and free the innocent. *Informally,* the courtrooms are almost always dark and empty; they're lit up and occupied only for the rare formal trial and to ratify decisions already made in judges' chambers, halls, and even in closets and restrooms (Nardulli, Eisenstein, and Flemming 1988, 373–374). In this chapter, we'll look closely at the criminal court structure, criminal court missions, and the roles of the courtroom work group.

■ THE CRIMINAL COURT STRUCTURE

Criminal courts in our federal system are arranged into three tiers at both national and state levels (Figure 7.1):

1. **Lower courts** (trial courts of limited jurisdiction): Have the power to decide the facts and apply the law in misdemeanor cases and conduct pretrial proceedings in felony cases
2. **Felony courts** (trial courts of general jurisdiction): Have the power to decide the facts and apply the law in felony cases

3. **Appellate courts:** Have the power to review trial courts' application of the law to the facts

 7-1 Your state's court system

Lower Courts

Lower courts (called by many different names like misdemeanor, superior, municipal, county, justice of the peace, and magistrate's courts) only have the power (**jurisdiction**) to decide misdemeanors and conduct preliminary proceedings in felony cases. That's why they're called **courts of limited jurisdiction.** Formally, defendants in lower criminal courts have the same rights as defendants in felony courts. In practice, most cases are tried less formally than in felony courts; and they're tried without juries. Lower criminal courts aren't **courts of record—** they don't keep written records of proceedings.

Lower courts decide minor (but by far the most numerous) cases, like traffic offenses, drunk and disorderly conduct, shoplifting, and prostitution. This makes them the first and only contact most people ever have with criminal courts (Forer 1984, 3).

In the 1800s, observers complained that in lower criminal courts in big cities judges rushed defendants through cramped, noisy, undignified courtrooms. Things were pretty much the same in the 1950s when Professor Caleb Foote (1956, 605) watched one Philadelphia magistrate decide fifty-five cases in 15 minutes. Four defendants were tried, convicted, and sentenced in 17 seconds!

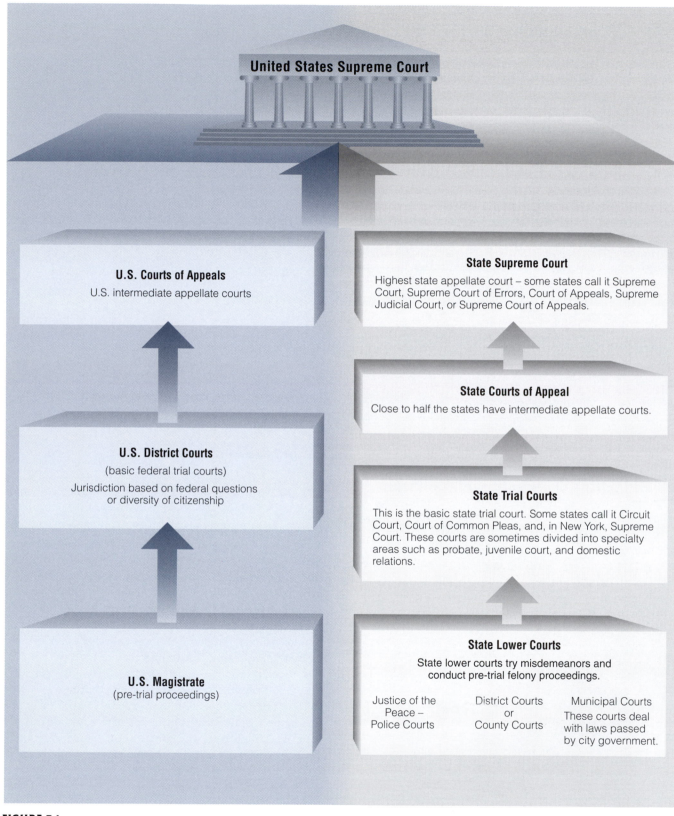

FIGURE 7.1

The Structure of Courts in the Federal System

The magistrate read off each of the four defendants' names, took one look at each, and said in turn, "Three months." In the 1970s, a sociologist who observed lower courts in another city for three months found judges decided 72 percent of the cases in less than a minute each (Mileski 1971, 479).

Observers in the 1990s told much the same stories. Describing a New York criminal court in 1991—where most cases were decided in less than 4 minutes—Professor Harry I. Subin (1991) wrote:

> [The court is] overwhelmed by a flood of cases . . . [and, therefore] accomplishes very little. It does not dispense justice. It simply disposes of each day's business in any way it can, so it can be ready to dispose of the next day's business. And because substantive action would slow things down, the court very rarely conducts legal proceedings or imposes punishment on the guilty.

Is speed necessarily bad? Obviously, the observers quoted here think so. A lot of judges also complain about it. According to one experienced trial judge, "For many years I have been dismayed by the fact that cases were allocated only fifteen to twenty minutes." The emphasis on speed, according to critics, has produced "assembly-line justice" rather than the deliberation that justice requires.

But empirical studies suggest otherwise. Stephen J. Schulhofer (1985, 562) observed lower criminal courts in Philadelphia for several months. After allowing for individual differences among judges, prosecutors, and defense attorneys, he found judges conduct misdemeanor trials according to genuine adversarial proceedings. Schulhofer found that even though it took only an average of 25 (and often less than 10) minutes to decide these cases, judges listened carefully to witnesses—often taking notes—and they took the time they needed to decide cases fairly and accurately. Ostrom and Hanson (2000) examined case processing in court systems in every part of the country. The study challenged the idea that speed and justice conflict, concluding: "[C]ourts can exercise considerable control over how quickly cases move . . . without sacrificing either advocacy or due process" (2).

7-2 Ostrom and Hanson's complete study

According to Schulhofer (1985), judges and attorneys in lower criminal courts take the rules of evidence seriously. Attorneys raise objections, and judges sustain them even when it slows down the proceedings. For example, in a simple assault case, one judge sustained several defense objections to the prosecutor's direct examination. At the end of the trial, the judge accused the prosecutor of ineptitude, saying he found it "hard to be-

lieve that this case went on for half an hour or an hour" (in fact, the trial had lasted 22 minutes) (562).

Thomas W. Church, Jr. (1985) pronounced the adversary system alive and well in four lower courts he observed in the Bronx, Detroit, Miami, and Pittsburgh. Church noted

> the obvious distaste many lawyers working in a prosecuting attorney's office seem to have for the defense side in general, a feeling often reciprocated by defense attorneys. (Possibly the most graphic evidence of this antipathy came during the summer I was conducting interviews in Miami when the annual prosecutor-public defender softball game degenerated into a fist fight.) After years of scholars' debunking the "adversary myth," it may be that the adversary system is in need of . . . bunking." (453)

Besides deciding minor criminal cases, lower criminal courts conduct four important pretrial proceedings in both misdemeanor and felony cases:

1. They decide whether to release defendants on bail.
2. They assign lawyers to indigent (poor) defendants.
3. They preside over preliminary hearings to test the government's case against defendants.
4. They decide whether confessions, searches, and seizures can be admitted as evidence.

Felony Courts

Felony courts (usually called district or circuit courts) are where felony cases are tried (Chapter 8). They're **courts of general jurisdiction,** meaning they can decide all felony cases from capital murder to theft and also review the decisions of lower courts. Felony courts are courts of record, and they follow the rules of the adversary process more than proceedings in lower courts.

Appellate Courts

The main distinction between the trial (lower criminal and felony) courts and appeals courts is appellate courts don't decide questions of guilt or innocence. In fact, the law doesn't require defendants to appear (and many defendants don't even show up voluntarily) when their cases are being heard in the appellate courts. Appellate courts decide cases by reviewing how the trial courts applied the law to the facts. Proceedings in the appellate court are the most formal of all three levels of courts.

Most states and the federal judiciary have two levels of appellate court—intermediate (usually called courts of appeals) and last resort (usually called supreme courts). The intermediate courts review the objections of defense and prosecution, the rulings trial courts have made on the objections, and whether the government has proved its case beyond a reasonable doubt. Supreme courts review the most serious cases—like death penalty cases—the most complicated legal questions, and all constitutional questions.

 7-3 Appellate courts in your state

■ CRIMINAL COURT MISSIONS

We all know courts are supposed to administer justice according to the rule of law. That's their formal mission, what we'll call their **due process mission** (Chapter 1). But courts also have informal missions. One is **crime control**—the public expects courts to make sure guilty people are convicted and sentenced to punishment. Another is **social justice**—doing what's "best" for victims and offenders. A third informal mission stems from the reality that courts are legal institutions *and* social organizations made up of a professional **courtroom work group**—prosecutors, judges, and defense lawyers. Their mission is to keep the organization running smoothly, efficiently, and above all harmoniously. This informal mission, we'll call it the court's **organizational mission**, dominates the everyday operations of our criminal courts (see Chapter 8 on plea bargaining). A final mission—we'll call it the **career mission**—focuses on providing the work group an avenue to advance their own careers either within the group or in private law practice or political office. We'll discuss this final mission when we look more closely at the roles of the courtroom work group. But, first, we'll examine the other four missions.

The Due Process Mission

The due process mission of the criminal courts consists of making sure the process of turning suspects first into defendants and then defendants into offenders and finally sentencing offenders to punishments is fair. In the words of the Constitution, fair means the criminal process won't "deny any person life, liberty, or property without due process of law." The best way to obey that constitutional command is to stick to **adjudication**—decision making in open court according to the adversary process. Fairness is more important than convicting guilty people, because in our constitutional system the ends don't justify the means—at least not formally (Chapter 1).

The adversary process used to be called the "sporting theory of justice," because it's a lot like a sporting event. There are two teams—the people's and the defendant's. Prosecutors represent the people's team (also called the government's, the state's, and the commonwealth's team).

The defense counsel represents the defendant's team. Both fight hard to win. It's ok for them to fight hard but they have to fight fair. Fighting fair means fighting according to the rules (the Constitution and statutes). Under the rules, it's fair for the lawyers on both sides to tell only their side of the story and to spin it as best they can to their advantage. But they have to back up their spinning with evidence (Chapter 8).

The judge is the umpire. She interprets and enforces the rules impartially as the law commands (and we hope in practice, too). Juries decide the *facts*—what the story really was—and whether they add up to guilt beyond a reasonable doubt (Chapter 8). This image reflects the highest ideals of American justice—an open, fair, impartial, dignified conflict that sorts out the guilty from the innocent, punishes the guilty, and sets the innocent free (Pound 1912, 302–328).

According to the adversary system, if all goes according to plan, competition over the facts guarantees (or at least greatly improves the odds) the true story will win. But in practice, the adversary system doesn't operate according to plan, mainly because the sides aren't evenly matched and because judges aren't neutral. Individual lawyers vary in their talents, skills, training, and experience. More money can hire better lawyers. Guilt or innocence can depend on who has the best lawyer more than on the facts of the case (Chapter 8). Judges aren't always impartial, especially when they're up for election. And as we're about to see, the organizational missions of the courtroom work group are contrary to the inefficient, time-consuming, adversary process (Glueck 1965; Rosett and Cressey 1976, 53–55).

The Crime Control Mission

The rules of the adversary process limit, but don't eliminate, the crime control mission of courts. The crime control mission responds to public opinion and is shaped by the "nasty, brutish" side of life seen in criminal courts. According to one judge, "There's no use kidding yourself. We have a particular type of clientele in this court: The criminal court is a cesspool of poverty." The public expects criminal justice to punish these "bad" people. Prosecutors are supposed to be ruthless; defense lawyers shouldn't "get their clients off on technicalities"; and judges shouldn't be "soft on criminals" or "handcuff the police" in their fight against crime (Levin 1977, 60).

The Social Justice Mission

This is how one judge describes the social justice mission: "You have to consider what type of person the defendant is. I try to glean from the background, the kind of woman he is married to, from the nature of his offense, from his relationship to his children and from his associations" (Levin 1977, 129–130). With social justice in mind, one judge granted probation to an armed robber because the victim provoked the defendant and the defendant's wife was a "neatly dressed woman in her twenties who appeared mature and seemed to have a settling effect on the defendant." Due process can get in the way of social justice when individual cases don't fit neatly into the rigid rules of the adversary process. These cases need the room provided by discretion so courts can take into account mitigating and aggravating circumstances (Levin 1977, 129–130; Padgett 1985, 753–800).

Social justice and crime control are combined in Miami Florida's Drug Courts, created to deal with the huge number of drug cases in Dade County. The idea behind the court was that "an effective and flexible program of court-supervised drug treatment could reduce demand for illicit drugs and hence involvement in crime and reinvolvement in the court system" (Goldkamp and Weiland 1993). The Miami Drug Court accepts only first-time offenders charged with third-degree felony drug possession. John S. Goldkamp and Doris Weiland studied a sample cohort of defendants for eighteen months. They found Drug Court defendants were rearrested less than other felony drug defendants and when they were rearrested the length of time to their first rearrest was two to three times longer than other defendants. Drug Court defendants *did* fail to appear more often than other defendants but this was because courts ordered them to appear far more often than other defendants.

The Organizational Mission

Courts are complex social organizations that place a high premium on accomplishing their mission of smooth, efficient, and harmonious decision making. Chief Judge Lawrence H. Cooke of the New York State Court of Appeals shows obvious pride in the part he played in carrying out the organizational mission of the court in this summary of his achievements:

> New York has become one of the few states where the courts are disposing of more cases than they are taking on. We've made the courts more manageable. The courts are working much better than they did, they're producing much more, and they're more nearly up to date than they were six years ago. (Margolick 1984, 10)

This mission is difficult to accomplish in adversary proceedings, especially when courts face heavy criminal caseloads, which most of them do. So, discretion and negotiation, not adversary proceedings and written rules, are the means to accomplish the organizational mission. But it's not just necessity and convenience that encourage the use of discretion and negotiation; they're more pleasant, too, as we're about to see in the operations of the courtroom work group.

■ THE COURTROOM WORK GROUP

The courtroom work group—judges, prosecutors, and defense attorneys—carries out the organizational mission of deciding (disposing of) cases. This is a difficult mission to accomplish in adversary proceedings, especially because there are so many criminal cases in most courts.

The courtroom work group has a lot more in common than the due process mission suggests. Decision making takes place within a close working and personal environment. Judges, prosecutors, and defense attorneys see one another regularly and have similar backgrounds and career ambitions.

After interviewing more than five hundred judges, prosecutors, and defense attorneys in major cities throughout the country, Paul B. Wice (1985) concluded:

> Despite their locations in a hectic urban setting, the criminal courts which I visited seemed like traditional villages. The high level of intimacy and frequency of interaction between nearly all of the courtroom work group made many defendants and outsiders unfamiliar with the court's inner workings incredulous as to the possible existence of adversary proceeding. Although the "kibitzing" is curtailed during the time when court is in session, it is never completely absent. In the hallways, around the snackbars, in the courtrooms during recesses, and before and after the day's business, the friendly joshing never seems to end. Whether this exaggerated conviviality serves as a type of necessary social lubricant to disguise actual tensions, or is an accurate measure of their camaraderie, is difficult to discern. Whichever purpose it serves, it is an omnipresent style of interaction that typified almost every city visited. (48)

In the courtroom work group, defendants are outsiders even to their lawyers. Once defendants are charged, judges, prosecutors, and defense lawyers usually agree defendants are guilty of *something*. All the group has to do is agree on a punishment. This is usually not hard to do because:

- There's a large volume of cases, and they all have deadlines.
- Most cases are routine.
- The group definitely prefers friendly negotiation to disputation.
- The pull of other business makes negotiation attractive.

Against the strong pull of these realities, due process, crime control, and social justice definitely have to compete with the time and effort the group commits to informal decision making. The mission to dispose of cases and the desire to maintain good work group relationships softens formal role conflicts among prosecutors, defense counsel, and judges (Nardulli 1979; Wice 1985, 110–113, 152).

According to James Eisenstein and Herbert Jacob (1977):

> Pervasive conflict is not only unpleasant; it also makes work more difficult. Cohesion produces a sense of belonging and identification that satisfies human needs. It is maintained in several ways. Courtroom work groups shun outsiders because of their potential threat to group cohesion. The work group possesses a variety of adaptive techniques to minimize the effect of abrasive participants. For instance, the occasional defense attorney who violates routine cooperative norms may be punished by having to wait until the end of the day to argue his motion; he may be given less time than he wishes for a lunch break in the middle of a trial; he may be kept beyond usual court hours for bench conferences. Likewise, unusually adversarial defense or prosecuting attorneys are likely to smooth over their formal conflicts with informal cordiality. Tigers at the bench, they become tame kittens in chambers and in the hallways, exchanging pleasantries and exuding sociability. (24–25)

The "justice" negotiated behind the scenes in the courthouse corridors, judges' chambers, or even the restrooms is far more frequent than the criminal trial that looms so large on TV and movie screens. "Justice by consent" dominates the reality of criminal courts, not the criminal trial. This reality that due process, crime control, and social justice have to fit in with the work group's organizational and personal agenda confuses those who aren't part of it, often to the point of exasperation. Deals prosecutors and defense attorneys make and judges approve are inconsistent (or so they appear to be) with both due process and crime control (Levin 1977, 3; Rosett and Cressey 1976, 2).

As parts of an organization, judges, prosecutors, and defense attorneys don't oppose one another in competition for the truth. They're a team, negotiating the best settlement possible with minimal dispute and maximum harmony within the courtroom work group. They have the largely thankless task of doing what they can to balance an array of competing, often irreconcilable, demands and values. Such balancing rarely satisfies anyone, because no one gets everything he or she wants—that's what settlement, as opposed to victory, means. In the adversary system, the goal is victory, and there's always a winner—or at least it seems that way from the outside. In negotiation, the goal is settlement, and the result is always at best "only half a loaf." Don't think negotiation and settlement have to mean injustice. They usually represent the best outcome possible in the real world (Nardulli, Eisenstein, and Flemming 1988, 373–374).

Judges

"The decision as to who will make the decisions affects what decisions will be made," Jack Peltason (1955), scholar of federal courts, wrote in 1955. This statement is still true. Even though we pride ourselves on being a "government of laws" and not individuals, judges play a major policymaking role in American criminal justice. The personal characteristics of judges affect decision making, so we need to know something about these characteristics (Slotnick 1995, 200).

States and the federal government select judges by three methods: popular election, appointment, and the merit plan. Thirty-two states elect judges—some in partisan, others in nonpartisan, elections. Thirty-seven states and the federal government appoint judges. The president nominates and the Senate approves federal judges; governors appoint state judges. Twenty-two states select judges according to the merit system, or the Missouri Bar Plan. (Missouri created the merit plan idea in 1940 to overcome the widespread use of political patronage in judicial selection.) Under the merit system, a commission made up of lawyers, citizens, and an incumbent judge draws up the list of nominees. From this list, governors appoint judges to fill a short initial term. After it expires, judges have to be elected (Bureau of Justice Statistics 1988, 64).

Supporters of the merit system argue that impartial decision making depends on knowing the law and the ability to judge according to the law. Elections and their dependence on party loyalty stand in the way of impartial decision making. Supporters of the elective system promote its democracy, arguing elected judges are responsive and responsible to the community they serve. Voters will (and should) throw out judges who don't respond to community values (Hall and Aspin 1987, 340; Nagel 1975, 31–32; Scheb 1988, 170–174).

Whether elected or appointed, interest groups—political parties, bar associations, businesses, police unions, civil rights organizations—try their best to influence the selection of judges, because they want policy to benefit their particular interests. Members of women's and minority groups, like other interest groups, seek the appointment of women and minority judges who will represent their interests. Minority groups especially feel the need for representation on state courts, because they're most likely to come in contact with state criminal justice and they make up such a small proportion of judges compared with their percentage in the general population (Figure 7.2).

In 2000, 18 percent of federal district court judges were women—double the percentage in 1990. We don't have complete numbers for state judges, but limited data show similar progress. For example, the majority of the Massachusetts supreme court are women, and one-third of all judges are women. Still, there are fewer

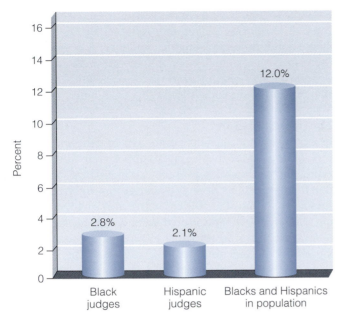

FIGURE 7.2
Percentage of Black and Hispanic Judges, 1997
SOURCE: ABA Task Force on Minorities in the Judiciary 1997.

women judges at the top, fewer with life tenure, and fewer minority women. Does gender matter in decision making? The little available research suggests it doesn't (ABA Commission on Women and the Legal Profession 2001).

 7-4 Selection of judges in your state

Prosecutors

Judges are the most visible and certainly look like they're the most important members of the courtroom work group. But, looks are probably deceiving. According to Professor of Criminal Justice Candace McCoy (1998), prosecutors are the most powerful members:

> The prosecutor is the government's representative and advocate in all phases of criminal adjudication. Except for the daily operations of public police, prosecution is the most powerful component of the criminal justice process because of the number of offenders and victims it affects and because it dominates decision making about the legal course of every case. In the United States, the prosecutor reviews the cases of all defendants arrested by the police, exercises independent investigatory powers, determines the factual and legal sufficiency of each case and whether to dismiss or pursue it, officially files the charges, negotiates the conditions of guilty pleas, and serves as the trial attorney whose client is the state. (457)

Prosecutors are a vital link between police and courts and courts and corrections. Police bring arrests to prosecutors, not to judges. Prosecutors, not judges, decide whether these cases ever get to court (Chapter 8). Enormous power results from this connection. By deciding not to charge, prosecutors can stop a police investigation in its tracks and render courts and corrections powerless. Even when they charge, they shape the course of events inside the work group by what crimes they decide to charge defendants with, what plea arrangements they make with defense attorneys, and what sentences they recommend to judges (Buchanan 1989, 2–8; Greenwood et al. 1973; Jacoby 1980).

Prosecution in the United States is local. Counties elect prosecutors. In 1996 (the latest available figures), 2343 local prosecutors' offices employed about 71,000 attorneys, investigators, and support staff—an increase of 25 percent over 1992. About 75 percent of chief prosecutors held full-time positions (Bureau of Justice Statistics 1998a).

Prosecution is local because American colonists hated the appointment of prosecutors by English kings thousands of miles away. The colonists also opposed private prosecutors because they denied equal access to justice. As soon as the Revolution was over, the new United States put into effect locally elected prosecutors paid for with public funds (McCoy 1998, 458).

The federal system is different. The president appoints federal prosecutors (U.S. attorneys) for all ninety-four federal districts. Despite this uniform centralized formal system, informal practice varies dramatically among the districts, especially, "considering that the U.S. attorneys in each district are drawn from the ranks of the party faithful with close ties to local political constituencies" (McCoy 1998, 458).

Prosecutors pursue multiple and conflicting missions. Formally, they're the chief law enforcement officer in the criminal courts. More than sixty years ago, U.S. Supreme Court Justice George Sutherland described their function in a classic statement:

> The mission of the prosecutor is not that he shall win a case, but that justice shall be done. As such, he is in a peculiar and very definite sense the servant of the law, the twofold aim of which is that guilt shall not escape or innocence suffer. He may prosecute with earnestness and vigor—indeed, he should do so. But, while he may strike hard blows, he is not at liberty to strike foul ones. (*Berger v. U.S.* 1935)

Along with pursuing justice, prosecutors are also office administrators, formulating policy and managing cases and their office staff. They're also careerists. They have their eye on gaining higher public office, entering high-paying prestigious private practice, or maybe just keeping their comfortable work group relations until they retire. We'll look at each of these missions as well as the structure and management of prosecutors' offices.

The law enforcement mission

Most of us have the image of prosecutors as law enforcers. This isn't surprising because it's how we most often see and hear about them in the news and in TV drama. In the real world, prosecutors' power to choose what crimes and suspects to prosecute is an essential part of law enforcement. Prosecutors use various standards to measure how successfully they're accomplishing their law enforcement mission. For example, they may decide welfare fraud deserves high priority and measure their success in dealing with it by either the number of convictions, the ratio of convictions to acquittals, or the types and lengths of sentences offenders get. If prosecutors see themselves as the people's representative, public opinion influences their decisions. So, if welfare recipients "ripping off the taxpayers" arouse the public, prosecutors prosecute welfare-related offenses. If the community believes drunk drivers are "getting off too easy," the representative-of-the-people-type prosecutors seek a high conviction rate and harsh sentences for drunk drivers (Carter 1974; Mellon, Jacoby, and Brewer 1981, 52; Neubauer 1974, 45).

Other prosecutors see themselves as public interest lawyers, experts elected by the public to control crime as their professional judgment dictates. So, *they* and not the public decide what crimes to prosecute, what sentences to ask for, and how to measure success. They work to serve the community's *interest,* not to satisfy the public's *desires.* When asked how he views the public, one prosecutor who considers himself a trustee of the public's best interest replied, "With a jaundiced eye" (Mellon, Jacoby, and Brewer 1981).

Prosecutors may be law enforcement officers, but they don't always get along with local police departments. This is nothing new. More than seventy years ago, President Hoover's National Commission on Law Observance and Enforcement found "frequent lack of cooperation between investigating and prosecuting agencies in the same locality." Why? Prosecutors work in different surroundings from the police. The police work on the streets; prosecutors work in and around the criminal courts with other lawyers. Prosecutors focus on **legal guilt**—enough *admissible* evidence to win cases; police officers act on **factual guilt**—when they "know" individuals are guilty. Legal rules and the professional legal subculture prosecutors work in can seem not just like a rebuke to police work but a system that sacrifices the interests of victims, cops, and the public by making "deals" with criminals and their lawyers (see Chapter 8 on plea bargaining). For prosecutors, who see the world through the eyes of the work group, a plea of guilty to a lesser crime than the offender really committed might be enough. To police, who see the world through the eyes of the police working personality (Chapter 6), the government should prosecute, convict, and punish criminals for the crimes they actually committed, not make deals for something less (Feeley and Lazerson 1983, 229–232; Feeney 1981, 4–6; Forst 1981, 1–3).

The justice mission

Prosecutors aren't just law enforcement officers, as officers of the court they're also supposed to do justice. Doing justice includes protecting defendants' constitutional rights—remember prosecutors can fight hard but they have to fight fair. Doing justice also includes tailoring the law to suit individual defendants' needs. Sometimes, this means deciding *not* to prosecute—like diverting drunk drivers into alcohol treatment. Or, it might mean asking for a sentence of probation for a first-time drug offender.

The organizational mission

Prosecution offices are organizations and as such their missions are efficiency, economy, and smooth-working relations among staff and between staff and other public agencies and the community. As heads of this organization, prosecutors put a premium on cases and crimes that produce the greatest impact for the quickest and most economical processing. Prosecutors as administrators also favor rules that foster routine, regular, and predictable results. So, they emphasize the uniformity of cases, rather than the uniqueness of individuals (Nardulli 1979, 108–111).

The career mission

Prosecutors want to get ahead in the legal profession. If they want to be career prosecutors, they build friendly relationships with their superiors and members of related agencies, mainly the police, public defenders, and judges. If they want to move up the political ladder, making the right political connections influences their decision making. If it's private practice they're after, they seek the goodwill of members of private law firms (Carter 1974, 71–74).

Structure and management

Prosecution management varies according to jurisdiction size, geography, resources, and technology. Every jurisdiction has a chief prosecutor, usually elected to a four-year term. In small jurisdictions, prosecutors work alone or with a few assistants who know one another personally and who work together closely. These prosecutors usually have their own private practices, too. In large jurisdictions, prosecutors' offices are large agencies with lots of assistant district attorneys (ADAs) whom chief prosecutors rarely see and probably don't even know. Chief prosecutors (DAs or county attorneys) in states,

Police-prosecutor teams have overcome some of the problems arising out of their different interests. The teams—police investigators and prosecutors—work closely from the early stages of investigation all the way to conviction. Maine created an entirely new agency, the Bureau of Intergovernmental Drug Enforcement to require police-prosecutor cooperation. The agency was responsible for "the integration and coordination of investigative and prosecutorial functions in the State with respect to drug law enforcement." For the first time, state law "mandated that prosecutors and investigators team up to create a more efficient and effective drug law enforcement strategy. It's not an investigation and then a trial; it's a unitary process, a case throughout," according to Assistant U.S. Attorney for Maine John Gleason (Buchanan 1989, 2–3).

The agency has reduced basic misunderstandings arising from the different worlds of police and prosecutors. According to bureau supervisor Dan Ross (Buchanan 1989):

> We have had to change some of our ideas because the attorney's perspective is that of the courtroom. Officers may not be concerned with how things appear in court because they tend to concentrate on just the facts. But the attorney has to care because appearances are so important in getting a conviction. (2–3)

For example, to get evidence in drug cases, police officers in Maine depended heavily on informants. Prosecutors didn't want to call informants as witnesses because jurors react negatively to informant witnesses. Once they worked together, police realized this and got evidence to back up what informants told them. Prosecutors also benefit from the teamwork. One prosecutor said, "The insights I have gained into case investigation translate into better courtroom performance." For example, prosecutors working closely with drug cops learned officers often have to decide on the spot to search when they've got limited information. Knowing this, prosecutors can make more effective arguments for the good faith exception to the search warrant requirement, an area, according to one

prosecutor in Maine, "where prosecutors are sometimes weak" (Buchanan 1989, 4).

Laconia, New Hampshire, adopted a police-prosecutor cooperation approach to test its effectiveness in battling quality-of-life crimes that don't get publicity but use up the lion's share of police budgets (Chapter 5). In Laconia, a prosecutor with an office in the police department prosecutes all misdemeanor arrests. Officers consult with the prosecutor about filing criteria and investigative practices, and the prosecutor lets police know how cases are decided in court. Knowledge about case dispositions has helped cops' decision making enough to close legal loopholes in cases of driving while intoxicated (DWI), disorderly conduct, theft, and assault. According to the chief of police in Laconia, the close contact between police and prosecutors has also reduced the number of lawsuits against the police. The chief says, "A higher degree of legal awareness has developed, and it is reflected in the officers' actions on the street" (Buchanan 1989, 7).

A New York police-prosecutor program to prepare felony cases was supposed to reduce the number of felony cases dropped or thrown out. Did it? To find out, James Garofolo (1991, 439–449) examined felony arrests and interviewed prosecutors and liaison officers in a sample of six county prosecutor's offices and the New York State Police. Four of the counties instituted the liaison program; two didn't. The program had little effect on felony case attrition and liaison officers had little effect on whether cases produced convictions. But, liaison officers *did* cut down case "slippage"—conviction for an offense less than the charge, such as from a Class E felony to a Class A misdemeanor. And, it improved communication between prosecutors and arresting officers.

Questions

1. Summarize the findings of the studies discussed.
2. List those that favor cooperation and those that don't.
3. What would you recommend as a wise public policy regarding cooperation? Why? Support your answer with information you have acquired.

and U.S. attorneys in federal jurisdictions, hardly ever appear in court. They set general office policy, deal with the public, and manage relations with other criminal justice agencies. Some chief prosecutors are career prosecutors, but most eventually wind up in private practice, become judges, or run for higher political office (Bureau of Justice Statistics 1992a, 1).

Most assistant prosecutors have just graduated from law school. They're usually appointed because of the law school they graduated from and where they ranked in their class—and their political connections. Democrats usually appoint assistant prosecutors who are Democrats; Republicans appoint Republicans. Most assistant prosecutors don't make prosecution a career. They stay fewer than five years and then go into private practice. "You're not supposed to stay too long. Sixty percent leave after three years. The longer you stay the less career value is the ADA [assistant district attorney] experience," said one (Wice 1985, 63). When they leave, most assistant prosecutors don't go to prestigious corporate law firms. They usually stay in criminal law practice, often becoming defense attorneys. A few become judges, but they hardly ever run for political office.

Assistant prosecutors operate according to two systems. Under the **zone system,** or horizontal case assignment, assistants are assigned to manage one stage of the prosecution—drafting criminal charges, working on pretrial motions, trying cases, or handling appeals. Under the **case system,** or vertical case management, assistants are assigned to manage all stages of specific defendants' cases from charge at least through trial and often through appeal. Zone system assistants get to be experts in criminal procedure (arraignment, preliminary hearing, pretrial motions, and trial); case system assistants become experts in criminal law (homicide, rape, burglary) (Jacoby 1980, 3).

Defense Counsel

Defense lawyers, like the other members of the courtroom work group (and all other criminal justice professionals for that matter), pursue formal and informal missions. We're all familiar with their formal mission to defend their clients. Their informal mission is to bargain with prosecutors to get the best deal for their clients. Another important informal organizational mission is to get along with the courtroom work group. They, too, have to focus on their career missions.

Defending accused persons

"In all criminal prosecutions, the accused shall enjoy the right to . . . have the Assistance of Counsel for his defense." So the Bill of Rights to the U.S. Constitution commands. To this the U.S. Supreme Court has added: Defendant's have the right to *effective* counsel (Chapter 8). And

the lawyer's code of ethics says defense lawyers have to "zealously" defend their clients. So, formally, defense lawyers have the constitutional duty and professional responsibility to make sure the government proves every element of its case beyond a reasonable doubt, based on evidence that was legally obtained and without any help from the accused.

An effective and zealous defense can go so far as to "actually frustrate the search for truth. Indeed, defense counsel may be ethically required to do so," says Rodney J. Uphoff (1995, 16). This may be especially true when lawyers *know* their clients' are guilty. One defense lawyer in Arthur Lewis Wood's (1967) classic study of the defense bar summed up the formal mission this way:

> It's a criminal lawyer's function to get a criminal off or help him get a lighter sentence. He's helping him preserve his freedom. Whether it's good for society to have a criminal loose is another question. It may not be good for society, but that is the lawyer's job. It's his duty to the client; everybody knows it. His job is to preserve his client's freedom. (67)

The work group mission

In the 1960s, Abraham Blumberg (1967, 22) called the practice of criminal defense law "a confidence game." According to Blumberg, organizational pressures generated by the courtroom work group lead criminal defense lawyers to abandon their role of zealous advocate for the accused. Relationships with judges and prosecutors, he believed, outweigh the needs of clients. To maintain good relations, judges, prosecutors, and defense lawyers join together in an "organized system of complicity" (20).

It's true defense lawyers, especially public defenders, aren't just lawyers, they're members of the courtroom work group. According to one observer, they're "surrogates of the prosecutor, a member of their 'little syndicate.'" The government pays public defenders, so it's no surprise some people view them as agents of the government—a suspicion shared by indigent defendants. The "friendly adversary" relationship between defense counsel and their supposed opponents—prosecutors—feeds this suspicion. Opponents, after all, aren't supposed to be friends (Caspar 1972, 107, 110–111).

David W. Neubauer (1974), who has studied day-to-day decision making in criminal justice systems in "middle America," puts it this way:

> If they are friendly adversaries, then we begin to suspect something is amiss. For example, if you visit most courtrooms, you will see the prosecution and defense exchange pleasantries before, after, and during the court appearances. You may even see two lawyers strenuously arguing their case in court, and then

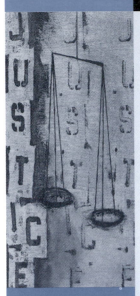

Professor Alan Dershowitz is a Harvard Law School professor who has defended many high-profile defendants. Consider the following passages from Dershowitz's *The Best Defense* (1982):

> Attorneys who defend the guilty and the despised will never have a secure or comfortable place in any society. Their motives will be misunderstood; they will be suspected of placing loyalty to clients above loyalty to society; and they will be associated in the public mind with the misdeeds of their clients. They will be seen as troublemakers and gadflies. The best of them will always be on the firing line, with their licenses exposed to attack.
>
> There will never be a Nobel Prize for defense attorneys who succeed in freeing the guilty. Indeed there are few prizes or honors ever bestowed on defense lawyers for their zealousness. The ranks of defense attorneys are filled with a mixed assortment of human beings from the most noble and dedicated to the most sleazy and corrupt. It is a profession that seems to attract extremes. The public sometimes has difficulty distinguishing between the noble and the sleazy; the very fact that a defense lawyer represents a guilty client leads some to conclude that the lawyer must be sleazy. Being so regarded is an occupational hazard of all zealous defense attorneys.
>
> The zealous defense attorney is the last bastion of liberty—the final barrier between an overreaching government and its citizens. The job of the defense attorney is to challenge the government; to make those in power justify their conduct in relation to the powerless; to articulate and defend the right of those who lack the ability or resources to defend themselves. (Even the rich are relatively powerless—less so, of course, than the poor—when confronting the resources of a government prosecutor.)
>
> One of the truest tests of a free country is how it treats those whose job it is to defend the guilty and the despised. In most repressive countries there is no independent defense bar. Indeed, a sure sign that repression is on the way is when the government goes after the defense attorneys. Shakespeare said, "The first thing we do, let's kill all the lawyers." Hitler, Stalin, the Greek colonels, and the Chinese Cultural Revolutionaries may not have killed all the lawyers first, but they surely placed defense attorneys—especially vigorous and independent ones—high on their hit lists.
>
> One of the surest ways of undercutting the independence of defense attorneys is to question the propriety of their representing the guilty. Those who argue that defense attorneys should limit their representation to the innocent, or indeed to any specific group or category, open the door to a system where the government decides who is, and who is not, entitled to a defense. Granting the power to the government, to the bar, or to any establishment, marks the beginning of the end of an independent defense bar—and the beginning of the end of liberty.
>
> The role of the defense attorney who defends guilty clients is the hardest role in the criminal justice system to explain to members of the public. In 1980 I traveled to China to advise the People's Republic on its criminal justice system. Most Chinese lawyers seemed to understand the need for free and independent judges and prosecutors. But hardly anyone—even those lawyers who had suffered most under the Cultural Revolution—seemed willing to justify the actions of a defense attorney representing a client whom he knew to be guilty and "counter-revolutionary." (Every society has its own favorite epithets for those it most despises.) "Why should our government pay someone to stand in the way of socialist justice?" was the question I was most often asked. I tried to explain that justice—whether socialist, capitalist, or anything else—is a process, not only an end; and that for the process to operate fairly, all persons charged with crime must have the right to a defense. Since not all defendants are created equal in their ability to speak effectively, think logically, and argue forcefully, the role of a defense attorney—trained in these and other skills—is to perform those functions for the defendant. The process of determining whether a defendant should be deemed guilty and punished requires that the government be put to its proof and that the accused have a fair opportunity to defend.
>
> I also tried to explain to the Chinese lawyers that laws that are today directed against counterrevolutionaries may tomorrow be directed at them. As H. L. Mencken once put it: "The trouble about fighting for human freedom is that you have to spend much of your life defending sons of bitches; for oppressive laws are always aimed at them originally, and oppression must be stopped in the beginning if it is to be stopped at all."
>
> To me the most persuasive argument for defending the guilty and the despised is to consider the alternative. Those governments that forbid or discourage such representation have little to teach us about justice. Their systems are far more corrupt, less fair, and generally even less efficient than ours. What Winston Churchill once said about democracy can probably also be said about the adversary system of criminal justice: It may well be the worst system of justice, "except [for] all the other [systems] that have been tried from time to time."
>
> The late Supreme Court Justice Felix Frankfurter once commented that he knew of no title "more honorable than that of Professor of the Harvard Law School." I know of none more honorable than defense attorney.

Questions

1. What reasons does Dershowitz give for being a defense attorney? Do you agree with them?

2. A common question people ask defense attorneys is, "How can you defend these people?" Does Dershowitz answer the question?

3. Would you defend a guilty person? (Refer to the Defense Counsel section.) Why or why not? Defend your answer.

having lunch together. Some commentators interpret such actions to mean that the defense has closer ties to the prosecution than to the client, and the client suffers. (78)

Can lawyers vigorously defend clients they've never seen before and probably will never see again, especially when it might antagonize professional peers they have ongoing relationships with? Some empirical evidence suggests defense lawyers *can* wage a hard fight in the adversary system, drive a hard bargain in plea-negotiating sessions, and *still* maintain close professional, peer, and personal relationships with prosecutors and judges. Defense lawyers shouldn't (and most don't) take personally either the fights over defending clients in court or the arguments for clients out of court. In fact, quite the opposite, because it's the heart of the adversary system (McIntyre 1987, 148).

I saw this firsthand when I was a first-year law student. On the advice of my brilliant criminal law professor, Claude Sowle, I went to watch a criminal trial. An inexperienced young prosecutor prosecuted and an experienced defense lawyer defended a teacher accused of murdering his wife. They went at each other so hard the judge finally said, "Boys, boys control yourselves or I'm gonna hold you both in contempt." Then came a lunch break and I saw an astonishing thing: the defense lawyer put his arm around the kid prosecutor, told him what a good job he was doing, and they went off to lunch together. After lunch, they came back and slugged it out for the rest of the afternoon.

How can this be? The answer lies in something else Professor Sowle taught us by his brutal attacks on our arguments and reasoning—don't take it personally and if you can't learn not to, don't be a lawyer. Confrontation, argument, and conflict are part of being a lawyer. One judge said, "Yesterday two lawyers started arguing about their case in the corridor after the hearing. That just shouldn't happen. Lawyers have to know how to channel disagreement" (McIntyre 1987).

The career mission

Many criminal defense lawyers have more immediate concerns than defending their clients' rights or maintaining good working relationships with prosecutors and judges. They're trying to make a living. According to one study, most criminal defense lawyers practice criminal law because it's the only way they can make a living in the law. They didn't graduate at the top of their law school classes, so they couldn't get jobs in large law firms or in corporations. They went into general practice and let minor criminal work help pay their bills. This is especially true of the majority of private criminal defense attorneys. These lawyers form an outer ring, beyond the elite corporate lawyers, with the less elite but still middle-status lawyers such as personal injury and labor lawyers who oppose corporations (Ladinsky 1963, 128).

Some don't like their work, and they don't believe it accomplishes anything noble for anybody: "It's not a very acceptable way of earning a living—at least according to many other lawyers. You are always dealing with shady characters. I take criminal cases but I would just as soon get away from it" (Ladinsky 1963, 64).

Other defense lawyers look at defense work—especially the trial experience they can get as public defenders—as a good credential to obtain positions in prestigious corporate law firms. In a sense, these lawyers treat criminal defense work as an apprenticeship for private law practice. Except in high-paying public defender's offices like the one in Los Angeles, where some attorneys in the mid-1990s were earning close to $100,000 a year, most public defenders leave public defense work after a few years and go into private practice. A lot of prosecutors go to the same private law firms defenders enter (Barker 1993, 83; Platt and Pollock 1974).

Knowledge and Understanding Check

The criminal court structure

✔ Identify and describe the three tiers of criminal courts.
✔ List and describe the formal and informal missions of the lower criminal and felony courts.
✔ Do you have a constitutional right to appeal a lower court's decision to a higher court? Explain.
✔ Describe the practice of appellate court review.

The courtroom work group

✔ Identify the members of the courtroom work group.
✔ List and explain the missions of the courtroom work group.
✔ How are judges selected?
✔ What is the demographic makeup of judges?
✔ List and describe the formal and informal missions of prosecutors.
✔ List and describe the formal and informal missions of defense attorneys.

KEY TERMS

adjudication	courts of limited jurisdiction	jurisdiction
appellate courts	courts of record	legal guilt
career mission	crime control	lower courts
case system	due process mission	organizational mission
courtroom work group	factual guilt	social justice
courts of general jurisdiction	felony courts	zone system

INTERNET PROJECT

Ineffective defense lawyer or ineffective defense system? Enter the key words "ineffective counsel." Summarize the author's arguments. Do you agree? Back up your answer with information in your text and the articles you find on Infotrac.

CHAPTER 8

Charge, Trial, and Guilty Pleas

AP/Wide World Photos

CHAPTER OUTLINE

PROSECUTOR JAVIER ALCALA [WHO WANTS TO GET TOUGH ON A YOUNG GUY CHARGED WITH POSSESSION OF MARIJUANA]: **The guy owns a .22.**

PUBLIC DEFENDER YOLANDA TREVINO: **He doesn't own a .22. A .22 was in his house. You're jumping to all kinds of conclusions.**

ALCALA: **Call it wild speculation.**

JUDGE RONALD LISK [TO ALCALA]: **Are you going to dismiss the felon-with-a-gun charge?**

ALCALA: **No.**

JUDGE LISK: **I'll give four months in county jail.**

ALCALA: **Four months?!**

JUDGE LISK: **He's not exactly [John] Dillinger [the notorious gangster].**

ALCALA: **They've [the cops] spent more time investigating the case than he'll spend in jail!**

TREVINO: **That's right.**

Instead of judges or juries handing down verdicts, the fates of hundreds of thousands of defendants [95 percent] a year are negotiated in two-minute conversations over the telephone, in hallways or parking lots like this one where both jokes and sharp exchanges punctuate the talks but where ultimately, a cordial businesslike atmosphere prevails in front of judges like Judge Lisk. These decisions are the backbone of California's jammed judicial system.

CHRISTOPHER H. SCHMITT (1991A, B)

■ INTRODUCTION

Only one out of ten people arrested for committing a felony goes to prison. Table 8.1 shows the decisions and decision makers who determine whether arrested suspects go free or become defendants and possibly convicted offenders. Figure 8.1 shows the funnel effect of decision making after arrest. In this chapter, we examine the decision making behind this funnel effect, including the decision to charge, what occurs during the defendant's first appearance in court, the trial, and the disposition of cases through guilty pleas.

 8-1 Latest statistics and an in-depth description of the steps in the criminal justice process in Monroe County, Indiana.

THE DECISION TO CHARGE

More than fifty years ago, prosecutor and Supreme Court Justice Robert Jackson (1940) said the power to charge people with crimes gives prosecutors "more control over life, liberty, and reputation than any other person in America" (32–33). Why? Because prosecutors have near total discretion to make three decisions:

1. To charge and—just as important—not to charge suspects with crimes
2. The specific crime to charge suspects with, like first- or second-degree murder
3. Whether to transfer the case from the criminal justice system to social services, like drug treatment, known as **diversion**

The **decision to charge** starts formal court proceedings (**adjudication**). Once adjudication starts, prosecutors represent the government in all the following proceedings:

1. Deciding whether to bail or detain defendants
2. Presiding over grand jury reviews and presenting the government's case in preliminary hearings
3. Presenting the government's case in trials
4. Negotiating guilty pleas with defense lawyers
5. Negotiating sentences with judges and defense lawyers

Let's look further at what influences the decision to charge; how race and gender affect the decision to charge; the consequences of being charged with a crime; and what's involved in testing the government's case.

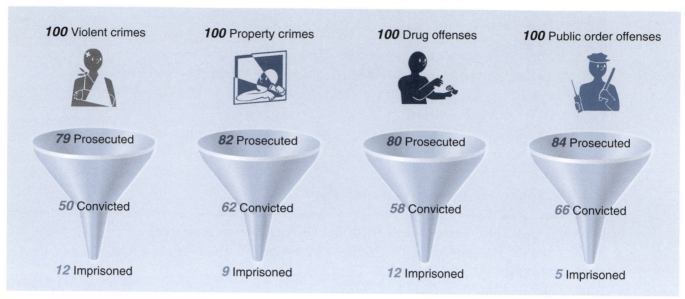

FIGURE 8.1
The Funnel Effect After Arrest
SOURCE: Bureau of Justice Statistics, 1992b, Table 5.53.

TABLE 8.1	
Decisions and Decision Makers from Arrest to Prison	

Decision Makers	Decisions
Prosecutor	• Charge with a crime • Divert to social service agency • Dismiss case • Test case by grand jury or judge • Plea-bargain • Try case • Recommend sentence
Judge	• Set bail • Assign counsel • Bind defendant over for trial • Rule on motions and objections before, during, and after trial • Sentence defendants
Bail bondsman	• Put up money bail • Pursue defendants who fail to appear
Grand jury	• Indict • "No bill" or dismiss charge
Defense counsel	• Advise defendant how to plead • Plea-bargain with prosecutor • Develop strategy to defend client's interest
Defendant	• Plead guilty or not guilty • Accept plea bargain
Court personnel	• Conduct bail investigation • Conduct pre-sentence investigation and report
Trial jury	• Convict • Acquit

Influences on the Decision to Charge

"Let the punishment fit the crime," the famous eighteenth-century Italian criminal law reformer Cesare Beccaria urged. In other words, focus on behavior the law defines as criminal and fit the punishment to the behavior. Ironically, modern prosecutors have stood Beccaria's idea on its head: They fit the crime to the punishment. They decide how much punishment the "badness" of the act and the "sinisterness" of the suspect deserve, and then they look for a crime to fit the deserved punishment. The bottom line: The decision to charge is the most discretionary decision (meaning it's the least subject to review) in all of criminal justice (Albonetti 1986, 624).

Most experts believe prosecutors need this broad discretion because not all arrests *should* turn into criminal charges. Some victims don't want prosecution. In other cases, there might not be enough evidence to prove defendants are guilty beyond a reasonable doubt. Maybe counseling or other noncriminal responses are better. Maybe resources can be spent better on prosecuting other cases (Gottfredson and Gottfredson 1988, 113–114).

What criteria do prosecutors use in deciding whether to charge and what to charge suspects with? Empirical research (Gottfredson and Gottfredson, 1988, 119–128; Miller et al. 2000, 661–663) points to four criteria we're familiar with by now. One is formal—the **strength of the case** against the suspect. Three are informal—seriousness of the offense, the criminal history of the suspect, and the relationship between the suspect and the victim.

Let's look at the formal legal criterion—the strength of the case. Legally, the strength of the case means the amount of evidence against the suspect. All the research puts this criterion at the top of the list of influences on prosecutors' decision to charge. So, answers to the questions, Are there witnesses? Are they believable? Will they show up in court? Is there physical evidence? and Is it admissible? are all important. If the evidence adds up to what prosecutors believe is proof beyond a reasonable doubt they'll charge suspects; if it doesn't, they won't.

The research repeatedly shows that whether law enforcement officers violated suspects' constitutional rights (got evidence by illegal searches and seizures and by coerced confessions) practically *never*—in less than one-tenth of 1 percent of all cases—enters into prosecutors' decision to charge. Prosecutors' concern isn't that police got evidence *illegally*; it's whether there's *enough* evidence to prove suspects are guilty beyond a reasonable doubt. For every one case prosecutors drop because police violated suspects' constitutional rights, *twenty* are dropped because the police didn't get enough evidence to prove they're guilty (Forst 1995, 363–365).

According to sociologist Donald Black (1989), "The strength of the case is a sociological as well as a legal question" (24). Black calls this sociological question the **social structure of the case.** In their charging decision, prosecutors have to answer the questions:

> **Who allegedly killed whom? That is, what were the characteristics of the alleged victim and the accused? Was this an upward or a downward murder (was the social status of the accused below or above the social status of the victim)? Or was it a lateral murder (between equals)? If lateral, at what status level were the principals: low, intermediate, or high? And what was the relational structure of the crime? Were the victim and the accused acquainted? If so, how well? Who are the witnesses for each side? . . . Anyone who ventures into the legal world without knowing how to assess the sociological strengths and weaknesses of a case has a disadvantage. Any law school that does not offer a course on this subject is denying its students valuable knowledge about how the law actually works. (Black 1989, 24)**

Prosecutors are wary of charging in cases where there's some kind of relationship between suspects and victims. For example, New York City prosecutors decided not to charge in more than half the assault cases in which suspects and victims had some kind of prior relationship (Vera Institute of Justice 1977). Why? According to one assistant district attorney:

> This woman was charged on the complaint of her common-law husband. She then filed a complaint against him for assault. I don't know which of them called the police first. The charge against her was reduced in the Complaint Room to assault in the third degree [a misdemeanor]. Because they were both com-plainants in court, I was able to speak to them both. They told me they did not wish to continue prosecution. They told me that they were both drinking and apparently they both started to insult each other. It wasn't clear who struck first, but the common-law husband struck his wife with a shovel, hitting her in the eye, and she struck him in the arm with an exacto knife, causing injury. Neither said they were injured seriously, though the arresting police officer had written up her assault against her husband as assault in the second degree, while his assault against her was a third-degree assault. She was also charged with possession of a weapon as a misdemeanor, which was also dropped because the husband refused to testify as to how the knife was used. The knife was not classified as a dangerous instrument per se.
>
> When I had satisfied myself that neither had been injured seriously, I looked at their past records. He had one previous arrest ten years ago, I don't recall for what, and she had no prior arrests. I felt that since there had not been problems with the law, and neither one had any sort of record, there was no reason to keep this case in court. (31–32)

This case shows a mix of the formal and informal criteria we've been examining. Of course, the relationship is important, but so is the seriousness of the offense—there weren't any serious injuries. The strength of the case also played a part in the decision—the victim didn't want her husband convicted and she wouldn't make a good witness because she wasn't entirely innocent herself. Whether the suspect had a criminal history was also considered—he had only one prior arrest and that was ten years ago; she had none.

Race, Gender, and the Decision to Charge

Do improper criteria like race and gender infect the decision to charge? Rarely, say some researchers. Celesta A. Albonetti (1986, 639) found race had no effect, and gender had only a little (women had a 7 percent better chance than men of having charges against them dropped) in the Washington, D.C. trial courts. Barbara Boland and her colleagues (1989) reported the strength of the case against the defendants (number of witnesses, amount of physical evidence, use of a weapon), not defendants' race or gender, affected the decision to charge in a nationwide sample of jurisdictions. W. Boyd Littrell (1979, 32–33) found little evidence of race or gender influencing the decision to charge in the New Jersey jurisdictions he examined.

Other researchers, however, say race, gender, and ethnicity *do* infect the decision to charge. Cassia Spohn, John Gruhl, and Susan Welch (1987, 175–181) examined the decision to charge Black, White, and Hispanic female

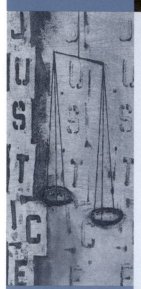

Charging Factors in Rape

Professor Susan Estrich (1987) of the Harvard Law School relates the following incident in her essay on sexual assault and the legal system, *Real Rape*:

> The man telling me this . . . story is an assistant district attorney in a large Western city. He is in his thirties, an Ivy League law school graduate, a liberal, married to a feminist. He's about as good as you're going to get making decisions like this. This is a case he did not prosecute. He considers it rape—but only "technically." This is why.
>
> The victim came to his office for the meeting dressed in a pair of tight jeans. Very tight. With a see-through blouse on top. Very revealing. That's how she was dressed. It was, he tells me, really something. Something else. Did it matter? Are you kidding!
>
> The man involved was her ex-boyfriend. And lover; well, ex-lover. They ran into each other on the street. He asked her to come up and see *Splash* on his new VCR. She did. It was not the Disney version—of *Splash*, that is. It was porno. They sat in the living room watching. Like they used to. He said, "Let's go into the bedroom where we'll be more comfortable." He moved the VCR. They watched from the bed. Like they used to. He began rubbing her foot. Like he used to. Then he kissed her. She said no, she didn't want this, and got up to leave. He pulled her back on the bed and forced himself on her. He did not beat her. She had no bruises. Afterward she ran out. The first thing she did was flag a police car. That, the prosecutor tells us, was the first smart thing she did.
>
> The prosecutor pointed out to her that she was not hurt, that she had no bruises, that she did not fight. She pointed out to the prosecutor that her ex-boyfriend was a weight lifter. He told her it would be nearly impossible to get a conviction. She could accept that, she said; even if he didn't get convicted, at least he should be forced to go through the time and expense of defending himself. That clinched it, said the D.A. She was just trying to use the system to harass her ex-boyfriend. He had no criminal record. He was not a "bad guy." No charges were filed.
>
> Someone walked over and asked what we were talking about. About rape, I replied; no, actually about cases that aren't really rape. The D.A. looked puzzled. That was rape, he said. Technically. She was forced to have sex without consent. It just wasn't a case you prosecute. (8–9)

Table 8.2 shows the rank order of factors that prosecutors interviewed by researchers at the Battelle Law and Justice Study Center considered most important in deciding whether to charge suspects with rape or a

TABLE 8.2

Factors in Filing Rape Charges

Rank	Factor	Percent Choosing
1	Use of physical force	82.0
2	Proof of penetration	78.0
3	Promptness of reporting	71.3
4	Extent of suspect I.D.	67.3
5	Injury to victim	63.3
6	Circumstances of initial contact	61.3
7	Relationship of victim and accused	60.7
8	Use of weapon	58.0
9	Resistance by victim	54.0
10	Witnesses	36.0
11	Suspect's previous record	31.3
12	Age of victim or suspect	24.7
13	Alcohol or drug involvement	12.7
14	Victim's previous arrest record	10.7
15	Sexual acts other than intercourse	9.3
16	Location of offense	4.0
17	Accomplices	3.4
18	Race of victim and suspect	0.7
19	Occupation of suspect	0.7

SOURCE: Battelle Law and Justice Study Center 1977.

lesser charge. Notice that more than half the prosecutors considered the use of force, the proof of penetration, the promptness of reporting, the extent of suspect identification, whether there was injury to the victim, the circumstances of the initial contact, the relationship between the victim and the accused, the use of a weapon, and resistance by the victim important. Most important to prosecutors' decision to charge was resistance by the victim, then came consent, and finally were personal characteristics of the victim and the offender, such as race, occupation, and criminal record.

Questions

1. Do you agree with the rankings in Table 8.2?
2. Do they indicate prosecutors take mainly formal or informal legal factors into account when charging rape?
3. Do you agree with the prosecutor's decision in the case Professor Estrich relates?
4. Legally, rape requires the intent to penetrate sexually against the will and without the consent of the victim. Does the charging decision in rape indicate prosecutors follow the law, or do organizational, community, professional, and other informal interests mainly influence their decisions?

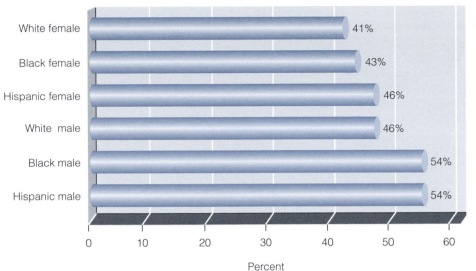

FIGURE 8.2

Percentage of Cases Charged

SOURCE: Walker, Spohn, and Delone 2000, Table 5.5.

and male defendants in over 33,000 Los Angeles cases. Controlling for age, seriousness of the offense, criminal history of the defendant, and whether defendants were armed, they found discrimination in favor of women and against Hispanics and Blacks (Figure 8.2). Race, gender, and ethnicity only matter in borderline cases, they found. Where the evidence is strong enough to definitely charge or too weak to charge at all, race and gender have no effect.

What are we to make of these conflicting findings among respectable researchers? According to Spohn and her colleagues (1987), we shouldn't get too comfortable with reassuring findings that race, ethnicity, and gender don't infect decision making, especially in highly discretionary, low visibility decisions like charging suspects with crimes. "While [our] findings are certainly not definitive, even for [Los Angeles], they do call for the kind of scrutiny in the pretrial stages that has been so rightly given to the convicting and sentencing stages" (187).

Consequences of the Decision to Charge

The decision to turn suspects into defendants by charging them with crimes has far-reaching consequences, even if the charges don't end up in convictions. The consequences for the defendants can include losing time at work or maybe even getting fired; getting locked up during court proceedings; and suffering damages to their reputation even if they're acquitted. After he was acquitted, one former U.S. Secretary of Labor asked bitterly, "How do I get my reputation back?"

Becoming a criminal defendant is a form of "degradation ceremony," to borrow Erving Goffman's phrase. According to Abraham S. Blumberg (1970):

The accused is confronted by definitions of himself which reflect the various worlds of the agent-mediators yet are consistent for the most part in their negative evaluation of him. The agent-mediators have seized upon a wholly unflattering aspect of his biography to reinterpret his entire personality and justify their present attitude and conduct toward him. Even an individual with considerable personal and economic resources has great difficulty resisting pressures to redefine himself under these circumstances. For the ordinary accused of modest personal, economic and social resources, the group pressures and definitions of himself are simply too much to bear. He willingly complies with the demands of agent-mediators, who in turn will help "cool him out." (69)

Testing the Government's Case

Formally, the prosecutor's power to charge is limited by the requirement that the government test its case before the case goes to trial. Test the case means an independent review of the prosecutor's decision to charge to make sure there's enough evidence to put the community and the defendant to the time and expense (and for defendants, the additional burden of stigma and stress) of criminal prosecution. The two testing devices are the preliminary hearing and the grand jury review.

In the **preliminary hearing,** lower court judges hear a preview of the government's evidence in open court and defense counsel can challenge the evidence. If judges decide there's enough evidence to go to trial, they **bind over** the defendant. The judge's "bind over" becomes the formal charge. In the **grand jury review,** prosecutors present evidence in secret to grand jurors (selected the same way trial juries are chosen) who decide if there's enough evidence to go to trial. If a majority of the grand jury decides there's enough evidence to go to trial, they "indict" the defendant. The **indictment** becomes the formal charge. We won't spend any more time on these testing devices because they're mainly formal proceedings ratifying what the courtroom work group (Chapter 7) has already—or will soon—work out informally among themselves (Miller et al. 2000, 682–683).

If defendants are bound over by a preliminary hearing judge or indicted by a grand jury, they're arraigned. **Arraignment** is a formal public proceeding consisting of bringing defendants to court, reading the charges against them, and demanding they plead not guilty, guilty, or **nolo contendere** (no contest) to the charges. The arraignment and plea to charges formally set the stage for the criminal trial. Informally, they provide the opportunity either to start, continue, or ratify a plea agreement.

■ THE FIRST APPEARANCE

After prosecutors file charges, defendants make their **first appearance** in court. (Don't confuse the first appearance with the arraignment; the first appearance comes before the arraignment, and defendants don't plead at the first appearance.) The first appearance judge does three things:

1. Reads the charges against defendants and informs them of their rights
2. Appoints lawyers for indigent (poor) defendants
3. Decides whether to bail or detain defendants prior to trial and sets the initial terms for bail or detention

Appointment of Defense Counsel

The U.S. Constitution guarantees every criminal defendant the right to a lawyer (Chapter 7), but it doesn't say anything about how to put that right into practice. The U.S. Supreme Court has filled in some of the blanks. We've already seen that when the Court says counsel it means *effective* counsel (Chapter 7). What about defendants who can't afford a lawyer (most defendants in criminal cases)? Do they have a right to a lawyer without having to pay for one? Yes, according to the Supreme Court—at least in felony cases and in misdemeanor cases if the punishment includes jail time.

How poor do defendants have to be to qualify as **indigent** (the legal term for defendants who are entitled a lawyer because they can't afford to pay for one)? The Supreme Court hasn't answered this question. States make their own rules, and first appearance judges apply the rules. There are three kinds of indigent defense:

1. **Public defenders,** full-time defense lawyers paid for by local taxpayers
2. **Assigned counsel,** lawyers in private practice selected from a list on a rotating basis either for a fee or **pro bono** (donated time)

3. **Contract attorneys,** private attorneys under contracts with local jurisdictions to represent indigent defendants for an agreed-upon fee

How does defense of the poor work in practice? Only 5 percent of all indigent defendants see a lawyer before their first appearance. This means poor defendants usually don't get any legal advice before they're interrogated, have to stand in lineups, or are charged with crimes. Furthermore, the most inexperienced and least-trained lawyers usually defend the poorest defendants (Court 1993). Despite these discouraging facts, some empirical evidence suggests that for poor defendants lucky enough to have lawyers, public defenders do as well for their clients as private defense counsel do for theirs. Roger A. Hanson and his colleagues (1992) analyzed a random sample of 4000 felony cases from nine courts and interviewed 125 defense attorneys. They found public defenders:

■ Disposed of their cases as fast as private lawyers
■ Were as successful as private lawyers at obtaining favorable outcomes for their clients
■ Were compensated and trained as well as prosecutors
■ Received about the same level of support as prosecutors in the same jurisdictions

Former public defender David Lynch (1994) disagrees. Lynch studied defense lawyers in two counties and found the courtroom work group corrupts the relationship between public defenders and their clients:

> **I have witnessed countless criminal defendants who claimed they were being "sold out" by their lawyers. Many asked the court, almost always unsuccessfully, to appoint new counsel. Some later filed collateral attacks, alleging coercion, to the entry of their guilty pleas. These allegations were almost always found to be unsubstantiated. Like mental institution inmates yelling "conspiracy," prison inmates yelling "conspiracy" were never taken credibly, even though the similarities of their tales of woe should have made people wonder. (124)**

The Vera Institute of Justice (2001), a New York City criminal justice research institute, designed and implemented an experiment in public defender service, the Neighborhood Defender Service of Harlem (NDS) in 1990. NDS put its offices in a Harlem neighborhood "far from the courthouse, and made community involvement the core of its approach to defense." It used a "team-approach that united lawyers, community investigators, and caseworkers as equal partners in the process." Vera's evaluation of the NDS experiment showed NDS clients got "substantially shorter" jail and prison sentences than poor clients represented by traditional lawyers for the poor. NDS, now on its own, had represented more than three thousand clients by 2001.

8-2 NDS and Vera Institute's evaluation

Bail and Detention

Almost all misdemeanor defendants and nearly two-thirds of all felony defendants remain free after they're charged (Figure 8.3). Let's look at the history of bail, the money bail system, potential bias in bail decisions, preventive detention, and defendant misconduct while on bail.

Bail

Bail, the release of defendants until their cases are decided, is ancient. More than two thousand years ago, the Greek philosopher Plato (1926) wrote that a "defendant shall provide three substantial securities [individuals] who guarantee to produce him at the trial, and if a man be unable or unwilling to provide these securities, the court must take, bind and keep him, and produce him at the trial of the case" (2:261).

The Eighth Amendment to the U.S. Constitution bans "excessive bail," but the U.S. Supreme Court hasn't done much in the way of telling us what "excessive" means. So, the kinds and amounts of bail are left mainly up to the states. In 1682, the Pennsylvania constitution included a provision copied by the rest of the states. It commanded all prisoners are "bailable" except in capital cases "where proof is evident" (Miller et al. 2000, 616). By 1900, money had replaced individuals to guarantee defendants would show up in court. At first, defendants had to put up the full amount of bail. If defendants showed up for their court date they got their money back. Soon, the money bail system replaced the demand for the full amount or direct financial surety.

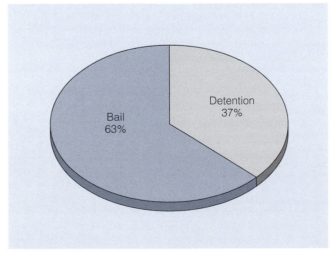

FIGURE 8.3
Pretrial Release and Detention, 1996
SOURCE: Bureau of Justice Statistics 1999.

The money bail system

Under the **money bail system,** defendants pay bondsmen (most of them are men) 10 percent of the total amount of bail; bondsmen are legally liable for the full amount if defendants don't appear. Even if defendants show up, they don't get their 10 percent back—it's the bondsmen's fee. Technically, when defendants fail to appear on private bail bonds, courts can collect the full amount from the bondsmen, who then can recoup the amount paid from defaulting defendants. In practice, this rarely happens. Intricate and entrenched informal rules ensure that bondsmen won't forfeit the amount of bail bonds (Schlesinger 1986, 182).

Bondsmen in Connecticut, for example, avoid forfeiture in several ways. They can compromise by agreement with the court to reduce the forfeited amount. They can also get delays from the court to look for defendants. Finally, they can find and bring their customers to court. From his observations of a Connecticut lower court, Malcolm M. Feeley (1979, 96–111) calculated bondsmen lost only about 3 percent of the face amount of bond forfeitures.

Formally, the amount of bail money is supposed to be just enough to make sure defendants show up in court. Extensive empirical research during the 1960s challenged the fairness of the money bail system in practice (Miller et al. 2000, 617). First, poor defendants were kept in jail, whereas affluent defendants were freed on bail (Foote 1965; Freed and Wald 1964; Goldfarb 1965). Some spent more time in jail waiting for trial than the length of the sentence for the crimes they were charged with (Miller et al. 2000, 618). Also, it's expensive to run jails, and local communities had to pay for feeding, housing, supervising, and caring for sick, detained defendants. Furthermore, detention affected the outcome of poor defendants' cases, because they couldn't help their lawyers as well as defendants out on bail. Many were sentenced to jail and prison instead of probation. Also, they tended to be sentenced to longer terms than bailed defendants because they couldn't show they were working, maintaining community ties, and obeying the law while they waited for trial (Rankin 1964, 641).

 8-3 Bail and 9/11

This research and the political temper of the 1960s led to a powerful bail reform movement. The heart of the movement was to shift bail decision making away from money and toward the characteristics of individual defendants. In 1961, the Manhattan Bail Project set off a wave of changes throughout the country. The Project staff personally interviewed arrested defendants to find out if they had ties to the community that would ensure they showed up in court. If they did, they were released solely on their promise to appear in court. Release in exchange for a promise to appear is called **release on recognizance (ROR).** Evaluation of the program was promising. According to Chris Eskridge's (1983) survey of research:

> From the data now available, it appears likely that [pretrial release] programs in general are able to ensure the appearance of an accused individual for the appointed court hearings at least as well as the traditional money bail system, and probably a bit better due to the screening ability of programs. (99–100)

Many states and the federal government passed laws shifting decision making away from money to ROR and other nonmoney conditions of release on bail.

 8-4 The Bail Reform Act of 1966

Race and gender bias in bail decisions

Empirical research about bail decisions backs up what we've found about decision making by police and prosecutors: Most of the time, judges decide bail according to three appropriate criteria:

1. The seriousness of the charges against defendants
2. The strength of the prosecution's case against defendants
3. The criminal history of defendants (Goldkamp 1985, 8–9; LaFave and Israel 1984, 2:114; Wice 1974)

Still, some research challenges these findings. E. Britt Patterson and Michael J. Lynch (1991) examined how judges decided bail according to a bail schedule in a large western city. **Bail schedules** are lists setting the amount of bail a defendant has to pay according to the offense defendants are charged with. Judges can raise or lower the amount on the schedule. What did they find? Whites, particularly White women, were more likely to receive bail *below* the schedule than non-Whites. When they controlled for seriousness of the offense and criminal history of the defendant, they found non-Whites and men had about the same chance as Whites and women to receive bail above the amount on the schedule. However, Whites and women were significantly more likely than non-White men to receive bail *below* the schedule (Figure 8.4).

Patterson and Lynch (1991) concluded, "Although minorities were not treated more harshly than whites, they were discriminated against because they were not given the same benefit of the doubt as were whites" (129).

 8-5 Riverside County, California's bail schedule

Preventive detention

Whether getting individuals to vouch for defendants, demanding money from them, or getting promises from them, the *purpose* of bail is clear—making sure defendants come to court. Beginning in the 1980s, there was a growing demand to add a second purpose to bail—protecting public safety by preventing defendants on bail from committing crimes. In line with public safety, the federal government and many states have amended their bail laws to provide for **preventive detention** (detaining

FIGURE 8.4
Race and Gender Differences in Bail Schedules
SOURCE: Patterson and Lynch 1991.

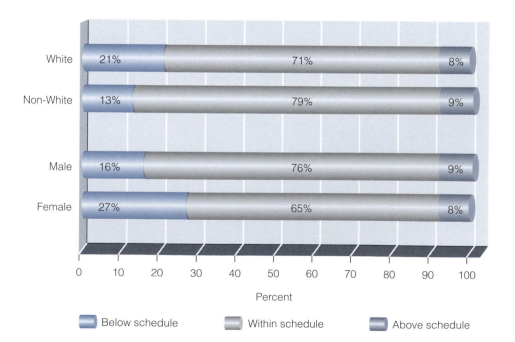

defendants to protect public safety). South Dakota is typical. Its bail statute used to make appearance in court the purpose of bail. However, in the 1980s, South Dakota amended its bail statute to include conditions based on the "risk that defendants will pose a danger to any person in the community" (Miller et al. 2000, 631–632).

8-6 Your state's bail statute

Setting conditions to ensure public safety may include banning defendants from certain neighborhoods or places or carrying weapons and requiring them to report to court periodically. But if judges decide these conditions (or others) won't protect the community, they can lock up defendants before and during trial. For example, the U.S. Bail Reform Act of 1984 directs judges to order defendants jailed if after a hearing they decide "no conditions or combination of conditions will reasonably assure . . . the safety of any other person and the community" (U.S. Code 1999. Title 18, §3142(f)).

Preventive detention provided the government with a useful tool in investigating the September 11, 2001, attacks on the World Trade Center and the Pentagon. For example, on November 9, 2001, a federal court ordered Mujahid Menepta preventively detained without bail. Menepta was an Oklahoma friend of Zacarias Moussaoui, who federal agents suspected was supposed to be the twentieth hijacker in the September 11 attack on the World Trade Center. The preventive detention order was issued after Jeffrey Whitney, a Bureau of Alcohol, Tobacco, and Firearms agent testified Menepta "is dangerous and poses a flight risk." Whitney told the court Menepta was born with the name Melvin Lattimore but changed his name to Mujahid Menepta after he converted to Islam in 1989. Menepta defended Moussaoui (whom he met in a mosque), telling a newspaper reporter, on October 9, 2001, "I think he's a scapegoat" (Thomas 2001).

8-7 U.S. Bail Reform Act

In *U.S. v. Salerno* (1987), the U.S. Supreme Court examined whether the preventive detention provision of the U.S. Bail Reform Act of 1984 violates the U.S. Constitution. The government charged "Fat Tony Salerno" and "Tony Ducks Carollo," two of New York's most famous Mafia family bosses, with twenty-nine counts of racketeering and conspiracy to commit murder (Toobin 2001, 58). At the arraignment, the government asked the judge to detain Fat Tony and Tony Ducks because no release condition could guarantee the safety of the community.

Fat Tony argued the preventive detention provision violated his constitutional rights because detaining him was punishment before conviction. A majority of the U.S. Supreme Court disagreed, writing that preventive detention is a "regulatory device," not punishment. The Constitution allows for balancing individual liberty and community safety. In this case, according to the Court, the need for public safety outweighed Salerno's interest in pretrial release.

Justice Marshall strongly dissented:

> It is a fair summary of history to say that the safeguards of liberty have frequently been forged in controversies involving not very nice people. Honoring the presumption of innocence is often difficult; sometimes we must pay substantial social costs as a result of our commitment to the values we espouse. But at the end of the day the presumption of innocence protects the innocent; the shortcuts we take with those whom we believe to be guilty injure only those wrongfully accused and, ultimately, ourselves.
>
> Throughout the world today there are men, women, and children interned indefinitely, awaiting trials which may never come or which may be a mockery of the word, because their governments believe them to be "dangerous." Our Constitution, whose construction began two centuries ago, can shelter us forever from the evils of such unchecked power. Over 200 years it has slowly, through our efforts, grown more durable, more expansive, and more just. But it cannot protect us if we lack the courage and the self-restraint to protect ourselves. Today, a majority of the Court applies itself to an ominous exercise in demolition.

8-8 *United States v. Salerno*, the Supreme Court opinion

Defendant misconduct during pretrial release

How big is the problem of defendants failing to show up for their court dates and committing crimes while they're on bail? (Goldkamp 1979, 53–59; Thomas 1976; Toborg 1981). Seventy-eight percent of all bailed defendants show up for all their court appointments (Hart and Reaves 1999, 26–27). Seventeen percent of those who miss their appointments, or fail to appear (FTA), show up later. So, 95 percent of all bailed defendants eventually show up in court. Defendants charged with violent crimes do even better—98 percent eventually show up. Drug case defendants don't do as well—92 percent eventually show up. Still, most FTA defendants aren't fugitives. They forgot a date, got confused about where they should go, or missed the scheduled time. Sometimes they were given the wrong time, date, or courtroom.

What about freed defendants committing crimes while they're on bail? Britt, Gottfredson, and Goldkamp (1992, 62–78) studied the value of monitoring the use of drugs by defendants on bail as a means to reduce not only their drug use but also their pretrial misconduct. They selected a control group and an experimental group of similar defendants on bail from a computerized case-tracking system in Pima and Miracopa counties in Arizona. The computerized system included information about prior record, court appearance history, offense, living arrangements, bail decision, failure to appear, and criminal behavior while on bail. The control group received normal supervision; the experimental group received drug monitoring during pretrial release.

No significant differences in failure to appear or re-arrest rates between the two groups occurred in Pima County, except members of the monitored group were *slightly less* likely to get rearrested for the possession of drugs. In Miracopa County, arrests and failure to appear rates were *higher* in the monitored group than in the control group. On the basis of their findings, the authors concluded that

> **systematic drug testing and monitoring in the pretrial setting . . . is not likely to achieve significant or major reductions in pretrial misconduct. At the same time that these programs fail to achieve their stated goal of reducing rates of pretrial misconduct, they carry a heavy price tag. In both Pima County and Miracopa County the cost of drug testing programs averaged from $400,000 to $500,000 per year. Given the high financial costs of these programs, including the testing and staffing required to accomplish them, it seems reasonable to question the effectiveness and cost-effectiveness of drug testing the released pretrial population. (Britt, Gottfredson, and Goldkamp 1992, 77)**

■ TRIAL

Criminal trials are the high point of formal criminal justice. They're public morality plays pitting good against evil, displaying the gory details of the horrors people are capable of inflicting on each other. But less than 3 out of 100 felony arrests ever get to trial. Practically no misdemeanor arrests do; they're decided by the courtroom work group. The bottom line: Court proceedings just ratify formally and publicly what the courtroom work group has already decided informally in private (Chapter 7). Let's look more closely at the missions of criminal trials, the role of juries, what constitutes a fair trial, and proving guilt.

Criminal Trial Missions

Criminal trials are powerful symbols. The "right" outcome is first and foremost a symbol of justice: Crime doesn't pay; the criminal justice system frees the innocent, punishes the guilty, and satisfies the victims. Of course, the "wrong" outcome is a powerful symbol, too—a symbol of injustice in which the wicked win, the innocent lose, the victims are frustrated, and wealth and power can buy "fancy lawyers" or shape outcomes to their liking. For good or ill, then, the trial teaches a public, visible, and potent lesson about the integrity, fairness, and effectiveness of the criminal justice process.

Second, criminal trials are searches for the truth. According to the adversary process (Chapter 7), the government has to prove defendants are guilty beyond a reasonable doubt. Third, trials are supposed to send messages to officials throughout the criminal justice system about the vast majority of cases that never get to trial. Expectations about what happens in trials shape police decisions to arrest, prosecutors' decisions to charge, defense lawyers' willingness to negotiate, and defendants' decisions to plead guilty. They all know "juries do not merely determine the outcome of the cases they hear; their decisions profoundly influence the 90 to 95 percent of cases that are settled through informal means" (Kalven and Zeisel 1966, 31–32; Silberman 1978, 283). Juries are the people's representatives in the "halls of justice," guarding against undue, improper, and vindictive government action. Leading jury experts have called this the "halo effect."

Juries

Trial by jury has ancient roots. In the Magna Carta of 1215, King John promised that "no free man shall be taken or imprisoned or in any way destroyed except by the lawful judgment of his peers." The Sixth Amendment to the U.S. Constitution guarantees the right to a trial "in all criminal prosecutions by an impartial jury of the State and district" where the crime was committed. In jury trials, juries decide the facts—whether the government's evidence proves defendants are guilty beyond a reasonable doubt. Their **verdict** (from the Latin to tell the truth) is their decision on that important question. Judges decide the law, meaning they apply the rules of the adversary system (Chapter 7). Defendants who don't want juries to decide the facts can have **bench trials,** in which judges decide both the facts and the law. Let's look at juries as a reflection of community values, the power they exercise through jury nullification, and how juries are selected.

The jury as a political institution

According to the famous nineteenth-century French observer Alexis de Tocqueville, "the [U.S.] jury is, above all, a political institution, and it must be regarded in this light in order to be understood." De Tocqueville's observation is still true; but it must be qualified. In clear-cut cases, formal law, not informal politics, governs. But, in cases that can go either way, extralegal influences enter the jury room and affect jurors' deliberations and decisions (Levine 1992, 14).

"I just stuck to the facts," most jurors say about their vote. And empirical studies show they're not lying. But, unconsciously their value judgments affect their interpretation of the facts—but only in *close* cases. We call this unconscious influence of value judgment the **liberation hypothesis**. According to Harry Kalven and Hans Zeisel (1966, 163–167) in their classic study of the jury, determining the truth and making value judgments are intertwined. The facts in close cases are not clear-cut. The chance of reading the facts in two sharply contrasting ways is heightened because of the adversary process—the prosecution spins the facts only toward "guilty," and the defense spins them only toward "not guilty."

According to the liberation hypothesis, the combination of the lack of clear-cut evidence and the fact spinning of the adversary process "liberate" jurors to resolve doubts in favor of their personal values. This can lead to verdicts based on personal prejudice, but it's more likely their verdicts reflect the values of their community—as they should. Community values range across a broad spectrum, including views about the crime problem; the value of punishment; moral standards; police power; and surely after "9/11," terrorism (Levine 1992, 16).

Social scientists (Dolan 2001) already see some signs of the effects of the September 11, 2001, attacks on jury decision making. Jury consultant Arthur H. Patterson says their research shows juries are *usually* "calm and dispassionate, capable of logically shifting through evidence and evaluating it evenhandedly." "But at the moment [October 2001], America's jury pool is *not* calm or dispassionate. At this time, most jurors are angry and fearful and very sensitized to terrorism, injury, and death." (B2). Patterson sees signs that in ambiguous cases, juries will trust government witnesses, like police officers, more than defense witnesses, and they'll give the prosecution—not the defense—the benefit of the doubt.

Jury nullification

Jury nullification, the power of juries to ignore the law and decide cases according to informal extralegal considerations, "fits neatly into a tradition of political activism by U.S. juries." It's also part of our history. William Penn benefited from nullification in 1670 when an English jury acquitted him for following his conscience in practicing his Quaker beliefs, a crime under English law. During colonial times, John Peter Zenger also violated the law by publishing material that criticized the British government. Zenger's lawyer told the jury they had the right "beyond all dispute to determine the law and the facts." The jury followed his suggestion and acquitted Zenger (Holden, Cohen, and de Lisser 1995, 4).

In the first video of an actual jury deliberation ever made (Levin and Hertzberg 1986), we see jurors agonizing over whether to nullify the law in the case of a man who clearly was guilty of carrying a handgun—his lawyer even told the jury his client was guilty. But he also told them, "You should acquit him anyway." Why? He didn't intentionally break the law because he didn't know it was illegal for him to have it. He told the police he had the gun and even went home and brought it back to the police when they asked him to. He was mildly retarded and obviously didn't know much of what was going on in court. And finally, the prosecutor never should have prosecuted him in the first place. The juries' verdict: "Not guilty."

Jury selection

The Sixth Amendment guarantees the right to an *impartial* jury. According to the U.S. Supreme Court, this means jurors have to be selected at random, from a "fair cross section of the community." To satisfy the random selection requirement, jurisdictions make a **jury list**, names taken from *one* of a variety of sources—voter registration lists, actual voter lists, tax rolls, telephone directories, or even lists of driver's license registrations. The jury list excludes minors, people who can't speak or write English, convicted felons, and recent residents. According to the Supreme Court, fair cross section doesn't mean jurors have to "mirror the community and reflect the various distinct groups in the population." For example, a jury doesn't have to include an 8 percent Hispanic makeup just because the community population is 8 percent Hispanic. It only bans the exclusion of recognized races, ethnic groups, or sexes from the *chance* to participate; it doesn't say they have to *actually* sit on juries (*Holland v. Illinois,* 1990; *Taylor v. Louisiana* 1975).

Many states "excuse" some potential jurors from jury duty—and jury service *is* a duty not a choice. Excuses include poor health, old age, economic hardship, and distance. Members of some occupations, like doctors, government workers, and members of the military, are also excused in many states (LaFave and Israel 1984, 2:708).

 8-9 Your state's jury selection process

Martin A. Levin (1988, 89–124), a political scientist who has studied juries, argues juries can't represent the community for two reasons: They're drawn from unrepresentative lists, and attorneys can remove prospective jurors by **peremptory challenge** (removing a prospective juror without a reason). According to Levin, multiple-source lists, including voters, public utility customers, driver's licenses, telephone directories, and tax rolls, would produce more representative jurors.

The **jury panel** consists of people from the jury list who are actually called for jury duty. Next comes the **voir dire,** the process of questioning the prospective jurors to pare the panel to actual juries. The voir dire gives prosecutors and defense counsel the chance to get the jurors they want and to exclude the ones they don't. They can remove jurors either by challenge for cause or peremptory challenge. In the **challenge for cause,** both prosecution and defense can object to as many prospective jurors as they like, as long as they can show prejudice to the judge's satisfaction, such as women in rape cases, bar owners in drunk-driving cases, and white men in a black gang-rape case. The prosecution and the defense also have a specific number of **peremptory challenges** they can use to remove prospective jurors without having to give a reason why.

Most of us think of juries as having twelve members and their verdicts as being unanimous. That was true for centuries but not anymore. Since 1970, U.S. Supreme Court decisions have allowed states to relax this standard. This occurs most often in misdemeanor cases, but seven states also use eight- and six-member juries in noncapital felonies. Two states also allow less than unanimous verdicts (11–1 and 10–2) in noncapital felony cases (Bureau of Justice Statistics 2001, 261).

Fair Trial

Fair trials require an atmosphere that doesn't prejudice the jury against defendants. In a notorious case, the State of Ohio tried Dr. Sam Sheppard for brutally murdering his socialite wife. The newspapers were filled with "evidence" (actually rumors) about Sheppard's "guilt"; nearly all editorials were against him, and reporters even disrupted the trial proceedings to scoop "sensational" stories. The jury convicted him, but the U.S. Supreme Court overruled the verdict, finding Sheppard couldn't get a fair trial in such a "carnival atmosphere" (*Sheppard v. Maxwell* 1966).

To guarantee an atmosphere that minimizes prejudice, trial judges can transfer the trial to a calmer location (**change of venue**). They can also **sequester the jury** (put them in hotel rooms under guard where they can't read newspapers, watch TV, or talk on the telephone) (Phillips 1977, 218). Trial judges can also put gag orders on the press and lawyers and even keep reporters out of the courtroom. Judges can also remove "unruly" spectators and "troublesome" members of the press. However, judges have less freedom to control disruptive defendants, because the Sixth Amendment guarantees defendants the right to be present at their own trials. But they can remove defendants if it's impossible to proceed with them in the courtroom. More often judges keep disruptive defendants in the courtroom gagged and bound to keep "order in the court" (*Illinois v. Allen* 1970).

Proving Guilt

Although it's probably not obvious to most outsiders, the elaborate rules for every procedure in the criminal trial—choosing jurors; opening statements of lawyers; examining and cross-examining witnesses; introducing and presenting evidence; closing arguments of lawyers; charging the jury, and jury deliberations—are all aimed at deciding whether defendants are guilty (Chapter 7). Whether they're guilty depends on proving guilt beyond a reasonable doubt.

Proof beyond a reasonable doubt

Proof beyond a reasonable doubt is the burden prosecutors have to carry in order to turn defendants into offenders. Defendants don't have to prove their innocence, and they don't have to help the state prove its case. They can even throw roadblocks in the way of the government's efforts to prove its case. In other words, defendants are innocent until proven guilty; they enjoy a presumption of innocence (Chapter 1). To win acquittal, all defendants have to do—and only if they choose to—is cast a reasonable doubt on the government's case (Black 1983, 635; *In re Winship* 1970).

According to the U.S. Supreme Court in the landmark case *In re Winship*, defendants have a constitutional right to proof beyond a reasonable doubt because it reduces the risk of convicting innocent people. Criminal defendants have so much to lose—property, liberty, and sometimes life itself—as well as suffering the stigma of being labeled "criminals," that without the right to proof beyond a reasonable doubt, conviction would deny them due process of law (Chapter 2). Less than proof beyond a reasonable doubt also weakens the criminal law's moral force and casts doubt on the courts' capacity to condemn guilty and vindicate innocent people (*In re Winship* 1970).

How much proof is proof beyond a reasonable doubt? Courts, including the U.S. Supreme Court, have struggled to define it. Here's one judge's struggle to instruct the jury on what proof beyond a reasonable doubt means:

> The phrase "beyond a reasonable doubt" has no technical or unusual meaning. You can arrive at the real meaning of it by emphasizing the word "reasonable." A reasonable doubt is a doubt for which a valid reason can be assigned. It's a doubt which is something more than a guess or a surmise. It's not a conjecture or a fanciful doubt. It's a reasonable doubt. It's not a doubt which is raised by somebody simply for the sake of raising doubts, nor is it a doubt suggested by the ingenuity of counsel or any of the jurors which is not justified by the evidence or lack of the evidence. A reasonable doubt is a doubt based on reason and not on the mere possibility of innocence. It is a doubt for which you can in your own mind conscientiously give a reason.

A reasonable doubt, in other words, is a real doubt, an honest doubt, a doubt which has its foundation in the evidence or the lack of evidence. It's the kind of doubt which in the serious affairs which concern you in everyday life you would pay heed and attention to. "Now, of course, absolute certainty in the affairs of life is almost never attainable and the law does not require absolute certainty on the part of the jury before you return a verdict of guilty. The state does not have to prove guilt beyond all doubt or to a mathematical or absolute certainty. What the law does require, however, is that after hearing all the evidence, if there's something in that evidence or lack of evidence which leaves in the minds of the jury as reasonable men and women a reasonable doubt about the fault of the accused, then the accused must be given the benefit of that doubt and acquitted. Any conclusion reasonably to be drawn from the evidence which is consistent with the innocence of the accused must prevail. If there's no reasonable doubt, then the accused must be found guilty. The test is one of reasonable doubt, a doubt based on reason and common sense. (*State v. Vicente* 2001, 630)

After he was convicted, Ruperto Vicente appealed complaining about the judge's "drumbeat repetition" in the instructions about reasonable doubt. Although the court agreed the instruction was long, it didn't prejudice the jury.

 8-10 *State v. Vicente*

Opening statements

In their **opening statements** prosecutors and defense lawyers give an overview of their side of the case. Prosecutors use the opening statements to give the jury a road map of what they're going to prove. This helps juries follow the case because prosecutors can't always present their evidence in a logical order. If they can follow the case, jurors are less likely to get confused, bored, and irritated by evidence that doesn't make sense without the opening statement. Defense lawyers can use their opening statement to take advantage of weaknesses in the prosecution's view of the case. Defense lawyer Seymour Wishman (1981) reports this incident from his own experience:

> The D.A., overly confident, had made a mistake in his opening statement. Instead of giving a general statement broadly outlining the kind of evidence he would present to the jury, he had been specific, naming witnesses and the details of what each would say. He had a strong case, but he was taking an unnecessary risk: I might be able to poke holes in some of his facts, and if I could, my performance would have more impact than it would have had otherwise. (169–170)

Calling and examining witnesses

Both the defense and prosecution have broad powers to **subpoena** (command by a court order) witnesses to testify. Ordinary witnesses usually get travel money and a small daily fee (rarely enough to pay them for lost wages). Expert witnesses (fingerprint specialists, psychiatrists, psychologists and so on) are well paid for their testimony.

The rules for **direct examination** (examination of witnesses on the side of the case the lawyers represent) differ from **cross-examination** (examination of witnesses on the opposing side). Answers to questions on direct examination call for narratives, like the answer to "Where were you on October 8 at about 8:00 P.M.?" In direct examination, lawyers can't ask **leading questions** (questions steering witnesses to the answers the lawyers want). Leading questions, which call for simple "yes" or "no" answers, during cross-examination are common.

Criminal law professor George P. Fletcher (1988), a respected writer on criminal law, describes the differences between direct and cross-examination this way:

> Lawyers at trial are directors as well as performers in presenting their client's version of the truth. They make theatrical decisions about the order in which to present their witnesses, they coach them like directors in rehearsal, and they lead their witnesses gently through their parts. Their presentation of the truth reflects art and rhetoric as well as rational argument (116). Their role [in direct examination] stops short of prompting their witnesses when they do not perform as expected. Prompting falls under the ban against asking "leading questions." A lawyer disappointed in his witness may not try to put words in his mouth. He cannot ask (assuming that the witness would be prepared to answer "yes"), "Isn't it true that you saw the gunman smiling as he was shooting?" He must try to elicit this testimony without giving away the script. But when they turn into critics on cross-examination, lawyers can ask all the leading questions they want and insist, often contemptuously, that the witness answer "yes" or "no." (231)

Fletcher describes defense attorney Barry Slotnick's skill in leading witnesses in cross-examination in the trial of Bernhard Goetz, the "subway vigilante" case in New York City in 1986. Slotnick wanted to establish that Goetz fired shots against four youths in rapid succession, not pausing between shots:

> The tactic became clear on the cross-examination of . . . Victor Flores, who claimed actually to have seen Goetz fire at two of the youths as they were running toward him and away from Goetz. He heard four shots "one after another." On cross-examination, Slotnick took advantage of his legal option to restate Flores's testimony in his own language and ask Flores to answer "yes" or "no" whether that was his view of what

happened. Thus he reformulated Flores's first statement about the pattern and rapidity of the shots by asking, "And the three shots or the four shots . . . that you hear in rapid succession after the first shot, were all going in your area, is that correct?" Having gained Flores's assent to the phrase "rapid succession," Slotnick began using the label over and over again in cross-examination. The jury heard Flores say "yes" to this description so often—five more times—that the words came to seem like his own. (Fletcher 1988, 121–122)

Slotnick made his intention clear by a question he asked just for the jury's benefit:

So it is fair to say that as far as your witnessing what occurred, the fact that he might have walked over to a rear seat and shot somebody and said something to them, like "you don't look bad, here's another," something like that, that really never happened? (Fletcher 1988, 121–122)

Admissible evidence

The law of evidence recognizes two types of evidence, **physical evidence** (weapons, stolen property, and fingerprints) and **testimonial evidence** (witnesses' spoken, written, or symbolic words). Lawyers can't use just any evidence they want to present. Evidence has to help prove the elements of the crime (**relevant evidence**). But even relevant evidence isn't admissible in three instances: if its power to damage the defendant is greater than its power to prove the government's case; if the government got it illegally like in an unreasonable search (Chapter 6); or if it's **hearsay evidence** (evidence not known directly by the witness, like a police officer who testifies to the facts of a robbery told to him by the bank teller who actually witnessed it).

Closing arguments

After both sides have presented all their evidence, they make their **closing arguments**. The experienced prosecutor Steven Phillips (1977) explains the importance of the closing argument:

It is one of the few arts left in which time is of no consequence. Standing before 12 people, a lawyer can be brief or lengthy—the choice is his own; there are no interruptions, and a captive audience. All that matters are those 12 people; they must be persuaded, or everything that has gone before is in vain. Summation is the one place where lawyers do make a difference; if an attorney can be said to "win" or "lose" a case, the chances are that he did so in his closing argument to the jury. (196–197)

Charging the jury

After the closing arguments, the judge charges the jury. The charge is given in the form of **jury instructions**.

Jury instructions explain the role of the jury—to decide whether facts prove the elements of the crime; explain the law—define the elements of the crime they have to apply the facts to; and explain what proof beyond a reasonable doubt means. This sounds simple enough but in reality the often long, complex, and technical legalese found in instructions demand a lot—maybe too much—from jurors. According to prosecutor Steven Phillips (1977):

A judge's charge to the jury is an amazing exercise in optimism. For two or three hours he reads to twelve laymen enough law to keep a law student busy for a semester. Twelve individuals, selected more or less at random, sit there, unable to take notes or ask questions. Somehow, just by listening, it is presumed everything spoken by the judge will take root in their collective intelligence. (213)

Jury deliberations

After the charge, the jury retires to a room to decide whether the prosecution proved its case beyond a reasonable doubt. When they've decided, they go back to the courtroom to reenact the centuries old scene of giving the court their verdict. Formally, judges have the last word—if the verdict is "Guilty," they turn defendants into offenders by entering a judgment of guilty; if the verdict is "Not guilty," they turn defendants into ordinary individuals by entering a judgment of acquittal.

■ GUILTY PLEAS

The vast majority of defendants don't go to trial; they plead guilty. As in all other criminal justice decisions, the numbers vary from place to place—from an average high of over 90 percent to an average low of about 75 percent (Ostrom and Hanson 2000, 7). Pleading guilty isn't a recent practice in disposing of criminal cases. More than 90 percent of defendants were pleading guilty in Essex County, England 450 years ago! (Samaha 1974). Yet, no one paid much attention to how rare formal decision making by trial is and how common informal decision making by guilty plea is until the 1960s, when disposition by guilty plea came under careful scrutiny and intense criticism (Alschuler 1979, 211; Pound and Frankfurter 1922, 93; Rosett and Cressey 1976; Sanborn 1986, 111).

All guilty pleas aren't alike. In **straight pleas** ("mercy of the court" pleas), defendants throw themselves on the mercy of the court by pleading guilty, hoping for some "mercy" from the sentencing judge *afterwards*. In **negotiated pleas**, defendants arrange some kind of deal for a reduced charge or sentence *beforehand* and then plead guilty. We'll look at straight pleas, negotiated pleas, what the Constitution has to say about guilty pleas, and plea-bargaining reform.

Straight Pleas

Most pleas are straight (mercy of the court) pleas (Boland and Forst 1985, 10–15; Heumann 1979a, 651; Rubenstein, Clarke, and Wright 1980, 81). Why do defendants plead guilty without a promise of getting something in return? Rubenstein, Clarke, and Wright (1980) tried to answer this question by analyzing data from police, jail, and court records in Alaska. They also interviewed every judge, prosecutor, and criminal defense attorney in Anchorage, Fairbanks, and Juneau, asking why defendants give up their right to jury trial without getting anything from the state. The strength of the case against them (**dead bang cases**) was the most common reason. One experienced defense lawyer described a dead bang case:

> Well, where you've got a nineteen-year-old kid who's ripped off somebody else's stereo and he confessed to it, what do you gain from going to trial? You can go to jury trial and your client gets on the stand and says, "I didn't do it," and you say, "Well, you confessed to it, and we found the stereo in your house." You know what's going to happen then? I mean, your client is either going to have to perjure himself, or he's not going to take the stand. And, if he doesn't take the stand, and if it takes you four days to try the case, you have nothing to argue at the end. The judge is going to say, "What happened here? Why did you waste thousands of dollars putting us all through this?" You know, they're going to pay a price for this—it's only natural. (Rubenstein, Clarke, and Wright 1980, 81)

Another reason for a straight plea is what we might call the "boy scout" reason—hoping that cooperating without bargaining will speak well for the defendant at sentencing:

> Now if the guy is a "boy scout" [said one defense lawyer] I might advise him to enter a guilty plea. Keep the image consistent that way. Take this guy charged with a first-offense burglary in a dwelling. He confessed when he was arrested and he helped the cops retrieve the property. He had no real defenses. If he had exercised all his constitutional rights it would have hurt him. He'd have gone to jail. I could advise him that if he continued in the cooperative mode in which he had already begun when I started representing him he'd have the best chances of probation. He got straight probation and a suspended imposition of sentence. He could never have gotten that disposition if he had exercised his constitutional rights. (Rubenstein, Clarke, and Wright 1980, 85)

Negotiated Pleas

In negotiated pleas, defendants make a deal—they plead guilty in exchange for either fewer or lesser charges (**charge bargaining**) or a lesser sentence (**sentence bargaining**) (McDonald 1979, 385–392). A combination of formal state law, informal **local legal culture** (attitudes, values, and expectations regarding law and the legal system), public opinion, and the courtroom work group determine whether the norm is charge bargaining or sentence bargaining. In states with fixed sentence laws—like 20 years for armed robbery—the only choice is charge bargaining; in indeterminate sentencing states—like 0 to 25 years for armed robbery—sentence bargaining might be the norm (Chapter 9).

History and tradition shape the effect of local legal culture on plea-bargaining norms. In Detroit, for example, charge bargaining is the norm because the city has a history of banning prosecutors from participating in sentencing. In Washington, D.C., sentence bargaining predominates because there's a history of making prosecutors "make a pitch" to the court for a particular sentence (Church 1985, 449–518; Friedman 1984, 6; Heumann 1979a, 211–212).

Public opinion affects local legal culture, too. Cases the public doesn't care about are probably going to be decided by plea; sensational cases will probably go to trial. The distinguished former U.S. Attorney General Edward Levi gave this advice to U.S. attorneys:

> [Consider] what the public attitude is toward prosecution under the circumstances of the case. There may be situations where the public interest might be better served by having the case tried rather than by being disposed of by means of a guilty plea—including situations in which it is particularly important to permit a clear public understanding that "justice is done" or in which a plea agreement might be misconstrued to the detriment of public confidence in the criminal justice system. For this reason, the prosecutor should be careful not to place undue emphasis on factors which favor disposition of a case pursuant to a plea agreement. (Heumann 1979a, 213–214)

According to James Eisenstein and Herbert Jacob, the courtroom work group also contributes to the local legal culture's influence on plea bargaining. They found defense attorneys, prosecutors, and judges have created norms for the "way things are done." Members of the work group rarely try to do things differently. They'll feel a lot discomfort if they insist on going to trial when negotiating is the "way things are done" (Eisenstein and Jacob 1977, 286; Nardulli, Eisenstein, and Flemming 1988).

The courtroom work group (prosecutors, defense lawyers, and judges) have different emphases when they bargain but they've all got the same criteria in mind when they negotiate (Albonetti 1990, 316–318; Alschuler 1968, 50; Champion 1989, 253–263; Forst 1995, 366–368; Mather 1979; Miller et al. 1978, 60–61), and by now four of the criteria won't surprise you:

■ Strength of the case
■ Seriousness of the offense
■ Dangerousness of the defendant
■ Relationship between the defendant and the victim
(see "Decision to Charge")

Let's look at these criteria and the roles of prosecutors, defense counsel, and judges in negotiated pleas.

Strength of the case

We begin with the strength of the case because prosecutors, defense lawyers, and judges repeatedly tell researchers (and when they talk to my class, my students) this is the most important of all the criteria. According to Herbert Miller and his associates in their study of plea bargaining, "Virtually all prosecutors regard weak cases as prime targets for plea negotiations." This isn't surprising given that we're talking about lawyers here. Of all the criminal justice professionals, lawyers are most in touch with the use of evidence to prove a case (McDonald 1985, 65; Miller et al. 1978, 62).

What makes a strong case? Maybe the defendant really *did* commit the crime, but lawyers know there's a huge gap between committing a crime and proving it—especially proving it beyond a reasonable doubt, the highest standard of proof known to our law. **Factual guilt**—what we know to be true outside court—isn't good enough; only **legal guilt**—what we can prove in court—counts. A St. Louis prosecutor ignored this distinction when he charged a defendant with murder on no more proof of *legal* guilt than a photograph a pawnbroker took of the defendant pawning the dead woman's TV set the day after her apartment was burglarized and she was murdered. When asked if he was worried that the defendant might be innocent, he replied he knew the defendant was guilty because:

> I sent two of my best investigators who are Black and competent men out on the street to check out the case. They went down to the section of town where this guy hangs out and they talked to the people down there about his involvement in this crime. They found out that the street talk says he's guilty. The guys down there on wise-guy alley say he did it, so I know he is guilty. (Miller et al. 1978, 93)

Here are three common reasons why cases are weak:

1. Only shaky evidence connects defendants to crimes.
2. Defendants have committed criminal acts, but they didn't have the intent the law demands to make the act a crime.
3. Defendants have committed criminal acts with required intent, but evidence has disappeared or weakened since prosecutors charged them. Witnesses die; they move out of town; they forget what happened;

or they decide they don't want the defendant—especially if they know her—to suffer after all. (Miller et al. 1978, 106–107)

Any one or combination of these reasons may lead to bargained pleas or **sweet deals,** sometimes called settling for half a loaf. In other words, conviction on lesser charges without trial is better than going to trial and ending in conviction (if you're the defendant) or in acquittal (if you're the prosecutor) (Miller et al. 1978, 108).

Seriousness of the offense

How do prosecutors, defense lawyers, and judges decide how serious an offense is? The answer begins with the **going rates for crimes,** the local "market value" measured in jail time or fine amount for particular crimes. Market values aren't the same as the punishments spelled out in the state's criminal code. According to one Detroit judge familiar with the practice, "The system operates in terms of defense attorney and defendants' expectations—what is widely known as a rate. It's an expectation model" (Heumann 1978, 9). Judge Ronald Lisk clearly was referring to the going rate in Santa Clara County, California, when he said to the prosecutor and defense lawyer, "It's a kilo case, guys. Everybody goes to the joint for two years for a kilo case. Sorry, there's not much I can do" (Schmitt 1991a).

How is the going rate determined? According to Milton Heumann (1979b), there's an informal understanding among prosecutors, defense lawyers, and judges about what punishment cases deserve. Each community has its own going rates, which are

> products of the individual courthouse and community, and are not primarily shaped by state or national considerations. In one jurisdiction an armed robber may receive eight years after a trial and five years if he pleads; in another, the comparable figures may be seven and four, or ten and eight, and so on. (Heumann 1979b, 208, 210)

In fact, going rates even vary from court to court in the same state, county, and city or town. For example, the Pennsylvania criminal code punishes first-degree burglary as a felony with prison time. A number of years ago, the going rate in Montgomery County was a few days in jail; in neighboring Philadelphia it was automatic probation (Miller et al.1978, 80).

The going rate may not be in writing, but the price of not pleading guilty is clear. According to Heumann, "Defendants are told clearly by someone—usually their lawyers, but sometimes by judges, prosecutors, police officers, or others—that they had better plead guilty or they will be punished more severely if they go to trial" (1978, 7). Defendants can count on sentences in line with the going rate if they plead guilty.

Senior staff don't always help new lawyers learn how to incorporate informal local going rates into their decision making. In Delaware, Pennsylvania, the senior prosecutor instructed new prosecutors only to "Protect yourself. You're a lawyer first and a prosecutor second. Check with somebody. Don't be Mr. Nice-Guy. Don't make a fool of yourself or gain a reputation for poor judgment. Don't bring stuff into a judge and have it rejected" (Miller et al.1978, 82). But they learn fast not to go above or below the going rates. One new prosecutor learned this the hard way. In his first case, he asked for the maximum sentence. Laughter broke out, a senior prosecutor stepped up, took the file from the novice's hand, and made clear to the judge the state wanted considerably less (in other words, the going rate) than the maximum (83).

Dangerousness of the defendant

Until now, we've referred to the defendant's criminal history (their past criminal *behavior*) as the sole criterion related to defendants that affects decision making. Now we have to extend the criterion to include not just their "bad records" but also "bad defendants." We'll call this combination of bad records and bad people the dangerousness of the defendant (Institute for Law and Social Research 1977). Herbert Miller quotes an experienced prosecutor on the point:

> I've got the police department record. I can see where the kid lives, what kind of neighborhood it is. I find out the place where the guy is hanging around and whether there are other scum in the area. I've got his prior arrests and their dispositions. (Miller et al. 1978, 119)

A senior prosecutor in Delaware County, Pennsylvania, said prosecutors ask the arresting officer who brings them the case jacket "whether this guy is trouble." Sometimes the officer will "tell you that although he looks like trouble, he really is not a bad guy or vice versa. Sometimes the police can tell you that he is a known troublemaker" (Miller et al. 1978, 67–68). But, prosecutors don't always accept what officers tell them. A senior prosecutor from Dade County, Florida, said,

> If the policeman says I don't like this guy and want to bust his ass and doesn't explain himself any further, I am not satisfied that he really tried to make the case. But on the other hand if the policeman reports that this guy is only the wheel man and won't give us the names of the two robbers who pulled the job, then I am willing to go along with a request for a tougher deal. Or if they say, the defendant told one story to the policeman at the crime scene and is now telling a different story, then I'll take this information into account as a legitimate concern of the police. (Miller et al. 1978, 67–68)

Lawyers don't look at case strength and offense and offender seriousness in isolation. In weak cases involving serious offenses and "bad news" offenders, some kind of guilty plea is likely, even if it's only half a loaf. In Miller and his associates' national survey of plea bargaining, one prosecutor reflected this attitude when he admitted he wouldn't dismiss murder, drug, and robbery cases (no matter how weak) because of their seriousness.

Heavy caseloads

We've now been reminded several times that the work group wants to dispose of cases efficiently, quickly, and harmoniously. But the work group subculture isn't all that pushes members. Heavy caseloads drive them to dispose of cases and to do it quickly and smoothly. As *administrators*, prosecutors manage caseloads, which most of them believe are too heavy. "We are running a machine here. We know we have to grind them out fast," said one Los Angeles prosecutor. A Manhattan prosecutor echoed his Los Angeles counterpart, "Our office keeps eight courtrooms extremely busy trying 5 percent of the cases. If even 10 percent of the cases ended in a trial, the system would break down. We can't afford to think very much about anything else" (Zimring and Frase 1980, 506–507).

Although the courthouse work group believes heavy caseloads force them to plea bargain, empirical research casts doubt on their belief. No simple relationship exists between caseload pressure and guilty pleas. Comparing trial rates in districts with extremely high volume and those with minimal caseload pressures showed no significant differences in the percentage of cases disposed of by trial and those disposed of by guilty plea. In Connecticut, where court caseloads were cut in half with no corresponding reduction in personnel, numbers of guilty pleas didn't drop at all (Heumann 1978, 29–31).

Defense counsel and plea bargaining

Formally, defense counsel have to look at the effect their bargaining decisions have on their clients because plea bargaining is essential to their constitutional and professional duties to vigorously and effectively defend their clients (Chapter 7). As one expert put it:

> Experienced criminal lawyers know that one of defense counsel's most important functions, perhaps the most important, is working out with the prosecutor the best possible disposition of a client's case in situations in which there is no realistic prospect of acquittal. The lawyer not only may properly do this, but s/he violates the obligation to represent the client adequately if s/he does not. (Amsterdam 1984, 1:229)

But these formal professional duties run up against their informal connections to the work group. In his description of what he calls "workgroup pathologies,"

David Lynch (1994), who worked both as a prosecutor and a public defender, reveals how much closer to the work group public defenders feel than they do to most of their clients:

> Part of "doing time" was having to put up with the constant stress and abuse heaped on us by ill-tempered and antisocial clients, whose sole audience for their angry outbursts against "the system" was their public defenders, whom they often considered to be incompetent, hired cronies of the state. . . . This was the sort of individual we public defenders were expected to represent to the best of our abilities. This was the sort of individual who caused us to become cynical about our role as "liberty's last champion" (the logo on our office's baseball team shirts) and who tended to alienate us from our work. This was the sort of individual who made us love plea bargaining. Plea bargaining unfortunately plays right into the hands of alienated public defenders. . . . It makes cases "go away," taking with them some of the stress, work, combat, and (very important) the client—whose "companionship" one often wishes to minimize and whose guilt one often believes (correctly or incorrectly) to be so obvious. (121–122)

Lynch also felt the pressures of disposing of the heavy caseload, pressures he calls "client control":

> Defense attorneys knew all too well that if they brought too many cases to trial, they would be seen as either unreasonable and worthy of professional ostracism or as a fool who was too weak to achieve "client control." Many attorneys I knew became masters of the fine art of "chair therapy," in which a client who insists on a trial is made to sit in the hall of the courthouse (or in the courthouse lockup) for days on end during the courthouse trial terms, waiting for his day in court, until he accepts a deal. Some (usually unintentionally) resorted to "good cop/bad cop" routines, in which a resistant defendant is subjected to the screams of his or her attorney, followed by the lawyer's associate, who tries to calmly help the accused see the light. Usually, however, defense attorneys, aware that incredible trial penalties were attached to the "right" to a jury trial, only needed to tell a defendant of the unconscionable sentences that had been meted out to others who dared to create work for a judge. (123)

Still, don't overemphasize the desire for work group harmony and speed as an influence on plea bargaining. According to plea-bargaining expert Donald Newman:

> Negotiation can be quite adversary. The defense counsel may indicate to the prosecutor that he thinks the state has no evidence against his client except possibly a charge of disorderly conduct. The prosecutor in turn may state that he is not only going to push an armed robbery charge but plans to level a special count of being a habitual offender unless the defendant cooperates. Defense counsel then offers to have his client plead guilty to petty larceny with the prosecutor offering to reduce the charge to second-degree robbery. (Miller et al. 2000, 952)

Judges and plea bargaining

Judges enter into plea bargaining in one of two ways: They either participate during the negotiations or supervise after lawyers have struck bargains. Sometimes they do both (LaFave and Israel 1992, 928). Judicial participation in plea bargaining varies according to individual judges' styles and from jurisdiction to jurisdiction. Miller and his associates (1978) found four types of participation by judges:

1. They don't participate at all.
2. They gently lean on lawyers to move the bargaining along.
3. They put heavy pressure on lawyers to "force" guilty pleas.
4. They bargain with the lawyers over sentence recommendations.

Judges who refuse to participate at all just look over what the lawyers have already decided. These judges believe they can't supervise impartially a process they're an active part of. But are they always impartial? Most of these judges in Miller and his associates' study (1978, 244–245) found they agreed with prosecutors on sentencing in almost 100 percent of the cases. One judge admitted he'd never changed a prosecutor's recommendation. He occasionally told prosecutors the sentence wasn't in line with "going rates" to give them something to think about in future cases, but he never changed a recommendation in the current case.

Judges who gently lean on participants want to keep the flow of cases moving as smoothly and swiftly as possible. They have to "keep the pleas coming in" as one Oregon judge put it or "keep things from getting bogged down" as another said. "Gently leaning" usually means talking to the lawyers about the case, sometimes asking why the case was going to trial and expressing displeasure with the idea (Miller et al.1978, 246–248).

Only a few judges try to "force" lawyers into bargains. The ones who do say heavy caseloads are the single most important reason they strong-arm defense lawyers and prosecutors into bargains. These judges make sure "no stone was left unturned to arrive at a plea of guilty," including "arm twisting, forcing, jerking the defense attorney around, and coming down on the defendant" (Miller et al.1978, 249). A burglary case in New York City's criminal courts is an excellent example of arm-twisting by the judge. When the case was called, one of the two defendants didn't have a lawyer, so the judge just picked out a lawyer who happened to be in the courtroom. The district attorney offered a 2-to-4-year sentence in return for a guilty plea right then. The judge jumped in with, "After today, it's 3 to 6, after that it's 4 to 8. If they're ever going to plead, today is the time to do it." When the defense lawyer turned down the bargain (remember the judge had appointed him only moments before), the judge said, "We'll make it very easy. It's 4 to 8 after today. Let's play hardball" (Schulhofer 1985, 585).

Another hardball judge in Hartford, Connecticut, admitted he turned himself into a prosecutor

> when 835 cases were backlogged. He reduced the backlog to 299 cases by ordering the prosecuting attorney to select his two best assistants and setting up conferences at five-minute intervals day and night for six days. He enforced attendance of the prosecutor and defense attorney under threat of an arrest warrant. Under these conditions defense attorneys went to prosecutors and disposed of easy cases. The judge then ordered them into his chambers to discuss "sticky cases" and make a plea recommendation. They then marched back into court to recite the recommended disposition onto the record. He observed, somewhat ironically, that this practice "stinks" because a judge becomes a prosecutor. He did, however, indicate pleasure with the results. (Miller et al. 1978, 252)

Judges can participate in sentence bargaining either indirectly or directly. They bargain indirectly when they systematically impose heavier sentences on convicted defendants who demand a trial. Why the differential? Several reasons. Defendants who admit their guilt show remorse; remorse is the first step toward rehabilitation; and so they deserve a lesser penalty. Other judges abide by the slogan, "If you want to win big, you'd better be prepared to lose big," so defendants who "burden" the state with a trial have to pay a price if the state wins. One Chicago judge says defendants who "waste" taxpayers' money and the court's time "deserve more time in jail for the problems they create" (Miller et al. 1978, 263–264).

Judges who bargain directly can offer general recommendations like "I'll give prison time as opposed to probation" or "I'll sentence in the upper instead of the lower range of prison time" (Miller et al. 1978, 260). Or, they can offer specific sentences like five years prison time or a $200 fine. Those who keep their offers general are balancing two values—they want predictability, believing defendants have a right to know what's going to happen to them, but they also want to maintain their independence as judges by not being just another party in the bargaining process (Miller et al.1978, 250).

There is considerable opposition to judges participating in plea bargaining. The American Bar Association Standards say the "trial judge should not participate in plea discussions" (LaFave and Israel 1992, 928–929). Some statutes and court rules go so far as to ban judges from plea

bargaining. For example, the Federal Rules of Criminal Procedure say judges "shall not participate in any such discussions." One court interpreted this rule to ban sentencing judges from taking any part "in any discussion or communication regarding the sentence to be imposed prior to the entry of a plea of guilty, conviction, or submission to him of a plea agreement" (*U.S. v. Werker* 1976).

Guilty Pleas and the Constitution

When defendants plead guilty, they give up three constitutional rights:

1. Right against self-incrimination (Amendment V)
2. Right to trial by jury (Amendment VI)
3. Right to confront the witnesses against them

Generally, we can give up (waive) our constitutional rights but only if we know what our rights are *and* if we give them up voluntarily. Judges have to "address the defendant personally in open court" (**colloquy**) to make sure defendants have knowingly and voluntary waived their rights. To satisfy the knowingly requirement federal judges—and most state judges—have to make sure defendants understand the following:

1. The charge and the punishment for the crime they're pleading guilty to
2. They have a right to a lawyer
3. They have a right to plead not guilty, the right to a jury trial, the right to a lawyer at the trial, the right to confront and cross-examine witnesses, and the right against self-incrimination
4. Once the court accepts the guilty plea, there will be no trial because the defendant has given up that right

To satisfy the voluntariness requirement, judges have to satisfy themselves by "addressing the defendant personally in open court" that the plea isn't the result of threats or force or promises (except of course for those in the plea bargain). Before finally accepting the guilty plea, judges have one more thing they have to do—make sure there is a "factual basis" for the plea. What does factual basis mean? There has to be *some* evidence in addition to the plea itself that defendants are guilty.

 **8-11 Details on procedures for accepting guilty pleas in federal courts**

Plea-Bargaining Reform

The courtroom work group accepts and supports plea bargaining, arguing that it:

- Creates administrative efficiency by controlling court calendars and moving cases swiftly through the criminal process after arrest

YOU DECIDE

Can he claim he's innocent and still voluntarily and knowingly plead guilty?

North Carolina v. Alford 400 U.S. 25 (1970)

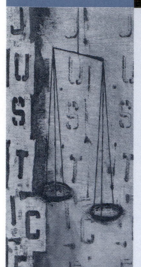

Facts

On December 2, 1963, Henry Alford was indicted for first-degree murder, a capital offense under North Carolina law. The court appointed an attorney to represent him, and this attorney questioned all but one of the various witnesses who Alford said would back up his claim of innocence. The witnesses, however, didn't support Alford's story; instead they gave statements that strongly indicated his guilt. Faced with strong evidence of guilt and no substantial evidentiary support for the claim of innocence, Alford's attorney recommended that he plead guilty but left the ultimate decision to Alford. The prosecutor agreed to accept a plea of guilty to a charge of second-degree murder, and on December 10, 1963, Alford pleaded guilty to the reduced charge.

Before the plea was finally accepted by the trial court, the court heard the sworn testimony of a police officer who summarized the State's case. Two other witnesses besides Alford were also heard. Although there was no eyewitness to the crime, the testimony indicated that shortly before the killing Alford took his gun from his house, stated his intention to kill the victim, and returned home with the declaration that he had carried out the killing. After the summary presentation of the State's case, Alford took the stand and testified he hadn't commit the murder but was pleading guilty because he faced the threat of the death penalty if he didn't. In response to his lawyer's questions, he acknowledged his lawyer had explained the difference be-

tween second- and first-degree murder and of his rights in case he chose to go to trial. The trial court then asked Alford if, in light of his denial of guilt, he still wanted to plead guilty to second-degree murder and Alford answered, "Yes, sir. I plead guilty on [because of] . . . the circumstances that he [Alford's attorney] told me." After getting information about Alford's prior criminal record, which was a long one, the trial court sentenced him to thirty years' imprisonment, the maximum penalty for second-degree murder.

Alford claimed his plea of guilty was invalid because it was the product of fear and coercion. On appeal, a divided panel of the Court of Appeals for the Fourth Circuit reversed on the ground that Alford's guilty plea was made involuntarily because North Carolina statutes encouraged defendants to waive constitutional rights by the promise of no more than life imprisonment if a guilty plea was offered and accepted. The Court of Appeals ruled that Alford's guilty plea was involuntary because its principal motivation was fear of the death penalty.

Opinion

As previously recounted, after Alford's plea of guilty was offered and the State's case was placed before the judge, Alford denied that he had committed the murder but reaffirmed his desire to plead guilty to avoid a possible death sentence and to limit the penalty to the thirty-year maximum provided for second-degree murder. Ordinarily, a judgment of conviction resting on a

---

- Saves tax dollars because negotiating costs less than trying cases, especially with a jury
- Ensures prompt correctional measures for defendants
- Promotes rehabilitation of defendants by requiring them to admit their guilt
- Reduces the humiliation and misery to defendants that can accompany a public trial
- Results in lesser punishment

But outsiders, including not only academics and criminal justice reformers whom we'd expect to find fault with it but also the public, have from time to time strongly opposed it. Criminal law professor George P. Fletcher (1995) sums up the attitude in his interesting book, *With Justice for Some:*

> Though roughly 90% of all cases are disposed of consensually without trial, there is something unseemly

about the prosecution's trading a lower charge in return for the defendant's cooperating and waiving his right to trial. The very idea that the authorities cut special deals with particular defendants offends the rule of law. Many legal systems on the Continent, Germany most strongly, have long rejected this kind of discretionary justice. . . . Germans refer to American-style discretionary justice as the . . . principle of expediency as opposed to the . . . principle of legality, which demands prosecution according to the extent of the perceived legal violation. Even-handed justice under the law should mean that everyone receives the same treatment: no leniency for those who promise something in return. (191)

The public agrees with Professor Fletcher. (So do most of my students. Every year when we discuss the

plea of guilty is justified by the defendant's admission that he committed the crime charged against him and his consent that judgment be entered without a trial of any kind. The plea usually includes both elements even though there is no separate, express admission by the defendant that he committed the particular acts claimed to constitute the crime charged in the indictment. Here Alford entered his plea but accompanied it with the statement that he had not shot the victim.

State and lower federal courts are divided on whether a guilty plea can be accepted when it is accompanied by protestations of innocence and hence contains only a waiver of trial but no admission of guilt. Some courts, giving expression to the principle that "our law only authorizes a conviction where guilt is shown," require that trial judges reject such pleas. But others have concluded that they should not "force any defense on a defendant in a criminal case," particularly when advancement of the defense might "end in disaster. . . ." They have argued that, since "guilt, or the degree of guilt, is at times uncertain and elusive," "an accused, though believing in or entertaining doubts respecting his innocence, might reasonably conclude a jury would be convinced of his guilt and that he would fare better in the sentence by pleading guilty. . . ." As one state court observed nearly a century ago, "reasons other than the fact that he is guilty may induce a defendant to so plead and he must be permitted to judge for himself in this respect."

Alford now argues in effect that the State should not have allowed him this choice but should have insisted on proving him guilty of murder in the first degree. The States in their wisdom may take this course by statute or otherwise and may prohibit the practice of accepting pleas to lesser included offenses under any circumstances. But this is not the mandate of the Fourteenth Amendment and the Bill of Rights. The prohibitions against involuntary or unintelligent pleas should not be relaxed, but neither should an exercise in arid logic render those constitutional guarantees counterproductive and put in jeopardy the very human values they were meant to preserve.

While most pleas of guilty consist of both a waiver of trial and an express admission of guilt, the latter element is not a constitutional requisite to the imposition of criminal penalty. An individual accused of crime may voluntarily, knowingly, and understandingly consent to the imposition of a prison sentence even if he is unwilling or unable to admit his participation in the acts constituting the crime.

Questions

1. Summarize the arguments the Court gives for its decision.
2. Do you think Henry Alford's plea was voluntary and knowing? Defend your answer using the discussion of the requirements for a plea in the text.

pros and cons of plea bargaining, they agree with Professor Fletcher. Do you?)

Critics also point to the unfairness of plea bargaining. Guilty defendants escape the full consequences of their wrongdoing by pleading guilty to crimes less serious than they've actually committed. Innocent defendants, on the other hand, plead guilty to crimes they didn't commit. For example:

> San Francisco defense attorney Benjamin Davis represented a man charged with kidnapping and forcible rape. The defendant was innocent, Davis says, and after investigating the case Davis was confident of an acquittal. The prosecutor, who seems to have shared the defense attorney's opinion on this point, offered to permit a guilty plea to simple battery. Conviction on this charge would not have led to a greater sentence

than thirty days' imprisonment, and there was every likelihood that the defendant would be granted probation. When Davis informed his client of this offer, he emphasized that conviction at trial seemed highly improbable. The defendant's reply was simple: "I can't take that chance." (Zimring and Frase 1980, 523)

These types of criticisms have led to some attempts to restrict and in a few cases ban plea bargaining entirely.

Ban on plea bargaining

In 1973, a distinguished panel appointed by President Richard Nixon (National Advisory Commission on Criminal Justice Standards and Goals 1973, 3.1) called for a total ban on plea bargaining by 1978. Alaska Attorney General Avrum Gross answered the call in 1975. A 1980 follow-up study to determine the effect found the ban had mixed results (Rubenstein, Clarke, and Wright 1980, 219–243; Rubenstein and Wright, 1979). Courts in Alaska didn't collapse under a crush of criminal trials. In fact, decision making actually speeded up after the ban. Why? Defendants continued to plead guilty at about the same rate, giving lawyers more time to prepare for cases that were going to trial.

But the ban wasn't a cure-all. Evils once blamed on plea bargaining were still there. Defendants' incomes still affected decision making. Defendants who went to trial still got stiffer punishments than those who pleaded guilty. Race, income, and employment status still infected sentencing decisions. The ban also took away some needed flexibility in charging and sentencing. For example, the ban stopped the practice of sentencing "clean kids" (first-time, nonviolent property offenses) to probation instead of prison. Professors Franklin Zimring and Richard Frase (1980) give a few more examples: "a shaky prosecution witness, a faulty police investigation, or an attractive defendant may provide irresistible inducements to bargain, and make negotiated settlements seem by far the most sensible recourse" (684).

A second follow up in 1991 by Teresa Carns (1991) also found mixed results. The Alaska courts still haven't broken down under the ban. The ban had definitely improved prosecutors' charging decisions. Tighter screening standards had led to a "dramatic increase in the number of cases not accepted for prosecution." On the other hand, despite the absolute formal ban on bargaining and an initial compliance with the ban, charge bargaining was routinely practiced.

8-12 Alaska's Plea Ban re-evaluated, the complete 1991 report

The finding that banning plea bargaining didn't break down the court blew a hole in the courtroom work group's cherished caseload hypothesis. According to the **caseload hypothesis,** the pressure to dispose of large numbers of criminal cases requires plea bargaining to keep the courts from breaking down. However, an evaluation of an experimental ban on plea bargaining in El Paso Texas, *supports* (modestly) the caseload hypothesis. Malcolm D. Holmes, Howard C. Daudistel, and William A. Taggart (1992), relying on annual numbers of felony cases pending at the beginning of each year; the number of cases added each year; jury trial dispositions each year; and convictions each year, found that although a majority of defendants still pled guilty, the number of jury trials went up, the rate of dispositions went down, and the number of convictions didn't change. The bottom line: Even a small increase in the number of trials slows down decision making.

Pretrial settlement conferences

Plea bargaining shuts out people with a vital interest in the case—victims, defendants, police officers, and sometimes judges—from the decision making. **Pretrial settlement conferences** try to make up for this important shortcoming. Dade County, Florida, set up an experiment with pretrial settlement conferences to restructure plea bargaining (Kerstetter and Heinz 1979). The Dade County pretrial settlement conferences took place in judges' chambers. Judges wore business suits instead of the forbidding black robes. Participants sat around the room or gathered about a table in an atmosphere more like a conference than a court proceeding.

Conference sessions were brief—from 10 to 25 minutes long. Topics included the seriousness of the case, the criminal history of the defendants, recommendations for punishment, and less frequently the personal backgrounds and circumstances of victims and defendants. Because most conferences generally lasted about 10 minutes, they only covered the topics superficially. Judges did most of the talking. In 40 percent of the cases, prosecutors didn't say anything about the facts of the case, and in over half the cases, prosecutors didn't say anything about defendants' prior records. Defense lawyers *did* discuss defendants' criminal history—usually to clear up misunderstandings—and defendants' personal characteristics in more than one-third of the cases. Police officers contributed facts relating to the crime in about 70 percent of the cases and added information about defendants' backgrounds in more than half the cases.

Most victims didn't come to the conference—two-thirds stayed away. Most who came were passive. Occasionally, they commented on the facts but practically never expressed views about disposition, except occasionally to approve what judges and lawyers recommended. Fear that victims would demand maximum sentences didn't materialize.

Two-thirds of the defendants came but, like victims, said little. If they said anything, it was usually about either the facts of the case or their background. They hardly ever mentioned recommended sentences.

The conferences didn't affect decision making. Before and after the experiment, the rate of cases going to trial, the sentences offenders got, and the time and expense of processing cases all stayed the same. However, the conferences did improve the attitudes of victims and police officers toward plea bargaining and the criminal justice system. Over half said they understood and approved of plea bargaining after they attended the conferences. Still, presettlement conferences clearly aren't a cure for whatever ails plea bargaining.

Knowledge and Understanding Check

The decision to charge
- ✔ What percentage of people arrested for a felony actually goes to prison?
- ✔ List and describe the formal and informal criteria prosecutors use in the decision to charge.
- ✔ Identify and describe the consequences of the decision to charge.

The first appearance
- ✔ List, describe, and trace the development of bail.
- ✔ List the three criteria most judges base their bail decisions on, and summarize some empirical challenges to the importance of these criteria.
- ✔ According to the research, how big are the problems of failure to appear and committing crimes while on bail?

Trial
- ✔ List and describe the missions of criminal trials.
- ✔ Discuss how community values can influence jury decision making.

- ✔ Describe jury selection.
- ✔ List and describe the steps involved in criminal trials to determine whether the defendant is guilty.

Guilty pleas
- ✔ Explain the difference between straight and negotiated guilty pleas.
- ✔ List and describe in detail the criteria courtroom work group members have in mind when they negotiate.
- ✔ What constitutional rights do defendants give up when they plead guilty? Under what conditions is it constitutional to plead guilty?
- ✔ Identify the arguments for reform in plea bargaining, and summarize the results of bans on plea bargaining.
- ✔ Summarize the results of pretrial settlement conferences.

KEY TERMS

adjudication	going rate for crimes	pretrial settlement conferences
arraignment	grand jury review	preventive detention
assigned counsel	hearsay evidence	pro bono
bail	indictment	proof beyond a reasonable
bail schedule	indigent	doubt
bench trial	jury instructions	public defenders
bind over	jury list	release on recognizance (ROR)
caseload hypothesis	jury nullification	relevant evidence
challenge for cause	jury panel	sentence bargaining
change of venue	leading questions	sequester the jury
charge bargaining	legal guilt	social structure of the case
closing argument	liberation hypothesis	straight pleas
colloquy	local legal culture	strength of the case
contract attorneys	"mercy of the court" pleas	subpoena
cross-examination	money bail system	sweet deals
dead-bang cases	negotiated pleas	testimonial evidence
decision to charge	nolo contendere	verdict
direct examination	opening statements	voir dire
diversion	peremptory challenge	
factual guilt	physical evidence	
first appearance	preliminary hearing	

INTERNET PROJECT

1. *Cases prosecuted in state courts:* How many cases were closed by state prosecutors last year? How many of these cases resulted in conviction? How many prosecutors were threatened with harm? How often did prosecutors' offices use DNA evidence? What was the breakdown among felony and misdemeanor cases, and what specific offenses fell into these two categories?

   a. Internet: *Prosecutors in State Courts, 1996*
   b. InfoTrac College Edition: Search using the key words "state prosecution cases."

2. *Plea bargaining:* Are you in favor of plea bargaining? Would you reform it? Ban it? Leave it alone?

   a. InfoTrac College Edition: Enter the key words "plea bargaining."

CHAPTER 9

Sentencing

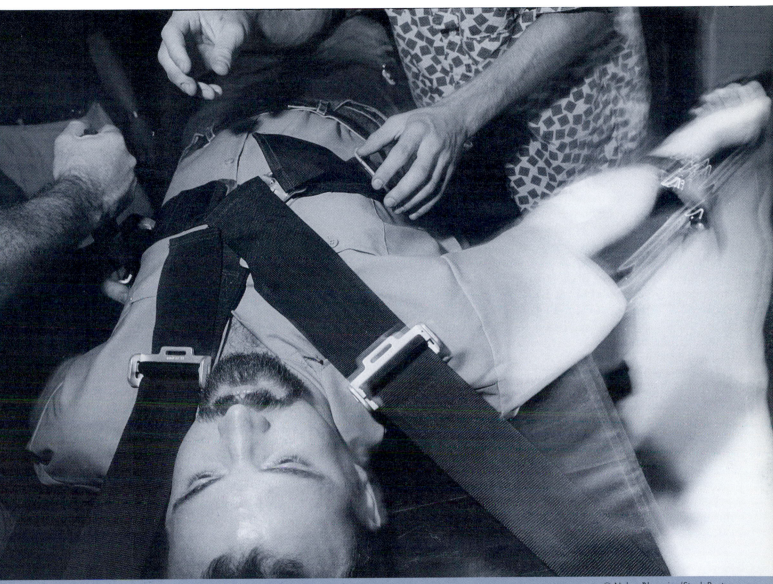

© Nubar Alexanian/Stock Boston

> I see him with solemn sorrow, adjusting the cap of judgment on his head.
> He addresses the consciences of the trembling criminals. . . .
> He acquaints them with the certainty of speedy death and consequently
> with the necessity of speedy repentance. The dreadful sentence
> is now pronounced. Every heart shakes with terror.
>
> EIGHTEENTH-CENTURY COURT OBSERVER (HAY 1975, 17–19)

■ INTRODUCTION

Every spring and fall, the scarlet-robed royal judges rode to all the county towns of eighteenth-century England to read proclamations, address the local bigwigs, and try all the felons held in the local jails. In the presence of the local bigwigs and surrounded by large crowds, they made their "jail delivery" a great spectacle. Nowhere was royal power more evident than when the judges put on their "black caps of death" to exercise their life and death power by pronouncing sentence on convicted felons (all felonies from murder to stealing were capital offenses). The judges took full advantage of the public spectacle to first strike terror by pronouncing the death sentence and then, at the last minute, temper justice with mercy by saving repentant convicts from the hangman's noose in a dramatic stay of execution.

Modern judges in the United States don't have the power of the eighteenth-century English judges, because the Constitution prohibits "cruel and unusual punishments." Judges have to share their power to sentence with legislatures, prosecutors, and corrections officials. Public demands to "get tough" on crime, reformers' dissatisfaction with judicial discretion, and scholars' research on the ineffectiveness of sentencing practices have produced reform laws limiting judges' sentencing power. Still, both certain justice and flexible mercy are parts of the practical reality of sentencing.

■ PURPOSES OF SENTENCING

Throughout history sentencing has had two basic goals: retribution and prevention. **Retribution** looks back at what criminals did and tries to make them "pay" for their wrongs by giving them their "just deserts." It's a means to vent society's outrage; in the words of a distinguished English judge, it's "right to hate criminals" and to express that hatred by hurting them to even the scales of justice.

Sometimes, retribution takes the form of the ultimate payment, life itself. Sometimes, it's mutilation, as in the Old Testament's "an eye for an eye." Today, it's prison time, or some other limit on the freedom to come and go as you please and enjoy the comforts of life. But, whatever form it takes, at the end of the day retribution is about inflicting pain because it's right to do so. It's right for society because it relieves our outrage and satisfies our basic urge to hurt what hurts us (like kicking the bike we fell off when we were kids). But, it's also right for criminals, because it treats them like full thinking individuals who can choose to do either right or wrong, accept responsibility if they make the wrong choice, and, by suffering pain for their wrong choices, "pay their debt to society" and become full members of the community again (Durham 1998, 131–153). In the words of Andrew von Hirsch, in his influential book *Doing Justice* (1976):

> [W]e should punish criminals simply for the crime committed. We should not do it either to reform them, or to deter them, or to deter others. In other words, punishment should fit the crime already committed, not the criminal—nor the crimes either the criminal or others might commit in the future.

Like retribution, **prevention** inflicts pain, too, but not to pay for past crimes; prevention looks forward and inflicts pain to stop criminals and criminal wannabes from committing crimes in the future. There are four types of prevention: special deterrence, general deterrence, incapacitation, and rehabilitation. The idea of prevention by deterrence was born in the eighteenth-century Enlightenment and is based on the English philosopher Jeremy Bentham's **philosophy of utility.** Utility starts with two assumptions about human nature: (1) people seek pleasure and avoid pain, and (2) they have the free will to choose their own actions.

In deterrence, the aim of punishment is to inflict just enough pain (or the threat of pain) to make criminals (or wannabes) avoid the pain of committing crimes. **Special deterrence** hopes to teach convicted criminals the lesson that "crime doesn't pay" by inflicting *actual* pain on them—pain that "costs" more than the pleasure they got from crime—so, when they get out of prison, they won't commit crimes. **General deterrence** "sends a message" to people thinking about committing crime that "crime *doesn't* pay." Whether that message gets through depends on three things—the swiftness, the certainty, and the severity of the punishment. According to deterrence theorists and researchers, swiftness and certainty are more important than severity. For example, knowing that you're really going to prison next week for one year—no ifs, ands, or buts—is more effective than maybe you'll go to prison for five years starting in the year 2030.

Incapacitation is based on the straightforward idea that criminals can't commit crimes while they're locked up. It's present-oriented because it's aimed at preventing locked up criminals from committing crimes they'd be committing if they weren't locked up. It isn't concerned with what they might do in the future when they get out. The ultimate incapacitation is, of course, death. The basic idea of **rehabilitation** is to change criminals into people who "work hard and play by the rules." Rehabilitation inflicts pain, but not on purpose, only as a necessary side effect of changing criminals.

In practice, none of these aims is either completely distinct from or in harmony with the others. So, punishment in specific cases is usually based on several conflicting aims. For example, a rapist goes to prison to suffer the pain of confinement for its own sake, to send him a message that rape doesn't pay, to incapacitate him so he won't be raping while he's in prison, to send a message to rapist wannabes that if they rape they'll go to prison, and to subject him to sex-offender treatment to rehabilitate him. In Kathleen Daly's (1994) study of sentencing in New Haven, Connecticut's courts, she writes:

> I read the sentencing transcripts many times before I could identify the category (or categories) in which a sentencing justification fell. . . . What I found was that judges combine various punishment theories. For example, the general deterrence aim of punishment—to send a signal to others that crime will not go unpunished—may shade in a desert- or retribution-based rationale. (Daley 1994, 182)

Daley gives this example of Dorothy who set two fires to her apartment after a fight with her boyfriend. At her sentencing, the judge said:

> This could have been a disastrous . . . incident for the people that lived in the house—undoubtedly something you didn't give a moment's thought to at the time you did this. But how many times do we pick up the paper and read about fires that are started by people motivated like you to retaliate against somebody else

for some grievance that result in serious injuries or deaths to people [retribution]. . . . This is the kind of conduct that we have an obligation to try to stop [special and general deterrence]. The only way that we know how to do it is to incarcerate the people that commit offenses like this [incapacitation], and this is the reason you are being incarcerated today: to demonstrate to you [special deterrence] and hopefully to other people who might be inclined to do the same thing [general deterrence] that kind of conduct is not going to be tolerated [retribution]. (Daley 1994, 184–185)

These punishments also raise difficult questions. Like, how much and what kind of pain is a rape worth? Or, how much pain exceeds the pleasure of satisfying the urge to rape? Does locking up a rapist really incapacitate him or just shift the pool of his victims? What sex-offender treatments work? And if so, who do they work for and under what circumstances? These, like so many other questions we've already encountered, and will encounter in the rest of the book, are all difficult and still unresolved.

■ HISTORY OF SENTENCING

Whether to fit sentences to the crime or tailor them to individual criminals has pestered officials, academics, and (in modern times) the public for more than a thousand years. In **determinate sentencing** (sometimes called fixed sentencing) legislatures focus on the crime and attach specific punishments to it, like fitting a sentence of 25 years to the crime of armed robbery. In **indeterminate sentencing** legislatures set only the outer limits of possible penalties, like 0 to 25 years for robbery. Corrections officials then tailor the actual time served using specialized programs to suit the individual offenders and release them when they're "corrected."

Both fixed *and* indeterminate sentencing are essential elements of criminal justice. Fixed sentences point to the desirability of the certainty, predictability, and even-handedness of formal rules in administering criminal justice. Indeterminate sentencing responds to the need for flexibility, the "play in the joints" of informal discretionary decision making that's essential to fair criminal justice. We can see the tension between fixed and indeterminate sentencing as early as A.D. 700 in the Roman Catholic Church's penitential books, sometimes laying down penance strictly according to the sin and at other times tailoring penance to suit individual sinners (Samaha 1978).

Determinate Sentencing, Pre-1878

In U.S. history, the controversy over fixed and indeterminate sentencing began during the 1630s in the Massachusetts Bay colony. The governor of the colony, the great

Puritan founder John Winthrop, maintained that both fairness and justice demanded wide judicial discretion. Each sentence, he said, should depend on a combination of the facts of the case, the background and character of the defendant, and the general needs of the community. So, Winthrop argued, poor people should pay lower fines than rich people, religious leaders should suffer harsher penalties than laypersons for committing morals offenses, and powerful colonists should receive more severe penalties for breaking the law than weak individuals. How could abuse of this wide discretionary power be avoided? Appoint wise judges whose personal prejudices don't infect their sentencing, Winthrop answered. The Massachusetts Bay Colony legislature wasn't convinced. It passed a fixed sentencing law banning judicial discretion in sentencing (Samaha 1989).

Fixed sentencing was common until the Revolution, when fixed but moderate penalties became the norm. States abolished the death penalty for many offenses. Corporal punishment (whipping), mutilation (cutting off ears and slitting tongues), and shaming (the ducking stool) remained on the books but were never used. By 1850, state laws established fixed prison terms for most felonies. However, early release for "good time" and other devices allowed the use of informal discretionary judgment to alter formally fixed sentences (Rothman 1971). Fixed sentencing remained the norm until the 1870s, when organized voices proclaimed the need for change.

Indeterminate Sentencing, 1878–1970

The modern history of sentencing grew out of dissatisfaction with legislatively fixed harsh prison sentences. A growing band of prison administrators complained that prisons were nothing more than warehouses for the poor, immigrants, and other "undesirables." They also claimed that imprisonment didn't work. Released prisoners soon returned to prison, and crime continued at unacceptably high rates no matter how many offenders were locked up. A high point in the debate about the ineffectiveness of fixed prison sentences was the National Prison Congress, where a large group of prison officials eager for reform gathered in 1870 in Cincinnati. Its "Declaration of Principles" was based on the idea that sentencing shouldn't just punish criminals; it should reform them. How? Get rid of fixed sentences and put indeterminate sentences in their place. A "mere lapse of time" to "pay" for past crimes shouldn't determine sentence length, the Congress proclaimed; "satisfactory proof of reformation" should determine how long to keep criminals in prison (Transactions of the National Congress of Prisons and Reformatory Discipline 1971).

New York enacted the first indeterminate sentencing law in 1878. It provided:

> Every sentence to the reformatory of a person convicted of a felony or other crime shall be a general sentence to imprisonment in the New York State reformatory at Elmira and the courts . . . shall not fix or limit the duration thereof. The term of . . . imprisonment . . . shall be terminated by the managers of the reformatory . . . but . . . imprisonment shall not exceed the maximum term provided by law for the crime for which the prisoner was convicted and sentenced. (Twentieth Century Fund 1976, 95)

By 1922, all but four states had adopted an indeterminate sentencing law.

Indeterminate sentencing laws were based on the confidence that professionals could transform criminals into hardworking individuals who played by the rules. A dedicated core of middle-class reformers accepted the findings (in fact, they were more beliefs than scientific findings) of contemporary social and physical scientists that both basic human "drives" and social "forces" controlled human behavior. According to these "findings," individuals didn't choose their actions; their heredity, physical characteristics, psyche, and environment thrust their behavior on them (Appier 1998, 16–17).

Indeterminate sentences weren't supposed to be "soft on crime"—far from it. According to the rehabilitation experts of the time, criminals were either corrigible or incorrigible. Reform measures could change the corrigibles—namely, first-time offenders under 30. The incorrigibles—over 30, repeat offenders—were hardened criminals beyond hope. What reform measures could change these criminals into hardworking citizens who obeyed the law? Professionals enforced strict rules and daily schedules of hard work, study, exercise, and healthy living habits. Prisoners who didn't comply got harsh punishment, like solitary confinement on a diet of bread and water, and/or whipping, hosing, and other corporal punishments.

Prison officials, parole officers, and reformers believed prisoners and parolees could easily fake reformation. So, they made prisoners prove they'd reformed by following prison rules. When prisoners were released from prison it was only conditionally (Chapter 10). Parolees had to clinch the proof their reformation was genuine by keeping a job, living a clean life, and staying out of even minor trouble with the law. Incorrigibles couldn't reform. But that didn't mean incorrigible prisoners could "get away" without working. They had to pay their own way, usually by forced hard labor inside prison because they refused to willingly earn their keep. If force didn't work, well then they should be killed (Samaha n.d.).

According to these tough reformers, judges trained in law weren't qualified to decide who was corrigible and incorrigible or when corrigibles could safely return to society. Only the new professionals—criminologists, physicians, psychiatrists, social workers, corrections officials—had the expertise and judgment to classify, treat, and proclaim which criminals had really turned into hardworking citizens who followed the rules and paid their own way (Lindsey 1925, 16, 96).

In indeterminate sentencing states, prison officials and parole boards had more discretionary power to decide actual sentences than legislatures and judges. But, judges could still make discretionary judgments. They could grant probation instead of imprisonment; suspend sentences in favor of community service; or pick confinement times within minimums and maximums prescribed by statutes, like 5 years under a statute that prescribed 0 to 10 years in prison. But, parole boards and corrections officers determined the exact date of release and the conditions and length of parole (Chapter 10).

Return to Fixed Sentencing, 1970–Present

Indeterminate sentencing remained dominant until the 1970s, when several forces combined to return to fixed sentencing. The country was in the midst of the biggest crime boom in history (Chapter 3). Prison riots in the late 1960s made rehabilitation look like nothing more than talk and exposed prisons as seething cauldrons of discontent erupting into extreme violence (Chapter 11). Prisoners' rights advocates challenged the broad informal discretionary powers of criminal justice officials. And a band of activist judges demanded that criminal justice officials justify their decisions in writing and empowered defendants to dispute their sentencing (Chapter 11).

At the same time, disillusionment with rehabilitation was spreading quickly among professionals. Several statistical and experimental studies strongly suggested poor people and Blacks got harsher sentences than Whites and more affluent Americans. Disillusionment and the troubling statistical studies led to the creation of a distinguished panel of the National Research Council to review sentencing practices. The panel concluded that by the early 1970s, a "remarkable consensus emerged among left and right, law enforcement officials and prisoners groups, reformers and bureaucrats that the indeterminate sentencing era was at its end" (Blumstein, Cohn, Martin, and Tonry 1983, 48–52).

What led to this remarkable consensus? A powerful alliance between civil libertarians and conservatives who agreed that the aim of sentencing is swift and certain punishment. But there the agreement ended. They disagreed over two fundamentals: the *length* and the *kind* of sentences. To civil libertarians, determinate sentencing meant short, fixed sentences, with programs to prepare prisoners for playing by the rules and paying their way in life. To conservatives, punishment meant long, fixed uncomfortable sentences (prisons aren't "country clubs").

The public was firmly on the side of the conservatives. Political scientist James Q. Wilson (1983b), in his best-selling *Thinking about Crime,* pointed to a public that was frustrated and fed up with judges who were "letting too many criminals off with a slap on the wrist."

The conservatives (Wilson 1983b) and the public view of fixed sentencing won. According to the National Council on Crime and Delinquency (1992):

> By 1990, the shift in goals of sentencing was complete. Virtually all new sentencing law was designed to increase the certainty and length of prison sentences to incapacitate the active criminal and deter the rest. (6)

By 1996 the United States was sentencing more people to prison for longer terms than almost any other country in the world.

■ TYPES OF FIXED SENTENCING

There are two variations of fixed sentences:

1. **Mandatory minimum sentences,** in which convicted offenders have to spend at least some time in prison
2. **Sentencing guidelines,** which base sentences on a combination of the severity of the crime and the criminal history of the offender

Mandatory Minimum Sentencing Laws

According to mandatory minimum sentence laws, offenders have to spend at least some time (the mandatory minimum laid out in the law) in prison. At least as far as the mandatory minimum is required, the laws take away both judges' and corrections officials' discretionary power in sentencing. Judges can't suspend the minimum, and they can't substitute probation for it. Prison and parole authorities can't release offenders until they've served the minimum.

Mandatory penalties have a long history. The Old Testament "an eye for an eye" is a mandatory penalty. The Anglo-Saxon king Alfred prescribed a detailed mandatory penalty code, including such provisions as

> If one knocks out another's eye, he shall pay 66 shillings, 6 1/3 pence. If the eye is still in the head, but the injured man can see nothing with it, one-third of the payment shall be withheld.

Mandatory minimums have had an on-and-off history in the United States (U.S. Sentencing Commission 1991, 14–16). They were used frequently during the 1800s, but then fell into disuse from 1900 to 1950. Then, fear of crime and illegal drugs became part of the Cold War in the

1950s. (Some members of Congress were convinced there was a Communist plot to get Americans "hooked" on an especially potent "pure Communist heroin" from China.) In 1956, Congress enacted a mandatory minimum drug law to make sure that offenders who did the drug crime would "do the time"—in this case, 5 years in prison for a first-time heroin sale. Congress repealed the 1956 law in 1970 (U.S. House of Representatives 1970, 11), because, it concluded that increased sentence lengths "had not shown the expected overall reduction in drug law violations." Further, they alienated youths from the general society; hampered the rehabilitation of drug law offenders; infringed on judicial discretion; and reduced the deterrent effect of drug laws. Prosecutors stopped charging offenders because even they believed the laws were too severe (U.S. Sentencing Commission 1991, 6).

The 1970 retreat from mandatory minimum sentences didn't last long. By 1991, forty-six states and the federal government had enacted mandatory minimum sentencing laws, mainly aimed at drug and weapons offenses. According to Senator Orrin Hatch:

> **The reason why we went to mandatory minimums is because of these soft-on-crime judges . . . who just will not get tough on crime, get tough especially on pushers of drugs that are killing our youth. And so that's why the mandatory minimums . . . within which judges have to rule, rather than allowing them to just put people out on probation who otherwise are killing our kids.** (*Frontline* 1999)

9-1 *Frontline, Snitch* transcript

Criminal justice officials told the U.S. Sentencing Commission (1991) that mandatory minimum sentences further five fundamental principles of criminal punishment.

1. *Equality*: Similar offenses receive similar sentences.
2. *Certainty*: Offenders and the public know that offenders will really do the minimum prison time the statute prescribes.
3. *Just deserts*: Violent and drug offenders, habitual criminals, and criminals who use guns to commit crimes deserve mandatory long prison terms.
4. *Deterrence*: Mandatory prison sentences deter crime by sending the strong message that those who "do the crime" really will "do the time."
5. *Incapacitation*: Mandatory prison terms protect public safety by locking up drug dealers and violent armed criminals. (15–16)

In 1990, Congress ordered the U.S. Sentencing Commission (1991) to evaluate federal mandatory minimum sentencing statutes. After studying presentence reports,

sentencing hearings, plea agreements, sentencing guideline worksheets, and a random sample of drug and firearms cases, the commission reported:

- Only 41 percent of defendants who qualify for mandatory minimum sentences actually receive them.
- Mandatory minimum sentences increase disparity in sentencing.
- Whites are less likely than Blacks and Hispanics to be indicted or convicted at the mandatory minimum.
- Whites are also more likely than Blacks and Hispanics to receive reductions for "substantial assistance" in aiding in the prosecution of other offenders. (76)

9-2 U.S. Sentencing Commission full report on mandatory minimum sentencing

Defendants who provide prosecutors with "substantial assistance" in investigating other offenders are eligible for an exception to the mandatory minimum sentences. The substantial assistance exception creates more than racial disparities. It also favors the very people the law was intended to punish ("drug kingpins") because underlings don't have anything to offer the government. Stanley Marshall, who sold less than one gram of LSD, got a 20-year mandatory prison sentence. Jose Cabrera, on the other hand, who the government estimated made more than $40 million from importing cocaine and who qualified for life plus 200 years, got 8 years because he provided "substantial assistance" in the case of Panamanian dictator–drug dealer Manuel Noriega.

According to Judge Terry J. Hatter, Jr., "The people at the very bottom who can't provide substantial assistance end up getting [punished] more severely than those at the top" (Wallace 1993, 11). Joey Settembrino (*Frontline* 1999), in prison serving a 10-year mandatory minimum for a cocaine deal, reflected on the irony:

> **They say that they want to get the big guy, they want to get the big fish, and that's why they go about getting all these little fish, because they eventually get the big fish. But what they don't realize is that when the big fish finally gets caught, he tells on the little fish, and he's free.**

Mandatory minimum sentences don't eliminate discretion either; they just shift it from judges to prosecutors. Prosecutors can use their discretion in a number of ways, including not charging defendants at all with mandatory sentence crimes (Chapter 8). Or, they can charge them with less serious mandatory minimum crimes. They can also manipulate the "substantial assistance" exception to suit their purposes. Although the Sentencing Commission recommended further study before drawing any final conclusions about the effectiveness of mandatory penalties, their findings suggest that mandatory minimum penalties aren't the easy answer to the crime problem that politicians promise and the public hopes (Campaign for an Effective Crime Policy 1993; Schulhofer 1993, 199).

9-3 National Public Radio's "This American Life" audios on mandatory minimum sentencing

One of the best-known, and most controversial, forms of mandatory minimum sentences are three-strikes laws.

Three-strikes laws

Despite the shortcomings of mandatory minimum sentences, they remain popular with the public and some professionals. The "three strikes and you're out" laws are especially popular. The basic idea behind these **three-strikes laws** is to lock up for life dangerous offenders who habitually prey on innocent people.

The catchy phrase may be new, but the idea behind three-strikes laws is almost five hundred years old. In sixteenth-century England and in the American colonies, statutes imposed harsh penalties on repeat offenders. In 1797, New York expanded habitual offenders to include all repeat offenders, not just offenders who repeated the same crime. The New York law ordered a sentence of mandatory life imprisonment "at hard labor or in solitude, or both" for all offenders convicted of their second felony—no matter what that second felony was. Habitual offender laws flourished even in the era of the indeterminate sentence. By 1968, every state had some form of habitual felon statute (Turner et al. 1995, 16).

The three-strikes laws are just habitual felon laws with a new name. By 1995, thirty-seven states had proposed some form of three-strikes legislation. Liberals and conservatives, Democrats and Republicans, and the public all favor them. Why are they so popular? Michael G. Turner, Jody L. Sundt, Brandon Applegate, and Francis T. Cullen (1995), in their survey of the enactment of three-strikes legislation, found several reasons:

■ Public dissatisfaction with the criminal justice system
■ The "panacea phenomenon"—the promise of a simple solution to a complex problem
■ The appeal of the catchy phrase—putting old habitual offender statute ideas into the language of modern baseball: "Three strikes and you're out" (Benekos and Merlo 1995, 3)

What effects have "three-strikes" laws had? There are several evaluations of California's 1994 three-strikes law (King and Mauer 2001), which mandates life in prison for *any* third felony (like auto theft, or even as in one case—stealing a pizza). The law was passed after the brutal sex-

ual assault and murder of Polly Klaas. By June 1, 2001, more than 50,000 offenders were in prison under the law (6271 for "three strikes" and 43,800 for "two strikes"). Joan Petersilia concluded that "the much higher imprisonment rates" brought about by the law "had no appreciable effect on violent crime, and only slight effects on property crime." The Sentencing Project, a research and advocacy group, analyzed official data on California two and three-strike sentencing and found the law

1. Has not significantly contributed to reducing crime
2. Has increased the number and severity of sentences for *non*violent crime
3. Is rapidly expanding an aging and costly prison population, a population that doesn't contribute to violent crime
4. Has no relation to California's 1990s crime bust (King and Mauer 2001)

9-4 Sentencing Project full report

Prior to its passage, a RAND Corporation study (Greenwood et al. 1994) found the California three-strikes legislation would reduce murder, rape, and aggravated assault by about 11 percent and other serious crimes like robbery and residential burglary. The study predicted that the cost of the law would be high, between $4.5 and $6.5 billion a year in 1994 dollars to pay for added prison space.

9-5 Full report of Rand's "three strikes" study

Sentencing Guidelines

Sentencing guidelines are fixed—but flexible—sentences based on balancing the seriousness of the offense and the criminal history of the offender. Guidelines establish narrow ranges of sentences; judges can sentence offenders within the ranges. Figure 9.1 on page 163 reproduces the Minnesota Sentencing Guidelines Grid for determining sentence ranges. The rows on the grid contain offenses, and the columns represent a score for criminal history. The bold line (disposition line) separates prison sentence ranges (above the bold line) from probation and other nonprison sentences (below the bold line). The numbers in the cells present the recommended sentence and the range of months over and below the recommended sentence judges can choose. For example, the recommended sentence for first-time aggravated robbery is 48 months; the judge can impose an actual sentence of 44 to 52 months. The range gives some room for judges to take into account differences in individual cases.

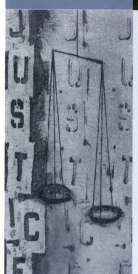

United States v. Brigham 977 F.2d 317 (7th Cir. 1992)

Facts

Agents of the Drug Enforcement Agency learned from an informant that Craig Thompson was in the market to buy 10 kilograms of cocaine. The DEA's undercover agents feigned willingness to supply him. During negotiations, Thompson said that he had just sold 17 kilograms and needed 10 more that very day to tide his organization over until the arrival of a shipment that he was expecting. Thompson and the agents did not trust one another. Jeffrey Carter, one of Thompson's goons, searched an agent; the agent's gun, normal in the business, did not trouble Carter, but a transmitter or recorder would mean big trouble. Carter was not very good at his job; he didn't find the concealed recorder. Thompson ultimately agreed to pay $30,000 per kilogram, a premium price for quick service. After the agents let on that they didn't trust Thompson any more than Thompson trusted them, Thompson agreed to let the agents hold his Rolls Royce as collateral until payment. In the agents' presence, Thompson called Tyrone Amos and told him to pick up "ten of those things today" at a suburban motel. Thompson and Carter would hand over the Rolls in a different suburb.

At the appointed time, less than five hours after the agents first met Thompson, one team descended on a restaurant to receive the Rolls Royce and another decamped to the motel to "deliver" the cocaine. Amos arrived at the motel in a car driven by Anthony Brigham. Amos and the agents at the motel had a conversation; Brigham stayed in the car. Carter had not appeared at the restaurant with the Rolls Royce, so everyone settled down to wait. Brigham looked around the parking lot but scrunched down in his seat when the agents' Corvette drove slowly by. At the restaurant, Thompson and the agents discussed future deals of 50–100 kilograms per month. At the motel, Brigham paced nervously in the lobby. After touring the parking lot again, lingering over the Corvette, Brigham joined Amos at a nearby gas station, where Amos placed a phone call. The two had a conversation and returned to the motel, where Amos told the agents that Carter and the Rolls were still missing. While Amos and one agent were dining together some distance from the motel, Thompson paged Amos with news that the Rolls had arrived. Back at the motel, the agents went through the motions of delivering cocaine. As Amos headed for the agents' car to retrieve the drugs from the trunk, Brigham moved his car to a location from which he could keep the delivery in sight. But there was no cocaine. Before Amos could open the trunk other agents moved in, arresting Amos and Brigham, just as they pinched Thompson and Carter at the restaurant.

All but Brigham pleaded guilty and provided valuable assistance to prosecutors. All but Brigham were sentenced to less than the "mandatory" minimums. Thompson received 84 months' imprisonment and Amos 75 months, after the prosecutor made motions under [the "substantial assistance" exception]. Carter, who was allowed to plead to a charge that did not carry a minimum term, received 4 years' probation, 4 months of which were to be in a work-release program run by the Salvation Army. That left Brigham, who went to trial, was convicted, and received the "mandatory" term of 120 months' imprisonment.

Opinion

Steep penalties await those who deal in drugs. Buying or selling 10 kilograms of cocaine—even agreeing to do so, without carrying through—means a minimum penalty of 10 years' imprisonment, without the possibility of parole. The "mandatory" minimum is mandatory only from the perspective of judges. To the parties, the sentence is negotiable. Did a marginal participant in a conspiracy really understand that a 10-kilo deal lay in store? A prosecutor may charge a lesser crime, if he offers something in return. Let's make a deal. Does the participant have valuable information; can he offer other assistance? Congress authorized prosecutors to pay for aid with sentences below the "floor." Let's make a deal.

Bold dealers may turn on their former comrades, setting up phony sales and testifying at the ensuing trials. Timorous dealers may provide information about their sources and customers. Drones of the organization—the runners, mules, drivers, and lookouts—have nothing comparable to offer. They lack the contacts and trust necessary to set up big deals, and they know little information of value. Whatever tales they have to tell, their bosses will have related. Defendants unlucky enough to be innocent have no information at all and are more likely to want vindication at trial, losing not only the opportunity to make a deal but also the two-level reduction the sentencing guidelines provide for accepting responsibility.

Mandatory minimum penalties, combined with a power to grant exceptions, create a prospect of inverted sentencing. The more serious the defendant's crimes, the lower the sentence—because the greater his wrongs, the more information and assistance he has to offer to a prosecutor. Discounts for the top dogs have the virtue of necessity, because rewards for assistance are essential to the business of detecting and punishing crime. But what makes the post-discount sentencing structure topsy-turvy is the mandatory minimum, binding only for the hangers on. What is to be said for such terms, which can visit draconian penalties on the small fry without increasing prosecutors' ability to wring information from their bosses?

Our case illustrates a sentencing inversion. Such an outcome is neither illegal nor unconstitutional, because offenders have no right to be sentenced in proportion to their wrongs. Still, meting out the harshest penalties to those least culpable is troubling, because it accords with no one's theory of appropriate punishments.

Was the evidence sufficient? Appellate judges do not serve as additional jurors. After a jury convicts, the question becomes whether any sensible person could find, beyond a reasonable doubt, that the defendant committed the crime. That is a steep burden, for 12 persons, presumably sensible and having a more direct appreciation of the evidence than the written record affords to appellate judges, have unanimously found exactly that.

Brigham emphasizes that "mere" presence at a crime does not implicate the bystander in that offense. Conspiracy is agreement, and what proof of agreement did the prosecutor present? Brigham arrived with Amos, conferred with Amos, and was in position to watch an exchange occur. No one testified that Brigham had any role in the exchange or Thompson's organization. Although the prosecutor portrayed Brigham as a lookout, he asks:

> What kind of lookout would be unarmed, without radio, pager, cellular phone, or any other way to give or receive alerts? What counter surveillance operative would hunker down in the car rather than keep a hawk-eyed watch? Thompson, Carter, and Amos, who reaped rewards for their assistance, were conspicuously absent at Brigham's trial. Had they no evidence to offer against him?

No one questions the rule that "mere presence" at the scene of a crime does not prove conspiracy. "Mere" presence differs from, say, "revealing" presence. Like many a weasel word, "mere" summarizes a conclusion rather than assisting in analysis. When the evidence does not permit an inference that the defendant was part of the criminal organization, the court applies the label "mere presence." So we must examine the evidence, taking inferences in the light most favorable to the jury's verdict, rather than resting content with slogans.

Brigham shows up on short notice with Amos, who the jury could conclude was there to receive 10 kilograms of cocaine from strangers whom Thompson and Amos do not trust. Is Amos likely to come alone? Is a companion apt to be ignorant of the nature and risks of the transaction? For almost three hours Brigham remains at the motel, generally observant and generally nervous; he follows Amos to a pay phone where a telephone call and conversation ensue. Amos reveals the contents of this conversation to the agents; the jury could conclude that he revealed it to Brigham too. While Amos and an agent go to dinner, Brigham keeps watch. After Amos returns, eye contact and a nod from Amos lead Brigham to take up position where he can watch the trunk of the agents' car. Just what was Brigham doing for three hours in the lobby and parking lot of the motel, if not assisting Amos? He was not exactly passing through while a drug deal went down around him. Brigham did not testify, and his lawyer offered no hypothesis at trial. At oral argument of this appeal the best his counsel could do was to suggest that Brigham might have believed that Amos was picking up counterfeit money rather than drugs. Tell us another! The jury was entitled to conclude that Brigham knew about, and joined, a conspiracy to distribute cocaine.

Thin the evidence was, but it was also sufficient. Evidence at sentencing shows that the jury drew the right inference. Amos related that he brought Brigham as a lookout. Brigham told the prosecutor that he was part of the organization and had been involved in some big-stakes transactions. But he was unable to provide enough information to induce the prosecutor to make the [substantial assistance] motion that unlocks the trap door in the sen-

tencing "floor." Pleading guilty would have produced the 10-year minimum term, so Brigham went to trial; he had nothing to lose and some chance of being acquitted. The evidence at sentencing showed that Brigham knew that Thompson's organization dealt in multi-kilogram quantities, which supports the judge's conclusion that Brigham qualifies for the 10-year minimum. All that remains is Brigham's argument that the judge should have invoked U.S.S.G. sec 5K2.0 to give him a break. Section 5K2.0 describes appropriate departures from the guidelines, but Brigham needed a departure from a minimum sentence prescribed by statute. That was available only on motion of the prosecutor. Brigham does not contend that in declining to make the motion the prosecutor violated the Constitution. . . . Wise exercise of prosecutorial discretion can prevent egregious sentencing inversions. How that discretion is to be exercised is a subject for the political branches. Brigham joined the conspiracy and received a sentence authorized by Congress. His judicial remedies are at a close.

AFFIRMED.

Dissent

I respectfully dissent. Taking all the evidence as described in the majority opinion as absolutely true, and viewing it in the light most favorable to the government, I still do not find that any sensible juror could find Brigham guilty of the crime of conspiracy beyond a reasonable doubt. At oral argument, counsel for Brigham could only suggest, in answer to a question from the bench as to what explanation he could give for Brigham's actions on the day in question, "that Brigham might have believed that Amos was picking up counterfeit money rather than drugs." An unbelievable scenario. The fact is, no one testified as to what exactly Brigham was doing or why he was doing it; no one, in spite of the marvelous totally cooperating witnesses who, if the government's theory is correct, could have nailed Brigham's hide to the jailhouse wall. But they didn't. And it is not Brigham's missing explanation that is fatal; it is the government's inability to explain that creates the problem.

Tell us another, indeed, but only if it is the government tale; the accused has absolutely no burden to explain anything. The government accuses, the defendant says "prove it," and the government says the suspicious activity is enough to convince and convict. And so it proved.

I would have directed a verdict of "not guilty" had I been the trial judge and I construe my role in review to be the same. I do not believe the evidence sufficient to convince a sensible juror of proof beyond a reasonable doubt. The existence of cooperating witnesses who knew all and told nothing virtually implies the missing witness analysis: you had the control, you didn't produce, I infer the testimony would have been adverse to you.

I would reverse.

Question

What exactly are Judge Easterbrook's objections to the mandatory minimum sentence he was obliged to impose in this case? Do you agree? Defend your answer.

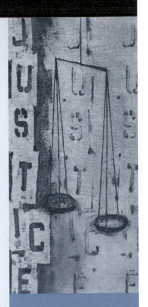

Should he get life for stealing a piece of pizza?

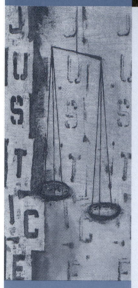

Slater 1995, B9

Jerry Dewayne Williams, 27, a 6-foot 4-inch Compton warehouser, was arrested near Craig's ice cream shop at the Redondo Beach Pier in July 1994 a few months after California passed its tough three-strikes law. According to prosecutors, Williams and a friend, a little drunk and maybe playing a game of "truth or dare," went up to four kids eating an extra-large pepperoni pizza. Williams and his friend asked for a piece; when the kids said no, they each took a piece anyway. His friend was never prosecuted, but a jury found Williams guilty of petty theft (stealing the slice of pizza).

Petty theft is ordinarily a misdemeanor, but Williams's prior convictions for robbery, attempted robbery, unauthorized use of a motor vehicle, and possession of a controlled substance made it a felony. So Judge Donald F. Pitts sentenced Williams to prison for 25 years to life. Williams was silent as Pitts pronounced the sentence. The reasons for Judge Pitts's sentence: Williams's five prior felony convictions, his "habit of finding trouble," and the "three strikes" law. Judge Pitts denied a defense lawyer Arnold Lester's motion that 25-years-to-life for stealing a piece of pizza was "cruel and unusual punishment." Williams became a poster child of "three strikes" opponents. "No matter how many pizza thieves it sends to prison,

this law is not going to make our streets safer," said Allan Parachini, spokesman for the American Civil Liberties Union.

But Heling Craig, part of a small contingent of Redondo Beach "three strikes" supporters, said Williams got what he deserved. "It's like, hey, this guy's had five chances and he still goes out and commits a crime." Prosecutors and supporters of the law agree with Heling Craig. They argue that "three strikes" offers two chances, and repeat offenders aren't being punished because of the third conviction but for their criminal history. Williams "is a habitual criminal, and that is what we are sentencing," said Deputy District Attorney Bill Gravlin, who prosecuted Williams. "The people of California are sick of revolving-door justice, they're sick of judges who are soft on crime. It is wrong to focus on the last offense." Williams's lawyer, Arnold Lester, "shook his head and disagreed.... Seems to me that society is going crazy in the punitive nature of these statutes."

Questions

1. List the arguments made for and against the three-strikes law.
2. Which side in the argument do you favor, and why?

9-6 Minnesota Sentencing Guidelines grid with commentary

What if judges want to sentence a first-time robber to more than 52 months or less than 44 months? This is called a **departure.** Judges can depart from the range when the "individual case involves substantial and compelling circumstances." What are "substantial and compelling circumstances"? Circumstances justifying downward departures include the victim was the aggressor in the crime (Kunume starts a fight with Jessica and Jessica stabs Kunume); the offender played only a minor role in the crime (Christian drives Charles to a convenience store so Charles can rob it); or the offender lacked the capacity of judgment due to physical or mental impairment (Ben is a borderline schizophrenic but not insane when he steals Amirthini's cell phone). Circumstances justifying upward departure include the victim was vulnerable (Keeley beat up an elderly man who has to use a walker); cru-

elty was inflicted on the victim (Eddie shot in the feet and the hands a victim he had just mugged); the crime was a major drug offense; or the crime was committed for hire (Brandon hired Jocelyn to shoot his wife). Judges who depart have to give written reasons for their departures. Defendants can appeal upward departures; prosecutors can appeal downward departures (Minnesota Sentencing Guidelines Commission 2001).

Terance D. Miethe and Charles A. Moore (1985, 357–361) evaluated the impact of the Minnesota sentencing guidelines. They found one major positive outcome—a shift in prison populations from property offenders to violent criminals—an outcome in line with the Minnesota legislature's intent to move property offenders into community corrections. But they also found that guidelines don't eliminate race, gender, marital status, income, and other biases from infecting sentencing decisions. Judges can hide their biases in their discretionary departure decisions. This is true even though their discretion is open to public view because they have to put their reasons for

Italicized numbers within the grid denote the range within which a judge may sentence without the sentence being deemed a departure. Offenders with nonimprisonment felony sentences are subject to jail time according to law.[1]

CRIMINAL HISTORY SCORE

SEVERITY LEVEL OF CONVICTION OFFENSE (Common offenses listed in italics)		0	1	2	3	4	5	6 or more
Murder, 2nd Degree (intentional murder; drive-by-shootings)	X	306 *299–313*	326 *319–333*	346 *339–353*	366 *359–373*	386 *379–393*	406 *399–413*	426 *419–433*
Murder, 3rd Degree Murder 2nd Degree (unintentional murder)	IX	150 *144–156*	165 *159–171*	180 *174–186*	195 *189–201*	210 *204–216*	225 *219–231*	240 *234–246*
Criminal Sexual Conduct, 1st Degree[2] Assault, 1st Degree	VIII	86 *81–91*	98 *93–103*	110 *105–115*	122 *117–127*	134 *129–139*	146 *141–151*	158 *153–163*
Aggravated Robbery 1st Degree	VII	48 *44–52*	58 *54–62*	68 *64–72*	78 *74–82*	88 *84–92*	90 *94–102*	108 *104–112*
Criminal Sexual Conduct 2nd Degree (a) & (b)	VI	21	27	33	39 *37–41*	45 *43–47*	51 *49–53*	57 *55–59*
Residential Burglary Simple Robbery	V	18	23	28	33 *31–35*	38 *36–40*	43 *41–45*	48 *46–50*
Nonresidential Burglary	IV	12[1]	15	18	21	24 *23–25*	27 *26–28*	30 *29–31*
Theft Crimes (Over $2,500)	III	12[1]	13	15	17	19 *18–20*	21 *20–22*	23 *22–24*
Theft Crimes ($2,500 or less) Check Forgery ($200–$2,500)	II	12[1]	12[1]	13	15	17	19	21 *20–22*
Sale of Simulated Controlled Substance	I	12[1]	12[1]	12[1]	13	15	17	19 *18–20*

☐ Presumptive commitment to state imprisonment. First Degree Murder is excluded from the guidelines by law and continues to have a mandatory life sentence. See section **II.E. Mandatory Sentences** for policy regarding those sentences controlled by law, including minimum periods of supervision for sex offenders released from prison.

▨ Presumptive stayed sentence; at the discretion of the judge, up to a year in jail and/or other nonjail sanctions can be imposed as conditions of probation. However, certain offenses in this section of the grid always carry a presumptive commitment to a state prison. These offenses include Third Degree Controlled Substance Crimes when the offender has a prior felony drug conviction, Burglary of an Occupied Dwelling when the offender has a prior felony burglary conviction, second and subsequent Criminal Sexual Conduct offenses, and offenses carrying a mandatory minimum prison term due to the use of a dangerous weapon (e.g., Second Degree Assault). See sections **II.C. Presumptive Sentence** and **II.E. Mandatory Sentences.**

[1]One year and one day

[2]Pursuant to M.S.• 609.342, subd. 2, the presumptive sentence for Criminal Sexual Conduct in the First Degree is a minimum of 144 months (see **II.C. Presumptive Sentence** and **II.G. Convictions for Attempts, Conspiracies, and Other Sentence Modifiers**).

Effective September 14, 2001

FIGURE 9.1

Minnesota Sentencing Guidelines

SOURCE: Minnesota Sentencing Guidelines Commission 2001.

departing in writing. And, prosecutors can even more easily hide their bias in their invisible reasons for charging and plea bargaining with defendants.

 9-7 You Decide: Was the sentence departure justified?

DISPARITY AND DISCRIMINATION IN SENTENCING

We've already learned from empirical research surveyed earlier in the book that decisions in criminal justice—arrest, charge, and disposition—depend on three appropriate criteria: seriousness of the offense, the criminal history of the offender, and the strength of the case. We've also learned that these are the *main* but not the *only* ingredients in decision making. Let's examine to what extent sentencing decisions are infected with inappropriate ingredients. Don't forget the distinction we've referred to earlier, the one between discrimination and disparity. **Sentencing discrimination** means the use of unacceptable criteria, usually race, ethnicity, or gender, to determine sentences. **Sentencing disparity** includes inequality of three different types:

1. *Different sentences for similar offenders.* Two burglars the same age, with similar records, break into stores after hours and each takes $100 from the cash register. One burglar goes to prison, the other gets probation.
2. *Similar sentences for different offenders.* Both a five-time burglar and a first-time burglar receive five years in prison.
3. *Similar offenders receiving different sentences for unimportant differences.* An armed robber who takes $1000 receives a 10-year sentence; another armed robber who takes $750 gets a 5-year sentence. (Schulhofer 1992, 835–836)

First, let's look at a tool judges use for determining sentences, the presentence investigation.

Presentence Investigation

Fixed sentencing *restricts* judicial discretion; it doesn't *eliminate* it. Judges can still use their discretion in sentencing. Also, because fixed sentences cover felonies, judges have lots of leeway in misdemeanor cases, which vastly outnumber felony cases. In other words, even in felony cases but still more so in the vast number of misdemeanor cases, judges don't just automatically apply sentences in statutes and guidelines; they use their discretion (Chapter 8). This leeway in sentencing allows judges to take into account the individual offender. Judges rely on the **presentence report (PSR),** which is based on a presentence investigation, to guide their discretion in sentencing.

The presentence report contains information about offenders' prior criminal record (criminal history); their social history; and, where there may be mental problems, a psychiatric evaluation. The first part of the PSR enumerates the facts of the case based on both the police report and the defendant's version of what happened. As you might expect, police and defendants' versions often conflict. Judges tend to accept the police version. (Critics say this is not fair to defendants.) The second part of the PSR includes the offender's prior criminal record, including prior convictions, dropped charges, and arrests. (Critics say histories shouldn't include arrests because they only require probable cause whereas convictions require proof beyond a reasonable doubt.) Social histories include family history, employment record, and education. Judges say social histories help them predict the offender's potential for rehabilitation and future behavior. Psychiatric evaluations include the defendant's history of mental illness, hospitalizations, treatment, and recommendations (Rosecrance 1985, 539–554).

The quality of information in PSRs can be a problem. Probation officers, who are in charge of presentence investigations and who write the PSRs, have to do these jobs while they're supervising heavy caseloads of probationers (Chapter 10). Always pressed for time, they can't always get all the information they need, or equally important, make sure the information they do get is correct.

Another problem is that probation officers have less influence on sentencing than the presentence investigation and report suggest. Based on his fifteen years of experience as a probation officer and on interviews with probation officers, Professor John Rosecrance (1985, 539–554; 1988, 236–256) concluded that they write presentence reports for three audiences: the court, the prosecutor, and the probation supervisor. They use the report to maintain their credibility, looking for cues from these audiences and providing them with recommendations their audiences want to hear. So, probation officers make recommendations not so much to influence their audiences' perceptions of defendants, but to legitimate the officers' own claim to being "reasonable."

Blacks and Disparity

Adult Black males account for less than 5 percent of the general population of the U.S. according to the 2000 census. But, they made up 18 percent of violent offenders, 26 percent of property offenders, and 42 percent of drug offenders sentenced in state courts in 1996, the latest figures available (Levin and Langan 2000).

9-8 "State Court Sentencing of Convicted Felons," full Bureau of Justice Statistics report

How do we explain this racial gap? Early research on the connection between race and sentencing suffered from two shortcomings. First, most sentencing research depended on **aggregate sentencing data** (lumping together data from all places studied). Aggregate data obscure local variations. For instance, conclusions based on all sentences in a state might hide racially determined sentences in particular counties; one county can obscure the racism of individual judges (Alabama Law Review Summer Project 1975, 676–746; Daley 1989, 136–168; Kruttschnitt 1984, 213–232; Nagel and Weitzman 1971, 171–198; Petersilia 1985, 15–35).

Martha A. Myers and Susette M. Talarico's (1987, 80–81) study of sentencing in Georgia clearly demonstrates the strengths of disaggregating data. They compared a random sample of 16,798 Georgia felons throughout the whole state with a comparable random sample of 1685 Georgia felons from Fulton and DeKalb counties. They found little systemwide different sentences of Black defendants:

> We expected that sanctions would be more severe in counties characterized by pronounced inequality, a sizeable percentage of black unemployed residents, and relatively high crime rates. In actuality, we found little evidence to support these expectations. . . . We found no consistent relationship with punitiveness in sentencing. Nor did the presence of large economically subordinate populations, whether black or unemployed, foster more severe sanctions. (Myers and Talarico 1987, 80–81)

But, after Myers and Talarico looked more closely at different communities, they found racial discrimination in specific communities where seriousness of the crime combined with the racial composition to create disparities. And, disparity might mean more leniency as well as more severity:

> There were many instances in which blacks received disproportionately lenient punishment. Although this pattern may suggest a paternalism that is just as discriminating as disproportionate punitiveness, it nevertheless indicates that courts in Georgia do not have a heavy hand with black defendants in the general systemic sense or in every context where differential treatment is observed. (Myers and Talarico 1987, 170–171)

Hispanics and Disparity

Gary D. Lafree (1985) analyzed 755 defendants in Tucson, Arizona, and El Paso, Texas, to find out whether there was discrimination in the sentencing of Hispanic defendants. He found major differences between the two cities in robbery and burglary sentences. In Tucson, there were no significant differences between sentences of Hispanics and non-Hispanics. In El Paso, on the other hand, Hispanics received longer sentences. Interviews with criminal justice officials suggested that the established Hispanic population in Tucson, versus the less-established Mexican American and Mexican national populations in El Paso, accounts for the difference. According to one El Paso prosecutor:

> We're sitting here on a border. Across the river from us, which is nothing more than an oversized mud puddle, is the city of Juarez, with over a million and a quarter residents. . . . Our police force is geared to the size of this city and what it can afford. El Paso does not have the economic base to support the city itself. In other words, we perceive El Paso as the city north of the Rio Grande, but bullshit, we're talking about another million and a quarter people that go back and forth like a tide. (Lafree 1985, 228)

Women and Disparity

Until the 1990s, most research on sentencing women showed a clear gender gap that favored women—they got more lenient sentences than men. Much of that research was based on data sets from the 1960s and 1970s before the move toward more fixed sentencing and more sophisticated research methods were developed to sort out the effects of gender from the effects of seriousness of offenses and criminal history of offenders.

Darrell Steffensmeier, John Kramer, and Cathy Streifel (1993, 411–446) analyzed later data from Pennsylvania during 1985 to 1987. Pennsylvania adopted sentencing guidelines in 1982 based on the combination of seriousness of offense and criminal history of offender. They applied regression analysis to sort out the effects of gender from offense and criminal history. They asked two important questions: Did gender affect the decision *whether* to sentence to incarceration? And did gender affect the decision of *how long* to incarcerate?

They found no gender gap in sentencing. The seriousness of the offense and the criminal history of the offender overwhelmed gender in both the decisions to sentence defendants to incarceration and how long the incarceration should be. So, here we have it again—the right reasons for decisions trump the wrong ones in criminal justice decision making. But gender wasn't completely irrelevant; men were 12 percent more likely to get prison sentences than women (Steffensmeier, Kramer, and Streifel 1993, 426–428).

What about downward departure decisions? Do judges give women breaks they don't give men? At first, it might look like they do. Steffensmeier and his colleagues found that 29 percent of women got a break in their departures contrasted to 15 percent of the men. But, when examined more closely, offense and history, not gender, were the reasons. In the words of one of the judges:

> Maybe some judges do give women a break because they feel sorry for the woman or because she has children. But the main thing for me is that sometimes you're comparing "apples and oranges." A woman coming before you in court may have the same prior record score or the same offense score as a man but her score involves all property offenses—no violent priors at all. And many times the woman's part in the offense is small, more the follower than the leader. I don't know where they find these guys but some of these women get hooked up with such losers you can hardly imagine it. Another thing that doesn't show up [in the official record] is that the women I see in court fairly often have health problems or mental problems. What are we going to do? The jails can't handle that. (Steffensmeier, Kramer, and Streifel 1993, 434)

Why did Steffensmeier and his colleagues find no gender gap while so much of earlier research did? The authors offer several possibilities. Maybe sentencing decisions have gotten more gender neutral because of greater concern about equal application of the law. Or, maybe Pennsylvania's sentencing guidelines led to greater equality by reducing judges' discretion. Part of the explanation is probably the more sophisticated statistical analysis that controlled for seriousness of offense and criminal history. Past studies with the fewest controls show the biggest gender gap (Steffensmeier, Kramer, and Streifel 1993, 435–437).

■ THE DEATH SENTENCE

"Thou shalt not kill!" commands the Old Testament. But, "Vengeance is mine," said the Old Testament God, and "not the Lord Chief Justice's," added the British playwright George Bernard Shaw. "Forgive thine enemies," the New Testament Jesus implored.

In North Carolina, visitors can hear or download audio clips of members of the media and public who have witnessed an execution. In Florida, photographs of the electric chair and execution gurney can be downloaded. And, in Oregon, an extensive narrative details how the condemned spend their last hours—and minutes. There's even a photo of a stopwatch to accompany the narrative. The Georgia Department of Corrections recently updated its death row site, which provides not only its always popular "virtual jail cell" tour but now also offers photos and a roster of condemned inmates. Until recently, you could go to the

Texas website and see the menu of death row prisoners' last meal.

 9-9 Execution tapes and NPR "Witnesses to Execution"

"I don't know if we'll ever go back to the death penalty as we knew it, as long as I'm governor," said Illinois governor George Ryan, who stopped all executions after thirteen men were sent to death row before being exonerated by new evidence. "Serious questions are being raised about the death penalty. . . ." U.S. Supreme Court Justice Sandra Day O'Connor (2001) told a group of Minnesota lawyers. Minnesota "must breathe a big sigh of relief every day," she told the audience (Minnesota has no death penalty).

These introductory paragraphs will give you some idea of the passion swirling around capital punishment, but all this passion is misleading. Let's look at some facts about the death sentence and some issues surrounding it.

The American public stands firmly behind the death penalty and an increasingly exasperated strong majority of the U.S. Supreme Court has repeatedly reminded stubborn defense lawyers that the U.S. Constitution doesn't forbid it. Yet, in the face of this strong public support and the clear rulings of the U.S. Supreme Court, the reluctance to actually kill criminals convicted of capital offenses is strong. On January 1, 2000, there were 3527 prisoners on death row—the highest number since 1951. The number of people waiting for execution has grown steadily since 1972 (Figure 9.2). But, the number of executions is low compared with the number of prisoners sentenced to death. Ninety-eight were executed in 1999, and they'd been waiting on death row an average of almost 12 years (Bureau of Justice Statistics 2000a, 1)!

Let's look more closely at the death penalty and constitutional issues, public opinion about the death penalty, the cost of executing prisoners, and four tough questions that should be asked when evaluating whether we should have the death penalty.

The Death Penalty and the Constitution

The Eighth Amendment to the U.S. Constitution prohibits "cruel and unusual punishments." The death penalty was well established before the Eighth Amendment was adopted and was widely practiced afterward. The U.S. Supreme Court didn't decide a single case challenging the constitutionality of the death penalty until 1890 in the case of William Kemmler. In 1889, shortly after New York introduced the electric chair to replace hanging, Kemmler was convicted and sentenced to death for murdering his wife in the state of New York. In 1885, the governor had asked the state legislature "whether the science of the present day cannot provide a means for

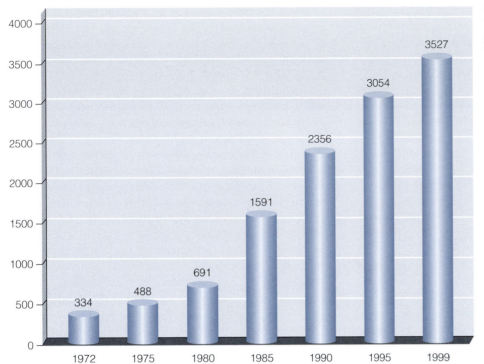

FIGURE 9.2
Prisoners on Death Row, 1972–1999
SOURCE: Bureau of Justice Statistics 2000d, Table 6.82.

taking life in a less barbarous manner" than hanging which "has come down to us from the dark ages." A commission appointed by the legislature found one—the newly invented electric chair. The commission reported that electrocution is "the most humane and practical method of execution known to modern science" (*In re Kemmler* 1890, 444).

The case of *In re Kemmler* (1890) came to the U.S. Supreme Court because Kemmler claimed electrocution was a cruel and unusual punishment—notice that he didn't argue that capital punishment itself was cruel and unusual, only the *method*. The Court agreed that electrocution was unusual but to violate the Eighth Amendment, it had to be unusual *and* cruel. But was it cruel? Absolutely not, said the Court. Punishments aren't cruel as long as they don't go further than "the mere extinguishments of life." The Court spelled out what this phrase means. First, death has to be instantaneous and painless. Second, it can't involve unnecessary mutilation of the body. According to the Court, beheading is cruel because it mutilates the body. Crucifixion is doubly cruel because it causes *lingering* death *and* mutilates the body.

9-10 Sounds and sights of executions (Don't visit if sounds and sights of executions upset you.)

In 1910 (*Weems v. U.S.*), the Court added the **principle of proportionality**—namely, that punishments should fit the crime—to the meaning of cruel. Paul Weems was convicted of falsifying a public document. The trial court sentenced him to 15 years of hard labor in chains and took away his civil rights for life. The U.S. Supreme Court overturned the sentence because the punishment was too harsh for the crime and therefore cruel. So far, the Court has taken the position that only the crime of murder fits the punishment of death. But, Louisiana has decided that the death penalty for raping a child under 12 is not cruel because it fits this monstrous crime.

9-11 Full opinions in *Weems v. U.S.* and Louisiana supreme court opinion in child rape case

The U.S. Supreme Court has also decided that the sentence of death doesn't violate three other provisions in the U.S. Constitution: It doesn't deny individuals life without due process of law (Fifth and Fourteenth Amendments) if both mitigating and aggravating circumstances are considered before the sentence is imposed. And, it doesn't deny equal protection of the law (Fourteenth Amendment) as long as the sentence isn't discriminatory; that is, race and other unacceptable criteria didn't play a part in the decision to impose the death sentence.

To meet these requirements, most death penalty states have passed **guided discretion death penalty statutes.** These statutes list the aggravating and mitigating circumstances that juries have to consider before they decide whether defendants should receive the sentence of death or life imprisonment. The usual aggravating circumstances include killing someone while committing some other felony; prior convictions for homicide; killing strangers; killing multiple victims; especially cruel killings; and killing law enforcement officers. Typical mitigating circumstances include no prior criminal history; mental or emotional stress; victim participation in the crime; and playing only a minor part in the murder. Defendants charged with capital crimes under guided discretion statutes are tried in two stages **(bifurcated trials)**. The first stage decides whether defendants are guilty; the second decides the sentence. It's during this second stage that juries consider the aggravating and mitigating circumstances before they decide whether defendants should receive the death penalty or life imprisonment.

The U.S. Supreme Court has also decided that sentencing juveniles (*Thompson v. Oklahoma* 1988) and retarded people (*Penry v. Lynaugh* 1989) to death isn't cruel and unusual and doesn't deny them either life without due process of law or equal protection of the laws. When he was 15, William Wayne Thompson, together with three older persons, shot his brother-in-law twice; cut his throat, chest, and abdomen; and broke his leg. Then they chained the body to a concrete block and threw it in a river. Thompson was convicted and sentenced to death. The Supreme Court ruled that the Constitution didn't stand in the way of the sentence. Johnny Paul Penry raped, beat, and then stabbed Pamela Carpenter with a pair of scissors. She died a few days later. Dr. Jerome Brown testified that Penry was mentally retarded, probably due to brain damage at birth, and that he had the mental age of a 6½-year-old and the social maturity of a 9- or 10-year-old. Penry was convicted and sentenced to death. The Supreme Court reversed his death sentence because the jury wasn't allowed to consider his mental retardation. However, the Court ruled that mental retardation shouldn't prevent his execution, just that the jury had to consider it. The case went back to Texas for a second sentencing trial. Penry was sentenced to death again, appealed to the Supreme Court again, and the Supreme Court overturned the second sentence because the Court said Texas still didn't allow the jury to fully consider Penry's retardation. In the meantime, the Texas legislature passed a statute banning the sentence of death of mentally retarded defendants. The governor vetoed the law.

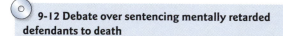

9-12 Debate over sentencing mentally retarded defendants to death

Public Opinion and the Death Penalty

Attitudes toward the death penalty shift with the mood of the country. In the conservative 1950s about two-thirds of the people favored it. Then, during the brief interlude of the mid-1960s liberalism, support slipped to 42 percent, the lowest in fifty years. The quick return to conservatism in the wake of the 1960s crime boom (Chapter 3) brought support back to 51 percent in 1969. Support continued to grow from the 1970s to the mid-1990s as the country's tough stand on punishment hardened. By 1994 support for the death penalty reached an all-time high—80 percent (Kohut 2001, 33).

After 1994, support began to falter for a number of reasons. First, DNA testing has struck home the obvious fact that human beings make mistakes, including sentencing innocent people to death (see "Fallibility" later). There is also a growing belief that the penalty isn't administered fairly; rich people can escape it and poor people can't. This is especially troubling because so many death penalty defendants are racial and ethnic minorities (see "Fairness" later). At the same time, there is growing doubt among the public that the death penalty prevents murder. For the first time in fifteen years, the ABC/Washington Post poll showed that a majority believes the death penalty doesn't prevent murder. Finally, religious beliefs are increasingly cited as the main reason for opposition among social conservatives, Catholics, and white evangelical Protestants (Kohut 2001, 33).

We should point out that support for the death penalty depends on the questions interviewers ask the people polled. The Gallup Poll, which has polled the public about the death penalty since the 1930s, had always asked just one question: "Are you in favor of the death penalty for a person convicted of murder?" In the last few years, they've also asked: "If you could choose between the following two approaches, which do you think is the better penalty for murder: the death penalty (or) life imprisonment, with absolutely no possibility of parole?" In Gallup's May 2001 poll, 65 percent favored the death penalty when asked only if they favored it for murder. Support dropped to 52 percent when they got to choose between death and life without any chance of parole (Newport 2001).

So, despite public uneasiness about the penalty, support remains over 50 percent even when those polled are given the choice between death and life with no chance of parole. One other thing, in that same poll, 81 percent supported the death penalty for Timothy McVeigh, including 58 percent of the people who said they were death penalty opponents! Obviously, a huge majority of the public has no problem with the death penalty in his case. Why? Three reasons: The public was convinced we weren't killing an innocent person (remember he confessed in public interviews); McVeigh himself said he wanted to die; and the crime was horrific (killing 168 innocent people, including many children). These findings led Frank Newport (2001) of the Gallup Poll to write:

We thus end up with a sociological hypothesis: Americans' support for the death penalty will increase to the degree that it is made clear that no mistake has occurred and that the death penalty is being applied to a truly guilty person. One corollary to this hypothesis: support may actually end up increasing in the years to come, rather than decreasing, as new DNA testing techniques become widely used. Why? Because, while this evidence may prove that some on death row are in reality innocent, it also may reduce any chance of a mistake in future cases.

○ **9-13 Newton's full report and audio of discussion of public opinion and the death penalty**

The Cost of the Death Sentence

For years we assumed the death penalty saved money. Not anymore. We've learned it's expensive to charge and try death sentence cases. In federal cases, the average cost of defending a negotiated death sentence is $192,333; the amount rises to $269,000 if the case goes to trial. Prosecuting a federal death penalty case costs an average of $365,000. These amounts don't include the cost of investigation, expert assistance, or law enforcement assistance (Judicial Conference of the United States 1998).

○ **9-14 Full report on costs of prosecuting and defending death cases**

Keeping prisoners on death row until they're executed is also high. According to an article in the *Columbus Dispatch*:

> The State of Ohio spent $1.5 million to kill one mentally ill man who wanted to be executed. Among the costs were: $18,147 overtime for prison employees and $2,250 overtime for State Highway Patrol officers at the time of the execution. This does not include overtime for 25 prison public information officers who worked the night of the execution. The state spent $5,320 on a satellite truck so that the official announcement of Wilford Berry's execution could be beamed to outside media, and $88.42 for the lethal drugs. Attorney General Betty Montgomery had 5 to 15 prosecutors working on the case. Between 5 and 10% of the annual budget for the state's capital-crimes section was devoted to the Berry case for 5 years. Keeping Berry in prison for his entire life would have cost approximately half as much. (Johnson 1999, A1)

In 1995, the estimated cost of one execution was $2 million. Asked why, the noted criminologist Frank Zimring

replied, "Lawyers cost more than prison guards" (Baldus 1995, 1035).

Four Tough Questions

The U.S. Supreme Court may have settled the constitutional questions surrounding the death penalty; the public may support it; and the cost might be worth it. But, let's examine four other questions about the sentence of death:

1. *The moral question:* Is it right?
2. *The utilitarian question:* Does it work?
3. *The fallibility question:* Does it kill innocent people?
4. *The fairness question:* Does it discriminate?

The moral question: Is it right?

Death penalty supporters point to two Old Testament passages: one from *Genesis,* "Whoever sheds the blood of man, by man shall his blood be shed" (Gen. 9:6); the other from Exodus, "Eye for eye, tooth for tooth, hand for hand, foot for foot, burn for burn, wound for wound, stripe for stripe" (Ex. 21:24–25). Opponents invoke the New Testament passage where Jesus admonishes the crowd before stoning an adulteress: "He that is without sin among you, let him first cast a stone at her" (John 8:7). They also point to the Old Testament in which God warns, "Vengeance is *mine*" (meaning it's not ours to inflict) (Deut. 32:35). Sister Helen Prejean (the nun who was the inspiration for the role played by Susan Sarandon in the movie *Dead Man Walking*) put the moral question this way: "When you hear of the terrible things people have done, you can say they deserve to die, but the key moral question is 'Do we deserve to kill?'" (*Frontline* 1996).

Supporters of capital punishment also rely on moral arguments to bolster their positions. According to Professor Ernest van den Haag:

> The life of each man should be sacred to each other man. . . . It is not enough to proclaim the sacredness and inviolability of human life. It must be secured as well, by threatening with the loss of their own life those who violate what has been proclaimed as inviolable—the right of innocents to live. (Bedau 1982, 331)

At the end of the day, the moral debate over capital punishment can't be a matter of science or logic; it boils down to values. Some people believe deeply it's wrong for the state to kill anyone for any reason; others believe just as deeply that it's wrong not to execute the worst criminals.

The utilitarian question: Does it work?

Way back in the 1600s, the tough-as-nails judge Sir Edward Coke said it made him "weep" that hanging 500 English felons in one year didn't reduce crime but instead encouraged it to grow by example. In the 1700s, both the great Italian criminologist Cesare Beccaria and the American reformer Benjamin Rush agreed with Lord Coke and opposed the death penalty at least in part because it didn't work to reduce crime. A hard core of abolitionists has crusaded against the death penalty ever since. The abolitionist crusade continued but the death penalty endured because of the strong public support for it, much of that support based on confidence that executions prevented murder.

The crusaders couldn't prove that killing criminals didn't reduce crime and the public couldn't prove it did. Then, in the 1950s, the distinguished and highly respected sociologist Thorsten Sellin (1959, 24; 1967) decided to study the deterrent effect of the death penalty. He compared homicide rates in states that had abolished the death penalty with carefully matched similar states next to and/or similar to states that retained the death penalty. He found that "Homicide rates are conditioned by other factors than the death penalty."

Other sociologists (Bowers 1974; Reckless 1969, 54) got similar results by comparing homicide rates before and after in (1) states that abolished the death penalty; (2) states that imposed a moratorium on the death penalty; (3) states with highly publicized executions; and, (4) states with mandatory death penalties against states with discretionary death penalties. They, too, found no deterrent effect. As if this weren't impressive enough social science evidence, Sellin even found that there is no statistical support for the proposition that law enforcement officials are safer in death penalty states than those in states without it. With this impressive array of studies, the sociologists seemed to have answered the deterrence question.

Then the accomplished University of Chicago economist Isaac Ehrlich (1975, 397) got into the debate in 1975 when he published the findings from his econometric study that "an additional execution per year . . . may have resulted, on average, in 7 or 8 fewer murders." Careful and responsible researcher that he is, he added this warning, "the weakness inherent in these predicted magnitudes is that they may be subject to relatively large prediction errors." Of course, the headline was more exciting than the warning. Death penalty supporters turned it into the bumper sticker "One execution saves eight innocent lives!" (Albert 1999, 354–355). Opponents pounced on it. And, both a cottage industry in death penalty research was born and an ideological battle broke out. The economists backing up Ehrlich's findings grew bolder. Steven K. Layson (1985, 68), in another elaborate econometric analysis based on homicide data from 1936 to 1977, concluded that every execution prevents eighteen murders!

The sociologists savaged the econometric analyses by pointing out all kinds of flaws. Even the U.S. Supreme Court joined the fray. Justice Thurgood Marshall (1976, 235) wrote in one dissenting opinion:

> The study is defective because it compares execution and homicide rates on a nationwide, rather than a state-by-state, basis. The aggregation of data from all States including those that have abolished the death penalty obscures the relationship between murder and execution rates. Under Ehrlich's methodology, a decrease in the execution risk in one State combined with an increase in the murder rate in another State would, all other things being equal, suggest a deterrent effect that quite obviously would not exist. Indeed, a deterrent effect would be suggested if, once again all other things being equal, one State abolished the death penalty and experienced no change in the murder rate, while another State experienced an increase in the murder rate.

The debate continues as you read this. Professor Craig J. Albert (1999, 354–355) has applied regression analysis to state-by-state homicide data from 1982 to 1994. His regression variables included economic conditions, demography (youth and race), population, and alcohol consumption. His conclusion: "The data do not support any conclusion that execution deters homicides." But, Professor Albert has enough caveats that we won't list here to assure us that his research isn't the last word on whether the death penalty reduces murders.

The fallibility question: Does it kill innocent people?

> In 8048 rape and rape-and-murder cases referred to the FBI crime lab from 1988 to mid-1995, a staggering 2012 of the primary suspects were exonerated owing to DNA evidence alone. Had DNA analysis not been available (as it was not a decade earlier), several hundred of the 2012 would probably have been tried, convicted, and sentenced for crimes they didn't commit. (National Institute of Justice 1996a)

Does this startling finding of the U.S. Department of Justice mean that innocent people are actually killed? If so, how many wrong executions are acceptable? Abolitionists quickly answer zero because, they argue, you can't say, "Whoops, wrong person, let's take this one back." It's too late for that. Supporters say, first, there's nothing to worry about because the last innocent person was executed in the 1930s. And second, that single mistake proves the death penalty is *almost* perfect, which is all we can expect from any human institution. Besides, they say the demand for perfection is only a smoke screen for death penalty opponents to hide their real motive, to get around the U.S. Supreme Court's firm majority position that sentences of death and capital punishment are constitutional.

We really don't know how many innocent people are executed. We hear and read about innocent people released at various stages in the criminal process—arrest, charge, trial, and conviction. We hear especially about close calls on death row—convicts who escape execution by days or sometimes even hours. As of February 2001, DNA tests had led to the release of eighty-two prisoners, ten of them on death row (LoLordo 2001, 3A). These releases have generated lots of news coverage and heated up the debate on the death penalty to furious proportions. Death penalty opponents argue these close calls are *too* close. Take the case of Florida half-brothers William Jent and Ernest Miller who came within 16 hours of execution. Supporters say they *prove* the system works (Radelet and Bedau 1998, 232). Calls for reform are growing louder as people from all parts of the religious, cultural, and political spectrum grow uneasy about the fallibility of the system. By the time you read these words, there may be a federal law providing for mandatory DNA testing in all capital cases.

 9-15 *Frontline*: A Case for Innocence and audio debate on mistakes

The fairness question: Does it discriminate?

You don't see wealthy people, or even middle class people, on death row. Since John Webster, a famous professor of medicine at the Harvard Law School, was sentenced to death and hanged in 1850, businesspeople, professors, lawyers, and doctors have escaped death row. Mostly unskilled workers (almost all men), including many Blacks and Hispanics, are found on death row. But, are they there *unfairly,* that is *because* they're poor, men, and Black, Hispanic or some other racial minority? There's not a single case in the twentieth century and so far in the twenty-first where a court decided a death sentence was based on class, sex, racial, or ethnic discrimination. Still, there's plenty of empirical evidence to cast doubt on whether there's no discrimination in death sentences (Black 1981, 94; Lewis 1979, 203–204).

The U.S. General Accounting Office (GAO) reviewed twenty-eight empirical studies of the death penalty to find out whether either the race of the defendant or the race of the victim mattered in the decision to impose a death sentence. What did the studies show?

1. *Race of the victim mattered.* Those who murder Whites are more likely to get sentenced to death than those who murder nonwhites. This finding was "remarkably consistent across data sets, states, data collection methods, and analytic techniques."
2. *Race of the defendant sometimes mattered and sometimes didn't.* The influence of the defendant's race varied across studies, like one study that showed Black defendants were more likely to get death sentences in rural areas but White defendants were more likely to get death sentences in urban areas.

The GAO published its results in 1990. All of the studies at that time were of southern states. Since then, law professor David Baldus and statistician George Woodworth (1998, 385, 399–400) examined both the period before and after the GAO study. Their study included all death penalty states that had imposed a death sentence (Kansas, New York, and New Hampshire hadn't done so at the time) and had an available study (total of 28 states). They found that in twenty-five of the twenty-eight states, there's evidence of race-of-the-victim disparities. There was some evidence of race-of-the-defendant disparity in ten states. Disparities aren't limited to the South: They were found in Philadelphia and in New Jersey in the 1990s.

 9-16 The complete Philadelphia study report

"The most in-depth and detailed study of race and the death penalty in North Carolina's history" found that between 1993 and 1997 "defendants whose victims are white are 3.5 times more likely to be sentenced to death than defendants whose victims are non-white." "Despite a generation of legal and cultural efforts to eliminate discrimination, these results show that racial bias still dramatically affects the most final of judgments—who gets the death penalty," according to law professor and principal investigator of the study, Jack Boger (Common Sense Foundation 2001).

 9-17 North Carolina study, full report and more recent research

Knowledge and Understanding Check

Purposes of sentencing
✔ Identify and explain the difference between the two main goals of punishment.
✔ List and describe the four types of prevention.
✔ Identify some of the difficult questions raised by punishment.

History of sentencing
✔ Explain the difference between and give an example of determinate and indeterminate sentences.
✔ Trace the development of and reasons for the shifts in sentencing from colonial times to 2002.

(continued)

Knowledge and Understanding Check (continued)

Types of fixed sentencing
- ✔ Identify the differences between mandatory minimum sentences and sentencing guidelines.
- ✔ List the strengths and weaknesses of mandatory minimum sentences.
- ✔ List the strengths and weaknesses of sentencing guidelines.

Disparity and discrimination in sentencing
- ✔ Explain the importance of presentence investigations in judges' decisions to sentence.
- ✔ Explain the difference between sentencing disparity and sentencing discrimination.

- ✔ List and give an example of the three types of sentencing disparity.
- ✔ Summarize the research on sentencing disparities and discrimination against Blacks, Hispanics, and women.

The death sentence
- ✔ What do the words "cruel" and "unusual" mean according to the U.S. Supreme Court?
- ✔ Why is the death penalty so expensive?
- ✔ According to the evidence, is the death sentence right? Does it work? Does it kill innocent people? Does it discriminate?

KEY TERMS

aggregate sentencing data
bifurcated trials
departure
determinate sentencing
fairness question
fallibility question
general deterrence
guided discretion death penalty
   statutes

incapacitation
indeterminate sentencing
mandatory minimum sentencing
moral question
philosophy of utility
presentence report (PSR)
prevention
principle of proportionality
rehabilitation

retribution
sentencing discrimination
sentencing disparity
sentencing guidelines
special deterrence
three-strikes laws
utilitarian question

INTERNET PROJECT

 What are the pros and cons of "mandatory minimum" sentences? Explain your answer based on the information you find.

1. There are several sites on the Internet with articles concerning mandatory minimum sentences. Using any search engine (Google, Yahoo, or MSN search), enter the key words "mandatory minimum sentence."

2. InfoTrac College Edition: Search on the key words "mandatory minimum sentences."

CHAPTER 10

Community Corrections

© Joel Gordon

CHAPTER OUTLINE

No other justice agency is involved with offenders as comprehensively as the probation department. Every other agency completes its work and then hands the case over to the next decision maker. The police arrest offenders and hand them over to the prosecutor who files charges; the prosecutor hands them to the judge who sentences; the judge finally hands them to the warden who confines. But the probation department interacts with all of these agencies, provides the data that influence each of their decisions, and takes charge of the offender's supervision at any point when the system decides to return the offender to the community.

JOAN PETERSILIA (1998, 570–571)

What does a probation officer do? To this day, I suffer a violent visceral pain whenever I hear some visiting academic discuss the "two hats" of the probation officer: cop or counselor. At last count, we wear at least 33 hats and the number is growing.

EDWARD J. COSGROVE (1994, 29)

The organized efforts of well-meaning sentimentalists who are unable to see anything but the welfare of the individual criminal and are interested only in the reform of the criminal to the exclusion of any consideration of his victims or of society as a whole have caused desperate criminals, convicted of serious offenses and sent to prison for long terms, to be set free wholesale again to prey upon society.

MAGAZINE ARTICLE 1927 (QUOTED IN WILCOX 1927, 1)

■ INTRODUCTION

Once convicted, criminals are sentenced and they move to the final stage of the criminal process—**corrections**. Corrections can take place in prisons and jails **(incarceration)**; in the community (probation and parole); or in a combination of confinement and community supervision (intermediate punishments). Incarceration—especially confinement in prisons—gets the lion's share of public attention, tax dollars, research efforts, and most textbook space (including the one you're reading at this moment). But most convicted offenders aren't in prison or jail; they're serving their sentences in the community. Almost 4 million adults were on probation at the beginning of 2001 and over 725,000 were on parole; 1.3 million were in prison and 600,000 were in jail (Bureau of Justice Statistics 2001c, Table 1). A small group of offenders (about 100,000) are sentenced to *intermediate punishments;* they remain in the community but under stricter supervision than ordinary probationers.

⊙ **10-1 Bureau of Justice Statistics report on corrections populations in 2000**

All **community corrections**—probation, parole, and intermediate punishments— have multiple and demanding missions:

- Punish offenders
- Protect the community
- Reduce crime
- Save money
- Relieve prison crowding
- Rehabilitate offenders

■ PROBATION AND PAROLE

Many people confuse probation with parole, so let's clear up the confusion before we discuss them.

1. **Probation** is a *substitute* for confinement in prison or jail; **parole** *follows* confinement in prison.
2. Probation is controlled by judges in local courts; parole is controlled by one state agency under the control of the governor.
3. In probation, local judges decide whether and under what conditions to release convicted offenders; in parole, a state parole board decides when and under

what conditions to release prisoners. (Petersilia 1998, 563)

Despite these differences, probation and parole have a lot in common:

1. They both take place in the community.
2. Their core missions are to hold offenders accountable for their crimes, protect public safety, and turn offenders into responsible people who support themselves and obey the law.
3. Probation offices and parole boards have the power to decide whether and when to release offenders into the community, the conditions of release, and whether to revoke release.

Let's look more closely at the history of probation and parole; their individual missions; the granting, conditions, and revocation of probation and parole; what the law says about probation and parole; their effectiveness; and the role of race, ethnicity, and gender in community corrections.

The History of Probation and Parole

Supervision in the community instead of confinement is an ancient practice. Justices of the peace in sixteenth-century England commonly released minor offenders from custody if the offenders promised to "be of good behavior" and some responsible person agreed to make sure they kept their promise. If they broke it, they were locked up. The "good behavior bond" was brought to the American colonies and continued in use after the Revolution in the new United States (Samaha 1981, 189–204). Let's look at the histories of probation and parole.

The history of probation
In the 1840s, a Boston shoemaker, John Augustus, earned the title of "first probation officer" by expanding on the good behavior bond. Augustus visited the Boston police court, where he saw "a ragged and wretched looking man" charged with being a "common drunkard." The man begged Augustus to save him from the House of Correction, "I'll never take another drink if you save me." Deeply moved, Augustus asked the judge to release the man into his custody for thirty days. During that time, Augustus fed the man and found him a job. After that, the man stopped drinking and supported himself (Champion 1988, 1–3).

Encouraged by his success, Augustus gave up shoe-making and gave the rest of his life to "saving" Boston criminals. Magistrates released two thousand people into his custody—mostly drunks, prostitutes, juveniles, and gamblers. Augustus treated them all the same; he took them into his home, found them jobs, and inspired them to "purify" their lives. He had great success, probably because of the powerful combination of his devotion to reform and his skill in selecting the right offenders.

He threw himself totally into his "calling," *and* he accepted only "good risks"—first-time, minor offenders who showed promise of success (National Probation Association 1983).

Probation was also a favorite of reformers during the great Progressive reform wave of the early 1900s. By 1930, the federal government and thirty-six states had enacted probation legislation. By 1940, all but the most rural areas in the country had embraced probation (Rothman 1980, 82–83).

The history of parole
Alexander Maconochie, a captain in the British Royal Navy, introduced the modern idea of parole when he was appointed superintendent of the infamous English penal colonies in New South Wales in 1840. Believing prisoners were capable of reform, he developed a plan to prepare them for their eventual return to society. He divided his system into three grades, with each offering more life outside prison. Prisoners could earn promotion through the grades by labor, study, and good behavior.

The third grade in Maconochie's system was what we call parole—conditional liberty with a "a ticket of leave." With ticket in hand, prisoners could live outside prison as long as they obeyed the conditions of release attached to the ticket. Violating the rules of release meant returning to prison and starting all over again through the ranks. So conditional liberty, like the grades inside prison, was tied to successfully living according to the rules outside prison walls (Wilcox 1927, 5–6).

The penologist Zebulon Brockway introduced parole to the United States when he became superintendent of the famous Elmira Reformatory in New York (Chapter 11). Brockway was determined to manage prison populations and reform prisoners. To accomplish these missions, he adopted a two-prong strategy: indeterminate sentences and parole releases (Chapter 9). Within a short time, parole came to include three elements, all based on the indeterminate sentence:

1. *Conditional release* from confinement before sentences expire
2. *Supervision* until sentences expire
3. *Revocation* for violations of the conditions of the release

Parole has always provoked controversy—usually heated controversy. Clair Wilcox (1927), in his masterful survey of parole in Pennsylvania in the 1920s, examined newspapers and magazine articles about parole. He found headlines like "Turning the Criminals Loose" and "Uplifters and Politicians Free Convicts" (1). Even Chief Justice and former U.S. President William Howard Taft piled on, telling the highly popular *Collier's Weekly* magazine:

> Paroles have been abused and should be granted with greater care. It is discouraging to read of the arrest and prosecution of one charged with a new felony who had

committed some prior offense, had secured parole after a short confinement and then had used his release to begin again his criminal life. (Wilcox 1927, 2)

These criticisms come from the 1920s, but they could just as easily have come from today. Most of us remember the outrage following the kidnapping and murder in 1993 of 12-year-old Polly Klaas, who was snatched from a slumber party by a parolee who had a criminal record of attacking children. Of course, the reality of parole is more complex than the critics admit. A closer look at the missions of probation and parole will give us insight into that reality.

The Missions of Probation and Parole

We've already noted the core missions of all community corrections:

1. *Punishment:* Hold offenders accountable for their crimes by punishing them.
2. *Protect public safety:* Make sure offenders don't commit new crimes against law-abiding people.
3. *Rehabilitate offenders:* Help offenders by connecting them with resources that turn them into responsible people who support themselves and obey the law.

Probation and parole have these same missions. Let's look at how probation and parole carry out these common missions.

The missions of probation

Until the end of World War II, the mission of probation was to show leniency to first-time, minor offenders. After the war, doubts that prison was "correcting" offenders led to the adoption of another mission—rehabilitation. Judges started putting repeat and even violent offenders on probation to reform them. By the 1970s, there was a backlash against probation. The public, fed up with crime and judges who were "soft on criminals," demanded probation accomplish a third mission—punish and protect the public from "felons on the streets." But there was a problem standing in the way of accomplishing the punish and protect mission—paying the high price of exploding prison populations (Clear and Braga 1995, 422).

Despite worries about its "softness," probation is still the punishment of choice, probably because the public's not willing to pay the high costs of confinement. According to Joan Petersilia (1995):

When the prison population began to overwhelm existing facilities, probation and "split sentences" (a jail sentence followed by a term on probation) became the de facto disposition of all misdemeanors. As prison overcrowding becomes a national crisis, the courts are being forced to use probation even more frequently. Many felons without criminal records are now sentenced to probation. (481)

Federal probation officer Edward J. Cosgrove (1994) describes the complexity created by the conflicting missions of rehabilitation and leniency and punishment and controlling prison populations:

When Gannon and Friday were the role models for police officers, probation officers were an extension of the law. We kept "order" by seeing that people just did the right things. In the '70s, rehabilitation was the goal of supervision. The medical model taught us to diagnose a problem and then provide treatment. Help meant counseling; understanding the hardships of poverty, illiteracy, and broken homes; rendering the necessary support to address these symptoms; and coping with the bad feelings and making changes.

As client needs seemed ever expanding, the '80s brought us the philosophy of reintegration. Probation officers could not expect to service all needs; so, the answer became brokering services: identify the problem and make the appropriate referral. By the end of the '80s, the pendulum had swung from primary care to clients to listening to the needs of the community. Mercy was not to be forgotten, but disparity must be eliminated. Guidelines achieved this with a focus on retributive justice, with scant attention focused to rehabilitation of the individual. The offender will be held accountable. Society will be protected. The Probation Service responded with the development of Enhanced Supervision. The goals were ranked: enforce court orders, provide risk control, address the correctional treatment needs of the offender.

What does a probation officer do? To this day, I suffer a violent visceral pain whenever I hear some visiting academic discuss the "two hats" of the probation officer: cop or counselor. At last count, we wear at least 33 hats and the number is growing. (29)

The missions of parole

From the brief history of parole sketched earlier, we can see a conflict between the original and ancient mission of rehabilitation and the more modern ones of punishment and public safety. Warren F. Spalding put it this way in an address to the American Prison Association in 1916:

A parole does not release the parolee from custody; it does not discharge him from the penal consequences of his act; it does not mitigate his punishment; it does not wash away the stain or remit the penalty. . . . Unlike a pardon, it is not an act of grace or mercy, of clemency or leniency. The granting of parole is merely permission to a prisoner to serve part of his sentence outside the walls of the prison. He continues to be in the custody of the authorities, both legally and actually, and is still under restraint. The sentence is in full force and at any time when he does not comply with the conditions upon which he was released, or does not conduct himself properly, he may be returned, for his own good and in the public interest. (Wilcox 1927, 21)

One mission Spalding doesn't mention is controlling prison populations. Beginning in the nineteenth century, when prisons became "warehouses for the poor," parole became a way to relieve prison crowding by making room for new prisoners.

The missions of parole aren't always in harmony. Releasing more prisoners reduces prison populations, but it may also increase the risk to public safety. Close supervision outside prison might enhance public safety, but it may interfere with rehabilitating offenders, too. Allowing the flexibility to rehabilitate offenders might at the same time endanger public safety. Now, let's turn to what determines who will get parole.

Granting Probation and Parole

Over 2 million offenders entered probation in 2000; over 400,000 entered parole (Bureau of Justice Statistics 2001b). Who decides whether offenders will spend their time behind bars or in the community? Who decides if and when offenders already behind bars will return to the community before the end of their sentences? These are the questions probation and parole authorities have to answer. Who are these authorities, and what criteria do they base their decisions on? Let's look at these questions and the answers to them.

Granting probation

Formally, probation is a criminal sentence imposed by judges. Probationers are in the custody of the state; they're legally accountable to the state and subject to conditions that limit their freedom and privacy. The judge can change the conditions of and revoke probation if probationers violate the conditions of their release. Informally, probation consists of discretionary decision making to accomplish the missions we discussed in the previous section. Probation isn't a **suspended sentence** (release of convicted offenders without conditions or supervision). The possibility of getting locked up is still "hanging over their heads," because at any time judges can revoke the suspension and send them to jail or prison (Allen et al. 1985, 81).

Formally, judges sentence offenders, but behind the sentencing decision is the influence of probation offices. Most judges' formal sentence only approves what probation officers have recommended in their presentence investigation report (Chapter 9). What criteria do probation officers use to decide? Two criteria don't surprise us—the more serious the offense and the longer the criminal history of the offender the less the chances of getting probation (Gottfredson and Gottfredson 1988, 194). Others are at least indirectly related to these. The Iowa Department of Corrections Scoring Guide (Iowa Department of Corrections n.d.) lists the following:

- *Employment*: Employment is a primary risk factor in that low levels of vocational achievement highly correlate with recidivism (committing another crime).
- *Education*: Overall academic achievement is germane to stability of a crime-free lifestyle.

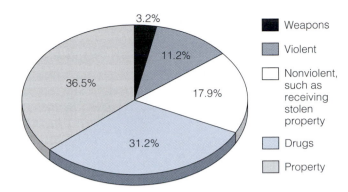

FIGURE 10.1
Felons Sentenced to Probation by Conviction Offense, 1996
SOURCE: Bureau of Justice Statistics 1999a.

- *Financial problems*: Financial problems . . . may be indicative of . . . inappropriate ways to get money.
- *Marital or equivalent situation*: A satisfying family or marital situation . . . [is] negatively correlated with criminal risk.

Do you think probation is for minor offenders? You're half right. Half of probationers committed misdemeanors; the other half committed felonies (Figure 10.1). And the numbers of felons on probation are growing (Bureau of Justice Statistics 2001b, Table 5). Joan Petersilia and her colleagues (1985) question this practice:

> Can probation accommodate more serious offenders, supervise them appropriately, and prevent them from threatening public safety? The most vital and fundamental question is whether traditional probation—based principally on the treatment/service role—should even be considered a legitimate sentencing alternative for convicted felons. (2)

Petersilia (1998) worries about the risk to both the public and to probation officers:

> How far from John Augustus's vision we have moved. In his autobiography Augustus wrote that "probation officers just need a good heart." Today it appears they believe they need much more. Two-thirds of parole and probation agencies now permit officers to carry weapons. . . . (578)

Are felons on probation a danger to public safety? Demands to get tough on crime and toughen up judges who are soft on criminals have produced a heated policy debate about whether felons should be on probation. This led researchers like Geerken and Hayes (1993, 557) to find out how much felons on probation contributed to the rates of burglary and armed robbery. They analyzed data on arrests, incarceration, and probation supervision for burglary and armed robbery in New Orleans. What did they find? Probationers accounted for 8 percent of burglary and armed robbery arrests. According to Geerken and Hayes:

[T]hese percentages are contrary to expectations and surprisingly low. They suggest that even the complete elimination of probation . . . would have a very negligible effect on the burglary and armed robbery rates since more than 90 percent of all burglaries and armed robberies were committed by persons not on probation . . . at the time of the arrest. . . . We argue . . . that since a low percentage of all burglary and armed robbery arrests are of persons on probation . . . at the time, policy changes tightening or eliminating . . . probation can affect only a small percentage of these crimes. (557)

Granting parole

The United States sentences more people to prison and keeps them there longer than any "major" country in the world (Chapter 11). But most prisoners spend less than two years in prison before they're released. They're released in three ways:

1. *Discretionary release:* Parole boards decide the date of release and set the conditions of their community supervision until their sentence expires.
2. *Mandatory release:* Legislatures and judges set the date of release and the conditions of their community supervision until their sentence expires.
3. *Expiration release:* Prisoners are released unconditionally when their sentence—less good time (Chapter 12)—expires.

In this section, we'll concentrate on discretionary release because mandatory and expiration release don't involve discretionary decision making.

Judges (with a lot of help from probation officers) make the probation decision; **parole boards** decide whether to release prisoners. State governors appoint about ten men and women to sit on the board, which has broad discretionary decision-making power. They review files (usually consisting of work done by probation officers); interview prisoners; and decide the date, conditions, and when necessary, the revocation of parole. They can also issue warrants and subpoenas; order the payment of **restitution** to victims and fees to the state to help pay the costs of their supervision; rescind release dates; restore (or continue to deny) prisoners' civil rights; and grant (or deny) final discharges from state custody (Petersilia 1998, 574).

What criteria drive the discretionary decision making of parole boards? An American Paroling Authorities' survey found these major criteria, listed here in order of importance to decision makers:

1. Seriousness of the offense the prisoner was locked up for
2. History of violence
3. Previous felony convictions
4. Possession of a firearm
5. Previous incarceration
6. Prior parole adjustment
7. Prison disciplinary record
8. Psychological reports
9. Victim input (Runda, Rhine, and Wetter 1994)

No surprises here. The ranking follows what we've learned throughout the criminal justice process: Seriousness of offense and criminal history top the list, followed by criteria indirectly related to the top two.

Parole boards use two methods of decision making in granting parole. In the **case study method**, "the board member, case worker, or parole agency collects as much information as possible, combines it in a unique way, mulls over the results, and reaches a decision" (Petersilia 1998, 575). Case studies were the standard method of decision making until attempts to restrict parole boards' discretion led to the adoption of the **risk assessment method**. This method is a statistically based prediction. Information is collected about the seriousness of the crime offenders are imprisoned for and their criminal history. The idea behind risk assessment is that the more serious the offense and the longer the criminal history the less the chances parolees will succeed in becoming law-abiding people who can support themselves. By 1994, half of the state parole boards had adopted a risk assessment method.

Supporters say decision making by risk assessment has several advantages. Predictions are based on objective legitimate criteria—the seriousness of the offense and criminal history. Because they're objective they're also fair; they prevent the infection of decision making based on gender, race, and class. They're also cheaper; imprisonment costs more than parole. And, they're best for the public; they confine the most dangerous offenders who've committed the worst crimes and release offenders who threaten public safety the least (Atkinson 1986, 54–55; Lombardi and Lombardi 1986, 86–87).

Objectively, which method is better? The empirical evidence shows the risk assessment method is *better* at predicting what drives all release decision making—the answer to the question, "Will parolees commit crimes when they're released?" But, how *much* better? When Stephen Klein and Michael Caggiano (1986) applied six widely used risk assessment models to recidivism data from Texas, California, and Michigan, they found, "They did not predict more than 10 percent of the variance on any of the measures of recidivism" (31). Kevin N. Wright, Todd R. Clear, and Paul Dickson (1984, 122–123) studied a risk assessment instrument developed for Wisconsin that the National Institute of Corrections called a "model system"; a number of other states had also adopted the instrument. They concluded that no matter what instrument was used, all predictions are "fairly weak."

The Conditions of Probation and Parole

Probation and parole don't mean probationers and parolees are free to do as they please. There are strings attached, because they're both offenders still under criminal sentences and in state custody. There are three types of conditions (Figures 10.2, 10.3):

PROB 7A
(Rev. 6/90)©

Conditions of Probation and Supervised Release

UNITED STATES DISTRICT COURT
FOR THE
_____

Name _____ Docket No. _____
Address _____
    Under the terms of your sentence, you have been placed on probation/supervised release (strike one) by the
Honorable _____ , United States District Judge for the District of _____ .
Your term of supervision is for a period of _____ , commencing _____ .
    While on probation/supervised release (strike one), you shall not commit another Federal, state, or local crime and shall not illegally possess a controlled substance. Revocation of probation and supervised release is mandatory for possession of a controlled substance.

CHECK IF APPROPRIATE:
☐ As a condition of supervision, you are instructed to pay a fine in the amount of _____ ; it shall be paid in the following manner _____ .
☐ As a condition of supervision, you are instructed to pay restitution in the amount of _____ to _____ ; it shall be paid in the following manner _____ .
☐ The defendant shall not possess a firearm or destructive device. Probation must be revoked for possession of a firearm.
☐ The defendant shall report in person to the probation office in the district to which the defendant is released within 72 hours of release from the custody of the Bureau of Prisons.

It is the order of the Court that you shall comply with the following standard conditions:
    (1)   You shall not leave the judicial district without permission of the court or probation officer;
    (2)   You shall report to the probation officer as directed by the court or probation officer, and shall submit a truthful and complete written report within the first five days of each month;
    (3)   You shall answer truthfully all inquiries by the probation officer and follow the instructions of the probation officer;
    (4)   You shall support your dependents and meet other family responsibilities;
    (5)   You shall work regularly at a lawful occupation unless excused by the probation officer for schooling, training, or other acceptable reasons:
    (6)   You shall notify the probation officer within seventy-two hours of any change in residence or employment;
    (7)   You shall refrain from excessive use of alcohol and shall not purchase, possess, use, distribute, or administer any narcotic or other controlled substance, or any paraphernalia related to such substances, except as prescribed by a physician;
    (8)   You shall not frequent places where controlled substances are illegally sold, used, distributed, or administered;
    (9)   You shall not associate with any persons engaged in criminal activity, and shall not associate with any person convicted of a felony unless granted permission to do so by the probation officer;
    (10) You shall permit a probation officer to visit you at any time at home or elsewhere, and shall permit confiscation of any contraband observed in plain view by the probation officer;
    (11) You shall notify the probation officer within seventy-two hours of being arrested or questioned by a law enforcement officer;
    (12) You shall not enter into any agreement to act as an informer or a special agent of a law enforcement agency without the permission of the court;
    (13) As directed by the probation officer, you shall notify third parties of risks that may be occasioned by your criminal record or personal history or characteristics, and shall permit the probation officer to make such notifications and to confirm your compliance with such notification requirement.

The special conditions ordered by the court are as follows:

    Upon a finding of a violation of probation or supervised release, I understand that the Court may (1) revoke supervision or (2) extend the term of supervision and/or modify the conditions of supervision.
    These conditions have been read to me. I fully understand the conditions, and have been provided a copy of them.

(Signed) _____   _____
Defendant   Date

_____   _____
U.S. Probation Officer/Designated Witness   Date

FIGURE 10.2
Conditions of Federal Probation

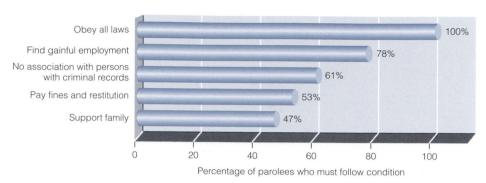

FIGURE 10.3
Parole Conditions
SOURCE: Petersilia 1998, 576.

- *Standard conditions*: Obey the law; don't carry a weapon; don't associate with criminals; report to your probation or parole officer; notify the office if you change your address; work or go to school; support your family; and don't leave the jurisdiction without permission.
- *Punitive conditions*: (Usually reserved for felony probationers) Pay your fines; report daily to your probation office; do community service; pay victims back (restitution); don't leave the house (house arrest); and get drug tests.
- *Treatment conditions*: Go through a substance abuse program; get family counseling; and go through job training.

The conditions in Figure 10.3 are common, but they're not realistic because the money and personnel aren't there to enforce them. "We design systems so that almost all parolees are likely to fail at some point. . . . Unfortunately parole [and probation] conditions serve as much to comfort agencies and parole boards, and help the release decision withstand public scrutiny, [as] to establish realistic expectations for the parolee" (Holt 1998, 10). You can substitute "probationer" for "parolee" because the criticism applies to both.

Revoking Probation and Parole

What happens if probationers and parolees violate the conditions of their probation? Judges and parole boards *can* send them to prison to serve the rest of their sentences. Revocation occurs for one of two reasons: **recidivism**—arrest or conviction for a new crime—or **technical violations**—violations of conditions that aren't crimes, like not notifying officers of a change of address. Judges and parole boards *can* revoke probation and parole; but they usually don't. Half of all probationers commit technical violations, but only 20 percent of these have their probation revoked.

Critics say the gap between technical violations and revocations is just one more example of criminals getting away with breaking the rules and threatening the safety of innocent people. But criminologists like Todd R. Clear and Anthony A. Braga (1995, 442) see it differently. They say technical violations only prove probationers' lack of

discipline, not that they're a threat to public safety. Just because a probationer doesn't tell her probation officer she moved doesn't mean she's going to commit a crime.

Probation, Parole, and the Law

Probationers and parolees are convicted offenders. So—according to the U.S. Supreme Court—they have fewer rights than law-abiding people. In the words of the Court, probationers and parolees are subject to "special restrictions" on their rights (*Griffin v. Wisconsin* 1987, 874–875). For example, probation and parole officers don't have to give *Miranda* warnings (*Minnesota v. Murphy* 1984). And, probationers and parolees have diminished rights against unreasonable searches and seizures guaranteed by the Fourth Amendment to the U.S. Constitution.

 10-2 *Minnesota v. Murphy* You Decide: Can officers enter probationers' and parolees' houses without warrants?

But *fewer* rights doesn't mean *no* rights. One right is related to revocation of probation and parole: they can't be revoked without due process of law (*Morrissey v. Brewer* 1973, 485–486) (Chapter 2). Due process guarantees the right to a hearing to decide whether probationers and parolees violated the conditions of their release and, if they did, whether the violation justifies revocation. The hearing has to provide suspected violators:

1. Written notice of the alleged violations
2. The right to see and hear the evidence against them
3. The opportunity to be heard in person and to present witnesses and documentary evidence
4. The right to confront and cross-examine the witnesses against them
5. A hearing panel made up of neutral members
6. A written statement by the hearing panel, including the evidence relied on and the reasons for revoking probation (*Morrissey v. Brewer* 1973, 487–489)

 10-3 *Morrissey v. Brewer*

The Effectiveness of Probation and Parole

Sixty percent of probationers successfully complete their sentence in the community; 43 percent of parolees successfully complete their conditional release (Bureau of Justice Statistics 2001b, Tables 5, 6). Not surprisingly, young, new offenders do best, and success goes down as time from release goes up (Bureau of Justice Statistics 1997, Table 3.6). What accounts for these numbers? Is it probation and parole supervision? Or, something else? Let's look at the research.

The Effectiveness of Probation

Many people think probation's a joke. Criminals, they believe, are walking around without supervision, free to commit more crimes and violate their probation. The truth is many probationers are low-risk offenders with no criminal history (Clear and Braga 1995, 430). In fact, some scholars argue these low-risk offenders would succeed without *any* supervision.

But we also know there's a subgroup of probationers who commit crimes at a high rate. James Byrne and Linda Kelly (1989) estimated this group at 10 percent, and that 60 percent of this group will be charged with new crimes within a year of their release. On the other hand, Joan Petersilia, Susan Turner, and James P. Kahan (1985) found that 65 percent of felons on probation in two California counties were rearrested for crimes like robbery and burglary.

Petersilia and her colleagues' study raised a storm of criticism of probation, but it only examined two counties in California and the state of Massachusetts. When Gennaro Vito (1986, 17–25) applied Petersilia and her colleagues' methodology to Kentucky, he found felony rearrest rates weren't 65 percent but 22 percent. Although, this is still higher than the public would like, it's not nearly as alarming as 65 percent. In their summary of recidivism studies, Geerken and Hayes (1993, 549–564) found recidivism ranged from Petersilia and her colleagues' high of 65 percent to as low as 12 percent for an average of about 40 percent. And, Michael Gottfredson and Don Gottfredson's (1992) long-term follow-up study of prisoners released in 1962, found two-thirds went back to jail or prison at least once *but* only 9 percent for serious felonies; the rest were for "nuisance" offenses.

Is it supervision that accounts for probation success or failure? We don't know the answer to this important question, because most researchers ignore the effects of supervision on ordinary probation. They're more interested in the effects of intermediate punishments (we'll discuss these later).

The effectiveness of parole

Less than half of all prisoners successfully completed parole in 2000 (Figure 10.4). Are recidivism rates affected by the amount of supervision? Empirical findings don't clearly answer this important question. A Connecticut

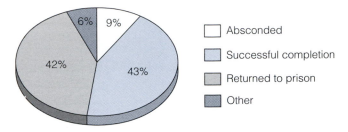

FIGURE 10.4
Adults Leaving Parole, 2000
SOURCE: U.S. Department of Justice 2001, Table 6.

court decision gave Howard R. Sacks and Charles H. Logan (1979) a unique opportunity to measure the effect of supervision on recidivism. In *Szarwak v. Warden* (1974), the Connecticut superior court ordered suspended sentences for all prisoners confined more than one year for committing unarmed robbery, burglary, or illegal possession of drugs.

 10-4 *Szarwak v. Warden*

The released prisoners became an experimental group in a natural experiment because eventually they would've been paroled. The control group consisted of prisoners released on parole at the ordinary time. What effect did parole have? Not much. Parolees avoided conviction for all offenses at a slightly higher rate (about 7 percent). But, parole had *no* significant effect on the seriousness of the offenses committed. And, the modest effects of parole supervision didn't last:

> Parole had no preventive effects after two (or three) years following release. Parole seems to affect recidivism while the parolee is on parole (and for a short period thereafter) but these effects soon begin to dissipate and tend to disappear by the time parolees have finished two years in the community. (Sacks and Logan 1979, 14–15)

They concluded, "Parole does not prevent a return to crime, but it does delay it" (20).

Sacks and Logan looked at parole supervision in general. But what about the *kind* of supervision? Does it matter? Yes, says Mark J. Lerner (1977); no, says Deborah Star (1979, 2–3, 52, 132; 1981). Lerner evaluated parole in New York State, where the public safety mission definitely comes first. At the time of Lerner's study, parole officers were "armed with .38 caliber revolvers [and] have even more extensive investigative and surveillance powers than those of policemen." Lerner divided 195 misdemeanor offenders into two groups, one in a control group released at the end of their sentences and the other released on parole. Based on arrests for two years after their release, Lerner found "parole supervision reduces criminal behavior of persons released from local correctional institutions" (Figure 10.5).

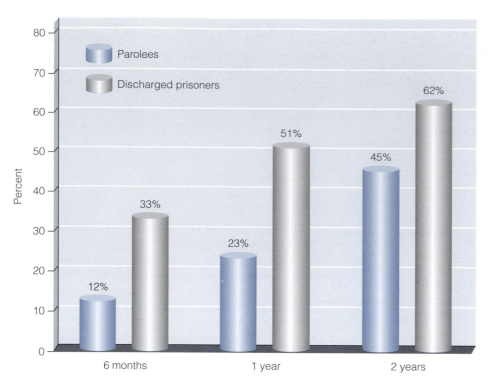

FIGURE 10.5
Percentage of Parolees and Discharged Prisoners Arrested
SOURCE: Adapted from Lerner 1997, 220, Table 1m.

Lerner (1977) concedes his study didn't try to explain *why* parole supervision reduced recidivism; he *speculated* the "effect is probably due to the deterrent or law-enforcement effect of parole supervision and not to the popular notions of rehabilitation" (220).

Star disagrees; her conclusion that the type of supervision doesn't matter is based on two experimental studies of parole by the California Department of Corrections. In the first, a group of felons (excluding prisoners convicted of murder, rape, and some other serious offenses) was randomly assigned to either an experimental group of parolees who received less supervision than a control group who received normal supervision. The experimental group had significantly fewer face-to-face contacts initiated by parole officers to check up on parolees than the control group. After six months, and again after one year, the researchers found no significant difference in either the frequency or the severity of criminal activity between the control group on regular parole and the experimental group on reduced supervision.

The second experiment (Star 1981, i–ii, 168, 251, 257)—the High Control Project—evaluated the effects of increased surveillance and investigation of parolees to control their criminal activities. The High Control Project differed from regular parole in four ways:

1. It emphasized control not service.
2. It emphasized investigating parolees' possible criminal activities *before* arrest. (Ordinary supervision stresses investigation *after* arrest.)
3. It targeted "high risk" cases.

4. It used parole officers specially trained in law enforcement.

The High Control Project relied on two tactics to test the effectiveness of high levels of control. In the first tactic, criminal investigation, high-control parole officers investigated parolees suspected of crimes, apprehended them, and helped to prosecute them. In the second tactic, **intensive supervision,** officers with reduced caseloads closely monitored parolees with serious prior criminal records to prevent them from committing new crimes.

Using a quasi-experimental design, high-control parolees were compared with regular parolees. The result? Neither aggressive criminal investigation nor intensified supervision made a difference. The researchers did find that criminal investigation in the High Control Project was better than ordinary parole in *verifying* criminal behavior after it took place, even if it didn't reduce the frequency and seriousness of criminal behavior.

Race, Ethnicity, Gender and Community Corrections

The same racial, ethnic, and gender *differences* we've seen in criminal behavior and in other parts of criminal justice are also true of probation and parole (there aren't any numbers for intermediate punishments) (Figure 10.6 on page 186). But, are these differences the result of discrimination injected into decisions to grant probation or parole, impose conditions, and revoke sentences? Unfortunately, there's not enough research in community corrections to answer this question.

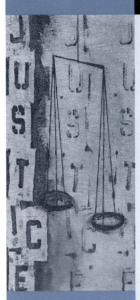

[The following is an excerpt from criminal justice researcher and past president of the American Society of Criminology, Joan Petersilia. In "A Crime Control Rationale for Reinvesting in Community Corrections," Petersilia suggests some policies for community corrections generally, and for parole especially. These suggestions are based on recent empirical research and stem from the debate over whether to spend our tax dollars on building more prisons or on crime prevention and supervision of offenders in the community.]

Last year Congress passed the most ambitious crime bill in our nation's history, the Violent Crime Control and Law Enforcement Act of 1994. It allocated $22 billion to expand prisons, impose longer sentences, hire more police, and to a lesser extent, fund prevention programs. But as part of the Republicans' "Contract with America," the House significantly revised the Act, and the money allocated to prevention programs was eliminated. The amended bill—whose price tag rose to $30 billion—shifted nearly all of the $5 billion targeted for prevention programs into prison construction and law enforcement. As a *Los Angeles Times* op-ed concluded of the whole matter: "what started out last legislative season as a harsh and punitive bill has gotten downright Draconian."

While such tough-on-crime legislation has political appeal, it finds almost no support among criminal justice practitioners and scholars. They are uniformly agreed that such efforts—which endorse an "enforcement model" to the sacrifice of all else—will do little to curb crime. In recent months, organizations as diverse as the International Association of Chiefs of Police (IACP), the U.S. Conference of Mayors, the American Bar Association (ABA), National Governors Association, the League of Cities, the RAND Corporation, the National Council on Crime and Delinquency (NCCD), the Campaign for an Effective Crime Policy (CECP), and the National Research Council have all voiced opposition to the approach.

Even prison wardens (who stand to benefit from an enforcement model) uniformly reject the crime-fighting solutions coming out of Washington. In a recent national survey of prison wardens, 85 percent of those surveyed said that elected officials are not offering effective solutions to America's crime problem. Chase Riveland, Washington State Director of Corrections, said that focusing only on prisons and ignoring the rest of the system is "drive-by legislation, at best." And Jerome Skolnick, President of the American Society of Criminology (ASC), spoke of the federal efforts in his 1994 Presidential Address and entitled it, "What *Not* to Do About Crime."

What is wrong with the current proposals? Some argue that they are racist, others argue that they cost too much, but nearly everyone agrees they have two major flaws: (1) they fail to prevent young people from entering and continuing a life of crime; and (2) they leave the vast majority of criminals, who are serving sentences on probation and parole rather than prison or jail, unaffected.

Criminologists have long observed that age 18 is the year of peak criminality. Analysis recently completed by Alfred Blumstein at Carnegie-Mellon showed that today we have the smallest cohort of 18-year-olds we will see for at least the next 15 years. Next year, the number is going to start going up, and the biggest growth will occur in the number of African American children who are now four to nine years old. Blumstein (1994) recently observed:

These young people are being less well educated and socialized, and as a result are easy recruits for the booming crack cocaine industry, where weapons are a business accessory for an increasing number of youths. The result will be a steep increase in juvenile and young adult violent crime, unless we begin investing in community-based programs to better socialize kids when their parents are not doing so. This is a population crying out for our attention, and, as a society, we need to find a means to divert them from becoming as violent as their big brothers.

As more young people are recruited into and retained in a criminal lifestyle, the ability of back-end responses (such as imprisonment) to increase public safety is severely limited because of the replenishing supply of young people who are entering into criminal careers.

The second, and equally important, reason that current federal efforts will fail is that they focus exclusively on prisons as a corrections strategy, ignoring the fact that most criminals are serving probation and parole sentences. In 1993 there were just under five million adult (convicted) criminals—or about one in every thirty-nine Americans. Seventy-two percent of all identified criminals were not in prison, but serving sentences in the community on probation or parole supervision. Even though we have quadrupled the number of prisoners in the past decade . . . the vast majority of offenders remain in the community amongst us (Bureau of Justice Statistics, 1995). If we are to effectively control crime—as opposed to exacting retribution and justice—we must focus our efforts where the offenders are, which is in the community reporting to probation and parole officers.

(continued)

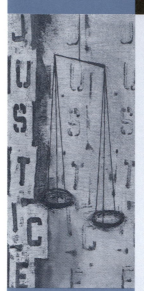

Despite the fact that both crime bills were touted by their proponents as comprehensive approaches to the crime problem, neither the 1994 Crime Act or the 1995 "Taking Back Our Streets" proposal *even mentions* probation or parole, much less provides funding or direction for revising programs or practices. Moreover, the federal bill will likely take money away from community corrections budgets, which are already at a dangerously low level, to fund the expanded prison space required to comply with federal mandates requiring state prisoners to serve 86 percent of their sentence (so-called "truth in sentencing").

This article addresses the public safety consequences of current probation and parole practices. It contends that current crime policies are neither comprehensive nor will they be effective unless we focus on the needs and risks posed by probationers and parolees. Whether we are able to control the crime propensities of *these* offenders is critical to the effectiveness of any anti-crime program.

Who Is on Probation and Parole? A Profile of the Population

The public misunderstands the safety risks and needs posed by offenders currently under community supervision.... To gauge the public safety risks of probationers and parolees, it is useful to consider the population as a whole in terms of conviction crimes.... [A]bout 16 percent of all adult probationers were convicted of violent crimes, as were 26 percent of parolees. This means that on any given day in the U.S. in 1991, there were an estimated 435,000 probationers and 155,000 parolees residing in local communities who have been convicted of violent crime—or over a half million offenders. If we compare that to the number of violent offenders residing in prison during the same year, we see that there were approximately 372,500 offenders convicted of violent crime *in* prison, and approximately 590,000 *outside* in the community on probation and parole! Overall, we can conclude that nearly three times as many violent offenders (1.02 million) were residing in the community as were incarcerated in prison (372,000). These numbers make painfully clear why a failure to provide adequate funding for community corrections invariably places the public at risk....

Despite the unprecedented growth in probation populations and their more serious clientele, probation budgets have not grown. From 1977 to 1990 prison, jail, parole, and probation populations all about tripled in size. Yet only spending for prisons and jails had accelerated growth in overall government expenditures. In 1990 prison and jail spending accounted for two cents of every state and local dollar spent—twice the amount spent in 1977. Spending for probation and parole accounted for two-tenths of one cent of every dollar spent in 1990—unchanged from what it was in 1977. Today, although nearly *three-fourths* of correctional clients are in the community, only about *one-tenth* of the correctional budget goes to supervise them.

The increase in populations, coupled with stagnant or decreasing funding, means that caseloads (the number of offenders an officer is responsible for supervising) keep increasing....

But neglect in funding has had serious consequences. As caseloads rise, there is less opportunity for personal contact between officer and offender, limiting any ability of the officer to bring about positive change in the offender, or refer the offender to appropriate community-based resources and programs (which incidentally are also being reduced). Court-ordered fines and restitution don't get paid, and community service doesn't get performed....

What Can We Do? A Proposal to Develop an Integrated Treatment/ Control Program for Drug Offenders

The grim situation described above is known to most of those who work in the justice system or study it. Until we curb the criminal activities of the three-fourths of criminals who reside in the community, real reductions in crime or prison commitments are unlikely. But just as there is growing agreement about the nature of the problem, there is also an emerging consensus about how to address it.

We need to first regain the public's trust that probation and parole can be meaningful, credible sanctions. During the past decade, many jurisdictions developed "intermediate sanctions" as a response to prison crowding. These programs (e.g., house arrest, electronic monitoring, and intensive supervision) were designed to be community-based sanctions that were tougher than regular probation, but less stringent and expensive than prison. The program models were good and could have worked, except for one critical factor: they were usually implemented without creating an organizational capacity to ensure compliance with the court-ordered conditions. Intermediate sanctions were designed with smaller caseloads enabling officers to provide both services and monitoring for new criminal activity, but they never were given the resources needed to enforce the sanctions or provide necessary treatment....

But not all programs have had this experience. In a few instances, communities invested in intermediate sanctions and made the necessary treatment and work programs available to offenders. And, most importantly, the programs worked: in programs where offenders both received surveillance (e.g., drug tests) and participated in relevant treatment, recidivism was reduced 20–30 percent. Recent program evaluations in Texas, Wisconsin, Oregon, and Colorado have found similarly encouraging results. Even in BJS's national probation follow-up study, it was found that if probationers were participating in or making progress in treatment programs, they were less likely to have a new arrest (38 percent) than either those drug offenders who had made no progress (66 percent) or those who were not ordered to be tested or treated (48 percent).

There now exists rather solid empirical evidence that ordering offenders into treatment and getting them to participate, reduces recidivism. So, the first order of business must be to allocate sufficient resources so that the designed programs (incorporating both surveillance and treatment) can be implemented. Sufficient monetary resources are essential to obtaining and sustaining judicial support, and achieving program success.

Once we have that in place, we need to create a public climate to support a reinvestment in community corrections. Good community corrections costs money, and we should be honest about that. We currently spend about $200 per year, per probationer, for supervision. It is no wonder that recidivism rates are so high. Effective treatment programs cost at least $12,000–$14,000 per year. Those resources will be forthcoming only if the public believes the programs are both effective and punitive.

Public opinion is often cited by officials as the reason for supporting expanded prison policies. According to officials, the public demands a "get tough on crime" policy, which is synonymous with sending more offenders to prison for longer terms. We must publicize recent evidence showing that offenders—whose opinion on such matters is critical for deterrence—judge some intermediate sanctions as *more* punishing than prison. Surveys of offenders in Minnesota, Arizona, New Jersey, Oregon, and Texas reveal that when offenders are asked to equate criminal sentences, they judge certain types of community punishments as *more* severe than prison.

One of the more striking examples comes from Marion County, Oregon. Selected nonviolent offenders were given the choice of serving a prison term or returning to the community to participate in the Intensive Supervision Probation (ISP) program, which imposed drug testing, mandatory community service, and frequent visits with the probation officer. About a third of the offenders given the option between ISP or prison chose prison.

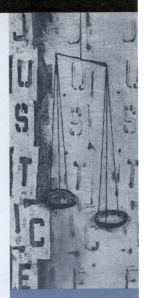

When Minnesota inmates and corrections staff were asked to equate a variety of criminal sentences, they rated three years of Intensive Supervision Probation as equivalent in punitiveness to one year in prison.

What accounts for this seeming aberration? Why should anyone prefer imprisonment to remaining in the community—no matter what the conditions? Some have suggested that prison has lost some of its punitive sting, and hence its ability to scare and deter. The length of time an offender can be expected to serve in prison has also decreased—the latest statistics show that the average U.S. prison term for those released to parole is 17 months. But more to the point, for less serious offenders, the expected time served can be much less. In California, for example, more than half of all offenders entering prison in 1995 are expected to serve six months or less. Offenders on the street seem to be aware of this, perhaps because of the extensive media coverage such issues are receiving.

For convicted felons, freedom, of course, is preferable to prison. But the type of program being advocated here—combining heavy doses of surveillance and treatment—does not represent freedom. In fact, as suggested above, such community-based programs may have more punitive bite than prison. . . .

It is important to publicize these results, particularly to policymakers, who say they are imprisoning such a large number of offenders because of the public's desire to get tough on crime. But it is no longer necessary to equate criminal punishment solely with prison. The balance of sanctions between probation and prison can be shifted, and at some level of intensity and length, intermediate punishments can be the more dreaded penalty.

Questions
Assume you are on the staff of a legislator. You've just received a copy of this article by Joan Petersilia.

1. On the basis of the article, how would you advise your legislator to vote on a proposal to spend more of the taxpayers' money on corrections? Support your advice with specific information and arguments from this article.
2. If you can't decide what advice to give, what questions do you want answered and what further information do you need before you advise your legislator?
3. In giving your advice, how would you use the mixed results of the empirical research discussed in The Effectiveness of Probation and Parole section?

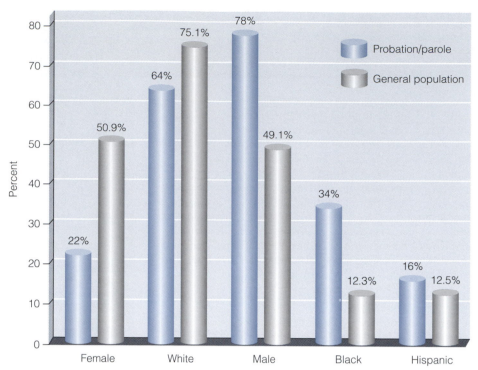

FIGURE 10.6
Probation, Parole, and General Population, 2000
SOURCES: Bureau of Justice Statistics 2001c; U.S. Census 2001, Table DP-1.

■ INTERMEDIATE PUNISHMENTS

For most of the twentieth century, convicted offenders were either locked up or put on probation. This **either/or corrections** (we can also call it **in-or-out corrections**) system ignored the reality that imprisonment is too harsh for a lot of criminal behavior, and for some offenders, probation is too lenient. In other words, probation and confinement weren't accomplishing the mission of doing justice—fitting the punishment to the crime and tailoring the penalty to suit the offender. **Intermediate punishments**, which are harsher than probation but milder than imprisonment, allow us to accomplish the mission of justice.

An ideal **graduated punishment system** would work like Figure 10.7. There are three important elements in the graduated punishment system depicted in Figure 10.7. First is the range of punishments, graduating in severity from the most lenient (probation) to the harshest (prison). Judges would choose the punishment that best fit the crime and the offender. Second, offenders wouldn't go straight to prison if they failed at a lower severity; they'd move up one level on the severity stairs. Third, the costs of punishment increase with the harshness of the punishment, from as low as $200 a year for each offender on routine probation to as high as $22,000 a year for every inmate in prison (Petersilia 1998, 582). Let's look more closely at these variations of intermediate punishments and their effectiveness.

Types of Intermediate Punishments

There is a fairly long list of intermediate punishments (Table 10.1). But they're only rarely used, despite the compelling justification for a graduated punishment system depicted in Figure 10.7. The latest numbers available when this book went to press were 121,251 offenders serving sentences for intermediate punishments (intensive supervision 104,028, electronic monitoring 15,095, and correctional boot camps 2128) (Bureau of Justice Statistics 2000e, Table 3.10).

Evaluating Intermediate Punishments

Intermediate punishments, especially ones that seem like they're really punishing offenders instead of coddling them—like correctional boot camps—are enormously popular with the public. But do they punish offenders? Do they deter crime? Do they rehabilitate offenders? Do they protect the public? There is a substantial amount of research (and mixed results) on the effectiveness of intermediate punishment programs, but we can boil it down into four findings researchers agree on:

1. *Intermediate punishments add tougher conditions to probation; they don't just divert offenders from prison.* This is good if the tougher conditions are added to offenders on probation who *deserve* harsher penalties and don't let serious prisoners out of prison. But it's not good if it's what we call **net widening**, meaning harsher penalties are added to offenders who need only ordinary supervision while intermediate punishments are

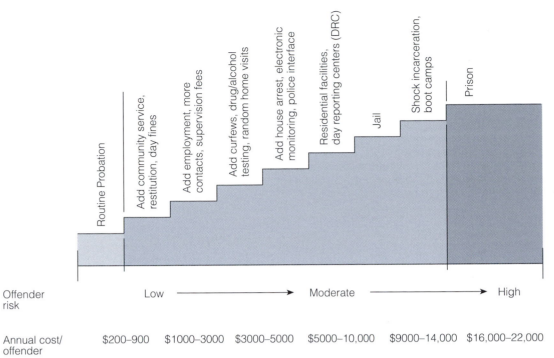

FIGURE 10.7

Model of a Graduated Punishment System

SOURCE: Petersilia 1998, 583, Table 21.4.

The labels on the graduated steps (from left to right) read:

- Routine Probation
- Add community service, restitution, day fines
- Add employment, more contacts, supervision fees
- Add curfews, drug/alcohol testing, random home visits
- Add house arrest, electronic monitoring, police interface
- Residential facilities, day reporting centers (DRC)
- Jail
- Shock incarceration, boot camps
- Prison

Offender risk	Low → Moderate → High

| Annual cost/offender | $200–900 | $1000–3000 | $3000–5000 | $5000–10,000 | $9000–14,000 | $16,000–22,000 |

TABLE 10.1

Intermediate Punishments

Type	Characteristics	Goals	Evaluation
Intensive supervision	1. Frequent contacts with officer (e.g., daily) 2. Less privacy and freedom (e.g., unannounced officer visits; drug testing) 3. Have to work, go to school, and/or get treatment	1. Public safety 2. Punishment 3. Reduce prison crowding 4. Save money 5. Rehabilitate offenders	1. More technical violations 2. Little or no effect on arrest rates 3. Little or no effect on kinds of crimes arrested for 4. Did justice by punishing appropriately (Petersilia, Turner, and Deschennes 1992, 19)
Home confinement/ Electronic monitoring	1. 24/7 surveillance 2. Ankle monitor	1. Confinement without imprisonment 2. Maintain family ties and employment 3. Save money 4. Public safety	1. Reduce costs 2. Participant found or kept employment 3. Participants supported their families 4. Younger participants failed more frequently than older participants 5. No reduction in jail populations 6. Technical problems with equipment
Correctional boot camps	1. Strict discipline 2. Physical training 3. Drill and ceremony 4. Military atmosphere 5. Physical labor 6. Punishment for minor violations	1. Deterrence 2. Punishment	1. Deterrence? Mixed empirical results 2. Succeed in punishing offenders
Fines	1. Money punishment	1. Pay debt to society (restitution) 2. Punishment 3. Deterrence	1. Mixed empirical results
Community service	1. Order to work on public property (e.g., clean parks, sweep streets, clean jails)	1. Punishment 2. Help community 3. Restitution 4. Rehabilitation	1. Few evaluations

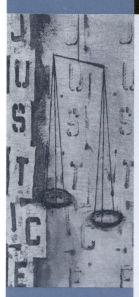

[Joan Petersilia (1990), a well-known criminal justice researcher and professor, gives her view in this excerpt.]

Are community sanctions punitive enough to convince the public that the "punishment fit the crime"? Having studied the development of these intermediate sanctions, I have discovered that some serious offenders feel that ISPs [intermediate sanctions programs, what in your text I refer to as intermediate punishments] are at least as punitive as imprisonment—if not more so. If this is true, then offenders' perceptions should be considered in structuring sanctions and in making sentencing decisions.

Punishment for Whom?

This country bases assumptions about "what punishes" on the norms and living standards of society at large. This practice overlooks two . . . facts: First, most serious offenders neither accept nor abide by those norms—otherwise, they wouldn't be offenders. Second, most of the people who even "qualify" for imprisonment today come from communities where conditions fall far below the living standards most Americans would recognize. If their values and standards differ, why should their perceptions of punishment be the same?

Nevertheless, criminal sanctions reflect society's values—negatively. The demand that serious criminals go to prison implies that prison imposes conditions that are intolerable and frightening to the law-abiding citizen. The belief that community sanctions are too lenient implies that no matter what conditions probation or parole impose, remaining in the community is categorically preferable to imprisonment.

When crime rates were lower and minor crimes could land a person in prison, many offenders might have shared these perceptions. Apparently, feelings are different among offenders who face prison sentences today. In several states, given the option of serving prison terms or participating in ISPs, many offenders have chosen prison. Pearson reports that about 15 percent of offenders who apply to New Jersey's ISP program retract their applications once they understand the conditions and requirements. Under the New Jersey structure, this means that they will remain in prison on their original sentences.

One of the more striking examples comes from Marion County, Oregon, which has been cooperating with researchers from the RAND Corporation in a randomized field experiment. Selected nonviolent offenders were given the choice of serving a prison term or returning to the community to participate in ISP. These offenders have been convicted, and the judge has formally imposed a prison term. After conviction, they were asked if they would agree to return to the community and participate in ISP, rather than go to prison. During the one-year study period, about a third of those eligible for the experiment have chosen prison instead of ISP.

What accounts for this seeming aberration? Why should anyone prefer imprisonment to remaining in the community—no matter what the conditions? Can we infer from this that prison conditions seem less "punishing" than ISP requirements to these offenders? To con-

sider this possibility, we first need to understand why imprisonment may have lost some of its punitive sting.

Has the Punitive Power of Imprisonment Diminished?

Zimring and Hawkins note that sanctions are most likely to deter if they meet two conditions: "the social standing is injured by the punishment," and "the individual feels a danger of being excluded from the group." It is hard to imagine that prison terms have either of these attributes for repeat criminals. Possessing a prison record is not as stigmatizing as in the past, because so many of the offender's peers (and other family members) also have "done time." A recent survey shows that 40 percent of youths in state training schools have parents who have also been incarcerated. Further, about a quarter of all U.S. black males will be incarcerated during their lives, so the stigma attached to having a prison record is not as great as it was when it was relatively uncommon.

In fact, far from stigmatizing, imprisonment evidently confers status in some neighborhoods. Particularly for gang-affiliated and career criminals, a prison sentence enhances status when the offender returns to his neighborhood, especially in the inner cities. California's Task Force on Gangs and Drugs reported that during public testimony, gang members themselves "repeatedly stated that incarceration was not a threat because they knew their sentences would be minimal." Further, some gang members considered the short period of detention as a "badge of courage, something to brag about when they return to the streets." And according to the California Youth Authority, inmates steal state-issued prison clothing for the same reason. Wearing it when they return to the community lets everyone know they have "done hard time."

As for employment opportunities, imprisonment has had increasingly less effect for the people in question. As William Julius Wilson makes painfully clear in The Truly Disadvantaged, employment opportunities have been shrinking for people of lower economic status, especially in urban areas, so the effect of a prison record may not be as dramatic as it was when jobs were more plentiful.

Some have argued that for poor people, prison may be preferred, but few scholars take such discussions seriously. It is undoubtedly true, however, that the quality of a person's lifestyle when free certainly has some bearing on the extent to which imprisonment is considered undesirable. The grim fact—and national shame—is that for most people who go to prison, the conditions inside are not all that different from the conditions outside. The prison environment may be far below the ordinary standards of society, but so is the environment they come from. As the quality of life that people can expect when free declines, the relative deprivation suffered while in prison declines.

Social isolation is another presumably punitive aspect of imprisonment. Again, the values of society surface in the belief that when a person goes to prison he is "among aliens." In prison, he is isolated from the kinds of people he would customarily (and by preference) be among. For today's inmates, that is less likely to be true. The newly admitted inmate will probably find friends, if not family, already there.

The warden of Pontiac Penitentiary described it thus: "When a new guy comes up here it's almost a homecoming—undoubtedly there are people from his neighborhood and people who know him. . . ." He goes on to recall how a ranking gang member, upon entry to prison, received a "letter from the ranking chief welcoming him into the family." As for real family, the warden in a Washington, D.C. jail recently noted that his facility currently contained three generations of a particular family at once. He remarked that, "It was like a family reunion for these guys." Some even suggest that prison serves as a buffer for offenders who find the outside world particularly difficult. One man, just released from a Massachusetts prison, said:

> I have literally seen guys who have been released walk out the door and stand on the corner and not know which direction to go. And they eventually go back to prison. As horrible as it is, prison provides some sort of community.

And, finally, the length of time an offender can be expected to actually serve in prison has decreased. . . . But more to the point, for marginal offenders (those targeted for prison alternatives), the expected time served can be much less. In California, Texas, and Illinois, two- to three-year prison terms often translate into less than six months actually served. In Oregon, prison crowding has created a situation in which a five-year sentence can translate into three to four months of actual time served. Particularly when the prison system is the subject of a court order and offenders are released because of a "cap," prison terms can be quite short. Offenders on the street seem to be aware of this, even more so with the extensive media coverage such issues are receiving.

For the above reasons, then, it seems at least plausible that prison terms (on average) are not perceived as being as severe as they were historically. No one has ever surveyed prisoners or ex-convicts to find out how punitive they think imprisonment is. However, one could say their actions answer that question implicitly: More than 50 percent of today's prison inmates have served a prior prison term. Add prior jail sentences, and the percentage rises to 80 percent. Knowing what it's like, 80 percent of them evidently still think that the "benefits" of committing a new crime outweigh the "costs" of being in prison. This implies a lot about how punitive prison is for these offenders. However, it does not explain why they would choose imprisonment over intensive probation.

Why Would Offenders Choose Prison Over ISPs?
For many offenders, it may seem preferable to get that short stay in prison over rather than spend five times as long in an ISP. But what about the relative conditions? If the speculations above have any validity, better a short time in conditions that differ little from your accustomed life than a long time in conditions that are very different from the "ordinary standards" of your community.

Taking Marion County, Oregon, as an example, consider the alternatives facing convicted offenders:

ISP
The offender will serve two years under this sanction. During that time, the offender will be visited by a probation officer two or three times per week, who will phone on the other days. The offender will be subject to unannounced searches of his home for drugs and have his urine tested regularly for alcohol and drugs. He must strictly abide by other conditions set by the court—not carrying a weapon, not socializing with certain persons—and he will have to perform community service and be employed or participate in training or education. In addition, he will be strongly encouraged to attend counseling and/or other treatment, particularly if he is a drug offender.

Prison
A sentence of two to four years will require that the offender serve about three to six months. During his term, he is not required to work nor will he be required to participate in any training or treatment, but may do so if he wishes. Once released, he will be placed on two years routine parole supervision, where he sees his parole officer about once a month. For these offenders, as for any of us, freedom is probably preferable to imprisonment. However, the ISP does not represent freedom. In fact, it may stress and isolate repeat offenders more than imprisonment does. It seems reasonable that when offenders return to their communities, they expect to return to their old lives. The ISP transforms those lives radically.

Their homes can be searched and they must submit regularly to urine testing. Offenders may well consider such invasions of their homes and lives more intrusive and unbearable than the lack of privacy in prisons—where it is an expected condition of life. The same is true of discipline and social isolation. By definition, imprisonment limits freedom of movement and activity, but once a person is in his own community, curfew and other restrictions may seem harder to take. Ironically, he may be less socially isolated from his peers in prison than in ISP.

Why Do Offenders' Perceptions Matter?
Having established the counter-intuitive fact that some serious offenders prefer imprisonment to ISPs, what are we to make of it? Whatever else, it does argue for reconsidering the range of sanctions this country has and the assumptions they reflect. The point is not to insist that on any absolute scale ISP is "worse" than prison. Rather, it is to suggest that the scale we currently use needs reexamining. For the people who are likely to come under either sanction, how society at large views those sanctions is largely irrelevant. How offenders view punishment ought at least to be considered. (23–27)

Questions
1. Why should the views of offenders about punishment matter?
2. What do offenders' attitudes suggest about the value of community punishments?
3. What would you recommend as a result of Petersilia's arguments?

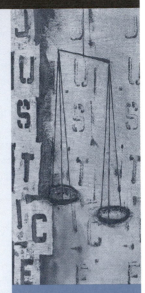

denied to prisoners whose crimes and history merit them. Unfortunately, net widening is a problem in most intermediate punishment programs. So, intermediate punishments haven't reduced prison populations. (Tonry and Lynch 1996)

2. *Intermediate punishments do justice by implementing a graduated punishment system.* Policy makers, judges, corrections personnel, and the public strongly support intermediate punishment for nonviolent offenders, especially first-time offenders. Offenders see intermediate punishments as tougher than being locked up, especially if they have to work and get regular drug tests. (Petersilia 1998, 583)

3. *Intermediate punishments can be cost-effective.* Intermediate punishments are cost-effective *if* they're managed well; directed at nonviolent offenders; and aren't net widening. (Tonry and Lynch 1996, 107, 137)

4. *Most intermediate punishment programs fail.* According to Michael Tonry and Mary Lynch (1996), "There is no free lunch. The failure of most intermediate sanctions to achieve promised reductions in recidivism, cost, and prison use were never realistic. . . . Intermediate sanctions can reduce costs and divert offenders from imprisonment, but those results are not easy to obtain" (137–138).

Knowledge and Understanding Check

Introduction
✔ How many offenders are serving in each type of community corrections?

Probation and parole
✔ Identify and describe three ways prisoners are released from prison.
✔ Trace the history of probation.
✔ Identify its conflicting missions.
✔ Summarize the results of evaluations of its effectiveness.
✔ Who gets probation? Who gets parole?
✔ What are the conditions of release for probation? for parole?
✔ How and when is probation revoked? How and when is parole revoked?

✔ Identify and explain the three usual measures of recidivism.
✔ Summarize the state of our knowledge about the effects of parole supervision on recidivism.
✔ Describe the differences in representation based on race, ethnicity, and gender in probation and parole.

Intermediate punishments
✔ What does either/or punishment mean?
✔ Explain how a graduated punishment system should work.
✔ Summarize the major research findings regarding intermediate punishments.

KEY TERMS

case study method
community corrections
community service
correctional boot camp
corrections
discretionary release
either/or corrections
expiration release

graduated punishment system
home confinement
incarceration
in-or-out corrections
intensive supervision
intermediate punishments
mandatory release
net widening

parole
parole boards
probation
recidivism
restitution
risk assessment method
suspended sentence
technical violations

INTERNET PROJECT

What are some of the current issues in probation? What solutions have been proposed to resolve them? How can examples from other countries help U.S. probation?
Suggested sites:
■ Bureau of Justice Statistics, Probation and Parole Populations: http://www.ojp.usdoj.gov/bjs/abstract/papp97.htm

■ Findlaw: http://laws.findlaw.com/US/000/97-634.html (*Tip:* Read the case of *Pennsylvania Department of Corrections v. Yeskey.*)
■ InfoTrac College Edition: Search using the key word "probation issues."

CHAPTER 11

Prisons, Jails, and Prisoners

© David Konte

CHAPTER OUTLINE

Turning the other cheek has lacked popular acceptance, so that at all times and all places, when human beings have violated the core interests of others, those others have felt it necessary or prudent and proper to respond in punitive ways. . . . Serious wrongs have usually elicited reactions, and the reactions have generally hurt. The Biblical injunction "an eye for an eye, a tooth for a tooth" was intended to limit . . . punishment, not to encourage severity (only an eye for an eye, not a crucifixion for stealing).

MICHAEL TONRY AND NORVAL MORRIS (TONRY 2000, VII)

Over the past twenty years, the fifty American states have engaged in one of the great policy experiments of modern times. In an attempt to reduce intolerably high levels of reported crime, the states doubled their prison capacity, and then doubled it again, increasing their costs by more than $20 billion per year. The states and the federal government have given up a lot to get to this point: that $20 billion could provide day care for every family that cannot afford it, or a college education to every high school graduate, or a living wage job to every unemployed youth.

WILLIAM SPELMAN (2000)

■ INTRODUCTION

What a difference a decade can make! In 1991 there were 700,000 Americans behind bars; by 2001 there were a record 2 million (Bureau of Justice Statistics 2001e). In 1990, 458 out of every 100,000 Americans were locked up; by 2000 there were 699, an increase of 70 percent and the highest proportion of a nation's people locked up in the world (Figure 11.1). The rates in some states are even higher (Louisiana at the top with 801) and some lower (Minnesota at the bottom with 128). There were 351 more prisons and jails and 528,000 more beds in 2000 than in 1990. In 1990, there were 44 *contracts* to build private prisons and jails for 15,000 prisoners. By 2000, there were 87,000 *prisoners* in 264 private prisons and jails. In 1990, there were almost 6000 crimes for every 100,000 people; by 2000 the rate had fallen to about 4000, a 33 percent drop (Chapter 3, Figure 3.5). (We'll discuss later whether the prison "boom" and prisoner crime "bust" are connected.)

 11-1 Prisoners 2000, complete report

In 1990, there were 44,000 women prisoners; by 2000 that number had almost doubled. Still, the numbers of women prisoners were dwarfed by the numbers of men in both 1990 (730,000) and 2000 (1,237,000) (Figure 11.2). The racial breakdown of prisoners stayed about the same—a little less than half were Black and about one-third were White in 1990 and in 2000. We don't know how many Hispanic prisoners there were in 1990 because they were counted as White, but in 2000, about one-sixth were Hispanic. The remaining small fraction of American Indians, Native Alaskans, Native Hawaiians, other Pacific Islanders, and Asians stayed about the same. The bottom line: There were far fewer women and White prisoners; far more Black prisoners; and somewhat more Hispanic prisoners than their percentages in the general population (Figure 11.3). The racial gap is even greater among women. Black women were three times more likely than Hispanic women and six times more likely than White women to be in prison (Bureau of Justice Statistics 2001e, Table 15).

When looked at by age group, 10 percent of Black men in their twenties and thirties are locked up compared with 2.9 percent of Hispanic men and 1.1 percent of White men in the same age groups (Bureau of Justice Statistics, 2001e, 11). Men between 20 and 35 and women between 25 and 40 dominate the prison population (Figure 11.2). The bottom line: There are huge gender and racial gaps in U.S. prison and jail populations.

About half of all prisoners are confined for violent offenses, a quarter for drug offenses, and another quarter for property crimes (Table 11.1).

Now that we've taken a brief look at who's confined and for what, let's take a more in-depth look at prisons, jails, and prisoners. We'll begin with the history of prisons in the United States, followed by an examination of the boom in the prison population. Then, we'll look individually at prisons, jails, and prisoners.

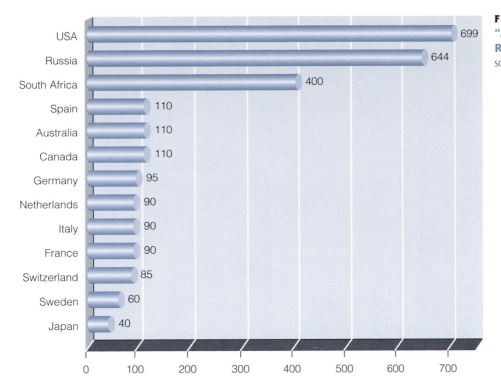

FIGURE 11.1
"Advanced Countries'" Imprisonment Rates
SOURCE: King and Mauer 2001.

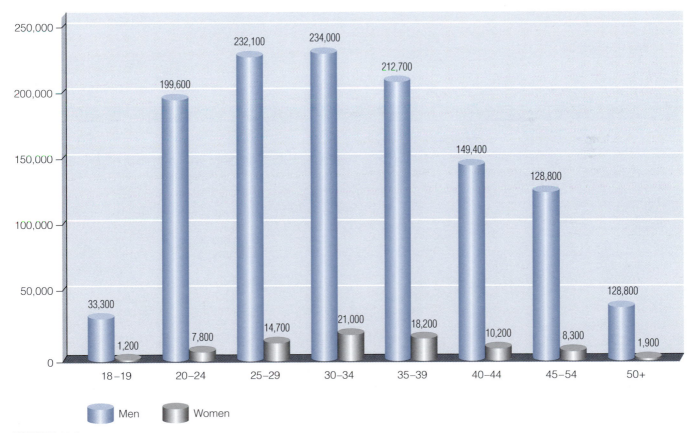

FIGURE 11.2
Prisoner Gender and Age, 2000
SOURCE: Bureau of Justice Statistics 2001e, Table 14.

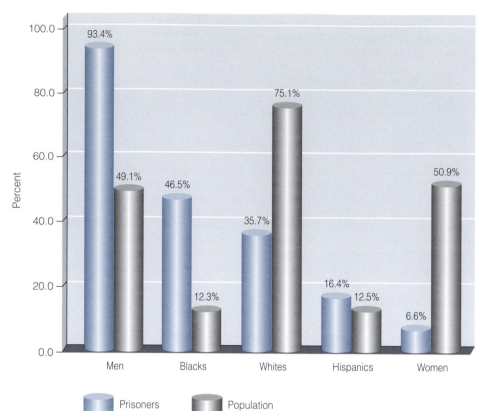

FIGURE 11.3
Prisoner Gender, Race, and Ethnicity, 2000

SOURCE: Bureau of Justice Statistics 2001e;
U.S. Census 2001, Table DP-1.

TABLE 11.1

Crimes Prisoners Confined For, 2000

Offenses	All	Male	Female	White	Black	Hispanic
Violent offenses	570,000	548,400	21,600	189,300	266,300	93,800
Murder*	141,500	134,900	6,600	44,000	70,700	22,900
Manslaughter	17,500	15,700	1,800	6,200	6,900	3,400
Rape	30,900	30,600	300	14,200	12,400	2,600
Other sexual assault	78,100	77,300	800	44,600	19,300	10,800
Robbery	161,800	156,600	5,200	33,800	97,300	26,200
Assault	115,100	109,700	5,400	35,800	50,500	23,800
Other violent	25,100	23,600	1,500	10,700	9,100	4,200
Property offenses	245,000	225,400	19,600	103,900	98,500	34,100
Burglary	116,600	112,900	3,800	49,200	47,200	16,200
Larceny	46,700	40,500	6,100	17,300	21,000	6,400
Motor vehicle theft	19,900	19,200	700	7,700	7,300	4,400
Fraud	31,700	24,100	7,600	16,000	12,000	2,800
Other property	30,100	28,700	1,400	13,600	11,000	4,200
Drug offenses	251,200	226,100	25,100	50,700	144,700	52,100
Public-order offenses**	120,600	112,800	7,800	51,500	42,100	21,300

NOTES: *Includes nonnegligent manslaughter.
**Includes weapons, drunk driving, court offenses, commercialized vice, morals and decency charges, liquor law violations, and other public-order offenses.
SOURCE: Bureau of Justice Statistics 2001e, Table 16.

■ THE HISTORY OF U.S. PRISONS

Punishment is as ancient as recorded history. One of the earliest known writings, the Code of Hammurabi, contains a list of penalties chipped in stone. These penalties strongly resemble the mandatory sentences of our own day (Chapter 9), except they don't include imprisonment. Prisons are ancient too. But until 1700, prisons weren't used for punishment; they confined suspects and defendants to make sure they showed up in court. Throughout most of North American colonial history prisons weren't used for punishment either. Capital punishment was an option but wasn't used frequently. Occasionally, early American judges sentenced offenders to whipping or mutilation, including cropping their ears or slitting their nostrils. Judges also used public shaming—stocks, ducking stools, pillories, dunce caps, or signs such as "I'm a fornicator" and the like. Less dramatic but still the punishments of choice were fines and restitution (Bowker 1982).

Let's look at the origins of the penitentiary, the correctional institution, and finally, modern-day prisons.

The Penitentiary, 1785–1890

Massachusetts, Pennsylvania, and New York each contributed to the development of what was known as the penitentiary, during the period from 1785 to 1890.

The Massachusetts system
Massachusetts was the first state to use prisons to punish convicted offenders. In 1785, the state passed a law allowing judges to sentence offenders to long-term confinement instead of the older punishments. The law named the Castle Island fortress built to guard Boston Harbor as the nation's first prison. According to the law, prisoners had to work at "hard labor," because "Whereas idleness is often the parent of fraud and cheating . . . confinement to hard labor may be a means of reclaiming such offenders." Convicts were ruled by a competent staff, including a doctor and a chaplain and subjected to military discipline and strict dietary and sanitary conditions. The basic idea was to remove offenders from a corrupting environment and make them work. Isolation and work was supposed to redeem their souls, reform their bodies, and instill in them the habits of law-abiding citizens. Armed with these, they'd be ready, willing, and able to pay their way and stay out of trouble (Hirsch 1992, 11).

The Pennsylvania system
The Pennsylvania Quakers soon stole the limelight from Massachusetts as prison innovators. The Quakers believed that inflicting pain for the sake of retribution was barbaric and cruel. To reclaim "fallen" citizens, the Quakers designed the Walnut Street Jail in Philadelphia. The jail was completed in 1790, followed by the Western Penitentiary in 1826 and the Eastern Penitentiary in 1830.

The Walnut Street Jail was the first **penitentiary** in the world. The basic idea of the penitentiary was to isolate offenders in their cells. In solitary confinement, they could think about what they did wrong and how they'd make it right by living useful lives when they went back into the world. To encourage prisoners to think, they weren't allowed to talk. They got adequate food, shelter, clothing, bedding, and medical care for free. (This was a major reform because before this prisoners had to pay for their keep in money.) And they worked—alone in their cells, making nails and cutting stones. Working all day in silent, solitary confinement and meditating in silent, solitary confinement the rest of the time was called the **Pennsylvania system.**

The Auburn system
In 1817, New York built its own version of the penitentiary based entirely on solitary confinement in small cells and a strict rule of silence. But since so many prisoners committed suicide or had mental breakdowns because of being locked up in tiny cells with nowhere to go and nothing to do, authorities modified the system. Under the **Auburn system** (named after the town where the penitentiary was built) or **congregate system,** prisoners worked in silent groups during the day and meditated and slept in solitary confinement at night. Anyone who broke the rules was whipped on the spot.

Except for working together and working alone, the Pennsylvania and Auburn penitentiary systems were alike. Prisons were separate worlds of huge, walled fortresses ruled by wardens with absolute power where breaking the rules of silence and work spelled instant, hard punishment. Both were considered humane—and they were, compared with capital punishment, mutilation, and whipping. Their missions were noble. They wanted to reform prisoners by means of silent meditation, hard work, healthy food, and proper religion. Once reformed, the penitentiary would send them back into the free world as people who worked for a living and obeyed the law instead of preying on others to survive.

The penitentiary system was part of a fundamental change taking place in the 1800s—the institutionalization of life outside the home. Historically, people worked, played, were educated, and were punished at home. After about 1820, these activities began to move from homes to bigger and impersonal buildings—factories, gymnasiums, hospitals, schools, "reformatories," and penitentiaries (Grob 1973; Rothman 1971).

However, most observers quickly noticed penitentiaries weren't accomplishing their mission of reforming prisoners. They also discovered reforming prisoners wasn't their only—maybe not even their primary—mission. If prisons weren't penitentiaries, then what were they? Custodial warehouses for criminals where despite the honest reform efforts and humanitarian rhetoric, warehouse keepers were sometimes awfully cruel. One prisoner from the Elmira Reformatory (a penitentiary for young offenders lavishly praised around the world for its reform ideals) reported what happened when he didn't finish a job:

> I knew I was in for a beating and I had a terror of what was coming. I refused to leave my cell. They stuck into the cell an iron rod with a two-foot hook on the end, heated red hot, and poked me with it. I tried to defend myself, but my clothing took fire, and the iron burned my breast. I finally succumbed, was handcuffed and taken to the bathroom. I asked Brockway [the famous born-again Christian superintendent] if I had not been punished enough. He laughed at me. I got half a dozen blows with the paddle right across the kidneys. The pain was so agonizing that I fainted. They revived me, and when I begged for mercy, Brockway struck me on the head with a strap, knocked me insensible. The next thing I knew I was lying on a cot in the dungeon, shackled to an iron bar. The next day I was again hoisted and beaten, returned to the dungeon, and after one day's rest, beaten again. Then I was put in the cell in Murderer's Row, where I remained for twenty-one days on bread and water. (Pisciotta 1983, 621)

The Correctional Institution, 1890–1970

The Progressive reformers attacked penitentiaries as cruel and barbaric, just as the creators of the penitentiary had attacked capital, corporal, and mutilation punishments as cruel and barbaric. The Progressives' mission was also to reform (now called rehabilitate) offenders into law-abiding people who worked to support themselves. Their strategy was to combine the tactics of humane treatment, counseling, vocational training, and discipline into a coherent, scientifically sound program.

The Progressives led a successful campaign to establish the indeterminate sentence (Chapter 9) and, the pillars of community corrections, probation and parole (Chapter 10). According to the Progressives, if they were going to accomplish their mission they had to first rid criminal justice of rigid formal decision making by legislators, lawyers, and judges. Next, they had to arm experts in the new social and medical sciences with discretionary decision making power to "diagnose," "treat," and "cure" offenders, who were "sick" with the "disease" of criminal behavior. The Progressive reforms became known as the **medical model of corrections.** According to the model, decisions as to whether to send offenders to prison in the first place; what kind of prison to send them to; and when to release them conditionally; and then finally from state custody should depend on prisoners' rehabilitation, not on their past crimes (Rothman 1980).

By the 1940s, the **correctional institution,** which was based on the mission of rehabilitation, had replaced

the penitentiary. In principle, correctional institutions were more humane and accommodating than "big houses," the name for old penitentiaries. They provided softer discipline; more yard and recreational privileges; more liberal visitation and mail policies; more amenities, such as movies; and more programs, like education, vocational training, and therapy (Irwin 1980, Ch. 2).

Not everyone agrees with this benign description of the correctional institution. According to prison scholar Robert Johnson (1996):

> The benefits of correctional institutions are easily exaggerated. To my mind, the differences between the Big Houses and correctional institutions are of degree rather than kind. Correctional institutions did not correct. Nor did they abolish the pains of imprisonment. They were, at bottom, simply more tolerable warehouses than the Big Houses they supplanted, less a departure than a toned-down imitation. Often, correctional institutions occupied the same physical plant as the Big Houses. Indeed, one might classify them as Big Houses gone soft. (74–75)

During the 1960s, politicians dragged the issue of correctional institutions (as they did crime, police, plea bargaining, and sentencing) into politics. Both conservatives and liberals attacked them—sometimes ferociously (American Friends Society 1971; Gaylin et al. 1978; Johnson 1996; Morris 1974; Sherman and Hawkins 1981). Liberals attacked correctional institutions because they put prisoners' *needs* over their *rights*. According to liberals, prison treatment programs were unjustified invasions of prisoners' privacy and autonomy. They also attacked the broad discretionary decision making of probation, parole, and prison officials as badly infected with individual, ethnic, racial, gender, and class discrimination.

Conservatives attacked correctional institutions as "soft on crime," describing them as "country clubs" where prisoners were freeloading on hardworking, honest people's money. With prisons like these, conservatives asked, how can we expect prisons to deter criminals and send a message to criminal wannabes that crime doesn't pay? It's surprising people aren't breaking *in* instead of breaking *out* of prison.

Academics joined the chorus of criticism by claiming indeterminate sentences for the purpose of rehabilitation didn't work and it was time to do *something* about it. Liberals and conservatives could agree with that. So could a frightened, frustrated, and angry public. And, so could politicians who saw criminal justice problems as red meat political issues (Chapter 1). And they had a point. The 1960s witnessed a wave of prison riots (Chapter 12), a huge crime boom (Chapters 1, 3), and high rates of recidivism.

There, the agreement ended. What to do became a heated controversy. Liberals wanted fewer people locked up, and they wanted those who were to stay behind bars for a short, fixed time. Further, liberals wanted prisoners' lives in confinement to be rich with programs to improve their chances of returning to productive and law-abiding lives outside prison. They called this process **reintegration.** Conservatives wanted long, fixed sentences under conditions that would punish offenders for their crimes (retribution), keep them from committing crimes (incapacitation or specific deterrence), and be unpleasant enough to make prisoners never want to come back (general deterrence) (Chapter 9).

Prisons, 1970–

The debate over prisons was hot and loud and political, but the future was with the conservatives. By the end of the 1970s, the dominant missions of prisons were retribution, incapacitation, and general deterrence. Rehabilitation remained but more as an incidental than a central mission.

The conservative victory accompanied (some say *caused*) four major changes in U.S. prisons:

1. Massive growth in prison populations (Figure 11.4 and next section)
2. Heavy reliance on prison time for drug offenses (see "Prisoners" later)
3. Increasing proportions of Black and Hispanic prisoners (see "Prisoners" later)
4. Rising power and influence of prison gangs (Chapter 12)

■ THE PRISON POPULATION BOOM

Commentators on American culture were surprised at the immediate and strong national unity that followed the attacks on the World Trade Center and the Pentagon on September 11, 2001. Maybe not as much noticed or dramatic, but still important to those of us who work in and study criminal justice, is the strength and unity of support for the prison population boom that began in 1975, following fifty years of stable prison populations. The conscious decision by all fifty states and the federal government to break with the past and grow prison populations sharply and quickly is remarkable enough. But it's nothing short of amazing to witness a quarter century of strong and unshakeable public support for spending more of its tax dollars on prisons during a time when its support for other government programs (except Social Security and Medicare) and the officials who administered them was falling.

It's easy to track the pattern of stability in prison populations from 1925 to 1975, which was broken by the boom in prison populations from 1975 to 2000 (Figure 11.4). It's quite another matter to *explain* this pattern. In the explanations that follow keep in mind one thing the experts agree on: Policy makers *decided* to increase prison populations, it didn't just happen. So, the question we

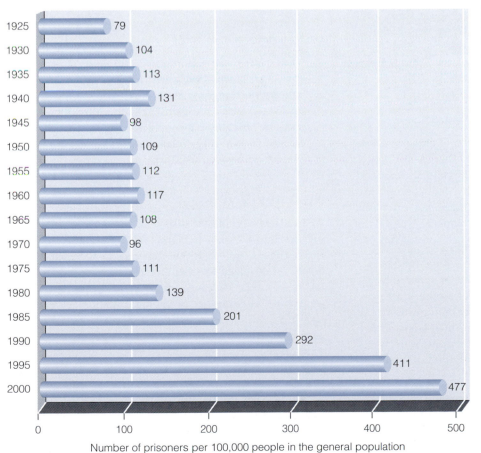

FIGURE 11.4
Prison Population Growth, 1925–2000
SOURCE: Bureau of Justice Statistics 2001g, Table 1; BJS 1995a; BJS 2001e.

Year	Value
1925	79
1930	104
1935	113
1940	131
1945	98
1950	109
1955	112
1960	117
1965	108
1970	96
1975	111
1980	139
1985	201
1990	292
1995	411
2000	477

Number of prisoners per 100,000 people in the general population

want to answer is, "Why *decide* to increase the prison population?" To find some answers, let's look at the public's response to crime, the role of political opportunism in the change, the impact of the drug war, the effects of a more efficient law enforcement system, and how racial and ethnic groups were affected by this change.

The Public's Response

The most common explanation for the imprisonment boom that began in the 1970s is the crime boom that began in the 1960s (Chapter 3). The public's reaction to the crime boom—"get tough on crime" by locking up criminals—was the combination of society's natural moral outrage and a rational desire to control crime (Di-Iulio 1996). Legislatures' and criminal justice agencies' decisions to "get tough" by locking up criminals followed. But, the "do the crime, do the time" response to crime wasn't invented in the 1970s. It's part of a long and distinguished sociological approach to crime control, explained by the great nineteenth-century sociologist Emile Durkheim's theory that punishment is a collective moral response to the violation of social norms (Chapter 2).

Still, rising crime rates are only part of the explanation for the prison population boom (Caplow and Simon 1999, 64). We've had other crime booms in the twentieth century—Prohibition in the 1920s and 1930s and 1950s drug offenses—and the public demanded a "lock 'em up" response then, too. But, none of these times produced explosions in prison populations. Significantly, the prison population boom and public support for it lasted right through the high-crime plateau of the 1980s *and* the crime bust of the 1990s (Chapter 3).

Political Opportunism

To another group of social scientists and penal experts with a distinguished history (conflict theorists, Chapter 2), morality may have driven the community's demand for punishment but the decision by legislatures and criminal justice agencies to increase prison populations was motivated by political opportunism. Politicians preyed on public outrage and fear to get votes. They exploited the crime boom as a symbol to

> channel anxieties about the social order spurred by the dismantling of racial and gender hierarchies, economic restructuring, and large scale immigration. From this perspective the mobilization of laws and resources for imprisonment is political opportunism rather than rational public policy. (Caplow and Simon 1999, 65)

But, there's more to the story of the decision making behind the prison population boom than political opportunism and community demands to control crime.

The Drug War

Another element in the story clearly is the decision to fight another war on drugs. Getting tough on crime can only raise prison populations if there are available offenders to lock up. Most murderers, rapists, robbers, burglars, and thieves aren't available to keep the population boom growing. Why? The worst criminals are already caught and locked up (or in rare cases, executed), leaving only a few roaming around uncaught, on probation, parole, or furlough. (Of course, when these few are discovered, they, their disgusting crimes, and criminal justice's failure to lock them up are blasted all over TV.) Also, sentences for violent offenses were lengthened. Keeping violent offenders locked up longer has also contributed to the prison population growth (Zimring and Hawkins 1991).

So, that left drug offenders to keep the prison populations growing—and they did. We won't tell here the story of devastation caused by the spread of "crack" cocaine in the 1980s and the violence associated with the trafficking of it. We'll concentrate on the response to it, which was to pass mandatory sentencing laws that created new drug crimes with stiff prison sentences and lengthened the sentences of drug laws already on the books (Chapters 3 and 9).

The result of tougher drug laws was that in any large city there was a pool of potential prisoners so large law enforcement officers could arrest as many as they had time and resources to go after. The same was definitely *not* true of violent and property crimes. According to Caplow and Simon (1999):

> Thus while more prison time for violent crime accounts for much of the growth in incarceration, a significant portion (how much is difficult to estimate) is associated with a . . . supply with few apparent constraints. This allows growth to continue, even if at a slower pace, during cycles when for whatever reason violent crime declines. (72)

System Efficiency

In 1960, state criminal justice agencies were inefficient offices run in highly personal ways by highly independent officials. By the 1980s, these same agencies had become modernized bureaucracies that could respond faster to public demand and political pressures. At the same time, the mission of criminal justice agencies was shifting from changing offenders into law-abiding citizens to controlling what was increasingly believed to be a permanent criminal class (see Chapter 1 on the pendulum swing between crime control and due process). So, the efficient, modern agencies could respond quickly to the public demand to control crime by locking up criminals (Caplow and Simon 1999, 97–110).

All criminal justice agencies—police, prosecution, defense lawyers, courts, and corrections—formed a rapid response team to satisfy public demand and political pressure for more incarceration. Police could make more arrests and make them stick because they were more efficient and knew the law better than they did in 1960. The courtroom work group could process greater numbers of defendants into offenders because they were more efficient (Chapter 7). Judges could no longer use their discretionary sentencing power to put the brakes on the new efficiency in locking up more people. Just the opposite was true: Mandatory sentencing laws and sentencing guidelines put the brakes on judges by restricting their discretion to sentence (Chapter 9).

Race and Ethnicity

What part—if any—did the infection of discriminatory decision making play in the prison population explosion? It's easy to document the disproportionate numbers of Black and Hispanic prisoners, and even how the disproportion increased (Figure 11.3). But *why* did it occur? One theory is the prison population reflects the reality that Blacks and Hispanics commit more crimes than Whites and other races and ethnic groups (Chapter 3). There's also research showing that street gangs are spreading from major to smaller cities, that they commit crimes routinely, and that their members are mainly Black (Decker and Van Winkle 1996; Klein 1995).

Other theories emphasize how tough it is to root out the infection of race and ethnicity from decision making that promotes locking up Blacks and Hispanics. Take minor offenses, where decision making is mainly discretionary. It's inevitable that race and ethnicity infect some police officers' decisions to arrest Blacks and Hispanics. Even if these arrests don't lead to jail time, arrest records can "tip sentencing decisions from probation to prison" after conviction for other offenses, and they can count as a strike in three-strikes laws (Caplow and Simon 1999, 90–91). According to Theodore Caplow and Jonathan Simon (1999):

> In the aggregate and over time, a systematic effect of subjecting African Americans to greater scrutiny for minor offenses will produce effects in the imprisonment rates (although how much of the racial disproportion they account for would be difficult to estimate). (91)

■ THE SIDE EFFECTS OF IMPRISONMENT

Most discussion and research about the decision to put our hopes and money in a crime policy based on locking up more offenders focuses on two direct effects of imprisonment—crime reduction and costs. As we'll shortly see, costs of imprisonment are measured by how much it costs to build prisons and maintain prisoners (see "Prisons"). Crime reduction is measured by how many prisoners return to crime when they leave prison (see "Prisoners" later and Chapter 12).

Here we'll discuss some of the side effects of the growth in imprisonment, or the "imprisonment binge" as some critics call it. We'll look at the effects of diverting resources from other services, diverting resources to other communities, the loss of income to offenders' communities, and offenders' imprisonment on their children. Let me warn you in advance that, important as this subject is, the research is scanty on these side effects. So, much of what follows isn't backed up by solid empirical proof.

Diverting Resources from Other Services

The billions of new dollars spent on prisons probably didn't come from more tax dollars but from cuts in other spending. For example, California built about a prison a year for twenty years and one university; it spent $34,000 on every prison inmate in 1997 but only $6,000 on every college student. Florida increased corrections spending over higher education by three to one. The bottom line, say Hagan and Dinovitzer (1999, 131), is "when we invest in prisons we often in effect make choices to disinvest in other social institutions as well as individuals who would otherwise receive assistance from them."

Diverting Resources to Other Communities

Towns all over the country are competing for new prisons, just as they once competed for new car plants. Prisons are a booming business that brings money and jobs; they're a community resource. But their resource is another community's loss. Most prisoners come from poor city neighborhoods. And most probationers and parolees are supervised in these neighborhoods, making it more likely that kids know a criminal than a doctor, lawyer, or teacher. According to Hagan and Dinovitzer (1999):

> As large numbers of inmates return to their communities, so too does the prison subculture, which . . . may be "intensely hostile to established authority.". . . It is a cruel irony that when young minority males are taken from their communities and imprisoned, they become a novel resource in the investment/disinvestment equation that shifts resources from one location to another, disadvantaging the minority community to the relative advantage of another community, usually in a majority group setting. (133)

YOU DECIDE

Does sending more people to prison reduce crime rates?

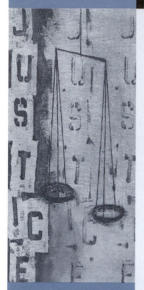

William Spelman, "Prisons and Crime," ed. Michael Tonry, *Crime and Justice: A Review of Research* (Chicago: University of Chicago Press), 419–494.

One of the great policy experiments in modern history was the fifty states' and the federal government's use of imprisonment to lower crime rates and make the public safer. Did the experiment work? "Yes," say some. "No," say others. "Not so fast," say others. Read the following excerpt from William Spelman's (2000) excellent survey of research on imprisonment and crime, and then you decide.

"What Recent Studies Do (and Don't) Tell Us about Imprisonment and Crime"

Over the past twenty years, the fifty American states have engaged in one of the great policy experiments of modern times. In an attempt to reduce intolerably high levels of reported crime, the states doubled their prison capacity, then doubled it again, increasing their costs by more than $20 billion a year. The states and the federal government have given up a lot to get to this point: that $20 billion could provide day care for every family that cannot afford it or a college education to every high school graduate, or a living wage job to every unemployed youth. But crime levels have (at last) responded, dropping to their lowest level in years. Thus recent history provides a prima facie [true if not proved otherwise] case for the effectiveness of prisons.

Not everyone has found this evidence persuasive. Some argue, quite convincingly, that recent crime reductions had nothing to do with the prison buildup. Crime has dropped because the number of poverty-stricken youth has dropped, or because police are more effective, or because of any number of other reasons. The correlation does not necessarily guarantee causation.

Perhaps more important, whether more prisons reduce crimes matters less than how much. Crime is not the only problem the American public is grappling with. Policy makers may decide to spend taxpayer dollars on child care, college education, job programs, or (for that matter) childhood immunization, infrastructure for decaying cities, subsidies to tobacco farmers, or B2 stealth bombers. (Occasionally, they can even decide that the best use of the money is to give it back to taxpayers.) It

is not enough to have a small effect on the crime problem if that means forgoing a big effect on an equally thorny social problem.

And prisons are no longer the only way to fight crime. Policy makers may decide to spend money on other agencies in the criminal justice system (e.g., more judges, better managed police, or better trained probation officers); on changes in the physical environment that make it more difficult to commit a crime; on education efforts that improve the public's capacity to intervene; on education and jobs programs that reduce would-be offenders' motivations to commit crimes; and on a host of other equally plausible alternatives.

With few exceptions, we have been unable to determine the benefit-cost ratios associated with these policies and programs. Nevertheless, we can be fairly sure that most do more good than harm; a few (childhood immunization is a classic case) may yield benefit-cost ratios as high as 5.0. Thus, it is no longer sufficient, if it ever was, to demonstrate that prisons are better than nothing. Instead, they must be better than the next best use of the money.

Better than nothing may be a minimal requirement but it has taken decades to establish whether even this is true. Sellin [Chapter 9] examined the effectiveness of the death penalty by comparing homicide rates over time between pairs of neighboring states, one with the death penalty and one without. Although Sellin's work was crude by today's standards, later studies became increasingly sophisticated as computers and knowledge of statistical methods became more widely available. The mold for most future studies was cast in 1973, however, when Ehrlich [Chapter 9] applied state of the art econometric methods and a plausible economic model to a cross section of American states. A raft of similar studies followed, each using similar methods, models, and data sets.

In 1978, the National Research Council (NRC) published an analysis of this burgeoning literature. Researchers reviewed the empirical studies, pointed out the principal objections to the most popular analysis

Loss of Income

It surprises many students to learn that offenders get their money illegally *and* legally. More than half of state prisoners had a job when they were arrested. Maybe it wasn't a "good" job or a "full-time job" but it was legal. And—like it or not—crime generates wealth too, sometimes bringing it in from the outside in the drug trade.

So, when offenders go to prison, their families and community lose an income producer. The reality is "many offenders drift back and forth over time between legal and illegal work" (Fagan and Freeman 1999).

Of course, illegal income is a mixed benefit—it brings bad behavior with it. But, keep in mind there's a high demand for illegal work. For example, the demand for ille-

methods, and showed that they provided inaccurate or biased results. . . . The rate of econometric studies dropped after the NRC report was published. The bar had been raised so high that, for a time, no one could jump it. Recently, however, the sheer expense of maintaining a million plus prison population has stimulated renewed attempts to use the quasi-experimental data. The new studies rely on new theoretical radical underpinnings; they employ new statistical methods . . . ; they recognize that statistical estimates can be fragile because crime has many causes and because the prison population may be both a cause and an effect of crime. Collectively, these studies have succeeded in overcoming many of the objections of previous efforts. Whether closer to the truth or not, they are certainly more defensible than the studies of the nineteen sixties and nineteen seventies.

Policy makers looking for a single best estimate are in error. We will never know enough about the relationship between prisons and crime to reduce our knowledge to a single point. Still, the recent studies suggest the best guess is [that doubling the prison population would reduce crime] in the neighborhood of 30 percent. Any figure between 20 and 40 percent can be defended and we should not be too surprised to find that the result is anywhere between 10 and 50 percent. Because theory is too weak to allow us to distinguish among different crime types and because the empirical estimates are not statistically significantly different from one another, the most prudent course would be to assume the percent for each crime type is about the same, on average. What then can we say about the cost effectiveness of further prison construction? As a back of the envelope analysis suggests, not much.

The ultimate futility of our analysis is at last revealed. We can be nearly certain the percent of reduction lies somewhere between 10 and 50 percent and we can be fairly sure it lies between 20 and 40 percent but we have no idea at all whether it is greater than or less than 26.5 percent. In a nutshell, then, what the studies of the past ten years tell us is that crime responds to prison capacity and that continued expansion of prisons nationwide will reduce the crime rate. What the studies do not tell us is whether the reduction is large enough to warrant continued expansion.

. . . It is critical that we stop considering prison expansion decisions in a vacuum. Even if we could be certain prison construction was cost effective, it may still be true that some other program or policy was more cost effective. Certainly many primary prevention programs at least appear to be worth their salt: Family intervention, Headstart, self paced education, and job apprenticeship programs are all examples. Many secondary prevention programs, including environmental design initiatives, community organizing, victim training, and even some offender rehabilitation programs have shown tremendous promise when applied to the offenders' victims and environments they fit best. It is easily conceivable that initiatives such as these will yield benefit-cost ratios much greater than the 1.5 to 2.0 ratio that is the best we can expect from continued prison expansion. Of a dullard, Samuel Johnson once proclaimed, "That fellow seems to me to assess the one idea and that is the wrong one." The criminal justice community possesses many ideas. If we are to serve the public well, we must stop pretending otherwise.

Questions

1. How much do *you* think doubling the prison population should have to reduce crime rates before you would support doubling the prison population? 10 percent, 20 percent? 30 percent? 40 percent? 50 percent? Defend your answer.
2. Would it be good enough for you to support doubling the population if you knew the percentages were anywhere from 10 to 50 percent? Defend your answer.
3. How would you rank the priorities in spending public money on increasing prison populations or other things like education, national defense, or lower taxes?
4. Does this survey of research influence your answer to question 3? Why? Why not?

gal drugs doesn't go to prison with the dealer. Plenty of substitutes are waiting in line to satisfy the demand. Sadly, the demand for legal jobs isn't as strong. So, when an offender leaves a legal job to go to prison, employers don't fill the job—it disappears (Wilson 1996). John Hagan and Ronit Dinovitzer (1999) summarize the problem this way:

Imprisonment is part of a process through which minority males in particular become embedded in social networks of crime that lead away from opportunities for legal work. At the same time that imprisonment weakens links into legal employment for these youth, the effect of the prison inmate culture is to strengthen their connection into gangs and the criminal underworld more generally.

The problem is that legal and illegal forms of work each create their own chainlike possibilities for future engagement and activity. . . . It is often the first job that establishes a mobility ladder within the same adjoining occupational networks. The chances of moving onward and upward in the labor market increase as a function of learning and being exposed to the new opportunities that employment in a work sector brings. Unfortunately, this is no less true of illegal work than it is of legal employment, and as individuals become involved in one or the other kind of setting, it is opportunities within that sector that are enhanced. Imprisonment can be a particularly consequential event in this kind of employment history. A number of studies now confirm that as time spent in prison increases . . . the subsequent likelihood of disengagement from the legal economy increases. This is not surprising given that even those who do not have criminal records have difficulty finding employment. (136)

The Effects on Offenders' Children

Two-thirds of women prisoners and more than half of men prisoners have children under 18. More than 1.5 million children have parents locked up in jails and prisons. The families left behind suffer financial, emotional, and psychological difficulties. "By getting tough on crime, the United States has also gotten tough on children," is the way Susan Phillips and Barbara Bloom (1998, 539) put it. Let's look, in turn, at how the incarceration of fathers and mothers affects the families they leave behind.

The effects of incarcerated fathers

We've already learned that many fathers involved in crime are also earning money legally. Even when they don't live in their children's homes, they buy them toys and diapers and "baby-sit" them. In their interviews with gang members, Decker and Van Winkle (1996) found all but one gang member with children saw their children every or nearly every day. Lanier (1993) found that 74 percent of 188 maximum security prisoners lived with their kids before they came to prison, and 75 percent said they spent a lot of time with them. That's the good news. The bad news is we don't have enough research to know if these fathers are a *good* influence on their children.

The effects of incarcerated mothers

Women represent a small part of the prison population, but their share is growing. More women are going to prison instead of receiving probation, and they're staying longer. This tougher attitude toward women offenders is captured in a comment by U.S. District Court Chief Judge Julian Cook, Jr. (1995) as he refused to consider

parental duties when he sentenced a pregnant mother of two small children convicted on a drug conspiracy charge:

> To grant her request would have the practical effect of establishing a precedent whereby the recent birth of a baby, coupled with the fear of being unable to identify an "adequate" family member to care for the minor children, would form the basis for vacating a term of incarceration in favor of probation. (145–147)

What are the consequences of sending more convicted mothers to prison? All we can say for sure in the sad absence of hard data is that locking women up will separate them from their children because most children live with their mothers. There's speculation that children of women in prison have problems of low self-esteem, lack of motivation, low achievement, and poor relationships with their peers. They feel guilt, shame, anxiety, sadness, grief, and isolation. When they reach adolescence they start "acting out," like getting involved with drugs and gangs. All this may be true but there's practically no empirical research to back it up (Hagan and Dinovetzer 1999, 146–148).

■ PRISONS

It's expensive to lock up offenders; in 1999, the last year for which we have data, the average cost was over $21,000 a year (Figure 11.5). The costs can be a lot higher (Alaska, $41,400!) or lower (Alabama, $8,500) (Camp and Camp, 2000, 87). Costs also vary a lot by the type of prison; the higher the security classification of the prison the higher the cost (Table 11.2). To better understand the issues surrounding prisons, we'll look at the various types of public prisons, private prisons, prison management, and corrections officers.

 11-2 Cost of locking up a prisoner in your state

Types of Prisons

There are many types of prisons in the United States. We'll concentrate on four—minimum security, medium security, maximum security, and supermaximum security (Figure 11.6). Notice the word *security* in all of them; it tells us security is the first mission of all prisons. Security against what? Three things: escape; harm to staff and other prisoners; and smuggling contraband into the prison. Security is the dominant criterion for building prisons and managing prisoners. The *amount* of security distinguishes the four types of prisons. We'll look at maximum security, medium and minimum security, and women's prisons.

FIGURE 11.5

Average Annual Inmate Cost, 1991–1999

SOURCE: Criminal Justice Institute 2001, 87.

Maximum security prisons

Maximum security prisons focus almost exclusively on security—preventing prisoners from escaping, hurting staff or each other, and keeping out contraband. Maximum security prisons can be traditional facilities, super-maxes, or new-generational facilities.

Traditional Traditional maximum security prisons are like fortresses, surrounded by thick, high walls or fences topped by electrified barbed or razor wire. Armed guards in fortified towers watch the walls at all times, using searchlights and even electronic devices to prevent prisoner escapes. Inside maximum security prisons, supervision, surveillance, and control are extensive. Prisoners are moved only in groups under close guard by officers.

In older maximum security prisons, large cell blocks arranged in tiers permit a single guard to observe hundreds of cells at one time. Bars replace doors and windows. Television surveillance makes it easier to watch prisoners, not only in their cells but also in the shower, at meals, and even in the toilet. Prisoners may be strip-searched before and after visits, and even visitors are subject to pat-downs. Officers take "head counts" throughout the day; anyone not accounted for prompts major efforts to locate the "missing" prisoner. Metal furniture built into the walls and floors improves security by preventing chairs and tables from being used as obstacles and weapons. Scraping, clashing, and echoing metal causes high noise levels. It's an understatement to say that prisons aren't quiet places.

TABLE 11.2	

Daily Cost to House Inmates in Minnesota

Security Level	Daily Cost per Prisoner
Oak Park Heights (level 6, maximum security for men)	$150.23
Shakopee (all women)	$104.27
St. Cloud (level 5, close security for men)	$96.09
Stillwater (level 5, close security for men)	$78.15
Average cost	$107.18

SOURCE: Daniel Storkamp 2001.

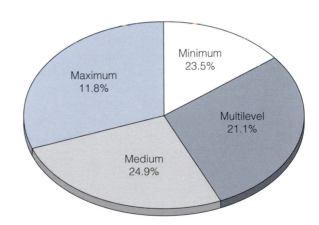

FIGURE 11.6

Breakdown of Percentage of Prisons by Security Level, 2000

NOTE: Percentages don't add up to 100 because intake and community facilities are not included.

SOURCE: Criminal Justice Institute 2001, 68.

"Supermaxes."   Prisons have always had "jails within prisons" (Riveland 1999, 1). Just because people are locked up doesn't stop some of them from trying to escape, assaulting others, and causing disturbances. As long as they threaten prison safety and order, administrators have to remove them from the general prison population. In the old days, they were put into special units called "the hole." Today, we call segregation in units away from the general prison population **special housing units** if the units are inside prisons.

Sometimes, whole prisons for "the worst of the worst" are built. These special prisons are called **supermaximum prisons,** or just **supermaxes.** The National Institute of Corrections defines supermax prisons this way:

> A freestanding facility, or a distinct unit within a freestanding facility, that provides for the management and security and control of inmates who have been officially designated as exhibiting violent or seriously disruptive behavior while incarcerated. Such inmates have been determined to be a threat to safety and security in traditional high security facilities and their behavior can be controlled only by separation, restricted movement, and limited access to staff and other inmates. (Riveland 1999, 3)

The legendary federal Alcatraz prison built in 1934 on an island off the coast of San Francisco was the first supermax prison, although it wasn't called that. Until 1963 when it closed, Alcatraz housed the nation's most notorious criminals, its "most sophisticated prison escape artists," prison riot leaders, and most violent prisoners. The prison was based on the philosophy of "lock 'em up and throw away the key."

Alcatraz introduced the **concentration model** of managing prisoners who most threatened prison security and safety. The model assumes it's easier to manage troublemakers if they're completely removed from the general prison population (Riveland 1999, 5). When Alcatraz was closed in 1963, rehabilitation was still the dominant penal policy. Alcatraz prisoners were then spread around the country in many different prisons, according to what sociologist and former Director of the Federal Bureau of Prisons David Ward (1994) calls the **dispersion model** of handling troublesome prisoners. Several assumptions lie behind the dispersion model. Spreading problem prisoners around prevents them from joining together to cause trouble. This relieves prison staff from having to spend all their time controlling the same troublemakers. It also allows the prison administration to break up cliques and gangs. And prisoners can participate in rehabilitation programs (Riveland 1999, 1).

By 1978, a combination of rising assaults on staff, prison unrest, and the "get tough on criminals" attitudes we discussed earlier led to a return to the concentration model. In that year, the U.S. Bureau of Prisons opened a "special high security control unit" in the federal prison at Marion, Indiana. The unit housed the nation's most dangerous prisoners. Assaults on staff and prisoners increased sharply around the country and at Marion in the early 1980s. At Marion, there were 54 serious inmate-on-inmate assaults, 8 prisoner killings, and 28 serious assaults on staff—not counting group disturbances.

On July 8, 1983, two prisoners armed with knives stabbed an officer they'd taken hostage. The next week, prisoners stabbed a general population prisoner five times because he had more privileges than they did. Several days later, while prisoners were returning to their cells from the dining hall, two prisoners attacked two officer escorts, stabbing one officer twelve times. After this stabbing, the prison was put on lockdown status—the temporary suspension of all activities, including recreation. Prisoners received sack lunches in their cells for breakfast, lunch, and dinner. As soon as these restrictions were lifted, one prisoner was stabbed and staff were threatened. The lockdown was reinstated. This pattern continued, more or less—lockdowns, some letup followed by prisoner violence, and then a reinstated lockdown (Ward 1990).

Marion remained the nation's only supermax until 1994, when the U.S. Bureau of Prisons opened the Administrative Maximum Penitentiary at Florence, Colorado. Florence (ADX) became the nation's (and probably the world's) state of the art supermax. According to the Office of Public Affairs of the Federal Bureau of Prisons:

> Florence (ADX) has been designed to operate in a humane, safe manner that is in accord with all applicable legal standards and sound correctional practices. . . . Unusually high security prisons are necessary at institutions like Marion and Florence because they confine the most serious escape and assault risks in the Bureau, as well as some equally dangerous inmates from a number of states. Most Marion inmates have demonstrated by highly assaultive, predatory, or serious escape-related behavior that they are in a stage of their institutional career where they cannot function in traditional, open population institutions of lower security. They are simply the most violent and dangerous inmates in the entire system, and most of them have proven it repeatedly. (Federal Bureau of Prisons 1993, 1)

So, according to the Bureau of Prisons (1993):

> An unfortunate but real aspect of modern correctional administration in America is that many prison populations include growing numbers of extremely violent, predatory individuals. This, in part, is due to the emergence of prison gangs that seek to control internal drug trafficking and other illicit activity, and rely on threats, intimidation, assault, and murder to accomplish their objectives. Another threat to prison security comes from major offenders, who have immense outside assets, or lead sophisticated criminal organizations with

resources that make violent, outside-assisted escapes a very real possibility. Furthermore, the lack of an enforceable Federal death penalty for murderous activity in prison means that, especially for inmates already serving life without parole, there is little effective deterrent to murder while incarcerated. (1)

Prisoners don't necessarily see what the Bureau of Prisons see when they look at supermaxes. One prisoner described life in supermax at Marion this way:

> Some men at Marion have grown up here in the harshest hole ever constructed. Deprived for so long of a normal existence, our measure of self-worth is gauged by our capacity to endure whatever physical or psychological torture is thrust upon us. Men along the tiers boast of surviving brutal riots, of running gauntlets of club-wielding guards, of being starved and beaten in places like San Quentin, Attica and Huntsville. It is both an indictment of society and a human tragedy that the state of imprisonment in America has been allowed to degenerate to this level. (Bingham n.d., 25)

Supermaxes fascinate and horrify (depending on your point of view) the press, the public, and politicians. According to Professor David A. Ward, author of a forthcoming definitive work on Alcatraz and nationally known prison expert, despite the small number of prisoners they have confined, Alcatraz (250 prisoners) and Marion (350 prisoners) supermaxes "have been responsible for more newspaper and magazine articles, more movies and television spots, more hearings before congressional committees, and more debates among criminologists and penologists than have been produced by all other federal prisons combined." Alcatraz confined some of the most notorious crime figures in our history—Al Capone, John Dillinger, Pretty Boy Floyd, and Baby Face Nelson.

According to Professor Ward, "Marion contained a small, special unit to hold the country's high-visibility spies, an 'avowed racist' serial killer, and the country's most famous prison writer, Jack Abbott, author of *In the Belly of the Beast*." Marion is the "end of the line" for the "worst of the worst" prisoners. In supermaxes, prisoners are locked in their cells for 23 hours a day. Whenever convicts leave their cells, they are handcuffed, their legs are chained, and three guards armed with nightsticks surround them. There are no programs and most prisoners are there indefinitely, many of them for the rest of their lives (Earley 1992, 30; Ward 1994, 81, 90).

Supermaxes cost a lot of money, about twice as much as maximum security prisons (Morris 2001, 394). Chase Riveland (1999) who headed the Washington State correctional system for over a decade and surveyed supermaxes for the National Institute of Corrections, explained why supermaxes are so expensive:

> These facilities are significantly more expensive to build than traditional general population prisons, due in part to the enhanced and extensive security features on locks, doors, and perimeters; reinforced walls, ceilings, and floors; and, frequently, the incorporation of advanced electronic systems and technology. Their operating costs have proven to be much greater also. Providing meals and other services at individual cell fronts, multiple-officer escorts and maintenance of the elaborate electronic systems are examples of things that add up quickly. The number of correctional officers required to assure both internal and external security, movement of inmates, security searches of cells, and the delivery of food and other supplies and services to individual cells generally drives staffing ratios—and therefore operating costs—much higher than those of general population prisons. (2)

Are supermaxes worth the price? Relying on anecdotes, supporters of supermaxes say they've reduced assaults and other serious incidents against prisoners and staff throughout the prison system, not just in the supermaxes. But, Commissioner Riveland says there's no hard data "comparing" these anecdotal claims of success with the costs of obtaining them. Further, in a long but important commentary on what we know about the impact of supermaxes, Commissioner Riveland writes:

> The cost, cost benefit, operating, legal, and ethical/moral issues of such facilities also raise a great deal of debate. Little is known about the impact of locking an inmate in an isolated cell for an average of 23 hours per day with limited human interaction, little constructive activity, and an environment that assures maximum control over the individual. Are potential negative effects greater after an individual has been in such a facility for three months, one year, three years, five years or more? Do extended isolation, absence of normal stimuli, and a controlling environment result in damage to an inmate's psyche? Research in this area is sparse. That which does exist tends to focus on the eventual recidivist criminal behavior—either in or out of prison—rather than on the potential psychological damage to the inmate....
>
> The impact of supermax facilities on staff working there has also been the subject of much discussion over the last several years ranging from the need to pick very experienced staff to the heightened levels of stress they experience. Having to deal on a daily basis with inmates proven to be the most troublesome—in an environment that prioritizes human control and isolation—presents line staff supervisors and facility and administrators with extraordinary challenges. Correctional administrators with experience in operating supermax facilities talk about the potential for creating a "we/they syndrome" between staff and inmates. The nature and reputation of the inmate and frequently

the behavior combined with ultra-control and rigidity magnify the tension between inmates and staff. When there is little interaction except in control situations, the adversarial nature of the relationships tends to be one of dominance and, in return, resistance on both sides. (Riveland 1999, 2)

New-Generation Maximum Security Prisons   Not all maximum security prisons fit the description of either the traditional or the supermax prisons. In the 1970s, a new idea for both building and managing maximum security prisons arose. **New-generation maximum security prisons** are based on the idea that offenders are sent to prison *as* punishment, not *for* punishment (Chapter 12). These prisons are built to allow both the architecture and management to contribute to a safe, humane confinement where the confinement itself is supposed to be the punishment. (See "Prison Management" later.)

New-generation prisons usually contain six to eight physically separated units within a secure perimeter. Each unit contains forty to fifty prisoners, with a cell for each inmate. Each also has dining rooms, a laundry, counseling offices, game rooms, and an enclosed outdoor recreation yard and work area. Because these units are only two levels high, there is continual surveillance from secure "bubbles," monitoring all prisoners' interactions with each other and staff. These self-contained units can keep many prisoners secure in groups small enough to participate in group activities. The design also permits specialization. One unit focuses on drug dependency. Another houses prisoners attending school. A third concentrates on work projects. Another is reserved for those with disciplinary problems (Ward and Schoen 1981, 9–11).

New-generation prisons are still maximum security prisons. For example, prisoners at Oak Park Heights (Minnesota's state-of-the-art new-generation prison) are under constant surveillance and can't move anywhere without officers. Prisoners do have some choices—they can work, go to school, or get treatment. But there are lots of things they *can't* do, like sit in their cells doing nothing (Table 11.3).

Medium and mimum security prisons

Most prisoners are not in maximum security prisons (Figure 11.6); they're confined in **medium security prisons** surrounded by barbed wire fences. Medium security prisons are less focused on security than maximum security prisons. Newer medium security facilities are commonly dormitories or other shared living quarters. Prisoners work without constant supervision. But, medium security prisons do have several security practices that resemble maximum security prisons—like head counts and surveillance (Singer 1983, 1204).

Minimum security prisons tend to be newer than maximum and medium security prisons; most were built

TABLE 11.3

Daily Schedule, Oak Park Heights New-Generation Maximum Security Prison

Time	Activity
6:30	Wake up
6:45–6:55	Live count—must show movement
7:00–7:20	Breakfast
7:35	Report to work
7:35–11:25	Work or program—receiving and orientation
11:25–11:40	Return to unit—stand-up count
11:40–12:15	Lunch
12:15	Return to work
12:15–3:25	Work or program—receiving and orientation
1:50–2:00	Education only—down to gym
2:00–3:30	Education only—mandatory gym
2:50–3:00	Verification count
3:25–3:35	Return to unit—verification count
3:35–4:50	Free time
4:50–5:00	Stand-up count
5:00–5:30	Dinner
5:30–8:30	Evening program
8:30–9:55	Evening program—free time
10:00	Stand-up count—inmates are locked
10:55–11:55	Shift change—live count
1:00	Live count
3:00	Live count
5:00	Live count

SOURCE: Minnesota Department of Corrections.

after 1950. Vocational training and treatment, not security, are their main focus. Minimum security prisoners are mainly first-time, nonviolent, white-collar and younger offenders who are not considered dangerous or likely to escape.

Minimum security prisons look a lot like college campuses, with low buildings surrounded by a recreational area. Critics call them country clubs or, in the case of federal minimum security prisons, "Club Fed" because of incarcerated Wall Street inside traders caught spending their afternoons there sunbathing and playing tennis.

Minimum security prisons emphasize trust and a normal lifestyle. Prisoners eat in small groups, often at tables for four, instead of at long rows of tables that all face in one direction, a common feature of maximum and medium security prisons. Minimum security prisoners also have some privacy, including private rooms with doors prisoners can lock.

Most minimum security prisons also offer some programs, including vocational training, academic education, and counseling. A fair number of prisoners are released for the day on work-study programs that allow them to hold jobs and attend neighboring schools and colleges. Some provide family visiting facilities for **conjugal visits** where prisoners can stay with their families for up to three days at a time (Singer 1983, 1203–1204).

Women's prisons

Most women's prisons combine maximum, medium, and minimum security levels in the same prison. Most of the time, a single cottage, dormitory, or wing is all that's needed to house maximum security women prisoners. At the other end of the security level, "honor cottages" confine minimum security prisoners. There are separate sections based on age groups, programs, and sentence lengths. Most women's prisons are less gloomy than men's because they tend to be located in rural settings, there's hardly any security equipment, and many have a cottage architecture and private rooms.

Private Prisons

Private prisons are built and managed by private companies under contract with the government. In 1989, Texas became the first state to open a private prison in the United States—four of them, in fact—two operated by Corrections Corporation of America and the other two by Wackenhut Corrections Corporation. By 2000, there were 264 private prisons in the United States.

Private participation in criminal justice is nothing new in our history. From colonial times until the 1850s, police patrols and detective work were private (Chapter 4). So was prosecution; until the 1850s, victims had to hire lawyers to prosecute their cases (Chapter 7). Private defense attorneys still play a major role (Chapter 7). Probation began as a private and often charitable operation in the middle of the nineteenth century (Chapter 10).

Private prison management isn't new either. In 1825, a merchant, Joel Scott, offered to pay the state of Kentucky $1000 to lease him all the prisoners in the inefficiently run and costly Frankfort prison. In return for the right to work the prisoners, Scott agreed to house, clothe, and feed them; and he promised further to pay the state half the profits made from the convict labor. This arrangement, which lasted until the 1880s, reported profits and no mistreatment of prisoners. Throughout the South and West, states followed Kentucky's example, contracting prisoners out to work in coal mines and factories and to build roads and railroads. Under pressure from organized labor and manufacturers who didn't hire contract prison labor, most states abandoned the contract labor system by 1900; these groups opposed the system because it competed unfavorably with free labor (McDonald 1992, 380).

Private companies have contracted with government to provide health care, prison industry, counseling, education, and food service for decades without controversy (Harding 2001, 267). We should keep this long history of private participation in criminal justice in mind as we discuss private prisons (and jails), which became a highly controversial issue in the 1980s when corporations got into the country's biggest growth industry—

imprisonment of adults for profit. When Corrections Corporation of America made a gutsy proposal to take over the whole state of Tennessee's corrections system in 1985, corrections professionals and policy makers set off a full-blown debate (McDonald 1992, 362). They raised several key issues:

1. Are private prisons constitutional?
2. Do they save money?
3. Do they work?

The constitutional question boils down to whether the state can give up its responsibility to punish criminals. No, say some, like Professor John DiIulio (Harding 2001):

> To remain legitimate and morally significant, the authority to govern behind bars, to deprive citizens of their liberty, to coerce (and even kill) them must remain in the hands of government authorities. Regardless of which penological theory is in vogue, the message that those who abuse liberty shall live without it is the brick and mortar of every correctional facility—a message that ought to be conveyed by the offended community of law abiding citizens through its public agents to the incarcerated individual. (274)

Yes, the state can delegate its power to punish, says Charles Logan (quoted in McDonald 1992), one of the pioneer researchers of private prisons:

> The state does not *own* the right to punish; it merely *administers* it in trust on behalf of the people and under the rule of law. Because the authority does not originate with the state it does not attach inherently or uniquely to it, and can be passed along to private agencies. (408)

Who's right? We don't know because the U.S. Supreme Court hasn't spoken on the matter.

We *do* know that more important than legalities to most legislatures and the public is whether private corporations can save tax dollars. On one side, we have those who *believe* private businesses can do everything better than government and, on the other side, those who *believe* businesses are only interested in growing and making money and so they can't possibly do what's best for the people. Unfortunately, we don't have hard evidence to back up either side (Harding 2001, 283–285).

The final and maybe the most important question is, "Do private prisons work?" First, we have to define what we mean by work. A prison that "works" is one where prisoners don't leave prison in *worse* shape than when they arrived. According to Richard Harding (2001):

> The prison experience is notorious for causing further deterioration in offenders' ability to cope upon release into the outside world. Public antagonism or

indifference to humanitarian issues and philosophical disillusionment with rehabilitation should not distract from this fundamental point. A penal objective . . . to suit the temper of our times would be to try to insure that prisoners do not undergo further social or character deformation while incarcerated. (325)

Do prisoners leave prison in worse shape than when they arrived? Once again, the answer as I write this is, we don't know. McDonald and his colleagues (1998) summed up the state of our knowledge this way:

Perhaps the most striking aspect of this research literature is that it is so sparse and that so few government agencies have chosen to evaluate the performance of their contractors formally. Even though there exist overall over a hundred privately operated secure confinement facilities [in the United States], there have been very few systematic attempts to compare their performance to that of public facilities. Most government agencies have been satisfied with monitoring compliance with the terms of the contracts. (65)

⊚ **11-3 You Decide: Should we privatize jails and prisons?** Full report of McDonald study

Prison Management

Prisons are run according to several management styles. Dr. George Beto, former director of the Texas Department of Corrections, adopted a **control model of management,** a style started during the 1800s at the famous Elmira Reformatory. The control model emphasized prisoner obedience, work, and education. Beto ran every prison in Texas as a maximum security prison. He believed prisoners needed order, and that only through order could they develop work and educational skills that would make their lives in prison more productive and also help them return successfully to life outside prison. Beto ran a tight prison. The warden made the rules, and they were enforced through a strict line of authority that ran from Beto through the assistant wardens all the way down to the most junior correctional officers. Prisoners *and* staff had to live and work according to rules spelled out in writing. Prisoners walked between painted lines in the corridors; loud talking was a punishable offense. Life in Beto's prisons was a busy routine of numbering, counting, checking, locking, and monitoring prisoner movement to and from work, training, education, and treatment.

Professor John DiIulio (1987), who studied prison management styles in Texas, Michigan, and California, found that under Beto's control model of management:

[O]fficers had a sense of mission, an esprit de corps, and an amazing knowledge of the prison's history. Treatment and work opportunities were offered on a regular basis and well administered. . . . In short, life

inside the Walls [the oldest prison in Texas] was in general safe, humane, productive, calm, stable, and predictable. (105)

Prisoners who broke the rules got the stick of quick and specific punishment—solitary confinement and heavier work. Prisoners who followed orders, worked, and "did their own time" got the carrot of the most liberal **good time** (time taken off prison time for good behavior) rules in American prisons—two days off for every productive, problem-free day served (DiIulio 1987, 107).

Despite Beto's masterful management, the control model has its shortcomings. In Texas, it suffered from the **building-tender system,** which relied on prisoners to help officers manage cell blocks. According to Dr. Beto:

In any contemporary prison, there is bound to be some level of inmate organization, some manner of inmate society. . . . The question is this: who selects the leaders? Are the inmates to select them? Or is the administration to choose them or at least influence the choice? If the former, the extent of control over organized and semi-organized inmate life is lessened; if the latter, the measure of control is strengthened. (DiIulio 1987, 112)

In practice, the building-tender system was a not very pretty prisoner-boss system: Race and ethnic prison gangs ran major parts of the Texas prison system; violence, exploitation, fear, and disruption followed (Martin and Ekland-Olson 1987).

At the other extreme, the Michigan prison system adopted a **responsibility management approach.** This model stresses the responsibility of prisoners for their own actions instead of administrative control of prisoners' behavior. All prisoners—even in maximum security prisons—should get a significant degree of freedom and then be held accountable for their actions. According to one Michigan administrator:

We go by the idea that prison should be as unrestrictive as possible. Don't misunderstand. Order comes first. You have to keep control. Security is number one through one thousand. But we don't have to smother people to keep things under control. We try to show inmates respect and expect it in return. We are more willing than Texas to give them air and then hold them accountable. . . . We attempt to operate safely in the least restrictive environment possible. . . . If Texas opts for the most restrictive, we opt for the least restrictive. (DiIulio 1987, 119–20)

The responsibility model isn't free of problems. For one thing, it requires enormous paperwork. Also, it caused animosity among officers toward the "brass" at corrections department headquarters in Lansing. According to one 30-year veteran officer:

I'd love to have a prison that could run the way the model says. But we've got a little problem: impulsive convicts and human nature. . . . This system deprives inmates of the right to safety in the name of giving them other rights. . . . A cellblock should be like a residential street. Would you want to live on a street where your neighbors were always shouting? Where most of what they shouted was vulgar and violent? Would you permit your neighbors to assault you and each other? (DiIulio 1987, 127)

Of course, it's not perfect, but Michigan prisons have provided more humane, safe, and secure confinement than many other state prisons.

Prison management reflects the personality and management style of prison wardens. Some believe it was George Beto's personality that accounted for the success of the control model in Texas prisons. Similarly, it isn't just the architecture of the new-generation prison at Oak Park Heights, Minnesota, that accounts for its low level of serious violence, suicide, and drug use. The architecture has its counterpart in the new management philosophy that accompanies it. Warden Frank Wood (and his successors) exemplified this new management philosophy, which requires personal interaction among the warden, inmates, and staff. Wood spent more than 25 percent of his time, in his words, "eyeball to eyeball" with inmates and staff. He personally conducted the final prisoner orientation meeting that makes them "understand their responsibilities and the prison's responsibilities to them."

Now retired, Wood still has great charisma. (When he entered the room at a recent retirement dinner for one of my colleagues all heads turned toward him, even those who didn't know he was.) He inspired many of his staff, several of whom are now wardens. They're firmly committed to the management style Wood started in the 1970s (Crist 2001). The following principles and practices guide this management style:

- "Staff should treat the inmates as we would want our sons, brothers, or fathers—and in women's prisons our daughters, sisters, and mothers—to be treated."
- If inmates don't work or go to school, they can't watch TV and "roam around their units"; they're locked in their cells.
- The response to troublemaking is individual—not group—punishment.
- Units are locked up on a random, regular basis for three to four days to "purge contraband."
- Every lock is tested every day.
- Inmates are kept very busy.
- The staff listen to every inmate request, however unimportant the requests may appear.
- Inmates are periodically rotated into the prison's mental health unit for observation and a change of environment, and for relief from nearby inmates and staff. (Ward 1987)

Corrections Officers

Corrections officers used to be called guards because of the misguided belief that their primary missions were protecting the public by preventing escape and controlling prisoners by keeping order. Newer thinking takes into account the reality that officers have to do a lot more than "merely opening and closing doors." Stan Stojkovic and Rick Lovell (1992) say corrections officers have to play the roles of "father, mother, babysitter, counselor, priest, and police officer to prisoners." Still, their primary missions remain to watch and guard prisoners. They watch them while they work, go to school, eat, exercise, relax, and sleep. They escort them to the doctor when they're sick or injured, to court when they have hearings, and to visits with their families on visiting day. They sit in towers to watch the prison walls and in cubicles to guard the areas inside prison and the gates between the outside world and prison (Jacobs 1983, 115–132).

The most important duty of officers is accounting for every prisoner at all times (called the **count**). Even one prisoner unaccounted for shuts down all operations and movement. Officers face disciplinary action for miscounting.

Guarding and watching prisoners is dangerous. Prisoners outnumber officers by as much as 50 to 1, so officers have to depend more on their communication skills than on their physical power to protect themselves, control prisoners, and prevent escape. On "ordinary" days, prisoners could assault and injure. During riots, prisoners might take them hostage, beat, rape, and kill them (Ross 1981, part I).

For officers on tower duty, it's also lonely and isolated. These officers have no contact with anyone except by telephone or walkie-talkie. They can't read, listen to the radio, or watch television. Tower guards remind prisoners as no one or nothing else can of the difference between the prisoners and those keeping them locked up (Toch 1978, 19–37).

To better understand the world of corrections officers, let's look more closely at the supervision hierarchy, women and minority corrections officers, officer training, and the growing power of their unions.

The supervision hierarchy

Sergeants, lieutenants, and captains supervise the line officers. Sergeants supervise cell blocks, work units, kitchens, and hospitals. They check correctional officers' work, assign them to specific tasks, and even fill in for absentees. In traditional prisons, social distance separates line officers from lieutenants and captains. True to the operations of any paramilitary organization, corrections officers receive orders from their superior officers and are expected to carry out efficiently and effectively.

Lieutenants act as prison police officers who keep the peace by stopping fights and other prison disturbances. They have to maintain order by "walking" prisoners to isolation or forcibly removing them from cells when necessary. When they're not settling disturbances, they go on preventive patrol, checking and "shaking down" prisoners for weapons and other contraband. Lieutenants police not only the prisoners but also the line officers. They search lower-ranking officers for contraband and weapons, just as they do prisoners. Lieutenants check on both prisoners and officers to make sure they're doing their jobs. Further, lieutenants write disciplinary reports, called "tickets," on officers, just as officers write them on prisoners. The few captains manage the loads of paperwork required by bureaucracy—personnel evaluations, budget preparations, and disciplinary committee reports.

Women and minority corrections officers

Traditionally, the process for selecting officers gave high priority to physical standards—height, weight, and general strength. So male officers always guarded male prisoners until the 1970s when affirmative action lawsuits and federal and state legislation started to change that. By 1986, 6 percent of corrections officers were women (Zimmer 1986, 1). By 1999, women made up one-third of the ranks (Bureau of Justice Statistics 2001e, Table 13).

Prison administrators resisted having women officers in men's prisons because they believed women's physical weakness would allow male prisoners to overpower and assault them. There has been little evidence to support this belief. In Illinois, none of the thirty-nine women officers and twenty-eight women trainees serving in medium and maximum security men's prisons were attacked by men prisoners (Hunter 1986, 12–13). And corrections officials in New York regard gender integration as a success, despite one knife attack on a woman officer in Attica (Jacobs 1983, 178–201).

A female correctional officer in San Quentin suggests that despite men's reluctance to have women colleagues, the presence of women officers has made male correctional officers less brutal:

> [Having women in the pen] brings about a calmer setting. It also forces male officers not to act as "big, bad and tough" because here they have this little 5'2", 115 lb. woman standing beside them, putting a guy that is 6'4", 230 lbs. in cuffs saying, "Come on now, act right," and not having any problem doing it. Whereas he might have to go in there with two or three other guys and tackle him down to cuff him. It also forces them to recognize that they can't go home and talk about how bad and mean they are and what a tough day they have had because some little chickie can do the same thing he is doing. (Owen 1985, 158)

About 25 percent of corrections officers are Black and about 6 percent are Hispanic, considerably less than their representation among prisoner populations but growing rapidly (Bureau of Justice Statistics 2001e, 3). Some say adding non-White officers will improve guard work, but it's not clear whether this is true. Psychologists Craig Haney, Curtis Banks, and Philip Zimbardo (1973) found:

> Although the black corrections officers are younger, more urban, better educated, and more liberal than their white colleagues, there were no consistent differences in their attitudes toward prisoners, staff, correctional goals, or their occupation. (163)

The famous Stanford Prison Experiment suggests the role officers play is far more important than their sex or race in determining how they do their work. In that experiment, some students acted as officers and others as prisoners. Some officers whatever their gender or race just enjoyed their dominant position and harassed prisoners:

> In less than a week the experience of imprisonment undid (temporarily) a lifetime of learning: human values were suspended, self-concepts were challenged and the ugliest, most base, pathological side of human nature surfaced. We were horrified because we saw some boys (guards) treat others as if they were despicable animals, taking pleasure in cruelty. (Owen 1985)

Training

The U.S. Bureau of Prisons conducts a prison officer training program that covers typical subjects like custodial care, disciplinary procedures, report writing, and other people-processing duties. But it does more. It offers a 40-hour introduction to interpersonal communications, with a 12-hour segment devoted to improving staff relations. According to some experts, training also ought to include "a liberal component" to help officers "to be more tolerant, more capable of accepting difference, and generally more sympathetic (in the best sense) to the prisoner's position" (Hawkins 1976, 105).

But training isn't a cure-all according to the Joint Commission on Correctional Manpower and Training. The commission maintains that "too often [officers] receive little useful direction from management or professionally trained staff, and they find themselves in something of a sink-or-swim situation." Gordon Hawkins (1976) says this problem is hard to solve because

> unfortunately, there is little scientific knowledge about handling offender populations, few principles for consistent practice, and almost no provision for assessing the value of particular measures in various situations. Custodial staff generally operate on the basis of lore which has made for continued improvements in practice in other fields and occupations. Very little has been written on group management practices with confined offenders. What there is has come mainly from social scientists and has little relevance for the line practitioner. (101)

11-4 You Decide: Do you want to be a corrections officer? Corrections officer as a career.

Corrections officers' unions

One of the side effects of the prison population boom is the dramatic reversal of fortune of corrections officers' unions. In 1980, the unions were weak, disorganized, and ineffective. Now they're a powerful force. For example, the California Correctional Peace Officers Association grew from a membership of 4000 to 23,000 officers. Their officers now make a lot more money than California schoolteachers and associate professors at the University of California. With its newfound power, the Illinois union was able to kill legislation to make Illinois prisons private (King 1998, 618–619).

■ JAILS

Don't confuse jails with prisons. A **jail** is a county or municipal facility for keeping adults while they wait for trial or for punishing them for less than a year after they're convicted. In contrast, prisons are state institutions where prisoners are locked up after they're convicted if their sentence is for more than a year. That's the formal definition. In practice, according to Professor Richard Frase (1998):

> Jails lie at the center of the criminal justice system. They are intimately related to every stage of pretrial and post trial procedure and are the detention facility that affects the community most directly and most frequently. . . . (474)

In addition to detention before and incarceration after conviction, jails hold all of the following people:

- Juveniles waiting to be transferred to juvenile facilities
- Adults waiting to be transferred to facilities in other counties, states, the federal government, or the military
- Adults waiting for mental facility commitment hearings
- Adults held as material witnesses
- Adults in protective custody
- Adults in contempt of court
- Probationers waiting for revocation hearings (Chapter 10)
- Parolees waiting for revocation hearings (Chapter 10)
- Felons waiting for transfer to prison after conviction
- Prison inmates waiting for trial on new charges, to testify as witnesses, or as plaintiffs in lawsuits against the government (Chapter 12) (Bureau of Justice Statistics 2001a, 2)

Looking at this long list of what jails do, it's easy to see why Professor Frase (1998) says jails are "at the center of the criminal justice system" and the "detention facility that affects the community most directly and most frequently." It's also easy to understand why he calls jails "the custodial dumping ground of last resort . . ." (474).

To better understand the role of jail in punishment of offenders, let's look at women incarcerated in jails, jail programs, jail conditions, and new-generation jails.

Women in Jail

Almost all of what we said about prison populations is true of jails, and what we're going to say about prisoners is true of the people detained in jail, so we won't repeat that here. But one difference does need emphasizing: According to the last jail census (Bureau of Justice Statistics 2001a, Table 5), most jails hold both men and women (90 percent men, 10 percent women), and the proportion of women in jails is growing (from 6 percent in 1983 to 11.2 percent in 1999). Despite their growing numbers, women in jail are at a disadvantage:

> Women are frequently denied access to the cafeteria and recreational facilities and confined to a specific floor, wing, or cell for the duration of their confinement. By far the most common medical problems of incarcerated women are gynecological or obstetric. . . . Yet medical services of jails, when provided, are usually [by] physicians accustomed to and primarily concerned with men. (Advisory Commission 1984, 14)

This quote comes from a 1984 report, but it was still true in 1995, even in separate jails for women (Gray, Mays, and Stohr 1995, 187).

Jail Programs

According to the latest jail census (Bureau of Justice Statistics 2001a, 10), jails offer a variety of programs for their detainees (Table 11.4).

However, the numbers and percentages in Table 11.4 don't tell us anything about the *quality* of these services. Notice, too, there's nothing in the census about exercise and recreation. The American Correctional Association Standards say jail inmates should receive at least one hour of exercise and exercise outside their cells (weather-permitting, outdoors) every day. The reason for the standard isn't to provide enjoyment but to maintain order. Idleness, especially without radios and TV sets to relieve it, raises tension and violence and weakens mental and physical health (Advisory Commission 1984, 21).

TABLE 11.4

Jail Jurisdictions with Programs, 1999

Program	Number	Percent
EDUCATION		
Secondary	1,545	55%
Basic adult	696	25
Special	303	11
Study release	260	9
Vocational	182	6
College	94	3
COUNSELING		
Religious/spiritual	1,960	70%
Alcohol	1,724	61
Drug	1,528	54
Psychological	1,306	47
Life skills	601	21
Domestic violence	488	17
Pretrial services	468	17
Job seeking	411	15
HEALTH CARE DELIVERY SYSTEM		
Fee-for-service	1,101	39%
On-site staff	882	31
Managed care	500	18
Local government physicians	338	12
MENTAL HEALTH SERVICES		
Screening at intake	2,152	78%
Psychotropic medication	1,832	66
24-hour care	1,309	47
Routine therapy/counseling	1,283	46
Psychiatric evaluation	1,044	38

SOURCE: Bureau of Justice Statistics 2001a, Table 15.

Jail Conditions

Some jails are modern, safe, clean, and efficiently and humanely administered. In 1975, Ronald Goldfarb, a leading jail expert, described one that wasn't:

> I was shocked to discover conditions [in the Atlanta jail] so horrible I could not believe them. The jail was far worse than the state prisons I had just seen. Inside a relatively modern exterior in a modest, busy part of town was a cramped, dark, dank interior. Large four-sided cages each held sixteen men, with disheveled beds and an open toilet. Inmates are kept inside these cages twenty-four hours a day throughout their often prolonged stays at the Atlanta jail. There is no privacy . . . and artificial air and light. A dismal atmosphere, a constant din, and a wretched stench pervaded the place. (27)

In 1998, a grand jury found the Atlanta jail still a lot like Goldfarb described it in 1975. "Hundreds of inmates sleep shoulder-to-shoulder on bedrolls crammed into every open space on the concrete floors. . . . The walls leak when it rains. Toilets don't work. Medical care is wanting. 'It's falling apart,' said one lawyer in a lawsuit against the jail." After hearing this kind of testimony, U.S. District Judge Marvin Shoob ordered the jail to make sweeping changes. By October 2000 when Sheriff Jackie Barrett took Judge Shoob on a tour of the jail Judge Shoob liked what he saw:

> During the tour, Barrett was able to show Shoob the ongoing renovation of the jail, now more than half finished. Shoob saw some cellblocks with drab walls and stained ceilings and some hallways with concrete floors. He was then taken to the renovated units with fresh coats of paint and newly tiled floors. Walls and ceilings are highlighted with paintings of flowers and butterflies. "The judge's involvement has been helpful to us," Barrett said. "We hope this will set a trend, set a model for other counties. It's been a good thing.
>
> [Former medical director of the jail Robert] Greifinger showed Shoob the medical records room, which he said was once so disorganized he could find only one out of five files he was seeking. The files, now color-coded and well-organized and categorized, are easy to locate, the doctor said. Greifinger then showed Shoob a small room used to clean dental equipment. When he was appointed in January, Greifinger said, equipment was dumped in a sink and hardly cleaned before being used on the next patient. "It was as if they were taking soiled instruments and reusing them in the next person's mouth," he said, noting that this could easily spread HIV, hepatitis and many other transmittable diseases. The room is now sparkling clean with proper sterilization equipment. Greifinger also noted that, previously, there were no sinks in the medical examination rooms, so doctors and nurses couldn't wash their hands between patients. "It seemed like the medical staff at the Fulton County Jail had not learned those basic hygienic lessons of the 19th century," he said. That has since been addressed. (Rankin 2000, 3b)

 11-5 The full details of the changes in the Atlanta jail

New-Generation Jails

The scene resembles a college dormitory with a student union lounge attached. At one end of a large, colorful room, a handful of young men are watching television; in another area, a second group watches a different set. Two inmates are playing ping-pong. A group of inmates goes up to the uniformed deputy, who is chatting amiably with someone, and asks him for the volleyball. He gives it to them, and they rush out the door to the recreation yard. Another man pads from the shower room to his private room, where he closes the door for privacy.

The area is bright, sunny, and clean. The furniture—sofas and chairs—is comfortable and clean. The carpet on the floor is unstained. No one has scratched his initials in the paint or on the butcher-block tables and desks. Windows allow a view of the outside. Despite all the activity, the room is relatively quiet. The television volume is low, and no one is shouting. (Gettinger 1984, 1)

This quote describes a **new-generation jail,** a concept supported by prestigious bodies like the Advisory Board of the National Institute of Corrections, the American Jail Association, the American Institute of Architects' Committee on Architecture for Criminal Justice, and the American Correctional Association. New-generation jails combine a new approach to architecture, management philosophy, operation, and training. This combination has changed a few jails. When the Federal Bureau of Prisons, traditionally an innovative force in American corrections, developed the new-generation jail concept based on the confinement model of prisons (lock people up *as* punishment not *for* punishment), the basic directive of the Bureau of Prisons was: "If you can't rehabilitate, at least do no harm." Three federal Metropolitan Correctional Centers (MCCs) were built in Chicago, New York, and San Diego to provide humane, secure detention (Weiner, Frazier, and Farbstein 1987, 40).

Architecturally, new-generation jails have a **podular design,** which allows constant surveillance (Figure 11.7) compared to traditional jails, which have a **linear design** (a corridor lined with cells) officers can see into only when they walk down the hallways (Figure 11.8). So, in traditional jails, officers can only control the area they see; prisoners control the rest. In new-generation jails, officers control most of the jail most of the time.

The podular design includes the following characteristics:

- Security concentration along the outside perimeter with impregnable walls and windows
- Restricted movement inside the jail—unit officers do not have keys; an officer in a control booth can allow movement in and out of the unit by closed-circuit TV and intercom
- Free movement and as few barriers as possible inside living units
- Living units with fewer than fifty prisoners to give officers an unobstructed view of the entire area
- Private rooms for prisoners
- Standard building materials for both cost and appearance

At first, new-generation jails were viewed as soft on criminals; critics accused them of providing inmates with a luxury motel at public expense. But the new jails report as much as 90 percent fewer violent incidents. Private rooms allow prisoners to go to their own rooms to cool off, thereby preventing violent responses to incidents. Homosexual rape has almost disappeared. Vandalism and graffiti have nearly vanished. For example, the jail at Pima, Arizona, reported:

- Damaged mattresses dropped from 150 a year to none.
- Repairs to TV sets dropped from two repairs a week to two repairs in two years.

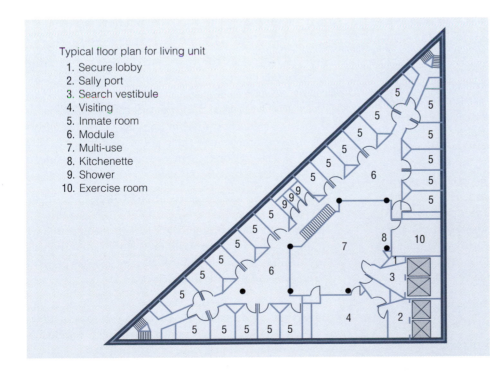

Typical floor plan for living unit

1. Secure lobby
2. Sally port
3. Search vestibule
4. Visiting
5. Inmate room
6. Module
7. Multi-use
8. Kitchenette
9. Shower
10. Exercise room

FIGURE 11.7
Podular Design
SOURCE: Federal Bureau of Prisons n.d

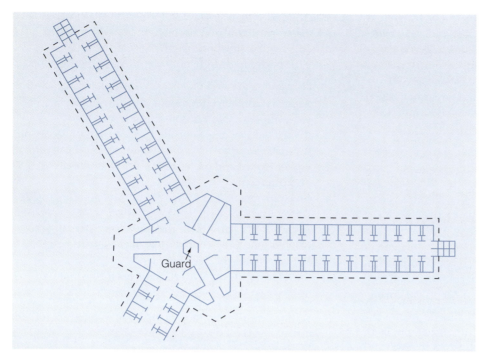

FIGURE 11.8
Linear Design
SOURCE: Federal Bureau of Prisons n.d.

■ Destroyed prisoner clothes dropped from an average 99 sets of clothes every week to 15 in two years. (Weiner, Frazier, and Farbstein 1987, 42)

These reductions have occurred without increases in construction and maintenance costs.

Architecture isn't the only reason for the success of new-generation jails; direct supervision has replaced old-style management. "You can't run a new-generation jail with old-generation management," said one new commander whose revamped podular design "had turned into a nightmare for staff and inmates." Direct supervision places officers in constant contact with prisoners, which allows officers to get to know prisoners and thereby recognize and respond to trouble before it escalates into violence. Negotiation and verbal communication replace physical force. Women officers, who make up 40 percent of direct supervision jails, are as effective in this role as male officers (Gettinger 1984, 20–21).

New-generation jails have had positive effects not only on prisoners and budgets but also on staff. Better surroundings benefit staff as much as, perhaps more than, prisoners, because in the long run staff spend more time in the jail than prisoners. According to Richard Weiner and his associates (1987), jails that are clean, vandalism- and graffiti-free, carpeted, less noisy, safe, and peaceful also help staff morale: "Officers and inmates [agree] that direct supervision works better than traditional approaches. Most of the officers acknowledged that what was good for the inmates helped them as well, by improving conditions and reducing tension" (42).

Stephen H. Gettinger (1984) reports:

The relatively pleasant atmosphere of the new-generation jail is designed with the officer in mind even more than the inmate. Without fear of assault, officers can relax and pay attention to their jobs. They are encouraged to mix actively with the inmates and are given authority to solve problems on their own. Officers learn leadership skills that will serve them well on the streets and equip them for management roles in the future. This job is more satisfying. (5)

Another side benefit to officer satisfaction is operating costs go down because staff absenteeism drops, in some places by as much as 40 percent.

Patrick G. Jackson and Cindy A. Stearns (1995) evaluated the new-generation jail in Sonoma County, California. Sonoma County built their jail after a federal court declared the conditions in the old jail unconstitutional. According to Jackson and Stearns:

[T]he cramped and poorly ventilated old jail was dirty, was loud, smelled, and, for most of the 225-or-so inmates and a much smaller staff, had all the negative trappings that go along with intermittent surveillance in linear facilities: a climate of fear, an absence of privacy, a lack of positive leadership, and so on. (205–206)

The new Sonoma County jail opened in 1991. A state-of-the art jail, it includes the two cornerstones of new-generation jails. First, it has podular architecture, including five two-tiered living quarters shaped in a semicircle facing an officers' station that is not enclosed by bars or glass barriers. Each "pod" contains a medical unit and a recreational area exposed to natural light, showers, carpeted floors, TV, and telephones. Wall-to-wall carpet and acoustical ceilings reduce noise, pastel-painted walls improve appearance, and plenty of inexpensive wood and plastic furniture replaces the harsh metal of traditional jails.

Second, it uses direct supervision. Correctional officers are trained extensively in interpersonal communications. They manage problems proactively. Continuous, direct, and personal supervision is supposed to put control of the jail in the hands of the officers, not the inmates. Inmates are managed by positive reinforcement, not by "brute force or steel bars" (Jackson and Stearns 1995, 207).

Jackson and Stearns (1995) measured the attitudes, perceptions, and behaviors of inmates in the old jail, before transfer, and in the new jail, after transfer. They found that women experienced the conditions of confinement in the new-generation jail differently from men. Men's perceptions of jail improved while women experienced increased dissatisfaction. The researchers suspect that the reason for this difference lies in the new-generation jail philosophy that

> seeks to lessen the development, breadth, intensity, and/or continuity of interpersonal networks or peer groups that might be perceived as supportive of inmate control of an institution. It is precisely these kinds of relationships between inmates that past research suggests has been of differential importance to female and male inmates. (215)

New-generation jails are a lot more expensive than traditional jails. Besides, they're harder to "sell" to the public because they're viewed as not harsh enough and therefore susceptible to the charge that they "coddle criminals." Also, administrators and managers remain skeptical of direct supervision, despite support among hard-line corrections officers and criminal justice professors (Logan and Gaes 1993, 256–257).

■ PRISONERS

We have good and recent numbers about the greatest change in prisoners—their vastly increased numbers. We also know that a growing proportion of prisoners are being locked up for drug offenses. We also have good and recent numbers about the main demographic constants—most prisoners are male, young, and Black or Hispanic, although women and Hispanic prisoners are making up a larger proportion of the prison population. Our other demographics, the latest official numbers, come from 1991 when the U.S. Bureau of Justice Statistics conducted a survey of state prisoners (Bureau of Justice Statistics

1993). According to the numbers in that survey, which probably haven't changed a lot, we can say:

- Most didn't live with both parents when they were growing up.
- Over a quarter had parents who abused alcohol and drugs.
- A third had a brother who served time in jail or prison.
- Less than half have been married.
- Almost three-quarters haven't graduated from high school.
- Most are not gang members.
- A third weren't employed when they were arrested.
- A third were using drugs and a third were drinking alcohol when they committed the crime they're serving time for.
- Less than half were making more than $10,000 a year at the time they committed the crime they're serving time for.
- Ninety-four percent have committed crimes (not counting minor offenses) before the crime they're serving time for.
- The number of older prisoners is increasing.

 11-6 Full survey of state prisoners

Women Prisoners

According to the American Correctional Association, women were historically imprisoned for either theft or drug offenses. Even the few violent crimes committed by women were special cases. Women convicted of murder or manslaughter had usually killed men who abused them. Women convicted of robbery did not ordinarily instigate the crime.

The traditional reasons given for the relatively small number of women prisoners compared with men have included the virtuous nature of women, their dependent status, and the code of chivalry. However, the reasons for the steep rise in the number of women prisoners since 1980 are *not* women's loss of virtue and dependence, nor the decline in chivalry. According to Barbara Owen and Barbara Bloom (1995), who profiled women prisoners in California, it's because of the growing numbers of women prosecuted and convicted of drug offenses, the increasingly harsh sentences for drug offenses, and the lack of both treatment and community sanctions for women drug offenders. In fact, Owen and Bloom argue that the "war on drugs" is really a war on women (166).

Recidivists

Most prisoners are **recidivists** (repeat offenders) who have served time in prison at least once before. Depending on the researcher, recidivism has a variety of meanings. It can include all crimes including juvenile offenses; all prior arrests; all criminal charges; all convictions; or only prior commitments to prison or jail. Nearly 85 percent of prisoners aren't first-time offenders; they were sentenced to either probation or incarceration as adults or juveniles. More than one-fifth of all prisoners have been convicted six or more times. More than 60 percent have already spent time incarcerated for prior offenses. More than half have been convicted of at least one violent crime (Beck 1989; Bureau of Justice Statistics 1988b; Greenfield 1985, 1).

The longer former prisoners remain out of prison, the less likely they are to return. Also, recidivism varies according to offense. Property offenders return to prison more frequently (36.8 percent) than violent offenders (31.5 percent). Burglars return most frequently, followed by robbers. Drug offenders, forgers, embezzlers, and sex offenders follow robbers; homicide is last with the lowest recidivist rates. The more times prisoners are confined, the greater the likelihood they'll return to prison. About one-quarter of all prisoners with no prior record will return to prison; 37 percent of all prisoners with one or two prior prison terms will return; and 42.7 percent of those with three or more prior terms will be back in prison (Immarigeon and Chesney-Lind 1992; Wallerstedt 1984, 2–3).

Recidivism also varies with age, gender, and race. The younger prisoners are when they leave prison, the greater the chance they'll be back. In Massachusetts, for example, 31 percent of prisoners under age 25 will return to prison; between the ages of 25 and 29, 28 percent recidivate. At 30 and older, only 17 percent return to prison.

Gender also affects recidivism. Men recidivate at substantially higher rates than women. In New York State, for example, 36 percent of released men return to prison; 12.1 percent of women return. Women are less likely to recidivate when support services are available in the community. Most imprisoned women have "serious economic, medical, mental health, and social difficulties which are often overlooked and frequently intensified" in prison (Immarigeon and Chesney-Lind 1992). Community programs more effectively enable women to lead law-abiding lives than does imprisonment. In Pennsylvania, for example, the Program for Women Offenders found that its services reduced recidivism. In a random sample of more than one thousand clients, 3.2 percent recidivated. Intermediate sanctions such as home confinement and intensive supervision may also provide alternatives to imprisonment, if they include direct services (Immarigeon and Chesney-Lind 1992.)

Whites recidivate at significantly lower levels than other races. In California, for example, 27.9 percent of released Whites returned to prison, whereas Blacks returned at a rate of 33.5 percent (Wallerstedt, 1984, 5).

Prisoners' Crimes

Half of all prisoners are violent offenders. The other half are divided among property (20%), drug (20%), and public order (10%) offenders (Bureau of Justice Statistics 2001e, 12). These overall percentages hide some important points related to gender, race, and ethnicity. First, it hides the relationship between the percentages of prisoners in each group and their representation in the general population (depicted in Figure 11.2). Second, it doesn't shed light on the effect of the prison population explosion on gender, race, and ethnicity. Figure 11.9 shows the contribution made by the four types of offenses to the increased numbers of men, women, Black, and Hispanic prisoners. Notice that drug offenses are responsible for more than one-third of the growth in women prisoners. Compare that to the contribution drug offenses made to the increase in men, Blacks, and Hispanics. Also, notice the contribution violent offenses made to the rise in Hispanic prisoners—58 percent compared to 50 percent of the increase in Black and 47 percent in White prisoners.

Let's put the 20 percent total for drug offenders in prison in perspective (Figure 11.9). In 1980, 1 out of every 16 prisoners was a drug offender; by 2000, 1 out of every 5 was a drug offender. In raw numbers, there were 19,000 drug offenders in prison in 1980; in 2000 there were 251,000 (Bureau of Justice Statistics 2001e, Table 16; King 1998, 608).

 11-7 *Prisoners in 1999, Prisoners in 2000,* full reports

Special Management Prisoners

The number of prisoners who need special treatment is growing. These **special needs prisoners** fall into three groups:

1. *Vulnerable:* A rapidly growing group of inmates who need protection from other prisoners to survive in prison
2. *Troublemaker:* Prisoners who need added restraints to protect other inmates, staff, or the security of the institution
3. *Mentally abnormal:* Prisoners with mental problems or retardation who can't function in the general population without assistance or who need professional treatment and medication

Special needs prisoners create problems for the prison administration. According to a report of the National Institute of Justice (1985), "Prisons must handle large numbers of people in standardized ways if they are to stay within their budgets and if equity issues are not to be raised" (National Institute of Justice 1985).

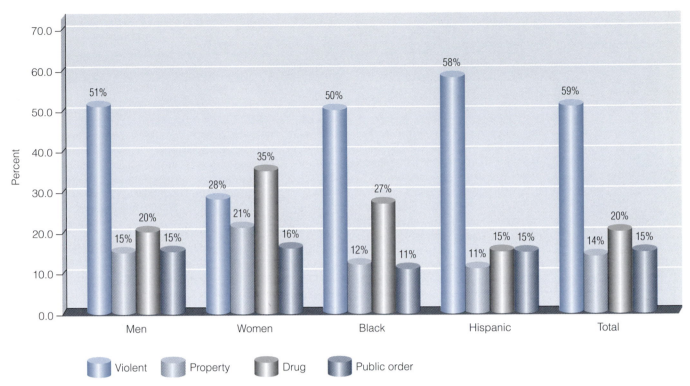

FIGURE 11.9
Percentage Growth of Prisoners by Offense, Gender, Race, and Ethnicity, 1990–1999

"You have three choices," said one prison administrator. "You can pitch your program to the majority of inmates, in which case the needs of special groups will not be met. You can tailor your efforts to the minority of special inmates, which means that the majority will suffer. Or you can run two separate programs" (National Institute of Justice 1985).

Length of Imprisonment

Earlier in the chapter, we stressed that we're sending many more people to prison. Here we look at another aspect of prisoners—how long we keep them there. Between 1985 and 1990, the average time prisoners actually stayed locked up increased only slightly—from 20 to 22 months. Between 1990 and 1999, the average increased to 28 months. Also, since 1990 the number of prisoners serving less than six months has dropped and the number serving at least ten years has risen. And, the projected length of actual time prisoners admitted in 1998 will serve has grown to 43 months (Bureau of Justice Statistics 1999a, 12; BJS 1999c).

Several factors affect the length of time prisoners serve. We've already discussed mandatory minimum sentences set by legislatures (Chapter 8). Judges and parole boards in indeterminate sentencing states still have discretion in deciding how long prisoners will stay locked up (Chapter 8). Forty states have good-time laws that allow

prisoners to reduce their sentences. There are three types of good-time release. Statutory good time is awarded at the time of sentencing; credits are deducted for misbehavior. In earned credit, prisoners start with no good time and earn it by positive behavior and participation in prison programs like education or vocational training. Special credits are awarded for exceptional acts like donating blood, for serving as subjects in medical experiments, or for exemplary behavior during emergencies. In most states, prisoners can get one day off their sentence for every good-time credit, but in some states they can get up to half their prison time off; in others, they get no days off (Criminal and Juvenile Justice Coordinating Council 1996).

The most common reasons for granting good time are that it's necessary to control prison populations and it helps rehabilitate prisoners. No empirical research supports either the control or rehabilitation of prisoners' hypotheses; empirical research does support the control prison population hypothesis. But research has demonstrated prisoners released early because of good time are no more likely to commit crimes than prisoners released after serving their full sentences (Criminal and Juvenile Justice Coordinating Council 1996).

The prison population explosion has made early release a controversial practice. More people are sentenced to prison for longer times, but prison administrators are coping with crowded prisons by releasing them early.

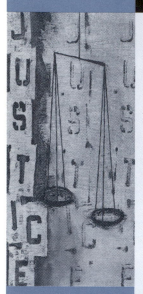

Most of the public, whatever their gender, race, or ethnic background, believes that violent and repeat offenders belong in prison. According to John DiIulio (1992), imprisonment is worth the cost. DiIulio and Anne Piehl analyzed prisoner self-report surveys that showed that the typical prisoner commits about twelve crimes a year. Crime depresses local business development and erodes local economic activity. According to some estimates, each street crime costs victims and society at least $2300 in pain, suffering, and economic loss. At the average of twelve street crimes a year, that amounts to $27,600 per year. That means it is cheaper in most states to lock up street criminals than to allow them to be free on the street, according to DiIulio (1992).

Moreover, imprisonment may also reduce crime, according to Patrick A. Langan 1991, 1568), a statistician for the Bureau of Justice Statistics. Langan examined admissions and releases to U.S. prisons to explain the steep rise in prison populations. He found that the increase in mandatory sentencing laws and the rise in the crime-prone age group population of the baby-boom era only partially explained the rise. More than half the increase, Langan found, was due to the increased use of imprisonment by sentencing judges. He also noted a decrease in crimes measured by victim surveys during the same period. Langan concluded:

> Whether rising incarceration rates have reduced crime . . . cannot be said with certainty. What is clear is that, since 1973, per capita prison incarceration rates have risen to their highest levels ever while crime rates measured in the National Crime Survey . . . have gradually fallen to their lowest levels ever. The changing age structure apparently does not explain most of the declines. Whatever the causes, in 1989, there were an estimated 66,000 fewer rapes, 323,000 fewer robberies, 380,000 fewer assaults, and 3.3 million fewer burglaries . . . between 1973 versus those of 1989. If only one-half or even one-fourth of the reductions were the result of rising incarceration rates, that would still leave prisons responsible for sizable reductions in crime. That possibility must be seriously weighed in debates about America's prisons. (1573)

"'Lock 'em Up' Is Bad Public Policy"

A group of academics and professionals representing such organizations as The Sentencing Project and the National Council on Crime and Delinquency (1991), on the other hand, advocates the greater use of alternatives to imprisonment in some cases. The National Council on Crime and Delinquency examined the strategy to reduce crime by increasing the probability and the length of imprisonment, particularly for drug of-

fenses. The research focused on Florida. According to researcher James Austin, "More than any state, Florida has dramatically followed this course of increasing the use of imprisonment for drug crimes." Florida has increased the use of imprisonment most dramatically—by over 300 percent from 1980 to 1989. Despite the increase in both prison building and the number of prison admissions, the Florida prison system has released prisoners at an even greater rate during the same period. The result is shorter prison terms, dropping from an average of 24 months in 1980 to 9 months in 1989.

According to the NCCD researchers:

> Based on the theories of deterrence and incapacitation, the sharp and huge rise in imprisonment should have produced a reduction in the crime rate. Instead, the crime rate rose 5 percent during the period. In fact, the steepest rise in crime accompanied the greatest rise in imprisonment, namely, between 1986 and 1989.

The war on drugs did not produce a reduction in drug offenses. Admissions to prison for drug offenses rose by 1825 percent over the decade, compared with an overall admission increase of 381 percent. For female drug offenders, the rise was even greater—more than 3000 percent. According to present data, the number of drug offenses continues to rise, not fall, despite the huge increase in prison admissions for drug offenses.

The explosion in the prison population creates a risk to public safety. Mandatory sentencing requires some prisoners to remain in prison, but it also forces the early release of ordinary prisoners. In one case, Charles Street, convicted of a violent crime, was released a year early. Following his early release, he murdered two Miami police officers. In another case, Robert and Harry Lebo were convicted for "molesting a crawfish trap." After their release, they were convicted of lobster theft. Under the habitual offender law, correctional authorities had to release two prisoners to make room for the Lebos. According to the researchers, "It is the worst of both worlds when nonviolent petty offenders are sentenced inappropriately to prison while dangerous criminals are released early."

Questions

1. What is the evidence for and against a tougher imprisonment policy?
2. Is the case for imprisonment stronger or weaker than the case against it, as presented here? Explain your answer.
3. Is it possible that both are correct? Is Florida perhaps an exception to the national data that Langan and DiIulio present? Defend your answer.

Knowledge and Understanding Check

The history of U.S. prisons
- Compare the Pennsylvania and Auburn, New York, systems of prison reform in the nineteenth century.
- Describe the Progressive reforms in prisons in the late nineteenth and early twentieth centuries.
- List four major changes in U.S. prisons since 1970.

The prison population boom
- Describe the trends in prison populations from 1925 to 2000.
- List and discuss the strengths and weaknesses of the four common explanations for the trends in prison population since 1970.

The side effects of imprisonment
- List and describe the direct and side effects of imprisonment.
- Summarize the state of what we know and don't know about each of the side effects of imprisonment.

Prisons
- Describe the trends and variations in prison costs since 1990.
- Identify and list the characteristics of the major types of prisons.
- Identify and describe three major issues in the debate over private prisons, and sum up the state of our knowledge on the three issues.

- Identify, describe, and list the strengths and weakness of the two prison management styles.
- Explain how personality has affected prison management.
- Describe the prison management hierarchy and how it operates.
- Identify and describe the missions and duties of corrections officers.
- Describe the trends in the numbers of women and minority corrections officers.
- Summarize the state of our knowledge about women officers in men's prisons.
- What do we know about the effect of training on prison officers' work?

Jails
- Why are jails called the center of the criminal justice system?
- Explain why women inmates in jails are at a disadvantage.
- Describe the nature and limits of jail programs.
- Compare new-generation with traditional jails, and list the strengths and weaknesses of each.

Prisoners
- Describe the general characteristics of the majority of prisoners in U.S. prisoners.
- Identify the main reasons for shortening prison terms.

KEY TERMS

Auburn system
building-tender system
concentration model
congregate system
conjugal visits
control model of management
correctional institution
count
dispersion model
good time laws
jail

linear design
lockdown status
maximum security prison
medical model of corrections
medium security prison
minimum security prison
new-generation jail
new-generation maximum security prison
penitentiary
Pennsylvania system

podular design
private prison
reintegration
recidivist
responsibility management approach
special housing units
special needs prisoners
supermaxes
supermaximum prison

INTERNET PROJECT

 Search under the key words "women's prisons" or variations such as "women prisoners." Scan the titles. What would you say are the major issues in women's prisons based on your scan? Pick one issue. Summarize the sides of the issue, proposed solutions, and evaluations of programs related to the issue.

CHAPTER 12

Prison Life

© William Murray

> **The standards of a nation's civilization can be judged by opening the doors of its prisons.**
>
> FYODOR DOSTOYEVSKY (1860)

> **The first duty of a prison . . . is to perform the function assigned to it by law . . . to insure that a sentence of imprisonment is a form of punishment. It must, however, be clear that it is the imprisonment, and not the treatment in prison, that constitutes the punishment. Men come to prison as a punishment, not *for* punishment.**
>
> SIR ALEXANDER PATERSON (1951, 23)

■ INTRODUCTION

What should life in prison be like? Ask my students and those at other colleges I've visited, and you'll hear some tough answers: "Torture chambers!" "Miserable!" "Horrible!" "Hellholes!" Listen to most people on the street and politicians who are only too happy to follow the public's lead, and you'll get similar answers. This is what we call the **punishment model of imprisonment** or the **confinement "plus" model of imprisonment.** It means locking criminals up isn't enough punishment; you have to add something more.

However, ask corrections professionals the same question, and you'll get a different answer. They'll remind you that most people locked up aren't there for life—they're going to get out. And probably sooner rather than later. Remember even in these tough times, prisoners are locked up less than two years on average (Chapter 11). Will torture, misery, and deprivation make them less dangerous and more productive when they're sitting beside us on the bus, going to the same movie, drinking at the same bar, or going to the same football game? Will it transform them from lawbreakers who prey on the rest of us into people who work hard, play by the rules, and pay their own way?

Corrections professionals will probably also ask you to consider the welfare of corrections officers—the "other prisoners"—who spend most of their time in prison, too (discussed in Chapter 11). What do you think their lives should be like? Does it matter that corrections professionals also have to spend their time in the "hellholes" you want for prisoners? Does it concern you that if the prisoners are miserable this makes the work of the professionals harder, too?

Unfortunately, the state of our knowledge doesn't help us answer the question "Does brutal punishment make prisoners more criminal or punish them into be-coming law-abiding, responsible people?" Nor does the empirical evidence give us a clear answer to the question "Do prison programs work?" One thing we do know: safe, secure, humane imprisonment makes the lives of corrections officers better, and in safe, secure, humane prisons the level of disorder, violence, and gang activity is lower than in brutal, unsafe prisons.

This is one reason why a number of corrections professionals—who know a lot more about these matters than the rest of us—recommend Sir Alexander Paterson's (1951, 23) **confinement model of imprisonment** as quoted in the chapter opener: Send offenders to prison *as* punishment, not *for* punishment. Disciplined, safe, secure, orderly confinement that provides the basic necessities of life *is* punishment, even if it's also *humane*. We don't have to *add* brutal, filthy, unsafe, disorderly conditions to confinement. What kind of lives do prisoners really lead behind bars? In this chapter, we'll look at the realities of male and female prison societies and the role of law in prison society.

■ MALE PRISON SOCIETY

Early prison researchers said there were two worlds where two completely separate societies existed—free society and the prison society. They called prisons **total institutions,** meaning they were isolated separate worlds with enough power to make prisoners give up their personalities and live completely regulated lives. Prison management created and maintained prison society inside prison walls.

To better understand the world of male prison society, let's look more closely at theories of how these prisons were created, the deprivations of imprisonment, how prisoners cope with stresses inside prison, violence behind bars, and programs for prisoners.

Indigenous and Importation Theories

This notion that prison society was created inside prison walls independent of the outside world we call the **indigenous theory** of prison life.

The early indigenous theory researchers concentrated on how prisoners adapted to life in prison. Donald Clemmer's 1940 classic *The Prison Community* introduced what he called the concept of **prisonization** (the process by which prisoners adapt to the prison world). Clemmer based his prisonization theory on detailed observations he made when he worked at Menard Penitentiary in Illinois. The standard explanation for how prisoners adapted to life in prison was the **inmate code,** the unwritten law based on the values of "noncooperation and hostility toward staff." In Kenneth Adams's (1992) words:

> The oppositional code, which governs inmate-staff interactions, was seen as a functional response to "reject their rejecters" and to salvage a sense of self-worth in the face of intense pressures. . . . (278)

Don't confuse this unwritten informal inmate code either with formal prison rules or the informal adaptations of the written rules of the prison to the lives of prisoners. The two cardinal principles of the inmate code are (1) do your own time and (2) never inform on another inmate. In a second classic, *Society of Captives,* Gresham Syke's (1958) study of life in a New Jersey prison during the 1950s, he identified five fundamental principles of the inmate code:

1. *Don't interfere with inmate interests:* Never rat on a con, don't be nosy, don't have a loose lip, don't put a guy on the spot.
2. *Don't quarrel with fellow inmates:* Play it cool, don't lose your head, do your own time.
3. *Don't exploit inmates:* Don't break your word, don't steal from cons, don't sell favors, don't welsh on bets.
4. *Maintain yourself:* Don't weaken, don't whine, don't cop out, be tough, be a man.
5. *Don't trust the guards or the things they stand for:* Don't be a sucker, guards are hacks and screws, the officials are wrong and the prisoners are right. (Clear and Cole 1994, 259)

Prisons have changed a lot since the indigenous theory was created by Clemmer and Sykes in the powerful classics and developed by their followers. Prisons got bigger and so did the proportion of the public locked up. The number of Black and Hispanic prisoners outpaced that of Whites, increasing an already disproportionate number of minorities in prison. Prison gangs got a lot bigger, their influence got stronger, and their connections with the outside world got firmer. More staff joined unions, and unions got a lot more powerful. The chance increased that courts would interference with prison management and life in prison. And, prisons and imprisonment became hot political issues.

All of these changes led to a new theory to explain prison society—the **importation theory**—based on the assumption that the roots of prison society lie outside prison. All prisoners bring with them a long history of life in public institutions—almost all have gone to school, many have spent time in juvenile and adult facilities, and some have been confined in psychiatric hospitals and other treatment facilities. They also bring to prison other individual attributes—their race, ethnicity, and criminal history. Once in prison, prisoners still watch TV, read magazines, listen to music, talk to visitors, bring lawsuits, and maintain contacts with gangs outside prison. All of these have broken down the clear lines (if there ever were any) between life inside and outside prison.

The "Pains of Imprisonment"

In his classic study of a maximum security prison, *Society of Captives,* Gresham Sykes (1958) identified five deprivations at the core of prison life:

- Goods and services
- Liberty
- Straight sexual relationships
- Autonomy
- Security

Recognizing these deprivations (Sykes called them **pains of imprisonment**) is essential to understanding the way prisoners deal with confinement. Researchers have confirmed Sykes's findings. They've also identified how painful these deprivations are and how prisoners handle them. Edward Zamble and Frank Porporino (1988) interviewed and surveyed 133 prisoners to identify the problems they faced in prison. Figure 12.1 shows the problems and the percentage of prisoners who identified each as the most significant problem they faced.

Let's look at a few important details behind Figure 12.1. First, based on inmates' own answers it looks like prison *is* "working." The pains prisoners are feeling are what they're supposed to feel for committing crimes. Second, the problems prisoners identify when they arrive in prison remain throughout their imprisonment, with one exception—inmates serving long sentences worry more about permanently losing their close relationships outside prison, finding friends inside prison with similar interests, and dealing with prison staff and bureaucracy. Also, Hispanics worry more about separation from family than other ethnic and racial groups, maybe because of the importance of family relationships in Hispanic culture (Adams 1992, 285).

Prisoners do develop coping skills to handle these deprivations. Two we'll look at are coping with the deprivation of goods and services by substituting their own prison economy and coping with the absence of straight sexual relationships by substituting them with consensual sex behind bars by some inmates.

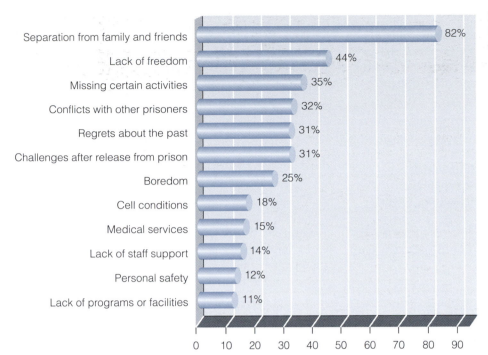

FIGURE 12.1

Most Difficult Problem Prisoners Face

SOURCE: Zamble and Porporino 1988.

The prison economy

Prisoners aren't supposed to be *comfortable* in confinement. As part of their punishment, they lose their freedom, their privacy, and also the "extras" connected to good things in life. They're supposed to live lives of **enforced poverty.** This means the state provides the bare essentials—plain food, clothing, and shelter. Prisons are supposed to be islands of poverty in a sea of plenty (Williams and Fish 1974, 40).

Of course, in movies, in the news, and on TV, prisons aren't exactly "islands of poverty." We see TV sets in prison cells and prisoners working out in well-equipped exercise rooms. We hear of "Club Feds" where "prisoners" play golf and lounge around swimming pools. We read of prisoners who are drunk on alcohol or high on other drugs. How can such comforts exist in these "islands of poverty"? Prisoners obtain some amenities legally. For example, they're allowed to receive gifts from friends and relatives. They can also buy some of the comforts of life from the prison commissary. Prisoners don't buy these—currency is banned—but with scrip or credit drawn on accounts supplied with money from the outside or that prisoners have earned in prison (discussed later in "Programs").

Still, the approved list of gifts and the stock of items in the commissary are hardly enough to satisfy the wants of most prisoners. Prisoners are well aware of all the comforts of life that they're *not* allowed to have. It's hard to satisfy their desires with available resources and within the enforced poverty of confinement. According to Susan Sheehan (1978), most of the men she studied in a New York prison were there "precisely because they were not willing to go without on the street. They are no more willing to go without in prison, so they hustle to obtain what they cannot afford to buy" (91).

Hustling contraband goods and services—mainly food, clothing, weapons, drugs, and prostitution—breaks prison rules and frustrates the goal of punishment by enforced poverty. Deprived of luxuries, prisoners do their best to get them. Getting what may seem like small luxuries eases the pain of imprisonment and promotes prison stability. Because contraband goods and services contribute to stability and therefore make prisons and prisoners easier to manage, they're tolerated by the authorities—at least to some extent.

Prisoners put great stake in these amenities and trouble comes when they don't get them. Trouble also brews when prisoner leaders lose the profits from controlling contraband goods and services. In some prisons, these leaders form symbiotic relationships with correctional officers. Both have an interest in maintaining stability, so they make trade-offs: Officers allow some illegal trafficking, usually in "nonserious" contraband such as food; prisoner leaders, in return, maintain peaceful cell blocks (Kalinich 1986).

Consensual sex

There's a ban on sex in all prisons. Why? Because suffering hardships is part of their punishment. Anecdotes about prison life for generations have told of routine consensual sex behind prison walls. The early records of Stillwater prison and the St. Cloud reformatory in Minnesota are full of celibacy code violations (Samaha, n.d.). But, the spread of AIDS has created a sense of urgency, spurring a demand for more knowledge about consensual sex in prison. Empirical research results vary as to how much consensual sex there is in prison—from rampant to infrequent. Here are some comments from Delaware prisoners commenting on sex in prison in 1994:

- "There's an unspoken ridicule of inmates who engage in sex today."
- "Sex still goes on in here. People I know don't use protection because it's not available. People are knowledgeable [about HIV] but still have sex."
- "Most people that do it are lifers . . . they don't care."
- "Just like on the streets; you can get sex anytime if you have money." (Saum, Spratt, Inciardi, and Bennett, 1997, 413)

Christopher Hensley (2000, 1–4) conducted face-to-face interviews with 174 male prisoners in Oklahoma prisons to "explore the amount of consensual homosexual activity in male prisons." The results of his study are depicted in Figure 12.2.

But, can we really know how much consensual sex there *really* is in prison? Methodological problems make it difficult. According to Christine Saum and her colleagues (1997) the major difficulty is inaccurate reporting because:

- Most incidents aren't recorded.
- Definitions of sex vary.
- Prisoners underestimate the amount of sex because they're afraid they'll get in trouble.
- Prisoners are embarrassed to admit they have sex with other men.
- Prisoners are afraid of being labeled weak or gay. (418)

Coping with Life's Stresses in Prison

In *The Felon* (1996), based on ex-convict turned sociologist John Irwin's interviews in Soledad men's prison in California, he writes that all new inmates ask themselves, "How shall I do my time?" Or, "What shall I do in prison?" A few can't cope at all; they either commit suicide or sink into psychosis. Irwin found those who can cope fit into two groups:

1. Those who identify with the world outside prison.
2. Those who identify primarily with the prison world. (426)

Jailers "who do not retain or . . . never acquired any commitment to outside social worlds tend to make a world out of prison." One jailer told Mark Fleisher (1989), who studied life in the maximum security federal penitentiary at Lompoc, California:

> Beating the system is the best game in town. Middle-class Americans will never understand it. You know, I feel "extracultural." I live on the same planet you do. We speak the same language, but that's where our similarity ends. That's right, I live outside this culture. This is your culture. This is your prison. You have to live with all the f——— rules in this society. I don't. You have to obey the rules, Mark. That's how you live. But, I don't have to obey anybody's f——— rules. The worst that can happen to me is that they put me back in prison. And who gives a f———! When they do that, you got to pay for me. I win. If this is all this society can do to me, then I'm gonna do whatever I want to do. How you going to stop me? I'm invincible. (8, 29)

Another jailer, this one in the federal prison at Leavenworth, Kansas, put it this way:

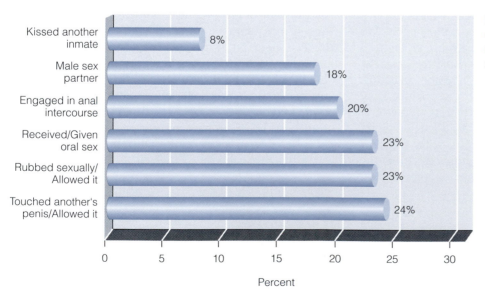

FIGURE 12.2
Amounts of Consensual Homosexual Activity in Oklahoma Men's Prisons
SOURCE: Based on Hensley 2000.

Kissed another inmate 8%
Male sex partner 18%
Engaged in anal intercourse 20%
Received/Given oral sex 23%
Rubbed sexually/Allowed it 23%
Touched another's penis/Allowed it 24%

Percent

As the years go by and you get older, you realize that your life is considered a failure by society's standards. . . . You're a jailbird. You don't have any money, no house, no job, no status. In society's eyes you're a worthless piece of shit, or you can say, "F——— society, I'll live by my own rules." That's what I did. I decided to live by my own standards and rules. They aren't society's but they are mine and that's what I've done. In your society, I may not be anybody, but in here, I am. (Johnson 1996, 164)

Prisoners who identify with the outside world adapt in two ways:

1. *Doing time:* Those who for the most part want to maintain their former life patterns and identities
2. *Gleaning:* Those who desire to make significant changes in their life patterns and identities and see prison as a chance to do this

"Time-doers" try to get through their prison terms with "the least amount of suffering and the greatest amount of comfort." They avoid trouble, find activities to occupy their time, secure a few luxuries, and make a few friends. The "gleaners" follow a plan of self-improvement. According to one gleaner:

I got tired of losing. I had been losing all of my life. I decided that I wanted to win for a while. So I got on a different kick. I knew that I had to learn something so I went to school, got my high school diploma. I cut myself off from my old . . . buddies and started hanging around with some intelligent guys who minded their own business. We read a lot, a couple of us paint. We play a little bridge and talk, a lot of the time about what we are going to do when we get out. (Irwin 1996, 430–431)

Deciding whether to be a time-doer, a gleaner, or a jailer can be difficult. Consider Piri Thomas, who was forced to decide whether to participate in a riot:

I stood there watching and weighing, trying to decide whether or not I was a con first and an outsider second. I had been doing time inside yet living every mental minute I could outside; now I had to choose one or the other. I stood there in the middle of the yard. Cons passed me by, some going west to join the boppers, others going east to neutral ground. . . . I had to make a decision. *I am a con. These damn cons are my people. Your people are outside the cells, home, in the streets. No! That ain't so. . . . Look at them go toward the west wall. Why in hell am I taking so long in making up my mind?* (Irwin 1996, 426)

In his review of the literature on coping, Kenneth Adams refers to research that asked inmates how they handle problems. Most male inmates choose "real-man strategies," relying heavily on personal strength and self-reliance. (We'll discuss "real-woman strategies" later.) Some long-term prisoners choose another coping strategy—minimum expectations based on focusing on today and not hoping for too much tomorrow. Hispanics sometimes join gangs as family surrogates to ease the pain of separation from their real families (Adams 1992, 286–287).

Violence

Racial and ethnic conflict, gangs and violent prisoners, and the prison economy can lead to violence against other prisoners. Assaults and homicides in maximum security prisons have grown to the point that "the possibility of being attacked or killed has loomed as the major concern of offenders incarcerated in these prisons or anticipating going to one." According to one prisoner in California during the 1990s:

I've been on the yard watching people get shot, watching people die. You know how hard it is coming out with tears in your eyes knowing that you're going to get hit, knowing that someone is going to physically hurt you, or try to kill you. . . . Eighty-two, 83, 84, people were dropping like flies, people getting stuck. After two or three years of that, it's hard. People on the outside say, ah, that doesn't happen. You weren't there, man. (Irwin and Austin 1997, 72)

Economic victimization occurs when violence or threats of it accompany gambling, fraud, loan sharking, theft, robbery, protection rackets, con games, delivery of misrepresented contraband, or failure to deliver promised goods. When promised commodities aren't delivered—or are not as promised—victims may retaliate. Drug trafficking is a good example. To get drugs into prisons requires sophisticated smuggling operations. Violence results if drugs are stolen, misrepresented, overpriced, or not delivered. Prisoners use violence to prevent these distribution irregularities from happening in the first place, or to retaliate for them if they do take place (Bowker 1983, 1230–1231).

Crowding is a common characteristic of prison life that probably accounts for some of the increased violence. On January 1, 2001, state prisons were between 100 and 115 percent full (Bureau of Justice Statistics 2001e, 1). The prison population boom (and the reasons for the boom) are behind crowded prisons (Chapter 11). But there's more to the explanation; it's the public's unwillingness to pay for more prisons.

Escalating prison violence is seen in the growing strength of gangs, racial and ethnic divisions, sexual assaults, prisoner-officer violence, and riots. We'll look at each of these, in turn, and how prisoners cope with violence.

 12-1 You Decide: What's the answer to prison crowding?

Gangs

Prison gangs are a part of prison life, despite strong prohibitions against them. Gang members rob, assault, and otherwise prey on members of other gangs and members of the general prison population. Prisons have always had violent prisoners, usually youths recently "graduated" from juvenile prison as well as unskilled, lower- and working-class criminals. Before the 1960s, a strong majority of prisoners opposed to violence kept them in check. Since then, however, the number of tough young prison graduates and unskilled prisoners has increased (Knox 1991, 283).

Gang members are already hostile to authority when they come to prison. Unlike with older prisoners, little rewards, like sneaking extra cups of coffee, don't satisfy gang members. Gang members care about status and gang rivalry, so they challenge authority. According to James Jacobs (1977) in his study of Stateville Prison outside Chicago:

> [W]hen a lieutenant was called to "walk" an inmate, he was often confronted with ten or twelve of the inmate's fellow gang members surrounding him, challenging his authority. One Stateville guard explained: "The inmate will say, 'I'm not going.' Then a group of his gang will gather around him. I'll have to call a lieutenant. Sometimes one of the leaders will just come over and tell the member to go ahead." (161)

Prison, in the eyes of many young prisoners, is the ultimate test of manhood. A man in prison is able to secure what he wants and protect what he has: "In here, a man gets what he can" and "nobody can force a man to do something he don't want to" are key elements of their belief system. Any prisoner who doesn't meet these standards isn't a man, "has no respect for himself," and so doesn't deserve respect (Irwin 1980, 193–194.)

The influence of prison gangs reaches beyond the prison. In about half the states, gangs have counterparts on the streets. In some of these states, prisons are bases for criminal gang activity in the community. In California, the Black Guerrilla Family is allied with a gang of younger Black prisoners called "Crips" (they cripple their victims), most of whom have been convicted of violent crimes. According to law enforcement officers, "leaders of the Black Guerrilla Family are directing a growing effort to take over part of Southern California's lucrative cocaine trade by using Crips as their soldiers" (*New York Times* 1985).

🔘 **12-2 Florida Department of Corrections "gang assessment tool"**

Race and ethnicity

During the 1960s and early 1970s, increased racial and ethnic consciousness, assertiveness, confrontation, solidarity, and violence marked U.S. society (Brakel 1982, 113). These developments were imported into male prison society, leaving men's prisons "fragmented, tense, and often extremely violent" (Irwin 1980, 181). (We'll see how different women's prison society is later in the chapter.)

Prison populations were also changing. By the late 1970s, Blacks, Hispanics, Native Americans, and other minorities in the general population were heading toward becoming the majority in American prisons. For example, by the early 1980s, 80 percent of Stateville's (Illinois' maximum security prison just outside Chicago) prisoner population was Black (Irwin 1980, 182).

With increased racial consciousness outside prison and among the minority prisoners in prisons came increased racial and ethnic hatred. Prisoners stick to their own race and ethnicity in choosing friends, cliques, and gangs. Of course, committing similar crimes, coming from the same neighborhood, doing time in another state prison or institution, living in the same cell block or working in the same prison workshop are also elements in individual and group relations in prison. But race and ethnicity is the overriding element in forming social groups in prisoner society (Irwin 1980, 1982).

Racial hatred between White and Black prisoners, their cliques, and gangs is the most volatile dynamic in prisons. Since the 1960s, Black prisoners have become more assertive. According to one Black prisoner at Stateville Prison in Illinois:

> In the prison, the black dudes have a little masculinity game they play. It has no name, really, but I call it whup a white boy—especially the white gangsters or syndicate men, the bad juice boys, the hit men, etc. The black dudes go out of their way to make faggots out of them. And to lose a fight to a white dude is one of the worst things that can happen to a black dude. And I know that, by and far, the white cats are faggots. They will drop their pants and bend over and touch their toes and get had before they will fight. (Robinson 1971, 29)

Another said: "Every can I been in that's the way it is. It's gettin' even I guess. You guys been cuttin' our b———s off ever since we been in this country. Now we're just gettin' even" (Jacobs, 1980, 16).

White prisoners become bigoted or more bigoted if they were already racially prejudiced before coming to prison. According to a white California prisoner:

> After 10:30, the voice dropped a decibel or two, and from the morass of sound Ron began to recognize certain voices by timbre and catch snatches of conversation. Above him, perhaps on the second tier, he picked up a gumboed black voice saying he'd like to kill all white babies, while his listener agreed it was the best way to handle the beasts—before they grew

up. A year earlier, Ron would have felt compassion for anyone so consumed by hate and whenever whites casually used "nigger" he was irked. Now he felt tentacles of hate spreading through himself—and half an hour later, he smiled when a batch of voices began chanting: "Sieg Heil! Sieg Heil!" (Bunker 1977, 92)

In the emphasis on Black and White prisoner conflicts we shouldn't overlook a third element—Hispanic prisoners. James B. Jacobs refers to this mix at Stateville, Illinois, maximum security prison:

> Afro-American, Caucasian-American and Mexican-American inmates lived side by side but maintained three distinct ethnic cultures. Inmates did not eat at the same table, share food, cigarettes or bathroom facilities with individuals of other ethnic groups. They would not sit in the same row while viewing television or even talk for more than brief interchanges with members of a different ethnic group. (Jacobs 1980, 13–14)

 12-3 Race and ethnic conflicts among Texas prison gangs

Sexual assault

Some prisoners are victims of sexual assault. More than 80 percent of the victims are young White men; 16 percent are Black; 2 percent are Hispanic. Most of the attackers are Black (80 percent); some are Hispanic (14 percent); and a few are White (6 percent). What explains these numbers? In Daniel Lockwood's (1980) study of sexual violence in prisons, one Black prisoner told Lockwood it's because Whites are weak:

> If you come in here alone then they [black prisoners] will try to crack on you for something. But if they know that you know people that have been here for awhile, then they know better. They try to pick on some of the weak ones. They like to pick on them. (29)

Another reason, according to Lockwood, is White prisoners are less organized, less likely to know other Whites in prison, and less willing to band together for protection. Also, class divisions among White prisoners are stronger than they are among Blacks. Middle-class Whites look down on other White prisoners they believe are their social inferiors. Some Whites don't even consider themselves criminals at all. All this isolates them and makes them more vulnerable to attacks (Lockwood 1980, 30).

Prisoners who don't respond to unwanted sexual approaches are going to become victims:

> You see a young pretty dude who doesn't come in here on a violent record. Now, he is probably in the worst situation than the guy that comes in here on a violent record. Because if you know that a guy has murdered

someone on the street, and has taken a life, and is in here for life, you are going to think three or—not just once but three or four times—before you go up against him. Somebody that shows he's timid, who is real quiet. That is basically it. Someone who is real quiet and withdrawn and looks scared. He looks frightened you know. He is most apt to be approached. (Lockwood 1980, 33–34)

In view of these Black perceptions of White physical weakness, weak group solidarity, and Black prisoners' pent-up rage against what they perceive as white oppression, Lockwood (1980, 33–34) was surprised to learn that

> sexual aggression in prisons is not more widespread. Even in men's prisons where sexual violence is most concentrated, estimates of the incidence of sexual assault run as low as less than 1 percent. In some prisons, of course, the numbers are higher. In New York State, 28 percent of the prisoners reported some form of aggression—threats, propositions, and some physical contact. Even here, however, only one prisoner reported actually being raped. (33–34)

These low numbers are probably one reason why personal safety was ranked eleventh out of the twelve problems prisoners said was the most important they face in prison (Figure 12.2).

Prisoner-officer violence

Prisoners don't just attack each other; they attack officers too. Officers take risks attempting to break up fights, managing intoxicated prisoners, and escorting them to segregation. These situations are known to provoke assaults. But not all violence is predictable, especially random violent acts like throwing dangerous objects at officers or dropping items from catwalks above as officers patrol cell blocks below (Bowker 1983, 1231).

Officers also attack prisoners. According to Todd R. Clear and George F. Cole (1994):

> Unauthorized physical violence against inmates by officers to enforce rules, uphold the officer-prisoner relationship, and maintain order is a fact of life in many institutions. Stories abound of guards giving individual prisoners "the treatment" outside the notice of their superiors. Many guards view physical force as an everyday operating procedure and legitimize its use. (275–276)

Riots

Riots are part of U.S. history; they're part of U.S. prison history too. Two modern examples are Attica State Prison in New York in 1970 and the bloody riot at New Mexico Penitentiary in 1980. Although riots like Attica and New Mexico rightly deserve their notorious reputation, riots are a rare part of prison life. Some riots are spontaneous;

others are planned in advance. A highly organized inmate force held together by racial solidarity and political consciousness planned and executed the famous Attica riot in 1971. To a considerable extent, that riot was a product of the 1960s—a political protest against "White oppression."

Other riots, like the bloody New Mexico riot in 1980, were spontaneous, disorganized outbursts. According to its historian, Mark Colvin (1982, 449), the New Mexico prison riot was the most brutal, destructive, and disorganized prison riot in U.S. history. In 36 hours, prisoners killed thirty-three fellow prisoners and beat and raped up to two hundred more. After drinking too much homemade whiskey, drunk prisoners overpowered four guards. Seven guards were taken hostage, beaten, stabbed, or sodomized before being released by their captors.

There was no plan. Prisoners stumbled on an open dormitory door, an open security grill, and blowtorches accidentally left behind by renovation crews. Storming through the prison, rioters tortured twelve inmates with blowtorches, set them on fire, and mutilated them. They beheaded one with a shovel. Their victims were suspected "snitches" (prisoners who inform on other prisoners' misbehavior), child rapists, and "mentally disturbed" prisoners whose screaming kept their killers awake at night (Colvin 1992).

Prisoners riot for complicated reasons. Some argue that riots break out when prison administrators take actions that disrupt existing prison society. This is particularly true when administrators try to alter power-sharing arrangements between staff and prisoners, arrangements that increase prisoners' status and comforts.

According to Colvin (1982), three situations create administrative disruptions:

1. *Discovering and exposing corruption,* such as narcotics traffic inside prisons
2. *Policy conflicts,* such as those between reformist, rehabilitation-oriented administrators and old-line, security-oriented staff
3. *Policy changes* brought about by new prison administrations, such as wardens who decide they're going to "crack down" on minority prisoner assertiveness (450)

If all three conditions occur simultaneously, trouble is almost certain to follow. Cohesion arising out of power, status, and wealth erodes badly. Conflict between prisoners' social structure and administrator's control structure erupts in various forms. Prisoner protests and strikes are organized to get back their privileges. If they do, order returns.

Sometimes, administrators don't give back lost privileges. Instead, for political or ideological reasons, they respond to protests with more restrictions. Prisoners' resentment grows, and administrators find it increasingly difficult to restore lost privileges. Hostility between guards and prisoners escalates; administrations change and guard turnover increases. Administrative actions don't restore order. On the contrary, they only raise tensions. As administrative staff divide into warring bureaucratic camps, prisoners' social structure disintegrates into self-protective, hostile cliques. Eventually, rioting breaks out.

Burt Useem and Peter Kimball (1989), in their stimulating study of prison riots, list the following eight popular theories of the causes of prison riots:

1. Violent, depraved prisoners
2. Prison conditions
3. Liberal judges giving prisoners too many rights
4. Radical prisoner organizations stirring up trouble
5. Prisoners crowded as if in cages
6. Racism
7. Gang plots
8. Prisoners' "cry for help" (3–4)

Coping with violence

Some older prisoners have established reputations for being tough; they can circulate throughout violent prisons without fear. Some young first-timers join gangs (**gangbanging**) for protection. But the majority of prisoners cope by avoiding most prisoners and most settings where large groups of prisoners congregate. According to John Irwin and James Austin (1997), they:

> shy away from most prisoners and settings where masses of prisoners congregate and withdraw into small groups or virtual isolation. Although they may occasionally buy from the racketeers, place bets, or trade commodities on a small scale with other unaffiliated prisoners, they stay out of the large-scale economic activities and dissociate themselves from the violent cliques and gangs. They stick to a few friends whom they have met in the cell blocks, at work, on the outside (homeboys), in other prisons, or through shared interests. Either alone or with their few trusted friends, they go to work and/or attend meetings of various clubs and formal organizations that the prison administration allows to exist in prison. Otherwise, they stay in their cells. (78)

Programs

If there's one thing prisoners have, it's "time on their hands." A few years ago, I visited a prison with a colleague who for seventeen years had also been Director of the Federal Bureau of Prisons. After we'd been there a while I said, "There's sure a lot of sitting around and sleeping going on here." He told me the average prisoner sleeps 17 hours a day. And this isn't new. In 1982, Chief Justice of the U.S. Supreme Court Warren Burger warned:

We can continue to have largely human "warehouses," with little or no education and training, or we can have prisons that are factories with fences around them . . . to accomplish the dual objective of training inmates in gainful occupations and lightening the enormous load of maintaining the prison system of this country. (Flanagan 1989, 135)

As we discuss prison programs, let's keep in mind that in too many prisons there are disappointingly few programs, or maybe it's more accurate to say there are too many programs with far too little money and staff (Lipton 1995, 4). It may surprise you to learn this, especially in view of two important missions prison programs are supposed to accomplish: rehabilitate prisoners and help manage prisons by keeping prisoners busy and out of trouble. (As my mother used to warn me—"Get busy, Joel. Idle hands tempt the Devil. Besides, it's good for what ails you.")

Why are there too many prisons either without programs or programs without enough support? The easy answer is the enthusiastic response to an article published in 1974, written by Robert Martinson, called "What Works? Questions and Answers About Prison Reform." It concluded: "With few and isolated exceptions, the rehabilitative efforts that have been reported so far have no appreciable effect on recidivism" (25). Martinson was one of three respected sociologists who had conducted the most extensive review of prison programs (231 programs) ever done. The professionals and the public saw the facts and concluded, " 'Nothing works,' so why do anything?"

But wait a minute; that answer sounds too simple. And it is. First, Martinson unforgivably spun the findings of the study. The study actually said, "the field of corrections has not *as yet* found satisfactory ways to reduce recidivism by *significant amounts*." (I added the italics so you can see the spin better.) Second, the article shored up the popular view that prison programs are "soft on crime" and so they undermine the prison mission to punish criminals. According to Douglas Lipton (1995), the principal author of the study Martinson worked on:

The phrase "nothing works" became a watchword and entered the corrections vocabulary. It was treated as fact. The belief that "nothing works" still has widespread acceptance and is one of the main reasons treatment programs are given low priority. (4)

Heated scholarly debate followed the knee-jerk reaction to the "nothing works" pronouncement. The outcome of this debate led to a more balanced assessment of the effectiveness of rehabilitation programs. Here's what two scholars deeply involved in rehabilitation research said:

Martinson's finding, which was picked up by the mass media (for example, "Big change in prisons" [*U.S. News and World Report*]" was used by critics of prison programs to argue against rehabilitation as a primary justification for incarceration. Soon, however, Martinson's critics pointed out that he was premature in dismissing *all* forms of intervention. Although few programs can succeed in rehabilitating *all* inmates, more *moderate* successes may be possible. (Gerber and Fritsch 1995, 120)

And,

Rather than ask, "What works for offenders as a *whole*?" we must increasingly ask, "Which methods work best for which types of offenders and under what conditions or in what types of setting?" (Palmer 1975)

The public and the politicians paid no attention to this debate. Let's not fall for the shallow spin of "nothing works," but instead follow the path of researchers like those just quoted in assessing prison programs.

Most people and some professionals in corrections probably agree with the distinguished National Academy of Science's definition of **rehabilitation** as "the result of any planned intervention that reduces an offender's further criminal activity" (Gaes et al. 1998, 4). But prison programs have broader missions than reducing recidivism, like reducing misbehavior in prison; contributing to peaceful, humane punishment; and improving prisoners' chances of getting a job when they get out of prison. Practically, rehabilitation programs are aimed at "correcting" deficiencies that have the strongest links to criminal behavior. We'll focus here on six types of programs—education, work, recreation, religious programs, financial assistance, and substance abuse. We'll also take a closer look at the debate over prison programs.

Education

Let's divide education into three categories: academic, vocational, and social (see "Cognitive Model of Rehabilitation" section later). Teaching prisoners to read and write is the oldest rehabilitation program; it's been a prison mission and a part of prison life since the birth of the reformatories in the 1870s (Chapter 11). By the 1930s, primary and secondary education had become primary rehabilitation programs. By the 1960s, college education had been added (Gaes et al. 1998, 57).

Academic education *can* reduce recidivism in three ways. First, education improves the chances of getting a job, and getting a job reduces the chances of recidivism. Second, the process of learning itself makes inmates more mature, conscientious, and committed to achievement. These qualities can lead to better decision making; better decision making reduces the chances of returning to prison. Third, the classroom is a chance for inmates to "interact with civilian employees in . . . a nonauthoritarian, goal-directed relationship" (Gaes et al 1998, 56–57).

12-4 *Adult Correctional Treatment* survey of research on prison programs

But *does* academic education reduce recidivism? Some research says yes, other research says no. Jorg Gerber and Eric Fritsch (1995) reviewed thirteen studies of primary and secondary education programs they determined were conducted rigidly enough to deserve consideration: nine of the studies found a *modest* relationship between the program and recidivism. As for college education, the answer was also mixed—there was a modest positive relationship in some studies and no relationship in others (123–130).

What about vocational education? Here the results are less mixed and more positive. According to Gerber and Fritsch (1995):

> Most of the research conducted in recent years shows a correlation between vocational training and a variety of outcomes generally considered positive for either society or correctional institutions: lower recidivism rates, lower parole revocation rates, better post release employment patterns, and better institutional disciplinary records. (131)

Besides the modest positive relationship between academic and vocational programs and recidivism, Gerber and Fritsch (1995) also found:

> a fair amount of support for the hypotheses that adult academic and vocational correctional education programs lead to fewer disciplinary violations during incarceration . . . increases in employment opportunities, and to increases in participation in education after release. (136–137)

But these positive effects depend on the following:

■ "The more extensive the educational program the more likely it is to achieve its stated objectives. For instance, research in New York State showed that inmates who earned their G.E.D. were less likely to recidivate than those who attended G.E.D. classes but did not earn the diploma."

■ "Programs that are separate from the rest of the prison are more likely to succeed. Successful programs had a designated area for providing vocational education and only vocational education."

■ "Programs that provide follow up after release are more likely to succeed. Successful programs had systematic procedures for providing rate placement services."

■ "Programs that are successful in attracting an appropriate audience are more likely to achieve their in-

tended objectives. For instance, the "Reading to Reduce Recidivism" program in Texas was hampered because it was designed for inmates who would serve short sentences and would be released quickly into the community, whereas the median sentence served by program participants was fifteen years."

■ "With respect to vocational education, programs that provide skills relevant to the contemporary job market are more likely to achieve their stated objectives. Administrators claim that their programs offer inmates saleable skills, which will enhance their probability of obtaining and maintaining employment in the free world. But critics often maintain that vocational training programs fail because what they teach bears so little relationship to an offender's subsequent life outside of prison." (Gerber and Fritsch 1995, 135–136)

The bottom line: There's reason for some optimism that academic and vocational education have a modest effect on reducing recidivism and misbehavior in prison and increasing job opportunities and further education after prison *if* they're designed, carried out, and followed up right.

Work

Education is the oldest rehabilitation *program*; work is the oldest prison *activity*. And, just as prisoners come to prison with major educational deficiencies they also bring deficiencies in their work history—poor to no work records, few if any marketable skills, and a poor to no work ethic (Gaes et al 1998, 62). So, work programs have multiple missions. Some of these missions are directed at inmates, such as developing positive attitudes toward work, self-discipline, and marketable skills. Two other missions are aimed at prison management:

1. Maintain order and safety by keeping prisoners busy and out of trouble.
2. Reduce the cost of imprisonment by using prison labor.

Prisons have to provide all the services most communities in the outside world have to provide—and more. So prisons have utilities (sewer and water, electricity, telephones), restaurants, bakeries, laundries, hospitals, mail delivery, fire protection, record keeping, and janitorial services.

Prisoners do most of the work to provide these services. Obviously, the resources of prisoner labor and time are in great supply in prisons. Prison jobs tell a lot about the prestige of the prisoners who hold them. The most prestigious are jobs closest to decision makers. Record keeping is the most prestigious because it puts inmates in charge of a valuable commodity—information (who's eligible for release or reclassification to lower or higher security prisons). Desk jobs are also desirable because they provide access to administrators and perhaps an opening to better food and other amenities; so are jobs that allow access to the commodities that prisoners can sell in the prison economy. The lowest prestige job is also the most available—janitorial work. This work is menial, like mopping floors, and there's no access to information, goods, and services (Clear and Cole 1994, 334).

Prison work also includes working in prison industries that produce for the outside world. Prison industries were a major part of prison life from 1900 to 1925. They were considered a major element in the rehabilitation of prisoners. Work was not only useful, it was also therapeutic, according to the Progressive prison reformers. But prison industries faced stiff opposition from labor and small business, because they took jobs away from union labor and profits away from small businesses. They ran into the firmly entrenched **principle of less eligibility** (prisoners can't make as much money as free workers).

Prison industries returned to prison life in the 1980s (Hawkins 1983, 98–103). By 2000, prisons were engaged in a long list of enterprises, including car repair, lumbering, ranching, meat processing, making flags, printing, data entry, telephone answering services, Braille translation, microfilming, and CD-ROM copying (*Corrections Compendium Journal* 2000, 8).

The major justification for returning prison industries to prison life is the idea that prisoners should pay for their imprisonment. But, this rarely happens; only a few prisoners work in prison industries. Further, many of the prison industry programs cost taxpayers more money than they save. People in charge of prison industries say that potential profits are eaten away by security and other concerns, such as rehabilitating inmates and protecting private businesses from unfair competition. "The goal is really to create work, reduce idleness, and help manage the prison," said Pamela Jo Davis, president of Florida's PRIDE (Prison Rehabilitative Industries and Diversified Enterprises) and chair of Correctional Industries Association, a national umbrella group for prison industries (Hoskinson 1998).

In 1997, 76,519 prisoners were working in prison industries, more than twice the number in 1980. Sales of products from prison industries more than tripled—from $392 million in 1980 to $1.62 billion in 1997. Nevertheless, according to a National State Auditors Association's evaluation of prison industries in thirteen states, many prison industries aren't self-sufficient (Hoskinson 1998).

Almost all evaluations of the effectiveness of work programs suffer from serious methodological flaws (Gaes et al. 1998, 63). But there's one rigorous and comprehensive study, conducted by the Federal Bureau of Prisons, that carefully matched a study group of prisoners who were employed in prison work programs and a control group that weren't. The results are promising:

> The study group inmates were more likely to be employed after release, more likely to successfully complete a halfway house stay, and are less likely to have their parole revoked. For example, at 12 months after release 6.6 percent of the study group participants had been revoked, compared to 10.1 percent of comparison group subjects. (Gaes et al. 1998, 64–65)

A long-term follow-up study examined which inmates were locked up for either a new crime or a technical parole violation. Inmates who had worked in prison industries were 24 percent less likely to recidivate than those who hadn't. Many of the study inmates were free for twelve years with no new offenses (Gaes et al. 1998, 66).

Economist Ann D. Witte (1975) studied work release in North Carolina and found that prisoners who participated in work-release programs were less likely to commit serious crimes than prisoners who didn't. According to Witte:

> There seems to be a number of possible ways in which work release might affect the seriousness of criminal activity. First, it provides a man with a stable work record and job experience. Second, it allows a man to support his dependents while in prison and hence could aid in keeping his family together. Third, it might provide new job skills. Fourth, it provides a man with money at the time of release and often with a job. Fifth, it allows a man to maintain contacts with the free community and limits at least somewhat his immersion in the prison community. Finally, it may change a man's attitude toward himself and toward society. (99)

The North Carolina experiment didn't fulfill all its possibilities. Nevertheless, Witte concluded:

> Work release should be considered a successful program: successful in the sense that men who have been on the work-release program decrease the seriousness of the criminal offenses which they commit after release from prison. This project found most support for work release affecting this decrease in seriousness of criminal activity by improving the work performance and the attitudes of men who participate in the program. (100)

Recreation

Most prisons have athletic teams; many prisoners work out in prison exercise rooms; virtually all watch movies; and some participate in drama, music, art, and journalism. Recreation is an important—and, of course, desired by most prisoners—part of prison life. Recreation programs are good for prisoners: They help to accomplish the mission of rehabilitation to the extent they teach inmates social skills like fair competition, working together

YOU DECIDE

Should prisoners get to lift weights and play team sports?

Several states are taking away the privileges or amenities of prisoners. For example, Georgia has removed its exercise bikes, foosball, pool, and Ping-Pong tables. "We got this all out of there," said Wayne Garner in 1995, commissioner of Georgia's Department of Corrections. Georgia Congressman Bob Barr, a Republican, supports the move: "I think prison is *for* punishment. I'm opposed to anything that detracts from the fundamental notion—one that ought to be hammered home every day—which is *they are there to be punished*" (emphasis added). Two of the most cherished privileges—team sports and weightlifting—are on the list of remaining privileges to be removed in a number of jurisdictions. Should they be removed too? (Winkeljohn 1998, 12E).

Many prison officials believe that "sports programs help condition inmates to behave better at the risk of losing their privileges. They say the games also provide a tension release, making inmates less aggressive." "I'm sure that's absolutely true," Bob Barr responds. "But," he adds, "Pavlov's dog can be made to respond to any number of positive stimuli" (Winkeljohn 1998, 12E).

On the other hand, one commentator asks:

Whatever happened to the constitutional provision which calls for the nation's citizens to not be submitted to cruel and unusual treatment? The state's punishment objective is accomplished by the deprivation of liberty in and of itself. If a person were held in a fabulous mansion, prohibited from leaving at any time and prohibited from seeing friends or family except at designated times, he would suffer punishment equal to any penitentiary. Those privileges sought to be terminated are minimal and only make conditions tolerable for the staff, more than the prisoners." (Morain 1998, B8)

Questions

1. Summarize the arguments for and against removing privileges for prisoners.
2. Think about what you have learned in this chapter. Would you recommend the removal of privileges? Why?
3. If you answered no to (2), what would you want to know before you changed your mind?

---

and building self-esteem. They're also part of the reward and punishment system that helps to enforce prison discipline. Few inmates want to lose the privilege of recreation. Finally, recreation definitely fits in with the philosophy of humane punishment. Perhaps nothing more humanizes prisons than allowing prisoners to participate in social activities they really enjoy. Of course, recreation programs also create safety risks. Fights can—and do—erupt during competitive sports, for example.

 12-5 Fit in prison? Pumping iron on the mainline

Religious programs

The scholarly literature doesn't pay much attention to religious programs in prison, but they exist in every prison. The First Amendment guarantees the "free exercise" of religion, so prisons have to provide religion programs. Like most other prison programs, religious programs help prisoners fill time, are supposed to aid in rehabilitation, and contribute to a humane punishment.

Todd Clear and his colleagues (1992) conducted one of the few national studies of religion in prison. Interviews with inmates indicated that religion helps prisoners by providing a psychological and physical "safe haven." Religion also enables inmates to maintain ties with family and religious volunteers. The study also found that participation in religious programs contributed both to helping prisoners adjust to prison and reducing disciplinary infractions.

Drug treatment

There's compelling evidence that drug use increases criminal activity among significant numbers of offenders (Gaes et al. 1998, 386). Almost two-thirds of state prisoners say they use drugs regularly; nearly half of federal prisoners say the same (Pelissier et al., in press). This has created enormous pressure on corrections departments to create drug treatment programs for prisoners. Most of these programs are **therapeutic communities (TCs)**, which isolate drug dependent prisoners from the general prison population. This isolation is supposed to increase group pressure on prisoners to commit themselves to the program and decrease peer pressure from outside the group to use drugs.

We'll look at the federal prison system because only a few state programs have been evaluated, and those evaluations have flaws (Pelissier et al., in press). In the federal therapeutic communities programs, each community contains about one hundred prisoners. Treatment lasts for half the day; during the rest of the day participants mingle with the general population, participating in normal prison activities—work, school, meals, recreation. The programs follow the cognitive model (discussed below). They try to "identify, confront, and alter attitudes, values, and thinking patterns that led to criminal behaviors and drug or alcohol abuse" (Pelissier et al., in press, 4).

Do the programs work? Bernadette Pelissier and her colleagues (in press, 12) compared participants with nonparticipants to find out how many were arrested or used drugs or alcohol within six months after they were released from prison. They found treated inmates were 73 percent less likely to be arrested and 44 percent less likely to use illegal drugs or alcohol than untreated inmates (13, 15).

But, treatment wasn't the only variable that was related to arrest and use. Older inmates, inmates with short criminal histories, inmates with full-time jobs, and those who lived with their spouses did better than their opposites. Researchers didn't (or maybe couldn't) sort out which of these elements contributed most to reduced arrests and drug and alcohol use. Also, the researchers didn't figure out how much each of the elements in the programs—cognitive skills, therapeutic community, or the intensity and quality of the treatment experience—contributed to the positive outcomes (Pelissier et al., in press, 16–20).

12-6 Pelissier et al., "Prison drug program outcomes" full report

Financial assistance

Some programs provide offenders released from prison with financial assistance in the form of employment compensation. One experimental program in Georgia and Texas, the Transitional Aid Research Project (TARP), gave a group of released prisoners small weekly payments, while control groups received no such payments. Released prisoners who received the aid were arrested less frequently and were also able to obtain better jobs than those who did not receive aid (Rossi, Berk, and Lenihan 1980).

Cognitive model of rehabilitation

"Target *thinking,* not *behavior*" is the core value of cognitive skills programs. The programs' mission is "rehabilitation through clearer thinking." They're based on a **cognitive model of rehabilitation** that's backed up by extensive research showing that "faulty thinking patterns" are related to recidivism. (Of course, we all have faulty thinking patterns, but for most of us they don't

lead us to prison.) The assumption behind the model is if you can correct prisoners' faulty thinking patterns you can reduce their recidivism. Prisoners' faulty thinking patterns include acting on impulse instead of thinking problems through; thinking about now instead of planning for the future; looking at the world through their eyes instead of seeing others' perspectives; acting before they think about the consequences of their actions; and thinking their bad actions are someone or something else's fault (Fabiano, Porporino, and Robinson 1990).

The Cognitive Thinking Skills program developed by Robert Ross and Elizabeth Fabiano is the most widely used program following the cognitive model. Coaches meet with groups of four to ten inmates for two hours, two to four times a week for thirty-five weeks. To keep participants motivated, coaches use a number of techniques, including role playing, videotaped feedback, modeling, group discussion, and games, that help avoid making the sessions like therapy or school.

Participants are tested to assess their cognitive skills and attitudes toward criminal behavior at the beginning and end of the thirty-five sessions. Results indicate statistically significant improvement in several areas: Participants

- Appreciate other people's perspectives better
- Accept criticism better
- Consider more options in resolving conflicts with others
- Have less negative attitudes toward law, courts, and police

Participants were satisfied with the program. Seventy-four percent said the program "was much better than any other program" they'd participated in. Three weeks after the program, 97 percent said they were using the skills they'd learned. Maybe most important, participants believed the program was "highly relevant to their lives" (Figure 12.3).

12-7 A detailed account of rehabilitation through clearer thinking

Did the program reduce recidivism? A follow-up showed that 19.7 percent of released inmates who completed the program were convicted of a new crime and returned to prison within a year compared with 24.8 percent of a control group of similar offenders who wanted to get in the program but couldn't. For offenders who completed the program in the community instead of prison the results were better: 8.4 percent of participants who completed the program in the community compared with the 24.8 percent who completed the program in prison were convicted. The bottom line: There was "some modest evidence of the effectiveness of the program" (Gaes et al.1998, 29).

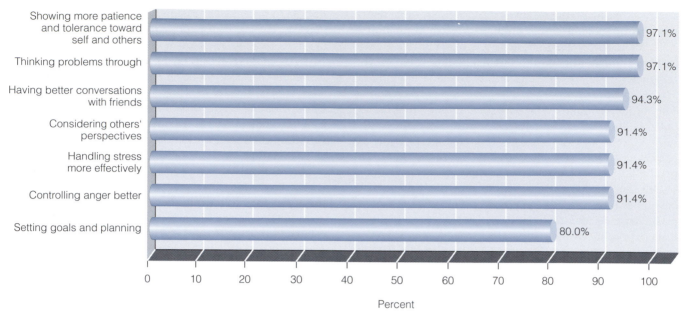

FIGURE 12.3

Areas Where Offenders Felt They Functioned Better

SOURCE: Fabiano, Porporino, and Robinson 1990.

12-8 Detailed description of the Delaware and North Carolina cognitive skills programs

Debate over prison programs

Education, vocational training, prison work, and religious programs are broadly supported, so they don't stir up much controversy. Recreation programs are a different story. They symbolize the deep division of opinion over the confinement model (prison *as* punishment) and punishment model (prison *for* punishment) discussed earlier in the chapter. Those who believe prisoners are supposed to suffer confinement *plus* more pain, resent recreation programs that allow prisoners to "work out," compete in sports, and watch movies.

Rehabilitation programs also arouse controversy, both from an ideological perspective—*Should* we rehabilitate prisoners?—and from a practical standpoint—*Can* we rehabilitate prisoners? We've already discussed how Robert Martinson's article started a war between rehabilitationists and retributionists. The truth is somewhere between nothing works and all treatments work. Ted Palmer (1992, 1–11) reviewed a wide range of rehabilitation programs. He found that between one-quarter and one-third of the programs "work" (reduce recidivism). In view of the discussion of prison programs included in this section, I think Palmer got it just about right: Rehabilitation programs work, *"but they don't work spectacularly."* Like the 1960s optimism that treatment was a panacea, the pessimism that "nothing works" is unwarranted.

Charles H. Logan of the University of Connecticut and Gerald G. Gaes of the Federal Bureau of Prisons (1993, 247) dismiss Palmer's study and other **meta-analyses** (studies of studies) of rehabilitation programs. Because of a host of definitional, methodological problems, and because of the pro-rehabilitation bias of most meta-analysis scholars, Logan and Gaes say the studies of studies of rehabilitation can't be trusted.

If we're just looking at whether prison programs turn prisoners into people who work hard and play by the rules, then the results of the research are mixed at best. But prison programs have missions besides rehabilitating prisoners. They also keep prisoners busy, and keeping them busy keeps them out of trouble—even if it doesn't turn them into law-abiding people. And, "constructive" activity is consistent with an orderly, safe, humane confinement. According to Logan and Gaes (1993):

"Constructive" activity is not defined here as "contributing to the betterment of inmates" but as activity that is, on its face, consistent with the orderly, safe, secure, and humane operation of a prison. Idleness and boredom can be considered wrong from a work ethic standpoint, or as unnatural because human beings are not meant to be idle, or as so fundamentally related to mischief as to be undesirable for that reason. In any case, prison programs can be defended as forms of constructive and meaningful activity and as antidotes to idleness, without invoking claims of rehabilitative effectiveness. This is not to say that it does not matter whether the programs have any rehabilitative effects; it would be fine if they did so. But when we say that the primary purpose of the prison is to punish through confinement, we become more interested in the operation of these programs inside the prison gates and less concerned about their effects beyond. (261)

LIFE IN WOMEN'S PRISONS

Most women prisoners are poor, undereducated, and unskilled Blacks or Hispanics with little or no work experience, locked up in Texas, California, and the federal prisons. They're also mostly young, single mothers with at least two children under 18. And, they have many medical, psychological, and financial problems and needs. According to Barbara Owen and Barbara Bloom (1995), "Substance abuse, compounded by poverty, unemployment, physical and mental illness, physical and sexual abuse, and homelessness, often propel women through the revolving door of the criminal justice system" (167).

More than 60 percent of women prisoners are serving time for nonviolent crimes, mainly drug offenses and minor property crimes. According to the U.S. Bureau of Justice Statistics, women are "substantially more likely than men to be serving time for a drug offense and less likely to have been sentenced for a violent crime." More than half of the increase in women prisoners is due to the imprisonment of drug offenders. According to Owen and Bloom, "the legal response to drug-related behavior has become increasingly punitive, resulting in a flood of less serious offenders into the state and federal prison systems." Since 1991, the number of women serving time for violent offenses actually has dropped. One-third of the women serving time for either murder or manslaughter had killed relatives (Owen and Bloom 1995, 168). In this section, we'll look at the culture of women's prisons and how female prisoners cope by "getting with the program."

The Culture of Women's Prisons

Women cope with prison life differently than men do. David A. Ward and Gene G. Kassebaum's (1965) pathbreaking study of the California Institution for Women demonstrated that women suffer from "affectional starvation," the need for personal relationships, and a "psychosexual" need for men. Ward and Kassebaum found that women prisoners met these needs by structuring their prison relationships around homosexual "family" relationships. But, unlike in men's prisons, female prisoners didn't coerce their partners into homosexual relationships. Of course, some women are "just playing around" with these relationships while others take them seriously.

Rose Giallombardo's (1966) study of the Federal Reformatory for Women supported Ward and Kassebaum's findings. Giallombardo showed that women reproduced outside family relationships in prison—father, mother,

daughter, sister. Unlike the subculture of men's prisons, women's prison subculture fostered mutuality and harmony, not competition and dissension.

Esther Heffernen (1972) found a heterogeneous population in the District of Columbia's Reformatory. For women who grew up in foster homes, prison became the center of their lives. They continuously struggled with staff and other inmates for control of their lives and to obtain illegal food, drugs, clothing, and letters. Women imprisoned for situational offenses, such as murder of an abusive husband, rejected any criminal self-identification, attempting to recreate conventional life inside prison and maintain contacts outside. These prisoners accepted rules and regulations and identified with the staff. Professional criminals tried to keep busy to pass time quickly and avoided trouble to get released as soon as possible to their former lives of crime.

Barbara Owen, in *Surviving the Mix: Struggle and Survival in a Women's Prison* (1998), conducted a combined ethnographic and survey study of the largest women's prison in the United States and probably the world. The Central California Women's Facility holds more than four thousand women. It has all levels of security, from the murderers on death row to the minor drug and property offenders. Two themes run throughout her research. First, when women enter prison, they realize the importance of developing some kind of program to help them cope with doing their time. Work assignments and personal relationships are essential elements in their program. Also important are privacy, material comforts, and acquiring skills. According to Owen (1998):

Most women want to do their time, leave the prison, and return to the free world. They want to avoid the mix of risky and self-defeating behaviors such as drug use and fighting or damaging relationships that interfere with one's program or limit freedom through placement in restrictive housing or the addition of time to one's sentence.

Some dip into the mix in the beginning of their prison terms, leaving when they establish a more productive program. Others invest permanently in the destructive spiral of the mix and its attendant activities. For a small minority of women, the lure of the mix, with its emphasis on the fast life and the excitement of drug use, fighting, and volatile intimate relationships, proves too hard to resist. (8)

For some, **"the mix"**—risky and self-defeating behaviors such as drug use and fighting or damaging relationships—is too tempting to overcome.

The second theme of Owen's research is the importance of personal relationships. The play family is one of these relationships. It contains interpersonal satisfactions, a combination of social and material responsibilities, and a sense of belonging. According to Owen (1998), the play family "creates the sense of community and protection that the . . . cliques and gang structure provide for male prisoners" (8).

"Getting with the Program"

As we saw in the last section, a program is essential to organizing a life around doing time. **"Getting with the program"** is the first step in learning how to do time. According to Barbara Owen (1998):

> Successful programming . . . involves settling down and developing a routine that provides satisfying . . . personal relationships and routine activities that offer constructive stimulation and protection from the dangers of the prison environment. (97)

Programming is to inmates what following a daily routine is to most people outside prison. According to one inmate:

> Programming means to me that I get up every morning, shower, brush my teeth, and get ready for work. I come to work, do my work. I go home for lunch, I come back. I get off, go home, shower and kick back. Either I read a book, or I kick back with some of my friends and bullshit. I stay in my room sometimes, but I go to the day room. It depends on the kind of mood I am in. I got in a fight once and lost my privileges for thirty days. This changed my whole attitude . . . as far as getting in trouble, going off on people. I have been able to come to myself, to sit in my room and think about my goals and stuff in life. (Owen 1998, 97)

Some women refuse to program. These women spend their time getting around expectations. Trying to get around the program leads to loss of jobs, time spent in detention, and loss of "good time" (reduction in sentence length).

■ LAW IN PRISON SOCIETY

Conviction for a crime results in a fundamental transformation in constitutional and legal status. It turns a defendant who at least formally is armed with all the rights of a free person into an offender stripped of constitutional rights (Chapter 9). But are defendants stripped bare, or are they left with some rights? The Thirteenth Amendment to the U.S. Constitution has something to say about this: It abolishes slavery, *"except as a punishment for crime whereof the party shall have been duly convicted."* Shortly after the amendment was adopted after the Civil War, a Virginia court in *Ruffin v. Commonwealth* (1871) explained what the Thirteenth Amendment means to prisoners:

> The bill of rights is a declaration of general principles to govern a society of freemen, and not of convicted felons and men civilly dead. Such men have some rights it is true, such as the law in its benignity accords to them, but not the rights of freemen. They are the slaves of the State undergoing punishment for heinous crimes committed against the laws of the land. While in this state of penal servitude, they must be subject to the regulations of the institution of which they are inmates, and the laws of the State to whom their service is due in expiation of their crimes.

The U.S. Supreme Court has gone so far as to say that "prison brutality . . . is part of the total punishment to which the individual is being subjected for his crime." These strong words don't mean prisoners have *no* rights; it does mean they have *minimal* rights.

According to the principle of **civil death,** a practice going back to ancient Rome, felons are treated as if they were dead when it comes to political and legal rights. The practice survives today in taking away felons' right to vote. But the details of this lost right are a mosaic of state and federal laws, summed up by The Sentencing Project (1998):

> In 46 states and the District of Columbia, felons are prohibited from voting while in prison. In addition, 32 states prohibit offenders from voting on parole and 29 bar voting while on probation. Felons are barred for life from voting in 14 states, a prohibition that can be waived only through a gubernatorial pardon or some other form of clemency. Only four states— Maine, Massachusetts, New Hampshire, and Vermont—allow prison inmates to vote.

So what rights do prisoners have? We'll look at the policy of hands-off prisons taken by the courts at various periods, an overview of which rights prisoners do maintain, their rights in practice, and how prison grievance procedures work when prisoners argue their rights have been violated.

Hands-Off Prisons

Until the 1960s, courts practically never interfered with prison life. Courts adopted a **hands-off doctrine**; prison administrators determined how prisons were run and the way prisoners were treated. According to the hands-off doctrine, the law didn't follow convicted offenders into prison; it left them at the prison gate. Prison conditions and prison society were none of the courts' business.

The main justification for this policy was that judges weren't qualified to run prisons. They weren't trained in prison administration, and they were far removed from prison life. So, it didn't make sense for judges to substitute their judgments for those of the experts—wardens and officers. Another reason for the doctrine was the mission of punishment. Prisons are supposed to be unpleasant. Finally, the doctrine was necessary for prison security. Prisoners' rights backed up by judicial intervention would have been a recipe for prison unrest and even riots (Baker et al. 1973, 454).

However, in the 1960s, a combination of forces led to limiting the hands-off doctrine. Prisoners' rights were added to the agenda of the civil rights movement. Black and Hispanic prisoners sued wardens and states over prison conditions and the treatment of minority prisoners. Disillusionment with rehabilitation shifted the emphasis from the *needs* of prisoners to their *rights*.

The prisoners' rights movement got help from a few activist federal judges who gave prisoners a forum by letting them bring their grievances to their courts. Having as respected a grievance forum as the federal courts generated great solidarity among prisoners, and this prisoner solidarity made the prisoners' rights movement even stronger. However, without the support of a new breed of prison lawyers—specialists who knew how to voice complaints and frame grievances in legal and constitutional terms—the prisoners' rights movement would have died "aborning." According to James B. Jacobs, a leading scholar of prisons and the rights of prisoners:

> A platoon, eventually a phalanx, of prisoners' rights lawyers, supported by federal and foundation funding, soon appeared and pressed claims. They initiated, and won, prisoners' rights cases that implicated every aspect of prison governance. In many cases the prisoners' attorneys were more dedicated and effective than the overburdened and inexperienced government attorneys who represented the prison officials. (Jacobs 1983, 39)

Overview of Prisoners' Rights

Ever since the 1960s, courts have made it clear that prisoners don't leave their constitutional rights at the prison gates—but, their rights are severely restricted. Too many people believe prisoners are always suing over every little thing they don't like and are winning their lawsuits. (We'll see later how far from reality this is.) In defining the limits of these rights, courts use a **balancing test of prisoners' rights**: they look at all the facts of each case and weigh the shrunken rights of prisoners against the prison's powerful missions of punishment, security, order, and discipline. It shouldn't surprise you to learn that the powerful prison missions almost always trump the shrunken rights of prisoners.

With all that said, here is the list of rights prisoners keep in shrunken form:

1. Access to the courts
2. Due process of law
3. Equal protection of the laws
4. First Amendment rights of free speech, association, and religion
5. The Eighth Amendment right against "cruel and unusual punishment"
6. Fourth Amendment rights against unreasonable searches and seizures

The right to go to court

Prisoners keep the right to go to court. The right to go to court includes the right to challenge the legality, the length, and the conditions of their confinement; the right to a lawyer, including a **jailhouse lawyer** (prisoners who help other prisoners on points of law); and access to law libraries, transcripts of their cases, and other materials they need to present their claims.

Due process of law

The Fifth and the Fourteenth Amendments guarantee that neither the federal government nor state governments can "deprive any person of life, liberty, or property without due process of law" (Chapter 2). Compared with free people, prisoners are "due" a lot less "life, liberty, and property" and a lot less process to protect them from deprivation of what little life, liberty, and property they have a right to. So, in determining whether state officials have deprived prison inmates of these rights, courts look at how *great* the deprivation of life, liberty, or property is and decide how *shrunken* the procedures to deprive inmates of life, liberty, or property can be.

According to the U.S. Supreme Court, "certain changes in conditions may be so severe or so different from ordinary conditions of confinement . . . the state authorities" can't make the changes "without complying with the minimum requirements of due process of law" (*Sandin v. Conner* 1995, 493). So, involuntarily committing an inmate to a mental hospital, forcing a prisoner to take antipsychotic drugs in prison, and taking away "good time" are severe enough to be protected by the due process clause. But most deprivations don't qualify. According to U.S. Supreme Court Justice David Breyer:

> Prison by design restricts the inmate's freedom. And one cannot properly view unimportant matters that happen to be the subject of prison regulations as substantially aggravating loss that has already occurred. Indeed, a regulation about a minor matter, for example, a regulation that seems to cabin the discretionary power of a prison administrator to deprive a inmate of, say, a certain kind of lunch may amount simply to an instruction to the administrator about how to do his job, rather than a guarantee to the inmate of a "right" to the status quo. Thus, this court has never held that comparatively unimportant prisoner "deprivations" fall within the scope of the Due Process Clause. . . . I recognize that, as a consequence, courts must separate the unimportant from the potentially significant. . . . It seems to me possible to separate less significant matters such as television privileges,

"sack" versus "tray" lunches, playing the state lottery, attending an ex-stepfather's funeral, or the limits of travel when on prison furlough, from more significant matters. . . . (*Sandin v. Conner* 1995, 499–500)

The Court also has decided some matters that might *seem* serious aren't serious enough to qualify for due process protection, like solitary confinement for thirty days or transferring prisoners from medium to maximum security prisons and even to supermaxes.

Assuming prison authorities have deprived prisoners of rights protected by due process, how *much* process are prisoners due? The Supreme Court has ruled that prisoners are definitely *not* entitled to the "full panoply of rights due" an ordinary person in a criminal trial. The state can satisfy the requirements of due process by providing prisoners:

1. An unbiased review board or committee
2. Notice of the proposed action and the grounds for it
3. An opportunity to "present reasons why the proposed action should not be taken (*Sandin v. Conner* 1995, 490)

Due process doesn't include the right to a lawyer or to confront the witnesses against them.

Equal protection of the laws

The Fourteenth Amendment guarantees all individuals, including prisoners, equal protection of the laws. However, we learned in Chapter 2 that the equal protection clause doesn't guarantee all groups will be treated exactly alike. Groups can be treated differently if there's a good reason for doing so. The most common equal protection claim prisoners make is racial and ethnic discrimination. In ordinary circumstances, race is never a good enough reason to treat people differently. But, prison's different. According to the Supreme Court, prison administrators have "the right, acting in good faith and in particularized circumstances, to take into account racial tensions in maintaining security, discipline, and good order" (*Lee v. Washington*, 1968, 334).

Free speech, association, and religion

Prisoners keep their First Amendment rights to expression, association, and religion only so far as they don't conflict with the prison's missions. In other words, courts balance prisoners' shrunken First Amendment rights against the broad need to accomplish the missions of prisons to punish prisoners and maintain security, safety, and discipline. So, prison administrators can censor the correspondence of prisoners. In *Procunier v. Martinez* (1974), the U.S. Supreme Court ruled that California's prison censorship rules were constitutional because they were designed to maintain security, order, and rehabilitation and because First Amendment freedoms were restricted only enough to ensure security, order, and rehabilitation.

Right against cruel and unusual punishment

The Eighth Amendment prohibits "cruel and unusual punishments." This prohibition is aimed specifically at the protection of prisoners. Nevertheless, the Eighth Amendment doesn't ban "every government action affecting the interests or well-being of a prisoner." According to the Court:

> Only the unnecessary and wanton infliction of pain constitutes cruel and unusual punishment forbidden by the Eighth Amendment. . . . It is obduracy and wantonness, not inadvertence or error in good faith, that characterize the conduct prohibited by the Eighth Amendment clause, whether that conduct occurs in connection with establishing conditions of confinement, supplying medical needs, or restoring official control over a tumultuous cellblock. The infliction of pain in the course of a prison security, therefore, does not amount to cruel and unusual punishment simply because it may appear in retrospect that the degree of force authorized or applied for security purposes was unreasonable. (*Whitley v. Albers*, 1986. 319)

In *Whitley v. Albers*, prisoners took a correctional officer hostage during a riot at the Oregon State Penitentiary and held him in the upper tier of a two-tier cell block. Prison officials developed a plan to free the hostage. According to the plan, the prison security manager entered the cell block unarmed. Armed prison officials followed him. The security manager ordered one of the officers to fire a "warning shot and to shoot low at any inmates climbing the stairs to the upper tier since he would be climbing the stairs to free the hostage." Assistant Warden Harold Whitley, after firing the warning shot, shot inmate Gerald Albers in the knee when Albers tried to climb the stairs. Albers contended that shooting him was cruel and unusual punishment. The Court agreed that, in hindsight the use of deadly force was probably excessive. But it wasn't "cruel and unusual punishment" if the officers acted in "good faith." Why? Because shooting him wasn't an "intentional and wanton infliction of pain" (313).

Right against unreasonable searches and seizures

The Fourth Amendment protects the people against unreasonable searches and seizures by any agent of the government (see Chapter 6). But the right of prisoners against unreasonable searches and seizures is extremely limited. (Some critics say it's nonexistent.) Surveillance, cell and strip searches, monitored visits, censored mail, and other restrictions on privacy are basic parts of prison life, justified on the grounds that prisoners are in prison as punishment; besides the invasions help to ensure secure, safe and orderly prisons.

In the leading case on the Fourth Amendment rights of prisoners, *Hudson v. Palmer,* the U.S. Supreme Court ruled that prisoners have no right to privacy in their cells.

Prisoners' Rights in Operation

Beginning in the late 1970s and continuing through the 1990s, the Supreme Court placed limits on prisoners' rights, returning to prison administrators much of the discretion they enjoyed during the hands-off era. Typical of this move is the important case of *Bell v. Wolfish* (1979), in which the Court ruled that prisoners had no right to a single cell. Justice Rehnquist wrote:

> The deplorable conditions and draconian restrictions of our Nation's prisons are too well known to require recounting here, and the federal courts rightly have condemned these sordid aspects of our prison systems. But many of these same courts have, in the name of the Constitution, become increasingly enmeshed in the minutiae of prison operations. Judges, after all, are human. They, no less than others in our society, have a natural tendency to believe that their individual solutions to often intractable problems are better and more workable than those of the persons who are actually charged with the running of the particular institution under examination. But under the Constitution, the first question to be answered is not whose plan is best, but in what branch of government is lodged the authority to initially devise the plan. This does not mean constitutional rights are not to be scrupulously observed. It does mean, however, the inquiry of federal courts into prison management must be limited to the issue of whether a particular system violates any prohibition of the Constitution, or in the case of a federal prison, a statute. The wide range of "judgment calls" that meet constitutional and statutory requirements are confined to officials outside the Judiciary Branch of Government.

Not only has the Supreme Court restricted the rights of prisoners and returned discretionary judgment to prison officials, but most prisoners fail in their lawsuits even when the Court has accepted they have rights against discretionary decision making by prison administrators. Most prisoners' cases never get beyond the earliest stages of the proceedings. In California, for example, the court terminated 80.4 percent of prisoners' cases shortly after they filed their suits and before prison administrators even responded. Nationwide, 68 percent of all prisoners' cases were dropped at this early stage. Due to early dismissal, only 4.2 percent of all cases filed ever get to trial (Thomas 1989, 27–54).

Even when prisoners succeed in getting their cases into court, they practically never "win." In one sample of 664 cases, only three court orders were issued regarding confinement conditions; only two prisoners were awarded minimal money damages. In a few more cases, seven temporary restraining orders and five preliminary injunctions were issued. Lawyers are probably a necessity; most cases that get to trial are cases of prisoners who

have lawyers. In the two cited cases awarded damages, the prisoner with a lawyer received $200; the one without a lawyer got only $6! (Thomas 1989, 27–54).

But Jack E. Call found that prisoners meet with greater success in prison crowding cases. Courts issued favorable rulings in 73.8 percent of all cases, 80 percent in federal district courts, and 66 percent in courts of appeals. According to Call (1988), many courts have made it clear that prison administrative discretion in managing prisons will not shield prisons from litigation involving "gruesome living conditions" (34–41).

To be fair, although prisoners win few victories in lower federal courts, court cases still affect life in prisons. Even a lost case can lead to prison reform. Prison administrators don't want courts to intrude into their domain, so they sometimes make changes to avoid the intrusions. Jim Thomas (1989), in his analysis of prisoner litigation, quotes one prison administrator on the effects of prisoner lawsuits:

> Where only a few years ago prisons operated without written rules and with only the most rudimentary record keeping systems, today prison authorities are engulfed in bureaucratic paper. There are regulations, guidelines, policy statements, and general orders; there are forms, files, and reports for virtually everything. (27)

Litigation has also increased centralization and oversight by correctional administrations.

Although, in the short term, court orders may reduce staff morale and even cause prison violence, court restrictions on crowding have increased prison and jail construction, according to Malcolm Feeley and Roger Hanson (1987). Court orders have also mitigated the most extreme abusive conditions in prisons. A detailed study of four major prison condition cases found that compliance, although grudging, slow, and incomplete, led all four states to spend substantial amounts of money responding to court orders. In some cases, new prisons were built following litigation. It is unlikely this would've occurred if prisoners hadn't sued their keepers (Harris and Spiller 1977).

Internal Grievance Mechanisms

Lawsuits aren't the only redress for prisoners who have grievances against prison administration. Every prison has some kind of internal grievance mechanism operated by prison officers and sometimes outside participants, including former prisoners. Although not totally supported by either prisoners or prison critics, internal grievance proceedings play a significant part in prison governance and life (Brakel 1983, 394).

Most state prison systems have broad powers to hear complaints. Illinois, for example, opens its Institutional

YOU DECIDE

Do prisoners have a right against unreasonable searches and seizures?

Hudson v. Palmer 468 U.S. 517 (1984).

Facts

Russell Palmer Jr., is an inmate at the Bland Correctional Center in Bland, Virginia, serving sentences for forgery, uttering, grand larceny, and bank robbery convictions. On September 16, 1981, Ted Hudson, an officer at the Correctional Center, with a fellow officer, conducted a "shakedown" search of Palmer's prison locker and cell for contraband. During the "shakedown," the officers discovered a ripped pillowcase in a trash can near the respondent's cell bunk. Charges against Palmer were instituted under the prison disciplinary procedures for destroying state property. After a hearing, Palmer was found guilty on the charge and was ordered to reimburse the State for the cost of the material destroyed; in addition, a reprimand was entered on his prison record.

Opinion

We have repeatedly held that prisons are not beyond the reach of the Constitution. No "iron curtain" separates one from the other. Indeed, we have insisted that prisoners be accorded those rights not fundamentally inconsistent with imprisonment itself or incompatible with the objectives of incarceration. For example, we have held that invidious racial discrimination is as intolerable within a prison as outside, except as may be essential to "prison security and discipline."

However, while persons imprisoned for crime enjoy many protections of the Constitution, it is also clear that imprisonment carries with it the loss of many significant rights. These constraints on inmates, and in some cases the complete withdrawal of certain rights, are "justified by the considerations underlying our penal system." The curtailment of certain rights is necessary, as a practical matter, to accommodate a myriad of "institutional needs and objectives" of prison facilities, chief among

which is internal security. Of course, these restrictions or retractions also serve, incidentally, as reminders that, under our system of justice, deterrence and retribution are factors in addition to correction.

We have not before been called upon to decide the specific question whether the Fourth Amendment applies within a prison cell. . . . We hold that society is not prepared to recognize as legitimate any subjective expectation of privacy that a prisoner might have in his prison cell and that, accordingly, the Fourth Amendment proscription against unreasonable searches does not apply within the confines of the prison cell. The recognition of privacy rights for prisoners in their individual cells simply cannot be reconciled with the concept of incarceration and the needs and objectives of penal institutions.

Prisons, by definition, are places of involuntary confinement of persons who have a demonstrated proclivity for anti-social criminal, and often violent, conduct. Inmates have necessarily shown a lapse in ability to control and conform their behavior to the legitimate standards of society by the normal impulses of self-restraint; they have shown an inability to regulate their conduct in a way that reflects either a respect for law or an appreciation of the rights of others.

The administration of a prison, we have said, is "at best an extraordinarily difficult undertaking." But it would be literally impossible to accomplish the prison objectives identified above if inmates retained a right of privacy in their cells. Virtually the only place inmates can conceal weapons, drugs, and other contraband is in their cells. Unfettered access to these cells by prison officials, thus, is imperative if drugs and contraband are to be ferreted out and sanitary surroundings are to be maintained.

Inquiry Board (IIB) to any prisoner who wants "resolution to complaints, problems, and grievances which [he or she has] not been able to resolve through other avenues available at the institution or facility" (Brakel 1982, 117). Let's look at some common grievances and grievance procedures.

Common Grievances and Disciplinary Violations
Grievances, such as these in Illinois, are common:

- Claims for early release
- Charges that guards issued disciplinary "tickets" improperly

- Complaints that work or program assignments were not right
- Claims that prisoners were classified wrong
- Charges that property was lost, stolen, or confiscated

Common disciplinary actions against prisoners include "tickets" for:

- Creating dangerous disturbances
- Disobeying a direct order
- Undertaking unauthorized movement
- Assaulting another prisoner or an officer
- Destroying or damaging property
- Possessing dangerous contraband
- Engaging in sexual misconduct (Brakel 1982, 117)

Determining whether an expectation of privacy is "legitimate" or "reasonable" necessarily entails a balancing of interests. The two interests here are the interest of society in the security of its penal institutions and the interest of the prisoner in privacy within his cell. The latter interest, of course, is already limited by the exigencies of the circumstances: A prison "shares none of the attributes of privacy of a home, an automobile, an office, or a hotel room."

We strike the balance in favor of institutional security, which we have noted is "central to all other corrections goals." A right of privacy in traditional Fourth Amendment terms is fundamentally incompatible with the close and continual surveillance of inmates and their cells required to ensure institutional security and internal order. We are satisfied that society would insist that the prisoner's expectation of privacy always yield to what must be considered the paramount interest in institutional security. We believe that it is accepted by our society that "loss of freedom of choice and privacy are inherent incidents of confinement."

Dissent

Prison guard Hudson maliciously took and destroyed a quantity of Palmer's property, including legal materials and letters, for no reason other than harassment. Measured by the conditions that prevail in a free society, neither the possessions nor the slight residuum of privacy that a prison inmate can retain in his cell can have more than the most minimal value. From the standpoint of the prisoner, however, that trivial residuum may mark the difference between slavery and humanity.

Personal letters, snapshots of family members, a souvenir, a deck of cards, a hobby kit, perhaps a diary or a training manual for an apprentice in a new trade, or even a Bible—a variety of inexpensive items may enable a prisoner to maintain contact with some part of his past and an eye to the possibility of a better future. Are all of these items subject to unrestrained perusal, confiscation or mutilation at the hands of a possibly hostile guard? Is the Court correct in its perception that "society" is not prepared to recognize any privacy or possessory interest of the prison inmate—no matter how remote the threat to prison security may be?

It is well-settled that the discretion accorded prison officials is not absolute. A prisoner retains those constitutional rights not inconsistent with legitimate penological objectives. There can be no penological justification for the seizure alleged here. There is no contention that Palmer's property posed any threat to institutional security. Hudson had already examined the material before he took and destroyed it. The allegation is that Hudson did this for no reason save spite; there is no contention that under prison regulations the material was contraband. The need for "close and continual surveillance of inmates and their cells," in no way justifies taking and destroying non-contraband property; if material is examined and found not to be contraband, there can be no justification for its seizure.

Questions
1. Which opinion do you support, the majority (which is regarded as "the law of the land") or the dissent? Explain your answer.
2. If you were deciding the law, what would you decide? What reasons would you give?

The Minnesota Department of Corrections gives all prisoners a written statement of ten procedures they're guaranteed in all grievance proceedings; they are:

1. A published list of the charges and penalties
2. A prompt and full statement of the nature of the alleged violation not later than five days after the prisoner is charged with a prison rule violation
3. The right to adequate notice prior to the hearing
4. The opportunity for a prisoner to appear in person before the disciplinary hearing board and be heard
5. The right to bring witnesses and present evidence to the hearing
6. The right to an impartial hearing board
7. The right to counsel or substitute counsel throughout the process
8. A written notice of the board's findings
9. The right to appeal to the warden or another designated person
10. The right to a record of the proceedings at the hearing for review and appeal (Minnesota Department of Corrections 1988)

Most prisoners complain about their classification and the amount of good time they're entitled to. For example, under the Illinois good-time rule, prisoners get their sentences reduced one day for every day of good time they served. Discipline violations can reduce this good time. Also in Illinois, prisoners are classified either as A, B, or C. Grade A entitles prisoners to maximum freedom and privileges; C is for maximum security and the least freedom. Disciplinary tickets might lead to downgrading a prisoner's security level. A challenge to a disciplinary ticket might, therefore, be grounds to grieve reduced good time and a security reclassification. For example, violating the Illinois prison rule against forced sexual contacts can reduce good time by 360 days *and* downgrade prisoners to grade C security for 360 days (Brakel 1983, 412).

Another ground for complaint is when administrators deny prisoners' requests to be put into protective custody. **Protective custody** means living in a segregation unit to protect them from other prisoners. One grievance arose when prison officials denied a request for protective custody to a 6'4" White man weighing 210 pounds against Black gang members. Prison officials argued he was big enough to protect himself (Brakel 1983, 414–415).

Missing prisoners' property is another source of complaint. Most commonly, these complaints arise because the administration has confiscated unauthorized property or contraband. Other common cases involve lost or stolen prisoner property. According to the prisoner, the administration didn't protect the property or didn't pay for damage or loss. Even though property cases don't usually involve a lot of money, they're important. First, they make up a considerable number of grievances filed. Second, items such as photographs, jewelry, and jackets may have sentimental value to the prisoner. These items may be all that provides individuality in an otherwise very impersonal and regulated place.

Grievance procedures and their effects

Grievance decision making is two-tiered. Members of a local grievance committee, drawn entirely from within the prison, initially decide for or against the prisoner. Prisoners can appeal decisions against them to a board made up of private citizens and correctional administrators. Proceedings are formal, governed by written rules and regulations. Prisoners have basic due process rights, usually including the right to be present at the hearing, sometimes the right to have witnesses and to challenge adverse evidence, and the right to have a decision in writing within a specified time period. This written decision has to give the reasons for the board's ruling. Prisoners have to go through the whole internal grievance procedure before they can take their cases to court, a requirement called **exhausting administrative remedies.**

Prisoners rarely win their grievance cases. One prisoner overestimated the win ratio when he said, "You don't win more than 1 in 10." In fact, it's less. One review of grievances in several cell blocks showed that prisoners won only 1 case out of 12 in one block, 1 of 19 in a sec-

ond, 1 of 25 in a third, and only 1 of 28 in a fourth. On appeal to a review board, the results were also low. In one maximum security prison, prisoners "won" 17 percent of the appeals and lost 75 percent. Another 8 percent had mixed results (Brakel 1982, 124–126).

Grievance procedures in prisons have several missions:

- Improve prison management and help identify problems
- Reduce inmate frustration and prison violence
- Aid prisoner rehabilitation
- Reduce the number of cases prisoners take to the courts
- Bring "justice" to prisons

Existing grievance mechanisms may or may not accomplish their missions. Research has raised several questions. To improve prison management by identifying problems, the first aim, prison administrators have to take the time periodically to review caseloads to determine what kinds of grievances prisoners have. Only by reviewing the grievances can something be done about them. This takes time and resources most prisons simply don't have. To achieve this aim might require prisoners to bring grievances more selectively; instead of using grievance procedures to express "rights consciousness" or harassment, they might have to "purify" their complaints. According to prison litigation expert Jan Brakel (1982, 129):

> The message to inmates should be that abusing the procedures for frivolous, repetitive grievances harms the chances of other inmates, and ultimately their own, of having important things changed.

Few prison officials go so far as to say grievance procedures eliminate violence from prisons. They may provide a "safety valve" for prisoner discontent and "keep the lid on" violent prison outbreaks, but there's no proof this is true. Correlations between violence levels and prison grievance mechanisms simply don't exist. Through grievance procedures, an inmate here and there might develop more respect for procedures and be willing to follow them. These inmates are probably "rehabilitated," in the sense that they're more ready to live inside (and outside) prison without breaking the rules. However, most prisoners don't see grievance mechanisms positively. In many cases, prisoners see them only as proof that institutions rig decisions to maintain the establishment against dissidents—in this case, prison officials against prisoners (Brakel 1982, 130).

Proving grievance mechanisms reduce the load of cases in courts is also difficult. Grievance mechanisms may reduce caseloads by resolving grievances inside prison but they're likely to increase litigation because prisoners who are more conscious of their rights are more apt to demand them. If they don't win in prison, they'll take their fights to the courts. The bottom line (as we've learned so many times in this book) is there's no empirical support for any of these speculations.

Finally, it's not clear that grievance mechanisms bring justice to prisons. For that to be the case, according to Jan Brakel (1982, 133), administrators and prisoners have to use them to their best advantage,

> instead of playing games with them, games of power, games of psychology, harassment games, legalistic games, passing time games, and so forth. At neither Vienna nor Stateville were the procedures used to full advantage—the staff failed to maximize both the problem-identification and the problem-disposition potential of the process, and far too many of the inmates abused the process with groundless or frivolous claims.

Several recommendations aim at bringing the reality of grievance mechanisms closer to their proclaimed missions. One suggests changing the composition of the grievance body. Prisoners and other critics commonly complain that prison officials dominate grievance mechanisms. They call for more outside participation, either by citizens or prisoners. However, although outsiders may be impartial, they're also naive and ignorant of prison society and can therefore be "conned" by both prisoners and administration. Prisoners aren't necessarily a good choice either. They can be partial and subject to intimi-

dation and physical danger if they rule against another prisoner.

Other reformers call for formal decision making, including written rules of procedure, adherence to decisions in prior cases, more documentation of proceedings, and putting decisions in writing. Some believe, however, that there's already enough "paper"; the real problem is how to use the documentation to achieve fair and just results. Demands for more investigation, more listening to the prisoners' side of the story, and so on accomplish little if all they do is add to an already heavily burdened grievance body (Brakel 1982, 136–137).

Perhaps the severest criticism is that too many frivolous and trumped-up grievances, or ones brought only to harass, are filed. Grievances have to be screened more carefully, but no one's quite sure how to do this. How does anyone decide, before hearings begin, whether a complaint has merit or is a farce—something "cooked up to obstruct the system, harass the staff, pass dead time"? Once proceedings begin, however, frivolous claims often come to light. At that point, they could be penalized, and such penalties might take several forms. Privileges such as movies, TV, or visits to the commissary could be taken away. Refiling restrictions could be imposed if present grievances are decided to be frivolous or spurious. Extreme cases might even call for the levy of fines (Brakel 1982, 139).

Knowledge and Understanding Check

Introduction
✔ Describe the difference between professionals' and nonprofessionals' views of what life in prisons should be like.
✔ Describe the difference between the confinement and punishment models of punishment.

Male Prison Society
✔ Describe the characteristics of most prisoners.
✔ Identify and describe the two major theories explaining prison society.
✔ What is a life of "enforced poverty," and how do inmates try to avoid it?
✔ Why is consensual sex prohibited in prisons, and how extensive is it?
✔ What do we know about rape in men's prisons?
✔ Identify the types of and discuss violence as part of life in prisons.
✔ List and describe the elements of the major types of prison programs.

✔ List the missions of each prison program, and discuss how effective each type is in accomplishing its missions.
✔ Describe the major issues in the debate over prison programs.

Life in Women's Prisons
✔ Describe women prisoners and the crimes they're in prison for.
✔ Describe the culture of women's prisons and compare it with that of men's prisons.
✔ What does "getting with the program" mean, and how do women prisoners do it?

Law in Prison Society
✔ Define, list the justifications for, and give the reasons for placing limits on the "hands-off" doctrine.
✔ Explain the balancing test to determine prisoners' rights.
✔ List six rights of prisoners, and describe each of them.
✔ Describe how prisoners' rights operate in practice.
✔ Identify the main grievances brought to and the procedures involved in internal grievance mechanisms.

KEY TERMS

balancing test of prisoners' rights
civil death
cognitive model of rehabilitation
confinement model of
    imprisonment
confinement "plus" model of
    imprisonment
enforced poverty
exhausting administrative
    remedies

gangbanging
"getting with the program"
hands-off doctrine
importation theory
indigenous theory
inmate code
jailhouse lawyer
meta-analyses
"the mix"
"nothing works"

pains of imprisonment
principle of less eligibility
prisonization
protective custody
punishment model of
    imprisonment
rehabilitation
therapeutic communities (TCs)
total institutions

INTERNET PROJECT

 InfoTrac College Edition: Investigate one of the following topics covered in Chapter 12 by selecting Search using the key words "consensual sex prisons," "women's prisons," or "prisoners' rights." What would you add to what was covered in the sections of the text related to these key words? Explain why.

Epilogue

As I was writing the last words of the last chapter of your book, I took a break to look at this morning's papers. Unbelievable as it may seem, I found a perfect article in *The New York Times* to close the book and give you some big things to think about. If you've read the book and listened to your instructor, I'm confident that by now, compared with most of the general public, you're kind of an expert in criminal justice. So you're in a position to give informed answers to the questions raised in the article: Should states cut back on the grand and expensive experiment in the punishment policy of the last thirty years? If so, where and how and who should they cut? And, is it politically possible to get support for cuts in criminal justice budgets?

The article describes the immediate problem of state budget crunches caused by the current recession, which will probably be over by the time you read this. But the questions are important even in the best of times. I'm also curious to know if your answers are different now than they would have been before you took this class and read your book. I'd really like to know the answer to this, so would you please take a little of your time and e-mail me your answer (*mailto:jbs1936@mn.rr.com*)? Thanks a lot and good luck.

Should we cut back on the grand and expensive punishment experiment?

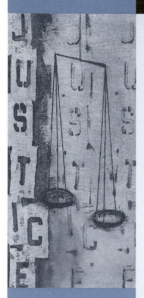

Fox Butterfield, "Tight Budgets Force States to Reconsider Crime and Penalties," *New York Times*, 21 January 2002. © 2001 by the New York Times Co. Reprinted by permission.

After three decades of building more prisons and passing tougher sentencing laws, many states are being forced by budget deficits to close some prisons, lay off guards, and consider shortening sentences. In the last month, Ohio, Michigan, and Illinois have each moved to close a prison, laying off guards in the process, prison officials say. Washington State is considering a proposal by Gov. Gary Locke to shorten sentences for nonviolent crimes and drug offenses and to make it easier for inmates to win early release, saving money by shrinking the prison population. Colorado and Illinois are delaying building prisons, and Illinois is cutting education for 25,000 inmates. California, which led the nation's prison building boom, will close five small, privately operated minimum security prisons when their contracts expire this year. Budget pressures are also adding momentum to a push to put a proposal on the California ballot in November that would reduce the number of criminals subject to the state's three-strikes sentencing law.

"I don't know of a correctional system in the country that isn't facing some of this," said Chase Riveland, a former director of Washington State prisons, now a consultant. Steven Ickes, an assistant director of the Oregon Department of Corrections, said, "My sense is that budget problems are making people ask fundamental questions about whether we can afford to keep on doing what we've been doing," locking up ever more criminals for longer periods. "We are going to have to make some tough choices about prisons versus schools, and about getting a better investment return on how we run our prisons so we don't have so many prisoners reoffending and being sent back."

Since the early 1970s, the number of state prisoners has increased 500 percent, growing each year in the 1990s even as crime fell. In that time, prisons were the fastest-growing item in state budgets—often the only growing item. More than two million inmates were in state and federal prisons and local jails, which cost more than $30 billion a year to run, Allen J. Beck, of the Bureau of Justice Statistics, said. In those years, said Franklin Zimring, director of the Earl Warren Legal Institute at the University of California, public pressure to get tough on crime made prison budgets virtually untouchable. But with crime having dropped or leveled off in the last nine years, this political pressure has abated, and with the economy in a decline, many states are having to cut spending to balance their budgets. "This means that prisons must now compete by everybody else's rules for scarce budget resources," Professor Zimring said.

But whether fiscal restraints will lead to a decline in the number of people in prison is less clear, Mr. Beck said. In the second half of 2000, he said, the number of inmates fell for the first time since 1972. "My best guess," Mr. Beck said, "is that the economic restraints are going to be offset by the rigidities of the sentencing laws of the 1990s, which required longer sentences. "What we may have is stability, with the prison population continuing to grow, but slowly, in keeping with the population of the United States."

The biggest change in response to the tight budgets has come in the three states that have moved to close prisons: Ohio, Michigan, and Illinois. Reginald Wilkinson, the director of the Ohio Department of Rehabilitation and Correction, said he had been ordered to cut his budget by 1.5 percent, or $19 million. At first, Mr. Wilkinson said, he feared he would have to close two prisons but found he could achieve the savings by closing one, the old Orient Correctional Institution, a maximum security prison in Columbus with 1,700 inmates. They are being transferred to 10 other prisons in Ohio. Some guards will also be transferred, but about 200 employees will be laid off, Mr. Wilkinson said. He is offering other guards incentives for early retirement. Guards account for about 80 percent of the cost of prisons.

In Michigan, where the prison department had to save $50 million, it closed a medium security prison in Jackson, 70 miles west of Detroit, along with a halfway house and a work camp. The prison agency also laid off 97 guards who worked in Jackson and cut 161 positions for sergeants, unit managers, and assistant deputy wardens at other prisons, said Matt Davis, a spokesman. To reduce costs further, Michigan is moving 250 to 300 prisoners who were temporarily housed in county jails back into prisons so more state guards do not have to be laid off, Mr. Davis said. But Wayne Kangas, the sheriff of Clinton County, where some of the state prisoners were housed, said the state's action would cost his county from $500,000 to $600,000 in lost revenues. "This will be a major problem for us," Sheriff Kangas said. "It's a real shock."

Illinois is closing the Joliet Correctional Center, an old prison that once held George Nelson, known as Baby Face, and is saving $5.4 million by eliminating classes for inmates beyond courses to pass a high school equivalency test, said Sergio Molina, a prisons spokesman. Illinois is also looking to save money with a new food program for inmates, Mr. Molina said.

In Washington, Governor Locke is asking the legislature to reduce sentences for nonviolent crimes and drug offenses and to release such prisoners faster for good behavior. Don Arlow, the budget and strategic planning chief for the Washington Department of Corrections, said these measures would reduce the number of inmates by 122 in a year. Governor Locke has also proposed to exempt inmates judged least likely to commit new crimes from supervision after they are released.

California will not renew licenses for five small private prisons for minimum security inmates later this year, said Stephen Green, a spokesman for the California Youth and Adult Correctional Agency. The state can do this because the number of inmates fell to 156,000, from 162,000, in 1999, Mr. Green said, and his agency expects a further drop of 3.1 percent this year. Inmates in the five private prisons will be transferred to regular state prisons. California has 6,700 inmates serving sentences of 25 years to life under the state's three-strikes law. Besides complaints that the law is overly punitive, there has long been criticism that it is an expensive way to combat crime, keeping people locked up long after their prime years for committing crime. As long as the California economy was doing well, this criticism was blunted. But Mr. Green said the budget deficit was making some legislators change their views, and he said he expected a proposal to require that the third strike be for a violent offense to be on the ballot this fall.

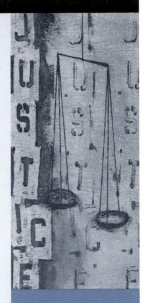

Appendix:
Constitution of the United States

Preamble

We the People of the United States, in Order to form a more perfect Union, establish Justice, insure domestic Tranquility, provide for the common defence, promote the general Welfare, and secure the Blessings of Liberty to ourselves and our Posterity, do ordain and establish this Constitution for the United States of America.

Article I

Section 1 All legislative Powers herein granted shall be vested in a Congress of the United States, which shall consist of a Senate and House of Representatives.

Section 2 The House of Representatives shall be composed of Members chosen every second Year by the People of the several States, and the Electors in each State shall have the Qualifications requisite for Electors of the most numerous Branch of the State Legislature.

No Person shall be a Representative who shall not have attained to the Age of twenty five Years, and been seven Years a Citizen of the United States, and who shall not, when elected, be an Inhabitant of that State in which he shall be chosen.

Representatives and direct Taxes shall be apportioned among the several States which may be included within this Union, according to their respective Numbers, which shall be determined by adding to the whole Number of free Persons, including those bound to Service for a Term of Years, and excluding Indians not taxed, three fifths of all other Persons. The actual Enumeration shall be made within three Years after the first Meeting of the Congress of the United States, and within every subsequent Term of ten Years, in such Manner as they shall by Law direct. The Number of Representatives shall not exceed one for every thirty Thousand, but each State shall have at Least one Representative; and until such enumeration shall be made, the State of New Hampshire shall be entitled to choose three, Massachusetts eight, Rhode Island and Providence Plantations one, Connecticut five, New York six, New Jersey four, Pennsylvania eight, Delaware one, Maryland six, Virginia ten, North Carolina five, South Carolina five, and Georgia three.

When vacancies happen in the Representation from any State, the Executive Authority thereof shall issue Writs of Election to fill such Vacancies.

The House of Representatives shall choose their Speaker and other Officers; and shall have the sole Power of Impeachment.

Section 3 The Senate of the United States shall be composed of two Senators from each State, chosen by the Legislature thereof, for six Years; and each Senator shall have one Vote.

Immediately after they shall be assembled in Consequence of the first Election, they shall be divided as equally as may be into three Classes. The Seats of the Senators of the first Class shall be vacated at the Expiration of the second Year, of the second Class at the Expiration of the fourth Year, and of the third Class at the Expiration of the sixth Year, so that one third may be chosen every second Year; and if Vacancies happen by Resignation, or otherwise, during the Recess of the Legislature of any State, the Executive thereof may make temporary Appointments until the next Meeting of the Legislature, which shall then fill such Vacancies.

No Person shall be a Senator who shall not have attained to the Age of thirty Years, and been nine Years a Citizen of the United States, and who shall not, when elected, be an Inhabitant of that State for which he shall be chosen.

The Vice President of the United States shall be President of the Senate, but shall have no Vote, unless they be equally divided.

The Senate shall choose their other Officers, and also a President pro tempore, in the Absence of the Vice President, or when he shall exercise the Office of President of the United States.

The Senate shall have the sole Power to try all Impeachments. When sitting for that Purpose, they shall be on Oath or Affirmation. When the President of the United States is tried, the Chief Justice shall preside: And no Person shall be convicted without the Concurrence of two thirds of the Members present.

Judgment in Cases of Impeachment shall not extend further than to removal from Office, and disqualification to hold and enjoy any Office of honor, Trust, or Profit under the United States: but the Party convicted shall nevertheless be liable and subject to Indictment, Trial, Judgment, and Punishment, according to Law.

Section 4 The Times, Places and Manner of holding Elections for Senators and Representatives, shall be prescribed in each State by the Legislature thereof; but the Congress may at any time by Law make or alter such Regulations, except as to the Places of choosing Senators.

The Congress shall assemble at least once in every Year, and such Meeting shall be on the first Monday in December, unless they shall by Law appoint a different Day.

Section 5 Each House shall be the Judge of the Elections, Returns, and Qualifications of its own Members, and a Majority of each shall constitute a Quorum to do Business; but a smaller Number may adjourn from day to day, and may be authorized to compel the Attendance of absent Members, in such Manner, and under such Penalties as each House may provide.

Each House may determine the Rules of its Proceedings, punish its Members for disorderly Behavior, and, with the Concurrence of two thirds, expel a Member.

Each House shall keep a Journal of its Proceedings, and from time to time publish the same, excepting such Parts as may in their Judgment require Secrecy; and the Yeas and Nays of the Members of either House on any question shall, at the Desire of one fifth of those Present, be entered on the Journal.

Neither House, during the Session of Congress, shall, without the Consent of the other, adjourn for more than three days, nor to any other Place than that in which the two Houses shall be sitting.

Section 6 The Senators and Representatives shall receive a Compensation for their Services, to be ascertained by Law, and paid out of the Treasury of the United States. They shall in all Cases, except Treason, Felony and Breach of the Peace, be privileged from Arrest during their Attendance at the Session of their respective Houses, and in going to and returning from the same; and for any Speech or Debate in either House, they shall not be questioned in any other Place.

No Senator or Representative shall, during the Time for which he was elected, be appointed to any civil Office under the Authority of the United States, which shall have been created, or the Emoluments whereof shall have been increased during such time; and no Person holding any Office under the United States, shall be a Member of either House during his Continuance in Office.

Section 7 All Bills for raising Revenue shall originate in the House of Representatives; but the Senate may propose or concur with Amendments as on other Bills.

Every Bill which shall have passed the House of Representatives and the Senate, shall, before it become a Law, be presented to the President of the United States; If he approve he shall sign it, but if not he shall return it, with his Objections to the House in which it shall have originated, who shall enter the Objections at large on their Journal, and proceed to reconsider it. If after such Reconsideration two thirds of that House shall agree to pass the Bill, it shall be sent together with the Objections, to the other House, by which it shall likewise be reconsidered, and if approved by two thirds of that House, it shall become a Law. But in all such Cases the Votes of both Houses shall be determined by Yeas and Nays, and the Names of the Persons voting for and against the Bill shall be entered on the Journal of each House respectively. If any Bill shall not be returned by the President within ten Days (Sundays excepted) after it shall have been presented to him, the Same shall be a Law, in like Manner as if he had signed it, unless the Congress by their Adjournment prevent its Return in which Case it shall not be a Law.

Every Order, Resolution, or Vote, to which the Concurrence of the Senate and House of Representatives may be necessary (except on a question of Adjournment) shall be presented to the President of the United States; and before the Same shall take Effect, shall be approved by him, or being disapproved by him, shall be repassed by two thirds of the Senate and House of Representatives, according to the Rules and Limitations prescribed in the Case of a Bill.

Section 8 The Congress shall have Power To lay and collect Taxes, Duties, Imposts and Excises, to pay the Debts and provide for the common Defence and general Welfare of the United States; but all Duties, Imposts and Excises shall be uniform throughout the United States;

To borrow Money on the credit of the United States;

To regulate Commerce with foreign Nations, and among the several States, and with the Indian Tribes;

To establish an uniform Rule of Naturalization, and uniform Laws on the subject of Bankruptcies throughout the United States;

To coin Money, regulate the Value thereof, and of foreign Coin, and fix the Standard of Weights and Measures;

To provide for the Punishment of counterfeiting the Securities and current Coin of the United States;

To establish Post Offices and post Roads;

To promote the Progress of Science and useful Arts, by securing for limited Times to Authors and Inventors the exclusive Right to their respective Writings and Discoveries;

To constitute Tribunals inferior to the supreme Court;

To define and punish Piracies and Felonies committed on the high Seas, and Offenses against the Law of Nations;

To declare War, grant Letters of Marque and Reprisal, and make Rules concerning Captures on Land and Water;

To raise and support Armies, but no Appropriation of Money to that Use shall be for a longer Term than two Years;

To provide and maintain a Navy;

To make Rules for the Government and Regulation of the land and naval Forces;

To provide for calling forth the Militia to execute the Laws of the Union, suppress Insurrections and repel Invasions;

To provide for organizing, arming, and disciplining, the Militia, and for governing such Part of Them as may be employed in the Service of the United States, reserving to the States respectively, the Appointment of the Officers, and the Authority of training the Militia according to the discipline prescribed by Congress;

To exercise exclusive Legislation in all Cases whatsoever, over such District (not exceeding ten Miles square) as may, by Cession of particular States, and the Acceptance of Congress, become the Seat of the Government of the United States, and to exercise like Authority over all Places purchased by the Consent of the Legislature of the State in which the Same shall be, for the Erection of Forts, Magazines, Arsenals, dock-Yards, and other needful Buildings;—And

To make all Laws which shall be necessary and proper for carrying into Execution the foregoing Powers, and all other Powers vested by this Constitution in the Government of the United States, or in any Department or Officer thereof.

Section 9 The Migration or Importation of such Persons as any of the States now existing shall think proper to admit, shall not be prohibited by the Congress prior to the Year one thousand eight hundred and eight, but a Tax or duty may be imposed on such Importation, not exceeding ten dollars for each Person.

The privilege of the Writ of Habeas Corpus shall not be suspended, unless when in Cases of Rebellion or Invasion the public Safety may require it.

No Bill of Attainder or ex post facto Law shall be passed.

No Capitation, or other direct, Tax shall be laid, unless in Proportion to the Census or Enumeration herein before directed to be taken.

No Tax or Duty shall be laid on Articles exported from any State.

No Preference shall be given by any Regulation of Commerce or Revenue to the Ports of one State over those of another: nor shall Vessels bound to, or from, one State be obliged to enter, clear, or pay Duties in another.

No Money shall be drawn from the Treasury, but in Consequence of Appropriations made by Law; and a regular Statement and Account of the Receipts and Expenditures of all public Money shall be published from time to time.

No Title of Nobility shall be granted by the United States: And no Person holding any Office of Profit or Trust under them, shall, without the Consent of the Congress, accept of any present, Emolument, Office, or Title, of any kind whatever, from any King, Prince, or foreign State.

Section 10 No State shall enter into any Treaty, Alliance, or Confederation; grant Letters of Marque and Reprisal; coin Money; emit Bills of Credit; make any Thing but gold and silver Coin a Tender in Payment of Debts; pass any Bill of Attainder, ex post facto Law, or Law impairing the Obligation of Contracts, or grant any Title of Nobility.

No State shall, without the Consent of the Congress, lay any Imposts or Duties on Imports or Exports, except what may be absolutely necessary for executing it's inspection Laws: and the net Produce of all Duties and Imposts, laid by any State on Imports or Exports, shall be for the Use of the Treasury of the United States; and all such Laws shall be subject to the Revision and Control of the Congress.

No State shall, without the Consent of Congress, lay any Duty of Tonnage, keep Troops, or Ships of War in time of Peace, enter into any Agreement or Compact with another State, or with a foreign Power, or engage in War, unless actually invaded, or in such imminent Danger as will not admit of delay.

Article II

Section 1 The executive Power shall be vested in a President of the United States of America. He shall hold his Office during the Term of four Years, and, together with the Vice President, chosen for the same Term, be elected, as follows:

Each State shall appoint, in such Manner as the Legislature thereof may direct, a Number of Electors, equal to the whole Number of Senators and Representatives to which the State may be entitled in the Congress; but no Senator or Representative, or Person holding an Office of Trust or Profit under the United States, shall be appointed an Elector.

The Electors shall meet in their respective States, and vote by Ballot for two Persons, of whom one at least shall not be an Inhabitant of the same State with themselves. And they shall make a List of all the Persons voted for, and of the Number of Votes for each; which List they shall sign and certify, and transmit sealed to the Seat of the Government of the United States, directed to the President of the Senate. The President of the Senate shall, in the Presence of the Senate and House of Representatives, open all the Certificates, and the Votes shall then be counted. The Person having the greatest Number of Votes shall be the President, if such Number be a Majority of the whole Number of Electors appointed; and if there be more than one who have such Majority, and have an equal Number of Votes, then the House of Representatives shall immediately choose by Ballot one of them for President; and if no Person have a Majority, then from the five highest on the List the said House shall in like

Manner choose the President. But in choosing the President, the Votes shall be taken by States, the Representation from each State having one Vote; A quorum for this Purpose shall consist of a Member or Members from two thirds of the States, and a Majority of all the States shall be necessary to a Choice. In every Case, after the Choice of the President, the Person having the greater Number of Votes of the Electors shall be the Vice President. But if there should remain two or more who have equal Votes, the Senate shall choose from them by Ballot the Vice President.

The Congress may determine the Time of choosing the Electors, and the Day on which they shall give their Votes; which Day shall be the same throughout the United States.

No person except a natural born Citizen, or a Citizen of the United States, at the time of the Adoption of this Constitution, shall be eligible to the Office of President; neither shall any Person be eligible to that Office who shall not have attained to the Age of thirty five Years, and been fourteen Years a Resident within the United States.

In Case of the Removal of the President from Office, or of his Death, Resignation or Inability to discharge the Powers and Duties of the said Office, the same shall devolve on the Vice President, and the Congress may by Law provide for the Case of Removal, Death, Resignation or Inability, both of the President and Vice President, declaring what Officer shall then act as President, and such Officer shall act accordingly, until the Disability be removed, or a President shall be elected.

The President shall, at stated Times, receive for his Services, a Compensation, which shall neither be increased nor diminished during the Period for which he shall have been elected, and he shall not receive within that Period any other Emolument from the United States, or any of them.

Before he enter on the Execution of his Office, he shall take the following Oath or Affirmation: "I do solemnly swear (or affirm) that I will faithfully execute the Office of President of the United States, and will to the best of my Ability, preserve, protect and defend the Constitution of the United States."

Section 2 The President shall be Commander in Chief of the Army and Navy of the United States, and of the Militia of the several States, when called into the actual Service of the United States: he may require the Opinion, in writing, of the principal Officer in each of the executive Departments, upon any Subject relating to the Duties of their respective Offices, and he shall have Power to grant Reprieves and Pardons for Offenses against the United States, except in Cases of Impeachment.

He shall have Power, by and with the Advice and Consent of the Senate to make Treaties, provided two thirds of the Senators present concur; and he shall nominate, and by and with the Advice and Consent of the Senate, shall appoint Ambassadors, other public Ministers and Consuls, Judges of the supreme Court, and all other Officers of the United States, whose Appointments are not herein otherwise provided for, and which shall be established by Law; but the Congress may by Law vest the Appointment of such inferior Officers, as they think proper, in the President alone, in the Courts of Law, or in the Heads of Departments.

The President shall have Power to fill up all Vacancies that may happen during the Recess of the Senate, by granting Commissions which shall expire at the End of their next Session.

Section 3 He shall from time to time give to the Congress Information of the State of the Union, and recommend to their Consideration such Measures as he shall judge necessary and expedient; he may, on extraordinary Occasions, convene both Houses, or either of them, and in Case of Disagreement between them, with Respect to the Time of Adjournment, he may adjourn them to such Time as he shall think proper; he shall receive Ambassadors and other public Ministers; he shall take Care that the Laws be faithfully executed, and shall Commission all the Officers of the United States.

Section 4 The President, Vice President and all civil Officers of the United States, shall be removed from Office on Impeachment for, and Conviction of, Treason, Bribery, or other high Crimes and Misdemeanors.

Article III

Section 1 The judicial Power of the United States, shall be vested in one supreme Court, and in such inferior Courts as the Congress may from time to time ordain and establish. The Judges, both of the supreme and inferior Courts, shall hold their Offices during good Behavior, and shall, at stated Times, receive for their Services a Compensation, which shall not be diminished during their Continuance in Office.

Section 2 The judicial Power shall extend to all Cases, in Law and Equity, arising under this Constitution, the Laws of the United States, and Treaties made, or which shall be made, under their Authority;—to all Cases affecting Ambassadors, other public Ministers and Consuls;—to all Cases of admiralty and maritime Jurisdiction;—to Controversies to which the United States shall be a Party;—to Controversies between two or more States;—between a State and Citizens of another State;—between Citizens of different States;—between Citizens of the same State claiming Lands under Grants of different States, and between a State, or the Citizens thereof, and foreign States, Citizens or Subjects.

In all Cases affecting Ambassadors, other public Ministers and Consuls, and those in which a State shall be a

Party, the supreme Court shall have original Jurisdiction. In all the other Cases before mentioned, the supreme Court shall have appellate Jurisdiction, both as to Law and Fact, with such Exceptions, and under such Regulations as the Congress shall make.

The Trial of all Crimes, except in Cases of Impeachment, shall be by Jury; and such Trial shall be held in the State where the said Crimes shall have been committed; but when not committed within any State, the Trial shall be at such Place or Places as the Congress may by Law have directed.

Section 3 Treason against the United States, shall consist only in levying War against them, or, in adhering to their Enemies, giving them Aid and Comfort. No Person shall be convicted of Treason unless on the Testimony of two Witnesses to the same overt Act, or on Confession in open Court.

The Congress shall have Power to declare the Punishment of Treason, but no Attainder of Treason shall work Corruption of Blood, or Forfeiture except during the Life of the Person attainted.

Article IV

Section 1 Full Faith and Credit shall be given in each State to the public Acts, Records, and judicial Proceedings of every other State. And the Congress may by general Laws prescribe the Manner in which such Acts, Records and Proceedings shall be proved, and the Effect thereof.

Section 2 The Citizens of each State shall be entitled to all Privileges and Immunities of Citizens in the several States.

A Person charged in any State with Treason, Felony, or other Crime, who shall flee from Justice, and be found in another State, shall on Demand of the executive Authority of the State from which he fled, be delivered up, to be removed to the State having Jurisdiction of the Crime.

No Person held to Service or Labour in one State, under the Laws thereof, escaping into another, shall, in Consequence of any Law or Regulation therein, be discharged from such Service or Labor, but shall be delivered up on Claim of the Party to whom such Service or Labor may be due.

Section 3 New States may be admitted by the Congress into this Union; but no new State shall be formed or erected within the Jurisdiction of any other State; nor any State be formed by the Junction of two or more States, or Parts of States, without the Consent of the Legislatures of the States concerned as well as of the Congress.

The Congress shall have Power to dispose of and make all needful Rules and Regulations respecting the Territory or other Property belonging to the United States; and nothing in this Constitution shall be so construed as to Prejudice any Claims of the United States, or of any particular State.

Section 4 The United States shall guarantee to every State in this Union a Republican Form of Government, and shall protect each of them against Invasion; and on Application of the Legislature, or of the Executive (when the Legislature cannot be convened) against domestic Violence.

Article V

The Congress, whenever two thirds of both Houses shall deem it necessary, shall propose Amendments to this Constitution, or, on the Application of the Legislatures of two thirds of the several States, shall call a Convention for proposing Amendments, which, in either Case, shall be valid to all Intents and Purposes, as part of this Constitution, when ratified by the Legislatures of three fourths of the several States, or by Conventions in three fourths thereof, as the one or the other Mode of Ratification may be proposed by the Congress; Provided that no Amendment which may be made prior to the Year One thousand eight hundred and eight shall in any Manner affect the first and fourth Clauses in the Ninth Section of the first Article; and that no State, without its Consent, shall be deprived of its equal Suffrage in the Senate.

Article VI

All Debts contracted and Engagements entered into, before the Adoption of this Constitution shall be as valid against the United States under this Constitution, as under the Confederation.

This Constitution, and the Laws of the United States which shall be made in Pursuance thereof; and all Treaties made, or which shall be made, under the Authority of the United States, shall be the supreme Law of the Land; and the Judges in every State shall be bound thereby, any Thing in the Constitution or Laws of any State to the Contrary notwithstanding.

The Senators and Representatives before mentioned, and the Members of the several State Legislatures, and all executive and judicial Officers, both of the United States and of the several States, shall be bound by Oath or Affirmation, to support this Constitution; but no religious Test shall ever be required as a Qualification to any Office or public Trust under the United States.

Article VII

The Ratification of the Conventions of nine States shall be sufficient for the Establishment of this Constitution between the States so ratifying the Same.

Amendment I [1791]

Congress shall make no law respecting an establishment of religion, or prohibiting the free exercise thereof; or abridging the freedom of speech, or of the press; or the right of the people peaceably to assemble, and to petition the Government for a redress of grievances.

Amendment II [1791]

A well regulated Militia, being necessary to the security of a free State, the right of the people to keep and bear Arms, shall not be infringed.

Amendment III [1791]

No Soldier shall, in time of peace be quartered in any house, without the consent of the Owner, nor in time of war, but in a manner to be prescribed by law.

Amendment IV [1791]

The right of the people to be secure in their persons, houses, papers, and effects, against unreasonable searches and seizures, shall not be violated, and no Warrants shall issue, but upon probable cause, supported by Oath or affirmation, and particularly describing the place to be searched, and the persons or things to be seized.

Amendment V [1791]

No person shall be held to answer for a capital, or otherwise infamous crime, unless on a presentment or indictment of a Grand Jury, except in cases arising in the land or naval forces, or in the Militia, when in actual service in time of War or public danger; nor shall any person be subject for the same offence to be twice put in jeopardy of life or limb; nor shall be compelled in any criminal case to be a witness against himself, nor be deprived of life, liberty, or property, without due process of law; nor shall private property be taken for public use, without just compensation.

Amendment VI [1791]

In all criminal prosecutions, the accused shall enjoy the right to a speedy and public trial, by an impartial jury of the State and district wherein the crime shall have been committed, which district shall have been previously ascertained by law, and to be informed of the nature and cause of the accusation; to be confronted with the witnesses against him; to have compulsory process for obtaining witnesses in his favor, and to have the Assistance of Counsel for his defence.

Amendment VII [1791]

In Suits at common law, where the value in controversy shall exceed twenty dollars, the right of trial by jury shall be preserved, and no fact tried by jury, shall be otherwise re-examined in any Court of the United States, than according to the rules of the common law.

Amendment VIII [1791]

Excessive bail shall not be required, nor excessive fines imposed, nor cruel and unusual punishments inflicted.

Amendment IX [1791]

The enumeration in the Constitution, of certain rights, shall not be construed to deny or disparage others retained by the people.

Amendment X [1791]

The powers not delegated to the United States by the Constitution, nor prohibited by it to the States, are reserved to the States respectively, or to the people.

Amendment XI [1798]

The Judicial power of the United States shall not be construed to extend to any suit in law or equity, commenced or prosecuted against one of the United States by Citizens of another State, or by Citizens or Subjects of any Foreign State.

Amendment XII [1804]

The Electors shall meet in their respective states, and vote by ballot for President and Vice-President, one of whom, at least, shall not be an inhabitant of the same state with themselves; they shall name in their ballots the person voted for as President, and in distinct ballots the person voted for as Vice-President, and they shall make distinct lists of all persons voted for as President, and of all persons voted for as Vice-President, and of the number of votes for each, which lists they shall sign and certify, and transmit sealed to the seat of the government of the United States, directed to the President of the Senate;—The President of the Senate shall, in the presence of the Senate and House of Representatives, open all the certificates and the votes shall then be counted;—The person having the greatest number of votes for President, shall be the President, if such number be a majority of the whole number of Electors appointed; and if no person have such majority, then from the persons having the highest numbers not exceeding three on the list of those voted for as President, the House of Representatives shall choose immediately, by ballot, the President. But in choosing the President, the votes shall be taken by states, the representation from each state having one vote; a quorum for this purpose shall consist of a member or members from two thirds of the states, and a majority of all states shall be necessary to a choice. And if the House of Representatives shall not choose a President whenever the right of choice shall devolve upon them, before the fourth day of March next following, then the Vice-President shall act as President, as in the case of the death or other constitutional disability of the President.—The person having the greatest number of votes as Vice-President, shall be the Vice-President, if such number be a majority of the whole number of Electors appointed, and if no person have a majority, then from the two highest numbers on the list, the Senate shall choose the Vice-President; a quorum for the purpose shall consist of two thirds of the whole number of Senators, and a majority of the whole number shall be necessary to a choice. But no person constitutionally ineligible to the office of President shall be eligible to that of Vice-President of the United States.

Amendment XIII [1865]

Section 1 Neither slavery nor involuntary servitude, except as a punishment for crime whereof the party shall have been duly convicted, shall exist within the United States, or any place subject to their jurisdiction.

Section 2 Congress shall have power to enforce this article by appropriate legislation.

Amendment XIV [1868]

Section 1 All persons born or naturalized in the United States, and subject to the jurisdiction thereof, are citizens of the United States and of the State wherein they reside. No State shall make or enforce any law which shall abridge the privileges or immunities of citizens of the United States; nor shall any State deprive any person of life, liberty, or property, without due process of law; nor deny to any person within its jurisdiction the equal protection of the laws.

Section 2 Representatives shall be apportioned among the several States according to their respective numbers, counting the whole number of persons in each State, excluding Indians not taxed. But when the right to vote at any election for the choice of electors for President and Vice President of the United States, Representatives in Congress, the Executive and Judicial officers of a State, or the members of the Legislature thereof, is denied to any of the male inhabitants of such State, being twenty-one

years of age, and citizens of the United States, or in any way abridged, except for participation in rebellion, or other crime, the basis of representation therein shall be reduced in the proportion which the number of such male citizens shall bear to the whole number of male citizens twenty-one years of age in such State.

Section 3 No person shall be a Senator or Representative in Congress, or elector of President and Vice-President, or hold any office, civil or military, under the United States, or under any State, who having previously taken an oath, as a member of Congress, or as an officer of the United States, or as a member of any State legislature, or as an executive or judicial officer of any State, to support the Constitution of the United States, shall have engaged in insurrection or rebellion against the same, or given aid or comfort to the enemies thereof. But Congress may by a vote of two thirds of each House, remove such disability.

Section 4 The validity of the public debt of the United States, authorized by law, including debts incurred for payment of pensions and bounties for services in suppressing insurrection or rebellion, shall not be questioned. But neither the United States nor any State shall assume or pay any debt or obligation incurred in aid of insurrection or rebellion against the United States, or any claim for the loss or emancipation of any slave; but all such debts, obligations and claims shall be held illegal and void.

Section 5 The Congress shall have power to enforce, by appropriate legislation, the provisions of this article.

Amendment XV [1870]

Section 1 The right of citizens of the United States to vote shall not be denied or abridged by the United States or by any State on account of race, color, or previous condition of servitude.

Section 2 The Congress shall have power to enforce this article by appropriate legislation.

Amendment XVI [1913]

The Congress shall have power to lay and collect taxes on incomes, from whatever source derived, without apportionment among the several States, and without regard to any census or enumeration.

Amendment XVII [1913]

Section 1 The Senate of the United States shall be composed of two Senators from each State, elected by the people thereof, for six years; and each Senator shall have one vote. The electors in each State shall have the qualifications requisite for electors of the most numerous branch of the State legislatures.

Section 2 When vacancies happen in the representation of any State in the Senate, the executive authority of such State shall issue writs of election to fill such vacancies: Provided, That the legislature of any State may empower the executive thereof to make temporary appointments until the people fill the vacancies by election as the legislature may direct.

Section 3 This amendment shall not be so construed as to affect the election or term of any Senator chosen before it becomes valid as part of the Constitution.

Amendment XVIII [1919]

Section 1 After one year from the ratification of this article the manufacture, sale, or transportation of intoxicating liquors within, the importation thereof into, or the exportation thereof from the United States and all territory subject to the jurisdiction thereof for beverage purposes is hereby prohibited.

Section 2 The Congress and the several States shall have concurrent power to enforce this article by appropriate legislation.

Section 3 This article shall be inoperative unless it shall have been ratified as an amendment to the Constitution by the legislatures of the several States, as provided in the Constitution, within seven years from the date of the submission hereof to the States by the Congress.

Amendment XIX [1920]

Section 1 The right of citizens of the United States to vote shall not be denied or abridged by the United States or by any State on account of sex.

Section 2 Congress shall have power to enforce this article by appropriate legislation.

Amendment XX [1933]

Section 1 The terms of the President and Vice President shall end at noon on the 20th day of January, and the terms of Senators and Representatives at noon on the 3d day of January, of the years in which such terms would have ended if this article had not been ratified; and the terms of their successors shall then begin.

Section 2 The Congress shall assemble at least once in every year, and such meeting shall begin at noon on the 3d day of January, unless they shall by law appoint a different day.

Section 3 If, at the time fixed for the beginning of the term of the President, the President elect shall have died, the Vice President elect shall become President. If the President shall not have been chosen before the time fixed for the beginning of his term, or if the President elect shall have failed to qualify, then the Vice President elect shall act as President until a President shall have qualified; and the Congress may by law provide for the case wherein neither a President elect nor a Vice President elect shall have qualified, declaring who shall then act as President, or the manner in which one who is to act shall be selected, and such person shall act accordingly until a President or Vice-President shall have qualified.

Section 4 The Congress may by law provide for the case of the death of any of the persons from whom the House of Representatives may choose a President whenever the right of choice shall have devolved upon them, and for the case of the death of any of the persons from whom the Senate may choose a Vice-President whenever the right of choice shall have devolved upon them.

Section 5 Sections 1 and 2 shall take effect on the 15th day of October following the ratification of this article.

Section 6 This article shall be inoperative unless it shall have been ratified as an amendment to the Constitution by the legislatures of three-fourths of the several States within seven years from the date of its submission.

Amendment XXI [1933]

Section 1 The eighteenth article of amendment to the Constitution of the United States is hereby repealed.

Section 2 The transportation or importation into any State, Territory, or possession of the United States for delivery or use therein of intoxicating liquors, in violation of the laws thereof, is hereby prohibited.

Section 3 This article shall be inoperative unless it shall have been ratified as an amendment to the Constitution by conventions in the several States, as provided in the Constitution, within seven years from the date of the submission hereof to the States by the Congress.

Amendment XXII [1951]

Section 1 No person shall be elected to the office of the President more than twice, and no person who has held the office of President, or acted as President, for more than two years of a term to which some other person was elected President shall be elected to the office of President more than once. But this Article shall not apply to any person holding the office of President when this Article was proposed by the Congress, and shall not prevent any person who may be holding the office of President, or acting as President, during the term within which this Article becomes operative from holding the office of President or acting as President during the remainder of such term.

Section 2 This article shall be inoperative unless it shall have been ratified as an amendment to the Constitution by the legislatures of three-fourths of the several States within seven years from the date of its submission to the States by the Congress.

Amendment XXIII [1961]

Section 1 The District constituting the seat of Government of the United States shall appoint in such manner as the Congress may direct:

A number of electors of President and Vice President equal to the whole number of Senators and Representatives in Congress to which the District would be entitled if it were a State, but in no event more than the least populous state; they shall be in addition to those appointed by the states, but they shall be considered, for the purposes of the election of President and Vice President, to be electors appointed by a state; and they shall meet in the District and perform such duties as provided by the twelfth article of amendment.

Section 2 The Congress shall have power to enforce this article by appropriate legislation.

Amendment XXIV [1964]

Section 1 The right of citizens of the United States to vote in any primary or other election for President or Vice President, for electors for President or Vice-President, or for Senator or Representative in Congress, shall not be denied or abridged by the United States, or any State by reason of failure to pay any poll tax or other tax.

Section 2 The Congress shall have power to enforce this article by appropriate legislation.

Amendment XXV [1967]

Section 1 In case of the removal of the President from office or of his death or resignation, the Vice President shall become President.

Section 2 Whenever there is a vacancy in the office of the Vice President, the President shall nominate a Vice President who shall take office upon confirmation by a majority vote of both Houses of Congress.

Section 3 Whenever the President transmits to the President pro tempore of the Senate and the Speaker of the House of Representatives his written declaration that he is unable to discharge the powers and duties of his office, and until he transmits to them a written declaration to the contrary, such powers and duties shall be discharged by the Vice President as Acting President.

Section 4 Whenever the Vice President and a majority of either the principal officers of the executive departments or of such other body as Congress may by law provide, transmit to the President pro tempore of the Senate and the Speaker of the House of Representatives their written declaration that the President is unable to discharge the powers and duties of his office, the Vice President shall immediately assume the powers and duties of the office as Acting President.

Thereafter, when the President transmits to the President pro tempore of the Senate and the Speaker of the House of Representatives his written declaration that no inability exists, he shall resume the powers and duties of his office unless the Vice President and a majority of either the principal officers of the executive department or of such other body as Congress may by law provide, transmit within four days to the President pro tempore of the Senate and the Speaker of the House of Representatives their written declaration and the President is unable to discharge the powers and duties of his office. Thereupon Congress shall decide the issue, assembling within forty-eight hours for that purpose if not in session. If the Congress, within twenty-one days after receipt of the latter written declaration, or, if Congress is not in session, within twenty-one days after Congress is required to assemble, determines by two thirds vote of both Houses that the President is unable to discharge the powers and duties of his office, the Vice President shall continue to discharge the same as Acting President; otherwise, the President shall resume the powers and duties of his office.

Amendment XXVI [1971]

Section 1 The right of citizens of the United States, who are eighteen years of age or older, to vote shall not be denied or abridged by the United States or by any State on account of age.

Section 2 The Congress shall have power to enforce this article by appropriate legislation.

Amendment XXVII [Proposed 1789; Ratified 1992]

No law, varying the compensation for the services of Senators and Representatives, shall take effect until an election of Representatives have intervened.

Glossary

A

adjudication: formal proceedings that take place in court.

adversary process: system in which criminal justice is viewed as a contest between the government and the individual.

aggregate sentencing data: lumping together data from all places studied.

alibi: a defense to criminal liability that places the defendant at a different location when the crime was committed.

anomie of influence: theory that people put rules aside to reduce their lack of success.

anomie theory: argues that crime is the result of the weakening of social norms.

appellate courts: courts of appeal jurisdiction; they have the power to review trial courts' application of the law to the facts.

arraignment: bringing defendants into open court to read charges against them and secure a plea from them.

arrest: a detention that amounts to a Fourth Amendment seizure.

asshole: anyone who questions police authority.

assigned counsel: lawyers in private practice selected by judges to represent indigent defendants on a case-by-case basis.

Auburn system: early prison system that imposed a rule of congregate work in absolute silence and solitary confinement at night; also known as a congregate system.

B

bail: release of defendants pending the final disposition of their cases.

balancing test of prisoners' rights: courts look at all the facts of each case and weigh the shrunken rights of prisoners against the prison's powerful missions of punishment, security, order, and discipline.

bench trial: defendants who don't want juries to decide the facts can have bench trials, in which judges decide both the facts and the law.

bifurcated trials: multistage trials in which defendants charged with capital crimes receive a verdict in the first stage and, if convicted, are sentenced during a second stage to death or life imprisonment.

bind over defendants: order that defendants stand trial.

biological explanation: explains crime by linking violent behavior to abnormal chromosomes.

broken windows theory: theory that neighborhoods can decay into disorder and even crime if no one attends faithfully to their maintenance.

building-tender system: prison management system that relies on prisoners to assist corrections officers in managing cell blocks.

C

career mission: providing the courtroom work group an avenue to advance their own careers either within the group or in private law practice or political office.

case attrition: process to sort out those people who shouldn't go any further in criminal prosecution from those who should.

caseload hypothesis: the pressure to dispose of large numbers of criminal cases requires plea bargaining to keep the courts from breaking down.

case study method: the board member, case worker, or parole agency collects as much information as possible, combines it in a unique way, mulls over the results, and reaches a decision.

case system: vertical case management, in which assistant prosecutors are assigned to manage all stages of specific defendants' cases from charge at least through trial and often through appeal.

cause in fact: "but for" the actions of the defendant, the result wouldn't have happened.

challenge for cause: the right of both sides to an unlimited number of objections to prospective jurors, as long as they can show prejudice to the judge's satisfaction.

change of venue: to guarantee an atmosphere that minimizes prejudice, trial judges can transfer the trial to a calmer location.

charge bargaining: plea negotiation in which prosecutors drop some charges or file less serious ones in exchange for a guilty plea.

civil death: a practice going back to ancient Rome, in which felons are treated as if they were dead when it comes to political and legal rights.

closing arguments: attorneys from both sides highlight the strong points of their case and the opposing side's weaknesses after both sides have presented all their evidence.

code of silence: don't ever tell on another cop.

cognitive model of rehabilitation: "target *thinking*, not *behavior*"; the program's mission is "rehabilitation through clearer thinking."

colloquy: a formal discussion in which judges attempt to determine whether defendants' guilty pleas are voluntary and knowing.

common law: the traditions, customs, and values of the English community translated into legal rules.

community corrections: probation, parole, and intermediate punishments.

community-oriented policing: citizen participation in setting police priorities and police operations.

community service: order to work on public property (e.g., clean parks, sweep streets, clean jails) as punishment for crimes.

community service mission: police mission devoted to providing both information and physical assistance to people in need.

concentration model: putting the most violent criminals in one prison to facilitate their management.

confinement model of imprisonment: model based on the belief that prisoners are sent to prison as punishment, not for punishment.

confinement plus model of imprisonment: based on the belief that locking criminals up isn't enough punishment; you have to add something more; also called the punishment model of imprisonment.

conflict perspective: conflict is normal; a view of law holding that the criminal law reflects the success of the most powerful groups in society to translate their values into law.

congregate system: the Auburn system; early prison system that imposed a rule of congregate work in absolute silence and solitary confinement at night.

conjugal visits: prisoners can stay with their families for up to three days at a time.

consensus perspective: view of law holding that the criminal law reflects a general agreement regarding the values of society.

consent search rule: a search must be conducted with voluntary agreement.

constable/night watch system: a police structure based in the local communities created by King William; it consisted of two elements—constables and night watch.

contract attorneys: private attorneys who operate under contracts with local jurisdictions to represent indigent defendants for a fee.

control model of management: prison management model that emphasizes prisoner obedience, work, and education.

correctional boot camp: places run like military boot camps to correct the behavior of the young, first-time offenders who are sentenced there.

correctional institution: type of prison developed during the early 1900s that was based on the penal philosophy of rehabilitation.

corrections: the most widely used label for the agencies and decision making related to the supervision of convicted criminals in custody.

counts: accounting for every prisoner at all times.

courtroom work group: prosecutors, judges, and defense lawyers who form a courtroom elite and whose primary goal is the efficient and harmonious disposition of cases.

courts of general jurisdiction: courts with the authority to hear and decide all criminal cases.

courts of limited jurisdiction: courts limited to hearing and deciding minor offenses and preliminary proceedings in felonies.

courts of record: courts that keep a formal written record of their proceedings.

crime control model: model that favors informal, discretionary decision making to efficiently, economically, accurately, and quickly separate the guilty from the innocent; criminal justice exists to reduce crime for the good of the whole society.

Crime Index: raw numbers and rates of eight serious crimes that track the movement, fluctuations, and trends in U.S. total rates.

crime-specific element: the idea that decision making differs according to the crime being contemplated and committed.

criminal event: a specific crime that an offender decides to commit.

criminal involvement: three stages: deciding to get into crime generally, continuing to be involved, and deciding to get out of crime.

criminal justice system: the collection of agencies that make up the whole of criminal justice.

criminal law: the formal definition of crime and punishment, describing what behavior is prohibited and prescribing the punishment for criminal behavior; the primary source of the actions of criminal justice agencies.

criminal law enforcement mission: consists of four missions—preventing crime, investigating crimes and identifying suspects, finding and catching suspects, and helping prosecutors build a case against defendants.

criminal omissions: the failure to act when there is a legal duty to act.

criminal procedure: informs public officials what power they have to enforce the list of criminal don'ts and what consequences they face for abusing that power.

cross-examination: examination of a witness by the opposing side.

D

damages: money awarded in noncriminal lawsuits for injuries; money awarded to plaintiffs in successful torts.

DARE: program in which specially trained officers go to schools to teach drug prevention.

dark figure in crime: offenses not reported or recorded in the UCR index.

dead-bang cases: cases in which a guilty verdict is virtually certain.

defense of qualified immunity: protects officers in torts whose actions are "objectively reasonable."

departure: when judges want to impose a sentence outside the range of punishment the law prescribes.

determinate sentencing: fixed sentencing, where legislatures fix the specific penalty for crimes.

determinist theories of crime: theories of criminal behavior positing that forces beyond the control of individuals determine how they behave.

differential association: theory that criminal behavior, like behavior in general, depends on the person's associations with other people.

differential response: approach in which the police response to routine calls differs from that to emergency calls.

diffusion of benefits: spread of crime reduction to areas around experimental hot spots targeted by police.

direct examination: first examination of a witness conducted by the side on whose behalf the witness was called.

Dirty Harry problem: when officers feel the need to resort to "dirty" means to catch criminals.

discretion: decisions based on individual judgment instead of formal rules.

discretionary release: parole boards decide the date of release and set the conditions of their community supervision until their sentence expires.

dispersion model: separating problem prisoners to multiple prisons around the country to prevent them from joining to cause trouble.

displacement: criminal activity moves to another location in response to police crackdowns.

diversion: transferring defendants into some alternative to criminal prosecution, such as alcohol or drug treatment programs.

doctrine of official immunity: limits the liability of officers for torts.

due process mission: says courts are supposed to administer justice according to the rule of law.

due process model: model that puts the formal legal process at the heart of decision making in criminal justice; criminal justice exists to guarantee fair procedures for every individual.

E

either/or corrections: practice of either incarcerating offenders or placing them on straight probation.

enforced poverty: the state provides only the bare essentials—plain food, clothing, and shelter—to prisoners.

entrapment: inducement by law enforcement officers to commit a crime for the purpose of prosecuting the offender.

excessive force: when officers use more than the amount of force necessary to get control of suspects and protect themselves and others.

exclusionary rule: prohibiting the use of illegally obtained evidence to prove guilt.

excuse: defense to criminal liability whereby defendants admit that what they did was wrong but that under the circumstances they were not responsible.

exhausting administrative remedies: requirement that prisoners have to go through the whole internal grievance procedure before they can take their cases to court.

expiration release: unconditional release at the end of the prison sentence.

ex post facto clause: a retroactive law.

external review of police misconduct: civilian review of police misconduct charges.

F

factual guilt: the defendant did commit the crime.

fallibility question: does the death penalty kill innocent people?

felonies: crimes punishable by one year or more in prison.

felony courts: trial courts of general jurisdiction; they have the power to decide the facts and apply the law in felony cases.

field interrogation: to stop, question, and sometimes search people who "don't look or act right."

first appearance: proceedings to read charges, set initial bail, and assign attorneys.

foot patrol: police patrolling on foot to increase contact with residents.

foreground forces in crime: positive attractions within the experience of criminality.

formal criminal justice: the law and written rules providing the framework of criminal justice; based on the U.S. and state constitutions, statutes, court decisions, and rule books.

Fourth Amendment frisk: consist of outer clothing pat downs for weapons and are less invasive than full-body searches.

Fourth Amendment stop: briefer detentions than arrests, and they take place in public.

full enforcement: the principle that law enforcement officers should enforce all criminal statutes with equal vigor.

G

gangbanging: affiliating with a gang in prison for protection.

general deterrence: utilitarian philosophy of sentencing that aims to prevent those in the general population from committing crimes.

general principles of criminal liability: the elements of crime prosecutors have to prove beyond a reasonable doubt.

general principles of justification and excuse: defenses to criminal liability.

"getting with the program": a program is essential to organizing a life around doing time; "getting with the program" is the first step in learning how to do time.

going rate for crimes: the local "market value" measured in jail time or fine amount for particular crimes.

good time: the number of days deducted from sentences for good behavior.

good-time laws: statutes that allow prisoners to reduce their sentences by a certain number of days for good behavior.

graduated punishment system: range of punishments, graduating in severity from the most lenient (probation) to the harshest (prison).

grand jury review: prosecutors present evidence in secret to grand jurors (selected the same way trial juries are chosen) who decide if there's enough evidence to go to trial.

guided discretion death penalty statutes: statutes requiring juries to administer capital punishment according to statutory guidelines on mitigating and aggravating circumstances.

H

"hands-off" doctrine: courts decline to interfere with the daily operations of prisons.

hardchargers: police willing to "rush into dangerous situations" who look for "the adrenaline high" from a dangerous call. They "volunteer" to handle incidents that "threaten their well-being."

hate crimes: crimes motivated by prejudice against a group (racial, ethnic, religious, the physically and mentally disabled, or sexual orientation).

hearsay evidence: information not directly known by the witness that is offered for its truth at trial.

home confinement: sentencing offenders to remain in their homes except for specified times and purposes.

hot spots patrol: location differentiates police response; problem areas receive the most attention.

hydraulic effect: shifting discretion from one agency to another produces a compression of discretion at one point in the system and an expansion somewhere else.

I

importation theory: theory that prison society has roots in conventions outside prison.

incapacitation: utilitarian philosophy of sentencing aimed at preventing sentenced offenders from committing crimes.

incarceration: corrections that take place in prisons and jails.

incident reports: officer's descriptions of a crime, witnesses, and suspects.

indeterminate sentencing: legislatures set only the outer limits of possible penalties.

indictment: formal accusation of a crime by a grand jury.

indigenous theory: theory that conditions inside prisons shape the nature of prison society.

indigent: poor defendants eligible to have defense counsel assigned to them by the courts.

informal criminal justice: discretionary decision making in day-to-day criminal justice.

inmate code: informal system of rules that determines right and wrong and good and bad within inmate society.

in-or-out corrections: either/or corrections.

intensive supervision: practice of subjecting probationers to more severe conditions and greater supervision than ordinary probation.

interest group theory: public and private groups, led by moral entrepreneurs or reformers, pressure legislators by a variety of means to purify society.

intermediate punishments: punishments that are less severe than incarceration but more severe than ordinary probation.

internal review: the most common and systematic accountability procedure for police misconduct.

irresistible impulse test: test of insanity that focuses on mental diseases and defects that affect defendants' willpower to control their actions.

J

jail: a county or municipal facility for keeping adults while they wait for trial or for punishing them for less than a year after they're convicted.

jailhouse lawyer: prisoners who help other prisoners on points of law.

jurisdiction: the power to decide by courts.

jury instructions: explanation to the jury of the law governing the case.

jury list: used by jurisdictions to satisfy the random selection requirement for jurors; it takes names from one of a variety of sources—voter registration lists, actual voter lists, tax rolls, telephone directories, or even lists of driver's license registrations and excludes minors, people who can't speak or write English, convicted felons, and recent residents.

jury nullification: the power of juries to ignore the formal law and decide cases according to informed extralegal considerations.

jury panel: those people called for jury duty who are not excused or exempted.

justification: defense to criminal liability that says the criminal behavior was justified under the circumstances.

K

Kansas City Preventive Patrol Experiment: tested the effectiveness of preventive patrol and found it wanting.

knock-and-announce rule: required of police before they enter a home.

knockdown force: sufficient use of force by police to bring a suspect to the ground.

know-nothings: ordinary people who aren't police and don't know anything about the world the police inhabit; officers generally treat these "good citizens" with courtesy and efficiency.

L

leading questions: cross-examination questions in which witnesses are essentially told how to answer.

legal cause: Asks the question: Is it fair to blame defendants for the results of actions that they set in motion?

legal guilt: guilt that the government has proved beyond a reasonable doubt by evidence according to the Constitution.

legalistic style of policing: style of policing that emphasizes formal criminal law enforcement and the minimization of discretionary decision making.

legitimate use of force: the force sometimes required by police to do their job.

liberation hypothesis: the assertion that in close cases the value judgments of jurors unconsciously affect their finding of the facts.

lifestyle-exposure theory: differences in victims' lifestyles account for the demographic differences in criminal victimization.

linear design: design found in traditional jails; a corridor lined with cells, officers can see into only when they walk down the hallways.

local legal culture: attitudes, values, and expectations of a particular court or jurisdiction regarding law and the legal system.

lockdown status: temporary suspension of all prison activities, including recreation.

lower criminal courts: courts of limited jurisdiction.

M

maintaining order: police mission devoted to keeping the peace by doing something to settle problems right now.

mandatory minimum sentence laws: determinate sentencing laws that require offenders to serve at least some time in prison.

mandatory release: conditional release from prison according to determinate sentencing laws and parole guidelines.

maximum security prison: prisons that focus mainly on security because they house the most dangerous and escape-prone prisoners.

medical model of corrections: based on treating instead of punishing criminals; views crime as illness and criminals as sick.

medium security prison: the second most secure prisons; they resemble maximum security prisons but with somewhat less constant supervision.

"mercy of the court" pleas: defendants throw themselves on the mercy of the court by pleading guilty, hoping for some "mercy" from the sentencing judge afterwards; straight pleas.

meta-analyses: studies of studies (of rehabilitation programs).

military model of policing: the structure in which law enforcement agencies resemble military organizations with their hierarchical command structure, uniforms, ranks, and call to a mission.

minimum security prison: the least secure prisons, where rehabilitation is stressed and relatively more freedom and privacy are allowed than in maximum and medium security prisons.

Miranda warnings: statements officers must read suspects to assure any incriminating statements made during their custody are voluntary.

"the mix": risky and self-defeating behaviors such as drug use and fighting or damaging relationships that interfere with one's program or limit freedom through placement in restrictive housing or the addition of time to one's sentence.

mobilize: the police go into action.

money bail system: defendants pay bondsmen (most of them are men) 10 percent of the total amount of bail; bondsmen are legally liable for the full amount if defendants don't appear.

monopoly of force: a defining feature of police work, in which officers know they have the power to back up their decisions with force.

moral question: is the death penalty right?

municipal police department: system that formalized police work, replacing the constable/night watch system; it was responsible to a central office and on duty "24/7."

N

National Crime Victimization Survey (NCVS): national survey of victims of violent crimes conducted by the U.S. Census Bureau.

negotiated pleas: guilty pleas in exchange for concessions from the government.

net widening: sentencing offenders to intermediate sanctions who would otherwise receive sentences of straight probation.

new-generation jail: jail in which both the architecture and the management style focus on the safe, humane confinement of inmates.

new-generation maximum security prison: based on the idea that offenders are sent to prison as punishment, not for punishment, these prisons are built to allow both the architecture and management to contribute to a safe, humane confinement where the confinement itself is supposed to be the punishment; they usually contain six to eight physically separated units within a secure perimeter.

nolo contendere: a plea of "no contest" to charges.

"nothing works": the belief that "nothing works" is one of the main reasons treatment programs in prison are given low priority.

O

objective basis: the facts required to justify and back up intrusive behaviors by police.

occupational crime: crimes committed by people who use their occupation as an opportunity to engage in criminal behavior.

opening statements: used by prosecutors and defense lawyers to give an overview of their side of the case.

opportunity theory: explanation that maintains that criminal behavior depends on the opportunities available.

organizational mission: mission by the courtroom work group to keep the courtroom running smoothly, efficiently, and above all harmoniously.

P

pains of imprisonment: deprivations of prison life, including goods and services, security, straight sexual relationships, liberty, and autonomy.

parole: release from incarceration while remaining in state custody according to specific conditions.

parole boards: agency that decides when to conditionally release prisoners before the end of their sentences.

penitentiary: early prisons in which prisoners had to remain silent to think about their crimes.

Pennsylvania system: early prison system that required solitary confinement and silence.

peremptory challenge: the right of both sides to a limited number of challenges to prospective jurors without cause or explanation.

petty misdemeanors: offenses punishable by fines or up to thirty days in jail.

philosophy of utility: utility starts with two assumptions about human nature: (1) people seek pleasure and avoid pain, and (2) they have the free will to choose their own actions.

physical evidence: one of two types of evidence the law recognizes, it includes weapons, stolen property, and fingerprints.

plain-view doctrine: object of seizure discovered inadvertently where an officer has a right to be.

podular design: jail design in which living units are pod-shaped, allowing officers to keep inmates under constant surveillance.

police corruption: form of occupational crime in which officers use their authority for private gain.

police crackdown: proactive strategy that sharply increases police presence.

police working personality: character traits of police officers revealed in their work.

predisposition test: test of entrapment that focuses on the intent of defendants who were not predisposed to commit crimes until the government improperly encouraged them.

preliminary hearing: held to determine whether there is probable cause to hold a revocation hearing to end an offender's probation.

preliminary investigations: collecting information at crime scenes and writing reports on what was learned.

presentence report (PSR): the report provided by the probation officer in a presentence investigation.

presumption of guilt: attitude of the crime control model that assumes those that remain in the system are probably guilty.

pretrial settlement conference: attempts to make up for the fact that plea bargaining shuts out people with a vital interest in the case—victims, defendants, police officers, and sometimes judges—from the decision making by including them.

prevention: the four types of prevention—special deterrence, general deterrence, incapacitation, and rehabilitation—look forward and inflict pain to stop criminals and criminal wannabes from committing crimes in the future.

preventive detention: detention of defendants who endanger either public safety or specific individuals.

preventive patrol: moving through the streets to intercept and prevent crime.

principle of economy: a reliance on the least expensive and invasive response to misbehavior.

principle of less eligibility: belief that prisoners should not earn as much as people working outside prison.

principle of proportionality: the sentence should fit the crime.

prisonization: process by which inmates adapt to the customs of the prison world.

private prison: built and managed by private companies under contract with the government.

privatization: private management of correctional facilities.

proactive patrol: police initiate action to control crime.

probable cause to arrest: the quantum of proof required to arrest.

probation: substitution for incarceration, in which those convicted face supervised release into the community.

problem-oriented policing: focuses on solving problems of crime, disorder, and fear by forming partnerships with residents, businesses, and other local agencies to get at the underlying causes of these problems.

pro bono assistance: appointment of counsel who voluntarily assist defendants without monetary compensation.

proof beyond a reasonable doubt: enough evidence legally obtained and properly presented that will convince an ordinary, reasonable person that a defendant is guilty.

protective custody: prisoners—often at their own request—are put into the segregation unit, where their movement is restricted to protect them from other prisoners.

psychoanalytic explanation: determinist intellectual theory of crime.

public defenders: defense attorneys who work full time in public defender offices to represent indigent defendants.

punishment model of imprisonment: theory that locking criminals up isn't enough punishment; you have to add something more.

Q

quality-of-life crime: belief that order is central to the quality of life and disorder leads to disorderly conduct, or quality-of-life crimes.

R

reactive patrol: police respond only after receiving calls for help from victims and witnesses.

reasonable suspicion to frisk: the quantum of proof required for a frisk.

reasonable suspicion to stop: the quantum of proof required for a stop.

recidivism: return to criminal behavior; when probationers are arrested for committing new crimes.

recidivist: repeat offender.

reform model of policing: the view that police are the front end, or gatekeepers, of the criminal justice system.

rehabilitation: utilitarian philosophy of punishment that aims at preventing future crimes by changing individual offenders.

reintegration: improving the chances of prisoners' returning to productive and law-abiding lives outside prison by making their lives in confinement rich with programs.

release on recognizance (ROR): release of defendants solely on their promise to appear at trial.

relevant evidence: evidence that relates to the elements of the crime.

responsibility management approach: prison management model that stresses the responsibility of prisoners for their own actions, not administrative control to ensure prescribed behavior.

restitution: paying back victims for the injuries and other losses caused by offenders; philosophy of sentencing based on requiring offenders to pay in money or service for the harm to individuals and society caused by their crimes.

retribution: philosophy of punishment that looks backward in time to punish for crimes already committed.

right-wrong test: tests whether a mental defect caused sufficient damage to defendants' capacity to reason that either they didn't know what they were doing or, if they knew what they were doing, they didn't know it was wrong.

risk assessment method: used to put inmates in a particular group according to the risk of their committing further crimes.

rotten apple theory: a single bad officer who is not reflective of the department.

routine activities theory: crimes are committed when there is a motivated offender, a suitable target, and the absence of a capable guardian.

S

search: examining persons or property to discover evidence, weapons, or contraband.

selective enforcement: the principle that law enforcement officers use discretionary judgment as to which laws to enforce.

sentence bargaining: plea negotiation in which defendants plead guilty with the understanding that the judge will show leniency.

sentencing discrimination: unacceptable criteria, such as race, ethnicity, and gender, influence sentencing.

sentencing disparity: the differences—not necessarily discrimination—in sentences among individuals.

sentencing guidelines: base sentences on a combination of the severity of the crime and the criminal history of the offender.

sequester the jury: put jurors in hotel rooms under guard where they can't read newspapers, watch TV, or talk on the telephone to avoid being prejudiced by outside sources.

service style of policing: style of policing that takes all requests for service seriously, regardless of whether they stem from criminal law violations, maintaining order, or simply providing information.

sex ratio of killing (SROK): number of homicides committed by women for every 100 homicides committed by men.

situational theories: explanations of criminal behavior based on the importance of location of targets and the movement of offenders and victims in time and space.

social control theories: theories that obedience to rules depends on institutions to keep the desire to break the rules in check.

social ecology: three community characteristics (low social economic status, racial or ethnic heterogeneity, and high residential mobility) lead to social disorganization and then to high-crime and delinquency rates.

social justice mission: courts responsibility to do what's "best" for victims and offenders.

social learning theories: theories that individuals at birth are blank slates and learn values and behavior.

social processes: interactions among members of families, peer groups, school, churches, and other social institutions.

social structure of the case: extralegal sociological considerations that affect decisions.

special deterrence: incapacitation of specific offenders.

special housing units: units that segregate inmates away from the general prison population are called special housing units if they are inside prisons.

special needs prisoners: the vulnerable, troublemakers, the mentally ill, and the elderly.

station queens: police who are wary of danger; they seek the refuge of inside to avoid the hazards of the streets.

statistical discrimination: attributing group stereotypes to individual members of the group.

straight pleas: pleas of guilty without negotiation.

strain theory: explanation of criminal behavior that focuses on the effects of frustration experienced by those who work hard yet fail to attain the American dream.

street crime: crimes committed by poor and minority criminals.

strength of the case: one of the main criteria for determining whether a case will be prosecuted.

strict liability offenses: crimes without intent, which carry light punishments such as fines.

subpoena: order of a court commanding that witnesses appear in court to present relevant testimony.

substantial capacity test: test of insanity that focuses on whether defendants have a mental disease or defect that causes a lack of substantial capacity to either appreciate the wrongfulness of their conduct or to conform their conduct to the requirement of the law.

supermaxes: supermaximum prisons.

supermaximum prison: "end of the line" prisons for the "worst of the worst" prisoners.

suspect: people who don't "fit" their surroundings.

suspended sentence: release of convicted offenders without conditions or supervision.

sweet deals: practice of prosecutors' settling for less than the initial charges because the case against a defendant is weak.

T

technical violations: breaking of probation rules that do not amount to crimes.

testimonial evidence: one of two types of evidence the law recognizes, it includes witnesses' spoken, written, or symbolic words.

therapeutic communities (TCS): programs that isolate drug dependent prisoners from the general prison population to increase group pressure on prisoners to commit themselves to the program and decrease peer pressure from outside the group to use drugs.

three-strikes laws: laws that lock up for life dangerous offenders who habitually prey on innocent people.

torts: noncriminal legal wrongs; private personal injury actions.

total institutions: prisons that are isolated separate worlds with enough power to make prisoners give up their personalities and live completely regulated lives.

trial courts: courts of general jurisdiction.

U

Uniform Crime Reports (UCR): FBI collection of data based on official police records of the numbers of crimes known to the police and the numbers of people the police arrest.

utilitarian question: does the death penalty reduce crime?

utilitarian theory of crime causation: theory based on the belief human nature seeks pleasure and avoids pain.

V

void-for-vagueness: rule that a law is invalid unless it clearly defines what it prohibits.

voir dire: examination of prospective jurors by the judge and the attorneys.

W

watchman style of policing: nonbureaucratic, informal style of policing in which officers focus on caretaking and maintaining order by means of discretionary decision making.

wedding cake model: criminal justice officials decide how to deal with cases by ranking criminal cases according to their serious.

white-collar crime: crimes committed by corporate officers and managers under the authority of the corporation.

Z

zone system: horizontal case assignment, in which assistants are assigned to manage one stage of the prosecution—drafting criminal charges, working on pretrial motions, trying cases, or handling appeals.

Bibliography

ABA Commission on Women and the Legal Profession. 2001. *The Unfinished Agenda: Women and the Legal Profession.* Chicago: American Bar Association.

ABA Task Force on Minorities in the Judiciary. 1997. *Directory of Minority Judges in the United States.* Chicago: American Bar Association.

Adams, Kenneth. 1992. "Adjusting to Prison Life." In *Crime and Justice: An Annual Review of Research*, ed. Michael Tonry. Chicago: University of Chicago Press.

Adamson, Patrick B. 1991. "Some Comments on the Origins of Police." *Police Studies* 14.

Advisory Commission. 1984. *Jails, Intergovernmental Dimensions of a Local Problem.* Washington, DC: Advisory Commission on Intergovernmental Relations.

Alabama Law Review Summer Project. 1975. "A Study of Differential Treatment Accorded Female Defendants in Alabama Criminal Courts." *Alabama Law Review* 27.

Albert, Craig J. 1999. "Challenging Deterrence: New Insights on Capital Punishment Derived from Panel Data." *University of Pittsburgh Law Review* 60.

Albonetti, Celesta A. 1986. "Criminality, Prosecutorial Screening, and Uncertainty: Toward a Theory of Discretionary Decision Making in Felony Case Processings." *Criminology* 24.

Albonetti, Celesta A. 1990. "Race and the Probability of Pleading Guilty." *Journal of Quantitative Criminology* 6.

Allen, Harry E., Chris W. Eskridge, Edward J. Latessa, and Gennaro Vito. 1985. *Probation and Parole in America.* New York: Free Press.

Alpert, Geoffrey P. 1987. "Questioning Police Pursuits in Urban Areas." *Journal of Police Science and Administration* 15.

Alpert, Geoffrey P., and Roger G. Dunham. 1990. *Police Pursuit Driving: Controlling Responses to Emergency Situations.* New York: Greenwood Press.

Alschuler, Albert W. 1968. "The Prosecutor's Role in Plea Bargaining." *University of Chicago Law Review* 36.

Alschuler, Albert W. 1979. "Plea Bargaining and Its History." *Law and Society Review* 13.

Alter, Jonathan. 2001 (November 5). "Time to Think About Torture." *Newsweek.*

American Academy of Political and Social Science. 1910. *The Administration of Justice in the United States.* Philadelphia: AAPS.

American Friends Society. 1971. *Struggle for Justice: A Report on Crime and Punishment in America.* New York: Hill and Wang.

Amsterdam, Anthony. 1984. *Trial Manual for the Defense of Criminal Cases.* Philadelphia: American Law Institute.

Anderson v. Creighton. 1987. 483 U.S. 635, 107 S.Ct. 3034, 97 L.Ed.2d 523 (1987).

Appier, Janis. 1998. *Policing Women: The Sexual Politics of Law Enforcement and the LAPD.* Philadelphia: Temple University Press.

Atkinson, Donald. 1986 (February). "Parole Can Work!" *Corrections Today.*

Baker, Donald P., et al. 1973. "Judicial Intervention in Corrections: The California Experience—An Empirical Study." *UCLA Law Review* 20: 454.

Baker, Mark. 1985. *Cops: Their Lives in Their Own Words.* New York: Fawcett.

Baldus, David C. 1995. "Symposium: The Capital Jury Project, Keynote Address." *Indiana Law Journal* 70.

Baldus, David C., and George Woodworth. 1998. "Race Discrimination and the Death Penalty: An Empirical and Legal Overview." In *America's Experiment with Capital Punishment,* eds. James R. Acker, Robert S. Bohm, and Charles S. Lanier. Durham, NC: Carolina Academic Press.

Barker, Emily. 1993 (January/February). "Paying for Quality." *American Lawyer* 83.

Barron v. Baltimore. 1833. 32 U.S. 7 Pet. 243.

Bator, Paul. 1963. "Finality in Criminal Law and Federal Habeas Corpus for State Prisoners." *Harvard Law Review* 76.

Battelle Law and Justice Study Center. 1977. *Forcible Rape: A National Survey of the Response by Prosecutors,* vol. 3. Washington, DC: National Institute of Law Enforcement and Criminal Justice.

Bayley, David H. 1998. *What Works in Policing.* New York: Oxford University Press.

Bayley, David H., and Egon Bittner. 1989. "Learning the Skills of Policing." In *Critical Issues in Policing,* eds. Roger C. Dunham and Geoffrey P. Alpert. Prospect Heights, IL: Waveland Press.

Beck, Allen J. 1989. *Recidivism of Prisoners Released in 1983.* Washington, DC: Bureau of Justice Statistics.

Becker, Howard. 1973. *Outsiders.* New York: Free Press.

Bedau, Hugo Adam. 1982. *Death Penalty in America*. New York: Oxford University Press.

Bell v. Wolfish. 1979. 441 U.S. 520.

Benekos, Peter J., and Alida V. Merlo. 1995 (March). "Three Strikes and You're Out!: The Political Sentencing Game." *Federal Probation*.

Berger v. United States. 1935. 195 U.S. 78.

Bernard, Thomas J. 1983. *The Consensus-Conflict Debate: Form and Content in Social Theories*. New York: Columbia University Press.

Bingham, T. D. n.d. "Maximum Transfer from Marion to Florence." *Prison Life* 25.

Bittner, Egon. 1970. *The Functions of the Police in Modern Society*. Cambridge, MA: Ogleschlager, Gunn & Black, Charles L., Jr. 1981. *Capital Punishment: The Inevitability of Caprice and Mistake,* 2d ed. New York: W. W. Norton.

Black, Donald J. 1980. *The Manners and Customs of the Police*. New York: Academic Press.

Black, Donald J. 1989. *Sociological Justice*. New York: Oxford University Press.

Black, Henry Campbell. 1983. *Black's Law Dictionary,* 5th ed. St. Paul: West.

Blackstone, Sir William. 1830. *Commentaries on the Laws of England*. London: T. Tegg. Pt. IV.

Blomberg, Thomas G., and Stanley Cohen, eds. 1995. *Punishment and Social Control: Essays in Honor of Sheldon L. Messinger*. New York: Aldine de Gruyter.

Blumberg, Abraham S. 1967. "The Practice of Law as Confidence Game: Organizational Co-Optation of a Profession." *Law and Society Review* 1.

Blumberg, Abraham S. 1970. *Criminal Justice*. Chicago: Quadrangle Books.

Blumenthal, Ralph. 1989 (August 22). "And Now a Private Midtown 'Police Force.'" *New York Times*.

Blumstein, Alfred. 1993. "Racial Disproportionality of U.S. Prison Populations Revisited." *University of Colorado Law Review* 64.

Blumstein, Alfred, Jacqueline Cohn, Susan Martin, and Michael Tonry. 1983. *Research on Sentencing: The Search for Reform*. Washington, DC: National Academy Press.

Boland, Barbara, and Brian Forst. 1985. "Prosecutors Don't Always Aim to Pleas." *Federal Probation* 49.

Boland, Barbara, et al. 1989 (June). *The Prosecution of Felony Arrests, 1986*. Washington, DC: BJS.

Bottomly, Keith. 1973. *Decisions in the Penal Process*. South Hackensack, NJ: Fred B. Rothman & Co., 1973.

Bowers v. Hardwicke. 1986. 478 U.S. 186.

Bowers, William J. 1974. *Executions in America*. Lexington, MA: Lexington Books.

Bowker, Lee H. 1982. *Corrections: The Science and the Myth*. New Haven, CT: Yale University Press.

Bowker, Lee H. 1983. "Prisons: Problems and Prospects." In *Encyclopedia of Crime and Justice,* ed. Sanford H. Kadish. New York: Free Press 3:1230–1231.

Boydstun, John. 1975. *San Diego Field Interrogation Final Report*. Washington, DC: Police Foundation.

Braithwaite, John. 1979. *Inequality, Crime, and Public Policy*. London: Routledge and Kegan Paul.

Brakel, Samuel. 1982 (January). "Administrative Justice in the Penitentiary: Report on Inmate Grievance Procedures." *American Bar Foundation Research Journal*.

Brakel, Samuel. 1983 (January). "Ruling on Prisoners' Grievances." *American Bar Foundation Research Journal*.

Brandl, Steven G., and James Frank. 1994. "The Relationship Between Evidence, Detective Effort, and the Disposition of Burglary and Robbery Investigations." *American Journal of Police* XIII.

Britt, Chester L. III, Michael R. Gottfredson, and John S. Goldkamp. 1992. "Drug Testing and Pretrial Misconduct: An Experiment on the Specific Deterrent Effects of Drug Monitoring Defendants on Pretrial Release." *Journal of Research on Crime and Delinquency* 29.

Brown, Craig M., and Barbara D. Warner. 1992. "Immigrants, Urban Politics, and Policing in 1900." *American Sociological Review* 57.

Brown, Michael K. 1988. *Working the Street: Police Discretion and the Dilemmas of Reform*. New York: Russell Sage.

Brown, Stephen E. 1984. "Social Class, Child Maltreatment, and Delinquent Behavior." *Criminology* 22.

Brownstein, Henry H. 1996. *The Rise and Fall of a Violent Crime Wave*. Guilderland, NY: Harrow and Heston.

Buchanan, John. 1989 (May/June). "Police-Prosecutor Teams: Innovations in Several Jurisdictions." *National Institute of Justice Reports*.

Buerger, Michael E. 1994. "The Problems of Problem-Solving: Resistance, Interdependencies, and Conflicting Interests." *American Journal of Police* XIII.

Buerger, Michael E., ed. 1992. *The Crime Prevention Casebook: Securing High-Crime Locations*. Washington, DC: Crime Control Institute.

Bunker, Edward. 1977. *Animal Factory*. New York: Viking Press, 92.

Bureau of Justice Statistics. 1988a (January). *Profile of State Prison Inmates, 1986*. Washington, DC: BJS.

Bureau of Justice Statistics. 1988b. *Report to the Nation on Crime and Justice,* 2d ed. Washington, DC: BJS.

Bureau of Justice Statistics. 1989a. *The Prosecution of Felony Arrests*. Washington, DC: BJS.

Bureau of Justice Statistics. 1989b (January). *The Redesigned National Crime Survey: Selected New Data, Special Report*. Washington, DC: BJS.

Bureau of Justice Statistics. 1992a. *Prosecutors in State Courts, 1990*. Washington, DC: BJS.

Bureau of Justice Statistics. 1992b. *Sourcebook of Criminal Justice Statistics, 1991*. Washington, DC: BJS.

Bureau of Justice Statistics. 1993. *Survey of State Prison Inmates, 1991*. Washington, DC: BJS.

Bureau of Justice Statistics. 1994. *Violence and Theft in the Workplace, 1987–1992*. Washington, DC: BJS.

Bureau of Justice Statistics. 1995a. *Prisoners in 1994*. Washington, DC: BJS.

Bureau of Justice Statistics. 1995b. *Probation and Parole, 1995*. Washington, DC: BJS.

Bureau of Justice Statistics. 1997. *Correctional Populations in the United States*. Washington, DC: Bureau of Justice Statistics.

Bureau of Justice Statistics. 1998 (March). *Violence By Intimates*. Washington, DC: BJS.

Bureau of Justice Statistics. 1998 (July). *Prosecutors in State Courts, 1996*. Washington, DC: BJS.

Bureau of Justice Statistics. 1999a (July). *Felony Sentences in the U.S. 1996*. Washington, DC: BJS.

Bureau of Justice Statistics. 1999b. *Pretrial Release and Detention, 1996*. Washington, DC: BJS.

Bureau of Justice Statistics. 1999c. *Prisoners in 1998*. Washington, DC: BJS.

Bureau of Justice Statistics. 2000a (December). *Capital Punishment 1999*. Washington, DC: BJS.

Bureau of Justice Statistics. 2000b. *Correctional Populations in the United States, 1997*. Washington, DC: BJS.

Bureau of Justice Statistics. 2000c. *Criminal Victimization in the U.S., 1999*. Washington, DC: BJS.

Bureau of Justice Statistics. 2000d (December 7). *Justice Expenditure and Employment Extracts*. Washington, DC: BJS.

Bureau of Justice Statistics. 2000e. *Sourcebook of Criminal Justice Statistics Online*. http:// www.albany.edu/sourcebook/.

Bureau of Justice Statistics. 2001a. *Census of Jails, 1999*. Washington, DC: BJS.

Bureau of Justice Statistics. 2001b. *Community Policing in Local Police Departments, 1997 and 1999*. Washington, DC: BJS.

Bureau of Justice Statistics. 2001c. *Criminal Victimization 2000*. Washington, DC: BJS.

Bureau of Justice Statistics. 2001d. *Prisoners in 1999*. Washington, DC: BJS.

Bureau of Justice Statistics. 2001e. *Prisoners in 2000*. Washington, DC: BJS.

Bureau of Justice Statistics. 2001f (August 28). "Probation and Parole in the United States, 2000—Press Release." Washington, DC: BJS.

Bureau of Justice Statistics. 2001g. *State and Federal Prisoners, 1925–1985*. Washington, DC: BJS.

Bureau of Justice Statistics. 2001h. *State Court Organization 1998*. Washington, DC: BJS.

Burrows v. State. 1931. 38 Ariz. 99, 297 P. 1029.

Butterfield, Fox. 1992 (November 13). "Study Cites Biology's Role in Violent Behavior." *New York Times*.

Butterfield, Fox. 1998 (March 19). "Reason for Dramatic Drop in Crime Puzzles the Experts." *New York Times*.

Butterfield, Fox. 2002 (January 21). "Tight Budgets Force States to Reconsider Crime and Penalties." *New York Times*.

Byrne, James M., and Linda Kelly. 1989. *Restructuring Probation as an Intermediate Sanction: An Evaluation of the Massachusetts Intensive Supervision Program*. Washington, DC: National Institute of Justice.

Call, Jack E. 1988. "Lower Court Treatment of Jail and Prison Overcrowding Cases: A Second Look." *Federal Probation* 52.

Camp, Camille Graham, and George M. Camp. 2000. *Corrections Yearbook 2000*. Middletown, CT: Criminal Justice Institute.

Campaign for an Effective Crime Policy. 1993 (October). "Evaluating Mandatory Minimum Sentences." Unpublished manuscript. Washington, DC: Campaign for an Effective Crime Policy.

Campbell, Angus, and Howard Schuman. 1969. "Racial Attitudes in Fourteen American Cities." *Supplemental Studies for the National Advisory Committee on Civil Disorders*. Washington, DC: Government Printing Office.

Caplan, Gerald M. 1983. *ABSCAM Ethics: Moral Issues and Deception in Law Enforcement*. Washington, DC: Police Foundation.

Caplow, Theodore, and Jonathan Simon. 1999. "Understanding Prison Policy and Population Growth." In *Prisons*, eds. Michael Tonry and Joan Petersilia. Chicago: University of Chicago Press.

Carlson, Jonathon C. 1987. "The Act Requirement and the Foundations of the Entrapment Defense." *Virginia Law Review*.

Carns, Teresa. 1991. *Alaska's Plea Bargaining Ban Re-Evaluated*. Alaska Judicial Council. (http://www.ajc.state.ak.us/Reports/pleafram.htm).

Carter, Lief H. 1974. *The Limits of Order*. Lexington, MA: Lexington Books.

Casper, Jonathan D. 1972. *American Criminal Justice*. Englewood Cliffs, NJ: Prentice-Hall.

Chambliss, William J. 1975. *Criminal Law in Action*. Santa Barbara, CA: Hamilton.

Chambliss, William J., and Robert Seidman. 1982. *Law, Order, and Power*, 2d ed. Reading, MA: Addison-Wesley.

Chamlin, Mitchell B., and John K Cochran. 1998. "Causality, Economic Conditions, and Burglary." *Criminology* 36.

Champion, Dean J. 1988. *Felony Probation: Problems and Prospects*. New York: Praeger.

Champion, Dean J. 1989. "Private Counsels and Public Defenders: A Look at Weak Cases, Prior Records, and Leniency in Plea Bargaining." *Journal of Criminal Justice* 17.

Chevigny, Paul. 1969. *Police Power: Police Abuses in New York City*. New York: Vintage.

Christopher Commission. 1991. *Report of the Independent Commission on the Los Angeles Police Department*. Los Angeles: Independent Commission on the Los Angeles Police Department.

Church, Thomas W., Jr. 1985. "Examining Local Legal Culture." *American Bar Foundation Research Journal* 3.

Clarke, Ronald V., and Marcus Felson, eds. 1993. *Routine Activity and Rational Choice*. New Brunswick, NJ: Transaction Publishers.

Clear, Todd R., and Anthony A. Braga. 1995. "Community Corrections." In *Crime*, eds. James Q. Wilson and Joan Petersilia. San Francisco: Institute for Contemporary Studies.

Clear, Todd R., and George F. Cole. 1994. *American Corrections*, 3d ed. Belmont, CA: Wadsworth.

Clear, Todd R., Bruce Stout, Linda Kelly, Harry Dammer, and Patricia Hardyman. 1992. *Prisons, Prisoners, and Religion*. New Brunswick, NJ: Rutgers University Press.

Clemmer, Donald. 1940. *The Prison Community*. New York: Holt, Rinehart, & Winston.

Cloward, Richard, and Lloyd Ohlin. 1960. *Delinquency and Opportunity: A Theory of Delinquent Gangs*. New York: Free Press.

Cohen, Fred. 1985. *Criminal Law Bulletin* 21.

Cohen, Lawrence E., and Marcus Felson. 1979. "Social Change and Crime Rate Trends: A Routine Activity Approach." *American Sociological Review* 44.

Colorado v. Connelly 1986. 479 U.S. 157.

Colorado Statutes. 1986. Section 18-1-704.5, 8b, C.R.S.

Colvin, Mark. 1982 (June). "The 1980 New Mexico Prison Riot." *Social Problems* 29.

Colvin, Mark. 1992. *The Penitentiary in Crisis: From Accommodation to Riot in New Mexico*. Albany, NY: State University of New York Press.

Common Sense Foundation. 2001 (April 16). "Landmark North Carolina Death Penalty Study Finds Dramatic Bias." Raleigh, NC: Common Sense Foundation.

Cook, Fay Lomax. 1979. "Crime Among the Elderly: The Emergence of a Policy Issue." In *Reactions to Crime*, ed. Dan E. Lewis. Beverly Hills, CA: Wadsworth.

Cook, Julian Abele, Jr. 1995. "Family Responsibility." *Federal Sentencing Reporter* 8.

Cooke, Jacob E. 1961. *The Federalist*. Middleton, CT: Wesleyan University Press.

Cordner, Gary W., and Robert C. Trojanowicz. 1992. "Patrol." In *What Works in Policing?* eds. Gary W. Cordner and Donna C. Hale. Cincinnati: Anderson.

Cornish, Derek B., and Ronald V. Clarke, eds. 1986. *The Reasoning Criminal: Rational Choice Perspectives on Offending*. New York: Springer-Verlag.

Corrections Compendium Journal. 2000 (September). Washington, DC: American Correctional Association.

Cose, Elliot. 1995. *The Rage of a Privileged Class*. New York: Harper Perennial.

Cosgrove, Edward J. 1994 (September). "ROBO-PO: The Life and Times of a Federal Probation Officer." *Federal Probation*.

Court, Andy. 1993 (January/February). "Is There a Crisis?" *American Lawyer*.

Criminal and Juvenile Justice Coordinating Council. 2000. "Working Paper No. 3, Executive Summary." http://www.cjjcc.org/download/wp03_es.pdf.

Criminal Justice Institute. 2001. *Corrections Yearbook 2000: Adult Corrections*. Middletown, CT: Criminal Justice Institute, Inc.

Criminal Justice Newsletter. 1996 (February 15).

Crist, David. 2001 (November 29). Lecture. University of Minnesota.

Cronin, Thomas E., Tania Z. Cronin, and Michael E. Milakovich. 1981. *U.S. vs. Crime in the Streets*. Bloomington, IN: Indiana University Press.

Cuddihy, William J. 1990. "The Fourth Amendment: Origins and Original Meaning. Unpublished dissertation. Claremont, CA: Claremont Graduate School.

Cullen, Francis T. 1983. *Rethinking Crime and Deviance Theory*. Totowa, NJ: Rowman and Allenheld.

Cumming, Elaine, Ian Cumming, and Laurel Edell. 1965. "Policeman as Philosopher, Guide, and Friend." *Social Problems* 12.

Cunningham William C., John J. Strauchs, and Clifford W. Van Meter. 1991. *Private Security: Patterns and Trends*. Washington, DC: National Institute of Justice.

Currie, Elliot. 1998. *Crime and Punishment in America*. New York: Metropolitan Books.

Dahrendorf, Ralf. 1958. "Out of Utopia: Toward a Reorientation of Sociological Analysis." *American Journal of Sociology* 64.

Daley, Kathleen. 1989. "Neither Conflict nor Labeling nor Paternalism Will Suffice; Intersections of Race, Ethnicity, Gender, and Family in Criminal Court Decisions." *Crime and Delinquency* 35.

Daley, Kathleen. 1994. *Gender, Crime, and Punishment*. New Haven, CT: Yale University Press.

Davis, Kenneth C. 1975. *Police Discretion*. St. Paul, MN: West.

Decker, Scott H., and Barrik Van Winkle. 1996. *Life in the Gang: Family, Friends, and Violence*. Cambridge: Cambridge University Press.

Dershowitz, Alan. 1982. *The Best Defense*. New York: Random House.

Dershowitz, Alan. 1994. *The Abuse Excuse and Other Cop-Outs, Sob Stories, and Evasions of Responsibility*. Boston: Little, Brown.

Dickerson v. U.S. 2000. 530 U.S. 428.

DiIulio, John. 1987. *Governing Prisons*. New York: Free Press.

DiIulio, John. 1992 (May 13). "The Value of Prisons." *Wall Street Journal*.

DiIulio, John. 1996. "Help Wanted: Economists, Crime and Public Policy." *Journal of Economic Perspectives* 10.

Dolan, Maura. 2001 (October 19). "Terrorism May Shift Jurors' Attitudes." *Los Angeles Times*.

Donohew, Lewis, Howard Sypher, and William Bukoski, eds. 1991. *Persuasive Communication and Drug Abuse Education*. Hillsdale NJ: Erlbaum Associates.

Dostoyevsky, Fyodor. 1860. *House of the Dead*. London: Heinemann.

Durham, Alexis. 1998. "Crime Seriousness and Punitive Severity: An Assessment of Social Attitudes." *Justice Quarterly* 5.

Durkheim, Emile. 1933. *The Division of Labor in Society*. New York: Free Press.

Durkheim, Emile. 1951. *Suicide: A Study in Sociology*. New York: Free Press.

Earley, Pete. 1992. *The Hot House*. New York: Bantam Books.

Eck, John E. 1983. *Solving Crimes: The Investigation of Burglary and Robbery*. Washington, DC: Police Executive Research Forum.

Eck, John E. 1992. "Criminal Investigation." In *What Works in Policing?* eds. Gary W. Cordner and Donna C. Hale. Cincinnati: Anderson.

Eck, John E., and William Spelman. 1987. *Problem Solving: Problem-Oriented Policing in Newport News*. Washington, DC: Police Executive Research Forum.

Ehrlich, Isaac. 1975. "The Deterrent Effect of Capital Punishment: A Question of Life and Death." *American Economic Review* 397.

Eisenstein, James, and Herbert Jacob. 1977. *Felony Justice*. Boston: Little, Brown.

Elias, Robert. 1986. *The Politics of Victimization*. New York: Oxford University Press.

Elton, Geoffrey R. 1973. *Tudor Policy and Police*. Cambridge, England: Cambridge University Press.

Elton, Geoffrey R. 1974. *England Under the Tudors*, 2d ed. London: Methuen.

Epstein, Gady, and Gail Gibson. 2001 (October 6). "O'Malley, Norris Criticizes FBI Investigation." *Baltimore Sun*.

Erikson, Kai T. 1966. *Wayward Puritans: A Study in the Sociology of Deviance*. New York: John Wiley & Sons.

Eskridge, Chris. 1983. *Pretrial Release Programming: Issues and Trends*. New York: Boardman.

Estrich, Susan. 1987. *Real Rape*. Cambridge: Harvard University Press.

Eve, Raymond A., and Susan Brown Eve. 1984. "The Effects of Powerlessness, Fear of Social Change, and Social Integration on Fear of Crime Among the Elderly." *Victimology* 9.

Fabiano, Elizabeth, Frank Porporino, and David Robinson. 1990. "Rehabilitation Through Clearer Thinking: A Cognitive Model of Correctional Intervention." Correctional Service of Canada. http://www.csc-scc.gc.ca/text/rsrch/briefs/b4/b04e.shtml.

Fagan, Jeffrey, and Richard Freeman. 1999. "Crime and Work." In *Crime and Justice: A Review of Research*, ed. Michael Tonry. Chicago: University of Chicago Press.

FBI. 2000. *Crime in the United States 1999*. Washington, DC: U.S. Department of Justice.

FBI. 2001. *Crime in the United States 2000*. Washington, DC: Government Printing Office.

Federal Bureau of Prisons. n.d. *Metropolitan Correctional Center*. Chicago.

Federal Bureau of Prisons. 1993 (June 16). "Florence Background Paper." Washington, DC: Office of Public Affairs.

Feeley, Malcolm M. 1979. *The Process Is the Punishment*. New York: Russell Sage.

Feeley, Malcolm M., and Roger Hanson. 1987. "What We Know, Think We Know, and Would Like to Know About the Impact of Court Orders on Prison Conditions and Jail Crowding." In *Prison and Jail Crowding: Workshop Proceedings*, eds. Dale K. Sechrest, Jonathan D. Caspar, and Jeffrey A. Roth. Washington, DC: National Academy of Sciences.

Feeley, Malcolm M., and Mark H. Lazerson. 1983. "Police-Prosecutor Relationships: An Interorganizational Perspective." In *Empirical Theories About Courts*, eds. Keith O. Boyum and Lynn Mather. New York: Longman.

Feeley, Malcolm M., and Austin D. Sarat. 1980. *The Policy Dilemma: Federal Crime Policy and Enforcement, 1968–1978*. Minneapolis: University of Minnesota Press.

Feeney, Floyd. 1981. *Case Processing and Police-Prosecutor Coordination*. Davis, CA: University of California, Davis, Center on Administration of Criminal Justice.

Felson, Marcus. 1998. *Crime in Everyday Life*, 2d ed. Thousand Oaks, CA: Pine Forge Press.

Finkelhor, David, et al. 1983. *The Dark Side of Families: Current Family Violence Research*. Beverly Hills, CA: Sage.

Flanagan, Timothy J. 1989. "Prison Labor and Industry." In *The American Prison: Issues in Research and Policy*, eds. Lynne Goodstein and Doris Layton MacKenzie. New York: Plenum Press.

Flanagan, Timothy J., and Dennis R. Longmire, eds. 1996. *Americans View Crime and Justice*. Thousand Oaks, CA: Sage.

Fleisher, Mark. *Warehousing Violence*. 1989. Newbury Park, CA: Sage, 8–29.

Fletcher, George P. 1978. *Rethinking Criminal Law*. Boston: Little, Brown.

Fletcher, George P. 1988. *A Crime of Self-Defense: Bernhard Goetz and the Law on Trial*. New York: Free Press.

Fletcher, George P. 1995. *With Justice for Some: Victims' Rights in Criminal Trials*. Reading, MA: Addison-Wesley.

Florida v. Royer. 1983. 460 U.S. 491.

Foote, Caleb. 1956. "Vagrancy-Type Law and Its Administration." *University of Pennsylvania Law Review* 104.

Foote, Caleb. 1965. "The Coming Constitutional Crisis in Bail." *University of Pennsylvania Law Review* 113.

Forer, Lois. 1984. *Money and Justice*. New York: W. W. Norton.

Forst, Brian. 1981. *Improving Police-Prosecutor Coordination*. Washington, DC: Institute for Law and Social Research.

Forst, Brian, ed. 1993. *The Socio-Economics of Crime and Justice*. Armonk, NY: M. E. Sharpe, Inc.

Forst, Brian. 1995. "Prosecution and Sentencing." In *Crime*, eds. James Q. Wilson and Joan Petersilia. San Francisco: Institute for Contemporary Studies Press.

Forst, Brian, F. J. Leahy, Jr., J. Shirhall, H. L. Tyson, and J. Bartolomeo. 1982. *Arrest Convictability as a Measure of Police Performance.* Washington, DC: National Institute of Justice.

Forst, Brian, Judith Lucianovic, and Sarah J. Cox. 1977. *What Happens After Arrest?* Washington, DC: National Institute of Law Enforcement and Criminal Justice.

Frase, Richard. 1998. "Jails." In *Handbook of Crime and Justice,* ed. Michael Tonry. New York: Oxford University Press.

Freed, Daniel J., and Patricia M. Wald. 1964. *Bail in the United States: 1964: A Report to the National Conference on Bail and Criminal Justice.* Washington, DC: Vera Institute of Justice.

Friedman, Lawrence M. 1984. *American Law.* New York: W. W. Norton.

Friedman, Lawrence M. 1985. *A History of American Law,* 2d ed. New York: Simon and Schuster.

Frontline. 1996. "Angel on Death Row." Washington, DC: Public Broadcasting System.

Frontline. 1999 (January 12). "Snitch." Washington, DC: Public Broadcasting System.

Fyfe, James J. 1982. "Blind Justice: Police Shootings in Memphis." *Journal of Criminal Law and Criminology* 73.

Gaes, Gerald G., Timothy J. Flanagan, Laurence L. Motuik, and Lynne Stewart. 1998. *Adult Correctional Treatment.* Washington, DC: U.S. Bureau of Prisons.

Garofalo, James. 1990. "The National Crime Survey, 1973–86: Strengths and Limitations of a Very Large Data Set." In *Measuring Crime: Large Scale, Long Range Efforts,* eds. Doris Layton MacKenzie, Phyllis Jo Baunach, and Roy R. Roberg. Albany, NY: State University of New York Press.

Garofolo, James. 1991. "Police, Prosecutors, and Felony Case Attrition." *Journal of Criminal Justice* 19.

Gaylin, Willard, Steven Marcus, David Rothman, and Ira Glasser. 1978. *Doing Good: The Limits of Benevolence.* New York: Pantheon.

Geerken, Michael R., and Hennessey D. Hayes. 1993. "Probation and Parole: Public Risk and the Future of Incarceration Alternatives." *Criminology* 31.

Geller, William A. 1985. *Crime File: Deadly Force.* Washington, DC: National Institute of Justice.

Geller, William A., and Kevin J. Karales. 1981. *Split-Second Decisions.* Chicago: Chicago Law Enforcement Study Group.

Geller, William A., and Michael S. Scott. 1992. *Deadly Force: What We Know and Don't Know.* Washington, DC: Police Executive Research Forum.

Gerber, Jorg, and Eric Fritsch. 1995. "Adult Academic and Vocational Correctional Education Programs: A Review of Current Research." *Journal of Correctional Rehabilitation* 22:1–2.

Gettinger, Stephen H. 1984. *New Generation Jails: An Innovative Approach to an Age-Old Problem.* Washington, DC: National Institute of Corrections.

Giallombardo, Rose. 1966. *Society of Women: A Study of a Women's Prison.* New York: Wiley.

Gibeaut, John. 1997 (May). "Sobering Thoughts: Legislatures and Courts Increasingly Are Just Saying No to Intoxication as a Defense or Mitigating Factor." *American Bar Association Journal.*

Glueck, Sheldon, ed. 1965. *Roscoe Pound and Criminal Justice.* Dobbs-Ferry, NY: Oceana Publications.

Goldfarb, Ronald. 1965. *Ransom: A Critique of the American Bail System.* New York: Harper and Row.

Goldfarb, Ronald. 1975. *Jails: The Ultimate Ghetto.* New York: Archer Press.

Goldkamp, John S. 1979. *Two Classes of Accused.* Cambridge, MA: Ballinger.

Goldkamp, John S. 1985. "Danger and Detention: A Second Generation of Bail Reform." *Journal of Criminal Law and Criminology* 76.

Goldkamp, John S., and Doris Weiland. 1993. *Assessing the Impact of Dade County's Felony Drug Court: Final Report.* Philadelphia: Crime and Justice Research Institute.

Goldstein, Herman. 1977: *Policing a Free Society.* Cambridge, MA: Ballinger.

Goldstein, Herman. 1984. *The Future of Policing.* Seattle: William O. Douglas Institute.

Gottfredson, Michael R., and Don M. Gottfredson. 1988. *Decision Making in Criminal Justice,* 2d ed. Sacramento, CA: Office of Attorney General of California.

Gottfredson, Michael R., and Travis Hirschi. 1990. *A General Theory of Crime.* Stanford: Stanford University Press.

Gottfredson, Stephen D., and Don M. Gottfredson. 1992. *Incapacitation Strategies and the Criminal Career.* Sacramento, CA: Office of Attorney General of California.

Gove, Walter, et al. 1986. "Are Uniform Crime Reports a Valid Indicator of the Index Crimes? An Affirmative Answer with Minor Qualifications." *Criminology* 23.

Gray, Tara, G. Larry Mays, and Mary K. Stohr. 1995. "Inmate Needs and Programming in Exclusively Women's Jails." *Prison Journal* 75:2.

Greenberg, David, ed. 1981. *Crime and Capitalism: Readings in Marxist Criminology.* Palo Alto, CA: Mayfield.

Greenberg, Martin S., R. Barry Ruback, and David R. Westcott. 1983. "Seeking Help from the Police: The Victim's Perspective." In *New Directions in Helping,* vol. 3, eds. Arie Nadler, Jeffrey D. Fisher, and Bella M. DePaulo. New York: Academic Press.

Greenfield, Lawrence A. 1985. *Examining Recidivism.* Washington, DC: Bureau of Justice Statistics.

Greenwood, Peter W., Jan Chaiken, and Joan Petersilia. 1977. *The Criminal Investigation Process.* Lexington, MA: D. C. Heath.

Greenwood, Peter W., and Joan Petersilia. 1975. *The Criminal Investigation Process, Vols. I–III.* Santa Monica, CA: Rand.

Greenwood, Peter W., C. Peter Rydell, Allan F. Abrahamse, and Nathan P. Caulins. 1994. *Three Strikes and You're Out: Estimated Benefits and Costs of California's New Mandatory-Sentencing Law.* Santa Monica, CA: Rand.

Greenwood, Peter W., Sorrel Wildhorn, Eugene C. Poggio, M. J. Strumwassder, and Peter DeLeon. 1973. *Prosecution of Adult*

Felony Defendants in Los Angeles County: A Policy Perspective. Santa Monica, CA: Rand.

Griffin v. Wisconsin. 1987. 483 U.S. 868.

Griswold v. Connecticut. 1965. 381 U.S. 479.

Griswold, David B. 1994. "Complaints Against the Police: Predicting Dispositions." *Journal of Criminal Justice* 22.

Grob, Gerald. 1973. *Mental Institutions in America*. New York: Free Press.

Grudt v. Los Angeles. 1970. 2 Cal.3d 575.

Hagan, John, and Ronit Dinovitzer. 1999. "Collateral Consequences of Imprisonment for Children, Communities, and Prisons." In *Prisons*, eds. Michael Tonry and Joan Petersilia. Chicago: University of Chicago Press.

Halberstam, David. 1998. *The Children*. New York: Random House.

Hall, John W. 1993. *Search and Seizure*, 2d ed. New York: Clark, Boardman, and Callaghan.

Hall, William, and Larry Aspin. 1987. "What Twenty Years of Judicial Retention Elections Have Told Us." *Judicature* 70.

Halper, Andrew, and Richard Ku. 1975. *An Exemplary Project: New York City Police Department Street Crimes Unit*. Washington, DC: Government Printing Office.

Haney, Craig, Curtis Banks, and Philip Zimbardo. 1973. "Interpersonal Dynamics in a Simulated Prison." *International Journal of Criminology and Penology* 1.

Hanson, Roger A., Brian J. Ostrom, William E. Hewitt, and Christopher Lomvardias. 1992. *Indigent Defenders Get the Job Done and Done Well*. Williamsburg, VA: National Center for State Courts.

Harding, Richard. 2001. "Private Prisons." In *Crime and Justice: A Review of Research*, ed. Michael Tonry. Chicago: University of Chicago Press.

Harris, M. Kay, and Dudley P. Spiller, Jr. 1977. *After Decision: Implementation of Judicial Decrees in Correctional Settings*. Washington, DC: U.S. Department of Justice.

Hart, Timothy C., and Brian A. Reaves. 1999. *Felony Defendants in Large Urban Counties, 1996*. Washington, DC: Bureau of Justice Statistics.

Hawkins, Gordon. 1976. *The Prison: Policy and Practice*. Chicago: University of Chicago Press.

Hawkins, Gordon. 1983. "Prison Labor and Prison Industries." In *Crime and Justice: An Annual Review of Research*, ed. Michael Tonry and Norval Morris. Chicago: University of Chicago Press.

Hay, Douglas. 1975. "Property, Authority, and the Criminal Law." In *Albion's Fatal Tree*, eds. Douglas Hay, Peter Linebaugh, John Rule, Edward P. Thompson, and Cal Winslow. London: Allen Lane.

Hay, Douglas. 1980. "Crime and Justice in Eighteenth- and Nineteenth-Century England." In *Crime and Justice: An Annual Review of Research*, eds. Norval Morris and Michael Tonry. London: Allen Lane.

Heffernen, Esther. 1972. *Making It in Prison: The Square, the Cool, and the Life*. New York: Wiley Interscience.

Hensley, Christopher. 2000. "Consensual Homosexual Activity in Male Prisons." *Corrections Compendium* 26:1.

Herbert, Steve. 1998. "Police Subculture Reconsidered." *Criminology* 36.

Heumann, Milton. 1978. *Plea Bargaining: The Experience of Prosecutors, Judges, and Defense Attorneys*. Chicago: University of Chicago Press.

Heumann, Milton. 1979a. "Author's Reply." *Law and Society Review* 13.

Heumann, Milton. 1979b. "Thinking About Plea Bargaining. In *The Study of Criminal Courts*, ed. Peter F. Nardulli. Cambridge, MA: Ballinger.

Hindelang, Michael. 1978. "Race and Involvement in Common Law Property Crimes." *American Sociological Review* 43.

Hindelang, Michael, Michael Gottfredson, and James Garofalo. 1978. *Victims of Personal Crime*. Cambridge, MA: Ballinger.

Hirsch, Adam Jay. 1992. *The Rise of the Penitentiary*. New Haven, CT: Yale University Press.

Hirschi, Travis. 1969. *Causes of Delinquency*. Berkeley: University of California Press.

Holden, Benjamin A., Laurie P. Cohen, and Eleena de Lisser. 1995 (October 4). "Color Blinded? Race Seems to Play an Increasing Role in Many Jury Verdicts." *Wall Street Journal*.

Holland v. Illinois. 1990. 493 U.S. 474 (1990).

Hollinger, Richard C., and John P. Clark. 1983. *Theft by Employees*. Lexington, MA: Lexington Books.

Hollinger, Richard C., and Lonn Lanza-Kaduce. 1988. "The Process of Criminalization: The Case of Computer Crime Laws." *Criminology* 26.

Holmes, Michael D., Howard C. Daudistel, and William A. Taggert. 1992. "Plea Bargaining Policy and State District Court Loads: An Interrupted Time-Series Analysis." *Law and Society Review* 26.

Holt, Norm. 1998. "Parole in America." In *Community Corrections: Probation, Parole, and Intermediate Sanctions*, ed. Joan Petersilia. New York: Oxford University Press.

Horney, Julie, and Ineke Haen Marshall. 1992. "Risk Perceptions Among Serious Offenders: The Role of Crime and Punishment." *Criminology* 30.

Hoskinson, Charles. 1998 (December 1). "Prison Industries Often in the Red." *Associated Press*.

Hough, Mike. 1987. "Offenders' Choice of Target: Findings from Victim Surveys." *Journal of Quantitative Criminology* 3.

Howe, Frederic C. 1910 (July). "A Golden Rule Chief of Police." *Everybody's Magazine*.

Hudson v. Palmer. 1984. 468 U.S. 517.

Hunter, Susan M. 1986. "On the Line: Working Hard with Dignity." *Corrections Today* 48:4.

Illinois v. Allen. 1970. 397 U.S. 337.

Immarigeon, Russ, and Meda Chesney-Lind. 1992. *Women's Prisons: Overcrowded and Overused*. San Francisco: National Council on Crime and Delinquency.

Inbau, Fred E., et al. 1980. *Criminal Law and Its Administration,* 4th ed. Mineola, NY: Foundation Press.

Ingraham, Barton L. 1980. "Reforming Criminal Procedure." In *Improving Management in Criminal Justice,* eds. Alvin W. Cohn and Benjamin Ward. Beverly Hills, CA: Sage.

In re Kemmler. 1890. 136 U.S. 436.

In re Winship. 1970. 397 U.S. 358.

Institute for Law and Social Research (INSLAW). 1977. *Curbing the Repeat Offender.* Washington, DC: INSLAW.

Iowa Department of Corrections. n.d. "Iowa Department of Corrections Scoring Guide." Mimeo produced by Iowa Department of Corrections.

Irwin, John. 1980. *Prisons in Turmoil.* Boston: Little, Brown.

Irwin, John. 1996. "The Prison Experience: The Convict World." In *Criminal Justice,* eds. George S. Bridges, Joseph G. Weis, and Robert D. Crutchfield. Thousand Oaks, CA: Pine Forge Press.

Irwin, John, and James Austin. 1997. *It's About Time: America's Imprisonment Binge,* 2d ed. Belmont, CA: Wadsworth.

Jackson, Patrick G., and Cindy A. Stearns. 1995. "Gender Issues in the New Generation Jail." *Prison Journal* 75.

Jackson, Robert. 1940. *Journal of the American Judicature Society* 34.

Jacobs, James B. 1977. *Stateville: The Penitentiary in Modern Society.* Chicago: University of Chicago Press.

Jacobs, James B. 1980. "Race Relations and the Prisoner Subculture." In *Crime and Justice: An Annual Review of Research,* eds. Norval Morris and Michael Tonry. Chicago: University of Chicago Press.

Jacobs, James B., ed. 1983. *New Perspectives on Prisons and Imprisonment.* Ithaca, NY: Cornell University Press.

Jacoby, Joan. 1980. *The American Prosecutor: A Search for Identity.* Lexington, MA: D. C. Heath.

Johnson, Alan. 1999 (February 28). "$88.42 in Drugs End Life of 'The Volunteer'; Wilford Berry's Case Cost Ohio $1.5 Million." *Columbus Dispatch.*

Johnson Robert. 1996. *Hard Time: Understanding and Reforming the Prison,* 2d ed. Monterey, CA: Brooks/Cole.

Judicial Conference of the United States. 1998 (September 15). *Federal Death Penalty Cases: Executive Summary.* Subcommittee on Federal Death Penalty Cases, Committee on Defender Services.

Kalinich, David B. 1986. *Power, Stability, and Contraband.* Prospect Heights, IL: Waveland Press.

Kalven, Harry, Jr., and Hans Zeisel. 1966. *The American Jury.* Chicago: University of Chicago Press.

Karmen, Andrew. 1990. *Crime Victims,* 2d ed. Pacific Grove, CA: Brooks/Cole.

Kathleen Daley. 1994. *Gender, Crime, and Punishment.* New Haven, CT: Yale University Press.

Katz v. U.S. 1967. 389 U.S. 347.

Katz, Jack. 1988. *Seductions of Crime: Moral and Sensual Attractions in Doing Evil.* New York: Basic Books.

Kelling, George L., and Catherine M. Coles. 1996. *Fixing Broken Windows.* New York: Free Press.

Kelling, George L., and David Fogel. 1978. "Police Patrol—Some Future Directions." In *The Future of Policing,* ed. Alvin W. Cohn. Beverly Hills, CA: Sage.

Kelling, George L., Tony Pate, Duane Dieckman, and Charles E. Brown. 1974. *The Kansas City Preventive Patrol Experiment: A Summary Report.* Washington, DC: Police Foundation.

Kennedy, Randall. 1998. *Race, Crime, and the Law.* New York: Vintage.

Kenyon, Jack P. 1986. *The Stuart Constitution,* 2d ed. New York: Cambridge University Press.

Kerstetter, Wayne A. 1985. "Who Disciplines the Police? Who Should?" In *Police Leadership in America: Crisis and Opportunity,* ed. William A. Geller. New York: Praeger.

Kerstetter, Wayne A., and Anne M. Heinz. 1979. *Pretrial Settlement Conference: An Evaluation.* Washington, DC: U.S. Department of Justice.

King, Roy D. 1998. "Prisons." In *Handbook of Crime and Punishment,* ed. Michael Tonry. New York: Oxford University Press.

King, Ryan S., and Marc Mauer. 2001 (August). *Aging Behind Bars: "Three Strikes" Seven Years Later.* Washington, DC: Sentencing Project.

Klein, Malcolm W. 1995. *The American Street Gang: Its Nature, Prevalence, and Control.* New York: Oxford University Press.

Klein, Stephen, and Michael Caggiono. 1986. *The Prevalence, Predictability, and Policy Implications of Recidivism.* Santa Monica, CA: Rand.

Klockars, Carl B. 1991a. "The Dirty Harry Problem." In *Thinking About Police,* 2d ed., eds. Carl B. Klockars and Stephen D. Mastrofski. New York: McGraw-Hill.

Klockars, Carl B. 1991b. "The Rhetoric of Community Policing." In *Thinking About Police,* 2d ed., eds. Carl B. Klockars and Stephen D. Mastrofski. New York: McGraw-Hill.

Knapp Commission. 1972. *Report on Police Corruption.* New York: George Braziller.

Knox, George W. 1991. *An Introduction to Gangs.* Berrien Springs, MI: Van de Vere Publishing Ltd.

Kohut, Andrew. 2001 (May 10). "The Declining Support for Executions." *New York Times,* 33.

Kruttschnitt, Candace M. 1984. "Sex and Criminal Court Dispositions: The Unresolved Controversy." *Journal of Research in Crime and Delinquency* 30.

Kruttschnitt, Candace M. 2001. "Women's Involvement in Serious Interpersonal Violence." *Aggression and Violent Behavior* 7.

Kyllo v. U.S. 2001. October Term 2000, Slip Opinion. http://a257.g.akamaitech.net/7/257/2422/11june20011200/www.supremecourtus.gov/opinions/00pdf/99–8508.pdf.

Ladinsky, Jack. 1963. "The Impact of Social Backgrounds of Lawyers on Law Practice and the Law." *Journal of Legal Education* 16.

LaFave, Wayne R., and Jerold H. Israel. 1984. *Criminal Procedure.* St. Paul, MN: West.

LaFave, Wayne R., and Jerold H. Israel. 1992. *Criminal Procedure,* 2d ed. St. Paul, MN: West.

LaFave, Wayne R., and Austin W. Scott, Jr. 1986. *Criminal Law,* 2d ed. St. Paul, MN: West.

Lafree, Gary D. 1985. "Official Reactions to Hispanic Defendants in the Southwest." *Journal of Research in Crime and Delinquency* 22.

Lafree, Gary D. 1998. *Losing Legitimacy.* New York: Westview.

Lambarde, William. 1583. *Eirenarcha.* London: Ralph Newbery.

Lane, Roger. 1992. "Urban Police and Crime in Nineteenth Century America." *Crime and Justice* 15.

Langan, Patrick A. 1991. "America's Soaring Prison Population." *Science* 251.

Langan, Patrick A., and Christopher Innes. 1986 (Fall). *Preventing Domestic Violence Against Women.* Ann Arbor, MI: The Criminal Justice Archive and Information Network.

Langworthy, Robert H. 1992. "Organizational Structure." In *What Works in Policing?* eds. Gary W. Cordner and Donna C. Hale. Cincinnati: Anderson.

Lanier, C. S. 1993. "Affective States of Fathers in Prison." *Justice Quarterly* 10.

Lanzetta v. New Jersey. 1939. 306 U.S. 451.

Layson, Stephen K. 1985. "Homicide and Deterrence: A Reexamination of the United States Time-Series Evidence." *Southern Economic Journal* 52.

Lee, Jennifer. 2001 (July 11). "Tracking Sales and Cashiers." *New York Times.*

Lee v. Washington. 1968. 390 U.S. 333.

Lenz, Timothy. 1986. "Group Participation in the Politics of Sentencing Reform." Ph.D. dissertation. University of Minnesota.

Leo, Richard. 1996. "Inside the Interrogation Room." *Journal of Criminal Law and Criminology* 86.

Lerner, Mark Jay. 1977. "The Effectiveness of a Definite Sentence Parole Program." *Criminology* 15.

Levin, Alan M., and Stephen J. Hertzberg. 1986 (April 8). "Inside the Jury Room." *Frontline.* Public Broadcasting System.

Levin, David A., and Patrick A. Langan. 2000. *State Court Sentencing of Convicted Felons, 1996.* Washington, DC: Bureau of Justice Statistics.

Levin, Martin A. 1977. *Urban Politics and the Criminal Courts.* Chicago: University of Chicago Press.

Levin, Martin A. 1992. "The American Judicial System: Should It, Does It, and Can It Provide an Impartial Jury to Criminal Defendants?" *Criminal Justice Journal* 11.

Levine, James P. 1992. *Juries and Politics.* Pacific Grove, CA: Brooks/Cole.

Levy, Leonard. 1968. *Origins of the Fifth Amendment.* New York: Oxford University Press.

Lewis, Peter W. 1979. "Killing the Killers: A Post–*Furman* Profile of Florida's Condemned." *Crime and Delinquency* 25.

Lincoln, Alan J., and Murray A. Strauss. 1985. *Crime and the Family.* Springfield, IL: Charles C. Thomas.

Lindsey, Edward. 1925. "Historical Sketch of the Indeterminate Sentence and Parole Systems." *Journal of Criminal Law and Criminology* 16.

Lipton, Douglas S. 1995. "CDate: Updating the Effectiveness of Correctional Treatment 25 Years Later." *Journal of Offender Rehabilitation* 22:1–2.

Littrell, W. Boyd. 1979. *Bureaucratic Justice: Police, Prosecutors, and Plea Bargaining.* Beverly Hills, CA: Sage.

Lockwood, Daniel. 1980. *Prison Sexual Violence.* New York: Elsevier/North Holland.

Logan, Charles H., and Gerald G. Gaes. 1993. "Meta-Analysis and the Rehabilitation of Punishment." *Justice Quarterly* 10.

LoLordo, Ann. 2001 (February 13). "DNA Testing Frees Va. Man Wrongly Imprisoned 18 Years; Release Comes Amid National Debate over Felons' Access to Tests." *Baltimore Sun.*

Lombardi, John H., and Donna M. Lombardi. 1986 (February). "Objective Parole Criteria: More Harm Than Good?" *Corrections Today.*

Lombroso-Ferrero, Gina. 1972. *Criminal Man.* Montclair, NJ: Patterson Smith.

Lynch, David. 1994. "The Impropriety of Plea Bargaining." *Law and Social Inquiry* 19.

M'Naughten's Case. 1843. 8 *Eng. Rep.* 718.

Manning, Peter K. 1995. "The Police: Mandate, Strategies, and Appearances." In *The Police and Society: Touchstone Readings,* ed. Victor E. Kappeler. Prospect Heights, IL: Waveland Press, Inc.

Manson v. Brathwaite. 1977. 432 U.S. 98.

Marcus, Paul. 1986. "The Development of Entrapment Law." *Wayne Law Review* 33.

Margolick, David. 1984 (December 30). "Cooke, About to Retire, Looks Back in Satisfaction." *New York Times.*

Margolick, David. 1994 (January 7). "Falsely Accused." *New York Times.*

Mars, Gerald. 1982. *Cheats at Work.* London: Allen and Unwin.

Marshall, Justice Thurgood. 1976. *Gregg v. Georgia.* 428 U.S. 227.

Martin, Steve J., and Sheldon Ekland-Olson. 1987. *Texas Prisons: The Walls Came Tumbling Down.* Austin, TX: Texas Monthly Press.

Martinson, Robert. 1974 (Spring). "What Works? Questions and Answers About Prison Reform." *The Public Interest.*

Marx, Gary T. 1982 (April). "Who Really Gets Stung? Some Issues Raised by the New Police Undercover Work." *Crime and Delinquency.*

Marx, Gary T. 1988. *Undercover: Police Surveillance in America.* Berkeley, CA: University of California Press.

Mastrofski, Stephen D. 1990. "The Prospects for Change in Police Patrol: A Decade of Review." *American Journal of Police* 9.

Mather, Lynn. 1974. "Some Determinants of the Method of Case Disposition: Decision Making by Public Defenders in Los Angeles." *Law and Society Review* 8.

Mather, Lynn. 1979. *Plea Bargaining or Trial? The Process of Criminal Case Disposition*. Lexington, MA: Lexington Books.

Matusow, Allen J. 1984. *The Unraveling of America: A History of Liberalism in the 1960s*. New York: Harper & Row.

Maxwell, Christopher, Joel H. Garner, and Jeffrey A. Fagan. 1991. *The Effects of Arrest on Intimate Partner Violence: New Evidence from the Spouse Assault Replication Program*. Washington, DC: National Institute of Justice.

McCoy, Candace. 1998. "Prosecution." In *The Handbook of Crime and Punishment*, ed. Michael Tonry. New York: Oxford University Press.

McDonald, Douglas. 1992. "Private Penal Institutions." In *Crime and Justice: A Review of Research*, ed. Michael Tonry. Chicago: University of Chicago Press.

McDonald, Douglas, Elizabeth Fournier, Malcolm Russell-Einhorn, and Stephen Crawford. 1998. *Private Prisons in the United States: An Assessment of Current Practice*. Cambridge, MA: Abt Associates, Inc.

McDonald, William F. 1979. "From Plea Negotiation to Coercive Justice: Notes on the Respectification of a Concept." *Law and Society Review* 13.

McDonald, William F. 1985. *Plea Bargaining: Critical Issues and Common Practices*. Washington, DC: National Institute of Justice.

McIntyre, Lisa J. 1987. *Public Defender*. Chicago: University of Chicago Press.

Mednick, Sarnoff A., and Karl O. Christiansen, eds. 1977. "A Review of Studies of Criminality Among Twins," and "A Preliminary Study of Criminality in Twins." *Biosocial Bases of Criminality*. New York: Gardner Press.

Meier, Robert F., and Terance D. Miethe. 1993. "Understanding Theories of Criminal Victimization." In *Crime and Justice: A Review of Research*, vol. 17, ed. Michael Tonry. Chicago: University of Chicago Press.

Mellon, Leonard, Joan Jacoby, and Marion Brewer. 1981. "The Prosecutor Constrained by His Environment: A New Look at Discretionary Justice in the United States." *Journal of Criminal Law and Criminology* 72.

Merton, Robert K. 1968. "Social Structure and Anomie." *Social Theory and Social Structure*, enlarged ed. New York: Free Press.

Meyer, Greg. 1991 "Nonlethal Weapons Versus Conventional Police Tactics: The Los Angeles Police Experience." Master's thesis. California State University Los Angeles.

Michael M. v. Superior Court of Sonoma County 1981. 450 U.S. 464.

Michigan v. Sitz. 1990. 496 U.S. 444.

Miethe, Terance D., and Charles A. Moore. 1985. "Socioeconomic Disparities Under Determinate Sentencing Systems: A Comparison of Preguideline and Postguideline Practices in Minnesota." *Criminology* 23.

Miethe, Terance D., and Robert F. Meier. 1994. *Crime and Its Social Context: Toward an Integrated Theory of Offenders, Victims, and Situations*. Albany, NY: State University of New York Press.

Mileski, Maureen. 1971 (May). "Courtroom Encounters: An Observation Study of a Lower Criminal Court." *Law and Society Review*.

Miller, Frank W., and Robert O. Dawson, George E. Dix, and Raymond I. Parnas. 2000. New York: Foundation Press.

Miller, Herbert S., et al. 1978. *Plea Bargaining in the United States*. Washington, DC: National Institute of Justice.

Milton, Catherine H. 1977. *Police Use of Deadly Force*. Washington, DC: Police Foundation.

Minnesota Sentencing Guidelines Commission. 2001. *Minnesota Sentencing Guidelines and Commentary*.

Minnesota v. Murphy. 1984. 465 US 420 (1984).

Miranda v. Arizona. 1966. 384 U.S. 436.

Misner, Gordon E. 1990 (December/January). "High-Speed Pursuits: Police Perspectives." *Criminal Justice, the Americas*.

Monkkonen, Eric H. 1992. "History of Urban Police." In *Modern Policing*, eds. Michael Tonry and Norval Morris. Chicago: University of Chicago Press.

Moore, Mark Harrison. 1992. "Problem-Solving and Community Policing." In *Modern Policing*, eds. Michael Tonry and Norval Morris. Chicago: University of Chicago Press.

Morain, Dan. 1998 (February 12). "More Inmate Privileges Fall in Get-Tough Drive." *Los Angeles Times*, B8.

Morris, Norval. 1951. "Somnambulistic Homicide: Ghosts, Spiders, and North Koreans. *Res Judicata* 5.

Morris, Norval. 1974. *The Future of Imprisonment*. Chicago: University of Chicago Press.

Morris, Norval, and Gordon Hawkins. 1967. *The Honest Politician's Guide to Crime Control*. Chicago: University of Chicago Press.

Morrissey v. Brewer. 1973. 408 U.S. 471.

Myers, Martha A., and Susette M. Talarico. 1987. *The Social Contexts of Criminal Sentencing*. New York: Springer-Verlag.

Nagel, Stuart S. 1975. *Improving the Legal Process*. Lexington, MA: Lexington Books.

Nagel, Stuart S., and Lenore J. Weitzman. 1971. "Women as Litigants." *Hastings Law Journal* 23.

Nardulli, Peter F. 1978. *The Courtroom Elite*. Cambridge, MA: Ballinger.

Nardulli, Peter F. 1979. "Organizational Analyses of Criminal Courts: An Overview and Some Speculation." In *The Study of Criminal Courts: Political Perspectives*, ed. Peter F. Nardulli. Cambridge, MA: Ballinger.

Nardulli, Peter F., James Eisenstein, and Roy B. Flemming. 1988. *The Tenor of Justice: Criminal Courts and the Guilty Plea*. Urbana, IL: University of Illinois Press.

National Advisory Committee on Criminal Justice Standards and Goals. 1973. *Police*. Washington, DC: U.S. Government Printing Office.

National Council on Crime and Delinquency. 1991 (June). *Escalating the Use of Imprisonment: The Case Study of Florida*. San Francisco: NCCD.

National Council on Crime and Delinquency. 1992. *Criminal Justice Sentencing Policy Statement*. San Francisco: NCCD.

National Institute of Justice. 1982. *The Effects of the Exclusionary Rule: A Study of California*. Washington, DC: Government Printing Office.

National Institute of Justice. 1983. *Report to the Nation on Crime and Justice*. Washington, DC: NIJ.

National Institute of Justice. 1985. *The Special Management Inmate*. Washington, DC: NIJ.

National Institute of Justice. 1996a. *Convicted by Juries, Exonerated by Science: Case Studies in the Use of DNA Evidence to Establish Innocence After Trial*. Washington, DC: NIJ.

National Institute of Justice. 1996b. *Measuring What Matters, Part I*. Washington, DC: NIJ.

National Law Journal. 1979 (September 10). "Pagano Case Points Finger at Lineups."

National Law Journal. 1990. December 25, 1989–January 1, 1990.

National Probation Association. 1983. *John Augustus, First Probation Officer*, reprint. New York: National Probation Association.

Neubauer, David W. 1974. *Criminal Justice in Middle America*. Morristown, NJ: General Learning Press.

Newman, Donald J. 1993. "The Development of Criminal Justice Higher Education." In *Discretion in Criminal Justice*, eds. Lloyd E. Ohlin and Frank J. Remington. Albany, NY: State University of New York Press.

Newport, Frank. 2001 (May 17). "What Can We Learn from Americans' Views About the Death Penalty?" Princeton, NJ: Gallup Poll.

Newsweek. 1982 (November 8). "Not Guilty Because of PMS?"

New York Times. 1985. June 2.

New York Times. 1992 (November 8). "Victims' Rights Amendments Pass in 5 States."

Nix, Crystal. 1987 (February 6). "Police Academy Adapts to Changing New York." *New York Times*.

Note. 1977. "Notes: Did Your Eyes Deceive You? Expert Psychological Testimony on the Unreliability of Eyewitness Identification." *Stanford Law Review* 29.

Note. 1983. *Notre Dame Law Review* 59.

O'Connor, Sandra D. 2001 (July 3). "Justice O'Connor Questions Death Penalty." *Washington Post*.

O'Donnell, Lawrence. 1983. *Deadly Force*. New York: William Morrow.

Ohlin, Lloyd E. 1993. "Surveying Discretion by Criminal Justice Decision Makers." In *Discretion in Criminal Justice: The Tension Between Individualization and Uniformity*, eds. Lloyd E. Ohlin and Frank J. Remington. Albany, NY: State University of New York Press.

Orfield, Myron W., Jr. 1987. "The Exclusionary Rule and Deterrence: An Empirical Study of Chicago Narcotics Officers." *University of Chicago Law Review* 54.

Ostrom, Brian J., and Roger A. Hanson. 2000. *Efficiency, Timeliness, and Quality: A New Perspective from Nine State Criminal Courts*. Washington, DC: National Institute of Justice.

Owen, Barbara. 1985. "Race and Gender Relations Among Prison Workers." *Crime and Delinquency* 31.

Owen, Barbara. 1998. *Surviving the Mix: Struggle and Survival in a Women's Prison*. Albany, NY: State University of New York Press.

Owen, Barbara, and Barbara Bloom. 1995. "Profiling Women Prisoners: Findings from National Surveys and a California Sample." *Prison Journal* 75.

Packer, Herbert L. 1964. "Two Models of the Criminal Process." *University of Pennsylvania Law Review*.

Packer, Herbert. 1968. *The Limits of the Criminal Sanction*. Palo Alto, CA: Stanford University Press.

Padgett, John F. 1985. "The Emergent Organization of Plea Bargaining." *American Journal of Sociology* 90.

Palmer, Ted. 1975. "Martinson Revisited." *Journal of Research on Crime and Delinquency* 12.

Pate, Anthony M., and Lorie A. Fridell. 1993. *Police Use of Force: Official Reports, Citizen Complaints, and Legal Consequences*. Washington, DC: Police Foundation.

Patterson, E. Britt, and Michael J. Lynch. 1991. "Biases in Formalized Bail Procedures." In *Race and Criminal Justice*, eds. Michael J. Lynch and E. Britt Patterson. New York: Harrow and Heston.

Paterson, Alexander, Sir. 1951. *Paterson on Prisons*. London: F. Mueller.

Pelissier, Bernadette, et al. In press. "Federal Prison Residential Drug Treatment Reduces Substance Use and Arrests After Release." *American Journal of Drug and Alcohol Abuse*.

Peltason, Jack. 1955. *Federal Courts in the Political Process*. New York: Random House.

Penry v. Lynaugh. 1989. 109 S.Ct 2934.

People v. Mills. 1904. 70 N.E. 786.

People v. Penman. 1915. 271 Ill. 82, 110 N.E. 894.

People v. Washington. 1987. 236 Cal.Rptr. 840.

Pereira, Joseph. 1992 (April 20). "In a Drug Program, Some Kids Turn in Their Own Parents." *Wall Street Journal*.

Perez, Douglas W. 1994. *Common Sense About Police Review*. Philadelphia: Temple University Press.

Petersilia, Joan. 1985. "Racial Disparities in the Criminal Justice System; A Summary." *Crime and Delinquency* 31.

Petersilia, Joan. 1989. "Influence of Research on Policing." In *Critical Issues in Policing,* eds. Roger C. Dunham and Geoffrey P. Alpert. Prospect Heights, IL: Waveland Press.

Petersilia, Joan. 1990. "When Probation Becomes More Dreaded Than Prison." *Federal Probation* 54.

Petersilia, Joan. 1995. "A Crime Control Rationale for Reinvesting in Community Corrections." *Prison Journal* 45.

Petersilia, Joan. 1998. "Probation and Parole." In *Handbook of Crime and Punishment,* ed. Michael Tonry. New York: Oxford University Press.

Petersilia, Joan, Susan Turner, and Piper Deschennes. 1992. "Intensive Supervision Programs for Drug Offenders." In *Smart Sentencing,* eds. James M. Byrne, Arthur J. Luritgio, and Joan Petersilia. Newbury Park, CA: Sage.

Petersilia, Joan, Susan Turner, and James P. Kahan. 1985. *Granting Felons Probation.* Santa Monica, CA: RAND Corporation.

Phillips, Steven. 1977. *No Heroes, No Villains: The Story of a Murder Trial.* New York: Random House.

Phillips, Susan, and Barbara Bloom. 1998. "In Whose Best Interest? The Impact of Changing Public Policy on Relatives Caring for Children with Incarcerated Parents." *Child Welfare* 77.

Pincus, Walter. 2001 (October 21). "Silence of 4 Terror Suspects Poses Dilemma." *Washington Post.*

Pisciotta, Alexander W. 1983. "Scientific Reform: The 'New Penology' at Elmira, 1876–1900." *Crime and Delinquency* 29.

Plato. 1926. *Laws.* Cambridge, MA: Harvard University Press, 2:261.

Platt, Anthony, and Randi Pollock. 1974. "Channeling Lawyers: The Careers of Public Defenders." In *The Potential for Reform of Criminal Justice,* ed. Herbert Jacob. Beverly Hills, CA: Sage.

Pletan v. Gaines. 1992. 494 N.W.2d 38.

Plucknett, Theodore F. T. 1956. *A Concise History of the Common Law,* 5th ed. London: Butterworth & Company.

Police Foundation. 1981. *Newark Foot Patrol Experiment.* Washington, DC: Police Foundation.

Pound, Roscoe. 1912. "The Administration of Justice in American Cities." *Harvard Law Review* 12.

Pound, Roscoe. 1921. "The Future of the Criminal Law." *Columbia Law Review* 21.

Pound, Roscoe, and Felix Frankfurter, eds. 1922. *Criminal Justice in Cleveland.* Cleveland: Cleveland Foundation.

Powell v. Alabama. 1932. 287 U.S. 45.

President's Crime Commission. 1967. *The Police.* Washington, DC: Government Printing Office.

President's Commission on Law Enforcement and Administration of Justice. 1967. *The Challenge of Crime in a Free Society.* Washington, DC: Government Printing Office.

Procunier v. Martinez. 1974. 416 U.S. 396.

Quinney, Richard. 1977. *Class, State, and Crime: On the Theory and Practice of Criminal Justice.* New York: David McKay Co.

Radelet, Michael L., and Hugo Adam Bedau. 1998. "The Execution of the Innocent." In *America's Experiment with Capital Punishment,* eds. James R. Acker, Robert S. Bohm, and Charles S. Lanier. Durham, NC: Carolina Academic Press.

Rankin, Charles. 1964. "The Effect of Pretrial Detention." *New York University Law Review* 39.

Rankin, Bill. 2000. "Judge Tours Spruced-Up Jail." *Atlanta Journal and Constitution.*

Ravin v. State. 1975. 537 P.2d 494 (Alaska).

Reckless, Walter. 1969. "The Use of the Death Penalty." *Crime and Delinquency* 15:43, 54.

Reiss, Albert J., Jr. 1980. "Victim Proneness in Repeat Victimization by Time of Crime." In *Indicators of Crime and Criminal Justice: Quantitative Studies,* eds. Steven E. Feinberg and Albert J. Reiss, Jr. Washington, DC: BJS.

Reiss, Albert, Jr. 1988. *Public Employment of Private Police.* Washington, DC: BJS.

Reiss, Albert J., Jr. 1992. "Police Organization." In *Modern Policing,* eds. Michael Tonry and Norval Morris. Chicago: University of Chicago Press.

Reiss, Albert J., Jr., and Jeffrey A. Roth. 1993. *Understanding and Preventing Violence.* Washington, DC: National Academy Press.

Remington, Frank. 1993. "The Decision to Charge, the Decision to Convict on a Plea of Guilty, and the Impact of Sentence Structure on Prosecution Practices." In *Discretion in Criminal Justice: The Tension Between Individualization and Uniformity,* eds. Lloyd E. Ohlin and Frank J. Remington. Albany, NY: State University of New York Press.

Remington, Frank, et al. 1976. *Criminal Justice Administration.* Indianapolis: Bobbs-Merrill.

Rennie, Ysabel. 1978. *The Search for Criminal Man.* Lexington, MA: Lexington Books.

Reuter, Peter, Robert MacCoun, and Patrick Murphy. 1990. *Money from Crime.* Santa Monica: Rand.

Rheinhold, Robert. 1989 (December 28). "Police, Hard Pressed in Drug War, Are Turning to Preventive Measures." *New York Times.*

Riveland, Chase. 1999. *Supermax Prisons.* Washington, DC: National Institute of Corrections.

Robinson, Billy "Hands." 1971 (September). "Love: A Hard Legged Triangle." *Black Scholar.*

Rosecrance, John. 1985. "The Probation Officers' Search for Credibility: Ball Park Recommendations." *Crime and Delinquency* 31.

Rosecrance, John. 1988. "Maintaining the Myth of Individualized Justice: Probation and Presentence Reports." *Justice Quarterly* 5.

Rosenbaum, Dennis P. 1986. *Community Crime Prevention: Does It Work?* Beverly Hills, CA: Sage.

Rosenbaum, Dennis P., Robert L. Flewelling, Susan L. Bailey, Christopher L. Ringwalt, and Deanna L. Wilkinson. 1994. "Cops in the Classroom: A Longitudinal Evaluation of Drug

Abuse Resistance Education (DARE)." *Journal of Research in Crime and Delinquency* 31.

Rosett, Arthur, and Donald Cressey. 1976. *Justice by Consent*. New York: J. B. Lippincott Co.

Rosett, Arthur, and Donald R. Cressey. 1976. *Justice by Consent*. New York: Harper & Row, Publishers.

Ross, Robert R. 1981. *Prison Guard/Correctional Officer: The Use and Abuse of the Human Resources of the Prison*. Toronto: Butterworths.

Rossi, Peter H., et al. 1974. "The Seriousness of Crimes: Normative Structure and Individual Differences." *American Sociological Review* 39.

Rossi, Peter H., Richard A. Berk, and Kenneth J. Lenihan. 1980. *Money, Work, and Crime: Experimental Evidence*. New York: Academic Press.

Rothman, David. 1971. *The Discovery of the Asylum*. Boston: Little, Brown.

Rothman, David. 1980. *Conscience and Convenience: The Asylum and Its Alternatives in Progressive America*. Boston: Little, Brown.

Rubenstein, Jonathan. 1973. *City Police*. New York: Farrar, Straus, and Giroux.

Rubenstein, Michael L., Steven Clarke, and Theresa Wright. 1980. *Alaska Bans Plea Bargaining*. Washington, DC: U.S. Government Printing Office.

Rubenstein, Michael L., and Theresa Wright. 1979. "Alaska's Ban on Plea Bargaining." *Law and Society Review* 13.

Ruffin v. Commonwealth. 1871. 62 Va. 790.

Runda, John, Edward Rhine, and Robert Wetter. 1994. *The Practice of Parole Boards*. Lexington, KY: Association of Paroling Authorities.

Russell, Katheryn K. 1998. *The Color of Crime*. New York: New York University Press.

Sack, Kevin. 2001 (October 28). "Focus on Terror Creates Burden for the Police." *New York Times*.

Sacks, Howard R., and Charles H. Logan 1979. *Does Parole Make a Difference?* Storrs, CT: University of Connecticut Law School Press.

Samaha, Joel. 1974. *Law and Order in Historical Perspective*. New York: Academic Press.

Samaha, Joel. 1978. "Discretion and Law in the Early Penitential Books." In *Social Psychology and Discretionary Law*, ed. Richard Abt. New York: W. W. Norton.

Samaha, Joel. 1979. "Hanging for Felony: The Rule of Law in Elizabethan Colchester." *Historical Journal* 21.

Samaha, Joel. 1981. "The Recognizance in Elizabethan Law Enforcement." *American Journal of Legal History* 25.

Samaha, Joel. 1989. "John Winthrop and the Criminal Law." *William Mitchell Law Review* 15.

Samaha, Joel. n.d. Unpublished summary of reformatory records of Stillwater Prison and St. Cloud Reformatory, Minnesota, 1900–1920.

Sampson, Robert J. 1987. "Urban Black Violence: The Effect of Male Joblessness and Family Disruption." *American Journal of Sociology* 93.

Sampson, Robert J. 1995. "Toward a Theory of Race, Crime, and Urban Inequality." In *Crime and Inequality*, eds. John Hagan and Ruth D. Peterson. Stanford, CT: Stanford University Press.

Sampson, Robert J., and Janet L. Lauritsen. 1997. "Racial and Ethnic Disparities in Crime and Criminal Justice in the United States." In *Ethnicity, Crime, and Immigration*, ed. Michael Tonry. Chicago: University of Chicago Press.

Sampson, Robert J., and William Julius Wilson. 1995. "Toward a Theory of Race, Crime, and Urban Equality. In *Crime and Inequality*, eds. John Hagan and Ruth D. Peterson. Stanford, CT: Stanford University Press.

Sanborn, Joseph. 1986. "A Historical Sketch of Plea Bargaining." *Justice Quarterly* 3.

Sandin v. Conner. 1995. 515 U.S. 472.

Saum, Christine A., Hilary Spratt, James A. Inciardi, and Rachael E. Bennett. 1997. "Sex in Prison: Exploring Myths and Realities." *Prison Journal* 75.

Savage, David, and Eric Lichtblau. 2001 (October 28). "Ashcroft Deals with Daunting Responsibilities."

Schanz, William T. 1976. *The American Legal Environment*. St. Paul, MN: West.

Scheb, John M. II. 1988. "State Appellate Judges' Attitudes Toward Judicial Merit Selection and Retention: Results of a National Survey." *Judicature* 72.

Schlesinger, Steven R. 1986. "Bail Reform: Protecting the Community and the Accused." *Harvard Journal of Law and Public Policy* 9.

Schmitt, Christopher H. 1991a (December 8). "A Look Inside Where Deals Are Made: 2-Minute Discussion Decides the Future of Many Defendants." *San Jose Mercury*.

Schmitt, Christopher H. 1991b (December 8). "Plea Bargaining Favors Whites as Blacks, Hispanics Pay Price." *San Jose Mercury*.

Schneckcloth v. Bustamonte. 1973. 412 U.S. 218.

Schneider, Victoria W., and Brian Wiersema 1991. "Limits and Use of the Uniform Crime Reports." In *Measuring Crime: Large Scale, Long Range Efforts*, eds. Doris Layton MacKenzie, Phyllis Jo Baunach, and Roy R. Roberg. Albany, NY: State University of New York Press.

Schroeder, William A. 1981. "Deterring Fourth Amendment Violations." *Georgetown Law Journal* 69:1361, 1378–86.

Schulhofer, Stephen J. 1985. "No Job Too Small: Justice Without Bargaining in the Lower Criminal Courts." *American Bar Foundation Research Journal* 3.

Schulhofer, Stephen J. 1992. "Assessing the Federal Sentencing Process: The Problem Is Uniformity, Not Disparity," *American Criminal Law Review* 29.

Schulhofer, Stephen J. 1993. "Rethinking Mandatory Minimums." *Wake Forest Law Review* 28.

Scott, Eric J. 1980. *Calls for Service: Citizen Demand and Initial Police Response.* Washington, DC: U.S. Department of Justice.

Sellin, Thorsten. 1959. "The Death Penalty." Appendix to American Law Institute, "Model Penal Code" (Tentative Draft No. 9).

Sellin, Thorsten. 1967. "The Death Penalty and Police Safety." *Capital Punishment.* New York: Harper and Row.

Shaw, Clifford. 1966. *The Jack-Roller.* Chicago: University of Chicago Press.

Sheehan, Susan. 1978. *A Prison and a Prisoner.* Boston: Houghton Mifflin.

Sheppard v. Maxwell. 1966. 384 U.S. 333.

Sherman v. United States. 1958. 356 U.S. 369.

Sherman, Lawrence W. 1978. *Scandal and Reform.* Berkeley, CA: University of California Press.

Sherman, Lawrence W. 1990 (March/April). "Police Crackdowns." *NIJ Reports.*

Sherman, Lawrence W. 1992. "Attacking Crime: Police and Crime Control." In *Modern Policing,* eds. Michael Tonry and Norval Morris. Chicago: University of Chicago Press.

Sherman, Lawrence W. 1995. "The Police." In *Crime,* eds. James Q. Wilson and Joan Petersilia. San Francisco: Institute for Contemporary Studies.

Sherman, Lawrence W., Patrick R. Gartin, and Michael E. Buerger. 1989. "Hot Spots of Predatory Crime: Routine Activities and the Criminology of Place." *Criminology* 27.

Sherman, Lawrence W., and Dennis P. Rogan. 1995. "Effects of Gun Seizures on Gun Violence: 'Hot Spots' Patrol in Kansas City." *Justice Quarterly,* 12.

Sherman, Lawrence W., Janell D. Schmidt, and Dennis P. Rogan. 1992. *Policing Domestic Violence.* New York: Free Press.

Sherman, Michael, and Gordon Hawkins. 1981. *Imprisonment in America: Choosing the Future.* Chicago: University of Chicago Press.

Shover, Neal, and David Honaker. 1992. "The Socially Bounded Decision Making of Persistent Property Offenders." *Howard Journal of Criminal Justice* 31.

Silberman, Charles. 1978. *Criminal Violence, Criminal Justice.* New York: Random House.

Simon, William, and John H. Gagnon. 1976. "The Anomie of Affluence: A Post-Mertonian Conception." *American Journal of Sociology* 82.

Singer, Richard G. 1983. "Prisons: Typologies and Classifications." *Encyclopedia of Crime and Justice.* New York: Free Press.

Sitz v. Department of State Police. 1993. 506 N.W.2d 209 (Mich. App.)

Skogan, Wesley G. 1990a. *Disorder and Decline.* New York: Free Press.

Skogan, Wesley G. 1990b. "Poll Review: National Crime Survey Redesign." *Public Opinion Quarterly* 54.

Skolnick, Jerome. 1994. *Justice Without Trial,* 3d ed. New York: Macmillan.

Skolnick, Jerome H., and David H. Bayley. 1986. *The New Blue Line.* New York: Free Press.

Skolnick, Jerome H., and James J. Fyfe. 1993. *Above the Law: Police and Excessive Use of Force.* New York: Free Press.

Slater, Eric. 1995 (March 3). "Thief Receives Sentence of 25 Years to life." *Los Angeles Times.*

Slevin, Peter, and Mary Beth Sheridan. 2001 (September 26). "Justice Dept. Uses Arrest Powers Fully: Scope of Jailings Stirs Questions on Detainees' Rights to Representation and Bail." *Washington Post.*

Slotnick, Elliot E. 1995. "Review Essay on Judicial Recruitment and Selection." In *Courts and Justice,* eds. G. Larry Mays and Peter R. Gregware. Prospect Heights, IL: Waveland Press.

Smith, Page. 1962. *John Adams.* New York: Doubleday.

Sparger, Jerry R., and David J. Giacopassi. 1992. "Memphis Revisited: A Reexamination of Police Shootings After the *Garner* Decision." *Justice Quarterly* 9.

Sparks, Richard. 1978. Testimony to House Subcommittee on Crime, Committee of the Judiciary, White Collar Crime, Second Session, 95th Congress, June 21, July 12 and 19th, and December 1.

Sparks, Richard F. 1981. "Surveys of Victimization—An Optimistic Assessment." In *Crime and Justice: An Annual Review of Justice,* eds. Michael Tonry and Norval Morris. Chicago: University of Chicago Press.

Sparrow, Malcolm K., Mark H. Moore, and David M. Kennedy. 1995. *Beyond 911: A New Era for Policing.* New York: Basic Books.

Spelman, William. 2000. "Prisons and Crime." In *Crime and Justice: A Review of Research,* ed. Michael Tonry. Chicago: University of Chicago Press.

Spitzer, Eliot. 1999. *The New York City Police Department's "Stop and Frisk" Practices.* Albany, NY: New York State Attorney General's Office.

Spohn, Cassia, and Jerry Cederblom. 1991. "Race and Disparities in Sentencing: A Test of the Liberation Hypothesis." *Justice Quarterly* 8.

Spohn, Cassia, John Gruhl, and Susan Welch. 1987. "The Impact of Ethnicity and Gender of Defendants on the Decision to Reject or Dismiss Felony Charges." *Criminology* 25.

Staples, Brent. 1999 (May 10). "Why Some Get Busted and Some Go Free." *New York Times.*

Star, Deborah. 1979. *Summary Parole.* California Department of Corrections.

Star, Deborah. 1981. *Investigation and Surveillance in Parole Supervision: An Evaluation of the High Control Project.* California Department of Corrections.

State v. Burrows. 1931.

State v. Damms. 1960. 100 N.W.2d 592 (Wis.).

State v. Furr. 1977. 235 S.E.2d 193 (N.C.).

State v. Metzger. 1982. 319 N.W.2d 459 (Neb.).

State v. Stewart. 1988. 763 P.2d 572 (Kansas).

State v. Vicente. 2001. 772 A.2d 680 (Conn.App.).

Staufenberger, Richard A. 1980. *Progress in Policing: Essays on Change.* Cambridge, MA: Ballinger.

Steffensmeier, Darrell, and Dana Haynie 2000. "Gender, Structural Disadvantage, and Urban Crime: Do Macrosocial Variables Also Explain Female Offending Rates?" *Criminology* 38.

Steffensmeier, Darrell, John Kramer, and Cathy Streifel. 1993. "Gender and Imprisonment Decisions." *Criminology* 31.

Stoddard, Ellwyn R. 1983. "Blue Coat Crime." In *Thinking About Police,* eds. Carl B. Klockars and Stephen D. Mastrofski. New York: McGraw-Hill.

Stojkovic, Stan, and Rick Lovell. 1992. *Corrections: An Introduction.* Cincinnati: Anderson.

Storkamp, Daniel. 2001. Personal correspondence. Minnesota Department of Corrections.

Stotland, Ezra. 1977. "White Collar Criminals." *Journal of Social Issues* 33.

Strachan-Davidson, James L. 1912. *Problems of the Roman Criminal Law.* Oxford: Clarendon Press.

Strauss, Murray, Richard Gelles, and Suzanne Steinmetz. 1980. *Behind Closed Doors: Violence in the American Family.* New York: Doubleday.

Subin, Harry I. 1991 (December 19). "230,000 Cases, Zero Justice." *New York Times.*

Substance Abuse and Mental Health Services Administration (SAMHSA) 2000. *1999 Annual Survey.* http://www.drugabusestatistics.samhsa.gov/.

Susla v. State. 1976. 247 N.W.2d 907.

Sutherland, Edwin H., and Donald R. Cressey. 1978. *Criminology,* 10th ed. Philadelphia: J. Lippincott.

Sykes, Gresham. 1958. *Society of Captives.* Princeton, NJ: Princeton University Press.

Szarwak v. Warden. 1974. 330 A.2d 466.

Taylor v. Louisiana. 1975. 419 U.S. 522.

Terry v. Ohio. 1968. 392 U.S. 1.

Texas Criminal Code. 1988. Section 9.42.

Thio, Alex. 1975. "A Critical Look at Merton's Anomie Theory." *Pacific Sociological Review* 18.

Thomas, Jim. 1989. "The 'Reality' of Prisoner Litigation: Repackaging the Data." *New England Journal on Criminal Law and Civil Confinement* 15.

Thomas, Jo. 2001 (November 10). "No Bail for Friend of Man Suspected of Preparing for Sept. 11 Hijackings." *New York Times.*

Thomas, Wayne H. 1976. *Bail Reform in America.* Berkeley, CA: University of California Press.

Thompson v. Oklahoma. 1988. 487 U.S. 815.

Tiffany, Lawrence P., et al. 1967. *Detection of Crime.* Boston: Little, Brown.

Toborg, Mary A. 1981. *Pretrial Release: A National Evaluation of Practices and Outcomes.* Washington, DC: National Institute of Justice.

Toch, Hans B. 1978. "Is a 'Correctional Officer,' By Any Other Name, a 'Screw'?" *Criminal Justice Review* 3.

Tonry, Michael. 1995. *Malign Neglect: Race, Crime, and Punishment in America.* New York: Oxford University Press.

Tonry, Michael, ed. 2000. *Crime and Justice: A Review of Research.* Chicago: University of Chicago Press.

Tonry, Michael, and Mary Lynch. 1996. "Intermediate Sanctions." In *Crime and Research: A Review of Research,* vol. 20, ed. Michael Tonry. Chicago: University of Chicago Press.

Toobin, Jeffrey. 2001 (November 5). "Crackdown." *New Yorker.*

Transactions of the National Congress of Prisons and Reformatory Discipline. 1971. Albany, NY: American Correctional Association.

Tunnell, Kenneth D. 1990. "Choosing Crime: Close Your Eyes and Take Your Chances." *Justice Quarterly* 7.

Tunnell Kenneth, and Larry K. Gaines. 1992. "Political Pressures and Influences on Police Executives: A Descriptive Analysis." *American Journal of Police* 11.

Turner, Michael G., Jody L. Sundt, Brandon Applegate, and Francis T. Cullen. 1995 (September). "'Three Strikes and You're Out' Legislation: A National Assessment." *Federal Probation.*

Twentieth Century Fund. 1976. *Fair and Certain Punishment.* New York: McGraw-Hill.

United States v. Brigham. 1992. 977 F.2d 317 (7th Cir. 1992).

United States v. Werker. 1976. 535 F.2d 198 (2d Cir. 1976), certiorari denied 429 U.S. 926.

Uphoff, Rodney J. 1995. "The Criminal Defense Lawyer: Zealous Advocate, Double Agent, or Beleaguered Dealer?" In *Courts and Justice,* eds. G. Larry Mays and Peter R. Gregware. Prospect Heights, IL: Waveland Press.

U.S. Census. 2001. Profile of General Demographic Characteristics: 2000. http//www2.census.gov/census_2000/datasets/demographic_profile/0_National_Summary/2khus.pdf.

U.S. Code. 1994. 42 U.S.C.A. §1983, subs. 1.

U.S. Code 1999. Title 18, §3142(f).

U.S. Department of Justice. 1978. *Response Time Analysis: Executive Summary.* Washington, DC: Government Printing Office.

U.S. Department of Justice. 2001 (August 26). Press release. Washington, DC: Government Printing Office.

Useem, Burt, and Peter Kimball. 1989. *States of Siege: U.S. Prison Riots, 1971–1986.* New York: Oxford University Press, 3–4.

U.S. House of Representatives. 1970. No. 1444, 91st Cong., 2d Sess. 11.

U.S. Sentencing Commission. 1991. *Mandatory Minimum Penalties in the Federal Criminal Justice System.* Washington, DC: U.S. Sentencing Commission.

U.S. v. Salerno. 1987. 481 U.S. 739.

Van Maanen, John. 1978. "The Asshole." In *Policing: A View from the Street,* eds. Peter K. Manning and John Van Maanen. New York: Random House.

Vera Institute of Justice. 1977. *Felony Arrests: Their Prosecution and Disposition in New York City's Courts.* New York: Vera Institute of Justice.

Vera Institute of Justice. 1988. *Community Policing in Action.* New York: Vera Institute of Justice, 11–12.

Vito, Gennaro. 1986. "Felony Probation and Recidivism: Replication and Response." *Felony Probation* 50.

Von Hirsch, Andrew. 1976. *Doing Justice: The Choice of Punishments.* New York: Hill and Wang.

Walker, Samuel. 1980. *Popular Justice.* New York: Oxford University Press.

Walker, Samuel. 1992a. "Origins of the Contemporary Criminal Justice Paradigm: The American Bar Foundation Survey, 1953–1969." *Justice Quarterly* 9.

Walker, Samuel. 1992b. *The Police in America,* 2d ed. New York: McGraw-Hill.

Walker, Samuel. 1993. *Taming the System: The Control of Discretion in Criminal Justice, 1950–1990.* New York: Oxford University Press, 1993, 18–20.

Walker, Samuel. 1994. *Sense and Nonsense About Crime and Drugs,* 3d edition. Belmont, CA: Wadsworth.

Walker, Samuel. 1998. *Popular Justice,* 2d ed. New York: Oxford University Press.

Walker, Samuel, and Vic W. Bumphus. 1992. "The Effectiveness of Civilian Review: Observations on Recent Trends and New Issues Regarding the Civilian Review of the Police." *American Journal of Police* XI.

Walker, Samuel, Cassia Spohn, and Miriam DeLone. 2000. *The Color of Justice.* Belmont, CA: Wadsworth.

Wallace, Henry Scott. 1993 (September). "Mandatory Minimums and the Betrayal of Sentencing Reform: A Legislative Dr. Jekyll and Mr. Hyde." *Federal Probation.*

Wallerstedt, John F. 1984. *Returning to Prison.* Washington, DC: BJS.

Wall Street Journal. 1994 (March 22). "Death at Work."

Ward, David A. 1987. "Control Strategies for Problem Prisoners in American Penal Systems." In *Problems of Long-Term Imprisonment,* eds. Anthony E. Bottoms and Roy Light. Brookfield, VT: Gower.

Ward, David A. 1990 (March 30). Personal conversation.

Ward, David A. 1994. "Alcatraz and Marion: Confinement in Super Maximum Custody." In *Escaping Prison Myths: Selected Topics in the History of Federal Corrections,* ed. John W. Roberts. Washington, DC: American University Press.

Ward, David A., and Gene G. Kassebaum. 1965. *Women's Prisons: Sex and Social Structure.* Chicago: Aldine.

Ward, David A., and Kenneth F. Schoen, eds. 1981. *Confinement in Maximum Custody.* Lexington, MA: Lexington Books.

Weems v. U.S. 1910. 217 U.S. 349.

Weiner, Richard, William Frazier, and Jay Farbstein. 1987 (June). "Building Better Jails." *Psychology Today.*

Weisburd, David, and Lorraine Green. 1995. "Policing Drug Hot Spots: The Jersey City Drug Market Analysis Experiment." *Justice Quarterly* 12.

Weiss, Mike. 1984. *Double Play: The San Francisco City Hall Killings.* Reading, MA: Addison-Wesley.

West, Cornell. 1994. *Race Matters.* New York: Vintage.

Whitley v. Albers, 475 US 312 (1986), 319.

Whitlock, Brand. 1914. *Forty Years of It.* New York: D. Appleton.

Wice, Paul. 1974. *Freedom for Sale.* Lexington, MA: Lexington Books.

Wice, Paul B. 1985. *Chaos in the Courthouse: The Inner Workings of the Urban Criminal Courts.* New York: Praeger.

Wilbanks, William. 1987. *The Myth of a Racist Criminal Justice System.* Monterey, CA: Brooks/Cole.

Wilcox, Clair. 1927. *Parole from State Penal Institutions.* Philadelphia: Pennsylvania State Parole Commission.

Williams, Hubert. 1993. "Foreword." In *Police Use of Force: Official Reports, Citizen Complaints, and Legal Consequences,* vol. I, eds. Anthony M. Pate and Lorie A. Fridell. Washington, DC: Police Executive Research Forum.

Williams, Virgil L., and Mary Fish. 1974. *Convicts, Codes, and Contraband.* Cambridge, MA: Ballinger.

Wilson v. Arkansas. 1995. 514 U.S. 927.

Wilson, James Q. 1968. *Varieties of Police Behavior.* Cambridge, MA: Harvard University Press.

Wilson, James Q. 1983a. *Crime File: Victims.* National Institute of Justice.

Wilson, James Q. 1983b. *Thinking About Crime,* rev. ed. New York: Basic Books.

Wilson, James Q., and George L. Kelling. 1982 (March). "Broken Windows." *Atlantic Monthly.*

Wilson, William Julius. 1996. *When Work Disappears: The World of the New Urban Poor.* New York: Knopf.

Wilson, Margo I., and Martin Daly. 1992. "Who Kills Whom in Spouse Killings? On the Exceptional Sex Ratio of Spousal Killings in the United States." *Criminology* 30.

Winkeljohn, Matt. 1998 (March 22). "Special Report: Sports in Prison." *Atlanta Journal and Constitution,* 12E.

Wishman, Seymour. 1981. *Confessions of a Criminal Lawyer.* New York: Times Books.

Witte, Ann Dryden. 1975. *Work Release in North Carolina: An Evaluation of Its Post-Release Effects.* Chapel Hill: University of North Carolina.

Wolfgang, Marvin E., Terence P. Thornberry, and Robert M. Figlio. 1987. *From Boy to Man, from Delinquency to Crime.* Chicago: University of Chicago Press.

Wood, Arthur Lewis. 1967. *Criminal Lawyer.* New Haven, CT: College and University Press.

Worden, Robert E. 1987. "The Causes of Police Brutality: Theory and Evidence." *And Justice for All*. Police Foundation.

Wright, James D. 1986. *The Armed Criminal in America*. Washington, DC: BJS.

Wright, Kevin N., Todd R. Clear, and Paul Dickson. 1984. "Universal Applicability of Probation Risk-Assessment Instruments." *Criminology* 22.

Wright, Richard T., and Scott H. Decker. 1994. *Burglars on the Job: Streetlife and Residential Break-ins*. Boston: Northeastern University Press.

Wright, Richard T., and Scott H. Decker. 1997. *Armed Robbers in Action*. Boston: Northeastern University Press.

Yant, Martin. 1991. *Presumed Guilty: When Innocent People Are Wrongly Convicted*. Buffalo, NY: Prometheus Books.

Zamble, Edward, and Frank Porporino. 1988. *Coping, Behavior, and Adaptation in Prison Inmates*. New York: Springer-Verlag.

Zimmer, Lynne E. 1986. *Women Guarding Men*. Chicago: University of Chicago Press.

Zimring, Franklin E., and Richard S. Frase. 1980. *The Criminal Justice System*. Boston: Little, Brown.

Zimring, Franklin E., and Gordon Hawkins. 1991. *The Scale of Punishment*. Chicago: University of Chicago Press.

Table of Cases

Name Index

Subject Index

Photo Credits